BULLINGER'S DECADES.

The Parker Society.

Instituted A.D. M.DCCC.XL.

For the Publication of the Works of the Fathers
and Early Writers of the Reformed
English Church.

THE DECADES

OF

HENRY BULLINGER,

MINISTER OF THE CHURCH OF ZURICH.

TRANSLATED BY H. I.

THE FIRST AND SECOND DECADES.

EDITED FOR

The Parker Society,

BY THE

REV. THOMAS HARDING, A.M.,

OF WORCESTER COLLEGE, OXFORD, AND VICAR OF BEXLEY, IN KENT.

CAMBRIDGE:

PRINTED AT

THE UNIVERSITY PRESS.

M.DCCC.XLIX.

CONTENTS.

ADVERTISEMENT.

One of the Parker Society's objects, as stated in the first of its Laws, is "the printing, as may appear desirable, of some of the Early English translations of the Foreign Reformers." Accordingly, the re-publishing of the English Version of the Decades of Bullinger was announced, as in the contemplation of the Council of the Society, in a List which was appended to the Second Annual Report; and the first volume is now, at length, presented to the subscribers. The edition, which is here reprinted, is that of 1587, which scarcely differs at all, in any material respects, from the former edition of 1584, and very little from that of 1577; but any important variations between the translation and the original Latin are carefully specified in the notes. The Version was made, as stated in the title-page, "by H. I. Student in Divinitie,"—"a person," according to Strype's testimony, "of eminency in the Church[1]."

These Decades, it is conceived, possess a peculiar claim on the regard of the members of the Church of England. For not only was Bullinger "well-deserving of this nation for his kind entertainment and harbour of our divines and scholars that fled abroad in Queen Mary's reign, and of note for that friendship and correspondence ever after maintained between him and them[2];" but several of his writings, as they became known here, were eminently appreciated by our theologians and religious persons of the era of the Reformation[3].

[1] Strype, Ann. book II. chap. 10, p. 145, Vol. II. part 2. ed. Oxf. 1824.

[2] Strype, Ann. ibid. p. 144. See also Strype, Mem. II. 1, pp. 531, 532, and Zurich Letters, Parker Soc. ed. pp. 41, 111, 127, 205, &c. 2nd ed.

[3] See Original Letters, Parker Soc. ed. pp. 5, 9, 54, 70, 618, 620, &c. Zurich Letters, 2nd ed. pp. 39, 110, 205, 468. Strype, Ann. chap. 21, p. 383, Vol. I. part 1, and part 2. chap. 46, p. 195, and chap. 48, p. 221. Jewel styled Bullinger, "*oraculum ecclesiarum.*" Zurich Letters, No. LXX. 1st series, p. 156. The University of Oxford, also, selected Bullinger's Catechism, as one of those books which the Tutors there were required to use, for the purpose of imparting sound religious principles to their pupils:—"ad informandum in vera reli-

And, above all, in the Convocation of the province of Canterbury, held in 1586, among the " Orders for the better increase of learning in the inferior Ministers," introduced by Whitgift, Archbishop of Canterbury, the following direction stands foremost :—" Every minister having cure, and being under the degrees of master of arts, and batchelors of law, and not licensed to be a public preacher, shall before the second day of February next provide a Bible, and Bullinger's Decads in Latin or English, and a paper book, and shall every day read over one chapter of the Holy Scriptures, and note the principal contentes thereof briefly in his paper booke, and shall every weeke read over one Sermon in the said Decads, and note likewise the chief matters therein contained in the said paper; and shall once in every quarter (viz. within a fortnight before or after the end of the quarter) shewe his said note to some preacher nere adjoyninge to be assigned for that purpose[1]." And, agreebly with this order, it is recorded by Strype, Dr. Theophilus Aylmer, Archdeacon of London, acted in his visitation in the early part of the year 1587,— " the Bishop's pious and painful son[2]."

Although a Memoir of Bullinger (together with indexes to the whole work) will be given in the last volume, it may be useful here to state briefly, that he was born at Bremgarten, near Zurich, on July 18, 1504 ; commenced his studies at the University of Cologne in 1519; began to unite himself to the divines of the Reformation in the course of 1524 ; was chosen pastor of Zurich, on the decease of Œcolampadius, in the close of 1531 ; dedicated to Rodolph Gualter and others his first volume of the Decades, March 1, 1549 ; and died September 17, 1575, in the 71st year of his age[3].

N.B.   The editing of these Decades having been commenced by the Rev. STEUART A. PEARS, the notes which have the initial (P) affixed to them, are due to his research.

gione juventutem." Wood. Hist. et Ant. Univ. Oxon. Lib. I. p. 296. quoted in Preface, p. iv. to "Sermons on the Sacraments by Henry Bullinger." Cambridge, 1840.

[1] Cardwell's Synodalia, Vol. II. p. 562. Oxf. 1842.   Strype's Whitgift, Vol. III. p. 194. App. No. 32.   Oxf. ed.

[2] Strype's Aylmer, p. 83. Oxf. ed.

[3] See Adami Vit. Germ. Theol. in vita Bullingeri; and "Bullinger," in Chalmers' Biograph. Dict.

FIFTY SERMONS

DIVIDED INTO

FIVE DECADES.

FIFTIE
GODLIE AND LEARNED
SERMONS, DIVIDED INTO

FIVE DECADES CONTAINING THE

chiefe and principall points of Christian Religi-
on, written in three severall Tomes or Sections,
by HENRIE BVLLINGER *Minister*
of the Church of TYGVRE *in*
Swicerland.

WHEREVNTO ARE ADDED CER-
TAINE EPISTLES OF THE SAME

Author concerning the Apparell of
Ministers and other indiffe-
rent things.

WITH A TRIPLE OR THREE-FOLD

Table verie fruitfull and ne-
cessarie[1].

Translated out of Latine into English, by

H. I. *Student in Diuinitie.*

MATTHEW. 17.

This is my beloued Sonne in whom I am well pleased: Heare him.

Imprinted at London by Ralph Newberie, dwelling
in Fleete street a little aboue the Conduit,

Cum gratia & priuilegio Regiæ Maiestatis.

1587.

[1 N.B. Notwithstanding what is here stated, the edition of 1587
has not this Table prefixed to it.]

A PREFACE

TO THE MINISTRY OF THE CHURCH OF ENGLAND, AND TO OTHER WELL DISPOSED READERS OF GOD'S WORD.

THAT just cause there is that all spiritual shepherds, and specially these of our time, should see carefully to the feeding of the flocks committed to their charge, may easily appear to him that shall but a little stay his consideration upon this matter. For first, the commandments of the Almighty touching this thing are very earnest, the authority of which should greatly enforce. Secondly, the rewards which he proposeth to vigilant and careful pastors are large and bountiful, the sweetness of which should much allure. Thirdly, the plagues and heavy judgments, which he denounceth against slothful and careless shepherds, are grievous and importable[1], the terror whereof should make afraid. Then the nature and condition of the sheep over whom they watch, the vigilancy of the wolf against whom they watch, the conscience in taking the fleece for which they watch, and this time and age wherein they watch, being rightly considered, will give them to understand sufficiently, that they have good occasion to watch.

How earnestly God commandeth, appeareth, Esay lviii. where he saith, "Cry aloud, spare not, lift up thy voice like a trumpet, shew my people their transgressions, and the house of Jacob their sins." And Esay lxii. "I have set watchmen upon thy walls, O Hierusalem, which all the day and all the night continually shall not cease: ye that are mindful of the Lord, keep not silence." And John xxi. "Feed my lambs, feed my sheep, and if ye love me, feed." And 2 Tim. iv. "Preach the word: be instant in season, out of season, improve[2], rebuke, exhort, &c." How sweetly with rewards he allureth, doth appear in the xii. of Daniel: "They that be wise shall shine as the brightness of the firmament,

Isai. lviii.

Isai. lxii.

John xxi.

2 Tim. iv.

Dan xii.

[1 i. e. unsupportable: "importable power."—Spenser. P.]
[2 i. e. reprove.]

1—2

and they that turn many to righteousness shall shine as the stars for ever and ever." And 1 Tim, iv. "Take heed to thyself and to doctrine; in them occupy thyself continually. For in so doing thou shalt save thyself and them which hear thee." How fiercely also he urgeth and driveth on the sluggish and careless shepherds with terrible plagues and whips threatened unto them, appeareth, Ezechiel iii., where he saith, "Son of man, I have made thee a watchman unto the house of Israel: therefore hear the word of my mouth, and give them warning from me: when I shall say unto the wicked, thou shalt surely die, and thou givest him not warning, nor speakest to admonish the wicked of his wicked way that he may live; the same wicked man shall die in his iniquity, but his blood will I require at thy hand." And Ieremie i. ver. 17: "Thou therefore, truss up thy loins, and arise, and speak unto them all that I command thee: be not afraid of their faces, lest I destroy thee before them." And 1 Cor. ix. ver. 16: "Though I preach the gospel, I have nothing to rejoice of[1]; for necessity is laid upon me, and woe is unto me, if I preach not the gospel: for if I do it willingly, I have a reward: but if I do it against my will, notwithstanding the dispensation is committed unto me."

Now the sheep, whereof spiritual shepherds have undertaken charge, are not beasts, but men: the very images of God himself endued with everliving souls, citizens with the saints and blessed angels, clothed with God's livery, beautified with his cognizance and all the badges of salvation, admitted to his table, and to no meaner dishes than the body and blood of the undefiled Lamb Christ Jesus; bought also and redeemed out of the wolf's chawes[2] with no less price than of that same blood more precious than any gold or silver. Sheep also of that nature they are, that, being carefully fed and discreetly ordered, they prove gentle and loving towards their shepherds, and serviceable towards the chief Shepherd Jesus Christ: but being neglected and left to themselves, they degenerate into bloody wolves, watching ever opportunity when they may rent in pieces their shepherds, and all other sheep which are not degenerated into their wolfish nature.

As for the spiritual wolf, against whom they watch, which

[1 So Tyndale's Versions, and Cranmer's Bible, 1539.]
[2 Chawes: jaws. P.]

1 Tim. iv.

Ezek. iii.

Jer. i.

1 Cor. ix.

is Satan, "He," as the apostle Peter witnesseth, 1 Epistle, 1 Pet. v.
cap. v. "never resteth, but as a roaring lion walketh about,
seeking ever whom he may devour." And for that cause also
is he called, Apoc. xx. ver. 2, " a dragon," which beast is Rev. xx.
naturally very malicious crafty, and watchful : so then, if the
spiritual shepherd must watch whiles the spiritual wolf doth
wake, he can promise unto himself no one moment of security,
wherein he may be careless.

God by his prophet Ezechiel, cap. xxxiv. saith : " Woe Ezek. xxxiv.
be unto the shepherds of Israel that feed themselves: should
not the shepherds feed the flocks ? Ye eat the fat, and ye
clothe you with the wool ; ye kill them that are fed, but ye
feed not the sheep." This sentence should awake the sleepy
and careless consciences of many shepherds. For as the priest
that serveth the altar is worthy to live upon the offerings,
and the soldier that ventureth is worthy his wages, and the
husbandman that toileth is worthy the harvest, and the
shepherd that feedeth the flock is worthy to be fed with
the milk, and clothed with the wool ; so, questionless, the
priest that serveth not is worthy no offerings, the soldier
that fighteth not is worthy no wages, the husbandman that
loitereth is worthy of weeds, and the shepherd that feedeth
not can with no good conscience require either the milk or
the fleece : but his due reward and just recompence is punishment, for that through his default the sheep are hunger-
starved and destroyed of the wolf.

But let the ministers of our time well weigh the condition
and manner of the time; and then, no doubt, they shall see
that it is high time to bestir them to the doing of their
duties. This time succeedeth a time, wherein was extreme
famine of all spiritual food, so that the sheep of this time can
never recover themselves of that feebleness whereinto they
were brought, but by some great and extraordinary diligence.
This time succeedeth a time, wherein the multitude of wolves
and ravenous beasts was so great, and their rage and fury so
fell in every sheepfold, that the good shepherds were either
put to flight, or pitifully murdered ; so that the sheep, being
committed to wolves, did either perish, or degenerate into
wolves : so that to regenerate them again into sheep requireth
no small labour. The church in this time is like land that
hath lain, time out of mind, unmanured, uncompassed, untilled;

by reason whereof it is so out of heart, that it requireth arms of iron and legs of brass to recover it again : or like a ship so worn with winds and tempests, so rent with rocks, so crackt and utterly decayed, that it seemeth a rare piece of cunning to make her take the seas again.

No remedy, then, but the ministry of this time, if there be any love or fear of God in them, if they would not have all things run to ruin, if they regard either God, themselves, or their brethren, must forthwith, without further delay, set themselves to feed their flocks, to teach, to exhort, to strengthen, to bind up, to build, to plant, to water, to set, to graff, to leave nothing undone that appertaineth to the feeding and fatting of the Lord's flocks, to the planting of the Lord's paradise, tilling of the Lord's husbandry, dressing of the Lord's vineyard, raising and rearing up of the Lord's temple. What great want there is in many to discharge their duties in this behalf, is very lamentable, and by some means (as much as is possible) to be supplied and remedied, rather than to be made a common theme and argument of railing, which at this day many do : wherein they shew themselves like unto those which find fault at other men's garments, not for that they love them, or mind to give them better, but for that they are proud of their own, and would scornfully shame and vex other. The cause of this great want needs not here to be disputed : but in very deed, any man may judge how unpossible it was for so populous a kingdom, abounding with so many several congregations, to be all furnished with fit and able pastors ; and that, immediately after such a general corruption and apostasy from the truth. For unless they should have suddenly come from heaven, or been raised up miraculously, they could not have been. For the ancient preachers of king Edward's time, some of them died in prison, many perished by fire, many otherwise ; many also fled into other countries, of whom some there died, and a few returned, which were but as an handful to furnish this whole realm. The universities were also at the first so infected, that many wolves and foxes crept out, who detested the ministry, and wrought the contempt of it everywhere : but very few good shepherds came abroad[1]. And whereas, since that

[[1] See Zurich Letters, reign of Q. Elizabeth, 2nd ed. Parker Soc. pages 24, 38, 42, 55, 61, 101, 104, 115, 427.]

time, now eighteen years, the universities being well purged, there was good hope, that all the land should have been over-spread and replenished with able and learned pastors; the devil and corrupt patrons have taken such order, that much of that hope is cut off: for patrons now-a-days search not the universities for a most fit pastor; but they post up and down the country for a most gainful chapman. He that hath the biggest purse to pay largely, not he that hath the best gifts to preach learnedly, is presented. The bishops bear great blame for this matter, and they admit (say they) unworthy men. See the craft of Satan, falsely to charge the worthiest pillars of the church with the ruin of the church, to the end that all church-robbers, and caterpillars of the Lord's vine-yard, may lie unespied. There is nothing that procureth the bishops of our time more trouble and displeasure, than that they zealously withstand the covetousness of patrons in re-jecting their unsufficient clerks. For it standeth them upon of all other, that the church of God doth prosper, in the decay and fall whereof they cannot stand, but perish. But howsoever it cometh to pass, certain it is, that many are far behind in those gifts which are necessary for their function; and small likelihood is there yet that the church shall be served with better, but rather with worse: for it seemeth not that patrons hereafter will bate one penny, but rather more and more raise the market.

The case standing thus, their labour surely is not worst bestowed, neither do they promote the glory of God or profit the church least, which to that end apply their endeavour, that the ministry which now is in place may come forward, and be better able to do their duties: I mean such as either set forth godly and learned treatises, or expositions of the holy scriptures, compiled by themselves in our mother tongue; or else such as translate the worthy works of the famous divines of our time. Both these sorts of men, no doubt, do much edify the godly, and do greatly help forward all those ministers which either not at all, or very meanly, understand the Latin tongue: so that amongst them are found many, which, by painful industry and diligent reading of such books, do God good service in the church; and so might all the rest of them do also, if sloth and worldly affairs did not hinder them. Some of that sort complain, that Calvin's manner of writing in his Institutions[1] is over deep and profound for them : Musculus also, in his Common Places, is very scholastical; the Commentaries of Marlorat[2] upon John, of Peter Martyr upon the Judges, of Gualter upon the small Prophets, and other many are translated and extant[3]; which altogether do handle most points of christian doctrine excellently well : but this sort of ministers for the most part are so bare bitten of their patrons[4], that to buy them all would deeply charge them. Therefore, questionless, no writer yet in the hands of men can fit them better than master Bullinger in these his Decades; who in them amendeth much Calvin's obscurity with singular perspicuity, and Musculus' scholastical subtlety with great plainness and even popular facility. And all those points of christian doctrine, which are not to be found in one, but handled in all, Bullinger packeth up all, and that in good order, in this one book of small quantity. And whereas divers of the ministry which lack knowledge, and some also which have knowledge but yet lack order, discretion, memory, or audacity, cannot, by reason of their wants, either expound, or exhort, or otherwise preach, but only read the order of service; the Decades of master Bullinger in this respect may do more good than shall perhaps at the first be conceived. For in very deed this book is a book of sermons; sermons in name, and in nature; fit to be read out of the pulpit unto the simplest and rudest people of this land : the doctrine of them very plain, without ostentation, curiosity, perplexity, vanity, or superfluity; very sound also, without popery, Ana-

[1 An English translation of this work, The Institution of the Christian Religion, appeared for the first time in 1561. See Introductory Notice to Calvin's Institutes, ed. Calv. Soc. p. lii.]

[2 Marlorat was a Protestant minister born in Lorraine : he wrote commentaries on Genesis, Psalms, Isaiah, and the New Testament, and was executed at Rouen by order of the Duke of Guise in 1562.—Moreri. P.]

[3 Cf. Zurich Letters, Second Series, Parker Soc. ed. p. 148.]

[4 " Burton similarly complained, in his odd way, that if our greedy patrons hold us to such hard conditions as commonly they do, they will make most of us work at some trade, as Paul did; at last turn taskers, maltsters, costermongers, grasiers, sell ale, as some have done, or worse."—Anatomy of Melancholy, Preface, quoted in Sermons on the Sacraments, by Henry Bullinger, Preface, p. v. note 6. Cambridge, 1840.]

baptism, Servetianism[5], or any other heresy; and in number fifty, every Decade containing (as the word importeth) ten; so that they may easily be so divided as there may be for every Sunday in the year one. Neither is it material what those fanatical fellows say, which can away with no homilies or sermons, be they never so sound, pithy, and effectual, to be read in churches. They are like physicians which forbid their patients all those meats which they may have and would do them good; and appoint them only such, as by no means they can obtain: for it will not yet be, that every parish shall have a learned able preacher resident and abiding in it. And in the mean time it cannot be denied, but that an homily or sermon, penned by some excellent clerk, being read plainly, orderly, and distinctly, doth much move the hearers, doth teach, confirm, confute, comfort, persuade, even as the same pronounced without the book doth.

Perhaps some hearers, which delight more to have their eyes fed with the preacher's action, than their hearts edified with his sermon, are more moved with a sermon not read: but to a good christian hearer, whose mind is most occupied on the matter, there is small odds. Better is a good sermon read than none at all. But nothing (say they) must be read in the open congregation, but the very canonical scriptures[6]. That rule is somewhat strait and precise. Then may not either the creed, called the Apostles' creed, or the Nicene creed, or the creed called Athanasius' creed, or any prayers which are not word for word contained in the canon of the scriptures, nor any contents of chapters, be read in the congregation. The church and congregation of the Colossians were enjoined by St Paul, Col. iv. ver. 16, to read amongst them the epistle written from Laodicea; which epistle (as Calvin thinketh[7]) was not written by Paul, but by the church of Laodicea, and sent to Paul, and is not contained in the canon of the scriptures. The church of Corinth also, and other churches of the godly, soon after the apostles' times (as

[5 Michael Servetus published his heretical work on the Trinity in 1531; he was burnt at Geneva in 1553. P.]

[6 See Hooker's Eccles. Pol. book v. § 20.]

[7 Falso putarunt a Paulo scriptam esse. Non dubito quin epistola fuerit ad Paulum missa.—Calvin. Comment. in loc.]

appeareth out of Eusebius, Lib. iv. cap. 23[1], and the writers
of the Centuries[2], Cent. ii. cap. 10) did use to read openly,
for admonition sake, certain epistles of Clement, and of Dionysius, bishop of Corinth. Master Bucer, in his Notes upon
the Communion Book in king Edward's time, writeth thus:
" It is better, that where there lacks to expound the scriptures unto the people, there should be godly and learned
homilies read unto them, rather than they should have no
exhortation at all in the administration of the supper[3]." And
a little after he saith : "There be too few homilies, and too
few points of religion taught in them : when, therefore, the
Lord shall bless this kingdom with some excellent preachers,
let them be commanded to make more homilies of the principal points of religion, which may be read to the people by
those pastors that cannot make better themselves[4]." And
that worthy martyr, doctor Ridley, bishop of London, speaking of the church of England that was in the reign of king
Edward (as he is reported by master Foxe, in his book of
Acts and Mon., To. ii. page 1940) saith thus[5] : " It had also
holy and wholesome homilies in commendation of the principal virtues which are commended in scripture, and likewise
other homilies against the most pernicious and capital vices
that use, alas!· to reign in this church[6] of England." So long,

[1 Ἐν αὐτῇ δὲ ταύτῃ (ἐπιστολῇ) καὶ τῆς Κλήμεντος πρὸς Κορινθίους
μέμνηται (Διονύσιος) ἐπιστολῆς, δηλῶν ἀνέκαθεν ἐξ ἀρχαίου ἔθους ἐπὶ τῆς
ἐκκλησίας τὴν ἀνάγνωσιν αὐτῆς ποιεῖσθαι. Λέγει γοῦν· Τὴν σήμερον οὖν
κυριακὴν ἁγίαν ἡμέραν διηγάγομεν, ἐν ᾗ ἀνέγνωμεν ὑμῶν τὴν ἐπιστολήν.
—Euseb. Hist. Eccles. Lib. iv. cap. 23. ed. Burton.]

[2 Hæc in multis etiam ecclesiis palam ac publice jam olim, et
apud nos quoque legi cognovimus.—Cent. 1. Lib. ii. 10. This is given
as a quotation from Eusebius, Lib. iii. cap. 16.]

[3 Præstat quidem, dum desunt qui scripturas populo viva voce rite
explicent, recitari populis pias et doctas homilias, quam ut nulla ei
doctrina atque exhortatio in administranda S. cœna exhibeatur.—Bucer. Script. Anglic. Bas. 1577, p. 465.]

[4 Est etiam nimis exiguus homiliarum numerus, paucique loci religionis nostræ his docentur. Cum itaque Dominus regnum hoc donarit
aliquot pereximiis concionatoribus, demandandum illis esset, ut Homilias plures, atque de præcipue necessariis locis componerent, quæ populis ab iis recitarentur pastoribus, qui ipsi meliores non possent
afferre.—Ibid. p. 466.]

[5 Vol. vii. 554, ed. 1838.]

[6 realm, Foxe.]

therefore, as none are read in the church but such as are sound, godly, and learned, and fit for the capacity of the people; and whiles they are not thrust into the church for canonical scriptures, but are read as godly expositions and interpretations of the same; and whiles they occupy no more time in the church than that which is usually left and spared, after the reading of the canonical scriptures, to preaching and exhortation; and whiles they are used, not to the contempt, derogation, or abandoning of preaching, but only to supply the want of it; no good man can mislike the use of them, but such contentious persons as defy all things which they devise not themselves.

And if it be said, there be already good homilies, and those also authorised, and likewise wholesome expositions of sundry parts of scripture to the same purpose: I grant there be so. But store is no sore. And as in meats, which are most dainty, if they come often to the table, we care not for them; so in sermons which are most excellent, if the same come often to the pulpit, they oftentimes please not: others are desired.

But, to end: these sermons of master Bullinger's are such as, whether they be used privately or read publicly, whether of ministers of the word or other God's children, certainly there will be found in them such light and instruction for the ignorant, such sweetness and spiritual comfort for consciences, such heavenly delights for souls, that as perfumes, the more they are chafed, the better they smell; and as golden mines, the deeper ye dig them, the more riches they shew; so these: the more diligently ye peruse them, the more delightfully they will please; and the deeper ye dig with daily study in their mines, the more golden matter they will deliver forth to the glory of God: to whom only be praise, for ever and ever. Amen.

FOUR GENERAL SYNODS OR COUNCILS[1].

SINCE the time of the apostles, many councils have been celebrated in sundry provinces. Those (councils) then were synods or assemblies of bishops and holy men, meeting together to consult for keeping the soundness of faith, the unity of doctrine, and the discipline and peace of the churches. Some of which sort the epistles of the blessed martyr Cyprian have made us acquainted withal[2].

The Nicene
council.

The first general or universal synod, therefore, is reported to have been called by that most holy emperor Constantine in the city of Nice, the year of our Lord 324[3], against Arius and his partners, which denied the natural deity of our Lord Jesus Christ. And thither came there out of all nations under heaven two hundred and eighteen[4] bishops and excellent learned men, who wrote the Creed commonly called the Nicene Creed.

Hitherto the creed of the Apostles sufficed, and had been sufficient to the church of Christ even in the time of Constantine: for all men confess that all the churches used no other creed than that of the Apostles (which we have made mention of and expounded in the first Decade), wherewith they were content throughout the whole world. But

[1 In his Latin Preface, Bullinger states that he prefixed to his Decades these Creeds of the most ancient councils and orthodox Fathers, that it might manifestly appear that the doctrine and faith of the Protestant churches, which was by many ill-reported of and most undeservedly condemned as heretical, was perfectly agreeable with the teaching of the apostles and of the primitive church.]

[2 viz. Councils at *Rome* and *Carthage* principally, in the matters of Novatus and Novatian, and concerning receiving back the lapsed into the communion of the church, and the validity of baptism by heretics.]

[3 More correctly, A.D. 325.—Mosheim, Eccles. Hist. Vol. I. p. 386, n. 1. ed. Soames, 1845.] ·

[4 The number should be 318: see Mosheim, ibid.; and Grier's Epit. of Gen. Councils, p. 33.]

for because in the days of Constantine the Great that wicked blasphemer Arius sprang up, corrupting the pureness of christian faith, and perverting the simple truth of doctrine taught by the apostles; the ministers of the churches were compelled of very necessity to set themselves against that deceiver, and in publishing a creed to shew forth and declare out of the canonical scriptures the true and ancient[5] confession of faith, condemning those novelties brought in of Arius. For in the creeds set forth by the other three general councils presently following neither was any thing changed in the doctrine of the apostles, neither was there any new thing added, which the churches of Christ had not before taken and believed out of the holy scripture: but the ancient truth, being wisely made manifest by confessions made of faith, was profitably and godly set against the new corruptions of heretics. Yet were the writings of the prophets and apostles the spring, the guide, the rule, and judge in all these councils; neither did the fathers suffer any thing to be done there according to their own minds[6]. And yet I speak not of every constitution and canon, but namely[7] of those ancient confessions alone, to which we do attribute so much as is permitted by the canonical scripture, which we confess to be the only rule how to judge, to speak, and do.

The second general council was held in the royal city Constantinople, under Gratian the emperor, in the year of our Lord 384. There were assembled in that synod (as witnesseth Prosperus Aquitanicus[8]) one hundred and eighty fathers or bishops, which condemned Macedonius and Eudoxius denying the Holy Ghost to be God[9].

The council of Constantinople.

And about the year of our Lord 434, in the very same

The council of Ephesus.

[5 Veram, id est veterem.—Lat.]

[6 See Goode's Divine Rule of Faith and Practice, Vol. I. pp. 141-156, and Vol. II. pp. 327-360.]

[7 specially; Lat. significanter.]

[8 Synodus Patrum CLXXX apud Constantinopolim celebrata est contra Macedonium, Spiritum-sanctum Deum esse negantem.—Prosper. Aquit. Chron. Opp. Par. 1711, col 735.]

[9 This Second General Council was assembled, A.D. 381, by the Emperor Theodosius the Elder, and was attended by 150 bishops, &c.—Mosheim, Eccles. Hist. Vol. I. p. 404. For the heresies of Macedonius and Eudoxius, see Routh, Scrip. Eccles. Opuscul. Vol. I. p. 417, &c.; and Hammond's Canons of the Church, p. 53.]

year that the blessed father Augustine died, when that godly prince Theodosius the Great was emperor, there came together at Ephesus the third synod, of two hundred priests or thereabouts, against Nestorius[1], which tare the mystery of the incarnation and taught that there were two Sons, the one of God, the other of man: whom this council condemned, together with the Pelagians[2], helpers of this doctrine as cousin to their own.

The council of Calcedon.

The fourth general council was assembled at Chalcedon, in the year of our Lord 454, under the emperor Martian; where six hundred and thirty fathers were gathered together, who according to the scriptures condemned Eutyches, which confounded the natures in Christ for the unity of the person[3].

Beda de ratione temporum[4], and many other writers, do join with these four universal councils two general synods more, the fifth and the sixth, celebrated at Constantinople. For the fifth was gathered together when Justinian was emperor, against Theodorus and all heretics, about the year of our Lord 552[5]. The sixth came together under Constantine the son of Constantius, in the year of our Lord 682. And there were assembled two hundred and eighty-nine bishops[6] against the Monothelites. But there was nothing determined in these synods, but what is to be found in the four first councils: wherefore I have noted nothing out of them.

[1 This council of Ephesus was held, A.D. 431, under Theodosius the Younger (not the Great).—Mosheim, Vol. I. p. 472; Grier, p. 74. For the heresy of Nestorius, see Hooker's Eccles. Pol. Book v. § 52. Augustine died August 28, 430.—Mosheim, Vol. I. p. 338, Soames' note.]

[2 una cum multis Pelagianis.—Lat.]

[3 The year of the assembling of this council was 451.—Mosheim, Vol. I. p. 481. For the heresy of Eutyches, see Hooker, Book v. § 52-54.]

[4 Bedæ de Sex Ætatibus Mundi, sive Chronicon, libellus. Opp. Tom. III. p. 116. Col. Agrip. 1612.]

[5 The year was 553.—Mosheim, Vol. II. p. 45; Hammond's Canons of the church, p. 113. "Contra Theodorum, et omnes hæreticos," are the words of Bede.]

[6 This council was held A.D. 680, under the Emperor Constantine Pogonatus. The number of attending bishops increased to near 200. —Mosheim, Vol. II. p. 101; Hammond's Canons, p. 125.]

THE NICENE CREED TAKEN OUT OF THE ECCLESI-
ASTICAL AND TRIPARTITE HISTORY.

WE believe in one God, the Father Almighty, maker of
of all things visible and invisible. And in one Lord Jesus
Christ, the Son of God, the only-begotten Son of the Father,
that is, of the substance of the Father; God of God, light of
light, very God of very God; begotten, not made, being of
the same essence and substance with the Father; by whom
all things were made, which are in heaven, and which are in
earth: who for us men and for our salvation came down,
was incarnate and manned (was made man). He suffered, and
rose again the third day, he ascended into heaven, and shall
come to judge the quick and the dead. And (we believe) in
the Holy Ghost. As for those that say, it was sometime
when he was not, and before he was born he was not; and
which say, because he was made of things not being (of
nothing) or of another substance, that therefore the Son of
God is either created, or turned, or changed, them doth the
holy catholic and apostolic church curse or excommunicate[3].

[7 Πιστεύομεν εἰς ἕνα Θεὸν, Πατέρα παντοκράτορα, πάντων ὁρατῶν
τε καὶ ἀοράτων ποιητήν. Καὶ εἰς ἕνα Κύριον Ἰησοῦν Χριστὸν, τὸν Υἱὸν
τοῦ Θεοῦ, γεννηθέντα ἐκ τοῦ Πατρὸς, μονογενῆ, τουτέστιν ἐκ τῆς οὐσίας
τοῦ Πατρός· Θεὸν ἐκ Θεοῦ, φῶς ἐκ φωτὸς, Θεὸν ἀληθινὸν ἐκ Θεοῦ ἀλη-
θινοῦ· γεννηθέντα, οὐ ποιηθέντα· ὁμοούσιον τῷ Πατρί· δι᾽ οὗ τὰ πάντα
ἐγένετο, τά τε ἐν τῷ οὐρανῷ, καὶ τὰ ἐν τῇ γῇ· τὸν δι᾽ ἡμᾶς τοὺς ἀνθρώπους καὶ διὰ τὴν ἡμετέραν σωτηρίαν κατελθόντα, καὶ σαρκωθέντα, ἐναν-
θρωπήσαντα, παθόντα καὶ ἀναστάντα τῇ τρίτῃ ἡμέρᾳ, ἀνελθόντα εἰς τοὺς
οὐρανούς· ἐρχόμενον κρῖναι ζῶντας καὶ νεκρούς. Καὶ εἰς τὸ Πνεῦμα τὸ
Ἅγιον. Τοὺς δὲ λέγοντας ἦν ποτὲ ὅτε οὐκ ἦν, ἢ οὐκ ἦν πρὶν γεννηθῆναι,
ἢ ἐξ οὐκ ὄντων ἐγένετο, ἢ ἐξ ἑτέρας ὑποστάσεως ἢ οὐσίας φάσκοντας
εἶναι, ἢ κτιστὸν, ἢ τρεπτὸν ἢ ἀλλοιωτὸν, τὸν Υἱὸν τοῦ Θεοῦ, τούτους ἀνα-
θεματίζει ἡ καθολικὴ καὶ ἀποστολικὴ τοῦ Θεοῦ Ἐκκλησία.—Socr. Hist.
Eccl. Lib. I. c. 8. ed. Reading. Cantab. 1720. P.]

THE CREED OF THE COUNCIL HELD AT CONSTANTIN-OPLE, TAKEN OUT OF A CERTAIN COPY WRITTEN IN GREEK[1] AND LATIN[2].

I BELIEVE[3] in one God, the Father Almighty, maker of heaven and earth, and of all things visible and invisible. And in one Lord Jesus Christ, the only-begotten Son of God, born of his Father before all worlds, light of light, very God of very God, begotten, not made, being of the same sub-

[1 Πιστεύομεν εἰς ἕνα Θεόν, Πατέρα παντοκράτορα, ποιητὴν οὐρανοῦ καὶ γῆς, ὁρατῶν τε πάντων καὶ ἀοράτων. Καὶ εἰς ἕνα Κύριον Ἰησοῦν Χριστόν, τὸν Υἱὸν τοῦ Θεοῦ τὸν μονογενῆ, τὸν ἐκ τοῦ Πατρὸς γεννηθέντα πρὸ πάντων τῶν αἰώνων· φῶς ἐκ φωτός, Θεὸν ἀληθινὸν ἐκ Θεοῦ ἀληθινοῦ· γεννηθέντα οὐ ποιηθέντα, ὁμοούσιον τῷ Πατρί· δι' οὗ τὰ πάντα ἐγένετο· τὸν δι' ἡμᾶς τοὺς ἀνθρώπους καὶ διὰ τὴν ἡμετέραν σωτηρίαν κατελθόντα ἐκ τῶν οὐρανῶν, καὶ σαρκωθέντα ἐκ Πνεύματος Ἁγίου, καὶ Μαρίας τῆς παρθένου, καὶ ἐνανθρωπήσαντα· σταυρωθέντα τε ὑπὲρ ἡμῶν ἐπὶ Ποντίου Πιλάτου, καὶ παθόντα, καὶ ταφέντα, καὶ ἀναστάντα τῇ τρίτῃ ἡμέρᾳ κατὰ τὰς γραφάς· καὶ ἀνελθόντα εἰς τοὺς οὐρανούς, καὶ καθεζόμενον ἐκ δεξιῶν τοῦ Πατρός· καὶ πάλιν ἐρχόμενον μετὰ δόξης κρῖναι ζῶντας καὶ νεκρούς· οὗ τῆς βασιλείας οὐκ ἔσται τέλος. Καὶ εἰς τὸ Πνεῦμα τὸ Ἅγιον, τὸ Κύριον, καὶ τὸ ζωοποιόν, τὸ ἐκ τοῦ Πατρὸς ἐκπορευόμενον, τὸ σὺν Πατρὶ καὶ Υἱῷ συμπροσκυνούμενον, καὶ συνδοξαζόμενον, τὸ λαλῆσαν διὰ τῶν προφητῶν· εἰς μίαν ἁγίαν καθολικὴν καὶ ἀποστολικὴν ἐκκλησίαν· ὁμολογοῦμεν ἓν βάπτισμα εἰς ἄφεσιν ἁμαρτιῶν· προσδοκῶμεν ἀνάστασιν νεκρῶν, καὶ ζωὴν τοῦ μέλλοντος αἰῶνος. Ἀμήν. P.]

[2 Credimus in unum Deum Patrem omnipotentem, factorem cœli et terræ, visibilium omnium et invisibilium: Et in unum Dominum Jesum Christum, Filium Dei, natum ex Patre ante omnia secula, Deum verum de Deo vero, natum, non factum, consubstantialem Patri: per quem omnia facta sunt, qui propter nos homines et salutem nostram descendit de cœlis, et incarnatus est de Spiritu Sancto ex Maria virgine, et inhumanatus est, et crucifixus est pro nobis sub Pontio Pilato, et sepultus est, et resurrexit tertia die, ascendit in cœlos, sedet ad dexteram Patris, iterum venturus est cum gloria judicare vivos et mortuos, cujus regni non erit finis: Et in Spiritum Sanctum, Dominum et vivificantem, ex Patre procedentem, cum Patre et Filio adorandum et conglorificandum, qui loquutus est per sanctos prophetas: Et unam sanctam catholicam et apostolicam ecclesiam: confitemur unum baptisma in remissionem peccatorum; exspectamus resurrectionem mortuorum, vitam futuri seculi. Amen.—Routh, Scriptor. Eccles. Opuscul. Vol. I. pp. 398, 9. Oxon. 1840.]

[3 Bullinger's copy reads Credo; confiteor; and exspecto; and Spiritum Sanctum Dominum vivificatorem.]

stance with the Father, by whom all things were made : who for us men, and for our salvation, came down from heaven, and was incarnate by the Holy Ghost and the virgin Mary, and was made man. He was also crucified for us under Pontius Pilate. He suffered and was buried: and he rose the third day, according to the scriptures. And he ascended into heaven, and sitteth on the right hand of God the Father: and he shall come again with glory to judge the quick and the dead; whose kingdom shall have no end. And (I believe) in the Holy Ghost, the Lord and giver of life, who, proceeding from the Father, is to be worshipped and glorified together with the Father and the Son ; who spake by the prophets : in one catholic and apostolic church. I confess one baptism for the remission of sins. I look for the resurrection of the dead; and the life of the world to come.

THE CONFESSION OF FAITH MADE BY THE SYNOD AT EPHESUS.

INASMUCH as because here I note all things briefly, I could not in writing place with these that large synodal epistle written by St Cyril to Nestorius[4], wherein is contained the full consent of the general council held at Ephesus. I have therefore rather chosen out of the 28th epistle of the same Cyril a short confession sent to the synod, and allowed by the whole council. Before the confession are set these words : " Even as in the beginning we have heard out of the divine scriptures, and the tradition of the holy fathers; so will we briefly speak, not adding any thing at all to the faith set forth by the holy fathers in Nice. For that doth suffice as well to all knowledge of godliness, as also to the utter forsaking of any heretical overthwartness."

And a little after this, the confession is set down in these words : " We acknowledge our Lord Jesus Christ, the only-begotten Son of God, to be perfect God and perfect man, of a reasonable soul and body ; born of the Father according to his Godhead before the worlds, and the very same according to his humanity born in the latter times of the virgin Mary

[4 See Routh, Scriptor. Eccles. Opusc. Vol. II. p. 17, &c. The epistle was written A.D. 430.]

for us, and for our salvation : for there was made an uniting of the two natures.   Wherefore we confess both one Christ, one Son, and one Lord.   And according to this understanding of the unconfounded unity, we acknowledge the holy virgin to be the mother of God, because that God the Word was incarnate and made man, and by the very conception gathered to himself a body taken of her.   But for the speeches uttered by the evangelists and apostles touching the Lord, we know that the divines do by reason of the two natures divide them, so yet as that they belong to one person ; and that they do refer them, some, because they are more agreeable to the Divinity, to the Godhead of Christ, and other some, (because they are) base, to his humanity."

To this confession Cyril addeth these words : " When we had read these holy words of yours (even in the synod to which the confession was sent), and did perceive that we ourselves were of the same opinion (for there is one Lord, one faith, and one baptism), we glorified God the Saviour of all (men), rejoicing together in ourselves, for that the churches both ours and yours do believe agreeably to the scriptures of God and tradition of the holy fathers[1]."

[1 .... ὡς ἄνωθεν ἔκ τε τῶν θείων γραφῶν ἔκ τε τῆς παραδόσεως τῶν ἁγίων πατέρων παρειληφότες ἐσχήκαμεν, διὰ βραχέων ἐροῦμεν, οὐδὲν τὸ συνόλον προστιθέντες τῇ τῶν ἁγίων πατέρων τῶν ἐν Νικαίᾳ ἐκτεθείσῃ πίστει· ὡς γὰρ ἔφθημεν εἰρηκότες, πρὸς πᾶσαν ἐξαρκεῖ καὶ εὐσεβείας γνῶσιν, πάσης καὶ αἱρετικῆς κακοδοξίας ἀποκήρυξιν.... Ὁμολογοῦμεν τοιγαροῦν τὸν Κύριον ἡμῶν Ἰησοῦν Χριστόν, τὸν Υἱὸν τοῦ Θεοῦ τὸν μονογενῆ, Θεὸν τέλειον καὶ ἄνθρωπον τέλειον ἐκ ψυχῆς λογικῆς καὶ σώματος· πρὸ αἰώνων μὲν ἐκ τοῦ Πατρὸς γεννηθέντα κατὰ τὴν Θεότητα, ἐπ᾽ ἐσχάτων δὲ τῶν ἡμερῶν τὸν αὐτὸν δι᾽ ἡμᾶς καὶ διὰ τὴν ἡμετέραν σωτηρίαν ἐκ Μαρίας τῆς παρθένου κατὰ τὴν ἀνθρωπότητα· ὁμοούσιον τῷ Πατρὶ τὸν αὐτὸν κατὰ τὴν Θεότητα, καὶ ὁμοούσιον ἡμῖν κατὰ τὴν ἀνθρωπότητα· δύο γὰρ φύσεων ἕνωσις γέγονε· διὸ ἕνα Χριστόν, ἕνα Υἱόν, ἕνα Κύριον ὁμολογοῦμεν.   Κατὰ ταύτην τὴν τῆς ἀσυγχύτου ἑνώσεως ἔννοιαν, ὁμολογοῦμεν τὴν ἁγίαν παρθένον Θεοτόκον, διὰ τὸ τὸν Θεὸν Λόγον σαρκωθῆναι, καὶ ἐνανθρωπῆσαι, καὶ ἐξ αὐτῆς τῆς συλλήψεως ἑνῶσαι ἑαυτῷ τὸν ἐξ αὐτῆς ληφθέντα ναόν.   Τὰς δὲ εὐαγγελικὰς καὶ ἀποστολικὰς περὶ τοῦ Κυρίου φωνὰς, ἴσμεν τοὺς θεολόγους ἄνδρας τὰς μὲν κοινοποιοῦντας, ὡς ἐφ᾽ ἑνὸς προσώπου, τὰς δὲ διαιροῦντας ὡς ἐπὶ δύο φύσεων· καὶ τὰς μὲν θεοπρεπεῖς κατὰ τὴν Θεότητα τοῦ Χριστοῦ, τὰς δὲ ταπεινὰς κατὰ τὴν ἀνθρωπότητα αὐτοῦ παραδίδοντας.—Ταύταις ὑμῶν ἐντυχόντες ταῖς ἱεραῖς φωναῖς, οὕτω τε καὶ ἑαυτοὺς φρονοῦντας εὑρίσκοντες, (εἷς γὰρ Κύριος, μία πίστις, ἐν βάπτισμα,) ἐδοξάσαμεν τὸν τῶν ὅλων Σωτῆρα Θεόν· ἀλ-

A CONFESSION OF FAITH MADE BY THE COUNCIL OF
　CHALCEDON, TAKEN OUT OF THE BOOK OF
　ISIDORE.

AFTER the rehearsal of the creeds set forth by the
synods of Nice and Constantinople, with a few words put
between, straightway the holy council of Chalcedon doth prescribe (their confession) in these words[2].

"We therefore, agreeing with the holy fathers, do with
one accord teach to confess one and the same Son, our Lord
Jesus Christ, and him (to be) perfect God in the Deity, and
the same also very man of a reasonable soul and body:
touching his Godhead (being) of one nature with his Father;
and the same, as touching his manhood, of one nature with
us, like to us in all things except sin: touching his Godhead,
born of his Father before the worlds; and the same in the
latter days made man for us and for our salvation. (We
teach) to consider, that he is one and the same Christ, the
Son, (our) Lord, the only-begotten Son, in two natures, neither

λήλοις συγχαίροντες, ὅτι ταῖς θεοπνεύστοις γραφαῖς καὶ τῇ παραδόσει
τῶν ἁγίων ἡμῶν πατέρων συμβαίνουσαν ἔχουσι πίστιν αἵ τε παρὰ ἡμῖν
καὶ αἱ παρὰ ὑμῖν ἐκκλησίαι.—Cyril. Alex. Opp. Par. 1638, Tom. v. P.
2, p. 106.]

[2 Ἑπόμενοι τοίνυν τοῖς ἁγίοις πατράσιν, ἕνα καὶ τὸν αὐτὸν ὁμολογεῖν
υἱὸν τὸν Κύριον ἡμῶν Ἰησοῦν Χριστὸν συμφώνως ἅπαντες ἐκδιδάσκομεν,
τέλειον τὸν αὐτὸν ἐν Θεότητι, καὶ τέλειον τὸν αὐτὸν ἐν ἀνθρωπότητι, Θεὸν
ἀληθῶς καὶ ἄνθρωπον ἀληθῶς τὸν αὐτὸν ἐκ ψυχῆς λογικῆς καὶ σώματος·
ὁμοούσιον τῷ Πατρὶ κατὰ τὴν Θεότητα, καὶ ὁμοούσιον τὸν αὐτὸν ἡμῖν κατὰ
τὴν ἀνθρωπότητα, κατὰ πάντα ὅμοιον ἡμῖν, χωρὶς ἁμαρτίας· πρὸ αἰώνων
μὲν ἐκ τοῦ Πατρὸς γεννηθέντα κατὰ τὴν Θεότητα, ἐπ᾽ ἐσχάτων δὲ τῶν
ἡμερῶν τὸν αὐτὸν δι᾽ ἡμᾶς καὶ διὰ τὴν ἡμετέραν σωτηρίαν ἐκ Μαρίας
τῆς παρθένου τῆς Θεοτόκου κατὰ τὴν ἀνθρωπότητα, ἕνα καὶ τὸν αὐτὸν
Χριστὸν, Υἱὸν, Κύριον, μονογενῆ, ἐκ δύο φύσεων ἀσυγχύτως, ἀτρέπτως,
ἀδιαιρέτως, ἀχωρίστως γνωριζόμενον· οὐδαμοῦ τῆς τῶν φύσεων διαφορᾶς
ἀνῃρημένης διὰ τὴν ἕνωσιν, σωζομένης δὲ μᾶλλον τῆς ἰδιότητος ἑκατέρας
φύσεως, καὶ εἰς ἓν πρόσωπον καὶ μίαν ὑπόστασιν συντρεχούσης, οὐκ εἰς
δύο πρόσωπα μεριζόμενον ἢ διαιρούμενον, ἀλλ᾽ ἕνα καὶ τὸν αὐτὸν Υἱὸν
καὶ μονογενῆ, Θεὸν, Λόγον, Κύριον Ἰησοῦν Χριστόν· καθάπερ ἄνωθεν οἱ
προφῆται περὶ αὐτοῦ, καὶ αὐτὸς ἡμᾶς ὁ Κύριος Ἰησοῦς Χριστὸς ἐξεπαί-
δευσε, καὶ τὸ τῶν Πατέρων ἡμῖν παραδέδωκε σύμβολον. Τούτων τοίνυν
μετὰ πάσης πανταχόθεν ἀκριβείας τε καὶ ἐμμελείας παρ᾽ ἡμῶν διατυπω-
θέντων, ὥρισεν ἡ ἁγία καὶ οἰκουμενικὴ σύνοδος, ἑτέραν πίστιν μηδενὶ ἐξεῖναι
προφέρειν, ἢ γοῦν συγγράφειν, ἢ συντιθέναι, ἢ φρονεῖν, ἢ διδάσκειν ἑτέροις.
—Labb. Conc. Par. 1671. Tom. IV. fol. 566, 7. P.]

2—2

confounded, nor changed, nor divided, nor separated; and
that the difference of the natures is not to be taken away
because of the unity, but rather, the property of both (his)
natures remaining whole and meeting together in one person
and one substance, that he is not parted or divided into two
persons, but is one and the same Son, the only-begotten Son,
God, the Word, (our) Lord Jesus Christ: even as the prophets
from the beginning (have witnessed) of him, as he himself hath
instructed us, and the confession of the fathers hath taught us.
These things therefore being ordered by us with all care and
diligence, the holy and universal synod doth determine, that
it should not be lawful for any man to profess any other
faith, or else to write, to teach, or speak to the contrary."

THAT THE DECREE OF THE SYNOD OF CHALCEDON IS NOT CONTRARY TO THE DOCTRINE OF THE BLESSED BISHOP CYRIL, TAKEN OUT OF THE FIFTH BOOK OF THE HOLY MARTYR VIGILIUS AGAINST EUTYCHES[1].

But now let us consider the last article in the decree
of the synod of Chalcedon: "We confess that Christ our Lord,

[1 Sed jam ultimum decreti capitulum videamus ex decreto synodi
Chalcedonensis: "Unum eundemque Christum Dominum unigenitum
(confitemur) in duabus naturis inconfuse, inconvertibiliter, indivise, in-
separabiliter cognoscendum, nusquam duarum naturarum diversitate
evacuata propter unionem, salva magis proprietate utriusque naturæ,
in unam personam atque substantiam convenientibus, non ut in duas
personas divisum aut segregatum, sed unum eundemque unigenitum
Filium Deum Verbum Dominum Jesum Christum." In hoc capitulo
hoc eis displicet, cur dixerint, "Salva proprietate utriusque naturæ;" vel,
"Non evacuata naturarum differentia:" quæ ut firma esse perdoceant,
consueta verborum prolixitate et inani assertione utentes, multa de
Cyrilli capitulis interponunt testimonia, quibus ille non duas in Christo
negat naturas, sed unam docet esse personam. Ne igitur soli eos
nostra disputatione refutemus, Cyrilli etiam nos verba ponamus; ut
quomodo Cyrillo teste nituntur, Cyrillo teste vincantur. Ex synodicis
Cyrilli ad Nestorium literis hæc sunt: "Non enim dicimus," inquit, "quod
divina natura conversa vel immutata facta sit caro, nec quod in totum
hominem, quod ex anima est et corpore, transformata sit; sed illud
magis, quod carnem animatam rationabile sibi copulaverit Verbum sub-
stantialiter, ineffabiliter et indeprehensibiliter factus sit homo, et nun-
cupatus sit etiam Filius hominis, non nudæ tantummodo voluntatis, sed

the only-begotten Son, is to be understood to be one and the self-same in (his) two natures, neither confounded, nor changed, nor divided, nor separated, not making void the difference of the two natures because of the unity, but keeping sound the property of both natures coming together into one person and substance, not as being divided or separated, but (as being) one and the same only-begotten Son, God, the Word, (our) Lord Jesus."

In this article this displeaseth them, because they said, " The property of both natures remaining sound ;" or, " The difference of the natures not being made void." And that they may persuade us that those things (which they mislike) are assuredly so, they, using their accustomed largeness of words and vain assertions, do bring in many testimonies out of the articles of Cyril, wherein he denieth not the two natures in Christ, but teacheth that there is but one person. To the intent therefore that we may not confute them with our disputation alone, let us set down also the words of Cyril, that even as they lean to the testimony of Cyril, so by the testimony of Cyril they may be overcome. In the synodal epistles of Cyril to Nestorius thus it is (written) : " For we do not affirm," saith he, " that the divine nature is turned or changed into flesh, nor yet that it is transformed into the

nec assumptione sola personæ, sed quod diversæ et quodammodo naturæ in unum convenerint. Unus tamen ex ambabus Christus et Filius, non evacuata aut sublata diversitate naturarum per conjunctionem; sed quia simul nobis effecerunt unum Dominum et Christum et Filium, id est, Divinitas et Humanitas per arcanam illam ineffabilemque copulationem ad unitatem." Quid hoc manifestius ? quid clarius ad consonantiam synodici decreti Chalcedonensis ex literis Cyrilli potuit demonstrari ? Ecce nec dicta dictis, nec sententiæ sententiis adversantur; sed sicut uno fidei sensu, ita iisdem pene usi sunt verbis. Dixit sancta synodus, Nusquam duarum naturarum diversitate evacuata: dixit beatus Cyrillus, Non evacuata aut sublata diversitate naturarum per conjunctionem. Dixit sancta synodus, Utrisque naturis in una persona convenientibus: dixit beatus Cyrillus, Non nudæ tantummodo voluntatis, sed nec assumptione sola personæ, sed quod diversæ quodammodo naturæ in unum convenerint. Dixit sancta synodus, Non in duas personas divisum, sed unum eundemque Christum: dixit beatus Cyrillus, Unus tamen ex ambabus, id est, naturis Christus Filius. Et iterum, Sed quia simul nobis effecerunt unum Dominum Christum et Filium, id est, Divinitas et Humanitas, &c.—Vigilius contra Eutychen. Tigur. 1539. p. 97.]

whole man, which consisteth of the body and soul; but we say rather, that the reasonable soul hath coupled to itself the substance of living flesh, that it is unspeakably and unconceivably made man, and is also called the Son of man, not of bare will alone, nor by the only taking on of the person, but because the two natures do after a certain manner come together in one, so that there is one Christ, and one Son of both (the natures) by joining them in one, not in making void or taking away the difference of the natures, but because they, that is, the Godhead and the manhood together, by that hidden and unspeakable knitting to the unity, have made to us one Lord, and (one) Christ, and (one) Son." What could be spoken more plainly than this? What could be shewed more clearly out of the epistles of Cyril to agree with the determination of the council of Chalcedon? For see, neither are words to words, nor sentence to sentence any thing contrary: but even as they had one meaning of faith, so use they in a manner the self-same words.

The holy synod said, "The difference of the two natures being no where made void;" St Cyril said, "The difference of the natures not being made void, or taken away, by joining them together." The holy synod said, "Both the natures meeting together in one person;" St Cyril saith, "Not of a bare will only, nor yet by the only taking on of a person, but because the two natures after a sort do meet together in one." The holy synod said, "Not being divided into two persons, but being one and the same Christ;" St Cyril said, "So that of two, that is to say (of two) natures in one Christ the Son;" and again, "Because they, that is, the Godhead and the manhood together, have made to us one Lord, (one) Christ, and (one) Son," &c.

THE CREED OF THE FIRST COUNCIL HELD AT TOLEDO, WHEN HONORIUS AND ARCADIUS WERE EMPERORS, TAKEN OUT OF THE BOOK OF ISIDORE[1].

About the year of our Lord 400.

WE believe in one very God, the Father Almighty, and the Son, and the Holy Ghost, maker of things visible and

[1 Credimus in unum Deum Patrem, et Filium et Spiritum Sanctum, visibilium et invisibilium factorem, per quem creata sunt omnia in

invisible, by whom all things were made in heaven and in earth. We believe, that there is one God and one Trinity of the divine substance. And that the Father himself is not the Son, but that he hath a Son, which is not the Father. That the Son is not the Father, but that the Son of God is of the nature of the Father. And also that the Holy Ghost is the Comforter, which neither is the Father himself, nor the Son, but proceeding from the Father and the Son. The Father therefore is unbegotten, the Son begotten, the Comforter not begotten but proceeding from the Father and the Son. The Father is he from whom this voice was heard out of heaven, "This is my beloved Son, in whom I am well pleased: hear him." The Son is he which said, "I went out from the Father, and came from God into the world." The Comforter is the Holy Ghost, of whom the Son said, "Unless I go away to the Father, the Comforter shall not

cœlo et in terra: hunc unum Deum et hanc unam esse divinæ substantiæ Trinitatem: Patrem autem non esse ipsum Filium, sed habere Filium qui Pater non sit: Filium non esse Patrem, sed Filium Dei de Patris esse natura: Spiritum quoque Paracletum esse, qui nec Pater sit ipse nec Filius, sed a Patre Filioque procedens. Est ergo ingenitus Pater, genitus Filius, non genitus Paracletus sed a Patre Filioque procedens. Pater est, cujus vox hæc est audita de cœlis, *Hic est Filius meus, in quo mihi bene complacui: ipsum audite.* Filius est qui ait, *Ego a Patre exivi, et a Deo veni in hunc mundum.* Paracletus Spiritus est, de quo Filius ait, *Nisi abiero ego ad Patrem, Paracletus non veniet ad vos.* Hanc Trinitatem personis distinctam, substantia unitam, virtute et potestate et majestate indivisibilem, indifferentem; præter hanc nullam credimus divinam esse naturam, vel angeli, vel spiritus vel virtutis alicujus, quæ Deus esse credatur. Hunc igitur Filium Dei, Deum natum a Patre ante omne omnino principium, sanctificasse uterum Mariæ Virginis, atque ex ea verum hominem sine virili generatum semine suscepisse, duabus duntaxat naturis, id est, Deitatis et carnis, in unam convenientibus omnino personam, id est, Dominum nostrum Jesum Christum: nec imaginarium corpus aut phantasmatis alicujus in eo fuisse, sed solidum atque verum: hunc et esurisse et sitisse et doluisse et flevisse et omnes corporis injurias pertulisse: postremo a Judæis crucifixum et sepultum tertia die resurrexisse: conversatum postmodum eum discipulis suis, et quadragesima post resurrectionem die ad cœlum ascendisse. Hunc Filium hominis etiam Dei Filium dici. Filium autem Dei Dominum Filium hominis appellamus. Resurrectionem vero futuram humanæ credimus carnis, animam autem hominis non divinam esse substantiam, aut Dei parem, sed creaturam dicimus divina voluntate creatam.—Labb. Concil. Par. 1671. Tom. II. col. 1227. P.]

come." We believe in this Trinity differing in persons (but) all one in substance, not divided nor differing in strength, power and majesty; (and) we believe, that beside this there is no divine nature, either of angel, or of spirit, or any power, which may be believed to be God.

We therefore believe, that this Son of God, being God begotten of his Father altogether before all beginning, did sanctify the womb of the virgin Mary, and that of her he took upon him very man, begotten without the seed of man, the two natures only, that is, of the Godhead and manhood, coming together into one person only, that is, our Lord Jesus Christ. Neither (do we believe) that there was in him an imagined or any phantastical body, but a sound and very (body), and that he both hungered, and thirsted, and taught[1], and wept, and suffered all the damages of the body: last of all, that he was crucified of the Jews, and was buried, and rose again the third day, and afterward was conversant with his disciples, and the fortieth day after his resurrection ascended into heaven. This Son of man, and also the Son of God, we call both the Son of God and the Son of man.

We believe verily, that there shall be a resurrection of the flesh of mankind; and that the soul of man is not of the divine substance, or of God the Father, but is a creature created by the will of God.

THE CREED OF THE FOURTH COUNCIL KEPT AT TOLEDO, TAKEN OUT OF THE BOOK OF ISIDORE[2].

As we have learned of the holy fathers, that the Father, and the Son, and the Holy Ghost are of one Godhead and

---

[1 "Docuisse" for "doluisse" is read in the Latin of Bullinger, by mistake: it ought to be "sorrowed."]

[2 Secundum divinas scripturas, doctrinam quam a sanctis patribus accepimus, Patrem et Filium et Spiritum Sanctum unius Deitatis atque substantiæ confitemur: in personarum diversitate Trinitatem credentes, in Divinitate unitatem prædicantes: nec personas confundimus, nec substantiam separamus. Patrem a nullo factum vel genitum dicimus: Filium a Patre non factum sed genitum asserimus: Spiritum vero Sanctum non creatum, nec genitum, sed procedentem ex Patre et Filio profitemur. Ipsum autem Dominum nostrum Jesum Christum, Dei Filium et Creatorem omnium, ex substantia Patris ante secula

substance, (so) is our confession, believing the Trinity in the difference of persons, and openly professing the unity in the Godhead; neither confound we the persons, nor divide the substance. We say, that the Father is made or begotten of none: we affirm, that the Son is not made, but begotten of the Father: and we profess that the Holy Ghost is neither created nor begotten, but proceeding from the Father and the Son. And (we confess) that the Lord himself Jesus Christ the Son of God, and the maker of all things, begotten of the substance of his Father before all the worlds, came down from his Father in the latter times for the redemption of the world, who (nevertheless) never ceased to be with the Father. For he was incarnate by the Holy Ghost and the glorious virgin Mary the holy mother of God, and of her was born alone the same Lord Jesus Christ, one in the Trinity, being perfect (man) in soul and body, taking on man without sin, being still what he was, taking to him what he was not: touching his Godhead equal with the Father, (and) inferior to his Father touching his manhood, having in one person the property of two natures. For (there are) in him two natures, God and man: and yet not two Sons or two Gods, but the same (God and man) one person in both natures, who

genitum, descendisse ultimo tempore pro redemptione mundi a Patre, qui nunquam desiit esse cum Patre. Incarnatus est enim ex Spiritu Sancto, et sancta gloriosa Dei genitrice Virgine Maria, et natus ex ipsa, solus autem Dominus Jesus Christus; unus de sancta Trinitate, anima et carne perfectum sine peccato suscipiens hominem, manens quod erat, assumens quod non erat: æqualis Patri secundum Divinitatem, minor Patre secundum humanitatem: habens in una Persona duarum naturarum proprietatem: naturæ enim in illo duæ, Deus et homo, non autem duo Filii et Dei duo, sed idem una Persona in utraque natura, perferens passionem et mortem pro nostra salute, non in virtute Divinitatis, sed infirmitate humanitatis. Descendit ad inferos, ut sanctos qui ibidem tenebantur erueret: devictoque mortis imperio resurrexit: assumptus deinde in cœlum, venturus est in futurum ad judicium vivorum et mortuorum: cujus nos morte et sanguine mundati remissionem peccatorum consecuti sumus: resuscitandi ab eo in die novissima in ea qua nunc vivimus carne: et in ea qua resurrexit idem Dominus forma percepturi ab ipso, alii pro justitiæ meritis vitam æternam, alii pro peccatis supplicii æterni sententiam. Hæc est catholicæ ecclesiæ fides: hanc confessionem conservamus atque tenemus: quam quisquis firmissime custodierit, perpetuam salutem habebit.
—Labb. Concil. Par. 1671. Tom. v. 1703. P.]

suffered grief and death for our salvation, not in the power of his Godhead, but in the infirmity of his manhood.   He descended to them below to draw out by force the saints which were held there.   And he rose again, the power of death being overcome.   He was taken up into the heavens, from whence he shall come to judge the quick and the dead. By whose death and blood we being made clean have obtained forgiveness of (our) sins, and shall be raised up again by him in the last day in the same flesh wherein we now live, (and) in that manner wherein the same (our) Lord did rise again, (and) shall receive of him, some in reward of their well-doing life everlasting, and some for their sins the judgment of everlasting punishment.   This is the faith of the catholic church, this confession we keep and hold, which whosoever shall keep stedfastly, he shall have everlasting salvation.

A DECLARATION OF THE FAITH OR PREACHING OF THE EVANGELICAL AND APOSTOLICAL TRUTH, BY THE BLESSED MARTYR IRENÆUS, TAKEN OUT OF THE THIRD CHAPTER OF HIS FIRST BOOK "CONTRA VALENT."

About the year of our Lord 185.

THE church, dispersed through the whole world even to the ends of the earth, hath of the apostles and their disciples received the belief, which is in one God the Father Almighty, which made heaven and earth, the sea, and all that in them is.   And in one Jesus Christ the Son of God, (who was) incarnate for our salvation.   And in the Holy Ghost, who by the prophets preached the mystery of the dispensation, and the coming of the beloved Jesus Christ our Lord, with his nativity of the virgin, and his passion, and resurrection from the dead, and his ascension in the flesh into the heavens, and his coming again out of the heavens in the glory of the Father to restore all things, and to raise up again all flesh of mankind : so that to Christ Jesus our Lord, both God, and Saviour, and King, according to the will of the invisible Father, every knee may bow, of things in heaven, and things in earth, and things under the earth, and that every tongue may praise him, and that he may judge rightly in all things, and that he may cast the spirits of naughtiness, with the angels which transgressed and became rebels, and wicked, unjust, mischievous, and blasphemous men, into eternal fire : and that to the just and holy ones, and such as have kept his commandments and remained in the love of him, partly from the beginning and partly by repentance, he may grant life, bestow immortality, and give glory everlasting. The church, although it be dispersed throughout the whole world, having obtained, as I have said, this confession and this faith, doth, as it were dwelling together in one house, diligently keep them, and likewise believe them, even as if it had one soul and the same heart; and doth preach, teach, and agreeably deliver these things, even as if it had all one mouth. For in the world the tongues are unlike, but the force of teaching is one and the same. Neither do the churches, whose foundation is laid in Germany, believe otherwise, or teach to the contrary : neither those in Spain, nor those in France, nor those in the east, nor those in Egypt, nor those in Libya, nor those which are in the world (beside): but even as the sun, (which is) the creature of God, is one and the self-same in all the world; so also the preaching of the truth shineth every where, and giveth light to all men, which are willing to come to the knowledge of the truth. And neither shall he, which among the chief overseers of the church is able to say much, speak contrary to this; for no man is above his master : neither shall he, which is able to say little, diminish this doctrine any whit at all. For seeing that faith is all one and the same, neither doth he, which is able to say much of it, say more than should be said : neither doth he, which saith little, make it ever a whit the lesser[1].

[1 Ἡ μὲν γὰρ ἐκκλησία, καίπερ καθ᾽ ὅλης τῆς οἰκουμένης ἕως περάτων τῆς γῆς διεσπαρμένη, παρὰ δὲ τῶν ἀποστόλων καὶ τῶν ἐκείνων μαθητῶν παραλαβοῦσα τὴν εἰς ἕνα Θεὸν Πατέρα παντοκράτορα, τὸν πεποιηκότα τὸν οὐρανὸν, καὶ τὴν γῆν, καὶ τὰς θαλάσσας, καὶ πάντα τὰ ἐν αὐτοῖς, πίστιν· καὶ εἰς ἕνα Χριστὸν Ἰησοῦν, τὸν Υἱὸν τοῦ Θεοῦ, τὸν σαρκωθέντα ὑπὲρ τῆς ἡμετέρας σωτηρίας· καὶ εἰς Πνεῦμα Ἅγιον, τὸ διὰ τῶν προφητῶν κεκηρυχὸς τὰς οἰκονομίας, καὶ τὰς ἐλεύσεις, καὶ τὴν ἐκ παρθένου γέννησιν, καὶ τὸ πάθος, καὶ τὴν ἔγερσιν ἐκ νεκρῶν, καὶ τὴν ἔνσαρκον εἰς τοὺς οὐρανοὺς ἀνάληψιν τοῦ ἠγαπημένου Χριστοῦ Ἰησοῦ τοῦ Κυρίου ἡμῶν, καὶ τὴν ἐκ τῶν οὐρανῶν ἐν τῇ δόξῃ τοῦ Πατρὸς παρουσίαν αὐτοῦ, ἐπὶ τὸ ἀνακεφαλαιώσασθαι τὰ πάντα, καὶ ἀναστῆσαι πᾶσαν σάρκα πάσης ἀνθρωπότητος, ἵνα Χριστῷ Ἰησοῦ τῷ Κυρίῳ ἡμῶν, καὶ Θεῷ, καὶ Σωτῆρι, καὶ Βασιλεῖ, κατὰ τὴν εὐδοκίαν τοῦ Πατρὸς τοῦ ἀοράτου, πᾶν γόνυ κάμψῃ ἐπουρανίων καὶ ἐπιγείων καὶ καταχθονίων, καὶ πᾶσα γλῶσσα ἐξομολογήσηται αὐτῷ, καὶ κρίσιν δικαίαν ἐν τοῖς πᾶσι ποιή-

Read further in the fourth chapter of his third book
Contra Valent. and you shall perceive that by the term of
apostolical tradition he meaneth the Creed of the Apostles.

A RULE OF FAITH, AFTER TERTULLIAN, TAKEN OUT OF HIS BOOK "DE PRÆSCRIPTIONIBUS HÆRETICORUM[1]."

About the
year of our
Lord 210.

THE rule of faith is, that we out of hand profess openly
what our belief is; which is that indeed whereby we believe

σηται· τὰ μὲν πνευματικὰ τῆς πονηρίας, καὶ ἀγγέλους παραβεβηκότας καὶ
ἐν ἀποστασίᾳ γεγονότας, καὶ τοὺς ἀσεβεῖς, καὶ ἀδίκους, καὶ ἀνόμους, καὶ
βλασφήμους τῶν ἀνθρώπων εἰς τὸ αἰώνιον πῦρ πέμψῃ· τοῖς δὲ δικαίοις,
καὶ ὁσίοις, καὶ τὰς ἐντολὰς αὐτοῦ τετηρηκόσι, καὶ ἐν τῇ ἀγάπῃ αὐτοῦ δια-
μεμενηκόσι, τοῖς ἀπ᾽ ἀρχῆς, τοῖς δὲ ἐκ μετανοίας, ζωὴν χαρισάμενος ἀφθαρ-
σίαν δωρήσηται, καὶ δόξαν αἰωνίαν περιποιήσῃ. Τοῦτο τὸ κήρυγμα παρει-
ληφυῖα, καὶ ταύτην τὴν πίστιν, ὡς προέφαμεν, ἡ ἐκκλησία, καίπερ ἐν ὅλῳ
τῷ κόσμῳ διεσπαρμένη, ἐπιμελῶς φυλάσσει, ὡς ἕνα οἶκον οἰκοῦσα· καὶ
ὁμοίως πιστεύει τούτοις, ὡς μίαν ψυχὴν καὶ τὴν αὐτὴν ἔχουσα καρδίαν, καὶ
συμφώνως ταῦτα κηρύσσει, καὶ διδάσκει, καὶ παραδίδωσιν, ὡς ἓν στόμα
κεκτημένη· καὶ γὰρ αἱ κατὰ τὸν κόσμον διάλεκτοι ἀνόμοιαι, ἀλλ᾽ ἡ δύναμις
τῆς παραδόσεως μία καὶ ἡ αὐτή· καὶ οὔτε αἱ ἐν Γερμανίαις ἱδρυμέναι ἐκκλησίαι ἄλλως πεπιστεύκασιν, ἢ ἄλλως παραδιδόασιν, οὔτε ἐν ταῖς Ἰβηρίαις,
οὔτε ἐν Κελτοῖς, οὔτε κατὰ τὰς ἀνατολὰς, οὔτε ἐν Αἰγύπτῳ, οὔτε ἐν Λιβύῃ,
οὔτε αἱ κατὰ μέσα τοῦ κόσμου ἱδρυμέναι· ἀλλ᾽ ὥσπερ ὁ ἥλιος τὸ κτίσμα τοῦ
Θεοῦ ἐν ὅλῳ τῷ κόσμῳ εἷς καὶ ὁ αὐτὸς, οὕτω καὶ τὸ κήρυγμα τῆς ἀληθείας
πανταχῇ φαίνει, καὶ φωτίζει πάντας ἀνθρώπους τοὺς βουλομένους εἰς ἐπί-
γνωσιν ἀληθείας ἐλθεῖν. Καὶ οὔτε ὁ πάνυ δυνατὸς ἐν λόγῳ τῶν ἐν ταῖς
ἐκκλησίαις προεστώτων ἕτερα τούτων ἐρεῖ· (οὐδεὶς γὰρ ὑπὲρ τὸν διδάσκα-
λον·) οὔτε ὁ ἀσθενὴς ἐν τῷ λόγῳ ἐλαττώσει τὴν παράδοσιν· μιᾶς γὰρ καὶ
τῆς αὐτῆς πίστεως οὔσης, οὔτε ὁ πολὺ περὶ αὐτῆς δυνάμενος εἰπεῖν ἐπλεό-
νασεν, οὔτε ὁ τὸ ὀλίγον ἠλαττόνησε.—Iren. adv. Hæres. Lib. I. cap. 3.
ed. Grabe. Oxon. 1702.]

[1 Regula est autem fidei, ut jam hinc, quid defendamus, profitea-
mur, illa scilicet qua creditur: Unum omnino Deum esse, nec alium
præter mundi conditorem, qui universa de nihilo produxerit per Verbum
suum primo omnium emissum. Id Verbum Filius ejus appellatum, in
nomine Dei, varie visum patriarchis, in prophetis semper auditum,
postremo delatum ex Spiritu Patris Dei et virtute in Virginem Mariam,
carnem factum in utero ejus, et ex ea natum, egisse Jesum Christum:
exinde prædicasse novam legem, et novam promissionem regni cœlorum: virtutes fecisse: fixum cruci: tertia die resurrexisse: in cœlos
ereptum sedere ad dexteram Patris: misisse vicariam vim Spiritus
Sancti, qui credentes agat: venturum cum claritate ad sumendos
sanctos in vitæ æternæ et promissorum cœlestium fructum, et ad pro-

that there is one God only, and not any other beside the maker of the world, which by his Word, sent out first of all, brought forth all things of nothing. That Word, being called his Son, being seen after sundry sorts of the patriarchs, being always heard in the prophets, and lastly by the Spirit and power of God the Father being brought into the virgin Mary, being made flesh in that womb and born of her, became Jesus Christ, (which) afterward preached the new law and the new promise of the kingdom of heaven, wrought miracles, sat at the right hand of the Father, was nailed to the cross, rose again the third day, was taken into the heavens, sitteth at the right hand of the Father, sent the power of the Holy Ghost to govern the believers in his own stead, shall come with glory to take the saints into the joy of eternal life and heavenly promises, and to condemn the wicked to everlasting fire, when both the parties are raised up and have their flesh restored again.

This rule, as it shall be proved, being ordained by Christ, hath among us no doubts at all, but those which heresies bring in, and which make men become heretics.

THE CREED OF THE BLESSED ATHANASIUS, BISHOP OF ALEXANDRIA, TAKEN OUT OF HIS BOOKS[2].

WHOSOEVER will be saved: before all things it is neces- *About the year of our Lord 333.* sary that he hold the catholic faith.

fanos judicandos igni perpetuo, facta utriusque partis resuscitatione cum carnis restitutione. Hæc regula, a Christo, ut probabitur, instituta, nullas habet apud nos quæstiones, nisi quas hæreses inferunt, et quæ hæreticos faciunt.—Tertul. Opp. de Præsc. Hær. cap. 13. ed. Semler. Tom. II. p. 13.]

[2 The best and latest critics, who have examined the thing most exactly, make no question but that this creed is to be ascribed to a Latin author, Vigilius Tapsensis, an African bishop, who lived in the latter end of the fifth century, in the time of the Vandalic Arian persecution: first, because this creed is wanting in almost all the manuscripts of Athanasius's works: secondly, because the style and contexture of it does not bespeak a Greek, but a Latin, author: thirdly, because neither Cyril of Alexandria, nor the council of Ephesus, nor pope Leo, nor the council of Chalcedon, have ever so much as mentioned it in all that they say against the Nestorian or Eutychian heresies: fourthly, because this Vigilius Tapsensis is known to have published

Which faith except every one do keep holy[1] and undefiled: without doubt he shall perish everlastingly.

And the catholic faith is this: that we worship one God
in Trinity, and Trinity in Unity.

Neither confounding the persons: nor dividing the substance.

For there is one person of the Father, another of the
Son, and another of the Holy Ghost.

But the Godhead of the Father, of the Son, and of the
Holy Ghost, is all one: the glory equal, the majesty co-
eternal.

Such as the Father is, such is the Son: and such is the
Holy Ghost.

The Father uncreate, the Son uncreate: and the Holy
Ghost uncreate.

The Father incomprehensible, the Son incomprehensible:
and the Holy Ghost incomprehensible.

The Father eternal, the Son eternal: and the Holy
Ghost eternal.

And yet there are not three eternals: but one eternal.

As also there be not three incomprehensibles, nor three
uncreated: but one uncreated, and one incomprehensible.

So likewise the Father is almighty, the Son is almighty:
and the Holy Ghost almighty.

And yet are they not three almighties: but one almighty.

So the Father is God, the Son is God: and the Holy
Ghost is God.

And yet they are not three Gods: but one God.

So likewise the Father is Lord, the Son Lord: and the
Holy Ghost Lord.

And yet not three Lords: but one Lord.

For like as we be compelled by the christian verity: to
acknowledge every person by himself to be God and Lord.

So are we forbidden by the catholic religion: to say
there be three Gods or three Lords.

several other of his writings under the borrowed name of Athanasius,
—with which this creed is commonly joined.—Bingham's Antiquities,
ed. 1840. Vol. III. 372. See also, for a full discussion of the question,
Waterland's works. P.]

[1 So also in the two Liturgies of Edward VI. See Parker Society's
edition, pages 38 and 229. The Latin is *integram*.]

The Father is made of none : neither created, nor begotten.

The Son is of the Father alone : not made, nor created, but begotten.

The Holy Ghost is of the Father and of the Son : neither made, nor created, nor begotten, but proceeding.

So there is one Father, not three Fathers : one Son, not three Sons : one Holy Ghost, not three Holy Ghosts.

And in this Trinity none is afore or after other : none is greater or less than other.

But the whole three persons be coeternal together : and coequal.

So that in all things, as is aforesaid : the Unity in Trinity, and the Trinity in Unity is to be worshipped.

He therefore that will be saved, must thus think of the Trinity.

Furthermore it is necessary to everlasting salvation : that he also believe rightly[2] in the incarnation of our Lord Jesus Christ.

For the right faith is, that we believe and confess : that our Lord Jesus Christ, the Son of God, is God and man.

God of the substance of the Father, begotten before the worlds : and man of the substance of his mother born in the world.

Perfect God and perfect man : of a reasonable soul, and human flesh subsisting.

Equal to the Father as touching his Godhead : and inferior to the Father touching his manhood.

Who although he be God and man : yet he is not two, but one Christ.

One, not by the conversion of the Godhead into flesh : but by taking of the manhood into God.

One altogether, not by confusion of substance : but by unity of person.

For as the reasonable soul and flesh is one man : so God and man is one Christ.

Who suffered for our salvation, descended into hell, rose again the third day from the dead.

He ascended into heaven, he sitteth on the right hand of

[2 fideliter, Lat.]

the Father, God Almighty: from whence he shall come to judge the quick and the dead.

At whose coming all men shall rise again with their bodies: and shall give account for their own works.

And they that have done good, shall go into life everlasting: and they that have done evil, into everlasting fire.

This is the catholic faith: which except a man believe faithfully[1], he cannot be saved.

THE CREED OF THE BLESSED DAMASUS, BISHOP OF ROME, TAKEN OUT OF THE SECOND TOME OF S. HIEROME HIS WORKS[1].

About the year of our Lord 376.

WE believe in one God the Father Almighty, and in one Jesus Christ our Lord the Son of God, and in the Holy Ghost.

[1 fideliter firmiterque, Lat.]

[2 Credimus in unum Deum, Patrem omnipotentem, et in unum Dominum nostrum Jesum Christum, Filium Dei, et in Spiritum Sanctum. Deum, non tres Deos; sed Patrem, et Filium, et Spiritum Sanctum, unum Deum colimus et confitemur: non sic unum Deum, quasi solitarium; nec eundem, qui ipse sibi Pater sit, ipse et Filius: sed Patrem esse qui genuit, et Filium esse qui genitus sit: Spiritum vero Sanctum non genitum neque ingenitum, non creatum neque factum, sed de Patre Filioque procedentem, Patri et Filio coæternum et coæqualem et cooperatorem: quia scriptum est, Verbo Domini cœli firmati sunt, id est, a Filio Dei, et spiritu oris ejus omnis virtus eorum. Et alibi: Emitte spiritum tuum, et creabuntur, et renovabis faciem terræ. Ideoque in nomine Patris et Filii et Spiritus Sancti unum confitemur Deum, quod nomen est potestatis, non proprietatis. Proprium nomen est Patri Pater; et proprium nomen est Filio Filius; et proprium nomen Spiritui Sancto Spiritus Sanctus. In hac Trinitate unum Deum colimus, quia ex uno Patre quod est unius cum Patre naturæ est, unius substantiæ, et unius potestatis. Pater Filium genuit, non voluntate, nec necessitate, sed natura. Filius ultimo tempore ad nos salvandos et ad implendas scripturas descendit a Patre, qui nunquam desiit esse cum Patre. Et conceptus est de Spiritu Sancto, et natus ex virgine: carnem et animam et sensum, hoc est, perfectum suscepit hominem; nec amisit quod erat, sed cœpit esse quod non erat; ita tamen, ut perfectus in suis sit, et verus in nostris. Nam qui Deus erat, homo natus est; et qui homo natus est, operatur ut Deus; et qui operatur ut Deus, ut homo moritur; et qui ut homo moritur, ut Deus resurgit. Qui, devicto mortis imperio, cum ea carne, qua natus et passus et mortuus fuerat, et resurrexit, ascendit ad Patrem, sedetque

We worship and confess God, not three Gods, but the Father, the Son, and the Holy Ghost, one God: one God, not so as though he were alone, nor as one which is himself Father to himself, and Son himself also; but him to be the Father which begot, and (him) to be the Son which was begotten; but the Holy Ghost to be neither begotten, nor created, nor made, but proceeding from the Father and the Son, co-eternal, co-equal, and working together with the Father and the Son: because it is written, "By the word of the Lord the heavens were established," that is, by the Son of God, "and by the breath of his mouth all the powers thereof;" and in another place, "Send forth thy breath, and they shall be created, and thou shalt renew the face of the earth." And therefore under the name of the Father, of the Son, and of the Holy Ghost, we confess one God, which is the name of the power, and not of the property. The proper name of the Father is the Father: and the proper name of the Son is the Son: and the proper name of the Holy Ghost is the Holy Ghost. In this Trinity of persons we worship one God (in substance), because that which is of one father is of one nature with the father, of one substance, and one power. The Father begat the Son, not by will or necessity, but by nature.

The Son in the last time came down from the Father to save us and to fulfil the scriptures, who (nevertheless) never ceased to be with the Father. And he was conceived by the Holy Ghost, and born of the virgin: he took upon him flesh, and soul, and sense; that is, he took on him very man, neither lost he what he was, but began to be what he was not; so yet that, in respect of his own properties, he is perfect God; and in respect of ours, he is very man. For he which was God is born man; and he which is born man, doth work miracles as God; and he that worketh miracles as God, doth die as a man; and he that dieth as man, doth rise again as God: who in the same flesh, wherein he was born and suf-

ad dexteram ejus in gloria, quam semper habuit et habet. In hujus morte et sanguine credimus emundatos nos; et ab eo resuscitandos die novissimo in hac carne qua nunc vivimus. Et habemus spem nos consecuturos præmium boni meriti, aut pœnam pro peccatis æterni supplicii. Hæc lege, hæc crede, hæc retine; huic fidei animam tuam subjuga; et vitam consequeris et præmium a Christo.—Hieronym. Opp. ed. Par. 1693-1706. Tom. v. col. 122.]

[BULLINGER.]

3

fered and died and rose again, did ascend to the Father, and
sitteth at his right hand in the glory which he always had,
and yet still hath.   By whose death and blood we believe
that we are cleansed; and that at the latter day we shall be
raised up again by him in this flesh wherein we now live.
And we hope that we shall obtain a reward for our good
deeds; or else the pain of everlasting punishment for our
sins.   Read this, believe this, hold this, submit thy soul to
this faith, and thou shalt obtain life and a reward at Christ's
hand.

Peter, bishop
of Alexan-
dria.

St Peter, bishop of Alexandria, taught and believed the
very same with the blessed Athanasius and Damasus, as it
may be gathered out of the thirty-seventh chapter of the
seventh book, and the fourteenth chapter of the eighth book,
of the Tripartite history [1].

THE IMPERIAL DECREE FOR THE CATHOLIC FAITH[2], TAKEN OUT OF THE TRIPARTITE HISTORY. Lib. IX. Cap. 7.

THE noble emperors, Gratian, Valentinian, and Theodosius, to the people of the city of Constantinople.   We will
all people, whom the royal authority of our clemency doth
rule, to be of that religion, which the religion brought in
by (Peter) himself doth at this time declare that St Peter
the apostle did teach to the Romans, and which it is evident
that bishop Damasus, and Peter the bishop of Alexandria,
a man of apostolical holiness, do follow: that is, that, according to the discipline of the apostles and doctrine of the
evangelists, in the equality of the majesty and in the holy

Catholics.

Trinity we believe that there is (but) one Godhead of the
Father, of the Son, and of the Holy Ghost.   Those which
keep this law, we command to have the name of catholic
Christians : but for the other, whom we judge to be mad and

Hereticks.

out of their wits, (we will) that they, sustaining the infamy

[1 Is (Petrus) Athanasii sudoribus particeps fuit.—Hist. Eccles.
Tripart. Lib. VII. cap. 37, p. 317.   Petro revertente de Roma cum
literis Damasi Romanæ urbis Antistitis, confirmantis consubstantia-
litatis fidem, et Petri Episcopi roborantis ordinationem.—Ibid. Lib.
VIII. cap. 14. Cassiodor. Opp. p. 329. Rotomag. 1679.]

[2 circa annum Domini, 382, Lat.]

of heretical doctrine, be punished first by God's vengeance, and after that by punishment according to the motion of our minds, which we, by the will of God, shall think best of.

Given the third of the Calends of March,
at Thessalonica; Gratian the Fifth,
Valentinian, and Theo-
dosius, Aug.
Coss[3].

FINIS.

[3 Impp. Gratianus, Valentinianus, et Theodosius, Augg. ad populum urbis Constantinopolitanæ. Cunctos populos, quos Clementiæ nostræ regit temperamentum, in tali volumus religione versari, quam divinum Petrum apostolum tradidisse Romanis religio usque nunc ab ipso insinuata declarat; quamque Pontificem Damasum sequi claret, et Petrum Alexandriæ episcopum, virum apostolicæ sanctitatis: hoc est, ut secundum apostolicam disciplinam evangelicamque doctrinam, Patris et Filii et Spiritus Sancti unam Deitatem sub pari majestate et sub pia Trinitate credamus. Hanc legem sequentes, Christianorum catholicorum nomen jubemus amplecti: reliquos vero, dementes vesanosque judicantes, hæretici dogmatis infamiam sustinere, divina primum vindicta, post etiam motus nostri, quem ex cœlesti arbitrio sumpserimus, ultione plectendos. Data III. Kalend. Martias. Thessalonicæ. Gratiano quinto et Theodosio Augg. Coss.—Hist. Eccles. Tripart. Lib. IX. cap. 7. ap. Cassiodor. Opp. Rotomag. 1679. p. 334.]

THE

FIRST DECADE OF SERMONS,

WRITTEN BY

HENRY BULLINGER.

***

OF THE WORD OF GOD; THE CAUSE OF IT; AND HOW,
AND BY WHOM, IT WAS REVEALED TO THE WORLD.

THE FIRST SERMON.

ALL the decrees of Christian faith, with every way how
to live rightly, well, and holily, and finally, all true and
heavenly wisdom, have always been fetched out of the testimonies, or determinate judgments, of the word of God;
neither[1] can they, by those which are wise men indeed, or
by the faithful and those which are called by God to the
ministry of the churches, be drawn, taught, or, last of all,
soundly confirmed from elsewhere, than out of the word of
God. Therefore, whosoever is ignorant what the word of
God, and the meaning of the word of God is, he seemeth to
be as one blind, deaf, and without wit, in the temple of the
Lord, in the school of Christ, and lastly, in the reading of
the very sacred scriptures. But whereas[2] some are nothing
zealous, but very hardly drawn to the hearing of sermons in
the church; that springeth out of no other fountain than this,
which is, because they do neither rightly understand, nor
diligently enough weigh, the virtue and true force of the
word of God. That nothing therefore may cause the zealous
desirers of the truth and the word of God to stay on this
point[3]; but rather that that estimation of God's word,
which is due unto it, may be laid up in all men's hearts; I
will (by God's help) lay forth unto you, dearly beloved, those
things which a godly man ought to think and hold, as concerning the word of God. And pray ye earnestly and continually to our bountiful God, that it may please him to give

[1 hodie, Lat.; at this time of day.]
[2 imo quod, Lat.; Yea, and that.]
[3 Ne quid remoretur, Lat.]

to me his holy and effectual power to speak, and to you the opening of your ears and minds, so that in all that I shall say the Lord's name may be praised, and your souls be profited abundantly.

First, I have to declare what the word of God is. *Verbum* in the scriptures, and according to the very property of the Hebrew tongue, is diversely taken. For it signifieth what thing soever a man will; even as among the Germans the word *ding* is most largely used. In St Luke, the angel of God saith to the blessed virgin: "With God shall no word[4] be unpossible;" which is all one as if he had said, all things are possible to God, or to God is nothing unpossible. *Verbum* also signifieth a word uttered by the mouth of man. Sometime it is used for a charge, sometime for a whole sentence, or speech, or prophecy: whereof in the scriptures there are many examples. But when *verbum* is joined with any thing else, as in this place we call it *verbum Dei*, then[5] is it not used in the same signification. For *verbum Dei*, "the word of God," doth signify the virtue and power of God: it is also put for the Son of God, which is the second person in the most reverend Trinity. For that saying of the holy evangelist is evident to all men, "The word was made flesh[6]." But in this treatise of ours, the word of God doth properly signify the speech of God, and the revealing of God's will; first of all uttered in a lively-expressed voice by the mouth of Christ, the prophets and apostles; and after that again registered in writings, which are rightly called "holy and divine scriptures." The word doth shew the mind of him out of whom it cometh: therefore the word of God doth make declaration of God. But God of himself naturally speaketh truth; he is just, good, pure, immortal, eternal: therefore it followeth that the word of God also, which cometh out of the mouth of God, is true, just, without deceit and guile, without error or evil affection, holy, pure, good, immortal, and everlasting. For in the gospel saith the Lord, "Thy word is truth[7]." And the apostle Paul saith, "The word of God is not tied[8]." Again, the scripture everywhere crieth: "The word of the Lord endureth for ever[9]." And

Marginal notes:
- Verbum, what it is.
- In English, a thing.
- The word of God, what it is.

[4] πᾶν ῥῆμα.—Luke i. 37.   omne verbum, Lat. and Vulg.]
[5] etiam sic, Lat.]
[6] John i. 14.]   [7] John xvii. 17.]
[8] 2 Tim. ii. 9.]   [9] Isai. xl. 8; 1 Pet. i. 25.]

Salomon saith: "Every word of God is purely cleansed. Add thou nothing to his words, lest peradventure he reprove thee, and thou be found a liar[1]." David also saith: "The sayings of the Lord are pure sayings, even as it were silver cleansed in the fire, and seven times fined from the earth[2]."

Of the causes and beginnings of the word of God. This you shall more fully perceive, dearly beloved, if I speak somewhat more largely of the cause or beginning, and certainty, of the word of God. The word of God is truth: but God is the only well-spring of truth: therefore God is the beginning and cause of the word of God. And here indeed God, since he hath not members like to mortal men, wanteth also a bodily mouth: yet nevertheless, because the mouth is the instrument of the voice, to God is a mouth attributed. For he spake to men in the voice of a man, that is, in a voice easily understood of men, and fashioned according to the speech usually spoken among men. This is evidently to be seen in the things wherein he dealt with the holy fathers, with whom, as with our parents Adam and Eva, Noe, and the rest of the fathers, he is read to have talked many and oftentimes. In the mount Sina the Lord himself preached to the great congregation of Israel, rehearsing so plainly, that they might understand those ten commandments, wherein is contained every point of godliness. For in the fifth of Deuteronomy thus we read: "These words," meaning the ten commandments, "spake the Lord with a loud voice, from out of the midst of the fire, to the whole congregation[3]." And in the fourth chapter: "A voice of words you heard, but no similitude did you see beside the voice[4]." God verily used oftentimes the means of angels, by whose ministry he talked with mortal men. And it is very well known to all men, that the Son of God the Father, being incarnate, walked about in the earth; and, being very God and man, taught the people of Israel almost for the space of three years[5]. But in times past, and before that the Son of God was born in the world, God, by little and little, made himself acquainted with the hearts[6] of the holy fathers, and after that with the

[1 Prov. xxx. 5, 6.]   [2 Psalm xii. 6.]
[3 Deut. v. 22.]   [4 Deut. iv. 8.]
[5 The duration of our Lord's ministry is now usually admitted to have been three years and a half.—See Greswell's Harmon. Evang., and Dr Robinson's Harmony of the Gospels.]
[6 insinuavit se Deus animis, Lat.]

minds of the holy prophets; and last of all, by their preaching and writings, he taught the whole world. So also Christ our Lord sent the Holy Ghost, which is of the Father and the Son, into the apostles, by whose mouths, words, and writings he was known to all the world. And all these servants of God, as it were the elect vessels of God, having with sincere hearts received the revelation of God from God himself, first of all, in a lively expressed voice delivered to the world the oracles and word of God which they before had learned; and afterward, when the world drew more to an end, some of them did put them in writing for a memorial to the posterity. And it is good to know how, and by whom, all this was done: for by this narration the true cause, certainty, and dignity of the word of God doth plainly appear.

The word of God revealed to the world by men.

There are not extant to be seen the writings of any man, from the beginning of the world, until the time of Moses, which are come to our knowledge; although it be likely that that same ancient and first world was not altogether without all writings. For by St Jude, the apostle, and brother of St James, is cited the written prophecy of our holy father Enoch, which is read to have been the seventh from our father Adam[7]. Furthermore, the writing, or history, of Job seemeth to have been set forth a great while before. But howsoever it is, all the saints in the church of God give to Moses, the faithful servant of God, the first place among the holy writers.

From the beginning therefore of the world, God, by his Spirit and the ministry of angels, spake to the holy fathers; and they by word of mouth taught their children, and children's children, and all their posterity, that which they had learned at the mouth of God; when they verily had heard it, not to the intent to keep it close to themselves, but also to make their posterity partakers of the same. For God oftentimes witnesseth, that "he will be the God of the fathers and of their seed for evermore[8]." This is most plainly to be seen in the history of Adam, Noe, and Abraham, the first and great grandfathers[9]. In the eighteenth of Genesis, verily, we read, that the angel of God, yea, and that more is, that

How and by whom the word of God hath been revealed from the beginning of the world.

[7] Jude, 14, 15.]   [8] Gen. xvii. 7.]
[9] genearcharum, Lat.]

Abraham.

even the Lord himself, did say to Abraham : " And shall I hide from Abraham what I mind to do ? since of Abraham shall come a great and mighty people, and all the nations of the earth shall be blessed in him ? And this I know, that he will command his children and his posterity after him, to keep the way of the Lord, and to do justice, judgment[1]," and the rest. Abraham therefore, a faithful and zealous worshipper of God, did not (even as also those old fathers of the first world did not) wax negligent at all herein, but did diligently teach men the will and judgments of God : whereupon of Moses, yea, and of God himself, he is called a prophet[2]. That devout and lively tradition of the fathers, from hand to hand, was had in use continually, even from the beginning of the world until the time of Moses.

Moreover, God of his goodness did provide that no age at any time should be without most excellent lights, to be witnesses of the undoubted faith, and fathers of great authority. For the world before the deluge had in it nine most excellent, most holy, and wise men; Adam, Seth, Enos, Kenam, Malaleel, Jared, Enoch, Methusalem, and Lamech. The chief of these, Adam and Methusalem, do begin and make an end of all the sixteen hundred and fifty-six years[3] of the world before the deluge. For Adam lived nine hundred and thirty years[4]: he dieth therefore the seven hundred and twenty-sixth year before the flood. And Methusalem lived nine hundred and sixty-nine years[5]: he dieth in the very same year that the flood did overflow ; and he lived together with Adam two hundred and forty-three years, so that of Adam he might be abundantly enough instructed as concerning the beginning of things, as concerning God, the falling and restoring again of mankind, and all things else belonging to religion, even as he was taught of God himself. These two fathers, with the rest above named, were able sufficiently enough to instruct the whole age in the true salvation and right ways of the Lord.

After the deluge God gave to the world again excellent men, and very great lights. The names of them are Noe, Sem, Arphaxad, Sale, Heber, Palec, Reu, Saruch, Nachor, Thare,

The clearest lights of the first world.

Adam and Methusalem.

[1 Gen. xviii. 17-19.]   [2 Gen. xx. 7.]

[3 Cf. Bullinger's Treatise, The Old Faith, translated in Coverdale's writings, &c. Parker Soc. ed. pp. 32, 36.]

[4 Gen. v. 5.]   [5 Gen. v. 27.]

Abraham, Isaac, and Jacob. Here have we thirteen most excellent patriarchs, among whom the first two, Noe and Sem, are Noe.
the chief; next to whom Abraham, Isaac, and Jacob, were more
notable than the rest. Noe lived nine hundred and fifty years
in all. He was six hundred years old when the flood drowned
the world[6]. He therefore saw and heard all the holy fathers of
the first world before the deluge, three only excepted, Adam,
Seth, and Enos. And also he lived many years together with
the other, which had both seen and heard them; so that he
could be ignorant in no point of those things which Adam had
taught. Noe dieth (which is marvel to be told, and yet very
true) in the forty-ninth year of Abraham's age[7]. Sem, the Sem.
son of Noah, lived many years with his father; for he lived
in all six hundred years. He was born to Noah about ninety-
six years before the deluge. He saw and heard, therefore,
not only his father Noe and his grandfather Lamech, but also
his great grandsire Methusalem, with whom he lived those
ninety-six years before the deluge. Of him he might be in-
formed of all those things which Methusalem had heard and
learned of Adam and the other patriarchs. Sem dieth, after
the death of Abraham, in the fifty-second year of Jacob, which
was thirty-seven years after the death of Abraham, in the
year one hundred and twelve of Isaac's age: so that Jacob,
the patriarch, might very well learn all the true divinity of
Sem himself, even as he had heard it of Methusalem, who was
the third witness and teacher from Adam. Furthermore,
Jacob the patriarch delivered to his children that which he Jacob.
received of God[8] to teach to his posterity. In Mesopotamia
there is born to Jacob his son Levi, and to him again is born
Kahad[9], which both saw and heard Jacob. For Kahad
lived no small number of years with his grandfather Jacob;
for he is rehearsed in the roll of them which went with
Jacob down into Egypt[10]: but Jacob lived seventeen years
with his children in Egypt. This Kahad is the grandfather Kahad.
Amram.
Moses.

[6 Gen. vii. 6.]

[7 There is some great miscalculation here; for Abraham, if born
at all before Noah's death, could only have been in his infancy.   Yet
Calvin also says, that "Abraham was nearly *fifty* years old, when his
ancestor Noe died."—Comment. in Gen. cap. ix. 28. But see note, p. 42.]

[8 a Deo per patres accepit.—Lat.]

[9 Kohath.—Vulg. Caath.]

[10 Gen. xlvi. 11.]

of Moses, the father of Amram, from whom Moses did perfectly draw that full and certain tradition by hand, as concerning the will, commandments, and judgments of God, even as Amram his father had learned them of his father Kahad, Kahad of Jacob, Jacob of Sem, Sem of Methusalem and of Adam the first father of us all: so now that Moses is from Adam the seventh witness in the world. And from the beginning of the world to the birth of Moses are fully complete two thousand three hundred and sixty-eight years of the world. And whosoever shall diligently reckon the years, not in vain set down by Moses in Genesis and Exodus, he shall find this account to be true and right[1].

The chief contents of the holy fathers' lively tradition.

Now also it behoveth us to know those chief principles of that lively tradition, delivered by the holy fathers at the appointment of God, as it were from hand to hand, to all the posterity. The fathers taught their children that God, of his natural goodness, wishing well to mankind, would have all men to come to the knowledge of the truth, and to be like in nature to God himself, holy, happy, and absolutely blessed: and therefore that God, in the beginning, did create man to his own similitude and likeness, to the intent that he should be good, holy, immortal, blessed, and partaker of all the good gifts of God; but that man continued not in that dignity and happy state; but by the means of the devil, and his own proper fault, fell into sin, misery, and death, changing his likeness to God into the similitude of the devil. Moreover, that God here again, as it were, of fresh began the work of salvation, whereby mankind, being restored and set free from all evil, might once again be made like unto God; and that he meant to bring this mighty and divine work to pass by a certain middle mean, that is, by the Word incarnate. For as, by this taking of flesh, he joined man to God; so, by dying in the flesh, with sacrifice he cleansed, sanctified, and delivered

[1 It is scarcely necessary to observe that the system of chronology here used differs considerably from the received system according to Usher. Bullinger followed the vulgar Jewish chronology, upon which the arrangements of Scaliger, Petavius, and Usher were afterwards founded. See Hales's Chronology, Vol. I. The difference does not materially affect the argument. P.—The line of the patriarchal tradition may be seen traced in Gray's Key to the Old Testament, pp. 80, 81. ed. 1797. Lond.]

mankind; and, by giving him his Holy Spirit, he made him like again in nature to God, that is, immortal, and absolutely blessed. And last of all, he worketh in us a willing endeavour aptly to resemble the property and conditions of him to whose likeness we are created, so that we may be holy both body and soul. They added moreover, that the Word should be incarnate in his due time and appointed age; and also, that there did remain a great day for judgment, wherein, though all men were gathered together, yet the righteous only should receive that reward of heavenly immortality.

So then, this is the brief sum of the holy fathers' tradition, which it is best to untwist more largely, and to speak of it more diligently, as it were by parts. First, therefore, the fathers taught, that the Father, the Son, and the Holy Ghost are one God in the most reverend Trinity, the maker and governor of heaven and earth and all things which are therein; by whom man was made, and who for man did make all things, and put all things under mankind, to minister unto him things necessary, as a loving Father and most bountiful Lord. Then they taught, that man consisted of soul and body, and that he indeed was made good according to the image and likeness of God; but that by his own fault, and egging forward of the devil, falling into sin, he brought into the world death and damnation, together with a web of miseries, out of which it cannot rid itself: so that now all the children of Adam, even from Adam, are born the sons of wrath and wretchedness; but that God, whose mercy aboundeth, according to his incomprehensible goodness, taking pity on the misery of mankind, did, even of his mere grace, grant[2] pardon for the offence, and did lay the weight of the punishment upon his only Son, to the intent that he, when his heel was crushed by the serpent, might himself break the serpent's head[3]: that is to say, God doth make a promise of seed, that is, of a Son, who, taking flesh of a peerless woman, (I mean, that virgin most worthy of commendations,) should by his death vanquish death and Satan, the author of death; and should bring the faithful sons of Adam out of bondage; yea, and that more is, should by adoption make them the sons of God, and heirs of life everlasting. The holy fathers, therefore,

[marginal notes] God. · Creation of the world. · Sin and death. · Grace, life, and redemption by Christ.

[2 promisisse, Lat.]　　　[3 Gen. iii. 15.]

Faith.

taught to believe in God, and in his Son, the redeemer of the whole world; when in their very sacrifices they did present his death, as it were an unspotted sacrifice, wherewith he meant to wipe away and cleanse the sins of all the world.

The lineal descent of Messias.

And therefore had they a most diligent eye to the stock and lineal descent of the Messias. For it is brought down, as it were by a line, from Adam to Noe, and from Noe by Sem even to Abraham himself: and to him again it was said, "In thy seed shall all the nations of the earth be blessed[1]:" in which words the promise once made to Adam, as touching Christ the redeemer and changer of God's curse into blessing, is renewed and repeated again. The same line is brought down from Abraham by Isaac unto Jacob[2]; and Jacob, being full of the Spirit of God, pointed out his son Juda to be the root[3] of the blessed Seed, as it is to be seen in the forty-ninth of Genesis. Lastly, in the tribe of Juda the house of David was noted, out of which that seed and branch of life should come.

The league of God.

Moreover, the holy fathers taught, that God by a certain league hath joined himself to mankind, and that he hath most straitly bound himself to the faithful, and the faithful likewise to himself again. Whereupon they did teach to be

The worship of God.

faithful to God-ward, to honour God, to hate false gods, to call upon the only God, and to worship him devoutly. Furthermore, they taught, that the worship of God did consist in things spiritual, as faith, hope, charity, obedience, upright dealing, holiness, innocency, patience, truth, judgment, and godliness. And therefore did they reprehend naughtiness and sin, falsehood, lack of belief, desperation, disobedience, unpatientness, lying, hypocrisy, hatred, despiteful taunts, violence, wrong, unrighteous dealing, uncleanness, riotousness, surfeiting, whoredom, unrighteousness, and ungodliness. They taught, that God was a rewarder of good, but a punisher and

Life eternal and the day of judgment.

revenger of evil. They taught, that the souls of men were immortal, and that the bodies should rise again in the day of judgment: therefore they exhorted us all so to live in this temporal life, that we do not leese[4] the life eternal.

This is the sum of the word of God revealed to the fathers, and by them delivered to their posterity. This is

[1 Gen. xxii. 18.] [2 per Isaacum *et* Jacobum, Lat. P.]
[3 genearcham, Lat.] [4 leese: lose.]

the tradition of the holy fathers, which comprehendeth all religion. Finally, this is the true, ancient, undoubted, authentical, and catholic[5] faith of the fathers.

The true historical narration delivered by the fathers to their children.

Besides this, the holy fathers taught their children, and children's children, the account of the years from the beginning of the world, and also the true historical course, as well profitable as necessary, of things from the creation of the world even unto their own times; lest peradventure their children should be ignorant of the beginning and succession of worldly things, and also of the judgments of God, and examples of them which lived as well godly as ungodly.

I could declare unto you all this evidently, and in very good order, out of the first book of Moses, called Genesis, if it were not that thereby the sermon should be drawn out somewhat longer than the use is. But I suppose that there are few, or rather none at all, here present, which do not perceive that I have rehearsed this that I have said, touching the tradition of the ancient fathers, as it were word for word, out of the book of Genesis; so that now I may very well go forward in the narration which I have begun.

So then, whatsoever hitherto was of the fathers delivered to the world by word of mouth, and as it were from hand to hand, that was first of all put into writing by the holy man Moses, together with those things which were done in all the time of Moses' life, by the space of one hundred and twenty years. And that his estimation might be the greater throughout all the world, among all men, and in all ages; and that none should but know, that the writings of Moses were the very word of God itself; Moses was furnished, and as it were consecrated by God, with signs and wonders to be marvelled at indeed, which the almighty by the hand, that is, by the ministry of Moses, did bring to pass: and verily, he wrought them not in any corner of the world, or place unknown, but in Egypt, the most flourishing and renowned kingdom of that age.

Moses in an history compileth the traditions of the fathers.

Those miracles were greater and far more by many, than that they can be here rehearsed in few words: neither is it needful to repeat them, because you, dearly beloved, are not unskilful or ignorant of them at all. After that also, God by

[5] authentica, orthodoxa, et catholica, Lat. P.]

other means procured authority to Moses. For many and oftentimes God had communication with Moses; and amongst the rest of his talk said he: "Behold, I will come to thee in a thick cloud, that the people may hear me talking with thee, and may believe thee for evermore[1]."

Neither was the Lord therewith content, but commanded Moses to call together all the people, six hundred thousand men, I say, with their wives and children. They are called out to the mount Sina, where God appeareth in a wonderful and terrible fashion; and he himself, preaching to the congregation, doth rehearse unto them the ten commandments. But the people, being terrified with the majesty of God, doth pray and beseech, that God himself would no more afterward preach to the congregation with his own mouth, saying, that it were enough, if he would use Moses as an interpreter to them, and by him speak to the church[2]. The most high God did like the offer; and, after that, he spake to the people by Moses whatsoever he would have done. And for because that the people was a stiff-necked people, and by keeping company with idolaters in Egypt was not a little corrupted, Moses now began to set down in writing those things which the holy fathers by tradition had taught, and the things also which the Lord had revealed unto him. The cause why he wrote them was, lest peradventure by oblivion, by continuance of time, and obstinacy of a people so slow to believe, they might either perish, or else be corrupted. The Lord also set Moses an example to follow. For whatsoever God had spoken to the church in mount Sina, the same did he straightway after write with his own finger in two tables of stone, as he had with his finger from the beginning of the world written the same in the hearts of the fathers[3]. Afterward also, in plain words, he commanded Moses to write whatsoever the Lord had revealed. Moses obeyed the Lord's commandment, and wrote them. The Holy Ghost, which was wholly in the mind of Moses, directed his hand as he writ. There was no ability wanting in Moses, that was necessary for a most absolute writer. He was abundantly instructed by his

[1 Exod. xix. 9.]
[2 Exod. xx. 19.]
[3 See Bullinger's treatise, The Old Faith, in Works of Bp. Coverdale, Parker Soc. Ed. pp. 27, 40.]

ancestors: for he was born of the holiest progeny of those
fathers, whom God appointed to be witnesses of his will, commandments, and judgments; suppose[4] Amram, Kahad, Jacob,
Sem, Methusalem and Adam. He was able, therefore, to
write a true and certain history, from the beginning of the
world even until his own time. Whereunto he added those
things which were done among the people of God in his own
life-time, whereof he was a very true witness, as one that
saw and heard them. Yea, and that more is, whatsoever he
did set forth in his books, that did he read to his people,
and amongst so many thousands was there not one found
which gainsayed that which he rehearsed: so that the whole
consent and witness-bearing of the great congregation did
bring no small authority to the writings of Moses.

Moses therefore contained in the five books, called the
five books of Moses, an history from the beginning of the
world, even unto his own death, by the space of two thousand
four hundred and eighty-eight years: in which he declared
most largely the revelation of the word of God made unto men,
and whatsoever the word of God doth contain and teach: in
which, as we have the manifold oracles of God himself, so we
have most lightsome[5] testimonies, sentences, examples, and
decrees of the most excellent, ancient, holy, wise, and greatest
men of the world, touching all things which seem to appertain
to true godliness, and the way how to live well and holily.
These books therefore found a ready prepared entrance of
belief among all the posterity, as books which are authentical,
and which of themselves have authority sufficient, and which,
without gainsaying, ought to be believed of all the world.
Yea, and that more is, our Lord Jesus Christ, the only-begotten Son of God, doth refer the faithful to the reading of
Moses; yea, and that indeed in the chiefest points of our
salvation: the places are to be seen, John v. Luke xvi.
In the fifth of Matthew he saith: "Do not think that I am
come to destroy the law and the prophets; for I am not come
to destroy them, but to fulfil them. For, verily, I say unto
you, though[6] heaven and earth do pass, one jot or tittle of
the law shall not pass, till all be fulfilled. Whosoever, therefore, shall undo one of the least of these commandments, and

The authority of Moses very great.

[4 puto autem, Lat.]
[5 clarissimorum, Lat.]
[6 donec prætereat.—Lat. as in Eng. Ver.]

shall teach men so, he shall be called the least in the kingdom of heaven[1]."

There have verily some been found, that have spoken against Moses, the servant of God. But God hath imputed that gainsaying as done against his divine majesty, and punished it most sharply. The proofs hereof are to be seen in Exod. xvi. and Numeri the xii. And first, of the people murmuring against Moses; then of Mary, Moses's sister, speaking against her brother. But to the people it was said: "Not against the ministers, but against the Lord, are your complaints[2]." As for Mary, she was horribly stricken with a leprosy[3]. Theotectus was stricken blind, and Theopompus fell to be mad, because he had unreverently touched the word of God[4]. For, although the word of God be revealed, spoken, and written by men, yet doth it not therefore cease to be that which indeed it is; neither doth it therefore begin to be the word of men, because it is preached and heard of men: no more than the king's commandment, which is proclaimed by the crier, is said to be the commandment of the crier. He despiseth God, and with God all the holy patriarchs, whosoever doth contemn Moses, by whom God speaketh unto us, and at whose hand we have received those things which the patriarchs from the beginning of the world by tradition delivered to the posterity. There is no difference between the word of God, which is taught by the lively expressed voice of man, and that which is written by the pen of man, but so far forth as the lively voice and writing do differ between themselves: the matter undoubtedly, the sense, and meaning, in the one and the other is all one. By this, dearly beloved, you have perceived the certain history of the beginning of the word of God.

[1] Matth. v. 17-19. Quisquis autem fecerit et docuerit, hic magnus vocabitur in regno cœlorum, Lat.; omitted by the translator.]

[2] Exod. xvi. 8.]

[3] Num. xii. 10. Miriam: Vulg. Maria.]

[4] Theotectus tragœdiarum scriptor, Lat. Theodectes, according to Suidas and Gellius x. 18, was a tragedian, and contemporary with Theopompus, who was an orator and historian, a pupil of Isocrates. Josephus, Lib. xii. cap. 2. Antiq. Jud., and Aristeas de LXX. Interp. relate the story referred to;—namely, that each of these writers was preparing to put forth a part of the scriptures, as their own composition, when they were visited, the former with blindness, the latter with madness, which lasted thirty days.—Ger. Vossius. Lib. i. c. 7. P.]

Now let us go forward to the rest; that is, to add the history of the proceeding of the word of God, and by what means it shined ever and anon very clear and brightly unto the world. By and by, after the departure of the holy man Moses out of this world into heaven, the Lord of his bountifulness gave most excellent prophets unto his church, which he had chosen to the intent that by it he might reveal his word unto the whole world. And the prophets were to them of the old time, as at this day amongst us are prophets, priests, wise men, preachers, pastors, bishops, doctors or divines, most skilful in heavenly things, and given by God to guide the people in the faith. And he, whosoever shall read the holy history, will confess that there flourished[5] of this sort no small number, and those not obscure, even till the captivity of Babylon. Amongst whom are reckoned these singular and excellent men, Phinees, Samuel, Helias, Heliseus, Esaias, and Jeremias. David and Sálomon were both kings and prophets. In time of the captivity at Babylon, Daniel and Ezechiel were notably known. After the captivity flourished, among the rest, Zacharias the son of Barachias. Here have I reckoned up a few among many: who, although they flourished at sundry times, and that the one a great while after the other, yet did they all, with one consent, acknowledge that God spake to the world by Moses, who (God so appointed it) left to the church in the world a breviary[6] of true divinity, and a most absolute sum of the word of God contained in writing. All these priests, divines, and prophets, in all that they did, had an especial eye to the doctrine of Moses. They did also refer all men, in cases of faith and religion, to the book[7] of Moses. The law of Moses, which is indeed the law of God, and is most properly called *Thora*[8], as it were the guide and rule of faith and life, they did diligently beat into the minds of all men. This did they, according to the time, persons, and place, expound to all men. For all the priests and pro-

The proceeding of the word of God.

The prophets.

The law.

[5 in populo sive ecclesia Dei, Lat.; in the people, or church, of God, omitted by the translator.]

[6 compendium, Lat.] [7 libros, Lat.]

[8 תּוֹרָה, a verbo ירה, instituere, docere.—Foster, Lex. Heb. P.— תורה, quam Legem vulgo vertimus, Hebræis ab indicando docendoque dicitur.—Bucer. in Psalm. ii. ed. Steph. 1554. p. 16. See also Hooper's Early Writings, p. 88, Parker Soc. Ed.]

[BULLINGER.]

4

phets, before the incarnation of Christ, did by word of mouth teach the men of their time godliness and true religion. Neither did they teach any other thing than that which the fathers had received of God, and which Moses had received of God and the fathers; and straightways after committing it to writing, did set it out to all us which follow, even unto the end of the world: so that now in the prophets we have the doctrine of Moses and tradition of the fathers, and them in all and every point more fully and plainly expounded and polished, being moreover to the places, times, and persons very fitly applied.

The authority of the holy prophets was very great.
Furthermore, the doctrine and writings of the prophets have always been of great authority among all wise men throughout the whole world. For it is well perceived by many arguments, that they took not their beginning of the prophets themselves, as chief authors; but were inspired from God out of heaven by the Holy Spirit of God: for it is God, which, dwelling by his Spirit in the minds of the prophets, speaketh to us by their mouths. And for that cause have they a most large testimony at the hands of Christ[1], and his elect apostles. What say ye to this moreover, that God by their ministry hath wrought miracles and wonders to be marvelled at, and those not a few; that at the least by mighty signs we might learn that it is God, by whose inspiration the prophets do teach and write whatsoever they left for us to remember?

Furthermore, so many commonweals and congregations gathered together, and governed by the prophets according to the word of God, do shew most evident testimonies of God's truth in the prophets. Plato, Zeno, Aristotle, and other philosophers of the gentiles, are praised as excellent men. But which of them could ever yet gather a church to live according to their ordinances? And yet our prophets have had the most excellent and renowned commonweals or congregations, yea, and that more is, the most flourishing kingdoms in all the world under their authority. All the wise men in the whole world (I mean those which lived in his time) did reverence[2] Salomon, a king and so great a prophet, and came unto him from the very outmost ends of the world. Daniel also had the preeminence among the wise men at Babylon,

[1] Dei Filio, Lat.; omitted.]
[2] tantum non adorarunt, Lat.; almost worshipped.]

being then the most renowned monarchy in all the world. He
was moreover in great estimation with Darius Medus, the son
of Astyages[3] or Assuerus, and also with Cyrus that most excellent king.   And here it liketh me well to speak somewhat
of that divine foreknowledge in our prophets, and most assured
foreshewing of things which were to come after many years
passed.   And now, to say nothing of others, did not Esaias
most truly foretell those things, which were afterward fulfilled
by the Jews in our Lord Christ?   Not in vain did he seem
to them of old time to be rather an evangelist than a prophet[4]
foretelling things to come.   He did openly tell the name of
king Cyrus one hundred and threescore years, at the least,
before that Cyrus was born[5]. Daniel also was called[6] of them
in the old time by the name of one which knew much[7].   For
he did foretell those things which are and have been done in
all the kingdoms of the world almost, and among the people
of God, from his own time until the time of Christ, and
further until the last day of judgment, so plainly, that he may
seem to have compiled a history of those things which then
were already gone and past. All these things, I say, do very
evidently prove, that the doctrine and writings of the prophets
are the very word of God : with which name and title they
are set forth in sundry places of the scriptures. Verily, Peter
the apostle saith, " The prophecy came not in old time by
the will of man : but holy men of God spake as they were
moved by the Holy Ghost."

    And although God did largely, clearly, plainly, and

Polyhistor.

*The word of
God revealed
by the Son
of God.*

[3 That Astyages, son of Cyaxares the first, is the Ahasuerus, and
Cyaxares the second, Astyages' son, the Darius the Mede, of scripture,
see Prideaux's Connect. Vol. I. pp. 72, 104, 120, ed. McCaul, Lond.
1845.]

[4 Ita ut a quibusdam evangelista quam propheta potius diceretur
(Esaias).—Augustin. de Civ. Dei. Lib. XVIII. cap. 29. Par. 1531. Tom. v.
Deinde etiam hoc adjiciendum, quod non tam propheta, quam evan-
gelista, dicendus sit (Isaias).—Hieron. Præf. in lib. Isai. Ed. Par.
1693-1706. Tom. I. col. 473.   See also Bullinger's treatise, The Old
Faith, ap. Works of Bp. Coverdale, Parker Soc. ed. p. 66.]

[5 Is. xliv. 28 ; xlv. 1.]

[6 recte appellatus est, Lat.]

[7 Quartus vero (Daniel), qui et extremus inter quatuor prophetas,
temporum conscius, et totius mundi philoïstoros, &c.—Hieron. Ep. L.
Secund. ad Paulinum. Ed. Par. 1706. Tom. IV. par. 2. col. 573.]

simply reveal his word to the world by the patriarchs, by Moses, by the priests and prophets; yet did he, in the last times of all, by his Son set it forth most clearly, simply, and abundantly to all the world. For the very and only-begotten Son of God the Father, as the prophets had foretold, descending from heaven, doth fulfil all whatsoever they foretold, and by the space almost of three years doth teach all points of godliness. For saith John: "No man at any time hath seen God; the only-begotten Son, which is in the bosom of the Father, he hath declared him[1]." The Lord himself, moreover, saith to his disciples: "All things which I have heard of my Father have I made known to you[2]." And again he saith: "I am the light of the world: whosoever doth follow me doth not walk in darkness, but shall have the light of life[3]." Our Lord also did teach, that to him, which would enter into heaven and be saved, the heavenly regeneration was needful[4], because in the first birth man is born to death, in the second to life; but that that regeneration is made perfect in us by the Spirit of God, which instructeth our hearts in faith, I say, in faith in Christ, who died for our sins, and rose again for our justification[5]. He taught that by that faith they which believe are justified; and that out of the same faith do grow sundry fruits of charity and innocency, to the bringing forth whereof he did most earnestly exhort them. He taught furthermore, that he was the fulfilling, or fulness, of the law and the prophets; and did also approve and expound the doctrine of Moses and the prophets. To doctrine he joined divers miracles and benefits, whereby he declared, that he himself was that light of the world, and the mighty and bountiful Redeemer of the world. And, to the intent that his doctrine and benefits might be known to all the world, he chose to himself witnesses, whom he called apostles, because he purposed to send them to preach throughout the world. Those witnesses were simple men, innocents, just, tellers of truth, without deceit or subtilties, and in all points holy and good; whose names it is very profitable often to repeat in the congregation. The names of the apostles are these: Peter and Andrew, James and John, Philip and Bartholomew,

The chief contents of Christ's doctrine.

The apostles of Christ.

[1 John i. 18.]   [2 John xv. 15.]
[3 John viii. 12.]   [4 John iii. 5.]
[5 Rom. iv. 25.]

Thomas and Matthew, James the son of Alphe, and Judas his brother, whose surname was Thaddæus, Simon and Judas Iscariot, into whose room (because he had betrayed the Lord) came St Matthias[6]. These had he, by the space almost of three years, hearers of his heavenly doctrine, and beholders of his divine works. These, after his ascension into the heavens, did he, by the Holy Ghost sent down from heaven, instruct with all kind of faculties. For, as they were in the scriptures passing skilful, so were they not unskilful, or wanting eloquence, in any tongue. And, being once after this manner instructed, they depart out of the city of Jerusalem, and pass through the compass of the earth, preaching to all people and nations that which they had received to preach of the Saviour of the world and the Lord Jesus Christ. And when for certain years they had preached by word of mouth, then did they also set down in writing that which they had preached. For some, verily, writ an history of the words and deeds of Christ, and some of the words and deeds of the apostles. Other some sent sundry epistles to divers nations. In all which, to confirm the truth, they use the scripture of the law and the prophets, even as we read that the Lord often-times did. Moreover, to the twelve apostles are joined two great lights of the world; John Baptist, than whom there was never any more holy born of women[7]; and the chosen vessel[8] Paul, the great teacher of the Gentiles[9].

John Baptist and Paul.

Neither is it to be marvelled at, that the forerunner and apostles of Christ had always very great dignity and authority in the church. For, even as they were the embassadors of the eternal King of all ages and of the whole world; so, being endued with the Spirit of God, they did nothing according to the judgment of their own minds. And the Lord by their ministry wrought great miracles, thereby to garnish the ministry of them, and to commend their doctrine unto us. And what may be thought of that, moreover, that by that word of God they did convert the whole world; gathering together, and laying the foundations of, notable churches throughout the compass of the world? Which verily by man's counsel and words they had never been able to have

The authority of the apostles very great.

[6 Matth. x. 2-4; Acts i. 26.]
[7 Matth. xi. 11.]   [8 Acts ix. 15.]
[9 1 Tim. ii. 7; 2 Tim. i. 11.]

brought to pass. To this is further added, that they which once leaned to this doctrine, as a doctrine giving life, did not refuse to die: besides that, how many soever had their belief in the doctrine of the gospel, they were not afraid, through water, fire, and swords, to cut off this life, and to lay hand on the life to come. The faithful saints could in no wise have done these things, unless the doctrine which they believed had been of God.

Although therefore that the apostles were men, yet their doctrine, first of all taught by a lively expressed voice, and after that set down in writing with pen and ink, is the doctrine of God and the very true word of God. For therefore the apostle left this saying in writing: " When ye did receive the word of God which ye heard of us, ye received it not as the word of men, but, as it is indeed, the word of God, which effectually worketh in you that believe[1]."

But now the matter itself and place require, that I gather also and plainly reckon up those books, wherein is contained the very word of God, first of all declared of the fathers, of Christ himself, and the apostles by word of mouth; and after that also written into books by the prophets and apostles. And in the first place verily are set the five books of Moses. Then follow the books of Josue, of Judges, of Ruth, two books of Samuel, two of Kings, two of Chronicles; of Esdras, Nehemias, and Hester one a-piece. After these come Job, David or the book of Psalms[2], Proverbs, Ecclesiastes, and Cantica. With them are numbered the four greater prophets, Esaias, Jeremias, Ezechiel, and Daniel: then the twelve lesser prophets, whose names are very well known: with these books the old Testament ended. The new Testament hath in the beginning the evangelical history of Christ the Lord, written by four authors, that is, by two apostles, Matthew and John; and by two disciples, Mark and Luke, who compiled a wonderful goodly and profitable book of the Acts of the Apostles. Paul to sundry churches and persons published fourteen epistles. The other apostles wrote seven which are called both canonical and catholic. And the books of the new Testament are ended with the

1 Thess. ii.

The roll of the books of the divine scriptures.

[1 1 Thess. ii. 13. Sermonem,—quo Deum discebatis, Lat.; and Erasmus' rendering.]

[2 Solomonis libelli tres, Lat.; omitted by the translator.]

Revelation of Jesus Christ, which he opened to the disciple whom he loved, John the evangelist and apostle; shewing unto him, and so to the whole church, the ordinance of God touching the church[3], even until the day of judgment. Therefore in these few and mean[4], not unmeasurable, in these plain and simple, not dark and unkemmed[5] books, is comprehended the full doctrine of godliness, which is the very word of the true, living, and eternal God[6].

Also the books of Moses and the prophets through so many ages, perils, and captivities, came sound and uncorrupted even until the time of Christ and his apostles. For the Lord Jesus and the apostles used those books as true copies and authentical; which undoubtedly they neither would, nor could, have done, if so be that either they had been corrupted, or altogether perished. The books also, which the apostles of Christ have added[7], were throughout all persecutions kept in the church safe and uncorrupted, and are come sound and uncorrupted into our hands, upon whom the ends of the world are fallen. For by the vigilant care and unspeakable goodness of God, our Father, it is brought to pass, that no age at any time either hath or shall want so great a treasure.

The scripture is sound and uncorrupted.

Thus much hitherto have I declared unto you, dearly beloved, what the word of God is, what the beginning of it in the church was, and what proceeding, dignity, and certainty it had. The word of God is the speech of God, that is to say, the revealing of his good will to mankind, which from the beginning, one while by his own mouth, and another while by the speech of angels, he did open to those first, ancient, and most holy fathers; who again by tradition did faithfully deliver it to their posterity. Here are to be remembered those great lights of the world, Adam, Seth, Methusalem,

[3 fata ecclesiæ, Lat.]   [4 sobriis, Lat.]

[5 unkemmed or unkempt: uncombed; impexis. —Lat. P.]

[6 The canon of Scripture received by the church of Rome, containing most of those books which we call apocryphal, was first set forth by the council of Trent; and afterwards confirmed by the bull of pope Pius IV. A.D. 1564. On this subject see Burnet on the 6th Article, with the notes in Page's Ed. 1839; and Bishop Cosin's "Scholastical History of the Canon of Scripture." P.]

[7 una cum lege et prophetis, Lat.; omitted.]

Noe, Sem, Abraham, Isaac, Jacob, Amram, and his son Moses, who, at God's commandment, did in writing comprehend the history and traditions of the holy fathers, whereunto he joined the written law, and exposition of the law, together with a large and lightsome[1] history of his own lifetime. After Moses, God gave to his church most excellent men, prophets and priests; who also, by word of mouth and writings, did deliver to their posterity that which they had learned of the Lord. After them came the only-begotten Son of God himself down from heaven into the world, and fulfilled all, whatsoever was found to be written of himself in the law and the prophets. The same also taught a most absolute mean how to live well and holily: he made the apostles his witnesses: which witnesses did afterwards first of all with a lively expressed voice preach all things which the Lord had taught them; and then, to the intent that they should not be corrupted, or clean taken out of man's remembrance, they did commit it to writing: so that now we have from the fathers, the prophets, and apostles, the word of God as it was preached and written.

These things had their beginning of one and the same Spirit of God, and do tend to one end, that is, to teach us men how to live well and holily. He that believeth not these men, and namely[2] the only-begotten Son of God, whom, I pray you, will he believe? We have here the most holy, innocent, upright-living, most praiseworthy, most just, most ancient, most wise, and most divine men of the whole world and compass of the earth, and briefly, such men as are by all means without comparison. All the world cannot shew us the like again, although it should wholly a thousand times be assembled in councils. The holy emperor Constantine gathered a general council out of all the compass of the earth; thither came there together, out of all the world, three hundred and eighteen most excellent fathers[3]: but they that are of the wisest sort will say, that these are not so much as shadows, to be compared to them, of whom we have received the word of God. Let us therefore in all things believe the word of God delivered to us by the scriptures.

[1 luculenta, Lat.]
[2 namely: especially; præsertim. P.]
[3 See before, page 12, where the number is inaccurately stated.]

Let us think that the Lord himself, which is the very living and eternal God, doth speak to us by the scriptures. Let us for evermore praise the name and goodness of him, who hath vouchedsafe so faithfully, fully, and plainly to open to us, miserable mortal men, all the means how to live well and holily.

To him be praise, honour, and glory for evermore. Amen.

OF THE WORD OF GOD; TO WHOM, AND TO WHAT END, IT WAS REVEALED; ALSO IN WHAT MANNER IT IS TO BE HEARD; AND THAT IT DOTH FULLY TEACH THE WHOLE DOCTRINE OF GODLINESS.

THE SECOND SERMON.

DEARLY beloved, in the last sermon you learned what the word of God is; from whence it came; by whom it was chiefly revealed; what proceedings[4] it had; and of what dignity and certainty it is.

Now am I come again, and, by God's favour and the help of your prayers, I will declare unto you, beloved, to whom, and to what end, the word of God is revealed; in what manner it is to be heard; and what the force thereof is, or the effect.

Our God is the God of all men and nations, who, according to the saying of the apostle, "would have all men to be saved, and to come to the knowledge of the truth [5]:" and therefore hath he, for the benefit, life, and salvation of all men, revealed his word, that so indeed there might be a rule and certain way to lead men by the path of justice into life everlasting. God verily, in the old time, did shew himself to the Israelites, his holy and peculiar people, more familiarly than to other nations, as the prophet saith: "To Jacob hath he declared his statutes, and his judgments to Israel: he hath not dealt so with any nation, neither hath he shewed them his judgments[6]:" and yet he hath not altogether been care-

To whom the word of God is revealed.

[4 progressus, Lat.]　　　　　[5 1 Tim. ii. 4.]
[6 Psal. cxlvii. 19, 20.]

less of the Gentiles. For as to the Ninivites he sent Jonas;
so Esaias, Jeremias, Daniel, and the other prophets bestowed
much labour in teaching and admonishing the Gentiles. And
those most ancient fathers, Noe, Abraham, and the rest, did
not only instruct the Jewish people which descended of
them, but taught their other sons also the judgments of God.
Our Lord Jesus Christ verily, laying open the whole world
before his disciples, said: "Teach all nations: preach the
gospel to all creatures[1]." And when as St Peter did not yet
fully understand, that the Gentiles also did appertain to the
fellowship of the church of Christ, and that to the Gentiles
also did belong the preaching of the glad tidings of salvation,
purchased by Christ for the faithful; the Lord doth instruct
him by a heavenly vision, by speaking to him out of heaven,
and by the message which came from Cornelius, as you know,
dearly beloved, by the history of the Acts of the Apostles[2].
Let us therefore think, my brethren, that the word of God
and the holy scriptures are revealed to all men, to all ages,
kinds[3], degrees and states, throughout the world. For the
apostle Paul, also confirming the same, saith: "Whatsoever
things are written, are written for our learning, that through
patience, and comfort of the scriptures, we may have hope[4]."

Let none of us therefore hereafter say, "What need I
to care what is written to the Jews in the old Testament, or
what the apostles have written to the Romans, to the Corinthians, and to other nations? I am a Christian. The prophets to the men of their time, and the apostles to those that
lived in the same age with them, did both preach and write."
For if we think uprightly of the matter, we shall see that the
scriptures of the old and new Testaments ought therefore to
be received of us, even because we are Christians. For Christ,
our Saviour and Master, did refer us to the written books of
Moses and the prophets. Saint Paul, the very elect instrument of Christ, doth apply to us the sacraments and examples
of the old fathers, that is to say, circumcision in baptism,
Coloss. ii.; and the paschal lamb in the supper or sacrament, 1 Cor. v. In the tenth chapter of the same epistle
he applieth sundry examples of the fathers to us. And in

[1 Matt. xxviii. 19.   Mark xvi. 15.]
[2 Acts x.]   [3 Sexubus, Lat.]
[4 Rom. xv. 4.]

the fourth to the Romans, where he reasoneth of faith, which justifieth without the help of works and the law, he bringeth in the example of Abraham; and therewithal addeth: "Nevertheless it is not written for Abraham alone, that faith was reckoned unto him for righteousness, but also for us, to whom it shall be reckoned if we believe[5]," &c.

"By that means," say some, "we shall again be wrapped in the law; we shall be enforced to be circumcised, to sacrifice flesh and blood of beasts, to admit again the priesthood of Aaron, together with the temple and the other ceremonies. There shall again be allowed the bill of divorcement, or putting away of a man's wife, together with sufferance to marry many wives." To these I answer: that in the old Testament we must consider that some things there are which are for ever to be observed, and some things which are ceremonial and suffered only till time of amendment[6]. That time of amendment is the time of Christ, who fulfilled the law, and took away the curse of the law. The same Christ changed circumcision into baptism. He with his own only sacrifice made an end of all sacrifices; so that now, instead of all sacrifices, there is left to us that only sacrifice of Christ, wherein also we learn to offer our own very bodies and prayers, together with good deeds, as spiritual sacrifices unto God. Christ changed the priesthood of Aaron for his own and the priesthood of all Christians. The temple of God are we, in whom God by his Spirit doth dwell. All ceremonies did Christ make void, who also in the nineteenth of Matthew did abrogate the bill of divorcement, together with the marriage of many wives. But although these ceremonies and some external actions were abrogated and clean taken away by Christ, that we should not be bound unto them; yet notwithstanding, the scripture, which was published touching them, was not taken away, or else[7] made void, by Christ. For there must for ever be in the church of Christ a certain[8] testimonial, whereby we may learn what manner of worshippings and figures of Christ they of the old time had. Those worshippings and figures of Christ must we at this day interpret to the church specially[9]; and

The writings of the old Testament are also given to Christians.

[5 Rom. iv. 23, 24.]
[6 Heb. ix. 10. tempus correctionis, Lat. So Vulgate.]
[7 i. e. or; vel, Lat.]   [8 i. e. a sure; certum, Lat.]
[9 spiritually, ed. 1577; spiritualiter, Lat. P.]

out of them we must, no less than out of the writings of the
new Testament, preach Christ, forgiveness of sins, and repentance. So then, to all Christians are the writings of the
old Testament given by God; in like manner as the apostle[1]
writ to all churches those things which bore the name or title
of some particular congregations.

To what end
the word of
God is re-
vealed.

And to this end is the word of God revealed to men,
that it may teach them[2] what, and what manner one God[3]
is towards men; that he would have them to be saved; and
that, by faith in Christ: what Christ is, and by what means
salvation cometh: what becometh the true worshippers of
God, what they ought to fly, and what to ensue. Neither is
it sufficient to know the will of God, unless we do the same
and be saved[4]. And for that cause said Moses: "Hear,
Israel, the statutes and judgments which I teach you, that ye
may do them and live[5]." And the Lord in the gospel, confirming the same, crieth: "Blessed are they which hear the
word of God and keep it[6]."

God's good-
ness to be
praised for
teaching us.

And here is to be praised the exceeding great goodness
of God, which would have nothing hid from us which maketh
any whit to live rightly, well, and holily. The wise and
learned of this world do for the most part bear envy or
grudge, that other should attain unto the true wisdom: but
our Lord doth gently, and of his own accord, offer to us the
whole knowledge of heavenly things, and is desirous that we
go forward therein; yea, and that more is, he doth further
our labour and bring it to an end. For "whosoever hath,"
saith the Lord himself in the gospel, "to him shall be given,
that he may have the more abundance[7]." "And every one
that asketh receiveth, and he that seeketh findeth, and to
him that knocketh it shall be opened[8]." Whereupon St
James the apostle saith: "If any of you lack wisdom, let
him ask of God, which giveth to all men liberally," that is,
willingly, not with grudging, "neither casteth any man in the

[1 apostles, 1577; apostoli, Lat.]
[2 De Deo et voluntate ejus, Lat. Omitted by the translator:
concerning God and his will.]
[3 What manner one; qualis, Lat. P.]
[4 ut salvi fiamus, Lat.]   [5 Deut. v. 1.]
[6 Luke xi. 28.]   [7 Matt. xiii. 12.]
[8 Luke xi. 10.]

teeth, and it shall be given him[9]." Where, by the way, we see our duty; which is, in reading and hearing the word of God, to pray earnestly and zealously that we may come to that end, for the which the word of God was given and revealed unto us. But as touching that matter, we will say somewhat more, when we come to declare in what manner of sort the word of God ought to be heard.

Now, because I have said that the word of God is revealed, to the intent that it may fully instruct us in the ways of God and our salvation; I will in few words declare unto you, dearly beloved, that in the word of God, delivered to us by the prophets and apostles, is abundantly contained the whole effect of godliness[10], and what things soever are available to the leading of our lives rightly, well, and holily. For, verily, it must needs be, that that doctrine is full, and in all points perfect, to which nothing ought either to be added, or else to be taken away. But such a doctrine is the doctrine taught in the word of God, as witnesseth Moses, Deut. iv. and xii. and Salomon, Proverb xxx.[11] What is he, therefore, that doth not confess that all points of true piety are taught us in the sacred scriptures? Furthermore, no man can deny that to be a most absolute doctrine, by which a man is so fully made perfect, that in this world he may be taken for a just man, and in the world to come be called for ever to the company of God. But he that believeth the word of God uttered to the world by the prophets and apostles, and liveth thereafter, is called a just man, and heir of life everlasting. That doctrine therefore is an absolute doctrine. For Paul also, declaring more largely and fully the same matter, saith: "All scripture, given by inspiration of God, is profitable to doctrine, to reproof, to correction, to instruction which is in righteousness, that the man of God may be perfect, instructed to all good works[12]."

Ye have, brethren, an evident testimony of the fulness of the word of God. Ye have a doctrine absolutely perfect in all points[13]. Ye have a most perfect effect of the word of God, because by this doctrine the man of God, that is, the

Marginal note: All points of true godliness are taught us in the holy scriptures.

[9 James i. 5.]   [10 pietatis rationem, Lat.]
[11 Deut. iv. 2; xii. 32.   Prov. xxx. 6.]
[12 2 Tim. iii. 16, 17.]
[13 Habetis omnes partes absolutæ doctrinæ, Lat.]

godly and devout worshipper of God, is perfect, being instructed, not to a certain few good works, but unto all and
every good work. Wherein therefore canst thou find any
want? I do not think that any one is such a sot, as to interpret these words of Paul to be spoken only touching the old
Testament; seeing it is more manifest than the day-light,
that Paul applied them to his scholar Timothy, who preached
the gospel, and was a minister of the new Testament. If so
be then, that the doctrine of the old Testament be of itself
full; by how much more shall it be the fuller, if the volume
of the new Testament be added thereunto! I am not so ignorant, but that I know that the Lord Jesus both did and spake
many things which were not written by the apostles. But
it followeth not therefore, that the doctrine of the word of
God, taught by the apostles, is not absolutely perfect. For
John, the apostle and evangelist, doth freely confess that the
Lord did many other things also, "which were not written in
his book;" but immediately he addeth this, and saith : "But
these are written, that ye might believe that Jesus is Christ
the Son of God and that in believing ye might have life
through his name[1]." He affirmeth by this doctrine, which
he contained in writing, that faith is fully taught, and that
through faith there is granted by God everlasting life. But the
end of absolute doctrine is to be happy and perfectly blessed.
Since then that cometh to man by the written doctrine of the
gospel; undoubtedly that doctrine of the gospel is most absolutely perfect.

I know, that the Lord in the gospel said, " I have many
things to tell you ; but at this time you cannot bear them :"
but therewithal I know too, that he immediately added this
saying : " But when the Spirit of truth shall come, he shall
lead you into all truth[2]." I know furthermore, that the
Spirit of truth did come upon his disciples; and therefore I
believe, that they, according to the true promise of Christ,
were led into all truth, so that it is most assuredly certain,
that nothing was wanting in them.

The Lord both spake and did many things which are not written.

[1 John xx. 30, 31.]

[2 John xvi. 12, 13. For this and the other texts, by which the
Romanists maintain patristical and ecclesiastical tradition, see the
treatise "Of Unwritten Verities" in Remains of Abp. Cranmer, Parker
Soc. ed. chap. IX.]

But some there are, which, when they cannot deny this, The apostles set down in writing the whole doctrine of godliness. do turn themselves and say, that "the apostles indeed knew all things, but yet taught them not but by word of mouth only, not setting down in writing all those things which do appertain to true godliness[3]." As though it were likely that Christ's most faithful apostles would, upon spite, have kept back any thing from their posterity. As though indeed he had lied which said, "These things are written, that in believing ye might have life everlasting." John therefore did let pass nothing which belongeth to our full instructing in the faith. Luke did omit nothing. Neither did the rest of the apostles and disciples of our Lord Jesus Christ suffer any thing to overslip them. Paul also wrote fourteen sundry epistles : but yet the most of them contained one and the selfsame matter. Whereby we may very well conjecture, that in them is wholly comprehended the absolute doctrine of godliness. For he would not have repeated one and the selfsame thing so often, to so many sundry men, if there had yet been any thing else necessary more fully to be taught for the obtaining of salvation. Those things undoubtedly would he have taught, and not have rehearsed one and the same thing so many times. Verily, in the third chapter of his epistle to the Ephesians he doth affirm, that in the two first chapters of the same his epistle he did declare his knowledge in the gospel of Christ. "God," saith he, "by revelation shewed the mystery unto me, as I wrote before in few words ; whereby when ye read ye may understand my knowledge in the mystery of Christ[4]." And this spake he touching that one and only epistle, yea, and that too touching the two first chapters of that one epistle. Whereunto when the most large and lightsome letters or epistles of St Paul himself, and also of the other apostles, are added, who, I pray you, unless he be altogether without sense, will once think, that the apostles have left in writing to us, their posterity, a doctrine not absolutely perfect ?

[3 Ex quibus omnibus...evidens (est)...quod non omnia, quæ ad religionem nostram pertinent, auctore Christo apostolorum ministerio consignata ecclesiæ, ... in scripturis explicata sint.—Albert. Pigh. Controversiarum præcipuarum, &c. Explicatio. Par. 1549. fol. 95. b. Controv. 3. de Ecclesia.]

[4 Ephes. iii. 3, 4.]

Against the lively and unfeigned[1] traditions of the apostles.

As for those which do earnestly affirm, that all points of godliness were taught by the apostles to the posterity by word of mouth, and not by writing, their purpose is to set to sale their own, that is, men's ordinances instead of the word of God.

But against this poison, my brethren, take this unto you for a medicine to expel it. Confer the things, which these fellows set to sale under the colour of the apostles' traditions, taught by word of mouth and not by writing, with the manifest writings of the apostles; and if in any place you shall perceive those traditions to disagree with the scriptures, then gather by and by, that it is the forged invention of men, and not the apostles' tradition. For they, which had one and the same Spirit of truth, left not unto us one thing in writing, and taught another thing by word of mouth. Furthermore, we must diligently search, whether those traditions do set forward the glory of God, rather than of men; or the safety of the faithful, rather than the private advantage of the priests. And we must take heed of men's traditions, especially since the Lord saith, "In vain do they worship me, teaching doctrines the precepts of men[2]." So that now the surest way is, to cleave to the word of the Lord left to us in the scriptures, which teacheth abundantly all things that belong to true godliness.

How the word of God is to be heard.

It remaineth now for me to tell, in what manner of sort this perfect doctrine of godliness and salvation, I mean, the very word of God, ought to be heard of the faithful, to the intent it may be heard with some fruit to profit them abundantly. I will in few words contain[2] it. Let the word of God be heard with great reverence, which of right is due to God himself and godly things. Let it be heard very attentively; with continual prayers between, and earnest requests. Let it be heard soberly to our profit, that by it we may become the better, that God by us may be glorified, and not that we go curiously about to search out the hidden counsels of God, or desire to be counted skilful and expert in many matters. Let true faith, the glory of God, and our salvation be appointed as the measure and certain end of our hearing and reading. For in Exodus Moses, the holy servant

[1 fained, 1577; confictas, Lat.]
[2 comprehendam, Lat.]

of God, is commanded to sanctify the people, and make them in a readiness to hear the sacred sermon, which God himself did mind to make the next day after. Moses therefore cometh, and demandeth of the whole people due obedience to be shewed, as well to God, as to his ministers. Then commandeth he them to wash their garments, to abstain from their wives. After that he appointeth certain limits, beyond which it was not lawful upon pain of death for them to pass[3]. By this we plainly learn, that the Lord doth require such to be his disciples, to hear him, as do specially shew obedience and reverence to him in all things. For he, being God, speaketh to us men : all we men owe unto God honour and fear. A man, unless he become lowly, humble, and obedient to God, is altogether godless. Then is it required at the hands of those, which are meet hearers of the word of God, that they lay apart worldly affairs, which are signified by the garments ; to tread under foot all filthiness and uncleanness of soul and body; to refrain for a season even from those pleasures which are lawful unto us. The Holy Ghost doth love the minds that are purely cleansed; which yet notwithstanding are not cleansed but by the Spirit of God. Needful it is to have a sincere belief in God, and a ready good-will and desire to live according to that which is commanded in the word of God. Moreover, we must be wise to sobriety[4]. Over curious questions must be set aside. Let things profitable to salvation only be learned. Last of all, let especial heed be taken in hearing and learning. For saith Salomon : " If thou wilt seek after wisdom as after gold, thou shalt obtain it[5]." Again he saith : " The searcher out of God's majesty shall be overwhelmed by his wonderful glory[6]." And again he saith : " Seek not things too high for thee, neither go about to search out things above thy strength ; but what God hath commanded thee, that think

[3 Exod. xix. 10—15.]

[4 Rom. xii. 3. Sapere ad sobrietatem : to think soberly, to sobriety, marg. Author. Ver.]

[5 Prov. ii. 4, 5.]

[6 Prov. xxv. 27, according to the Vulgate version, which is : " Qui scrutator est majestatis, opprimetur a gloria." "He that is a searcher of majesty (viz. of God), shall be overwhelmed by glory."— Douay Version. Calvin uses the text in the same sense, Instit. Lib. III. cap. 21. §. 2.]

[BULLINGER.]

5

thou always on: and be not over curious to know his infinite works; for it is not expedient for thee to see his hidden secrets with thine eyes[1]." Whereupon the apostle Paul saith: "Let no man think arrogantly of himself, but so think that he may be modest and sober, according as God to every one hath given the measure of faith[2]." And hereto belongeth that which the same apostle saith: "Knowledge puffeth up, and charity doth edify[3]."

The diseases and plagues of the hearers of God's word.

But chiefly we must beware of those plagues, which choke the seed of the word of God, and quench it without any fruit at all in the hearts of the hearers. Those plagues and diseases hath the Lord rehearsed, or reckoned up, in the parable of the sower[4]. For first of all, wanton and vain cogitations, which always lie wide open to the inspirations of Satan and talk of naughty men, are plagues to the word of God. Also voluptuous and dainty lovers of this world, who cannot abide to suffer any affliction for Christ and his gospel, do without any fruit at all hear God's word, although they seem to give ear unto it very joyfully. Furthermore, "the care of this world, and the deceit of riches," are most pestilent diseases in the hearers of the word of God. For they do not only hinder the seed, that it cannot bring forth fruit in their hearts; but also they do stir up and egg men forward to gainsay the word of God, and to afflict the earnest desirers of God's word. Here therefore we must take heed diligently, lest, being infected with these diseases, we become vain and unthankful hearers of the word of God.

We must pray continually, that the bountiful and liberal Lord will vouchsafe to bestow on us his Spirit, that by it the seed of God's word may be quickened in our hearts, and that we, as holy and right hearers of his word, may bear fruit abundantly to the glory of God, and the everlasting salvation of our own souls. For what will it avail to hear the word of God without faith, and without the Holy Spirit of God to work or stir inwardly in our hearts? The apostle Paul saith: "He which watereth is nothing, nor he which planteth; but it is God which giveth increase[5]." We have need therefore of God's watering, that the word of God may

What the power and effect of God's word is.

[1 Ecclesiast. iii. 21—23.]   [2 Rom. xii. 3.]
[3 1 Cor. viii. 1.]   [4 Matt. xiii. 1—23.]
[5 1 Cor. iii. 7.]

grow to a perfect age, may receive increase, yea, and may come also to the bringing forth of ripe fruit within our minds. The same apostle Paul saith: "To us also is the word of God declared, even as unto our fathers. But it availed them nothing to hear the word, because it was not joined with faith in them that heard it: for they died in the desert." And immediately after he saith: "Let us therefore do our best to enter into that rest, so that no man die in the same example of unbelief[6]." If therefore that the word of God do sound in our ears, and therewithal the Spirit of God do shew forth his power in our hearts, and that we in faith do truly receive the word of God, then hath the word of God a mighty force and wonderful effect in us. For it driveth away the misty darkness of errors, it openeth our eyes, it converteth and enlighteneth our minds, and instructeth us most fully and absolutely in truth and godliness. For the prophet David in his Psalms beareth witness, and saith: "The law of the Lord is perfect, converting the soul; the testimony of God is true, and giveth wisdom unto the simple; the commandment of the Lord is pure, and giveth light unto the eyes[7]." Furthermore, the word of God doth feed, strengthen, confirm, and comfort our souls; it doth regenerate, cleanse, make joyful, and join us to God; yea, and obtaineth all things for us at God's hands, setting us in a most happy state: insomuch that no goods or treasure of the whole world are to be compared with the word of God.

And thus much do we attribute to the word of God, not without the testimony of God's word. For the Lord by the prophet Amos doth threaten hunger and thirst, "not to eat bread and to drink water, but to hear the word of God[8]." For in the old and new Testaments it is said, "that man doth not live by bread only, but by every word that proceedeth out of the mouth of God[9]." And the apostle Paul saith, that "all things in the scriptures are written for our learning, that by patience and comfort of the scriptures we might have hope[10]." Also Peter saith: "Ye are born anew, not of corruptible seed, but of incorruptible, by the word of God which liveth and lasteth

[6 Heb. iii. 17, and iv. 2, 11.]
[7 Psal. xix. 7, 8.]
[8 Amos viii. 11.]
[9 Deut. viii. 3; Matt. iv. 4.]　　　[10 Rom. xv. 4.]

for ever. And this is the word which by the gospel was preached unto you[1]." The Lord also in the gospel beareth witness to the same, and saith: "Now are ye clean by the word which I have spoken unto you[2]." Again in the gospel he crieth, saying: "If any man loveth me, he will keep my saying, and my Father will love him, and we will come into him, and make our dwelling-place in him[3]." Jeremy saith also: "Thy word became my comfort[4]." And the prophet David saith: "The statutes of the Lord are right, and rejoice the heart[5]." Whereunto add that saying of the Lord's in the gospel: "If ye remain in me, and my words remain in you, ask what ye will, and it shall be done for you[6]." In another place also the prophet crieth, saying: "If ye be willing and will hearken, ye shall eat the good of the land; but if ye will not hear my word, the sword shall devour you[7]." Moreover Moses doth very often and largely reckon up the good things that shall happen to them which obey the word of God; Leviticus xxvi., Deut. xxviii. Wherefore David durst boldly prefer the word of God before all the pleasures and treasures of this world. "The fear of the Lord is clean, and endureth for ever; the judgments of the Lord are true, and righteous altogether: more to be desired are they than gold, yea, than much fine gold; sweeter also than honey, and the dropping honeycombs. For by them thy servant is plainly taught, and in keeping of them there is a great advantage. Therefore is the law of thy mouth more precious unto me than thousands of silver and gold. Unless my delight had been in thy law, I had perished in my misery[8]." To this now doth appertain that parable in the gospel, of him which bought the precious pearl; and of him also which sold all that he had, and bought the ground wherein he knew that treasure was hid[9]. For that precious pearl, and that treasure, are the gospel or word of God: which, for the excellency of it, is in the scriptures called a light, a fire, a sword, a maul which breaketh

[1 1 Pet. i. 23, 25.]   [2 John xv. 3.]
[3 John xiv. 23.]   [4 Jer. xv. 16.]
[5 Psal. xix. 8.]   [6 John xv. 7.]
[7 Isai. i. 19, 20.]
[8 Psal. xix. 9—11, and cxix. 72, 92.]
[9 Matt. xiii. 44—46.]

stones, a buckler [10], and by many other names like unto these.

Dearly beloved, this hour ye have heard our bountiful Lord and God, "who would have all men saved and to come to the knowledge of the truth," how he hath revealed his word to all men throughout the whole world, to the intent, that all men in all places, of what kind [11], age, or degree soever they be, may know the truth, and be instructed in the true salvation; and may learn a perfect way how to live rightly, well, and holily, so that the man of God may be perfect, instructed to all good works. For the Lord in the word of truth hath delivered to his church all that is requisite to true godliness and salvation. Whatsoever things are necessary to be known touching God, the works, judgments, will and commandments of God, touching Christ, our faith in Christ, and the duties of an holy life; all those things, I say, are fully taught in the word of God. Neither needeth the church to crave of any other, or else with men's supplies to patch up that which seemeth to be wanting in the word of the Lord. For the Lord did not only, by the lively expressed voice of the apostles, teach our fathers the whole sum of godliness and salvation; but did provide also, that it, by the means of the same apostles, should be set down in writing. And that doth manifestly appear, that it was done for the posterity's sake, that is, for us and our successors, to the intent that none of us nor ours should be seduced, nor that false traditions should be popped into any of our mouths instead of the truth. We must all therefore beware, we must all watch, and stick fast unto the word of God, which is left to us in the scriptures by the prophets and apostles.

Finally, let our care be wholly bent, with faith and profit to hear whatsoever the Lord declareth unto us: let us cast out and tread under foot whatsoever, by our flesh, the world, or the devil, is objected to be a let to godliness. We know what the diseases and plagues of the seed of God's word, sowed in the hearts of the faithful, are. We know how great the power of God's word is in them which hear it devoutly. Let us therefore beseech our Lord God to pour into our minds

[10 Psal. cxix. 105; Jer. xxiii. 29; Ephes. vi. 17; Psal. xci. 4.]
[11 sexus, Lat.]

his holy Spirit, by whose virtue the seed of God's word may be quickened in our hearts, to the bringing forth of much fruit to the salvation of our souls, and the glory of God our Father. To whom be glory for ever.

OF THE SENSE AND RIGHT EXPOSITION OF THE WORD OF GOD, AND BY WHAT MANNER OF MEANS IT MAY BE EXPOUNDED.

THE THIRD SERMON.

DEARLY beloved brethren, I do understand that, by means of my doctrine of the word of God, there are risen sundry thoughts in the hearts of many men, yea, and that of some there are sown abroad very ungodly speeches. For some there are which do suppose that the scriptures, that is, the very word of God, is of itself so dark, that it cannot be read with any profit at all[1]. And again some other affirm, that the word plainly delivered by God to mankind doth stand in need of no exposition. And therefore say they, that the scriptures ought indeed to be read of all men, but so that every man may lawfully invent and choose to himself such a sense as every one shall be persuaded in himself to be most convenient[2]. These fellows do altogether condemn the order received of the churches, whereby the minister of the church doth expound the scriptures to the congregation. But I, dearly beloved, if, as ye have begun, so ye will go forward, to pray to the Lord, do trust, by the hope that I have in God's goodness, that I am able plainly to declare, that to the godly the scripture is nothing dark at all, and that the Lord's will is altogether to have us understand it: then, that the scriptures

[1 Scripturæ plurimum frequenter obscuritatis habent, et se trahi accommodarique in diversam sententiam et eludi cauta expositione facile permittunt, etiam quantumvis claræ evidentesque appareant: adeo ut, nisi aptentur ad—ecclesiasticam—traditionis communem sententiam—fiant nobis in laqueum, etc.—Albert. Pigh. Controv. Præcip. Explicatio. Par. 1549. fol. 93. Controv. 3. de Ecclesia.]

[2 Hooker's Preface to Eccles. Pol. Vol. I. p. 180. ed. Oxf. 1820.]

ought always to be expounded.　Where also I will teach you
the manner, and some ready ways, how to interpret the scriptures.　The handling of these points shall take away the
impediments which drive men from the reading of the word
of God, and shall cause the reading and hearing of the word
of God to be both wholesome and fruitful.

　　And first of all, that God's will is to have his word un- God's will is
derstood of mankind, we may thereby gather especially, be- word under-
cause that in speaking to his servants he used a most common stood.
kind of speech, wherewithal even the very idiots[3] were acquainted.　Neither do we read that the prophets and apostles,
the servants of God and interpreters of his high and everlasting wisdom, did use any strange kind of speech : so that in
the whole pack of writers none can be found to excel them in
a more plain and easy phrase of writing.　Their writings are
full of common proverbs, similitudes, parables, comparisons,
devised narrations, examples, and such other like manner of
speeches, than which there is nothing that doth more move
and plainly teach the common sorts of wits among mortal
men.　There ariseth, I confess, some darkness in the scriptures, by reason of the natural property[4], figurative orna-
ments, and the unacquainted use of the tongues.　But that Difficulty in
difficulty may easily be helped by study, diligence, faith, and tures.
the means of skilful interpreters.　I know that the apostle
Peter saith, in the epistles of Paul "many things are hard
to be understood[5] :" but immediately he addeth, " which the
unlearned, and those that are unperfect, or unstable, pervert,
as they do the other scriptures also, unto their own destruction."　Whereby we gather, that the scripture is difficult or
obscure to the unlearned, unskilful, unexercised, and malicious
or corrupted wills, and not to the zealous and godly readers or
hearers thereof.　Therefore, when St Paul saith, " If as yet
our gospel be hid, from them it is hid which perish, in whom
the prince of this world hath blinded the understanding of the
unbelievers, that to them there should not shine the light of
the gospel of the glory of Christ, who is the image of God[6];"

　[3 Idiot: an uneducated person, ἰδιώτης.　P.]
　[4 ex idiomate, Lat.]
　[5 2 Pet. iii. 16.]
　[6 2 Cor. iv. 3, 4.　"Lest the light of the gospel of the glory of
Christ."—Cranmer's Bible, 1539.]

he doth not lay the blame of this difficulty on the word of
God, but upon the unprofitable hearers. Whosoever we are,
therefore, that do desire rightly to understand the word of
God, our care must be that Satan possess not our minds, and
close up our eyes. For our Saviour also in the gospel said:
"This is damnation, because the light came into the world, and
men loved darkness rather than light[1]." Besides that, the holy
prophets of God, and the apostles, did not call the word of
God, or the scriptures, darkness, obscureness, or mistiness, but
a certain brightness and lightsomeness. David saith: "Thy
word is a lantern unto my feet, and a light unto my paths[2]."
And what, I pray you, is more evident, than that, in making
doubtful and obscure things manifest, no man doth refer to
darkness and uncertainties? Things uncertain, doubtful, and
obscure, are made manifest by those things that are more
certain, sure, and evident. But, as often as any question or
controversy doth happen in matters of faith, do not all men
agree, that it ought to be ended and determined by the scriptures? It must therefore needs be, that the scriptures are
evident, plain, and most assuredly certain.

The word of God requireth an exposition. But, though the scripture be manifest and the word of
God be evident, yet, notwithstanding, it refuseth not a godly
or holy exposition; but rather an holy exposition doth give
a setting out to the word of God, and bringeth forth much
fruit in the godly hearer. And for because many do deny
that the scriptures ought to have any exposition, I will shew
by examples (which cannot be gainsaid) that they ought altogether to be expounded. For God himself, having often
communication with Moses by the space of forty days, and as
many years, did by Moses expound to the church the words
of the law, which he spake in Mount Sina to the whole congregation of Israel, writing them in two tables: which Moses
left to us the Deuteronomy, and certain other books, as commentaries upon God's commandments. After that, immediately followed the prophets, who, interpreting the law of
Moses, did apply it to the times, places, and men of their age;
and left to us, that follow, their sermons as plain expositions of
A solemn exposition of God's word. God's law. In the eighth chapter of Nehemias we read these
words: "Esdras the priest brought in the law, the book of
Moses, and stood upon a turret made of wood, (that is, in the

[1] John iii. 19.]   [2] Ps. cxix. 105.]

holy pulpit.) And Esdras opened the book before the congregation of men and women, and whosoever else had any understanding. And the Levites stood with him, so that he read out of the book, and the Levites instructed the people in the law, and the people stood in their place, and they read in the book of the law distinctly, expounding the sense, and causing them to understand the reading[3]." Thus much in the book of Nehemias. Mark here by the way, my brethren, that the lawful and holy ministers of the church of God did not only read the word of God, but did also expound it.

This manner of reading and expounding the scriptures, or word of God, our Lord Jesus Christ did neither abrogate nor contemn, when, coming in the flesh, he did as a true prophet and heavenly master[4] instruct the people of his church in the doctrine of the new Testament. For entering into the synagogue at Nazareth, he stood up to read; and there was delivered to him the book of the prophet Esay. So he opened the book, and read a certain notable place out of the sixty-first chapter. Then, shutting the book, he gave it to the minister again, and expounded that which he had read, declaring how that in himself now that prophecy was fulfilled[5]. Moreover, after that he was risen from death, he joined himself in company to the two disciples, which went to Emaus; with whom he talked of sundry matters: but at length, "beginning at Moses and all the prophets, he expounded to them whatsoever was written of himself throughout all the scriptures[6]." The apostles, following this example of the Lord, did themselves also expound the word of God. For Peter, in the second chapter of the Acts of the Apostles, doth expound the sixteenth Psalm of Christ's resurrection from the dead[7]. And Philip also doth plainly expound to the nobleman of Ethiope the prophecy of Esay, whereby he bringeth him to the faith of Christ and fellowship of the church[8]. Whosoever doth say, that Paul doth not every where interpret the holy scripture, he hath neither read nor

[3 Nehem. viii. 2—8.]

[4 Adeoque novi Testamenti aut christianæ ecclesiæ doctor:—Lat. omitted by the translator: and so a teacher of the new Testament, or of the christian church.]

[5 Luke iv. 16—21.]   [6 Luke xxiv. 15—27.]

[7 Acts ii. 25—31.]   [8 Acts viii. 30—38.]

seen the deeds nor writings of Paul. Thus have I, I hope, both plainly and substantially shewed, that the word of God ought to be expounded.

What their meaning is that will not have the scriptures expounded.

And for those which cry out against the exposition of the scriptures, and would not have the ministers of the word and churches to declare the scriptures in open and solemn audience, neither to apply them to the places, times, states, and persons, their fetch[1] is to seek somewhat else than the honour due unto God. They lead their lives far otherwise than is comely for godly men. Their talk is wicked, unseemly, and dishonest. Their deeds are mischievous and heinous offences. And this would they do without punishment, and therefore desire to have the exposition of the scriptures to be taken clean away. For if a man do read the words of the scripture only, not applying it to the states, places, times, and persons, it seemeth that he hath not greatly touched their ungodly and wicked life. Therefore, when they cry that sermons and expositions of the scriptures ought to be taken away from among men, and that the scriptures ought to be read simply without any addition; they mind nothing else but to cast behind them the law of God, to tread under foot all discipline and rebuking of sin, and so to offend freely without punishment: which sort of men the righteous Lord will in his appointed time punish so much the more grievously, as they do more boldly rebel against their God.

The scriptures are not to be corrupted with foreign expositions.

In the mean season, all the ministers of the church must beware, that they follow not herein their own affections any whit at all, or else corrupt the scriptures by their wrong interpretations; and so by that means set forth to the church their own inventions, and not the word of God. Some such like offence it seemeth that the teachers of the ancient people in old time did commit, because the Lord in Ezechiel accuseth them, saying: " Seemeth it a small thing to you to have eaten up the good pasture, but that ye must also tread the residue of your pasture under your feet? and to drink the clearer water, but that ye must trouble the rest with your feet? Thus my sheep must be fain to eat the thing that is trodden down with your feet, and to drink that which ye with your feet have defiled[2]." A sore offence is this, which the Lord according to his justice punisheth most sharply. We

[1 quærunt, Lat.] [2 Ezek. xxxiv. 18, 19.]

therefore, the interpreters of God's holy word, and faithful ministers of the church of Christ, must have a diligent regard to keep the scriptures sound and perfect, and to teach the people of Christ the word of God sincerely; made plain, I mean, and not corrupted or darkened by foolish and wrong expositions of our own invention.

And now, dearly beloved, the place and time require us to say somewhat unto you touching the interpretation of the holy scriptures, or the exposition of the word of God. Wherein I will not speak any thing particularly of the skilful knowledge of tongues, or the liberal sciences, which are things requisite in a good interpreter; but will briefly touch the generalities alone. And first of all ye must understand, that some things in the scriptures, or word of God, are so plainly set forth, that they have need of no interpretation, neither will admit any exposition: which if any man go about with his own expositions to make more manifest, he may seem to do as wittily as he, which with fagot-light and torches would help the sun at his rising to give more light unto the world. As for those things which are so set down, that they seem to require our help to expound them, they must not be interpreted after our own fantasies, but according to the mind and meaning of him, by whom the scriptures were revealed. For St Peter saith: "The prophecy came not in old time by the will of man; but holy men of God spake as they were moved by the Holy Ghost[3]." Therefore the true and proper sense of God's word must be taken out of the scriptures themselves, and not be forcibly thrust upon the scriptures, as we ourselves lust. And therewithal ye must mark a few certain rules, which I mean briefly to touch and to shew unto you, in those few words which I have yet to speak.

First, since the apostle Paul would have the exposition of the scriptures to agree fitly, and in every point proportionally with our faith; as it is to be seen in the twelfth to the Romans[4]: and because again in the latter epistle to the Corinthians he saith, "Seeing then that we have the same spirit of faith (according as it is written, I believed, and there-

The holy scriptures are not to be expounded according to men's fantasies.

The exposition of the scripture must not be contrary to the articles of our belief.

[3] 2 Pet. i. 20, 21. The translator has here omitted, "omnis scriptura prophetica non est privatæ interpretationis." "No prophecy of scripture is of any private interpretation." P.]

[4] Rom. xii. 6. Respondere proportioni fidei, Lat.]

fore have I spoken), we also believe, and therefore do we speak[1]:" let it therefore be taken for a point of catholic religion, not to bring in or admit any thing in our expositions which others have alleged against the received articles of our faith, contained in the Apostles' Creed and other confessions of the ancient fathers. For saith the apostle: "In defence of the truth we can say somewhat, but against the truth we are able to say nothing[2]." When therefore in the gospel after St John we read the saying of the Lord, "The Father is greater than I[3]," we must think, that it is against the articles of our faith to make or admit any inequality in the Godhead betwixt the Father and the Son; and therefore, that the Lord's meaning was otherwise than the very words at the first blush do seem to import. Again, when we read this saying of the apostle, "It cannot be that they which were once illuminated, if they fall away, should be renewed again into repentance[4];" let us not believe that repentance is to be denied to them that fall: for the catholic faith is this, that in every place, at every season, so long as we live on this earth, a full pardon of all sins is promised to all men which turn to the Lord. In like manner, when we read that the Lord took bread, and said of the bread, "This is my body[5];" let us presently remember, that the articles of our faith do attribute to our Lord the very body of a man, which ascended into heaven, and sitteth at the right hand of the Father, from whence it shall come to judge the quick and the dead; and let us think, that the Lord, speaking of the sacrament, would have us to expound the words of the sacrament sacramentally, and not transubstantially. Also in reading that saying of the apostle, "Flesh and blood cannot inherit the kingdom of God[6];" let us not by and by upon these words take it simply as the words do seem to signify, but sticking to the article of our faith, "I believe the resurrection of the body[7]," let us understand, that by flesh and blood are meant the affections and infirmities, not the nature and substance, of our bodies.

The exposition must not be repugnant to the love of God and our neighbour.

Furthermore, we read in the gospel, that the Lord doth gather a sum of the law and the prophets, saying: "Thou

[1 2 Cor. iv. 13.]   [2 2 Cor. xiii. 8.]
[3 John xiv. 28.]   [4 Heb. vi. 4—6.]
[5 Matt. xxvi. 26.]   [6 1 Cor. xv. 50.]
[7 hujus carnis, Lat.   Of this body.   See below, page 168.]

shalt love the Lord thy God with all thy heart, with all thy soul, and with all thy mind : this is the chief and great commandment. And the second is like unto it : Thou shalt love thy neighbour as thyself. In these two commandments hangeth the whole law and the prophets[8]." Matt. xxii. Upon these words of the Lord that holy man Aurelius Augustinus, in the thirty-sixth chapter of his first book *De Doctrina Christi*, saith : " Whosoever doth seem to himself to understand the holy scriptures, or any part thereof, so that [with] that understanding he doth not work these two points of charity towards God and his neighbour, he yet doth not understand the scriptures perfectly. But whosoever shall take out of them such an opinion as is profitable to the working of this charity, and yet shall not say the self-same thing which shall be proved that he did mean whom he readeth in that place ; that man doth not err to his own destruction, nor doth altogether by lying deceive other men[9]." Thus much writ Augustine. We must therefore, by all means possible, take heed that our interpretations do not tend to the overthrow of charity, but to the furtherance and commendation of it to all men. The Lord saith: " Strive not with the wicked[10]." But if we affirm that he spake this to the magistrates also, then shall charity towards our neighbours, the safety of them that are in jeopardy, and defence of the oppressed, be broken and clean taken away. For thieves and unruly persons, robbers, and naughty fellows, will oppress the widows, the fatherless, and the poor, so that all iniquity shall reign and have the upper hand. But in a matter so manifestly known I suppose it is not needful to use many examples.

Moreover, it is requisite in expounding the scriptures, and searching out the true sense of God's word, that we mark upon what occasion every thing is spoken, what goeth before,

In expounding the scriptures, we must mark that that

[8 Matt. xxii. 37—40.]

[9 Quisquis igitur scripturas divinas, vel quamlibet earum partem, intellexisse sibi videtur, ita ut eo intellectu non ædificet istam geminam caritatem Dei et proximi, nondum intellexit. Quisquis vero talem inde sententiam duxerit, ut huic ædificandæ caritati sit utilis, nec tamen hoc dixerit, quod ille, quem legit, eo loco sensisse probatur; non perniciose fallitur, nec omnino mentitur.—Aug. de Doct. Christ. I. 36. Par. 1531. Tom. III. fol. 5. P.]

[10 ne restiteritis malo, Lat. Matt. v. 39.]

goeth before
and followeth
after, and
also the cir-
cumstances.

what followeth after, at what season, in what order, and of
what person any thing is spoken. By the occasion, and the
sentences going before and coming after, are examples and
parables for the most part expounded. Also, unless a man do
always mark the manner of speaking throughout the whole
scriptures, and that very diligently too, he cannot choose in
his expositions but err very much out of the right way.
St Paul, observing the circumstance of the time, did thereby
conclude that Abraham was justified, neither by circumcision,
nor yet by the law. The places are to be seen in the fourth
to the Romans and the third to the Galatians. Again, when
it is said to Peter, " Put up thy sword into thy sheath : he
that taketh the sword shall perish with the sword[1];" we must
consider, that Peter bare the personage of an apostle, and not
of a magistrate : for of the magistrate we read, that to him
is given the sword to revengement[2].—But it would be over
tedious and too troublesome to rehearse more examples of
every particular place.

The exposi-
tion of God's
word must
be made by
the laying
together of
divers places.

There is also, beside these, another manner of interpreting
the word of God; that is, by conferring together the places
which are like or unlike, and by expounding the darker by
the more evident, and the fewer by the more in number.
Whereas therefore the Lord saith, " The Father is greater
than I;" we must consider, that the same Lord in another
place saith, " My Father and I are all one[3]." And whereas
James the apostle saith, that Abraham and we are justified
by works[4], there are many places in St Paul to be set
against that one. And this manner of interpreting did Peter

2 Pet. i.

the apostle allow, where he saith : " We have a right sure
word of prophecy, whereunto if ye attend, as unto a light
that shineth in a dark place, ye do well, until the day dawn,
and the day-star arise in your hearts."

That ancient writer Tertullian affirmeth, that " they are
heretics, and not men of the right faith, which draw some odd
things out of the scriptures to their own purpose, not having
any respect to the rest; but do by that means pick out unto
themselves a certain few testimonies, which they would have
altogether to be believed, the whole scripture in the mean

[1 Matt. xxvi. 52.]   [2 Rom. xiii. 4.]
[3 John xiv. 28, and x. 30.]
[4 James ii. 21, 24.]

season gainsaying it : because indeed the fewer places must be understood according to the meaning of the more in number[5]."

And finally, the most effectual rule of all, whereby to expound the word of God, is an heart that loveth God and his glory, not puffed up with pride, not desirous of vain-glory, not corrupted with heresies and evil affections; but which doth continually pray to God for his holy Spirit, that, as by it the scripture was revealed and inspired, so also by the same Spirit it may be expounded to the glory of God and safeguard of the faithful. Let the mind of the inter-preter be set on fire with zeal to advance virtue, and with hatred of wickedness, even to the suppressing thereof. Let not the heart of such an expositor call to counsel that subtle sophister the devil, lest peradventure now also he do corrupt the sense of God's word, as heretofore he did in paradise. Let him not abide to hear man's wisdom argue directly against the word of God. This if the good and faithful expositor of God's word shall do, then, although in some points he do not (as the proverb saith) hit the very head of the nail[6] in the darker sense of the scripture; yet notwith-standing that error ought not to be condemned for an heresy in the author, nor judged hurtful unto the hearer. And whosoever shall bring the darker and more proper meaning of the scripture to light, he shall not by and by condemn the unperfect exposition of that other : no more than he which is author of the unperfect exposition shall reject the more proper sense of the better expositor, but by acknow-ledging it shall receive it with thanksgiving.

The scriptures must be expounded with a zealous heart after earnest prayer.

Thus much hitherto have I said touching the sense and exposition of God's word : which, as God revealed it to men, so also he would have them in any case to understand it. Wherefore there is no cause for any man, by reason of a few difficulties, to despair to attain to the true understanding of the scriptures. The scripture doth admit a godly and religious interpretation. The word of God is a rule for all

[5] De scripturis ad sententiam suam excerpent, cetera nolentes intueri . . . . cum oporteat secundum plura intelligi pauciora. Sed proprium hoc est omnium hæreticorum. — Tertull. adv. Praxeam, cap. 20. Opp. ed. Semler. Tom. II. p. 183. Hal. Mag. 1828.]

[6] The proverb which Bullinger has adopted is "acu rem tetigisti."]

men and ages to lead their lives by : therefore ought it
by interpretation to be applied to all ages and men of all
sorts.   For even our God himself did by Moses in many
words expound and apply to his people the law, which he
gave and published in Mount Sina.   Furthermore, it was
a solemn use among the ancient prophets first to read, and
then by expositions to apply, God's law to the people.   Our
Lord Jesus Christ himself expounded the scriptures.   The
same did the apostles also.   The word of God therefore
ought to be expounded.   As for those which would not have
it expounded, their meaning is, because they would sin freely,
without controlling or punishment.   But whereas the scripture doth admit an exposition, it doth not yet admit any
exposition whatsoever : for that which savoureth of man's
imagination it utterly rejecteth.   For as by the Spirit of
God the scripture was revealed, so by the same Spirit it is
requisite to expound it.   There are therefore certain rules
to expound the word of God religiously by the very word
of God itself : that is, so to expound it, that the exposition
disagree not with the articles of our faith, nor be contrary
to charity towards God and our neighbour ; but that it be
thoroughly surveyed, and grounded upon that which went
before and followeth after, by diligent weighing of all the
circumstances, and laying together of the places.   And chiefly
it is requisite, that the heart of the interpreter be godly bent,
willing to plant virtue and pluck up vice by the roots, and
finally, always ready evermore to pray to the Lord, that he
will vouchsafe to illuminate our minds, that God's name may
in all things be glorified.   For his is the glory, honour, and
dominion, for ever and ever.   Amen.

OF TRUE FAITH; FROM WHENCE IT COMETH; THAT
    IT IS AN ASSURED BELIEF OF THE MIND, WHOSE
    ONLY STAY IS UPON GOD AND HIS WORD.

THE FOURTH SERMON.

In my last sermon I declared unto you, how that the
perfect exposition of God's word doth differ nothing from the
rule of true faith and the love of God and our neighbour.
For undoubtedly that sense of scripture is corrupted, which
doth square[1] from faith and the two points of charity.   I
have now therefore next to treat of true faith and charity
towards God and our neighbour; to the intent, that no man
may find lack of any thing herein.   And first, therefore, by
God's help, and the good means of your prayers, I will speak
of true faith.

This word "faith," or "belief," is diversly used in the common talk of men.   For it is taken for any kind of religion or
honour done to God: as we say, the Christian faith, the
Jewish faith, and the Turkish faith.   Faith, or belief, also is
taken for a conceived opinion of any thing that is told us: as
when we hear any thing rehearsed unto us out of the Indian
or Ethiopian history, we by and by say that we believe it;
and yet notwithstanding we put no confidence in it, nor hope
to have any commodity thereby at all.   This is that faith
wherewith St James saith that the devil believeth and trem-
bleth[2].   Last of all, faith is commonly put for an assured
and undoubted confidence in God and his word.   Among the
Hebrews faith taketh her name of truth[3], certainty, and assured
constancy.   The Latins call that faith, when that is done[4]
which is said.   Whereupon one saith, "I demand of thee
whether thou believest or no?"   Thou answerest: "I believe."   The defini-
"Do then that which thou sayest, and it is faith."   Therefore,   tions of
                                                                   faith.

[1 cum fide pugnat.]   [2 James ii. 19.]

[3 אֱמוּנָה *faithfulness*, from אָמַן to *prop, stay, support*, to *be firm.*
אֱמֶת *faithfulness, truth.*   See the Lexicons.]

[4 Fides, quod fiat, quod dicitur, Lat.   "Credamus, quia fiat
quod dictum est, appellatam fidem."—Cic. de Off. I. 7.]

[BULLINGER.]   6

in this treatise of ours, Faith is an undoubted belief, most firmly grounded in the mind.

This faith, which is a settled and undoubted persuasion or belief leaning upon God and his word, is diversly defined by the perfecter divines. St Paul saith: "Faith is the substance of things hoped for, the evidence of things not seen[1]." The substance, or *hypostasis*[2], is the foundation, or the unmoveable prop, which upholdeth us, and whereon we lean and lie without peril or danger. The things hoped for are things celestial, eternal, and invisible. And therefore Paul saith: Faith is an unmoveable foundation, and a most assured confidence of God's promises, that is, of life everlasting and all his good benefits. Moreover Paul himself, making an exposition of that which he had spoken, immediately after saith: "Faith is the argument of things not seen." An argument or proof is an evident demonstration, whereby we manifestly prove that which otherwise should be doubtful, so that in him, whom we undertook to instruct, there may remain no doubt at all.

But now, touching the mysteries of God revealed in God's word, in themselves, or in their own nature, they cannot be seen with bodily eyes; and therefore are called things not seen. But this faith, by giving light to the mind, doth in heart perceive them, even as they are set forth in the word of God. Faith, therefore, according to the definition of Paul, is in the mind a most evident seeing[3], and in the heart a most certain perceiving[4] of things invisible, that is, of things eternal; of God, I say, and all those things which he in his word setteth forth unto us concerning spiritual things.

To this definition of Paul's they had an eye which defined faith in this sort: "Faith is a grounded persuasion of heavenly things, in the meditation whereof we ought so to occupy ourselves for the assured truth's sake of God's word, that we may believe, that in mind we do see those things as well, as with our eyes we do behold things sensibly perceived

[1 Heb. xi. 1.]

[2 ὑπόστασις, proprie, *fundamentum, fulcrum*, &c. Schleusner Lex in voc. In this exposition of Heb. xi. 1, Bullinger and Calvin agree, in several parts, word for word. See Calv. Instit. Lib. III. cap. 2. §. 41.]

[3 saying, ed. 1587, Lat. evidentissima mentis *visio.*]

[4 Comprehensio, Lat.]

and easy to be seen[5]." This description doth not greatly
differ from this definition of another godly and learned man,
who saith: "Faith is a stedfast persuasion of the mind,
whereby we do fully decree with ourselves that God's truth
is so sure, that he can neither will, nor choose, but perform
that which he in his word hath promised to fulfil[6]." Again:
"Faith is a stedfast assuredness of conscience, which doth
embrace Christ in the same sort wherein he is offered unto
us by the gospel[7]." Another there is which after the same
manner almost defineth faith in this sort: "Faith is a gift
inspired by God into the mind of man, whereby, without
any doubting at all, he doth believe that to be most true
whatsoever God hath either taught or promised in the books
of both the testaments[8]." The very same author of this
definition, therefore, doth extend faith to three terms of
time: to the time past, the time present, and the time to
come. For he teacheth to believe that the world was made
by God, and whatsoever the holy scriptures do declare to
have been done in the old world; also that Christ dying for
us is the only salvation of them which believe: and that

[5 The editor has not succeeded in tracing this definition to its
source. The original Latin gives the definition thus: Fides est rerum divinarum persuasio, quarum cogitationi ita incumbere debemus,
propter oraculorum fidem, ut non minus ea cernere animo credamus,
quam oculis res sensu perceptas et aspectabiles cernimus.]

[6 This definition is thus given in the original Latin: Fides est
firma animi persuasio, qua nobiscum statuimus tam certam esse Dei
veritatem, ut non possit non præstare quod se facturum sancto suo
verbo recipit.—The editor has not been able to discover these exact
words in Calvin's writings; but similar definitions are found in his Institutes, Lib. III. cap. 2. § 42, and Vera Eccles. Reform. Ratio. Tom.
VIII. p. 275, ed. Amstel.]

[7 Fides, inquam, firma est conscientiæ certitudo, quæ Christum
amplectitur, qualis nobis per evangelium offertur.—Calvin. Vera Eccles. Reform. Ratio. Opp. Tom. VIII. p. 275. a.]

[8 A definition of Faith, almost the same as this, is found in Gropper's Enchiridion, attached to the edition of 1538 of the Canons of a
synod of the province of Cologne, and is as follows: Fides est donum
menti hominis divinitus infusum, quo citra ullam hæsitantiam credit
esse verissima, quæcunque divina eloquia docuerunt.— In Symbol.
Apost. fol. 49. Colon. In a later work, also, Gropper says: Fides
est præteritorum, præsentium, et futurorum.—Instit. Cathol. p. 232,
Colon. 1554.]

by the same God, at this day also, the world and church are governed or preserved, and that in Christ the faithful are saved : last of all, that that shall most assuredly light upon the ungodly and the godly, whatsoever the holy scriptures do either threaten or promise.

The description of true faith.

Out of all these definitions, therefore, being diligently considered, we may, according to the scriptures, make this description of faith : Faith is a gift of God, poured into man from heaven, whereby he is taught with an undoubted persuasion wholly to lean to God and his word ; in which word God doth freely promise life and all good things in Christ, and wherein all truth necessary to be believed is plainly declared. Which description of faith I will, by God's help, in this that followeth unfold into parts, and by assertion of places out of the scriptures will both confirm and make manifest unto you. Ye, as hitherto ye have done, so still give diligent ear, and in your hearts pray earnestly to God.

The beginning and cause of faith.

First of all, the cause or beginning of faith cometh not of any man, or any strength of man, but of God himself, who by his Holy Spirit inspireth faith into our hearts. For in the gospel the Lord saith : " No man cometh to me unless my Father draw him[1]." And again : " Flesh and blood," saith the Lord to Peter, confessing Christ in true faith, "hath not revealed this to thee, but my Father which is in heaven[2]." Whereunto the apostle Paul alludeth when he saith : " We are not able of ourselves to think anything as of ourselves, but all our ability is of God[3]." And in another place : " To you it is given for Christ, not only to believe in him, but also to suffer for his sake[4]." Faith therefore is poured into our hearts by God, who is the well-spring and cause of all goodness.

Faith is planted by the word of God.

And yet we have to consider here, that God, in giving and inspiring faith, doth not use his absolute power, or miracles, in working ; but a certain ordinary means agreeable to man's capacity : although he can indeed give faith without those means, to whom, when, and how it pleaseth him. But we read, that the Lord hath used this ordinary means even from the first creation of all things. Whom he meaneth to bestow knowledge and faith on, to them he sendeth teachers,

[1 John vi. 44.]   [2 Matt. xvi. 17.]
[3 2 Cor. iii. 5.]   [4 Phil. i. 29.]

by the word of God to preach true faith unto them. Not
because it lieth in man's power, will, or ministry, to give faith;
nor because the outward word spoken by man's mouth is able
of itself to bring faith : but the voice of man, and the preaching of God's word, do teach us what true faith is, or what
God doth will and command us to believe. For God himself
alone, by sending his Holy Spirit into the hearts and minds of
men, doth open our hearts, persuade our minds, and cause us
with all our heart to believe that which we by his word and
teaching have learned to believe. The Lord could by miracle
from heaven, without any preaching at all, have bestowed
faith in Christ upon Cornelius the Centurion at Cesaria[5] : but
yet by an angel he doth send him to the preaching of Peter;
and while Peter preacheth, God by his Holy Spirit worketh
in the heart of Cornelius, causing him to believe his preaching. Verily St Paul saith : "How shall they believe in him
of whom they have not heard? How shall they hear without a preacher? And how shall they preach if they be not
sent? So then, faith cometh by hearing, and hearing by
the word of God[6]." In another place also, "Who is Paul,"
saith he, "or what is Apollos, but ministers, by whom ye
have believed, according as God hath given to every one?
I have planted, Apollos watered, but God hath given increase.
So then he that planteth is nothing, nor he that watereth,
but God that giveth increase[7]." With this doctrine of St Peter
and St Paul doth that agree which Augustine writeth in the
preface of his book of Christian Doctrine, where he saith :
"That which we have to learn at man's hand, let every one
learn at man's hand without disdain. And let us not go
about to tempt him in whom we believe; neither, being deceived, let us think scorn to go to church, to hear or learn
out of books, looking still when we shall be rapt up into the
third heaven. Let us take heed of such like temptations of
pride, and let us rather have this in our minds, that even the
apostle Paul himself, although he were cast prostrate, and instructed by the calling of God from heaven, was nevertheless
sent to a man to be taught the will of God : and that Corne-

[5] Apud Cæsaream Stratonis, Lat.　　Strato's Tower was the
earlier name of Cæsarea Palæstina.—Relandi Palæstin. Illustr. Lib. III.
in voc. Cæsarea.]

[6] Rom. x. 14, 15, 17.]　　　　　　　　[7] 1 Cor. iii. 5—7.]

lius, although God had heard his prayers, was committed to
Peter to be instructed; by whom he should not only receive
the sacraments, but should also hear what he ought to believe,
what to hope for, and what to love: all which things notwithstanding might have been done by the angel," &c.[1]   The
same Augustine also, in his Epistle to the Circenses, saith:
" Even he worketh conversion and bringeth it to pass, who
by his ministers doth warn us outwardly with the signs of
things, but inwardly doth by himself teach us with the very
things themselves[2]."   Also in his treatise, the xxvi. upon John:
"What do men" (saith he) "when they preach outwardly?
What do I now while I speak?   I drive into your ears a
noise of words: but unless he which is within do reveal it,
what say I, or what speak I?   He that is without doth husband the tree, but he within is the creator of it[3]," &c.   This
said he.

We must
pray for true
faith.

But, even as the Lord his desire is, to have us believe his

[1 Quod per hominem discendum est, sine superbia discat; et per
quem docetur alius, sine invidia tradat quod accepit.   Neque tente-
mus eum cui credidimus, ne talibus inimici versutiis et perversitate
decepti, ad ipsum quoque evangelium audiendum atque discendum
nolimus ire in ecclesias, aut codicem legere, aut legentem prædican-
temque hominem audire, et exspectemus rapi usque in tertium cœlum,
sive in corpore, sive extra corpus, sicut dicit Apostolus, et ibi audire
ineffabilia verba, quæ non licet homini loqui, aut ibi videre Dominum
Jesum Christum, et ab illo potius quam ab hominibus audire evangelium.   Caveamus tales tentationes superbissimas et periculosissimas,
magisque cogitemus et ipsum Apostolum Paulum, licet divina et
cœlesti voce prostratum et instructum, ad hominem tamen missum
esse ut sacramenta perciperet atque copularetur ecclesiæ; et centu-
rionem Cornelium, quamvis exauditas orationes ejus eleemosynasque
respectas ei angelus nunciaverit, Petro tamen traditum imbuendum,
per quem non solum sacramenta perciperet, sed etiam quid credendum, quid sperandum, quid diligendum esse audiret.   Et poterant
utique omnia per angelum fieri.—August. ex Præf. in Lib. de Doctr.
Christiana. Par. 1531. Tom. III. fol. 2.]

[2 Hoc agit ille et efficit, qui per ministros suos rerum signis extrin-
secus admonet, rebus autem ipsis per seipsum intrinsecus docet.—Ad
Circenses. Ep. cxxx. Tom. II. fol. 124.]

[3 Quid faciunt homines forinsecus annunciantes?   Quid faci-
modo ego, cum loquor?   Strepitum verborum ingero auribus vestris.
Nisi ergo revelet ille qui intus est, quid dico, aut quid loquor?   Exte-
rior cultor arboris: interior est creator.—In Joh. cap. vi. Tract. 26.
Tom. IX. fol. 47.]

word, (for the prophet crieth out and saith, "To-day if ye
will hear his voice, harden not your hearts;[4]") so in like
manner he doth require of us all, which hear his word, that
we be not slack in praying. For, in hearing the word of
God, we must pray for the gift of faith, that the Lord may
open our hearts, convert our souls, break and beat down the
hardness of our minds, and increase the measure of faith bestowed upon us. Of this order of prayer there are many
examples in the holy scriptures. When the Lord in the
gospel said to one, "Canst thou believe? to him that believeth
all things are possible;" he made answer, saying, "I believe,
Lord, help thou mine unbelief[5]." The apostles also cry to
the Lord, and say: "O Lord, increase our faith[6]." Moreover,
this prayer, wherein we desire to have faith poured into us,
is of the grace and gift of God, and not of our own righteousness, which before God is none at all. This therefore is left
unto us for a thing most certain and undoubtedly true, that
true faith is the mere gift of God, which is by the Holy
Ghost from heaven bestowed upon our minds, and is declared
unto us in the word of truth by teachers sent of God, and is
obtained by earnest prayers which cannot be tired. Whereby
we learn, that we ought often and attentively to hear the
word of God, and never cease to pray to God for the obtaining of true faith.

But that this faith, inspired from heaven, and learned out *That faith is*
of the word of truth, doth put into man's mind an undoubted *an undoubted*
persuasion of
persuasion; that is, that whatsoever we believe in the word of *the mind.*
God, we do believe it most assuredly, without wavering or
doubting, being altogether as sure to have the thing, as faith
doth believe to have it (for I use this word persuasion, not as
it is commonly taken, but for a firm assent of mind, inspired
and persuaded by the Holy Ghost;) that this faith, I say, doth
put into man's mind this undoubted persuasion, I mean to
declare by the example of Abraham's faith, which Paul in the
fourth chapter to the Romans describeth in these words:
"Abraham, contrary to hope, believed in hope: and he fainted
not in faith, neither considered he his own body now dead,
when he was almost an hundred years old, nor the deadness
of Sarae's womb; he stackered[7] not at the promise of God

[4 Psal. xcv. 7, 8.]   [5 Mark ix. 23, 24.]   [6 Luke xvii. 5.]
[7 So in Tyndale's and Cranmer's Versions.]

through unbelief, but became strong in faith, and gave the glory to God, having a sure persuasion, that he, which had promised, was able also to perform[1]."

✓   In these words of the apostle there are certain notes to be observed, which do prove to us that faith doth bring an assured persuasion into the mind and heart of man; and so, that faith is an undoubted confidence of things believed, whereto the heart is made privy; that is, that true faith doth not fly to and fro from place to place in the heart of man, but that, being deeply rooted in Christ, it sticketh in the heart which is enlightened. First, saith the apostle, "Abraham, contrary to hope, believed in hope:" that is to say, there he had a constant hope, where notwithstanding he had nothing to hope after, if all things had been weighed according to the manner of this world. But hope is a most firm and undoubted looking after those things which we believe: so that we see that the apostle did make faith manifest by hope, and by the certainty of hope did declare the assured constancy of faith. After that saith he, "Abraham fainted not in faith, nor stackered at the promise of God through unbelief, but was strong in faith." There are two kinds of stackerings in mankind[2]: the one is that, which, being overcome by evil temptations, doth bend to desperation, and the despising of God's promises. Such was the stackering of those ten spies of the holy land, of whom mention is made in the thirteenth and fourteenth chapters of Numbers. The other stackering is rather to be called a weak infirmity of faith, which also is tempted itself; that now I may not make rehearsal to you, how that in us all, by the spot of original sin, is naturally grafted a certain kind of unbelief, and that man's mind is at no time so enlightened or confirmed, but that cloudy mists of ignorance and doubtings do sometimes arise:

[1 Rom. iv. 18—21.]

[2 Bullinger's words here are very much akin to Calvin's, who writes on Rom. iv. 19, as follows: Duplex enim est fidei debilitas: una, quæ tentationibus adversis succumbendo, excidere nos a Dei virtute facit: altera, quæ ex imperfectione quidem nascitur, non tamen fidem ipsam extinguit. Nam nec mens unquam sic illuminata est, quin maneant multæ ignorantiæ reliquiæ: nunquam sic est animus stabilitus, quin multum hæreat dubitationis.—Comment. in loc. Amstel. Tom. VII. p. 29.]

et notwithstanding, faith yieldeth not to temptation, neither
s drowned nor sticketh in the mire of stackering; but, laying
hold upon the promised word of truth, getteth up again by
truggling, and is confirmed. So we read, that, at the promise of God, this came into Abraham's mind: "What, shall
there a son be born to thee that art an hundred years old[3]?"
This was that infirmity, and stackering, or weakness, of faith.
But here the apostle, commending Abraham's faith, which
overcame and yielded not, teaching us also of what sort true
faith ought to be, that is, a firm and most assured persuasion,
saith: "Abraham fainted not in faith, neither considered his
own body dead[4], when he was almost an hundred years old,
nor the deadness of Sarae's womb." Lo, this thought came
into Abraham's mind: "Shall a son be born to me that am
an hundred years old?" But he fainted not in faith. The
faith of Abraham began not to droop by reason of this temp-
ation. For he considered not the weakness that was in himself, nothing answerable to the promise of God. What then?
He stackered not at the promise of God through unbelief:
that is, he gave no place to unbelief to be tempted of it; he
fell not to his own reasons and doubtful inquisitions, as unbelievers are wont to do. For God's promise being once set
before the eyes of his mind, to that, I say, he stuck unmove-
ably, casting off all doubts and reasons of his own. For
faith hath no respect at all to the weakness, misery, or lack,
which is properly in mankind; but setteth her whole stay in
the power of God. So then, I say, Abraham was strong in
faith, that is, he prevailed and got the upper hand in his
temptation. For this is an argument, to shew that he had
the upper hand[5]: "He fainted not, nor waxed weak in
faith."

It followeth in the apostle, "Abraham gave God the glory;"
to wit, in believing that God wisheth well to mankind, and that
he is a true God and almighty. For he giveth God his glory,
which attributeth to God the properties of God, and doth not
gainsay the word and promise of God. For John the apostle

[3 Gen. xvii. 17.]

[4 Now dead, 1577; jam emortuum, Lat.]

[5 Opponitur enim illi superiori, Lat. For there is opposed to that
which went before. Omitted by the translator.]

saith: "He that believeth not in God, maketh God a liar[1]."
Abraham therefore believed in God, and in believing gave
God the glory. The apostle Paul goeth forward and saith
"He was throughly persuaded, or certified, that he which
had promised was able also to perform." Paul used the
Greek word πληροφορηθείς, which is all one as if you should
say, being certified. For πληροφορέω doth signify, fully to
certify: whereupon πληροφορία is an assured faith given
unto us, which is made by way of argument, or by the thing
itself. And they call that πληροφόρημα, which we call a
certification; as when a thing by persuasions is so beaten into
our minds, that after that we never doubt any more. Therefore faith did certify Abraham, and with undoubted persuasions did bring him to the point never to doubt, but that God
was able to perform what he had promised: in faith therefore
he stuck unmoveable to the promise of God, being assuredly
certified that he should obtain whatsoever God had promised

It is certain therefore, and plainly declared by the word
of the apostle, that true faith is an undoubted persuasion in
the mind of the believer, even so to have the thing as his
belief is, and as he is said to have it in the express word of
God. Whereby also we learn, that faith is not the unstable

**Faith believ-
eth not every
thing what-
soever.**

and unadvised confidence of him which believeth every great
and unpossible thing. For faith is ruled and bound to the
word of God; to the word of God, I say, rightly and truly
understood. The godly and faithful, therefore, do not by
and bye out of the omnipotency of God gather what they
list; as though God therefore would do every thing because
he can do all things, or that faith should therefore believe
every thing, because it is written, "All things are possible
to him that believeth." For his faith is therefore a great
deal more[2], because that which he doth believe is so set
down and declared in the word of God, as he doth believe.
Furthermore, where the Lord in the gospel saith, "All things
are possible to him that believeth," we must not take that
saying to be absolutely spoken, but to be joined to the word
will, and glory of God, and the safety of our souls. For al

[1 1 John v. 10.]
[2 Nam *pius* ideo credit, quia, &c., Lat. The translator read *plus*.

things which God in his word hath promised, all things which God will have, and lastly, all things which make to the glory of God and the safeguard of our souls, "are possible to him that believeth." And for that cause the apostle both openly and plainly said: "Whatsoever God hath promised, that same he is able also to perform." For whatsoever he hath not promised, and whatsoever pleaseth not his divine majesty, or is contrary to the will and express word of God, that cannot God do; not because he cannot, but because he will not[3]. God could make bread of stones; but we must not therefore believe that stones are bread, neither are they bread therefore, because God can do all things. This ye shall understand better and more fully, where as[4] a little here-after I shall shew unto you, that true faith strayeth not nor wavereth, wandering to and fro, but cleaveth close and stick-eth fast to God and his word.

In the mean season, because we have shewed out of Paul's words, by the example of Abraham, that faith is a substance and undoubted persuasion in the heart; and because many do stiffly stand in it, that man is not surely certain of his salvation[5]: I will add a few examples out of the gospel, whereby they may plainly perceive, that faith is a most sure ground and settled opinion touching God and our salvation. And first, verily, the centurion, of whom mention is made in the gospel, had conceived a stedfast hope that his servant should be healed of the Lord. For he understood how great and mighty things he promised to them that believe. He gathered also by the works of Christ, that it was an easy matter for him to restore his servant to health again. There-fore he cometh to the Lord, and among other talk saith: "It is no reason that thou shouldest come under my roof; yea, do but say the word, and my servant shall be made whole." These words do testify, that in the heart and mind of the centurion there was a sure persuasion of most assured health,

Examples of undoubted Faith.

[3 Non quod non possit omnia, sed quod nolit omnia, Lat.]

[4 i. e. where, ubi, Lat.]

[5 Hujus temporis hæreticorum error est, posse fideles eam no-titiam habere de sua gratia, ut certa fide statuant sibi remissa esse peccata.—Bellarm. de Justif. Lib. III. cap. 3. p. 949. Colon. Agrip. 1619.]

which by a certain comparison he doth make manifest and more fully express. "For I myself am a man under the authority of another; and under me I have soldiers; and I say to one, Go, and he goeth; and to another, Come, and he cometh; and to my servant, Do this, and he doeth it." When the Lord perceived this certification of his mind by his words most full of faith, he crieth out, "that in all Israel he hath not found so great faith[1]." The same again in the gospel speaketh notably of the woman's faith which was sorely plagued with the bloody flux. And that faith was an undoubted persuasion in her heart once illuminated, we may thereby understand, because she (being first indeed stirred up by the works and words of the Lord) thought thus within herself: "If I do but touch his garment, I shall be whole;" and therefore, pressing through the thickest of the throng, cometh to the Lord[2].

But why heap I together many examples? Doth not the only[3] faith of the Chananitish or Syrophenician woman declare more plainly than that it can be denied, how that faith is a most assured persuasion of things believed? For being over-passed, and, as it were, contemned of the Lord, she wavereth not in faith; but following him, and hearing also that the Lord was sent to the lost sheep of the house of Israel, she goeth on to worship him. Moreover, being put back, and, as it were, touched with the foul reproach of a dog, she goeth forward yet humbly to cast herself prostrate before the Lord, requesting to obtain the thing that she desired. She would not have persevered so stiffly, if faith had not been a certification in her believing mind and heart. Wherefore the Lord, moved with that faith of hers, cried: "Woman, great is thy faith; be it done to thee even as thou wilt[4]."

It is manifest therefore, by all these testimonies of the holy scripture, that faith is a stedfast and undoubted persuasion in the mind and heart of the believer.

Whereunto faith leaneth, and what the object or foundation of faith is.

This being now brought to an end, let us see what it is, whereupon man's faith doth lean; and also, how we may clearly perceive, that faith is not a vain and unstable opinion (as a

[1 Matt. viii. 5—10.]   [2 Matt. ix. 20—22.]
[3 una, Lat.]   [4 Matt. xv. 22—28; Mark vii. 26.]

little before we were about to say) of any thing whatsoever,
conceived in the mind of man, but that it is tied up and contained within bounds, and, as it were, certain conditions.   In
the definition therefore of faith we said, that faith bendeth
to God-ward, and leaneth on his word.   God therefore, and
the word of God, is the object or foundation of true faith.
The thing whereon a man may lean safely, surely, and without all manner doubting, must needs be stedfast and altogether
unmoveable; which doth give health, which doth preserve,
and which doth fill up or minister all fulness unto us: for
this doth faith seek and request.   But this is not elsewhere
than in God.   On God alone therefore doth true faith bend
and lean.   God is everlasting, chiefly good, wise, just, mighty,
and true of word.   And that doth he testify by his works
and word.   Wherefore in the prophets he is called a strong
and unmoveable rock, a castle, a wall, a tower, an invincible
fortress, a treasure, and a well that never will be drawn dry[5].
This everlasting God can do all things, knoweth all things, is
present in all places, loveth mankind exceedingly, doth provide
for all men, and also governeth or disposeth all things.   Faith
therefore, which is a confidence of God's good-will and of his
aid in all necessities, and of the true salvation of mankind,
bendeth on God alone, and cannot lean to any other creature,
in whom the things are not that faith requireth.

And even as God is true of word, and cannot lie, so is his
word true and deceiveth no man.   In the word of God is
expressed the will and mind of God.   To the word of God
therefore hath faith an eye, and layeth her ground upon God's
word; touching which word the Lord in the gospel said :
" Heaven and earth shall pass, but my word shall not pass[6]."
The word of God here is compared with the most excellent
elements.   Air and water are feeble and unstable elements :
but heaven, although it turn and move, doth keep yet a
wonderful and most stedfast course in moving, and stedfast
are all things therein.   The earth is most stable and unmoveable.   Therefore, if it be easier for these things to be loosed,
which cannot be undone, than for the word of God to pass; it
followeth, that God's word in all points is most stable, un-

[5 2 Sam. xxii. 2, 3; Psal. xxxi. 2, 3; Prov. xviii. 10; Isai. xxxiii. 6;
Jer. xvii. 13.]   [6 Mark xiii. 31.]

moveable, and not possible to be loosed. "If" (saith the Lord in Jeremy) "ye can undo the league that I have taken with the day, or the covenant that I have made with the night, so that it neither be day nor night at the appointed time, then may my covenant be of none effect which I have made with David[1]." But not the whole world, laying all their strengths together, is able to make it day when it is once night, nor cause the day to break one hour sooner than the course of heaven doth command. Therefore not all this world, with all the power and pomp thereof, shall be able once to weaken or break, to change or abolish, so much as one tittle in the word of God, and the truth of God's word. Faith therefore, which resteth upon a thing most firm or sure, cannot choose but be an undoubted certification. And since God's word is the foundation of faith, faith cannot wander to and fro, and lean to every word whatsoever: for every opinion conceived without the word of God, or against God's word, cannot be called true faith. And for that cause St Paul, the apostle of Christ, would not ground the true or christian faith upon any carnal props or opinions of men, but upon the truth and power of God. With his words will I conclude this place: "Faith" (saith he) "cometh of hearing, and hearing by the word of God[2]." "By the word of God," he saith, and not by the word of man. Again, to the Corinthians: "My preaching" (saith he) "was not in enticing words of man's wisdom, but in the shewing forth of the Spirit, and of power; that your faith should not be in the wisdom of man, but in the power of God[3]." Whereby also we learn, that some there are, which against all reason require faith at our hands; that is, they would have us to believe that which they are not able to shew out of God's word, or that which is clean contrary to the word of God.

To the better declaring of this that I have said availeth that short abridgement of God's word and of faith, which we in the definition of faith have closely knit up together. There are there rehearsed two chief points of faith and of the word:

Two chief points of faith. and first of all, that God in Christ doth freely promise life and every good thing. For God, who is the object or mark

[1 Jer. xxxiii. 20, 21.]   [2 Rom. x. 17.]
[3 1 Cor. ii. 4, 5.]

and foundation of faith, being of his own proper nature everliving, everlasting[4], and good, doth of himself, from before all
beginning, beget the Son like to himself in all points; who,
because he is of the same substance with the Father, is himself also, by nature, life, and all goodness. And to the end he
might communicate to us, his sons and brethren, both life
and all goodness, he became man; and being conversant, very
God and man, among men, he testified that God the Father, True faith
seeketh all
through the Son, doth pour himself wholly with all good good things
in God
things into the faithful, whom he quickeneth and filleth with through
Christ.
all goodness, and last of all doth take them up to himself
into the blessed place of everlasting life; and that he doth
frankly and freely bestow this benefit, to the end that the
glory of his grace may in all things be praised. This doth
true faith believe; and hereunto belong no small part of the
scriptures, which testify, that God in Christ doth communicate
to the faithful life and godliness. John the apostle crieth out
and saith: "In the beginning was the Word, and the Word
was with God, and God was the Word. And the Word became
flesh, and dwelt among us. And we saw the glory of God,
as the glory of the only-begotten Son of the Father, full of
grace and truth. And of his fulness have all we received[5],"
&c. For the Lord himself, in the Gospel after St John, said:
"Verily I say unto you, whatsoever things the Father doth,
the same also doth the Son. For even as the Father doth
raise the dead to life and quickeneth them, so also doth the
Son quicken whom he will: for neither judgeth the Father
any man, but hath committed all judgment to the Son, that
all men may honour the Son even as they honour the Father.
He that honoureth not the Son, the same honoureth not the
Father which hath sent him. Verily, verily, I say unto you,
he that heareth my word, and believeth on him that sent me,
hath life everlasting, and shall not come into judgment, but is
escaped from death unto life[6]." With these words of the
gospel agreeth that saying of St Paul: "In Christ are laid
up all the treasures of wisdom and knowledge. Because in
him dwelleth all fulness of the Godhead bodily, and ye in
him are fulfilled[7]." But that these great benefits of God are

[4] vivus, æternus, Lat.]
[5] John i. 1, 14, 16.   Conspeximus gloriam *ejus*, Lat.]
[6] John v. 19, 21—24.]   [7] Col. ii. 3, 9.]

freely bestowed upon the faithful, Paul, that vessel of election, declareth in these words : " Blessed be God, who hath chosen us in Christ before the foundations of the world were laid, and hath predestinated us into the adoption of children through Jesus Christ unto himself, according to the good pleasure of his will, to the praise of the glory of his grace, wherein he hath made us accepted in the beloved ; through whom we have redemption in his blood[1]," &c. And again : " All have sinned, and have need of God's glory, but are justified freely through his grace, by the redemption which is in Christ[2] :" and so forward. True faith therefore doth believe, that life and every good thing doth freely come to it from God through Christ : which is the chief article of our faith, as in the articles of the belief is more largely laid forth.

True faith believeth the holy scriptures.

The second principal point of God's word and faith is, that in the word of God there is set down all truth necessary to be believed ; and that true faith doth believe all that is declared in the scriptures. For it telleth us, that God is ; what manner one he is ; what God's works are ; what his judgments, his will, his commandments, his promises, and what his threatenings are ; finally, whatsoever is profitable or necessary to be believed, that doth God's word wholly set down unto us, and that doth true faith receive, believing all things that are written in the law and the prophets, in the gospel and writings of the apostles. But whatsoever cannot be fetched or proved out of those writings, or whatsoever is contrary unto them, that do the faithful not believe at all : for the very nature of true faith is, not to believe that which squareth from the word of God[3]. Whosoever therefore believeth not the fables and opinions of men, he alone believeth as he should : for he dependeth only upon the word of God, and so upon God himself, the only fountain of all truth.

The matter, the argument, and the whole sum of faith is briefly set out unto us in the articles of the christian faith, whereof I will speak at another time. I have this hour declared unto you, dearly beloved and reverend[4] bre-

[1 Ephes. i. 3—7. Qua caros nos reddidit per dilectum, Lat. and Erasmus' rendering.]

[2 Rom. iii. 23, 24.] [3 Quæ cum verbo Dei pugnant, Lat.]

[4 honorandi, Lat. And there is no et (and) in the original.]

thren in the Lord, the definition of faith; which to the end that I may surely fasten in every one's mind, and that all may understand what faith is, I repeat it here again, and therewithal conclude this sermon. Faith is a gift of God, poured into man from heaven, whereby he is taught with an undoubted persuasion wholly to lean to God and his word; in which word God in Christ doth freely promise life and every good thing, and wherein all truth necessary to be believed is plainly declared. Let us all pray to God our Father through his only-begotten Son our Lord Jesus Christ, that he will vouchsafe from heaven to bestow true faith upon us all, that we, by it knowing him aright, may at the last obtain life everlasting. Amen.

THAT THERE IS ONE ONLY TRUE FAITH, AND WHAT THE VIRTUE THEREOF IS.

THE FIFTH SERMON.

BEING cut off with the shortness of time, and detained by the excellency of the matter, I could not in my last sermon make an end of all that I had determined to speak touching faith: now therefore, by the grace of the Holy Spirit, I will add the rest of the argument which seemeth yet to be behind. Pray to the Lord that that, which by man's voice is brought to your ears, may by the finger of God be written in your hearts.

True faith is ignorant of all division; for "there is," saith the apostle, "one Lord, one faith, one baptism, [one] God[5] and Father of all[6]." For there remaineth, from the beginning of the world even unto the end thereof, one and the same faith in all the elect of God. God is one and the same for ever, the only Well of all goodness, that can never be drawn dry. The truth of God, from the beginning of the world, is one and the same, set forth to men in the word of God. Therefore the object and foundation of faith, that is, God and the

Faith is one alone.

[5 unus Deus, Lat.]　　　　　　[6 Ephes. iv. 5, 6.]

[BULLINGER.]　　　　　　　　　　　　　　7

word of God, remain for ever one and the self-same. In one and the self-same faith with us have all the elect ever since the first creation of the world believed, that unto us through Christ all good things are freely given, and that all truth necessary to be believed is declared in the word of the Lord: wherefore the faithful of the old world have always settled their faith on God and his word; so that now, without all doubt, there cannot be any more than one true faith.

There are many and sundry religions, but no more than one true faith.

I know very well, that in the world there are sowed many and sundry faiths, that is to say, religions. For there is the Indian faith[1], the Jewish faith, the faith of the Mahometists, and the faith of the Georgians[2]; and yet notwithstanding there is but one true christian faith, the abridgement whereof is contained in the articles of our belief, and is taught at the full in the sacred scriptures of both the Testaments. I know also that there are sundry beliefs of men, resting upon sundry things, and believing that which is contrary to true faith: but yet, nevertheless, there remaineth but one true belief in God and his word, (which is) an undoubted persuasion and confidence of things most true and assuredly certain.

Faith doth increase and decrease.

This confidence doth grow with increase in the minds of the faithful, and, contrarily, decreaseth again and utterly faileth. And for that cause the apostles besought the Lord, saying: "Lord, increase our faith[3]." And Paul the apostle doth in his writings everywhere wish to the faithful the increase of the spirit and faith. David also before him prayed, saying: "O God, create a clean heart within me, and take not thy Holy Spirit from me[4]." For he had seen how that from Saul, whom he succeeded in the kingdom, the good Spirit of God was departed, and that instead thereof the wicked spirit had entered into his mind, which tormented him very pitifully. Hereunto belongeth that saying in the gospel: "To every one that hath shall be given, and from him that hath not

[1 Indiana fides, Lat.]
[2 fides Georgiana, Lat. The Georgians are a branch of the Greek Church. Mosheim's Eccles. Hist. Book IV. Cent. 16. Sect. 3, Ch. 2. § 10. ed. Soames. Smith and Dwight's Missionary Researches in Armenia, Letter 8.]
[3 Luke xvii. 5.]
[4 Ps. li. 10, 11.]

shall be taken away that which he hath not," or that he maketh no account of, "and shall be given to him that hath[5]." Neither was it in vain that the Lord said to Peter, "I have prayed for thee, Peter, that thy faith fail not[6]." For Paul speaketh of some in his time, that "made shipwreck of their own faith, and overthrew the faith of other[7]." And to what end, I pray you, do we daily hear the word of God, and make our humble petitions to the Lord, but because we look for increase of godliness, and his aid to keep us that we fall not from true faith? Verily Paul to the Thessalonians saith : "We pray earnestly day and night to see you personally, and to supply that which is wanting in your faith[8]." And a little before he said : "For this cause I sent Timotheus, that I might be certified of your faith, lest by any means the tempter had tempted you, and so our labour had been of none effect[9]." The same apostle also, in his Epistle to the Ephesians, saith : "Christ gave some apostles, some prophets, some pastors and teachers, to the restoring of the saints, unto the building of the body of Christ, until we all meet together in the unity of faith, and the acknowledging of the Son of God, unto a perfect man, unto the measure of age of the fulness of Christ, so that now we be no longer children[10]." Therefore, so long as we live, we learn, that our faith may be perfect[11]; and if so be at any time it shall be weakened by temptations, that then it may be repaired, and again confirmed. And in this diversity, (I mean) in this increase and weakness of faith, there is no partition or division; for the self[12] root and substance of faith doth always remain, although it be at some time more, and at some time less. In like manner, faith is not therefore changed or cut in sunder, because one is called general faith, and another particular[13] faith.

General and particular faith.

[5 Luke xix. 26, where the reading of the copies is either *that which he hath*, or, *that which he seemeth to have*.]

[6 Luke xxii. 32.]

[7 1 Tim. i. 19; 2 Tim. ii. 18.]

[8 1 Thess. iii. 10.]

[9 1 Thess. iii. 5.]

[10 Ephes. iv. 11—14.]

[11 may not be perfect, 1587; ut perficiatur fides nostra, Lat.]

[12 self-same, 1577.]

[13 specialis, Lat.]

For general faith is no other than that which believeth that all the words of God are true, and that God hath a good-will to mankind : particular faith believeth nothing contrary to this ; only that, which is common to all, the faithful applieth particularly to himself, believing that God is not well minded toward others alone, but even unto him also. So then it bringeth the whole into parts, and that which is general into particularities. For whereas by general faith he believeth that all the words of God are true ; in the same sort by particular faith he doth believe that the soul is immortal, that our bodies rise again, that the faithful shall be saved, the unbelievers destroyed, and whatsoever else is of this sort taught to be believed in the word of God.

Faith inspired and faith gotten.

Moreover, the disputation touching faith poured into us, and faith that we ourselves get; touching formal faith, and faith without fashion[1]; I leave to be beaten out of them which of themselves do bring these new disputations into the church. True faith is obtained by no strength or merit of man, but is poured into him of God, as I declared in my last sermon : and though man obtain it by hearkening unto the word of God, yet nevertheless it is wholly imputed to the grace of God; for unless this grace do work inwardly in the heart of the hearer, the preacher that laboureth outwardly doth bring no profit at all. We read in the third chapter of St Augustin's book *De Prædestinatione Sanctorum*, that once he was in an error, because he thought that that faith, wherewith we believe in God, is not the gift of God, but that it was in us as of ourselves, and that by it we do obtain the gifts of God, whereby we may in this world live rightly and holily[2]. But this he confuteth in that book at large, and that substantially. So then true faith, which bendeth on God alone[3], and is directed by the word of God, is formal

Formal faith.

[1] de fide *infusa* et *acquisita*, de fide *informi* et *formata*, Lat The reader who is so disposed may find these points stated in Andr Vega. de Justificat. Colon. 1572. Quæst. I. pp. 727, 728.]

[2 Cum similiter errarem, putans fidem, qua in Deum credimus non esse donum Dei, sed a nobis esse in nobis, et per illam nos im petrare Dei dona, quibus temperanter et juste et pie vivamus in ho seculo.—August. de Præd. Sanct. c. 3. Par. 1531. Tom. VII. fol. 253.]

[3 in unum Deum tendit, Lat.]

enough, or sufficiently in fashion[4]. Verily, the form of faith is engraven in the heart of the faithful by the Holy Ghost. And although it be small, and doth not grow up to the highest degree, yet notwithstanding it is true faith, having force in it as it were a grain of mustard-seed. The thief, that was crucified with our Lord, believed in the Lord Jesus, and was saved, although the force of faith was strong in him but a very small season, and brought not forth any great store of fruit of good works: finally, that faith of the thief was not any whit diverse or contrary from the faith of St Peter and St Paul, but was altogether the very same with theirs, although their faith brought forth somewhat more abundantly the fruit of good works. Peter and Paul were frankly and freely justified, although they had many good works: freely was the thief justified, although his good works were very few or none at all. Let us hold therefore, that true faith is one alone, which notwithstanding doth increase and is augmented, and, again, may decrease and be extinguished.

There remaineth now for me to declare the virtue and effect of true faith. This hath the holy apostle Paul done[5] very excellently well, yea; and that most absolutely too. But although, in the eleventh chapter to the Hebrews, he had said very much, he is compelled notwithstanding to confess that he cannot reckon up all: therefore at this time I mean to rehearse a few virtues of faith, leaving the rest, dearly beloved, to be sought out and considered of yourselves.

The power and effect of faith.

True faith before all things bringeth with it true knowledge, and maketh us wise indeed. For by faith we know God, and judge aright of the judgments and works of God, of virtues and vices. The wisdom that it bringeth with it is without doubt the true wisdom. Many men hope that they can attain to true wisdom by the study of philosophy: but they are deceived as far as heaven is broad[6]. For philosophy doth falsely judge and faultily teach many things touching God, the works of God, the chief goodness, the end of good and evil, and touching things to be desired and eschewed. But the very same things are rightly and truly taught in the word of God, and understood and perceived by faith. Faith therefore is the true wisdom, and maketh us wise indeed. For

Faith is the true knowledge that maketh men wise.

[4 Satis est *formalis* aut *formata*, Lat.]
[5 ante me, Lat. ; done before me.]   [6 toto cœlo, Lat.]

Jeremy also saith: "Behold, they have cast away the word of the Lord; what wisdom therefore can there be left in them[1]?" The wisdom of Salomon is worshipfully thought of throughout the whole compass of the world; and yet we read that the Lord, in the gospel after St Matthew, uttered this sentence against the Jews: "The queen of the south shall rise in judgment with this generation and shall condemn it; because she came from the ends of the world to hear the wisdom of Salomon: and behold, there is one in this place greater than Salomon[2]." Christ is preferred before Salomon, and the wisdom of Christ before the wisdom of Salomon. But it is well known, that the wisdom of Christ, the Son of God, cannot be attained to without faith. Faith therefore bringeth with it the most excellent wisdom. But herein this wisdom of ours deserveth a singular praise, because they that desire it are not sent to foreign nations, with great cost and labour, to learn it; as to the priests of Egypt, the gymnosophists of India[3], the philosophers of Greece, or to the rabbins of the Jews. God hath dispersed the word of God throughout the whole world, so that now the word of faith is in the hearts of all the faithful. For Paul the apostle saith: "Thus saith the justice that is of faith, Say not in thy heart, Who shall ascend into heaven? that is, to fetch Christ down from above. Or; Who shall descend into the deep? that is, to bring Christ from the dead again. But what saith he? The word is nigh unto thee, even in thy heart: this same is the word of faith, which we preach; for if thou confess with thy mouth the Lord Jesus, and dost believe with thy heart that God hath raised him from the dead, thou shalt be saved[4]."

Faith therefore doth not only make us wise, but happy also; the Lord himself bearing witness thereunto, and saying to his disciples: "Happy are the eyes that see the things that ye see. For I say unto you, that many prophets and kings have desired to see the things that ye see[5], and to hear the

---

[1 Jer. viii. 9.]   [2 Matt. xii. 42.]

[3 Gymnosophistæ, Lat. A sect of Indian philosophers, who wore no clothing, and practised the severities of standing alternately on one foot, and of fixing their eyes on the sun.—Plin. H. N. vii. 2. med. § 2 Schelleri Lex. totius Latin. sub voc.]

[4 Rom. x. 6—9.]

[5 et non viderunt, Lat. and have not seen them: omitted.]

things that ye hear, and heard them not[6]." We shall there-How man may attain to the chief goodness.
fore find in faith a most certain determination of the most
notable question stirred in, since the beginning of the world,
of learned and most excellent wits; which is, by what means
a man may live, be happy, attain to the chief goodness, be
joined to the chief goodness, and so be justified? There have
been, yea, and yet are, divers opinions touching this matter,
contrary the one to the other. But we do briefly and truly
affirm, that by true faith a man doth live, is happy, attaineth
to the chief goodness, is conjoined to the chief goodness,
and also justified: so that God dwelleth in us, and we in
him; and that by faith we are both happy and blessed.
What, I pray you, could have been spoken more excellently,
worthily, or divinely, touching true faith? For see; faith
quickeneth us, maketh us happy, joineth us to the chief
goodness, so that he[7] in us and we in him may live; and
faith doth also fully justify us.

But now it is best to hear the testimonies out of the
scriptures. Faith maketh us happy. For to St Peter, con-Faith maketh happy.
fessing the Lord Jesus by true faith, it is said: "Happy art
thou, Simon, the son of Jonas. Flesh and blood hath not
revealed this to thee, but my Father which is in heaven[8]."
St Paul, for the proof of faith, bringeth in that sentence of
David: "Happy are they whose iniquities are forgiven, and
whose sins are covered. Blessed is the man to whom the
Lord shall impute no sin[9]." Faith quickeneth or maketh Faith quick-eneth.
alive. For "the just liveth by faith[10]." This doth Paul very
often in his writings allege out of the prophets. The same
Paul also saith: "The life which now I live in flesh, I live
by faith in the Son of God, who loved me and gave himself
for me[11]." Faith joineth us to the eternal and chief goodness, Faith joineth to God.
and so maketh us to enjoy the chief goodness, that God may
dwell in us and we in God. For the Lord Jesus himself in
the gospel saith: "He which eateth my flesh, and drinketh
my blood, dwelleth in me, and I in him. As the living Father
sent me, so also I live by the Father, and he that eateth me
shall live by me[12]." But to eat and drink the Lord is to

[6] Luke x. 23, 24.]   [7] Deus, Lat.]
[8] Matt. xvi. 17.]   [9] Rom. iv. 7, 8; Ps. xxxii. 1, 2.]
[10] Gal. iii. 11; Heb. x. 38.]   [11] Gal. ii. 20.]
[12] John vi. 56, 57.]

believe in the Lord, that he hath given himself to death for us. Whereupon John the apostle saith : "We have seen and do witness, that the Father hath sent the Son the Saviour of the world. Whosoever shall confess that Jesus is the Son of God, God dwelleth in him and he in God[1]." Wherefore also Paul said : "I live now; not I, but Christ liveth in me[2]."

Faith justi-
fieth. Moreover faith doth justify. But for because the treatise thereof cannot be fitly and fully made an end of this hour, I mean to defer it till the next sermon that shall be.

At this present, dearly beloved, ye must remember, that there is but one true faith, that is, the christian faith. For although there be said to be many faiths, that is, religions ; yet notwithstanding there is only but one true and undoubted faith. And that doth increase, and again decrease, in some men. As for those in whom it is rightly and godly observed, in them it sheweth forth sundry virtues. For it bringeth with it true wisdom ; finally, it quickeneth, and maketh us blessed and happy indeed. To God, the Father, the author of all goodness and of our felicity, be all praise and glory, through Jesus Christ our Lord, for ever and ever. Amen.

THAT THE FAITHFUL ARE JUSTIFIED BY FAITH WITHOUT THE LAW AND WORKS.

THE SIXTH SERMON.

BEING ready here, dearly beloved, to speak unto you of faith, which without works doth justify them that believe, I call upon the Father, which is in heaven, through his only-begotten Son Jesus Christ our Lord, beseeching him to open my mouth and lips to the setting forth of his praise, and to illuminate your hearts, that ye, acknowledging the great benefit of God, may become thankful for it, and holy indeed.

And first of all, I will speak certain things, chiefly neces-
Justification. sary to this argument or treatise, touching this term of justification. The term of justifying, very usual and common

[1 1 John iv. 14, 15.]   [2 Gal. ii. 20.]

among the Hebrews, and of a large signification, is not at
this day so well understood of all men as it ought to be.
To justify is as much to say as to quit from judgment and
from the denounced and uttered sentence of condemnation. It
signifieth to remit offences, to cleanse, to sanctify, and to give
inheritance[3] of life everlasting. For it is a law term belonging to courts where judgment is exercised. Imagine therefore, that man is set before the judgment-seat of God, and
that there he is pleaded guilty; to wit, that he is accused and
convinced of heinous offences, and therefore sued to punishment or to the sentence of condemnation. Imagine also, that
the Son of God maketh intercession, and cometh in as a mean,
desiring that upon him may be laid the whole fault and
punishment[4] due unto us men, that he by his death may
cleanse them and take them away, setting us free from death,
and giving us life everlasting. Imagine too, that God, the
most high and just judge, receiveth the offer, and translateth
the punishment together with the fault from us unto the neck
of his Son; making therewithal a statute, that whosoever
believeth that the Son of God suffered for the sins of the
world, brake the power of death, and delivered us from damnation, should be cleansed from his sins and made heir of life
everlasting. Who therefore can be so dull of understanding,
but may perceive that mankind is justified by faith?

But that there may be no cause of doubt or darkness
left in the mind of any man; that which I have already
spoken generally, by the parable and similitude fetched from
our common law, I will here particularly bring into certain
parts, confirming and manifestly proving every one of them
severally out of the holy scriptures, so that even to the
slowest[5] wits the power of faith and work of justification may
be most evident.

And first, I will shew unto you, that this term of justifi- What it is
cation is taken in this present treatise for the absolution and   to justify.
remission of sins, for sanctification, and adoption into the
number of the sons of God. In the thirteenth of the Acts,
the apostle Paul saith: "Be it known unto you, men and
brethren, that through this Lord Jesus Christ is preached

[3 hæredem constituere, Lat.]
[4 omnis culpa et pœna, Lat.]
[5 vel tardis ingeniis, Lat.]

unto you the forgiveness of sins; and by him all that believe are justified from all things, from which they could not be justified by the law of Moses[1]." See, in Christ is preached unto us the forgiveness of sins; and he that believeth that Christ preached forgiveth sins[2] is also justified. It follow-eth therefore, that justification is the remission of sins. In the fifth chapter to the Romans saith the same apostle: "Being justified by the blood of Christ, we shall be saved from wrath through him[3]." But the blood of Christ washeth away sins. Justification, therefore, is the washing away or forgiveness of sins. And again, in the same chapter, saith he more plainly: "Judgment entered by one offence unto condemnation, but the gift of many sins unto justification[4]." He maketh justification the contrary to condemnation: there-fore, justification is the absolution and delivery from condem-nation. What say ye to this moreover, that he doth plainly call justification a gift, that is, the forgiveness of sins? Here-unto also belong those words of his: "Even as by the sin of one condemnation came on all men; so by the righteous-ness of one good came upon all men to the justification of life[5]." Here again is the justification of life made the con-trary of condemnation unto death set as a pain upon our heads because of the transgression: justification of life there-fore is an absolution from sins, a delivery from death, a quick-ening or translating from death to life. For in the fourth to the Romans the same apostle expoundeth justification by sanctification[6], and sanctification by the remission of sins. For in treating of faith, whereby we are justified, or which God imputeth to us for righteousness without works, he saith: "Even as David also doth expound the blessedness of that man, to whom the Lord imputeth righteousness without works, saying: Blessed are they whose iniquities are forgiven, and whose sins are covered[7]." What could be more plainly spoken

[1 Acts xiii. 38, 39.]
[2 qui credit annunciato Christo, remittenti peccata, Lat.]
[3 Rom. v. 9.]   [4 Rom. v. 16.]   [5 v. 18.]
[6 beatificationem, Lat. This is the term which Bullinger employs in this Treatise of Justification, and which the translator, rather un-happily, has rendered *sanctification*. The idea intended by Bullinger is expressed in Rom. iv. 7, which he quotes. — Cf. Calvin, Instit. Lib. iii. cap. 11. § 4. & 22.]
[7 Rom. iv. 7.]

than this? For he doth evidently expound justification by sanctification, and sanctification by remission of sins. Furthermore, what else is sanctification but the adoption whereby we are received into the grace and number of the sons of God? What is he therefore that seeth not, that in this treatise of St Paul justification is taken for adoption? especially, since in the very same fourth chapter to the Romans he goeth about to prove that an inheritance is due to faith, whereunto also he doth attribute justification. By all this it is made manifest, that the question of justification containeth nothing else but the manner and reason of sanctification; that is to say, whereby and how men have their sins forgiven, and are received into the grace and number of the sons of God, and, being justified, are made heirs of the kingdom of God.

And now, let us try whether that which we have said be taught in the scriptures: that Christ before the judgment-seat of God, when sentence of condemnation was to be pronounced against us for our offences, took our sins upon his own neck, and purged them by the sacrifice of his death upon the cross; and that God also laid upon Christ our fault and punishment, so that Christ alone is the only satisfaction and purging of the faithful. This doth the apostle Paul teach most expressly, where he saith: "Who shall lay anything to the charge of God's elect? It is God that justifieth. Who shall condemn? It is Christ that died; yea rather, it is he which is raised up, and is at the right hand of the Father, making intercession for us[8]." And again he saith: "Christ redeemed us from the curse of the law, while he was made the curse for us; (for it is written, Cursed be every one that hangeth on the tree;) that upon the gentiles might come the blessing of Abraham through Jesus Christ[9]," &c. This did the apostle teach out of the writings of Moses. And Moses in his books doth oftentimes make mention, that the sins are laid upon the heads of the beasts which were sacrificed. But those sacrifices bare the type or figure of the death and sacrifice of Christ. Esaias also in his fifty-third chapter saith expressly: "He verily hath taken on him our infirmities, and borne our pains. He was wounded for our iniquities, and smitten for our sins. For the pain of our punishment was laid upon him, and with his stripes are we healed. We all went astray like

Christ hath taken on himself and cleansed our sins.

[8 Rom. viii. 33, 34.]   [9 Gal. iii. 13, 14.]

sheep, every one turned his own way; but the Lord hath thrown upon him all our sins." And immediately after: "He hath taken away the sins of the multitude, and made intercession for the transgressors[1]." Than these words, I think, nothing can be brought more to the matter, or more fit for our present purpose. To this alludeth St Peter when he saith: "The Lord himself bare our sins in his body upon the cross, that we, being dead to sin, may live to righteousness; by the sign of whose stripes we are made whole[2]." Hereunto alluded St John, the forerunner of the Lord, when he said: "Behold the Lamb of God, that taketh away the sins of the world[3]." Moreover, the apostle Paul beareth witness hereto, saying: "Him that knew not sin he made sin for us, that we through him might be made the righteousness of God[4]." Also in his epistle to the Colossians he saith: "It pleased the Father, that in Christ all fulness should dwell; and by him to reconcile all things unto himself, having set peace through the blood of his cross by him, both things in earth and things in heaven[5]." These, I suppose, are testimonies sufficiently evident to prove, that upon Christ are laid our sins, with the curse or condemnation due unto our offences; and that Christ by his blood hath cleansed our sins, and by his death hath vanquished death and the devil, the author of death, and taken away the punishment due unto us.

The pain and offence of sin are taken away by Christ.

Yet because there be some, and those not a few, which deny that Christ by his death hath taken from us sinners both fault and punishment[6], and that he became the only satisfaction of the whole world; I will therefore now allege certain other testimonies, and repeat somewhat of that that I have before recited, thereby to make it manifest, that Christ, the only satisfaction of the world, hath made satisfaction both for our fault and punishment. Esaias verily witnessed, that

[1 Isai. liii. 4—6, 12.]
[2 1 Pet. ii. 24.   Cujus ejusdem vibice, Lat.]
[3 John i. 29.]   [4 2 Cor. v. 21.]   [5 Col. i. 19, 20.]
[6 pœnam et culpam, Lat.   Fingunt sibi (Romanenses theologi) distinctionem pœnæ et culpæ: *culpam* remitti fatentur Dei misericordia; sed culpa remissa *pœnam* restare, quam persolvi Dei justitia postulat.—— Calvin, Instit. Lib. iii. cap. 4. § 29.   See also Burnet's Expos. of the Thirty-nine Articles, ed. Page. Art. xxii. p. 285, and Palmer's Letters to Dr Wiseman, Let. II.]

both the fault of our offence and the punishment were taken away, when he saith: "He bare our infirmities, and was wounded for our iniquities:" finally, "the discipline of peace" (that is, the discipline, or chastising, or punishment, bringing peace; or the penalty of our correction, that is, the punishment due to us for our offences,) "was laid on his neck." Mark also what followeth: "and with the blueness of his stripes[7] are we healed[8]." This doth evidently teach, that by the pain of Christ our punishment is taken away. For look what pain, penalty, punishment, or correction was due to us, and the same was laid on the Lord himself: and for that cause was the Lord wounded, and received stripes; and with them he healed us. But he had not yet healed us at all, if we should yet look for wounds, stripes, and strokes, that is to say, punishment for our sins. The death of Christ, therefore, is a full satisfaction for our sins. But what, I pray you, should Christ avail us, if yet we should be punished for our offences? Therefore, when we say, that he did bear all our sins in his body upon the cross, what else do we mean, I pray you, but that the Lord by death, that was not due unto him, took from us God's vengeance, that it might not light on us to our punishment? Paul, as often as he maketh mention of our redemption made by Christ, is wont to name it ἀπολύ-τρωσιν[9]; by which word he understandeth not, as the common sort do, redemption barely and simply, but the very price and satisfaction of redemption. Wherefore also he writeth, that Christ himself did give himself to be the ἀντί-λυτρον[10] for us; that is to say, the price wherewith captives are redeemed from their enemies in the war. For that which we do commonly call ransoms, the Greeks do name λύτρα. So then that is ἀντίλυτρον, when man for man, and life for life, is redeemed. But upon them, that are thus ransomed and

[7 livore ejus, Lat. and Vulg.]

[8 Isai. liii. 4, 5.]   [9 Rom. iii. 24; Eph. i. 7.]

[10 1 Tim. ii. 6. This passage is almost word for word Calvin's, as follows: "Ac quoties de redemptione per eum facta meminit Paulus, vocare solet ἀπολύτρωσιν, quo non simpliciter *redemptionem* indicat, qaliter vulgo intelligitur; sed *pretium* ipsum et satisfactionem redemptionis," (the French version adds, que nous appellons Rançon en François). "Qua ratione et Christum ipsum se pro nobis ἀντίλυτρον dedisse scribit."—Calvin. Instit. Lib. III. cap. 4. ed. Amstel. and Vol. II. p. 221. ed. Calvin Translat. Soc. 1845.]

set at liberty, there is no punishment afterward laid, by reason of the translation thereof from one to another. Furthermore, this is the new covenant that God in his Christ hath made with us, " that he will not remember our iniquities[1]." But how could he choose but remember our iniquities, if he ceased not to punish them ? So then, this remaineth not to be doubted of, that Christ our Lord is the full propitiation[2], satisfaction, oblation, and sacrifice for the sins, I say, for the punishment and the fault, of all the world : yea, and by himself alone ; for in none other is any salvation : " neither is there any other name given unto men whereby they must be saved[3]."

How punishment is laid on us.

I deny not, but that because of discipline, chastisement, and exercise, divers sorts of punishments are laid upon men's necks, and that they are diversely afflicted and vexed because of their offences. But those afflictions, howsoever they be patiently suffered of the faithful, do not yet wash sins away, nor make satisfaction for misdeeds. St Peter saith : " Marvel not that ye are tried by fire, which thing is done for your trial[4], as if any new thing should happen unto you ; yea, rather rejoice herein, that ye are partakers of the afflictions of Christ, that in the revelation also of his glory ye may rejoice and be glad[5]." This, I say, is the end and use of afflictions. And by this means the glory of Christ endureth pure and uncorrupted.

God hath appointed that he that believeth should have eternal life and be justified.

It remaineth now for me to prove out of the holy scriptures, that God the Father hath ordained, that he, whosoever doth believe in the only-begotten Son of God, shall be made partaker of Christ his righteousness ; that is, shall be justified by him, be absolved from his sins, and be made heir of life everlasting. Esaias therefore saith : " In the acknowledging of him, or in his knowledge, shall my righteous servant justify the multitude, whose sins he himself shall bear[6]." But what

[1 Heb. viii. 12.]

[2 propitiationem, Lat. portion, ed. 1587.]

[3 Acts iv. 12.]

[4 This is Erasmus' rendering, which Bullinger adopts : Ne miremini, dum per ignem exploramini, quæ res ad experimentum vestri fit, perinde quasi, &c. The Vulgate is different.]

[5 1 Pet. iv. 12, 13.]

[6 ch. liii. 2. Potest hic tam active quam passive legi dictio דעת, id est, cognitio vel scientia.—Calv. Comment. in loc. Jesai. Accord-

else is the acknowledging or knowledge of Christ, but true
faith? Moreover, the Lord Jesus himself in the gospel after
St John saith: "And as Moses lift up the serpent in the
wilderness, even so must the Son of man be lift up; that whosoever believeth in him should not perish, but have life everlasting[7]." There was none other remedy in the desert against
the envenomed bitings of the serpents, but the contemplation
or beholding of the serpent lift up and hanged aloft. No
plaster did cure them that were poisoned[8], no oblation made
to God, not prayer itself offered to God, not any work, nor
any way else: the only beholding of the serpent made the
poison harmless that then had crept into all their limbs. In
like manner, nothing at all doth save us from death but only
faith in Christ: for by faith we behold and see Christ lifted
up upon the stake of the cross, as it is to be seen in the sixth
chapter of John. It followeth in the words of our Saviour:
"God so loved the world, that he gave his only-begotten Son;
that whosoever believeth should not perish, but have life everlasting. For God sent not his Son into the world to condemn
the world, but that the world through him might be saved.
He that believeth on him is not condemned: but he that
believeth not is condemned already, because he believeth not
in the name of the only-begotten Son of God[9]." By these
words now the third time is faith beaten into our heads, by
which we are made partakers of the Son of God, of his life,
salvation, redemption, and all good things beside. In the
sixth chapter of the Gospel after John our Lord again saith:
"This is the will of the Father which sent me, that every
one that seeth the Son, and believeth in him, should have
life everlasting, and I will raise him up at the last day[10]."
Nothing can be alleged to make more for our present argument than these words of his. For he saith plainly, that
the will of God the Father is, that we should believe in the
Son, and by this belief have our salvation. Whereupon John,
the evangelist and apostle, in his canonical epistle dareth
burst forth into these words: "He that believeth not God
maketh him a liar, because he believed not the record that

ingly, Bullinger introduces here Calvin's *two* renderings, cognitione
sui, vel in scientia sua. The latter is the rendering of the Vulgate.]

[7] ch. iii. 14, 15.]   [8] Wisd. xvi. 12.]
[9] John iii. 16—18.]   [10] John vi. 40.]

God gave of his Son. And this is the record, that God hath given unto us eternal life, and this life is in his Son. He that hath the Son hath life : and he that hath not the Son of God hath not life[1]." Dearly beloved, note this. The eternal and unchangeable will of God is, that he will give eternal life unto the world. But he will give the life through Christ, who is naturally life itself, and can give life. The very same God also will that we obtain and have life in us, and that we have it no other ways than by faith. For the apostle Paul taught, that Christ doth dwell in our hearts by faith[2]. Moreover, the Lord himself also witnesseth, and saith, " He that eateth me shall live by me[3]." But ye know, dearly beloved, that to eat Christ is to believe in him. And therefore we knit up this place with these words of St Peter : " To this Christ do all the prophets bear witness, that whosoever believeth in him shall receive forgiveness of sins through his name[4]."

We have in these a most ample testimony of the whole sacred scriptures. By these I have evidently enough declared, that God hath appointed, that whosoever doth believe in Christ, being cleansed from his sins, shall be made heir of life everlasting.

This will I make more evident yet, by declaring how that

Men are jus-tified by faith alone.

faith alone, that is, that faith for itself, and not for any works of ours, doth justify the faithful. For itself I say, not in respect that it is in us a quality of the mind, or our own work in ourselves ; but in respect that faith is the gift of God's grace, having in it a promise of righteousness and life ; and in respect that, naturally, of itself, it is a certain and un-doubted persuasion resting upon God, and believing that God, being pacified by Christ, hath through Christ bestowed life and all good things on us. Therefore faith for Christ, and by the grace and promise of God, doth justify : and so faith, that is, that which we believe, and wherein our confidence is settled, God, I say, himself by the grace of God[5] doth justify us through our redemption in Christ : so that now our own works or merits have no place left to them at all, I mean, in justi-

[1 1 John v. 10—12.]
[2 Ephes. iii. 17.]
[3 John vi. 57.]
[4 Acts x. 43.]
[5 ipse inquam Deus, ipsa Dei gratia, Lat.]

ication : for otherwise good works have their place in the faithful, as we in place convenient do mean to shew.   For *Christ compared with Adam.* Paul, the teacher of the Gentiles, doth in the way of opposition compare Christ with Adam, and sheweth that of Adam, and so of our own nature and strength, we have nothing but sin, the wrath of God, and death.   And this doth he shew under the name of Adam, to the intent that no man should seek for righteousness and life in the flesh.   And again, on the other side, he declareth that we by Christ have righteousness, the grace of God, life, and the forgiveness of all our sins.   In this opposition, he doth earnestly urge and often repeat this word, " of one[6]," to no other end verily, but that we should understand, that faith alone doth justify.

To the Galatians he doth very evidently use this kind of *God's testament.* argument.   " To the last will and testament of a man, if it once be proved, nobody doth add or take any thing away." Reason therefore doth rightly require, that no man put to or take away any thing from the testament of God.   But this is the testament which God confirmed ; that his will is, to bestow the blessing upon Abraham's seed, not in many, or by many, but through one.   " For he saith not, And to the seeds, as though he spake of many; but as speaking of one he saith, And to thy seed, that is, Christ[7]."   Therefore, it is a detestable thing to augment or diminish any thing in this testament of God.   Christ alone is the only Saviour still : men can neither save themselves nor other.

Again, in the same epistle to the Galatians he saith : " We *We are not justified by* know that man is not justified by the works of the law, but *the works of the law, but* by faith in Jesus Christ[8] ; insomuch as no flesh shall be jus- *by faith.* tified by the works of the law[9]."   This is now the third time that Paul saith, that men are not justified by the works of the law : in the which clause he comprehendeth all manner of works of what sort soever.   So then, no kind of works do justify.   But what is it then that justifieth ?   Faith in Christ, and that verily alone.   For what else can those words import, " We know that man is not justified but by faith in

[6 Rom. v. 12, &c.]

[7 Gal. iii. 16.   *in* semine tuo, Lat.]

[8 Et nos in Jesum Christum credidimus, ut justificaremur ex fide Christi, et non ex operibus legis, Lat.   Omitted by the translator.]

[9 Galat. ii. 16.]

[BULLINGER.]

8

Christ?" For the force of these two speeches is all one, "Faith alone doth justify;" and, "It is certain that we are not justified but by faith in Jesus Christ[1]." He addeth the example of the apostles: "And we have believed in Jesus Christ, that we might be justified by faith in Jesus Christ, and not by the works of the law." In like manner also Peter argueth by an example in the Acts of the Apostles, and saith: "We believe that through the grace of our Lord Jesus Christ we shall be saved, even as they." Acts xv.

Moreover, in the very same chapter to the Galatians he saith: "I despise not the grace of God; for if righteousness come of the law, then Christ is dead in vain." For, if we in ourselves had had any thing whereby we might be saved, what needed the Son of God to take our flesh, to suffer, and to die? But for because the Son of God, being incarnate, did suffer and die, and died not in vain; therefore in our flesh there was nothing that could obtain salvation for mankind. Wherefore the only Son of God is our Saviour for ever, and by true faith maketh us partakers of his salvation.

Christ died not in vain.

Paul in the very beginning of his epistle to the Romans doth prove that all men are sinners; that in men there remaineth no strength for them to be saved by; and that the law of God itself doth dig up[2] the knowledge of offences, that is, doth apply them, bring them to light, and make them manifest, but doth not take them away, blot them out, or utterly extinguish them; and that therefore God, for his own goodness' sake, to the end that the work that he hath made should not altogether perish, doth justify the faithful freely by faith in Jesus Christ. I will rehearse a few of the apostle's own words. "The righteousness of God," saith he, "is declared without the law, being witnessed notwithstanding by the law and the prophets; the righteousness of God, I say, cometh by faith in Jesus Christ unto all and upon all them that believe. For there is no difference: for all have sinned, and have need of the glory of God, but are justified freely by his grace through the redemption that

All men are sinners.

[1 Cf. Calvin. Comment. in loc. cit. Maneat igitur illud constitutum: hic propositionem esse exclusivam, Nos non aliter justificari quam fide; aut, Non nisi fide justificari: cui ista æquipollet, Nos sola fide justificari.]

[2 eruere, Lat.]

is in Christ Jesu; whom God hath set forth to be a propitiation through faith in his blood[3]." These words of the apostle, I suppose, are most manifest to them that believe. He plucketh justification from our own merits and strength, and attributeth it to grace, whereby the Son of God is given to the world unto the punishment of the cross, that all they that believe that they are redeemed by the blood of the Son of God may be justified. Again the apostle immediately after addeth: "Therefore we hold, that man is justified by faith without the works of the law." Upon the neck of this again he argueth thus: "Is he the God of the Jews only? Is he not also of the Gentiles? Yes, even of the Gentiles also. For it is one God that shall justify circumcision by faith, and uncircumcision through faith[4]." To be God, is nothing else but to be life and salvation. But God is the God of the Gentiles also, and not of the Jews alone: therefore God is the life and salvation of the Gentiles. This life and salvation he doth communicate to us, not by the law or through circumcision, but by faith in Christ; therefore faith alone doth justify. This may be proved by the example of Cornelius the centurion, who, as soon as St Peter had preached unto him, and he once believed, was by and by justified, when as yet he had not received circumcision, or the law; when as yet he had not sacrificed, nor merited righteousness by any work that he did: for he was freely justified in faith through Jesus Christ. For Peter concluded his sermon to him in these words: "To this Christ do all the prophets give witness, that through his name whosoever believeth in him shall receive remission of sins[5]."

God justifieth as well the Gentiles as the Jews by faith.

After all this, the apostle Paul bringeth forth that notable and singular example of our father Abraham, teaching by what means our father Abraham was justified. For, this being once truly declared, it cannot choose but be plain and manifest to every one, by what means God's will is to justify all men: for the sons cannot be justified any other way than the father before them was justified. Abraham therefore was not justified by circumcision, or receiving of the sacrament; for it is said that he was justified before he was circumcised.

By what means our father Abraham was justified.

[3 Rom. iii. 21—25.]   [4 Ibid. v. 28—30.]
[5 Acts x. 43.]

Afterward was added the sign of circumcision, as "the seal of the righteousness of faith," that is, the sign or sealing that all the seed of Abraham is justified by faith[1]. The same our father Abraham was not justified by the law: for the law was four hundred and thirty years[2] added to the promise, not to take away sin or to work justification, but to make sin appear, and to make us altogether empty; and, when we are once made empty, to send, and as it were compel us to fly, to Christ. Again, Abraham was not justified by his works: and yet, in that most excellent patriarch are found to be good works; yea, and those too good works of true faith, which are both notable and many in number, such and so many as you shall scarcely find in any other. Nevertheless, yet the apostle saith: "What shall we say then that Abraham our father as pertaining to the flesh (who, I say, is our father touching the flesh) did merit or find?"——for both those significations hath the Greek word εὑρηκέναι[3]. For, "if Abraham were justified by works, then hath he to boast; but not before God." For God is only just, and he that only justifieth: all men are corrupt; yea, even Abraham is a sinner, and every man standeth in need of the glory of God. For which cause also the prophet did plainly forbid to boast in any thing, but in the mercy of God. Wherefore Abraham boasted not against God; he acknowledged himself to be a sinner, and that he was to be justified freely, and not for his own merits' sake. The apostle goeth forth and saith: "For what saith the scripture? Abraham believed in God, and it was reckoned unto him for righteousness." Two things are here affirmed: first, that Abraham believed in God; secondly, that that was imputed to him for righteousness. By this it followeth, that Abraham was justified by faith, and not by works. And that doth the apostle prove after this manner: "To him that by works doth merit righteousness righteousness is not imputed. But to Abraham is righteousness imputed: therefore he merited not righteousness by works." Again: "To him verily that worketh not, but believeth, his faith is counted for

[1 Rom. iv. 10—12.]

[2 Galat. iii. 17.   post annos, Lat.]

[3 εὑρηκέναι, quod *invenisse* reddunt, significat, teste Budæo, *mereri*.—Bucer. Enarr. Epist. ad Rom. in loc. cit. p. 226, Basil. 1562.]

righteousness. But Abraham believed in God; therefore his faith was reckoned for righteousness[4]."

In the same chapter the same apostle bringeth forth other arguments, altogether as strong as these, to prove that faith justifieth without works. "If they," saith he, "which are of the law be heirs, then is faith but vain, and the promise made of none effect[5]." They are of the law, which seek to be justified by the works of the law. But faith resteth upon the mercy of God. What place then shall grace and the mercy of God have left unto them, if we by works do merit justification? What shall I need to believe, that by the blood of Christ I shall be justified, if God by my works be at one with me again, who for my sins was angry with me? Finally, salvation and righteousness are promised of God. But then the promise endeth, when our own merits begin to come in place. For the apostle to the Galatians saith : "If inheritance be of the law, then is it not now of the promise. But God gave the inheritance to Abraham by promise[6]." Therefore that the promise might remain stable, faith justifieth, and not merits.

Neither is faith nor the promise of none effect.

Again, in the fourth chapter to the Romans he saith : ' Therefore by faith is the inheritance given, that it might be by grace, that the promise might be sure to all the seed ; not to that only that is of the law, but to that also that is of the faith of Abraham." He rehearseth here two causes, for which he attributeth justification to faith, and not to works. The first is, that justification may be of free gift, and that the grace of God may be praised. The latter is, that the promise and salvation may remain stedfast, and that it may come upon the Gentiles also : but it should not be given to the Gentiles, if it were due only to the law and circumcision, because the Gentiles lack them both. Finally, the hope of our salvation ought to be stedfastly established : but it should never be surely grounded, or safely preserved, if it were attributed to our own works or merits ; for in them is always something wanting. But in God and in the merit of the Son of God can nothing be lacking. Therefore our salvation is surely confirmed, not to be doubted of, and assuredly certain, if that we seek for it by faith in the Son of God, who is our righteousness and salvation.

Justification of free gift.

[4 Rom. iv. 1—5.]   [5 Ibid. v. 14.]
[6 Gal. iii. 18, 22.]

To all these I will yet add another testimony out of St Paul, which is indeed both most evident and easy to be perceived. In his epistle to the Ephesians he saith: "By grace are ye saved through faith, and that not of yourselves; it is the gift of God: not of works, lest any man should boast himself. For we are the workmanship of God, created in Christ Jesus into good works, which God hath before ordained that we should walk in them[1]."

More than this I will not say, neither will I at large expound the words of Paul. For these testimonies are more clear than the noon-day, and do most evidently testify, that we are justified by faith, and not by any works.

Faith sheweth forth and expresseth itself by good works.

But, reverend[2] brethren in the Lord, good works here come into no jeopardy to be little set by, because of this doctrine, which teacheth that faith alone doth justify. Thus did the apostles of Christ teach; why then should we not teach so too? As for them that think this doctrine, whereby we do constantly affirm that faith alone without works doth justify, to be contrary to religion, let them blame the apostles of Christ, and not find fault with us. Moreover, whereas we

Faith only justifieth.

say, that the faithful are justified by faith alone, or else by faith without works, we do not say, as many think we do, that faith is post alone[3], or utterly destitute of good works: for wheresoever faith is, there also it sheweth itself by good works; because the righteous cannot but work righteousness. But before he doth work righteousness, that is to say, good works, he must of necessity be righteous: therefore the righteous doth not attain to righteousness that goeth before by works that follow after. Wherefore that righteousness is attributed to grace: for the faithful are freely by grace justified in faith, according to that saying, "The just shall live by his faith;" and after that they are justified, they begin to bring forth the works of righteousness. Therefore in this discourse I mean not to overthrow good works, which have their due place and dignity in the church among the faithful before the face of God: but my mind is, by all the means I may, to prove that the grace of God, and increase of the Son of God, is overthrown and trodden under foot, when we join our merits and works to the merit of Christ

[1 Ephes. ii. 8—10.]   [2 honorandi, Lat.]

[3 fidem esse solam, Lat.]   [4 meritum, Lat.]

and to faith, by which we take hold on Christ. For what
can be more manifest than this saying of the blessed apostle?
"If we be saved by grace, then not now works[5]; for then
grace is no more grace. But if we be saved by works, then
is it now no grace[6]; for the work is no more work." Rom. xi.
Wherefore these two, grace and merit or work, cannot stand
together. Therefore, lest we should overthrow the grace of
God, and wickedly deny the fruit of Christ his passion, we do
attribute justification unto faith only, because that faith attributeth it to the mere grace of God in the death of the Son of
God.

And yet for all this we acknowledge that we are created, *Of good
works.*
according to the doctrine of Paul, unto good works; to those
good works, I say, which God hath before ordained[7], which
he in his word hath appointed, and doth require us to walk
in the same: in which although we walk, and are become
rich in good works, yet notwithstanding we do not attribute
to them our justification; but, according to the doctrine of the
gospel, we humble ourselves under the hand of him that saith:
"So ye also, when ye have done all things that are commanded you, yet say, We are unprofitable servants; we have
done no more than we ought to do[8]." So then, as often as
the godly doth read, that our own works do justify us, that
our own works are called righteousness, that unto our own
works is given a reward and life everlasting; he doth not by
and by swell with pride, nor yet forget the merit of Christ:
but, setting a godly and apt interpretation upon such-like
places, he doth consider that all things are of the grace of
God, and that so great things are attributed to the works of
men, because they are received into grace, and are now become the sons of God for Christ his sake; so that at the last,
all things may be turned upon Christ himself, for whose sake
the godly know that they and all theirs are in favour and
accepted of God the Father.

In this that I have said (which is a little indeed in respect
of the largeness of the matter, but sufficiently long enough in
respect of one hour's space appointed me to speak in,) I have
declared unto you, dearly beloved, the great effect of faith;
that is to say, that it justifieth the faithful; where, by the way,

[5 ex operibus, Lat.]   [6 jam non ex gratia, Lat.]
[7 Ephes. ii. 10.]   [8 Luke xvii. 10.]

I have rather briefly touched, than at large discoursed upon, the whole work of justification, both profitable and necessary for all men to know. Now, therefore, I pass over this, and come to the rest.

Faith the root of all good works.

True faith is the well-spring and root of all virtues and good works: and first of all, it satisfieth the mind and desire of man, and maketh it quiet and joyful. For the Lord in the gospel saith: "I am the bread of life: he that cometh to me shall not hunger; and he that believeth in me shall not thirst at any time[1]." For what can he desire more, which doth already feel, that by true faith he possesseth the very Son of God, in whom are all the heavenly treasures, and in whom is all fulness and grace? Our consciences are made clear and quiet, so soon as we perceive that by true faith Christ, the Son of God, is altogether ours; that he hath appeased the Father in our behalf; that he doth now stand in the presence of the Father, and maketh intercession to him for us. And for that cause saith Paul: "Being justified by faith, we have peace with God through our Lord Jesus Christ[2]." Through the same Christ, also, by faith we have a free passage unto the Father[3]. Wherefore we pray to the Father in his Son's name, and at his hand we obtain all things that are available to our behoof. Very well therefore said the apostle John: "And this is the confidence that we have in him, that, if we ask any thing according to his will, he heareth us. And if we know that he heareth us, whatsoever we ask, we know also that we have the petitions that we requested at his hands[4]." They that want faith do neither pray to God, nor yet receive of him the things that are for their welfare. Moreover, faith maketh us acceptable to God, and doth command us to have an eye to the well using of God's good gifts.

Faith the victory of all Christians.

Faith causeth us not to faint in tribulations: yea also, by faith we overcome the world, the flesh, the devil, and all adversities; as the apostle John saith: "For all that is born of God overcometh the world: and this is the victory that vanquisheth the world, even your faith. Who is he that overcometh the world, but he that believeth that Jesus is the Son of God[5]?" Paul saith: "Some were racked, not caring,

[1 John vi. 35.]   [2 Rom. v. 1.]
[3 Ephes. ii. 18.]   [4 1 John v. 14, 15.]
[5 1 John v. 4, 5.]

by faith, to be set at liberty, that they might obtain a better resurrection.   Other some were tried with mocks and stripes, with fetters and imprisonments; were stoned, were hewed in pieces, were slain with the edge of the sword: they wandered in sheep-skins and goat-skins, comfortless, oppressed, afflicted, (of whom the world was not worthy,) wandering in deserts and mountains, and in the dens and caves of the earth[6]."   For the Lord himself in the gospel said: "This spake I unto you, that ye might have peace in me.   In the world ye have affliction; but be of good confidence, I have overcome the world[7]."   Faith therefore both shall be, and is, the force and strength of patience.   Patience is the prop[8], uplifting, and preservation of hope.   Of faith springeth charity.   Charity "is the fulfilling of the law[9]," which containeth in it the sum of all good works.   But unless we have a true faith in God, there is no charity in us.   "Every one that loveth him that begat," saith John the apostle, "loveth him also that is born of him[10]."

The hour is past a good while since, and no man is able in many hours, so substantially as it requireth, to declare the whole effect of faith.

Ye have heard, dearly beloved, that true faith is the justification of the church or faithful of God; that it is, I say, the forgiveness of all sins, a receiving into the grace of God, a taking by adoption into the number of the sons of God, an assured and blessed sanctification[11], and finally, the well-spring of all good works.   Let us therefore in true faith pray to God the Father, in the name of our Lord Jesus Christ, that he will vouchsafe to fill our hearts with this true faith; that in this present world, being joined to him in faith, we may serve him as we ought; and, after our departure out of this life, we may for ever live with him in whom we believe.   To him be praise and glory for ever.   Amen.

[6 Heb. xi. 35—38.]
[7 John xvi. 33.]
[8 *Hœc* fulcit, &c., Lat.   This (faith) is the prop, &c.]
[9 Rom. xiii. 10.]   [10 1 John v. 1.]
[11 beatificationem, Lat.]

OF THE FIRST ARTICLES OF THE CHRISTIAN FAITH CONTAINED IN THE APOSTLES' CREED.

THE SEVENTH SERMON.

In my two last sermons I entreated of true faith and the effects thereof; and among the rest in one place I said, that the articles of the christian faith are, as it were, a brief summary of true faith: now therefore I think it to be not beside the purpose, and part of my duty, to lay before you those twelve articles of our belief. For they are the substance and matter of true faith, wherein faith is exercised: which because it is the ground[1] of things hoped for, here is plainly and briefly declared in these articles what things those are that are to be hoped for. But let no man at this present look for at my hand the busy[2] and full discourse of the articles of our faith: I will but briefly go through them, touching only the most necessary points. They are in another place handled more at large by several parts. Pray ye with me to the Lord, that he will vouchsafe to shew to us his ways, to guide and preserve us in them, to the glory of his own name, and the everlasting salvation of our souls.

The Apostles' Creed. First, I have to say somewhat touching the common name, whereby the articles of our faith are usually called the Symbol or Creed of the Apostles. A symbol is as much to say as a conferring together, or else a badge[3]. The articles are called a conferring together, because, by the laying together of the apostles' doctrine, they were made and written to be a rule and an abridgement of the faith preached by the apostles, and received of the catholic or universal church. But what he was that first did thus dispose and write these articles, it is not known, nor left in writing of the holy scriptures. Some there are that do attribute it to the apostles themselves, and therefore do call it by the name of the Apostles' Creed. St Cyprian, the martyr, in his exposition of the Apostles' Creed, saith: "Our ancestors have a saying, that after the Lord's ascension, when by the coming of the Holy Ghost the fiery tongues sat upon every one of the apostles, so

[1 substantia, Lat.]   [2 operosam, Lat.]
[3 et collatio, et indicium, Lat.]

that they spake both divers and sundry languages, whereby
there was no foreign nation nor barbarous tongue to which they
seemed not sufficiently prepared to pass by the way ; they had a
commandment from the Lord, to go unto all nations to preach
the word of God.   When therefore they were in a readiness
to depart, they laid down among themselves a platform of
preaching for them all to follow, lest peradventure, being
severed one from another, they should preach divers things
to them that were converted to the faith of Christ. Wherefore
being there all together, and replenished with the Holy Ghost,
they gathered one every one's several sentence, and made
that breviary (as I said) to be a pattern for all their preach-
ings to be framed by, appointing it for a rule to be given to
them that should believe[4]." This saith Cyprian. But whether
they were of the apostles' own making or no, or else that
other, the apostles' disciples, made them, yet this is very well
known, that the very doctrine of the apostles is purely contained and taught in them.   These twelve articles are called
also a badge, because by that sign, as it were by a badge,
true Christians are discerned from false.

Now I will declare what order I will use in expounding
them unto you. This whole breviary, or abridgement of faith,
may be divided into four parts; so that the three first parts
may make manifest the mysteries of the three Persons in one
Godhead; and that the fourth may lay forth the fruits of
faith, that is to say, what good things we look for by faith,
and what good things God bestoweth on them that put their
trust in him.   And yet, this notwithstanding, I will proceed

The partition
of the Apos-
tles' Creed.

[4 Tradunt majores nostri, quod post ascensionem Domini, cum
per adventum sancti Spiritus super singulos quosque apostolos ig-
neæ linguæ sedissent, ut loquelis diversis variisque loquerentur, per
quod eis nulla gens extera, nulla linguæ barbaries inaccessa videretur
et invia, præceptum eis a Domino datum, ob prædicandum Dei verbum, ad singulas quemque proficisci nationes.   Discessuri itaque ab
invicem normam prius futuræ sibi prædicationis in commune consti-
tuunt, ne forte alius ab alio abducti diversum aliquid his, qui ad fidem
Christi invitabantur, exponerent.   Omnes ergo in uno positi, et
Spiritu sancto repleti, breve istud futuræ sibi (ut diximus) prædicationis indicium, conferendo in unum quod sentiebat unusquisque, com-
ponunt, atque hanc credentibus dandam esse regulam statuunt.—
Cypr. Expos. in Symb. Apost. in init. ed. Oxon. 1682.   This tract is
not Cyprian's, but was written by Ruffinus.]

herein even orderly so as the twelve articles are placed or set down.

The first article of christian faith is this: "I believe in God, the Father Almighty, maker of heaven and earth." And this first article of the Creed containeth two especial points: for first we say generally, I believe in God; then we descend particularly to the distinction of the Persons, and add, the Father Almighty. For God is one in substance, and three in Persons. Wherefore, understanding the unity of the substance, we say plainly, I believe in God: and again, keeping and not confounding the Persons, we add, In the Father Almighty, In Jesus Christ his only Son, and in the Holy Ghost. Let us therefore believe that God is one, not many, and pure in substance; but three in Persons, the Father, the Son, and the Holy Ghost. For in the law it is written: "Hearken, Israel: The Lord our God is one Lord[1]." And again, in the gospel we read that the Lord saith: "Baptize them in the name of the Father, of the Son, and of the Holy Ghost[2]."

God is one in substance, and three in Persons.

By the way, this is singularly to be marked of us; that, when we pray, we say, "Our Father which art in heaven, give us this day our daily bread;" but that, when we make confession of our belief, we say not, We believe, but, "I believe." For faith is required of every one of us, for every particular man to have without dissimulation in his heart, and without double meaning to profess it with his mouth. It was not enough for Abraham to have faith for all his seed; neither will it avail thee any thing for another to believe, if thou thyself art without faith: for the Lord requireth faith of every particular man for himself. Wherefore, so oft as we confess our faith, every one of us by himself doth say, "I believe." But what it is to believe, I have declared already in my fourth sermon.

I believe in God.

It followeth in the confession, "I believe in God." God is the object and foundation of our faith, as he that is the everlasting and chief goodness, never weary, but alway ready at our need. We therefore believe in God; that is to say, we put our whole hope, all our safety, and ourselves wholly into his hands, as unto him that is able to preserve and bestow on us all things that are requisite for our behoof.

[1 Deut. vi. 4.]   [2 Matt. xxviii. 19.]

Now it followeth that that God, in whom we rest, and God is called a Father. unto whose tuition we do all commit ourselves, is "the Father Almighty." Our God is therefore called Father, because from before all beginning he begat the Son like to himself. For the scripture calleth God "the Father of our Lord Jesus Christ." "He," saith the apostle, "is the brightness of the glory of God, and the lively image[3] of the substance of the Father: to whom he said, Thou art my Son, this day have I begotten thee." And again: "I will be his Father, and he shall be my Son[4]." Also God is called Father in respect of the likeness that he hath with our earthly father; to wit, because of our creation, the favour, love, good-will, and carefulness wherewith he is affected towards us. For God hath created us, God loveth us, God regardeth our affairs, and is careful for us; yea, and that more exceedingly too than any earthly father is. For saith David: "Even as the father pitieth his children, so doth the Lord pity them that fear him: for he knoweth our estate, remembering that we are but dust[5]." Esaias also in his 49th chapter saith: "Can a woman forget her own infant, and not pity and be fain over[6] the son of her own womb? But admit she do forget; yet will not I forget thee." In this is declared God's good-will to us-ward: and we, confessing that God is our Father, do also profess that God to us is both gentle, liberal, and merciful, who wisheth us all things that are available to our health, and purposeth nothing to us-ward but that which is good and wholesome; and, last of all, that at his hand we receive what good soever we have, either bodily or ghostly.

God is called Almighty, because by his might he can do God is called Almighty. all things; because he is Lord of all things, and hath all things subject to his commandment. For the same cause also is he called the Lord of hosts. Heaven, earth, and whatsoever is therein, stars, all elements, men, angels, devils, all living creatures, all things created, are in the power of the most high and everlasting God. Whatsoever he commandeth, that they do: nothing is able to withstand his will. What he

[3 expressa imago, Lat.; Erasmus' rendering. The Vulgate has only *figura*.]

[4 Heb. i. 3, 5.]

[5 Psal. ciii. 13, 14.]

[6 eximie afficiatur erga, Lat.]

will, that must of necessity be done: and also these things he useth even as his own will and pleasure is, and as his justice and man's salvation do require. First we confessed, that God doth will us well; and now we acknowledge, that whatsoever he will, that he is able to bring to pass. For we say that God is Almighty, that is, that there is nothing but he can do it, which is profitable and necessary for us men, as he that is Lord of all, and our strong helper.

God is the maker of heaven and earth.

But that God is our good Father, liberal, gentle, merciful, strong, almighty, Lord of all, and our defender and deliverer, it is to be seen by his wonderful works. For he is the "maker of heaven and earth." And in the making of heaven and earth he hath declared the great love that he beareth to mankind. For when as yet they were not, neither were able with deserts and good turns to provoke God to do them any good; then God first of his own mere and natural goodness made heaven and earth, a most excellent and beautiful palace, and gave it them to dwell in, putting under man's dominion all the creatures of this whole world. But how great power he shewed in the making of all these things, it is evident by this, that "he spake the word, and they were made; he commanded, and they were created[1]." Which if thou bring into parts, and severally examine what he made in those six days, in what order, with what beauty, to how great commodity of mankind, and finally how almost with no labour at all he brought them all forth, as it is at large written by Moses in the first of Genesis, thou shalt be compelled to be amazed at the good-will and power of God. And yet, by the way, we must think the Creator of all things to be such an one, as by his Son, that is, by his eternal Wisdom, hath created all things both visible and invisible; yea, and that of nothing too: and doth moreover at this very present sustain, nourish, rule, and preserve all things by his everlasting Spirit, without which every thing would presently fall to ruin, and come to nought. We do herein therefore confess also the providence of our eternal God, and his exceeding wise government.

And thus in this first part I have declared unto you that which is proper to the Father. For he is a Father; yea, he is the Father of our Lord Jesus Christ, and our Father also,

[1 Psal. xxxiii. 9, and cxlviii. 5.]

being Lord of all things, maker of heaven and earth, governor and preserver of all things, by whom all things are,
and in whom all things consist; who from before all beginning begot the eternal Son, equal with the Father, being of
one substance, power, and glory with the Father, by whom
also he made the world. From both them proceedeth the Holy
Ghost, as David witnesseth, and saith : " By the word of the
Lord the heavens were made, and by the breath of his mouth
all the host thereof[2]."

Now followeth the second part, wherein are contained all *The second article of our belief.*
the mysteries of Jesus Christ, our Lord, the Son of God.
For the second article of the christian faith is thus word for
word : " And in Jesus Christ, his only Son, our Lord." This
article also comprehendeth two things : the first is, that we
believe in the Son of God ; the second, what the Son of God
is.   For we confess that we believe, that is, that we put our
whole hope and confidence of life and salvation, as well in the
Son as in the Father. And therefore we say plainly, " I believe *To believe in the Son of God.*
in Jesus Christ," even as before we said, " I believe in God,"
&c.   For the Lord Jesus himself, in the fourteenth chapter
of John, saith : " Let not your heart be troubled : ye believe
in God, believe also in me."   Again : " This is the work of
God, that ye believe in him whom he hath sent[3]."   And
again : " This is eternal life, to know thee, the true God only,
and him whom thou hast sent, Christ Jesus[4]."   Moreover, in
the gospel after St John we read, that the Lord, speaking to
the blind whose eyes he opened, said : " Dost thou believe in the
Son of God ?" and that the blind, having received his sight,
answered : " Who is he, Lord, that I may believe in him ?"
Whereunto the Lord replied : " Thou hast seen him, and he it
is that talketh with thee."   And that then again the blind
said, " I believe, Lord ;" and therewithal he worshipped him[5].
Therefore let us also believe and worship ; let us believe that
Jesus is the very Son of God the Father, being of one power
with the Father, although in Person he differ from the Father :
which David testifying saith, " The LORD said to my Lord,
Sit thou at my right hand," &c.[6]

But if we declare at large, who that Son of God is, in *Who the Son of God is.*

[2 Psal. xxxiii. 6.]   [3 John vi. 29.]
[4 John xvii. 3.]   [5 John ix. 35—38.]
[6 Psal. cx. 1.]

whom we believe, then must we note three things especially. The first is, that he is called the only Son. If he be the Son, yea, and that too the Son of God, then is his nature and substance a divine nature and substance. For in this signification doth the apostle call him "the brightness of the glory of the Father, and the lively image of his substance." Very well therefore do the holy fathers say, that the Son is of the same substance and being with[1] the Father. Whereunto belongeth that, that he is called the only Son; and in another place, the only-begotten and first-begotten Son. For we also are called sons, not by participation of nature, or likeness of substance, or naturally, but by adoption. And therefore the Jews were not offended, because he called himself the Son of God, in that sense that all the faithful are called, and are, the sons of God; but because they did perceive, that he did more extol himself in saying that he is the natural Son of God, equal to God, and God himself. For thus we read in the fifth of John: "Therefore the Jews sought the more to kill Jesus; not only because he had broken the sabbath, but said also that God was his Father, and made himself equal with God." Again, where the Lord in the tenth chapter said, "I and my Father are one; then the Jews took up stones to stone him withal: but Jesus answered, Many good works have I done unto you; for which of them do ye stone me?" To which the Jews replied: "For thy good works' sake we stone thee not, but for thy blasphemy, and because thou, being a man, makest thyself God." These are most evident testimonies of the natural Godhead of Christ, which whosoever believeth not, he hath not the Father[2]. For he that honoureth the Son, honoureth the Father; and he that is without the Son hath not the Father: and unless the Son were God by nature, he could not be the Saviour of the world.

Consubstantial and co-essential. The only Son.

Now the second thing that is to be marked is, that the name of the only-begotten Son of God is opened, and he is called "Jesus Christ." The name is expressly set down, that we may know who it is in whom we believe, lest peradventure we might be deceived in the person. It is Jesus: which name was given unto him by God's appointment from heaven, even

Jesus.

[1] consubstantialis et coessentialis, Lat.]
[2] 1 John ii. 23.]

as also it was prefigured in duke Josue and in Jesus the high priest. The angel, in the gospel after St Matthew, instructing Joseph, saith: "Mary shall bring forth a son, and thou shalt call his name Jesus. For he shall save his people from their sins[3]."

So then this Son of God, Jesus, is the Saviour of the world, who forgiveth sins, and setteth us free from all the power of our adversary the devil: which verily he could not do, unless he were very God. He is also called Christ, which is all one as if you say, Anointed. The Jews call him Messias; which word is a title proper to a kingdom or priesthood[4]. For they of old were wont to anoint their kings and priests: they were anointed with external or figurative ointment or oil. But very Christ was anointed with the very true ointment, that is, with the fulness of the Holy Ghost: as is to be seen in the first and third chapters after St John. Most properly therefore is this name Christ attributed to our Lord. For, first, he is both King and Priest of the people of God. Then the Holy Ghost is poured fully by all means and abundantly into Jesus, from whom, as it were by a lively fountain, it floweth into all the members of Christ. For this is that Aaron, upon whose head the oil was poured, " which ran down to his beard, and the nethermost skirts of his garment[5]:" for " of his fulness we have all received[6]."

Christ.

The last thing that is to be noted now in this second article is, that we call the Son of God "our Lord." The Son of God verily is for two causes properly called our Lord: first, in respect of the mystery of our redemption. For Christ is the Lord of all the elect, whom he hath delivered from the power and dominion of Satan, sin, and death, and hath made them a people of his own getting for himself[7]. This similitude is taken of lords, which with their money buy slaves for their use, or else which in wars reserve captives, whom they might have slain, or which deliver men condemned from present death. So then by this, lords are, as it were, deliverers, redeemers, or saviours[8]. Hereunto verily alludeth

Christ is our Lord.

[3 ch. i. 21.]   [4 tam regni, quam sacerdotii, Lat.]
[5 Psal. cxxxiii. 2.]   [6 John i. 16.]
[7 populum acquisitionis, Lat. 1 Pet. ii. 9.]
[8 Dominus redemptoris et assertoris vocabulum est.—Erasm. Colloq. Inquisit. de Fide. Opp. Lugd. Bat. 1703. Tom. I. col. 729.]

[BULLINGER.]

9

Paul, where he saith: "Ye are bought with a price: become not (therefore) the servants of men[1]." And St Peter saith "Ye are redeemed, not with gold and silver, but with the precious blood of the unspotted Lamb[2]." Moreover, Christ is called Lord in respect of his divine power and nature, by which all things are in subjection to the Son of God. And for because this word "Lord" is of a very ample signification, as that which containeth both the divine nature and majesty, we see that the apostles in their writings use it very willingly Paul to the Corinthians saith: "Although there be many lords, yet have we but one Lord Jesus Christ, by whom al things are, and we by him[3]."

The third article of our belief.

Now the third article of christian faith is this: "Which was conceived by the Holy Ghost; born of the virgin Mary.' In the second article we have confessed, that we believe in Jesus Christ, the Son of God, our Lord: wherein we have as it were in a shadow, confessed, that we believe assuredly that God, the Father, hath for us and our salvation given to the world his Son, to be a Saviour and Redeemer; for hitherto belong those names, Jesus, and Lord. Now therefore in thi third article I have to declare the manner and order how he came into the world; to wit, by incarnation. This article containeth two things; the conception of Christ, and his nati vity: of both which I will orderly speak, after that I have briefly declared unto you the causes of the Lord his incarna tion.

The causes of the Lord his incarnation.

Men were in a miserable taking, and all mankind should utterly have perished for sin, which we have all drawn from the first man Adam: for the reward of sin is death. And for that cause we, that were to be cast into hell, could no enter into heaven, unless the Son of God had descended unto

Immanuel.

us, and, becoming God with us[4], had with himself drawn u into heaven. Therefore the chief cause of his incarnation is to be a Mediator betwixt God and men, and by intercession to join, or bring into one, them that were severed. For

A mediator.

where a mediator is, there also must needs be discord and parties. The parties are God and men: the cause of dis cord is sin. Now the office of the mediator is to bring t

[1 1 Cor. vii. 23.]   [2 1 Pet. i. 18, 19.]
[3 1 Cor. viii. 5, 6.]
[4 Immanuel, Lat.]

agreement the parties disagreeing : which verily cannot be done, unless that sin, the cause of this variance, be taken clean away. But sin is neither cleansed nor taken away, except that blood be shed, and death do follow. This witnesseth Paul in his ninth chapter to the Hebrews. The mediator ought therefore to take on him our flesh and blood, that he might both die and shed his blood. Furthermore it is needful, that this advocate, or mediator, be indifferently common to both the parties, whom he hath to reconcile : wherefore our Lord Christ ought to be very God and very man. If he had been God alone, then should he have been terrible to men, and have stood them in little stead : if he had been mere man, then could he not have had access to God, which is a consuming fire. Wherefore our Lord Jesus Christ, being both God and man, was a fit Mediator for both the parties. Which thing the apostle witnessing saith : "One God, and one Mediator of God and men, the man Christ Jesus, who gave himself the price of redemption for all[5]." The same apostle, in the second and ninth chapters to the Hebrews, speaketh many things belonging to this place. And in the second chapter, rehearsing another cause of Christ his incarnation, he saith : " It became him in all things to be made like unto his brethren, that he might be merciful and a faithful High Priest in things concerning God, for to purge the people's sins. For in that he himself was tempted, he is able to succour them that are tempted." Another cause, wherefore our Lord was incarnate, was, that he might instruct us men in all godliness and righteousness ; and finally, that he might be the light of the world, and an ensample of holy life. For Paul saith : "The grace of God that bringeth salvation hath appeared unto us, teaching us to renounce ungodliness, and to live holily[6]." To conclude : he therefore became one with us by the participation of nature, that is to say, it pleased him to be incarnate for this cause, that he might join us again to God, who for sin were separated from God ; and receive us into the fellowship of himself, and all other his goodness beside.

The next is for us to declare the manner of his incarnation. This article of faith standeth on two members. The first is,

The manner of Christ his conception.

[5 1 Tim. ii. 5, 6.]
[6 Tit. ii. 11, 12.]

"He was conceived by the Holy Ghost." All we men, Christ excepted, are conceived by the seed of man, which of itself is unclean; and therefore we are born sinners; and Paul saith, "We are born the sons of wrath[1]." But the body of Christ, I say, our Lord, was not conceived in the virgin Mary by Joseph, or by any seed of man, but by the Holy Ghost: not that the Holy Ghost was in place of the seed; for nothing is begotten of the Spirit, but what is spiritual. Neither hath our Lord a phantastical[2], but a very true body, and of the same substance with us. So then our Lord was conceived in the womb of the virgin by the Holy Ghost. For the Holy Ghost by his eternal power did bring to pass, that, the virginity of the mother being uncorrupted, she, I say, being made with child, conceived of her blood, and gave a pure and very human body to the Son of God; as is declared at large by the angel Gabriel in the first chapter of St Luke: of which place I mean to speak elsewhere more largely: I do now pass it over untouched.

God himself straightways after the beginning of the world did foretell, that such should be the manner of that conception. For he said not, The seed of the man shall tread down the serpent's head, but "the seed of the woman[3]." Moreover the Lord by the prophets saith: "I will raise up seed to David." But Moses' law for the raising up of seed to the brother departed is well known: for if the brother died without issue of children, his brother remaining alive was compelled to marry the deceased brother's wife, and of her to beget children, which were called and counted, not by the name of him that was living, but of the dead brother[4]. Wherefore, when there was not to be found a man of David's line, that was sufficiently meet to beget on the virgin the Son of God, the Saviour of the world, God himself raiseth up seed to David, and by his Holy Spirit maketh the virgin with child; who, although she were not with child by a man of

[1 Ephes. ii. 3.]

[2 The Docetæ, an early heretical sect, maintained, that the incarnation and sufferings of our Lord were not real, but phantastical.— See Routh's Reliq. Sacr. Tom. I. p. 461. ed. Oxon. 1846; also Calvin. Instit. Lib. II. cap. 13.]

[3 Gen. iii. 15.]

[4 Deut. xxv. 5, 6.]

David's line, yet because she was a daughter of David's stock, and because, God so working, she of her own substance gave substance to the Son of God, this her child Christ both is, and is called, the Son of David. What doth that argue moreover, that David in the 110th Psalm saith, "In the mighty power of holiness the dew of thy birth is to thee of the womb of the morning;" or, "The dew of thy birth is to thee of the womb of the morning in the mighty power of holiness?" That is to say, By a certain mighty power of holiness, and marvellous means, shalt thou be born. For thy birth shall be like unto the engendering of the dew, which cometh of the pure morning, as it were a child born of the womb. For as in the day-time the sun draweth out of the earth a vapour, which, by reason of the smallness of the heat which draweth it upward, is by the coldness of the temperate night-evenings drawn down again, and resolved into water; so God, that is the Sun of righteousness, took blood of the earth, that is, of the body of the untouched virgin Mary, and by a wonderful means did holily and purely bring to pass, that of her unspotted womb should be born and conceived the most holy Son of God.

The causes, why this conception of the Son of God in the womb of the holy virgin is most pure, are these. He that is conceived in the womb of a virgin is God; but God is a consuming fire, which cannot take or suffer any uncleanness in itself. Another cause is this: God came to cleanse our uncleanness, that is, the uncleanness of us men. He himself verily ought to be exempt from all original spots, and in all points most holy, to the end that, being the only unspotted sacrifice offered up for the sins of all the world, he might clean take away all the sins of the world. For that which is itself defiled cannot cleanse the thing that is defiled; but rather the spot or filthiness doth double his uncleanness by the coming to of that other unclean thing. *The causes why Christ his conception is pure.*

The second member of this third article is: He was "born of the virgin Mary." The Lord was born of Mary his mother, yet she a virgin still. He is therefore very man, which is born of woman. Moreover his birth is pure: for he was born of the virgin, so that together she was a mother, and yet a virgin too. For Esaias saith: "Behold, a virgin shall *Of the birth of Christ.*

conceive, and bring forth a son[1]." A virgin, saith he, shall do
both, conceive and bring forth; so that nevertheless she may
remain a virgin still.   The birth, therefore, of the Son of
God is most pure.   Also his birth is a true birth, verily and
indeed.   For he taketh flesh of the substance and womb of
the virgin: in which signification also our Lord Jesus Christ
is called the Son of David.   He could not be called David's
son, unless he had taken very human substance of Mary, a
maid or daughter of the stock of David.   Which that the
apostle John might most properly signify and express, he
saith: "The Word was made flesh[2]."   And the apostle Paul
saith: "He doth nowhere take on him the angels, but the
seed of Abraham[3]."   And in the same place again he affirmeth,
that the Lord "was made like to his brethren in all things,
sin excepted."   To the Philippians he saith: "When he was
equal with God, he made himself of no reputation, taking on
him the form of a servant, and made in the likeness of men,
and found in figure as a man[4]."   Again, the apostle John
beareth witness, and saith: "Every spirit, that confesseth
that Jesus Christ is come in the flesh, is of God; and every
spirit, which confesseth not that Jesus Christ is come in the
flesh, is not of God[5]."   Luke, in his second chapter, hath at
large set forth the manner of his nativity; and I do mean
elsewhere to speak of it at the full.   Let us therefore confess,
that Jesus Christ was "conceived by the Holy Ghost, and
born of the virgin Mary."

The fourth
article of our
belief.   The fourth article of christian faith is this: "He suffered
under Pontius Pilate, was crucified, dead, and buried: he descended into hell."   In this fourth article is declared the end,
use, and chiefest commodity of the Lord his incarnation.   For
he became man, that he might suffer and die, and, by dying
and suffering, might redeem us from eternal death and the
torments of hell, and make us (being once cleansed) heirs of
life everlasting.   For this is the end of the Lord his death,
as I will by and by shew you, and as Paul doth at large declare in the ninth chapter to the Hebrews.

[1 Isai. vii. 14.]   [2 John i. 14.]
[3 Heb. ii. 16, 17.   assumit, Lat.; Erasmus' rendering.   The Vulgate has _apprehendit._]
[4 ch. ii. 6—8.]   [5 1 John iv. 2, 3.]

This article also is divided into his parts. First, we con- Christ did suffer.
fess that our Lord suffered in very deed, and not phantastically
to the appearance only[6]; and that he suffered verily the
calamities and miseries of this world, and after that again the
torments of the slaughter-men, and death itself in most bitter
pangs. He suffered therefore both in soul and body; yea,
and that too in many fashions. For Esaias saith: " He is a
man of sorrows, and hath felt calamities. He beareth our infirmities, and hath carried our sorrows[7]." For the Lord himself also in the gospel said: "My soul is heavy, even unto the
death[8]." But verily he suffered all this for us; for in him
was neither sin, nor any cause else why he should suffer.

Secondarily, in this article is noted the time, and Pontius Christ suffer-
ed under
Pontius
Pilate.
Pilate the judge under whom the Lord died, and redeemed
the world from sin, death, the devil, and hell. He suffered
therefore in the monarchy of the Romans, under the emperor
Tiberius, when as now, according to the prophecy of Jacob,
father of Israel[9], the Jewish people obeyed foreign kings, because there were no more kings or captains of the stock of
Judah to have the rule over them: for he foretold, that
then the Messias should come[10]. What may be thought of
that moreover, that the Lord himself, oftener than once in
the gospel, did foreshew that he should be delivered into the
hands of the Gentiles, and by them be put to death?

In the third point of this article we do expressly declare
the manner of his death; for we add: "He was crucified," and
died on the cross. But the death of the cross, as it was most
reproachful, so also was it most bitter or sharp to be suffered;
yet took he that kind of death upon him, that he might make
satisfaction for the world, and fulfil that which from the
beginning was prefigured, that he should be hanged on the
tree. Isaac was laid on the pile of wood to be offered up in
sacrifice. Moses also stuck the serpent on the stake of wood,
and lift it up to be beheld. And the Lord himself said: " I,
when I shall be lift up from the earth, will draw all men unto
me[11]." Finally, he died on the cross, giving up his ghost to
God. For he died verily and indeed, as you shall straightway perceive: where I have briefly to declare unto you,

[6] non putative.]   [7] Isai. liii. 3, 4.]
[8] Mark xiv. 34.]   [9] Jacobi Israelis, Lat.]
[10] Gen. xlix. 10.]   [11] John xii 32]

what the fruit of Christ his death is. First, we were accursed because of sin: he therefore took our curse upon himself, being lift up upon the cross, to the end he might take our curse away, and that we might be blessed in him. Then also, the heritage bequeathed to us by will could not come unto us, unless he which bequeathed it did die. But God bequeathed it: who, that he might die, became man, and died according to his human nature, to the end that we might receive the heritage of life. In another place again Paul saith: " Him that knew not sin did God make sin for us, that we by him might be made the righteousness of God[1]." Our Lord therefore became man, by the sacrifice of himself to make satisfaction for us; on whom, as it were upon a goat for sin-offering, when all the sins of the whole world were gathered together and laid, he by his death took away and purged them all: so that now the only sacrifice of Christ hath satisfied for the sins of the whole world. And this verily is the greatest commodity of Christ his death taught everywhere by the apostles of Christ. Next after that, also, the death of Christ doth teach us patience and the mortification of our flesh: yea, Christ, by the participation of himself, doth by his Spirit work in us, that sin may not reign in us. Touching which thing the apostle Paul teacheth many things in the sixth chapter to the Romans. The Lord in the gospel saith: " If any man will follow me, let him deny himself, and take up his cross, and follow me[2]." These, and a few more, are the fruits of the Lord his passion, or the death of Christ.

Our Lord was buried.   Fourthly, in this article is added: " He was buried." For our Lord died verily and indeed upon the cross. The very truth of his death was proved by the soldier, which thrust him through the side. After that, he was taken down from the cross, and laid in a sepulchre. In the gospel are expressed the names of them that buried him, Joseph and Nicodemus. There is also shewed the manner how they buried him. The fruit of this his burial the Saviour himself hath taught in these words: " Verily, verily, I say unto you, unless the seed of corn cast into the earth do die, it remaineth alone; but if it die, it bringeth forth much fruit[3]." Whereupon the apostle exhorteth us to be buried with Christ in his

[1 2 Cor. v. 21.]   [2 Matt. xvi. 24.]
[3 John xii. 24.]

death, that we may rise again in the newness of life[4]; yea, that we may live and reign with him for evermore. If, therefore, our bodies also be buried at any time, let us not therefore be troubled in mind; for the faithful are buried, that they may rise with Christ again.

The fifth part of this fourth article some do put severally by itself, for the fifth article of our faith. I for my part do see no cause why it should be plucked from that that goeth before; nor why it should make by itself a peculiar article of our faith. The words are these: "He descended into hell." Touching this there are sundry opinions among the expositors of the holy scriptures. Augustine, in his book *De Fide et Symbolo*[5], doth neither place these words in the rule of belief, nor yet expound them. Cyprian saith thus: "It is to be known verily, that in the creed of the Latin church this is not added, 'He descended into hell;' nor yet is this clause received in the churches of the east: but yet the sense of that clause seemeth to be all one with that, where it is said, 'He was buried.'[6]" This saith he. So then Cyprian's opinion seemeth to be, that to descend into hell is nothing else but to be laid in the grave, according to that saying of Jacob: "Ye will bring my grey hairs with sorrow to hell, or the grave[7]."

But there are some that think this assertion to be without lawful proof. For it is not likely that they would wrap a thing once already plainly spoken immediately after in a darker kind of speech. Nay rather, so often as two sentences are joined together that signify both one thing, the latter is always an exposition of the first[8]. But in these two

He descended into hell.

[4 Rom. vi. 4.]

[5 August. Opp. Par. 1531. Tom. III. p. 31. "The descent into hell is not in the creed expounded by St Augustine, De Fide et Symbolo."—Pearson on the Creed. Oxf. ed. 1820. Vol. II. p. 278.]

[6 Sciendum sane est, quod in ecclesiæ Romanæ symbolo non habetur additum, *Descendit ad inferna;* sed neque in orientis ecclesiis habetur hic sermo: vis tamen verbi eadem videtur esse in eo quod sepultus dicitur.—Cypr. Expos. in Symb. in loc. p. 22. ed. Oxon. 1682.]

[7 Gen. xlii. 38. ad inferos, Lat. and Vulgate. Ainsworth translates the passage: Ye shall bring down my grey hairs with sorrow unto hell. See also Hutchinson's Works, p. 57. Parker Soc. ed.]

[8 Bullinger here, almost word for word, adopts Calvin's argument,

speeches, " He was buried," and "He descended into hell," the
first is the plainer, and the latter the more intricate. Augustine,
in his ninety-ninth epistle to Evodius, turmoileth himself pitifully in this matter[1].   To Dardanus, *de Dei Præsentia*, he
writeth, that the Lord went into hell, but that he felt no torment[2]. We shall more agreeably to the truth seem to understand this article, if we shall think that the virtue of Christ
his death did flow even to them that were dead, and profited
them too : that is to say, that all the patriarchs and holy
men, that died before the coming of Christ, were for the
death of Christ preserved from death everlasting; as St Peter
also maketh mention, " that the Lord went in the Spirit,
and preached unto the spirits that were in prison[3]."   For
verily they by the death of Christ were made to know the
sentence of condemnation justly pronounced against them,
because, when they lived, they believed not with Noe and
them that were with him in the Saviour that was to come.
Or else otherwise, by the lower parts, or by hell, we understand not the place of punishment appointed for the wicked,
but the faithful that are departed, even as also by the higher
parts[4] we understand them that yet are remaining alive.
Wherefore the soul of Christ descended into hell, that is to
say, it was carried into Abraham's bosom, wherein all the

which is: Nam quoties loquutiones duæ rem eandem exprimentes
simul connectuntur, posteriorem esse prioris exegesin convenit.—
Calvin. Instit. Lib. II. cap. 16. § 8.]

[1 Opp. Par. 1531. Tom. II. fol. 86.]

[2 This statement seems to be gathered out of the following passage in the Epistle of Augustine referred to: Non enim facile alicubi
scripturarum inferorum nomen positum invenitur pro bono.   Unde
etiam quæri solet, Si non nisi pœnalia recte intelliguntur inferna, quomodo animam Domini Christi pie credamus fuisse in inferno.   Sed
bene respondetur, ideo descendisse ut quibus oportuit subveniret.
Unde beatus Petrus eum dicit solvisse *dolores inferni, in quibus impos-
sibile erat teneri eum*.   Porro si utraque regis et dolentium et requies-
centium * * * in inferno esse credenda est, quis audeat dicere Dominum Jesum ad pœnales inferni partes venisse tantummodo, nec
fuisse apud eos qui in Abrahæ sinu requiescunt ? ubi si fuit, ipse est
intelligendus paradisus, quem lationis animæ illo die dignatus est
polliceri.   Quæ si ita sunt, generale paradisi nomen est, ubi feliciter
vivitur.—August. Epist. 57. Tom. II. ed. Par. 1531.]

[3 1 Pet. iii. 19.   inobedientibus ac in carcere detentis, Lat.]

[4 per superos, Lat.]

faithful already departed were gathered together. Therefore, when he said to the thief that was crucified with him, "This day shalt thou be with me in paradise," he promised him the fellowship of life and of the blessed souls. Touching Abraham's bosom, our Lord spake at large in the sixteenth chapter of the gospel after St Luke. For whereas the Lord is said to have descended, that cometh to pass by the manner of speaking: for otherwise it is evident by Luke, that Abraham's bosom is a place severed a great way from hell, and placed up aloft. But to inquire or reason over curiously of these things is rather the point of a curious fool than of a godly-minded man. We confess in this article, that the souls are immortal, and that they immediately after the bodily death do pass to life, and that all the saints from the beginning of the world, being sanctified by faith through Christ, do in Christ and by Christ receive the inheritance of life everlasting.

I would add to these the fifth article, but that the hour is now already spent. We will therefore defer it unto the next sermon. And now let us all together pray to God, our Father which is in heaven, that he will vouchsafe us his Spirit to inspire us with that true and quickening faith which is in the Father and Son: in the Father, as the maker of all things; in the Son, as the Saviour of the whole world, who therefore came down from heaven, and was incarnate in the womb of the most holy virgin Mary, to the end he might be the Mediator betwixt God and men, and reconcile or make them at one again betwixt themselves; and that he might have wherewithal to make an oblation to appease God's justice, and to purge our sins which he bare on his body, yea, which he took away, and made all the faithful heirs of life everlasting.

Let us now give praise to the grace of God, and thanks to the Son of God: to whom alone all honour and glory is due for ever and ever. Amen.

OF THE LATTER ARTICLES OF CHRISTIAN FAITH CONTAINED IN THE APOSTLES' CREED.

THE EIGHTH SERMON.

LET us first of all pray to our God, that he will vouchsafe to grant us an happy, speedy, and very fruitful proceeding in the declaration of the other articles of christian belief.

The fifth article of our belief.

The fifth article of our belief is: "The third day he rose again from the dead." And this article, verily, of our belief is in a manner the chief of all the rest. Neither are the apostles so busily occupied in declaring and confirming the other, as they are in this one. For it had not been enough, if our Lord had died only, unless he had also risen from the dead again. For if he had not risen from the dead, but had remained still in death, who should have persuaded us men, that sin was purged by the death of Christ, that death was vanquished, Satan overcome, and hell broken up for the faithful by the death of Christ? Yea verily, we have foolish fellows[1] that would never cease to blaspheme the very God, to make a mock of our hope, and to say: "Tush, who did ever return from the dead, to tell us whether there be a life in another world after this or no, and what kind of life it is? Because therefore we cannot find, that any man did ever return from the dead, that is to be doubted of, which these babblers[2] do tattle touching the life of the world to come." That the Lord therefore might declare to the whole world, that after this life there is another, and that the soul dieth not with the body, but remaineth alive; he[3] returned the third day alive again to his disciples: and at that instant shewed them, that sin was purged, death disarmed, the devil vanquished, and hell destroyed. For the sting of death is sin: or the reward of sin is death: the devil hath the power of death[4], and shutteth in hell for sins. Now therefore, in that Christ riseth alive again from the dead, death could have no domi-

The glorious resurrection of Christ.

[1 absurdi nostri homines, Lat.]
[2 spermologi, Lat.; Erasmus' rendering, not the Vulgate's, in Acts xvii. 18.]
[3 Dominus noster, Lat.]
[4 1 Cor. xv. 56; Rom. vi. 23; Heb. ii. 14.]

nion over him: and because death, by suffering the Lord to pass, is broken, it must needs follow, that the devil and hell are vanquished by Christ; and lastly, that sin, the strength and power of them all, is purely purged. It is evident, therefore, that the resurrection of our Lord Jesus Christ doth, as it were, certify and by seal assure us of our salvation and redemption, so that now we cannot any longer doubt of it.

We confess, therefore, in this article, that our Lord Jesus Christ is risen again, and that he is risen again for our behoof; that is to say, that he hath wiped away our sins, and that for us he hath conquered death, the devil, and hell, according to the saying of the apostle: "God hath saved us, and hath called us with an holy calling, not according to our works, but according to his own purpose and favour, which was given unto us through Jesus Christ before all beginning, but is declared openly now by the appearing of our Saviour Jesus Christ, who hath verily put out death, and brought forth life, light, and immortality by the gospel[5]." There are many more like this in the fourth of his epistle to the Romans, and in the fifteenth of his first to the Corinthians. For the Lord also in the gospel after St John saith: "I am the resurrection and the life: he that believeth in me, although he be dead, shall live; and every one that liveth and believeth in me shall not die for ever[6]."

Now also let us throughly consider every word of this article severally by itself. We confess the Lord his resurrection. But a resurrection is to rise again. That riseth which falleth. The body of Christ fell, therefore the body of Christ riseth; yea, it riseth again, that is to say, the very same body of Christ, which before it fell did both live and stir, doth now rise again; it doth, I say, both live and stir again. For truly said Tertullian of the resurrection of the flesh, that "this word resurrection is not properly spoken of any thing, save of that which first fell. For nothing can rise again but that that fell. For by rising again, because it fell, we say the resurrection is made; because this syllable 're' is never added but when a thing is done again[7]." Wherefore

What a resurrection is.

[5 2 Tim. i. 9, 10.   ante tempora æterna, Lat.; Erasmus' rendering; the Vulgate has, tempora secularia.]

[6 John xi. 25, 26.]

[7 Resurrectionis vocabulum non aliam rem vindicat, quam quæ

the women in the gospel, when they went to anoint the body
of the Lord, which hung upon the cross, did hear the angel
of the Lord say : " Why seek ye the living among the dead?
He is not here, but is risen[1]," &c. This history of the Lord's
resurrection is set forth in the twenty-fourth after Luke, and
the sixteenth after Mark. Peter the apostle also, in the second
of the Acts, affirming the Lord's resurrection by the testimony
of David[2], doth expressly shew that the Lord is verily risen
again.

Out of or from the dead.

After this we say again, that he is risen out of or from
the dead : which member doth express the truth both of
his death and resurrection. For the body or flesh dieth, or is
destroyed ; but, being dead, is raised up again : this body,
therefore, or flesh, is raised up again ; as though he that
maketh confession of his belief should say, Our Lord died
even in the very same condition of nature that other mortal
men do die in ; but he tarried not, nor yet stuck fast among
the dead. For the very same mortal flesh, which he had
taken unto him, and by dying had laid aside, he now taketh
again immortal ; as David had foretold before, saying :
" Because thou shalt not leave my soul in hell, nor suffer
thy Holy One to see corruption[3]." For Christ is the first-
begotten of them that rise again, in whom, as in the head,
there ought to be declared in what sort the resurrection of
all Christ his members shall be in the day of judgment.

*He was cru-
cified, dead,
taken down
and laid in
his grave
upon Good
Friday,
where his
body lay all
Saturday,
that is,
Easter-even,
and on Sun-
day, which
is Easter-day,
in the morn-
ing he rose
again from
death to
life.*

And we confess that this resurrection was made the third
day ; I mean the third day after his death. For upon the
day of preparation[4] he is taken down from the cross and
carried into a sepulchre, where his body resteth the whole
sabbath-day ; and about the beginning of the first day of
sabbaths[5], which, I say, is the first day of the week, and

cecidit. Surgere enim potest dici et quod omnino non cecidit ; quod
semper retro jacuit : resurgere autem non est nisi ejus quod cecidit.
Iterum enim surgendo, quia cecidit, resurgere dicitur : re enim syllaba
iterationi semper adhibetur.—Tertul. Adv. Marcion. Lib. v. cap. 9. ed.
Semler. Tom. i. p. 347.]

[1 Luke xxiv. 5, 6.]

[2 in prima illa concione sua, Lat. Omitted by the translator : in
that his first sermon.]

[3 Psal. xvi. 10.]

[4 in die parasceves, Lat. Mark xv. 42.]

[5 John xx. 1. diei primi sabbatorum, Lat. ; Erasmus' render-

among us at this day is called Sunday[6], in the morning he
arose again from the dead. Whereas therefore in the twelfth
chapter of the gospel after St Matthew we read that the Lord
said, "As Jonas was three days and three nights in the
belly of the whale, so shall the Son of man be in the heart
of the earth three days and three nights;" yet notwithstanding, in the sixteenth and twentieth chapters, expounding himself as having spoken that by synecdoche, he saith : "I must
go to Hierusalem, and suffer many things of the scribes and
elders, and be killed, and raised up again the third day[7]."

The sixth article of our faith is: "He ascended into
heaven, and sitteth at the right hand of God, the Father
Almighty." That body, which is of the same substance with
our bodies, taken out of the virgin Mary, and taken verily of
the substance of the virgin, which hung upon the cross, and
died, and was buried, and rose again; the very same body, I
say, ascended into the heavens, and sitteth at the right hand
of God the Father. For after that by the space of forty
days our Lord had abundantly enough instructed his disciples
touching the truth of his resurrection and the kingdom of
God, he was taken up into heaven.

The sixth article of our belief.

By that ascension of his he declareth to the whole compass
of the earth, that he is Lord of all things, and that to him
are subject all things that are in heaven and in earth; that
he is our strength, the power of the faithful, and he of whom
they have to boast against the gates of hell. For he, ascending into heaven, hath led captivity captive; and, by spoiling
his enemies, hath enriched his people, on whom he daily
heapeth his spiritual gifts. For he sitteth above, that, by
pouring his virtue from thence into us, he may quicken us
with the spiritual life, and deck us with sundry gifts and
graces, and, lastly, defend the church against all evils. For
God is our Saviour, King, and Bishop[8]. Whereupon, when
as once the Capernaites were offended, because the Lord had
called himself the bread of life that came down from heaven
to give life unto the world, he saith : "Doth this offend you?

The glorious ascension of Christ.

ing, not the Vulgate's. The first day of the sabbaths, Cranmer's
Bible.]
　　[6 dominica, Lat.]
　　[7 ch. xvi. 21, and xx. 18, 19.]
　　[8 pontifex, Lat.]

What therefore if you shall see the Son of man ascend thither where he was before[1]?" As if he should say : Then verily ye will gather, by my quickening, resurrection, and glorious ascension into the heavens, that I am the bread of life, brought down from heaven, and now again taken up into the heavens, there to remain the Saviour, Life, and Lord of heaven and earth. Moreover, St Peter the apostle in the Acts saith : " Let all the house of Israel know for a surety, that God hath made the same Jesus, whom ye have crucified, Lord and Christ[2]."

The force of Christ his ascension into heaven.

Furthermore, he did not only rise again from death, and come to his disciples, but also ascended into heaven as they beheld and looked on him, to the end that we thereby might be assuredly certified of eternal salvation. For by ascending he prepared a place for us, he made ready the way ; that is, he opened the very heavens to the faithful. God hath placed in heaven the very humanity that he took of us : which is indeed a lively and unreproveable testimony, that all man-kind[3] shall at the last be translated into heaven also. For the members must needs be made conformable to the head. Christ, our Head, is risen again from the dead ; therefore we, his members, shall also rise again. And even as a cloud took away the Lord from the sight of his disciples; so shall we that believe be carried in the clouds to meet the Lord, and shall wholly in soul and body be, and for ever dwell, in heaven with our Head and Lord, Christ Jesus. And this doth John evidently teach him that readeth his fourteenth chapter, where the Lord saith : " I go to prepare a place for you, and will come again to you, and take you unto myself, that whereso-ever I am, ye may also be." Paul the apostle also witness-eth, and saith : " We that live, and shall be remaining in the coming of the Lord, shall be carried in the clouds together with them that are raised up from the dead, to meet the Lord in the air[4]."

We confess therefore in this article, that Jesus Christ, being taken up into heaven, is Lord of all things, the King and Bishop, the deliverer and Saviour of all the faithful

[1 John vi. 61, 62.]
[2 ch. ii. 36. hunc Jesum, Lat.]
[3 rather, "our whole manhood." totum hominem, Lat.]
[4 1 Thess. iv. 17.]

in the whole world. We confess, that in Christ, and for Christ, we believe the life everlasting, which we shall have in this body at the end of the world, and in soul so soon as we are once departed out of this world.

But now, by the way, we must weigh the very words of this article. " He ascended," we say. Who ascended, I pray you? He that was born of the virgin Mary, that was crucified, dead, and buried, that rose again from the dead: he (I say) ascended verily both body and soul. But whither ascended he? Into heaven. Heaven in the scriptures is not taken always in one signification. First, it is put for the firmament, and that large compass[5] that is over our heads, wherein the birds fly to and fro, and in which the stars are placed, that are called the furniture and host of heaven. For saith David: " God is clothed with light, as with a garment: he spreadeth forth the heaven as it were a curtain." He saith also: " I shall see thy heavens, the work of thy fingers, and the moon and stars which thou hast laid." And again: " Which covereth the heaven with clouds, and prepareth rain for the earth." And again: " The heavens declare the glory of God, and the firmament sheweth forth the works of his hands[6]." Then also, heaven is taken for the throne and habitation of God: and lastly, for the place, seat, and receptacle of them that are saved, where God giveth himself to be seen and enjoyed of them that be his. For David, witnessing again, saith: " The Lord hath prepared his seat in heaven[7]." Whereupon the Lord in the gospel saith: " Swear not by heaven; for it is God's seat[8]." And the apostle Paul saith: " We know, if our earthly mansion of this tabernacle be destroyed, that we have a dwelling-place for ever in heaven, builded by God, not made by hands[9]." And therefore, in this signification, heaven is called the kingdom of God, the kingdom of the Father, joy, happiness, and felicity, eternal life, peace and quietness. And although God indeed be not shut up in any place, (for he saith, " Heaven is my seat, and the earth the footstool of my feet[10];)" yet, because the glory of God doth most of all shine in the heavens, and because that in heaven he giveth himself to be seen and enjoyed of them

He ascended into heaven.

[5 extentione, Lat.]   [6 Psal. civ. 2. viii. 3. cxlvii. 8. xix 1.]
[7 Psal. ciii. 19.]   [8 Matt. v. 34.]
[9 2 Cor. v. 1.]   [10 Isai. lxvi. 1.]

that are his, (according to that saying, "We shall see him even as he is[1];" and again, "No man shall see me," saith the Lord, "and live[2];") therefore God is said to dwell in heaven.   Moreover Christ our Lord, touching his divinity, is not shut up in any place; but, according to his humanity once taken, which he drew up into heaven, he is in the very local place of heaven; neither is he in the meantime here in earth and every where bodily, but, being severed from us in body, remaineth in heaven.   For he ascendeth, which, leaving that which is below, doth go to that above.   Christ therefore, leaving the earth, hath placed a seat for his body above all heavens.   Not that he is carried up beyond all heavens; but because, ascending up above all the circles[3] into the utmost and highest heaven, he is taken, I say, into the place appointed for those that are saved.   For Paul the apostle, speaking plainly enough to be understood, saith: "Our conversation is in heaven, from whence we look for the Saviour to come[4]," &c.   In the same manner also Luke the evangelist saith: "And blessing them, he departed from them, and was carried into heaven[5]."

But why do I make so much ado about expounding that which is most evidently declared in the very Creed by that

He sitteth at the right hand of God the Father Almighty.

which followeth?   For the next is: "He sitteth at the right hand of God, the Father Almighty."   For by this we understand what kind of place heaven is, and what our Lord doth in heaven.   It is not surely for our frailty over-narrowly to seek out or discuss the secrets of heaven; and yet it is not against religion to inquire after that that is taught us in the scriptures, and so perfectly to remember it as it is taught us.   Our Lord is simply said to sit; and that too to sit at the right hand of the Father Almighty.   Let us therefore see[6] what the right hand of the Father is, and what it is to sit at the right hand of the Father.

The definition of God's right hand taken here for the place's name.

The right hand of the Father in the scripture hath two significations.   First, the right hand of God is the place appointed for them that are saved, and the everlasting felicity in

[1 1 John iii. 2.]

[2 Exod. xxxiii. 20.]   [3 supra omnes orbes, Lat.]

[4 Phil. iii. 20.]   [5 ch. xxiv. 51.]

[6 ex scripturæ testimoniis, Lat. Omitted by the translator: From the testimonies of scripture.]

heaven.   This did St Augustine set down to be marked long
before us; who, in the twenty and sixth chapter of his book
de Agone Christiano, writeth, that "the right hand of the
Father is the everlasting felicity given to the saints; even as
also the left hand is most rightly called the continual misery
allotted to the ungodly: not so that by this means, that I
have said, the right or left hand is to be understood in respect
of God himself, but in respect of his creatures' capacity[7]."   And
this did St Augustine speak according to the scriptures.   For
David saith: "The path of life shalt thou make known to me:
the fulness of joys is in thy sight; and at thy right hand is
gladness for ever[8]."   What else is this, than if he had said;
Thou shalt bring me into life, I say, into the very heavens,
where I shall be filled with joys, both by seeing and beholding
thee, and also by enjoying thee: at thy right hand in eternal
blessedness are joys everlasting?   In the gospel also we read,
that the sheep are placed by the Judge at the right hand, and
the goats at the left[9].   And when the right hand is taken in
this sense, then "to sit" doth signify to rest from all labours,
and to live quietly and in happy state.   For that saying in
the prophet is very well known, "A man shall sit under his
vine[10]:" as if he should have said, All things shall be at peace,
in safety, and at quiet.   So then this that I have said is
meant by the right hand of the Father: and where we confess, that the Son doth sit at the right hand of the Father Almighty, we do acknowledge, that our Lord, being delivered
from all trouble and mortal infirmities, doth now in his
humanity both rest and rejoice in the very local place of
heaven, where we believe that both our souls and bodies
shall be and live for ever.   For the Lord himself in the
gospel witnesseth, that in his Father's house there are many
mansions, which he goeth to prepare, that they may have
a place; and although he did depart, yet that he would return to them again, and take them unto himself, that where

To sit is to be at rest and enjoy felicity.

[[7] Dextera Patris est beatitudo perpetua, quæ sanctis datur; sicut
sinistra ejus rectissime dicitur miseria perpetua, quæ impiis datur: ut
non in ipso Deo, sed in creaturis, hoc modo, quo diximus, intelligatur
dextera et sinistra.—August. de Agon. Christ. cap. xxvi. Op. Tom. III.
fol. 164. Par. 1531.]

[[8] Psal. xvi. 11.]   [[9] Matt. xxv. 33.]
[[10] Micah iv. 4.]

he is, they also might be in the same place with him[1]. Wherefore we believe, that Christ is at rest in heaven, where he hath
prepared a place of rest for us also, to remain in joys everlasting.   And for because our bodies shall not be every where
in felicity, but in the only appointed place; therefore saith
St Augustine truly, that "Christ our Lord, according to the
measure of his very body, is in some one place of heaven[2]."
And St Cyprian saith: "To sit at the right hand of the
Father is the mystery of his flesh taken up into heaven[3]."

God's right hand the name of his power; and in this signification to sit is to reign.

Secondarily, the right hand of God is put for the virtue,
kingdom, protection, deliverance, and power of God.   For
David saith: "The Lord's right hand is high: the Lord's
right hand doth mighty things[4]."   And Moses said: "Thy
right hand, O Lord, is magnified in power: thy right hand, O
Lord, hath broken the enemy[5]."   And when the right hand is
put in this sense, then "to sit" doth signify to reign, to
deliver, to use power, and do the office of a prince.   For
saith David: "The LORD said unto my Lord, Sit thou at my
right hand, till I make thine enemies thy footstool[6]."   And
the prophet Zachary saith: "Behold the man that is called
the Branch: he shall bud out of his place, and build the temple of the Lord, and sit and rule upon his throne, and be a
priest upon his seat[7]."   In this sense the right hand of God
is infinite, and contained in no measure of place.   Whereas[8] we
confess, that our Lord doth "sit" at the right hand of the
Father, we do profess, that the Son is exalted above all
things, having all things subject under himself, as Paul,
in his first chapter to the Ephesians, saith; and finally, that
the Son, being so exalted, can do all things, doth reign in
the universal church, doth deliver them that are his, doth
make intercession to the Father in heaven, and in the
power of his Godhead is present in all places.   For therefore did the Creed add almightiness to this sitting of his,

[1 John xiv. 2, 3.]

[2 Non dubites (Christum esse) in loco aliquo cœli propter veri
corporis modum.—August. Op. Par. 1679—1700. Lib. ad Dardan.
Tom. II. col. 692.]

[3 Sedere ad dexteram Patris carnis assumptæ mysterium est.—
Cypr. (Ruffin.) Expos. in Symb. fol. 25. Oxon. 1682.]

[4 Psal. cxviii. 16.]   [5 Exod. xv. 6.]
[6 Psal. cx. 1.]   [7 ch. vi. 12, 13.]
[8 et cum, Lat.   And whereas, 1577.]

where it is said, "He sitteth at the right hand of the Father
Almighty." And in St Matthew the Lord saith: "To me is
given all might in heaven and in earth: go therefore, and
bring all nations unto me[9]."

So then I suppose that briefly thus I have well declared
what manner of place heaven is; to wit, a place of quietness,
joy, and everlasting felicity, wherein the Son of God doth sit,
doth dwell, and is in his humanity, as we also, that are the
members of Christ, shall be in the very same place without
all dolour and grief in joy for evermore. And although our
Lord be delivered from all grievous business, yet we mean not
that he sitteth idly leaning on his elbows[10]. For he is a King,
a Priest, and very God in the very temple of God: he cannot
choose therefore, of his natural property and office, but work
salvation in the elect, and do all things that lie God, a king,
and priest, in hand to do. So then now we all know what
our Lord doth, as he sitteth in heaven. Neither is it any
trouble to him at all to do and work that which he doth;
for he worketh not of compulsion, but naturally, and of his
own accord.

Thus, and no otherwise, did the ancient interpreters of
the holy scriptures handle this article of our belief; some of
whose testimonies I will here allege. St Hierome, in his
exposition of Paul's first chapter to the Ephesians, saith:
"He hath declared the power of God by the similitude of a
man: not because a seat is placed, and God the Father sitteth
thereon, having his Son sitting there with him; but because
we cannot otherwise conceive how the Son doth judge and
reign, but by such words applied to our capacity. As therefore to be next to God, or to depart far from him, is not to be
understood according to the distance of places, but after men's
merits, because the saints are heard by him, but the sinners
(of whom the prophet saith, 'Behold, they that get themselves
from thee shall perish,') are removed far enough from coming
near him at all; even so likewise, to be either at the right
or left hand of God is to be taken so, that the saints are at
his right hand, and sinners at his left. As our Saviour himself
also in the gospel, affirming the same, doth say, that at the
right hand are the sheep, and the goats at the left. More-

*St Hierome
of the right
hand of the
Father.*

[9 ch. xxviii. 18, 19.]
[10 non otiosum desidere, Lat.]

over, this very word 'to sit' doth argue the power of a kingdom, by which God is beneficial to them on whom he doth vouchsafe to sit; insomuch as verily he doth rule them, and hath them always in his guiding, and doth turn to his own beck or government the necks of them that before ran out of way at random and at liberty[1]."

St Augustine of the right hand of the Father.

St Augustine, in his book *de Fide et Symbolo*, saith: "We believe that he sitteth at the right hand of God the Father. Yet not so therefore, as though we should think that God the Father is comprehended within the limits of a man's body; so that they that think of him should imagine, that he hath both a right and a left side: and whereas it is said, that the Father sitteth, we must not suppose that he doth sit with bended hams; lest peradventure we fall into the same sacrilege, for which the apostle accurseth them that have changed the glory of the incorruptible God into the similitude of a corruptible man. For a detestable thing it is to place God in such a likeness in a christian church: and much more wicked is it to place it in the heart, where the temple of God is verily and indeed, if it be cleansed from earthly desires and error. We must therefore understand, that 'at the right hand' is as much to say as in greatest happiness, where righteousness and peace and gladness is: even as also the goats are placed at the left hand, that is, in misery for their iniquities to their pain and torment. Whereas God therefore is said to sit, thereby is not meant the placing of his limbs, but his judicial power, which his majesty never

[1 Per humanam similitudinem Dei potentiam demonstravit: non quo solium ponatur, et Deus Pater in eo sedeat, secumque Filium habeat residentem; sed quo nos aliter judicantem atque regnantem nisi per nostra verba intelligere nequeamus. Sicut ergo proximum esse Deo, vel ab eo procul recedere, non secundum locorum spatia, sed juxta merita, sentiendum est; quod sancti juxta eum sint, peccatores vero (de quibus ait propheta, dicens, Ecce qui elongant se a te peribunt) ab omni ejus vicinia submoveantur; sic et in dextris vel in sinistris Dei esse accipiendum est, quod sancti a dextris ejus sint, peccatores vero a sinistris: Salvatore quoque id ipsum in evangelio comprobante, quum oves a dextris, hædos esse memoret a sinistris. Sed et ipsum verbum, *sedere*, regni significat potestatem, per quam beneficium ejus Deus tribuit, super quibus sedere dignatur; quod scilicet regat eos, et in curru suo habeat, et ad nutum proprium vaga prius et libera colla convertat.—Hieron. Comment. in Ep. ad Ephes. cap. i. Par. 1706. Tom. iv. par. 1, col. 335.]

wanteth in bestowing worthy rewards on those that are worthy of them[2]." And so forth.

The blessed bishop Fulgentius, in his second book to king Trasimundus, saith: "The Lord, to shew that his humanity is local, saith to his disciples, 'I ascend to my Father and to your Father, my God and your God.'" And by and by after: "Declaring the incomprehensibility of his Godhead, he saith to his disciples, 'Behold, I am with you always, even unto the end of the world[3].'"

The blessed martyr and bishop of Trent, Vigilius, in his first book against heresies, saith: "This was to go to the Father, and to depart from us; to take away out of this world the nature which he took of us. Thou seest therefore, that it was proper to the same nature to be taken away, and to depart from us; according to the words of the angels which said, 'This Jesus, who is taken up from you, shall come again, even as ye see him go into heaven.' For see the miracle, see the mystery of both his properties: the Son of God in his humanity is departed from us; according to his divinity he saith to us, 'Behold, I am with you always, even unto the end of the world.' If he be with us, how saith he,

St Fulgentius. His humanity is local, that is, contained in space of place; but his Godhead incomprehensible, as that that is every where, and is not contained in any place.

St Vigilius.

[2 Credimus etiam quod sedet ad dexteram Dei Patris: nec ideo tamen quasi humana forma circumscriptum esse Deum Patrem arbitrandum est, ut de illo cogitantibus dextrum aut sinistrum latus animo occurrat: aut id ipsum quod sedere Pater dicitur, flexis poplitibus fieri putandum est; ne illud incidamus sacrilegium quo execratur apostolus eos qui commutaverunt gloriam incorruptibilis Dei in similitudinem corruptibilis hominis. Tale enim simulacrum Deo nefas est Christiano in templo collocare; multo magis in corde nefarium est, ubi vere est templum Dei, si a terrena cupiditate atque errore mundetur. 'Ad dexteram' ergo intelligendum est dictum esse in summa beatitudine, ubi justitia et pax et gaudium est: sicut ad sinistram hædi constituuntur, id est, in miseria propter iniquitates, et labores atque cruciatus. Sedere ergo quod dicitur Deus, non membrorum positionem, sed judiciariam significat potestatem, qua illa majestas nunquam caret semper digna dignis tribuendo.—De Fide et Symb. c. 7. Par. 1531. Tom. III. fol. 31.]

[3 (Dominus) ut localem ostenderet humanitatem suam, dicit discipulis suis: Ascendo ad Patrem meum et ad Patrem vestrum, Deum meum et Deum vestrum.—Immensitatem vero suæ divinitatis ostendens discipulis dicit: Ecce ego vobiscum sum omnibus diebus, usque ad consummationem seculi.—Fulgent. Op. Venet. 1742. ad Trasimund. Lib. II. cap. xvii. p. 50.]

' The time shall come, when ye shall desire to see one of the days of the Son of man, and ye shall not see it?' Both he is with us, and not with us; because them, whom he hath left and departed from in his manhood[1], he hath not left nor forsaken in his Godhead[1]."[2] This saith he.

The seventh article. Christ a Judge.

The seventh article of our faith is this: " From thence he shall come to judge the quick and the dead." In the former articles there is set forth and confessed the divine goodness, bountifulness, and grace in Christ: now also shall be declared the divine justice, severity, and vengeance that is in him. For there are two comings of our Lord Jesus Christ. First he came basely in the flesh, to be the Redeemer and Saviour of the world: at the second time he shall come gloriously to judgment, to be a judge and revenger that will not be entreated against all unrepentant sinners and wicked doers. And he shall come out of heaven, from the right hand of the Father, in his visible and very human body, to be seen of all flesh, with the incomprehensible power of his Godhead, and being attended on by all the angels. For the Lord himself in the gospel saith: " They shall see the Son man coming in the clouds of heaven with great power and glory, and he shall send his angels with the great sound of a trump[3]," &c.

To judge, what it is.

But now, to " judge" is to sit in the tribunal-seat, to hear and discuss matters, to take up strifes, to determine and give

[1 The words *manhood* and *Godhead* are transposed in ed. 1577.]

[2 Hoc erat ire ad Patrem et recedere a nobis, auferre de hoc mundo naturam, quam susceperat ex nobis. Vides ergo eidem naturæ proprium fuisse ut auferretur et abiret a nobis, quæ in fine temporum reddenda est nobis, secundum attestantium vocem angelorum, Hic Jesus qui receptus est a vobis, sic veniet, quemadmodum vidistis eum euntem in cœlum. Nam vide miraculum, vide utriusque proprietatis mysterium: Dei Filius secundum humanitatem suam recessit a nobis; secundum divinitatem suam ait nobis, Ecce ego vobiscum sum omnibus diebus usque ad consummationem seculi. Si nobiscum est, quomodo ait, Venient dies quando desideretis diem unum Filii hominis, et non videbitis? Sed et nobiscum est, et non est nobiscum; quia quos reliquit et a quibus discessit humanitate sua, non reliquit nec deseruit divinitate sua.—Vigil. adv. Eutych. in Cassandr. Op. Par. 1616. Lib. I. p. 518.]

[3 Matt. xxiv. 30, 31.]

sentence, and lastly, to defend and deliver, and again, to chastise and punish, and by that means to keep under and suppress injury and malice. We believe therefore, that our Lord Jesus Christ in that day shall deliver all the godly, and destroy all the wicked; according to the words of the apostle, who saith: " Our Lord shall be revealed from heaven with the angels of his power, with a burning flame, and shall lay vengeance on them that have not known God[4];" and again, " The same just Judge shall give a crown of righteousness to all them that love his coming[5]."

The manner of this judgment the writings of the evangelists and apostles do tell us shall be in this sort. When once the wickedness of this world shall come to the full, and that antichrist shall have deceived the world, so that there is but little faith remaining, and that the wicked shall say, Peace and quietness; then shall a sudden destruction come. For our Lord, the Judge, shall send his archangel, to blow the trump, and to gather together from the four winds all flesh to judgment: by and by after shall the Judge himself, our Lord Jesus Christ, follow with all the host of heaven: and he shall descend out of heaven into the clouds: and, sitting aloft in the clouds as in a judgment-seat, shall be easily seen of all flesh. For they that shall be then living at the day of judgment, shall in a very prick[6] of time be changed, and stand before the Judge; and all the dead shall in a moment rise up again. Then shall the Judge divide the sheep from the goats, and, according to justice shall give judgment with the sheep[7] and against the goats, saying, "Come, ye blessed," &c., and, " Go, ye cursed," &c. Presently after shall follow execution. For the sheep shall by and by be caught up into the clouds to meet the Lord in the air, and shall ascend with him joyfully into heaven to the right hand of God the Father, there to live for ever in glory and gladness. The bottom of the earth shall gape[8] for the wicked, and shall suck them all up horribly, and send them down to hell, there to be tormented for ever with Satan and his angels. All this shall be

The picture of the last judgment.

[4 2 Thess. i. 7, 8.]   [5 2 Tim. iv. 8.]

[6 in puncto, Lat. 1 Cor. xv. 52. Erasmus, in puncto temporis. Vulgate, in momento.]

[7 pro ovibus, Lat.]

[8 dehiscet ima tellus, Lat.]

done, not by any long, troublesome, or changeable process
as is used in our courts of law, but even in the twinkling o
an eye.   For then shall all men's hearts be laid open, and
every man's own conscience shall accuse himself.   This i
more at large set out in Matt. xxiv. and xxv., Wisd. iii. an
v., 1 Cor. xv., 2 Cor. v., 1 Thess. iv., v., Rom. ii., 2 Pet. ii
&c.

The quick and dead are judged.
Now we do simply confess, that the quick and the dea
shall be judged.   This do some expound of the godly an
ungodly.   But the Symbol or Creed was ordained for th
most simple of understanding; and simple things are fittes
for to teach simple men.   Therefore we say simply, that th
dead are all they, that from the beginning of the world eve
until the last day are departed out of this mortal life: and
the living are they, which at that day shall be alive in thi
world.   For the apostle saith: " Behold, I tell you a mystery
we shall not all sleep, but we shall all be changed by the las
trump, in a moment of time, and in the twinkling of an eye.
For the trump shall sound, and the dead shall rise again incorruptible, and we shall be changed[1]."   And again, in anothe
place, the same apostle saith: " This I say unto you in the
word of the Lord, that we, which shall live and be remaining
at the coming of the Lord, shall not prevent them which ar
asleep.   Because the Lord himself shall come down out o
heaven with a great noise, and the voice of an archangel
and the trump of God: and first shall the dead in Christ ris
up again; then shall we, which shall be alive and be remaining
be caught up together with them in the clouds into the air t
meet the Lord: and so shall we be with the Lord for evermore[2]."

The reward and punishment is most certain.
We confess therefore in this seventh article, that we
believe there shall be an end of all things in this world, and
that the felicity of the wicked shall not endure for ever.   For
we believe that God is a just God, who hath given all judgment unto his Son, to repay to every one in that day according to his works, pains to the wicked that never shall be
ended, and to the godly joys everlasting.   And so in this
article we profess, that we look for a deliverance, a ceasing

[1 1 Cor. xv. 51, 52. *per* extremam tubam, Lat. and Erasmus. The
Vulgate has, in novissima tuba.]
[2 1 Thess. iv. 15—17.]

from troubles, and the reward of life everlasting. For how should he destroy them that believe in him, his people and his servants, who in the most true gospel saith, " Verily, I say unto you, that ye, which have followed me, in the re- generation, when the Son of man shall sit on the seat of his majesty, ye also shall sit upon twelve seats judging the twelve tribes of Israel[3]?" There are most certain rewards and pe- nalties appointed for the godly and ungodly in the word of truth. He cannot lie that said to Esay: " Say to the righteous, that it shall go well with him ; for he shall enjoy the fruit of his study. But woe be to the wicked : it shall be evil with him; for he shall be rewarded according to the works of his own hands[4]." And thus much touching the second part of the Creed. Now are we come to the third part.

The eighth article of our belief is this : " I believe in the Holy Ghost." This third part of the Creed containeth the property of the third Person in the reverend Trinity. And we do rightly believe in the Holy Ghost, as well as in the Father and the Son. For the Holy Ghost is one God with the Father and the Son : and rightly is faith in the Holy Ghost joined to faith in the Father and the Son. For by him the fruit of God's salvation, fulfilled in the Son, is sealed to us, and our sanctification and cleansing is bestowed on us, and derived from him to us, by the Holy Ghost. For the apostle saith : " God, which anointed us, is he also which hath sealed us, and hath given the earnest of the Spirit in our hearts[5]." And again : " Ye were indeed defiled with naughtiness; but now ye are cleansed, and sanctified, and lastly justified, through the name of the Lord Jesus, and by the Spirit of our God[6]." The Father indeed doth sanctify too, but by the blood of Jesus Christ, and poureth the same sanctification out of him into us by the Holy Ghost : so that it is, as it were, the property of the Holy Ghost to sanctify ; whereupon he is called Holy or the Sanctifier. Therefore, so often as we hear the Holy Ghost named, we must by and by think of the power in working, which the scripture attributeth

The eighth article of our faith.

[3 Matt. xix. 28.]   [4 ch. iii. 10, 11.]
[5 2 Cor. i. 21, 22.]   [6 1 Cor. vi. 11.]

to him, and we must look after the benefits that from him do flow to us. For the power, operation, or action of the Spirit is that, whatsoever the grace of God doth work in us through the Son: so that of necessity we must believe in the Holy Ghost. And in this eighth article we do profess, that we do verily believe, that all the faithful are cleansed, washed, re-generated, sanctified, enlightened, and enriched of God with divers gifts of grace for Christ his sake, but yet through the Holy Ghost. For without him there is no true sanctification: wherefore we ought not to attribute these gifts of grace to any other means; this glory belongeth to the Holy Ghost only. Of whom I will more largely and fully discourse in my other sermons.

The Father in Christ hath fully given us all heaven-ly treasures.

The hour is spent, which warneth me to wrap up briefly and make an end; therefore I exhort you all to have your faith religiously bent upon the Lord Jesus: for him hath the heavenly Father sent to us, in him hath he wholly expressed and shewed himself to us, and him doth the Holy Ghost print in our hearts and keep in our minds. And in Christ is all man's salvation and every part thereof contained; wherefore we must beware that we derive it not from any thing else. "It pleased the Father," saith the apostle, "that all fulness should dwell in the Son," and in him to recapitulate, and as it were, to bring into a sum, all points of salvation, that in him all the faithful may be fulfilled[1]. For if salvation be sought, then even by his very name are we taught that salvation is in his power: for he is called Jesus, that is, a Saviour. If we de-sire the Holy Spirit of God and his sundry gifts, we shall find them also in the anointing of Christ: for he is called Christ, the Anointed, I say, the Holy of holies, and the sanctifier, or else the anointer of us with his Spirit. If any man have need of strength and might, of power and deliverance, well, he hath to look for it in Christ his dominion: for Christ is Lord of all. In the same Christ we find redemption: for he hath redeemed us that were sold under Satan's yoke. In his con-ception we have purity; in his nativity we have sufferance[2]: for he became like to us, that he might suffer grief as well as

[1 Col. i. 19; Ephes. i. 10. ἀνακεφαλαιώσασθαι, id est, recapitulari. —Erasm. Annot. in loc. cit.]

[2 indulgentiam, Lat.]

we[3]. For in his passion we have forgiveness of sins, in his
condemnation we have absolution, satisfaction in his offering or
cleansing[4] sacrifice, cleansing in his blood, and an universal
reconciliation in his descending into hell.   In his burial we
have the mortification of our flesh, the newness of life; yea
rather, the immortality of the soul, and resurrection of our
bodies in his glorious resurrection.   We have also the inheritance of the heavenly kingdom, with the assured sealing
thereof, in his ascension and sitting at the right hand of the
Father.   And there is he our Mediator, Priest, and King, our
safeguard and our head, our defender and most sure rest[5].
From thence he poureth into us his Holy Spirit, the fulness of
all good things; and doth communicate himself wholly to us,
joining us unto himself with an indissoluble knot.   From thence
we do with confidence and joy look for him to be our Judge,
to be, I say, our patron and deliverer, which shall condemn
and send down headlong into hell all our enemies with Satan;
but shall take us and all the faithful of every age up into
heaven with himself, there to sing a new song, and to rejoice
in him for ever.   To him be glory for ever.   Amen.

OF THE LATTER ARTICLES OF CHRISTIAN FAITH CON-
TAINED IN THE APOSTLES' CREED.

THE NINTH SERMON.

LET us call to our Father in heaven, through our Lord
Jesus Christ, that he will vouchsafe to pour his grace into us,
that we may to our no small profit dispatch and expound the
last part of the articles of christian belief.

The ninth article of faith is this: "The holy catholic *The ninth*
church, the communion of saints."   After the confession of our *our belief.*
belief in the holy Trinity, and in the mystery of the Son of
God, our Lord Jesus Christ, and lastly in the Holy Ghost, the
sanctifier and restorer of all; now, in the fourth part, is
reckoned up the fruit and power, the effect and end, of faith,
and what doth come to, and is bestowed on, the faithful.
There cometh to them communion of God and all saints, sanc-

[3 condolere nobis, Lat.]   [4 expiatorio, Lat.]
[5 securitas, Lat.]

tification, remission of sins, the resurrection of the flesh, and
life everlasting. Of which I will speak in order as they lie, so
far forth as the bountiful Lord shall give me ability.

Now then here we have to rehearse[1] out of the eighth
article this word, "I believe :" we must (I mean) say, "I believe the holy catholic church." Some unlearned there are,
which hold opinion, that in this point of our confession we
should say, "I believe in the holy church." The reason that
leads them so to think is this; because they find written in
the Constantinopolitan Creed, "And in the Holy Ghost, the
Lord that giveth life, who proceedeth from the Father and
the Son, who together with the Father and the Son is to be
worshipped and glorified, who spake by the prophets in one
catholic and apostolic church[2]." For these words they do so
distinguish, that, as they do repeat out of the premises these
words, "I believe," and make this the sense, "I believe in the
Holy Ghost, the Lord ;" even so here again they do repeat
these words, "I believe," making this to be the sense, "I believe in one catholic and apostolic church[3]." But this is more
than needeth, yea, and against all godliness do they wrest these
words of the Creed : for this, "In one catholic and apostolic
church," is not referred to the verb, "I believe," but to the
Holy Ghost, because he spake by the prophets in one catholic
and apostolic church. For our meaning is, and we confess,
that one and the same Spirit did all things in both Testaments,
contrary to the opinion of them which imagined, that there
were two spirits contrary the one to the other.

Moreover St Cyprian, in his exposition of the Apostles'
Creed, saith : "He said not, In the holy church, nor, In the
remission of sins, nor, In the resurrection of the body. For if
he had added the preposition 'in,' then had the force of those
clauses been all one with the force of that that went before.
For in those words wherein our belief touching the Godhead
is set down, we say, 'In God the Father, in Jesus Christ his
Son, and in the Holy Ghost :' but in the rest, where the

Marginal notes:
We must not in our confession say, I believe in the church.

Cyprian.

[1 repetendum est, Lat.]

[2 locutus est per prophetas in unam catholicam, &c., Lat.]

[3 All this is comprised in that principle, I believe the catholic
church. And therefore the council of Nice said, I believe in the
church (πιστεύω εἰς τὴν ἐκκλησίαν), that is, I believe and trust the
same in all things.—Annot. of Rhiems Test. in 1 Tim. iii. 15.]

speech is not of the Godhead, but touching the creatures or
mysteries, the preposition 'in' is not added, that we may say,
'In the holy church;' but that the holy church is to be believed,
not as we believe in God, but as a congregation gathered
together to God; and that the forgiveness of sins is to be believed, not that we ought to believe in the forgiveness of sins;
and that the resurrection of the flesh is to be believed, not
that we ought to believe in the resurrection of the flesh.   So
then, by this syllable 'in' the Creator is discerned from the
creatures, and that that is God's from that that is man's[4]."
This saith Cyprian.

St Augustine, in his book *de Fide et Symbolo*, hath: " I Augustine.
believe the holy church," not, "I believe in the holy church[5]."
There are alleged also his words in his epistle *ad Neophytos*,
touching consecration, Distinct. 4, cap. 1: " We said not,
that ye had to believe in the church, as in God; but understand how we said, that ye, being conversant in the holy
catholic church, should believe in God[6]."

Much more evidently doth Paschasius, in the first chapter Paschasius.
of his first book *de Spiritu Sancto*, say: " We believe the
church, as the mother of regeneration; we do not believe in
the church, as the author of salvation.   He that believeth in

[4 Non dixit, in sanctam ecclesiam, nec in remissionem peccatorum, nec in carnis resurrectionem. Si enim addidisset IN præpositionem, una eademque vis fuisset cum superioribus. Nunc autem in
illis quidem vocabulis, ubi de divinitate fides ordinatur, in Deum
Patrem dicitur, et in Jesum Christum Filium ejus, et in Spiritum sanctum: in ceteris vero, ubi non de divinitate, sed de creaturis ac mys-
teriis sermo est, IN præpositio non additur, ut dicatur, in sanctam
ecclesiam, sed sanctam ecclesiam credendam esse, non ut in Deum, sed
ut ecclesiam Deo congregatam; et remissionem peccatorum credendam
esse, non in remissionem peccatorum; et resurrectionem carnis, non
in resurrectionem carnis. Hac itaque præpositionis syllaba Creator a
creaturis secernitur, et divina separantur ab humanis.—Cypr. (Ruffin.)
Expos. in Symb. Apost. fol. 26. Oxon. 1682.]

[5 Credimus et sanctam ecclesiam, utique catholicam.—August. de
Fid. et Symb. ed. Par. 1531. Tom. III. fol. 32.]

[6 Non ergo diximus, ut in ecclesiam, quasi in Deum crederetis:
sed intelligite nos dicere, et dixisse, ut in ecclesia sancta catholica
conversantes in Deum crederetis. — Gratian. Decret. Par. III. de
Consecr. Distinct. 4. can. 73.   The Sermo ad Neophytos, which is
quoted from, is not Augustine's. August. Opp. Tom. VI. Append.
p. 290.]

the church, believeth in man : for man hath not his being
of the church, but the church began by man.   Leave off
therefore this blasphemous persuasion, to think that thou
hast to believe in any worldly creature ; since thou mayest
not believe neither in angel nor archangel.   The unskilfulness
of some have drawn and taken the preposition 'in' from the
sentence that goeth next before, and put it to that that followeth, adding thereto also too too shamelessly somewhat
more than needed[1]."   This hath Paschasius in that book of
St Gregory. his, which St Gregory the Great, bishop of Rome, liked very
well of[2].

Thomas   What say ye to that moreover, that Thomas of Aquine,
Aquine. reasoning of faith, in the second book, Part. II. Artic. ix.
Quæst. 1, saith ?   " If we say, 'I believe in the holy church,'
we must understand, that our faith is referred to the Holy
Ghost, which sanctifieth the church ; and so make the sense
to be thus : 'I believe in the Holy Spirit, that sanctifieth the
church.'   But it is better, and according to the common use,
not to add at all the syllable 'in,' but simply to say, the holy
Pope Leo. catholic church : even as also pope Leo saith[3]."   This hath
Thomas.

[1 Credimus ecclesiam quasi regenerationis matrem ; non in ecclesiam credimus quasi in salutis auctorem.   Qui in ecclesiam credit, in
hominem credit : nam non homo ex ecclesia, sed ecclesia esse cœpit
ex homine.   Recede itaque ex hac blasphemiæ persuasione, ut in
aliquam humanam te æstimes debere credere creaturam ; cum omnino
nec in angelum nec in archangelum sit credendum.   Nonnullorum
imperitia, In, præpositionem hanc, velut de proxima vicinaque sententia, in consequentem traxit ac rapuit, et ex superfluo imprudenter ap-
posuit.—Paschas. de Spiritu Sancto, Lib. I. cap. i. in Biblioth. Patr.
Par. 1624. Tom. IX. col. 180.]

[2 Quod Paschasius hujus apostolicæ sedis diaconus, cujus apud
nos rectissimi et luculenti de sancto Spiritu libri extant, miræ sanctitatis vir fuerit, eleemosynarum maxime operibus vacans, cultor pauperum et contemptor sui.—S. Gregorii Dialog. IV. 40. Rom. 1613.
III. 926.   P.]

[3 Si dicatur, In sanctam ecclesiam catholicam, hoc est intelligendum, quod fides nostra refertur ad Spiritum sanctum qui sanctificat
ecclesiam, ut sit sensus : Credo in Spiritum sanctum sanctificantem
ecclesiam.   Sed melius est, et secundum communiorem usum, ut non
ponatur ibi, In, sed simpliciter dicatur, sanctam ecclesiam catholicam ; sicut etiam Leo Papa dicit.—Aquin. Sum. Tot. Theol. par. II.
Quæst. 1. Art. 9, p. 7, Tom. II. Venet. 1594.]

So now ye have heard the opinions of the ancient doctors of the church, Cyprian, Augustine, Gregory, Paschasius, pope Leo; and also of Thomas of Aquine, which taught now in the latter times. And, dearly beloved, ye do understand, by proofs taken out of the canonical scripture, that we must acknowledge and confess the holy catholic church, but not believe in the holy catholic church.

And now we have to see, what that is that is called the church, and what is called the catholic church. *Ecclesia*, which word we use for the church, is properly an assembly; it is, I say, where the people are called out, or gathered together, to hear somewhat touching the affairs of the commonweal. In this present treatise it is the company, communion, congregation, multitude, or fellowship of all that profess the name of Christ. Catholic is as much to say as this fellowship is universal, as that that is extended through all places and ages[4]. For the church of Christ is not restrained into any corner among the Donatists in Africa[5]: it stretcheth out itself through the compass of the world, and unto all ages, and doth contain all the faithful from the first Adam even unto the very last saint that shall be remaining before the end of the world. This universal church hath her particular churches; I mean, the church of Adam and of the patriarchs, the church of Moses and of the prophets before the birth of Christ, the christian church, which is so named of Christ himself, and the apostolical church gathered together by the apostles' doctrine in the name of Christ. And finally, it containeth these particular churches, as the church of Jerusalem, of Antioch, of Alexandria, of Rome, of Asia, of Africa, of Europe, of the east, of the west, &c. And yet all these churches, as it were members of one body under the only head Christ, (for Christ alone is the head of his church,

The catholic church.

[4 Here the translator has omitted: "For all saints are united, just as the members in one body, which depend on one head. Therefore the aggregate and whole multitude of the faithful is called the church." Sancti enim omnes ita uniuntur, ut membra in uno corpore, quæ ab uno dependent capite. Ergo universitas totaque multitudo fidelium dicitur ecclesia.]

[5 For their own body, on account of the sanctity of its bishops, they (the Donatists) claimed exclusively the name of a true, pure, and holy church. This pestilence scarcely extended beyond Africa.—Mosheim, Eccles. Hist. Cent. IV. Book II. part 2, chap. 5.]

not only triumphant, but militant also,) do make one only catholic church; in which there are not to be found either

The true church.

heresies or schisms: and for that cause it is called the true[1] church, to wit, of the right and true opinion, judgment, faith, and doctrine. For in the church only is true faith, and without the church of God is neither any truth, nor yet salvation.

So then in this article we confess, that all the faithful dispersed throughout the whole compass of the earth, and they also that at this time live in heaven, as many, I say, as are already saved, or shall even until the very end of the world be born to be saved, are one body, having gotten fellowship and participation with God and a mutual communion among themselves. And for because no man can be made one with God, unless he also be holy and pure even as

We believe the church to be holy.

God is holy and pure; therefore we believe that the church is holy, that is, that it is sanctified by God the Father in the blood of the Son and the gift of the Holy Ghost. We have heard testimonies enough in the former sermons; therefore this one of Paul shall be sufficient, which he writeth to the Ephesians: "Christ loved the church, and gave himself for it, to sanctify and to cleanse it in the fountain of water through the word, to make it unto himself a glorious church not having spot or wrinkle[2]," &c. By which words we understand, that the church is called undefiled and altogether clean

How the church is holy.

not in respect of itself, but because of Christ. For the church of Christ is so far forth holy, as that yet every day it doth go forward in profiting, and is never perfect so long as it liveth on the earth. And yet notwithstanding, the holiness of it is most absolutely perfect in Christ. Whereunto verily belongeth that notable saying of the Lord: "He that is washed hath no need but to wash his feet only, for he is wholly clean[3]." For the faithful are purely cleansed by Christ, who washeth them with his blood; but yet, because the flesh doth strive with the spirit so long as life remaineth on the earth, therefore the godly have need with faith and the Holy Ghost to wash and wipe their feet, that is, the

[1] orthodoxa, Lat.]

[2] ch. v. 25—27. mundatam lavacro aquæ, Lat. Erasmus' rendering.]

[3] John xiii. 10.]

reliques and spots wherewith they are distained by their daily conversation in this world.

But now, whereunto belongeth this that is added, "The communion of saints?" These words are neither read in Cyprian, nor Augustine, nor yet by them expounded[4]. Wherefore it is likely, that they were added for the better understanding of that which went before : for, that it might appear that the catholic church is the fellowship or company of the faithful, he added, "The communion of saints;" as if he should have said, which church is a communion of saints. Paul called them saints, which for their faith are sanctified by the blood and Spirit of God. Also this word "communion" is very evident and comfortable. For first, the meaning thereof is, that betwixt God and us there is a communion, that is, a fellowship and participation, and so, consequently, a parting betwixt us of all good and heavenly things. And then also we understand, that we are fellows and partakers with all the saints that are living either in heaven or on earth : for we are members of them under one head, Christ. For the apostle John saith: "That which we have seen and heard we declare unto you, that ye also may have fellowship with us, and that your fellowship may be with the Father, and his Son Jesus Christ[5]." Hereunto appertaineth that trim[6] similitude of the body and members under one head, which the apostle Paul handleth at large in deed. But what is he, that can worthily enough set forth the great goodness of God's gift and benefit, in that we are made fellow-partners of God, with whom we are most nearly conjoined, and have a part in all his good and heavenly things? What can be more delightful to our ears, than to hear, that all the saints, as well in heaven as in earth, are our brethren, and that we again are members, partners, and fellows with them? Blessed be God, which hath so liberally bestowed his blessing on us in Christ his Son.

To this place belongeth the discourse upon the sacraments ; of which, and of the church, I mean at another time more fully to entreat. This for the present time is sufficient. For this

The communion of saints.

[4 See Pearson on the Creed, Oxf. ed. 1820. Vol. II. p. 427.]

[5 1 John i. 3. societas vestra, Lat. But the Vulgate and Erasmus have nostra, as the Greek.]

[6 elegans, Lat.]

that I have said doth abundantly enough express and set out the fruit of faith in the Father, the Son, and the holy Ghost; to wit, that we have participation with God and all the saints, and that in this fellowship we are sanctified from all filth or uncleanness, being cleansed and holy in Christ our Lord.

The tenth article of our belief.

Now followeth the tenth article of our belief; which is, "The forgiveness of sins." The second fruit or commodity of our belief in God, the Father, the Son, and the Holy Ghost, is here set forth, that is, the remission of sins; which, although it be contained in sanctification spoken of in the last article, is in this place notwithstanding more lively expressed. Without the church, as it were without the ark of Noe, is no salvation: but in the church, I mean, in the fellowship of Christ and the saints, is full[1] forgiveness of all offences. That this may be the better understood, I will divide it into some parts.

The acknowledging and confessing of our sins.

First of all, it is needful to acknowledge and confess, that we are sinners, and that by nature and our own proper merits we are the children of wrath and damnation. For St John doth not in vain nor without a cause call every one a liar, that saith he hath no sin[2]. And God, which knoweth the hearts of men, hath commanded us even till the last gasp to pray, saying: "Forgive us our debts." Moreover, in the gospel we have two excellent examples of men openly confessing their sins to God; the prodigal son, I say, and the publican in St Luke[3]. Let us therefore think, that we are all sinners, as Paul also taught; yea, as he hath evidently proved in the first chapter to the Romans; and let us freely confess to God our sins with David in the 32nd and 51st Psalms, saying: "My sin have I made known to thee, and mine iniquity I have not hid. I have said, I will confess mine unrighteousness against myself; and thou hast forgiven the iniquity of mine offence." "Have mercy on me, O God, according to thy great mercy," &c. The Psalm is known.

Our sins are forgiven of God, not for our merits, but for Christ his sake.

Secondarily, let us believe, that all these sins of ours are pardoned and forgiven of God, not for the acknowledging and confessing of our sins, but for the merit and blood of the Son of God; not for our own works or merits, but for the truth and mercy, or grace, of God. For we do plainly profess,

[1 plenaria, Lat.]
[2 1 John i. 8.]
[3 ch. xv. 21, and xviii. 13.]

saying: "I believe the forgiveness of sins." We say not, I buy, or by gifts do get, or by works obtain, the forgiveness of sins; but, "I believe the forgiveness of sins." And the word "remission" or "forgiveness" doth signify a free pardoning, by a metaphor taken of creditors and debtors. For the creditor forgiveth the debtor, when he is not able to pay : therefore remission is a forgiving[4], according to the saying of our Saviour in the Gospel : "A certain lender had two debtors; and when they were not able to pay, he forgave them both[5]." Hereunto belongeth that also in the Lord's prayer : "And forgive us our debts ;" for our debts are our sins : them do we request to be remitted, that is, to be forgiven us. In this sense also saith St Paul : "To him that worketh is the reward reckoned not of grace, but of due debt; but to him that worketh not, but believeth on him that justifieth the ungodly, his faith is counted for righteousness : even as David describeth the blessedness of that man, unto whom God imputeth righteousness without works, saying, Blessed are they whose unrighteousnesses are forgiven, and whose sins are covered. Blessed is that man to whom the Lord will not impute sin[6]." Wherefore, in respect of us which have not wherewithal to repay, our sins are freely forgiven; but in respect of God's justice, they are forgiven for the merit and satisfaction of Christ.

Moreover, it is not the sins of a few men, of one or two ages, or a few and certain number of sins, are forgiven only ; but the sins of all men, of all ages, the whole multitude of sins, whatsoever is and is called sin, whether it be original, or actual, or any other else[7]; to be short, all sins are forgiven us. Which we do hereby learn, because the only sacrifice of Christ is effectual enough to wash away all the offences of all sinners, which by faith come to the mercy-seat of God's grace[8]. And yet by this we do not teach men to sin, because the Lord hath long since made satisfaction for sins : but if any man do sin, we teach him to hope well, and not to despair, but to flee to the throne of grace ; for there we say that Christ, sitting at the right hand of the Father, is "the Lamb of God that taketh away the sins of the world." And in the Creed verily it is

All sins are forgiven.

[4 remissio est donatio, Lat.]
[5 Luke vii. 41, 42.]   [6 Rom. iv. 4—8.]
[7 sive alienum sit, Lat.]
[8 ad thronum gratiæ, Lat.   Heb. iv. 16.]

expressly said, "I believe the forgiveness of sins," and not of sin.
For when we say "of sins," we acknowledge that God forgiveth
all sins.   For to let pass the proofs hereof out of the 3rd and
5th of Paul to the Romans, those out of St John, the apostle and
evangelist, shall be sufficient, who in his epistle testifieth, and
saith: "The blood of Jesus Christ cleanseth us from every sin[1]."
Lo, he saith from every sin. He, I say, that saith from every
one, excepteth none, unless it be that which the Lord himself
excepted; I mean, the sin against the Holy Ghost; for which
the very same St John forbiddeth us to pray[2].   Again also he
saith : "If we acknowledge our sins, God is faithful and just
to forgive us our sins, and to cleanse us from all our unrighteousness[3]."   The apostle thought it not enough to say barely,
"To forgive us our sins;" but, that he might declare the thing
as it is indeed so plainly that it might easily be understood, he
addeth moreover this saying : "And to cleanse us from all our
unrighteousness."   Lo, here he saith again, "from all unrighteousness."   And for because some caviller might peradventure make this objection, and say, This kind of doctrine
maketh men sluggish and slow to amendment; for men under
the pretence of God's grace will not cease to sin : therefore
John in his 2nd chapter answereth their objection, and saith :
"Babes, these things write I to you, that ye sin not: and if
any man sin, we have an advocate with the Father, Jesus
Christ the righteous.   And he is the atonement for our sins :
and not for our sins only, but also for the sins of all the
world[4]."   Wherefore it is assuredly true, that by the death
of Christ all sins are forgiven them that believe.

God alone,
and not man,
forgiveth
sins.

     Moreover, the Lord alone forgiveth sins.   For it is the
glory of God alone to forgive sins, and of unrighteous to
make men righteous.   Therefore, whereas men are said to
forgive sins, that is to be understood of their ministery, and
not of their power.   The minister pronounceth to the people,
that for Christ his sake their sins are forgiven : and in so
saying he deceiveth them not; for God indeed forgiveth the
sins of them that believe, according to that saying : "Whose
sins ye forgive, they are forgiven them[5]."   And this is done
so often as the word of the gospel is preached; so that there
be no need to feign, that auricular confession and private ab-

[1   1 John i. 7.]   [2   1 John v. 16.]   [3   1 John i. 9.]
[4   1 John ii. 1, 2.]   [5   John xx. 23.]

solution at the priest's hand is necessary for the remission of sins. For as auricular confession was not in use among the saints before the coming of Christ, so we read not that the apostles heard private confession, or used private absolution in the church of Christ. It is enough for us to confess our sins to God, who, because he seeth our hearts, ought therefore most rightly to hear our confessions. It is enough, if we, as St James teacheth us, do one to another betwixt ourselves confess our faults and offences[6]; and so, after pardon asked, return into mutual favour again. It is enough for us to hear the gospel, promising the forgiveness of our sins through Christ, if we believe. Let us therefore believe the forgiveness of sins, and pray to the Lord that he will vouchsafe to give and increase in us this same belief. These things were of old and in the primitive church effectual enough to obtain pardon and full remission of sins: and as they were, so are they undoubtedly at this day sufficient too.

Furthermore, the Lord doth so pardon our sins, not that they should not be any more in us, nor leave their reliques behind them, as a sting in our flesh, but that they should not be imputed to us to our damnation. Concupiscence sticketh fast and sheweth itself in our flesh, striving still with the good Spirit of God, even in the holy ones, so long as life lasteth on this earth. Here therefore we have need of long watching and much fasting, to draw from the flesh the nourishment of evil, and often prayers to call to God for aid, that we be not overcome of the evil. And if any man shall hap to fail for feebleness, and be subdued of temptation, let him not yield himself, by lying still, to be caught in the devil's net: let him rise up again by repentance, and run to Christ, believing that by the death of Christ this fall of his shall be forgiven him. And so often shall he have recourse to him, as he shall be vanquished by concupiscence and sin. For to this end shoot all the exhortations of the prophets and apostles, calling on still to return to the Lord.

How sins are forgiven.

Finally, the Lord doth so forgive our sins, that he will never once remember them again. For so he foretold us by Jeremiah, in his 31st chapter. He therefore doth not punish us. For he hath not only forgiven the fault, but also the punishment due for the sin. Now then, whereas the Lord

We make not satisfaction for punishment.

[6 James v. 16.]

sometime doth whip us with his scourges, and whippeth us for
our sins indeed (as the holy scripture doth plainly declare), he
doth it not to the intent, that with our affliction we should
make satisfaction for the sins we have committed; for then
should the death of Christ be of none effect: but the Lord
with whipping doth chastise us, and by whipping us doth let
us understand, that he liketh not of the sins, which we have
committed, and he doth freely forgive: by whipping us also
he maketh us examples to other, lest they sin too; and cutteth
from us all occasion of sinning; and by the cross doth keep
our patience in ure[1]. This thus far, touching the forgiveness
of sins. Of which I have said somewhat in my sermon of faith
that justifieth[2], and elsewhere.

The eleventh
article of our
faith. The eleventh article is this: " The resurrection of the
flesh." These two articles, this and the twelfth, shut up, as
briefly as may be, the most excellent fruit of faith, and sum
of all perfection; they wrap up, I say, the end of faith, in
confessing life everlasting, and the full and perfect salvation of
the whole man. For the whole man[3] shall be saved, as well
in soul as body. For as man by sin did perish both in body
and soul, so ought he to be restored again both bodily and
ghostly: and as he ought, so was he by Christ restored
again. The soul of man verily is a spirit, and dieth not at
all: the body is earthly, and therefore dieth and rotteth. For
which cause many hold opinion, that the bodies die, never to
be made partakers of joy or pain in the world to come. But
we in this article profess the contrary, acknowledging that
those our bodies, and so that flesh of ours, shall rise again,
and enter into life everlasting.

The resur-
rection of
our flesh. Of this word "resurrection," or rising again, I have spoken
in the exposition of that article, "The third day he rose
again from the dead." But now this word "flesh" doth a great
deal more significantly express the resurrection of this flesh[4]
than if we should say the resurrection of the body. Verily
Cyprian saith, that in some churches of the east this article
was thus pronounced: "I believe the resurrection of this
flesh[5]." And Augustine also, in the tenth chapter of his book

[1] i.e. in exercise and practice.   exercet, Lat.]
[2] See above, page 109.]   [3] See above, page 144.]
[4] hujus nostræ carnis, Lat.]
[5] Satis cauta et provida adjectione fidem symboli ecclesia nostra

de Fide et Symbolo, saith: "We must without doubting believe, that this visible, which is properly called flesh, shall rise again. The apostle Paul doth seem, as it were, with his finger to point at this flesh, when he saith, 'This corruptible must put on incorruption.' When he saith 'this,' he doth, as it were, put out his finger unto this flesh[6]." This hath Augustine. Moreover, St Hierome compelleth John, bishop of Hierusalem, openly to confess the resurrection of the flesh, not of the body only. "Flesh," saith he, "hath one definition, and the body another. All flesh is a body; but every body is not flesh. That is flesh properly, which is compact of blood, veins, bones, and sinews. A body, although it be called flesh, yet sometimes is said to be of like substance to the firmament, or to the air, which is not subject to touching or seeing; and oftentimes too may be both touched and seen. A wall is a body, but it is not flesh[7]." Thus much out of Hierome. Let us therefore believe, that men's bodies, which are taken of the earth, and which living men bear about, wherein they live, and are, which also die and turn into dust and ashes, that those bodies, I say, are quickened and live again.

But thou demandest, how this flesh, being once resolved into dust and ashes, and so into nothing, can rise again in the former shape and substance: as when it is torn with the teeth of beasts, or consumed to nothing with the flame of fire, and when in the grave[8] there is to be found but a small and

Whether the same bodies, that do putrefy, rise again.

docet, quæ in eo quod a ceteris traditur 'carnis resurrectionem,' uno addito pronomine tradit, 'Hujus carnis resurrectionem.'—Cypr. Expos. in Symb. Apost. fol. 28. Oxon. 1682. See also Becon's Works, Parker Soc. ed. Vol. II. page 49.]

[6 Hæc ergo visibilis, quæ caro proprie dicitur, sine dubitatione credenda est resurgere. Videtur enim Paulus apostolus eam tanquam digito suo ostendere, cum dicit, "Oportet corruptibile hoc induere incorruptionem." Cum enim dicit Hoc, in eam quasi digitum intendit.— Opp. Par. 1531. Tom. III. fol. 32.]

[7 Alia enim carnis, alia corporis definitio est. Omnis caro est corpus; non omne corpus est caro. Caro est proprie, quæ sanguine, venis, ossibus, nervisque constringitur: corpus quamquam et caro dicatur, interdum tamen æthereum vel aërium nominatur, quod tactui visuique non subjacet; sed plerunque visibile est atque tangibile. Paries est corpus, sed non caro, &c.—Hieron. Ep. xxxviii. ad Pam. adv. Error. Johan. Jerosol. ed. Par. Tom. IV. par. 2. col. 322.]

[8 in monumentis, Lat.]

little quantity of dusty powder? I refer thee to the omnipotency of God, which the apostle spake of where he saith:
"Christ hath transformed this vile body of ours, to make it
conformable to his glorious body, by the power wherein he
can make all things subject to himself[1]." Wherefore he that
in the beginning, when as yet there was not a man in the
world, could bring forth man out of the dust of the earth,
although the same man be again resolved into that out of
which he was taken, I mean, into earth, as the saying is,
"Dust thou art, and into dust shalt thou return again[2];" yet
notwithstanding, the same God again, at the end of the
world, is able to raise man out of the earth. For the Lord
in the gospel saith plainly: "The hour shall come, wherein
all they that are in the graves shall hear the voice of the
Son of God, and shall come forth; they that have done good
to the resurrection of life, and they that have done evil to
the resurrection of judgment[3]." And now by faith we are
throughly persuaded, as the apostle saith, "that he that
hath promised is able also to perform[4]." There are moreover lively examples of this matter, and most evident testimonies of the holy scripture. Jonas is swallowed up of the
whale in the Syrian[5] sea, but the third day after he is cast
up again alive upon the shore out of the beast's entrails;
which is a token, that the flesh shall verily rise again.
Wherefore, that is not hard to be believed that in the
Apocalypse[6] is said, that "the sea casteth up her dead."

[1 Phil. iii. 21. Erasmus, whose rendering Bullinger adopts, has
transfiguravit.]

[2 Gen. iii. 19.]

[3 John v. 28, 29.]

[4 Rom. iv. 21.]

[5 The Syrian Sea is that part of the Mediterranean about
Cæsarea.—Relandi Palæstina, Lib. iii. p. 675, ed. Traject. ad Rhen.
1714. in voc. Cæsarea. Cf. Calvin. Comm. in Jon. i. 3, p. 253, ed.
Amstel. 1667.]

[6 in theologia Domini, Lat. The sense, in which Bullinger gives
this name to the Apocalypse, is, not only because it is in some copies
called the Revelation of John the Divine (see Horne's Introduction,
Vol. iv. part 2, chap. 5, §. 1), but because (as he writes in his Comment. in Apocalyps. p. 1. Basil. 1570), est doctrina de rebus ecclesiæ
Christi revelata cœlitus a Christo in gloria, et compendium totius
pietatis, et prophetarum explicatio et summarium.]

The force of fire had no force to hurt the three companions of Daniel: yea, the rage of wild beasts (contrary to nature) abstained from biting Daniel himself: what marvel is it therefore, if at this day neither the force of fire, nor rage of wild beasts, is able to resist the power of God, being disposed to raise his creatures up again[7]? Did not our Lord Christ raise up Lazarus, when he had lien three days in the grave, yea, and stank too, to life again? Did not he himself, having once broken the tyranny of death, rise up again the third day from the dead? Did he not rise again in the same substance of flesh and form of body, wherein he hanged on the cross, and, being taken down from the cross, was buried? Not without good cause do we look back to Christ, which is called the first-begotten among the dead[8], so often as we think in what manner the resurrection of our flesh shall be. For the members shall rise again in the same order that the Head is risen up before them in: we verily shall not rise again the third day after our death; but in our manner and order shall we rise at the last day; yea, and that too in the very same body wherein now we live.

I will add a few testimonies to prove the resurrection of our flesh. Job, confessing his faith touching the resurrection of the dead, in his great weakness, affliction, and sickness, saith: "I know that my Redeemer liveth, and that in the last day I shall rise out of the earth, and shall be clad again with my skin, and in my flesh I shall see God: whom even I myself shall see, and my eyes shall behold, and none other. This hope is laid up in my bosom[9]." This testimony is so evident as that it needeth no larger an exposition.

No less evident are those testimonies out of Esay, chap. xxvi.; Ezech. xxxvii.; Psalm xvi.; Matt. xxii.; John v. vi. xi. Throughout the Acts in every place is often repeated the resurrection of the dead. St Paul, in the fifteenth chapter of his first epistle to the Corinthians, doth make a full discourse of this resurrection. In the fourth chapter of his second epistle he saith: "We which live are always delivered to death for

Testimonies of the true resurrection.

[7] Cf. Works of Bp. Jewel, Parker Soc. ed. Vol. ii. p. 867.]

[8] Coloss. i. 18. Rev. i. 5. primogenitus ex mortuis, Lat.]

[9] Job xix. 25—27. The last sentence of v. 27 is in the Vulgate as in Bullinger's Latin, "reposita est hæc spes mea in sinu meo:" and in the Douay Version, "This my hope is laid up in my bosom."]

Jesus' sake, that the life of Jesus also might appear in ou mortal flesh[1]." See now, what could be spoken more plainly than that the life of Christ shall be made to appear in thi mortal flesh of ours? For by and by after he saith: "W know that he, that raised up the Lord Jesus, shall raise u up also by the means of Jesus[2]." And in the fifth chapter again: "We must all appear before the judgment-seat o Christ," saith he, "that every man may receive the works o his body, according to that he hath done, whether it be good or evil[3]." Therefore these very bodies of ours shall rise again in the day of judgment.

And now, dearly beloved, I have to declare unto you in what manner our bodies shall rise again, and of what sort they shall be in the resurrection. In the shutting up and end of all ages, or of this world, our Lord Jesus Christ shall come to judgment with great majesty; and then, whomsoever that day shall find alive, they shall in a moment of time be changed; and first (I say) shall all they that died, from the first Adam to the last that shall die, rise up again, and in their own flesh stand among the living that are changed, before the tribunal-seat of Christ, looking for that last pro-nounced sentence in judgment. This doth Paul set down in these words: "Lo, I tell you a mystery; We shall not all verily sleep, but we shall all be changed in a moment of time, in the twinkling of an eye, at the sound of the last trump: for it shall sound, and the dead shall rise again incorruptibly, and we shall be changed. For this corruptible must put on incorruption, and this mortal must put on immortality[4]."

By this evident testimony of the apostle we may gather in what fashion our bodies shall be in that resurrection. Verily, our bodies shall be none other in the resurrection than now they be; this only excepted, that they shall be clean without all corruption and corruptible affection. For the apostle saith, "The dead shall rise again;" and, "We shall be changed." And again, pointing expressly and precisely to these very bodies which here we bear about, he saith, "This corruptible, this mortal, yea, this body, I say, and no other," as Job also witnessed, shall rise again: and that shall rise again incorrup-tible, which was corruptible; that shall rise again immortal,

In what sort our bodies shall rise again.

Of what fashion our bodies shall be in the resurrection.

[1 2 Cor. iv. 11.]　　　　[2 ibid. v. 14.]
[3 verse 10.]　　　　[4 1 Cor. xv. 51—53.]

which before the resurrection was mortal.   So then this body of ours in the resurrection shall be set free from all evil affections and passions, from all corruption; but the substance thereof shall not be brought to nought, it shall not be changed into a spirit, it shall not lose the own and proper shape. And this body verily because of that purification and cleansing from those dregs, yea, and rather because of these heavenly and divine gifts, is called both a spiritual body, and also a glorious and purified body.

A glorious body.

For Paul, in the third to the Philippians, saith: "Our conversation is in heaven, from whence we look for the Saviour, the Lord Jesus Christ, who shall change our vile body, that it may be made like unto his glorious body." See here, the apostle calleth not our resurrection from the dead a transubstantiation, or loss of the substance of our body, but a changing: then also, shewing what kind of body that changed body is, he calleth it a glorious body, not without all shape and void of fashion, but augmented in glory: yea, he setteth before us the very body of our Lord Jesus Christ, wherein he sheweth us what fashion our bodies shall have, being in glory.   For in plain words he saith: "He shall make our vile body like to his glorious body."   Let us therefore see what kind of body our Lord had after his resurrection.   It was neither turned into a ghost, nor brought to nothing, nor yet not able to be known by the shape and figure; for, shewing them his hands and feet, that were easily known by the print of the nails wherewith he was crucified, he said, "See, for I am even he[5]," to wit, clad again with the same body wherein I hung upon the cross.   For, speaking yet more plainly, and proving that that body of his was not a spiritual substance, he said: "A spirit hath not flesh and bones, as ye see that I have."   He hath therefore a purified body, flesh and bones, and the very same members which he had when as yet his body was not purified.   And for this cause did the same Lord offer to Thomas his side[6], and the scars of his five wounds, to be felt and handled; to the end that we should not doubt but that his very body was raised up again.   He did both eat and drink with his disciples, as Peter in the Acts[7] witnesseth before Cornelius, that all men might know, that the very self-same body that died rose from death again.

[[5] Luke xxiv. 39.]   [[6] John xx. 27.]   [[7] ch. x. 41.]

Now, although this body be comprehended within a certai
limited place, not dispersed all over and every where; althoug
it have a just quantity, figure, or shape, and a just weigh
with the own kind and nature[1]; yet notwithstanding it is fre
from every passion, corruption, and infirmity.   For the bod
of the Lord once raised up was in the garden, and not in th
sepulchre, when the women came to anoint it; it meeteth the
by the way as they return from the sepulchre, and offeret
itself to be seen of Magdalene in the garden; it goeth in com
pany[2] to Emaus with the two disciples that journeyed t
Emaus: in the mean time, while he was with them i
body, he was not among the other disciples; when they twai
are returned to the eleven, the Lord himself at evening i
present with them: he goeth before his disciples into Galilee
presently after he cometh into Jury again, where his bod
was taken up from mount Olivet into heaven.   All this dot
prove the certain verity of Christ his body.   But because th
body (although it be a true and very body, of the own prope
kind[3], place, disposition, and of the own proper shape an
nature) is called a glorified and glorious body, I will sa
somewhat of that glory, which verily is incident to the tru
shape and substance of the body once raised up again.

What a
glorious
body is.

First, glory in this sense is used for a lightsomeness an
shining brightness.   For Paul saith, that the children of Israe
for the glory of Moses' countenance, could not behold wit
their eyes the face of Moses[4]: so then a glorious body is
bright and shining body.   A very good proof of this did ou
Lord shew, even a little before his resurrection, when it please
him to give to his disciples a small taste of the glory to come
and for that cause took aside certain, whom he had chose
into the top of a certain hill, where he was transfigured befor
them, so that the fashion of his countenance did shine as th
sun, and his clothes were white and glistered as the light
The Lord verily had still the same bodily substance, and th
same members of the body, but they were transfigured.   Bu
it is manifest, that that transfiguration was in the accident
For light and brightness was added, so that, the shape an
substance of the countenance and body remaining as it wa

[1 sexum et suam naturam, Lat.]
[2 æquis passibus, Lat.]
[4 2 Cor. iii. 7.]

[3 sui sexus, Lat.]
[5 Matt. xvii. 2.]

the countenance and body did glister as the sun and the light.
And although we read not that the body of the Lord did
within those forty days, wherein he shewed himself alive again
to his disciples, make manifest and spread abroad the brightness which it had, and that by reason of the dispensation,
whereby also he did eat with his disciples, notwithstanding
that clarified bodies need not food or nourishment at all; yet
nevertheless his body shineth now in heaven, as John in the
first of the Apocalypse witnesseth: and the sacred scriptures
lay an assured hope before us, that even our bodies also shall
in the resurrection be likewise clarified. For the Lord himself in the gospel, alleging the words of Daniel, saith: "Then
shall the righteous shine as the sun in his Father's kingdom[6]."
For this cause the glorious bodies are called also clarified, of
the clearness of that heavenly brightness wherewith they
glister and are adorned.

Secondarily, glory and vileness are made contraries.
For Paul saith: "He shall change our vile body, to make it
in fashion like to his glorious body[7]." In these words vileness
and glory are set the one against the other. Vileness comprehendeth the whole pack of miseries and infirmities, passions
and affections, which for sin was laid upon the body: from
all which our bodies are purged in the resurrection of life; so
that then the glorious bodies are bodies drained from the
dregs of all corruption, passions, and infirmities, and clad with
eternity, heavenly feeling, and glory. For the apostle saith:
"It is sown in corruption; it riseth in incorruption: it is sown
in dishonour; it riseth in glory: it is sown in infirmity; it riseth
in power: it is sown a natural body; it riseth a spiritual body[8]."
The gifts therefore of the glorious and clarified bodies are
very great and many, as incorruption, glory, power, and the
quickening Spirit. For the apostle himself, shewing what he
meant by the natural[9] and spiritual body, addeth this immediately, and saith: "There is a natural body, and there is a
spiritual body; as it is written, The first man Adam was made
a living soul; and the last Adam was made a quickening spirit."
And yet again more plainly he saith: "Howbeit, that is not
first which is spiritual, but that which is natural, and then that

Glorious bodies rest free from vileness.

[6] Matt. xiii. 43; Dan. xii. 3.]   [7] Phil. iii. 21.]
[8] 1 Cor. xv. 42—44.]
[9] animale, Lat.]

which is spiritual. The first man is of the earth, earthy : the second man is the Lord from heaven. As is the earthy, such are they that are earthy : and as is the heavenly, such are they also that are heavenly. And as we have borne the image of the earthy, so shall we bear the image of the heavenly." So then Paul calleth that natural body an earthy body, which we have of our first father Adam, whose quickening is of the soul, and by it doth live. And he calleth the spiritual body an heavenly body, which we have of Christ, and made to the likeness of the body of Christ; which although it be a very body indeed, and the flesh thereof be very flesh indeed, yet notwithstanding it is quickened and preserved by the Spirit of Christ, and needeth not any power vegetative.

The natural and spiritual body.

Although therefore these very bodies and members, which now we bear, shall after the resurrection be in heaven; yet nevertheless, because they are clarified and cleansed from all corruption and feeling of the natural body, there shall not be verily any natural or corruptible sense or affection, nor use of the carnal body and members. And this doth the Lord affirm against the Sadducees (that dreamt of marriages in heaven, or rather by that absurdity made a mock of the resurrection), where he saith : " The sons of this world marry wives, and give in marriage; but they that shall be thought worthy of that world and of the resurrection from the dead, do neither marry wives, nor give in marriage; neither can they die any more. For they are equal to the angels, and are the sons of God, as soon as they be the sons of resurrection[1]." To which effect also Paul saith : " Flesh and blood cannot inherit the kingdom of God." And lest peradventure any man should mistake his words, and think that he spake of the substance of the flesh, he addeth immediately this for interpretation thereof, and saith : " Neither shall corruption inherit incorruption[2]." Wherefore flesh and blood, that is to say, the affections and lusts of the flesh, shall not be in the elect that live in heaven. For the joys of heaven do differ a great deal from the joys of the earth, and are so far forth of another condition, that they cannot admit such corrupt creatures to be inheritors of them ; and for that cause

Flesh and blood shall not be in heaven.

Sensu animali. Animalis.

[1 Luke xx. 34—36. cum sint, Lat.]
[2 1 Cor. xv. 50.]

the corruptible bodies must first be purged from all corruption, and by that means purely clarified. The Turks therefore are deceived, that look for earthly joys[3].

Moreover, the bodies of the wicked shall also rise again. For Paul, in the Acts, saith : "I believe all that is written in the law and the prophets, hoping in God that the resurrection of the dead, which they themselves look for also, shall be both of the just and unjust[4]." See here, the apostle saith of the unjust also. But in this resurrection there shall not be taken out of their bodies the infirmity, corruption, dishonour, and misery; for even then that very body, rising again in dishonour, shall by the judgment and power of God be surely shut in dishonour and corruption, and so be condemned for ever to bear endless torments, and in death and corruption shall neither die nor yet corrupt: that even as on earth are found certain bodies that do endure even in the fire, so the cursed bodies of the wicked shall not be worn out, nor broken with any torments whatsoever; for every minute they shall receive new strength to suffer, and so by continual suffering shall abide their deserved punishments for ever and ever and without all end. For the Lord in the gospel saith, "They that have done evil shall rise again to the resurrection of damnation[5];" that is, to an enduring and everlasting damnation. And Daniel before him said: "And the multitude of them that sleep in the dust of the earth shall awake, some to everlasting life, and some to shame and perpetual contempt[6]." And in the gospel, again, the Lord saith: "Their worm dieth not, and their fire is not quenched." And the very same words used Esay before him in his 66th chapter[7]. We must always therefore have that saying of the Lord in our hearts: "Fear him that can destroy both the body and the soul in hell[8]." Thus much hitherto touching the resurrection of the flesh.

The last article of our belief, which with good luck shutteth up the rest, is this: "And life everlasting." We have heard and understood, that the souls of men are immortal,

The bodies of the wicked shall also rise again.

The twelfth article of our belief.

[3 See Sale's Prelim. Discourse to his translation of the Koran, Sect. IV.]

[4 ch. xxiv. 15.]

[5 John v. 29.]

[6 Dan. xii. 2.]

[7 Mark ix. 44; Isai. lxvi. 24.]

[8 Matt. x. 28.]

[BULLINGER.]

12

and that our bodies do rise again in the end of the world.
We have confessed that this is our belief. It followeth now,
in the latter end of the Creed, whither it is that the immortal
soul and body raised up again shall come. Therefore in our
confession we say, "And life everlasting;" that is, I believe
that I shall have life, and live for ever, both in body and
soul. And that everlastingness verily is perpetual and hath
no end, as a little before is proved out of the holy scriptures.

Life ever-lasting.

Moreover, the souls are made partakers of this eternal
life immediately after they are departed out of the bodies, as
the Lord himself witnesseth, saying: "He that believeth in
the Son of God shall not come into judgment, but hath
escaped from death to life[1]." As for the bodies, they are
buried and do putrefy; and yet so, notwithstanding, that they
shall not be without life for ever: but they shall then at
length be received into eternal life, when, being raised up,
they shall after the time of judgment be caught into the air,
there to meet Christ, that they may for ever be with the
Lord. For then do the souls return out of heaven, every
one to his own body, that the whole, perfect, and full man
may live for ever both in soul and body. For the soul of
Christ dying on the cross did out of hand depart into paradise, and the third day after returned to the body, which
rose again and ascended into heaven. Even as, therefore,
eternal life came to the Head Christ, so shall it also come
to all and every member of Christ.

Now, whereas Paul, citing Esay, saith, "What the eye
hath not seen, nor the ear heard, nor hath at any time come
into the heart of man, that hath the Lord prepared for them
that love him[2];" I suppose verily, if all were said touching
eternal life, that might be spoken by all the men of all ages that
ever were or shall be, yet that scarcely the very least part
thereof hath or shall be throughly touched. For howsoever
the scripture doth with eloquent and figurative speeches, with
allusions and hard sentences[3], most plainly shew the shadow of
that life and those joys; yet, notwithstanding, all that is
little or nothing in comparison to speak of, until that day do
come wherein we shall with unspeakable joy behold God himself, the Creator of all things, in his glory; Christ our Savi-

[1 John v. 24.]   [2 1 Cor. ii. 9; Is. lxiv. 4.]
[3 ænigmatibus, Lat.]

ɔur in his majesty; and finally, all the blessed souls, angels,
patriarchs, prophets, apostles, martyrs, our fathers, all nations[4], all the host of heaven, and lastly, the whole divine and
heavenly glory.   Most truly therefore said Aurelius Augustine, *Lib. de Civitat. Dei*, XXII. cap. 29: "When it is demanded of me, what the saints shall do in that spiritual
body; I answer, not that which I now see, but that that I
believe.   I say therefore, that they shall see God in that
spiritual body."   And again: "If I should say the truth, I
know not in what sort that action, quietness, and rest shall
be.   For the peace of God doth pass all understanding[5]."
To be short, we shall see God face to face, we shall be filled
with the company of God, and yet be never weary of him.
And the face of God is not that countenance that appeareth   The face of
in us; but is a most delectable revealing and enjoying of   God.
God, which no mortal tongue can worthily declare.   Go to
then, dearly beloved brethren; let us believe and live, that
when we shall depart from hence we may in very deed have
trial[6] of those unspeakable joys of the eternal life to come,
which now we do believe.

Hitherto have I, throughout the four last articles, declared unto you the fruit and end of christian faith.   Faith
leaneth upon one God, the Father, the Son, and the Holy
Ghost, which sanctifieth the faithful, and purgeth and halloweth
a church to himself: which church hath a communion with
God and all saints; all the offences of which church God
pardoneth and forgiveth; and doth preserve it both soul and
body.   For as the saints' souls cannot die, so God raiseth up
their bodies again, and maketh them glorious and everlasting,
to the end that the whole man may for ever live in heaven
with the Lord: to whom be praise and glory world without
end.   Amen.

[4 et omnem gentem nostram, Lat.   And all our race.]
[5 Cum ex me quæritur, quid acturi sint sancti in illo corpore
spiritali; non dico quod jam video, sed dico quod credo.   Dico itaque,
quod visuri sint Deum in ipso corpore...
Illa quidem actio, vel potius quies, atque otium quale futurum sit,
si verum velim dicere, nescio.—Ibi est enim pax Dei, quæ, sicut ait
apostolus, superat omnem intellectum.—Opp. Par. 1531, Tom. v.
fol. 310.]
[6 experiamur, Lat.]

OF THE LOVE OF GOD AND OUR NEIGHBOUR.

THE TENTH SERMON.

IT remaineth, since I have in some sermons discoursed o
true faith, that I do now also add one sermon touching lov
towards God and our neighbour. For in my fourth sermo
I promised, so soon as I should have done with the expositio
of faith, that then I would speak of love toward God and ou
neighbour; because the exposition of the scriptures ought no
to go awry out of faith and charity, which are, as it were, th
right and holy marks for it to draw unto. Ye, as hitherto y
have done, so cease not yet to pray, that this wholesome doc
trine may be by me taught as it should be, and by you re
ceived with much increase and profit.

Love and charity.

And, first of all, I will not curiously put any differenc
between charity and love. I will use them both in one an
the same sense. St Augustine, *De Doctrina Christiana*, saith
" I call charity a motion of the mind to delight in God for h
own sake, and to delight in himself and his neighbour fo
God's sake[1]." And therefore I call love a gift given to ma
from heaven, whereby with his heart he loveth God befor

Love, from whence it is.

and above all things, and his neighbour as himself. Lov
therefore springeth from heaven, from whence it is poure
into our hearts. But it is enlarged and augmented, partly b
the remembrance and consideration of God's benefits, partl
by often prayer, and also by the hearing and frequenting
the word of Christ. Which things themselves also are the gif
of the Spirit. For the apostle Paul saith : " The love of Go
is poured out into our hearts by the Holy Ghost which
given us[2]." For verily the love of God, wherewith he love
us, is the foundation and cause of our love wherewith we lo
him; and of both these jointly consisteth the love of o
neighbour. For the apostle saith : " We love him because
first loved us." And again : " Every one that loveth hi
which begot, loveth him also that is born of him[3]."

[1 Caritatem voco motum animi ad fruendum Deo propter ipsu
et se atque proximo propter Deum.—De Doct. Christ. Lib. III. cap.
Vol. III. fol. 11.]

[2 Rom. v. 5.]   [3 1 John iv. 19; v. 1.]

Hereby we gather again, that this gift of love cannot be *Double charity.* divided or severed, although it be double. For he that loveth God truly, hateth not his neighbour : and yet, nevertheless, his love, because of the double respect that it hath to God and our neighbour, standeth of two parts. And because of his double charity the tables of God's law are divided into twain : the first whereof containeth four commandments touching the love of God, the second comprehendeth six precepts touching the love of our neighbour. Of which I will speak in their own place. But at this time, because the love of God and of our neighbour are twain, I will first speak of the love of God, and then of the love of our neighbour. "In these two commandments," saith the Lord, "hang the law and the prophets[4]."

With that which we call the love of God, we love God *The love of* entirely well ; we cleave to God as the only, chief, and eternal *God.* goodness ; in him we do delight ourselves and are well pleased ; and frame ourselves to his will and pleasure, having evermore regard and desire of him that we love[5]. With love we love God most heartily. But we do heartily love the things that are dear unto us, and the things that to us seem worthy to be desired ; and we love them entirely indeed, not so much for our commodity, as for because we do desire to join, and, as it were, for ever to give and dedicate ourselves wholly to the thing that we so dearly love. So verily we desire for ever to be joined with God, and are in charity fast linked unto him ; as the apostle saith : "God is charity ; and he that dwelleth in charity dwelleth in God, and God in him[6]." And that is the way whereby we cleave to God, as to the only chief and eternal goodness, in whom also we are delighted, and that not a little. In him we rest, thinking assuredly that without him there is no good at all ; and again, that in him there is to be found all manner of goodness. Wherefore our hearty love is set on no good thing but God : and in comparison of him whom we love, we do lightly[7] loathe and tread under foot all things else that

[4 Matt. xxii 40.]

[5 "Here be many propositions together, which we will explain fitly and one by one a little more fully :" omitted. P.—Plurima hic simul sunt proposita, quæ sigillatim et per partes copiosius paulo exponemus.]

[6 1 John iv. 16.]

[7 facile, Lat.]

seem to be good in the whole world; yea, verily, the love o

By the love
of God all
evils are
overcome.

God in us doth overcome all the evils which otherwise seem
invincible.　Let us hear Paul with a vehement motion pro
claiming this, and saying: "Who shall separate us from th
love of God? shall tribulation, or anguish, or persecution
or hunger, or nakedness, or peril, or sword? (As it is written
For thy sake are we killed all the day long, and are counted
as sheep for the slaughter.)　Nevertheless in all these thing
we overcome through him that loved us.　For I am sure tha
neither death, nor life, nor angels, nor rule, nor power, no
things present, nor things to come, nor height, nor depth, no
any other creature shall be able to separate us from the lov
of God which is in Christ Jesu our Lord[1]."　Hitherto have
recited the words of Paul.

The love of
God fashion-
eth us to the
will and
pleasure of
God.

　　The love of God worketh in us a will to frame ourselve
wholly to the will and ordinances of him whom we do heartil
love.　Yea, it is pleasant and sweet to him that loveth God
do the thing that he perceiveth is acceptable to God, if it b
done.　He that loveth doth in mind reverence him whom h
loveth.　His eye is never off him whom he loveth.　He do
always, and in all things, wish for his dearling whom he lovet
His only joy is, as oft as may be, to talk with God, and aga
to hear the words of God speaking in the scripture.　For t
Lord in the gospel saith: "If any man love me, he will ke
my word: he that loveth me not doth not keep my words
Again: "Abide ye in my love.　If ye keep my comman
ments, ye shall abide in my love, even as I also have kept m
Father's commandments, and do abide in his love."　An
again: "If any man love me, he will keep my word; and m
Father will love him, and we will come to him, and make o
dwelling in him[2]."

The manner
how to love
God.

　　But now let us hear Moses, the servant of God, declarin
and teaching us the way and manner how to love God;
wit, how great love ought to be in the elect.　"Thou shalt
saith he, "love the Lord thy God with all thy heart, wi
all thy soul, and with all thy strength[3]."　The very san
words, in a manner, did our Lord in the gospel repeat, an
said: "Thou shalt love the Lord thy God with all thy hear

[1] Rom. viii. 35—39.]　　　[2] John xiv. 23, 24; xv. 9, 10.]
[3] Deut. vi. 5.]

with all thy soul, with all thy strength, and with all thy mind[4]." By this we understand, that the greatest love that may be is required at our hands to God-ward; as that which challengeth man wholly, how big soever he be, and all the parts of man, as peculiar unto itself. In the mind is man's understanding. In the heart is the seat of his affections and will. The strength of man containeth all man's ability, as his very words, deeds, counsel, riches, and his whole substance. Finally, the soul is the life of man. And we verily are commanded to employ all these upon the love of God, when we are bidden to love God with all our soul, with all our strength, with our whole mind, and our whole heart. Nothing is overslipped, but all is contained in this. We are God's wholly and altogether; let us altogether therefore and wholly love God. Let nothing in all the world be dearer to us than God: let us not spare for God's sake any thing of all that which we possess, how dear to us or good soever it be; but let us forsake, spend, and give it for God's sake, and as the Lord by his word appointeth: for in doing so we love God before and above all things.

We are also commanded to stick to God only, and to embrace him alone. For to whom we do wholly owe all that we have, to him is all the whole sincerely, simply, and fully to be given. Here are they condemned, whosoever will at once love God and the world together. The Lord requireth the whole heart, the whole mind, the whole soul, and all the strength; finally, he requireth all whatsoever we are, or have in possession: he leaveth nothing therefore for thee to bestow on other. By what right then wilt thou give to the flesh, the devil, to other gods, or to the world, the things that properly are God's own? And God verily alone is the chiefest, eternal, greatest, mightiest creator, deliverer, preserver, most gentle, most just, and best of all. He alone doth give, hath given, and is able to give to man all that is expedient for the safeguard of his body and soul. God alone doth minister to man ability to live well and blessedly: and therefore God deserveth to be loved alone, and that too before and above all other things. This love of God doth bless all the haps and chances of men, and turneth them to their profit, according to that saying: "To them that love God all

God alone to be loved.

[4 Matt. xxii. 37.]

things work for the best[1]." This love of God also containeth
this; that it suffereth us not to honour, worship, reverence,
fear, or call upon any, neither to trust in, obey, or stick to any
other, but to the one and only God, to whom all glory is due.

Who is our
neighbour.   But now, before we speak of the love of our neighbour, it
is requisite that we first shew who it is that is our neighbour;
touching which I see some men to doubt and stick uncertainly.
For some there are, that take their kinsfolks to be their
neighbours: other some there are, that think that their
benefactors are their neighbours, and judge them strangers
that do them any harm.   But our Lord Jesus Christ telleth
us, that every one, yea, though he be our enemy, is nevertheless our neighbour, if he stand in need of our aid or counsel.
For he imagineth that a Jew, lighting among thieves, and
lying on the high-way half dead, and covered with wounds
and swelling dry blows[2], was not regarded of his own countrymen, a Levite and a priest, that passed by him; but at last
was taken up and healed by a Samaritan.   Now there was
a deadly enmity between the Jews and the Samaritans; yet
notwithstanding, this Samaritan doth good to the Jew, because
he saw that the case and necessity of the afflicted man did so
require.   Now therefore the Lord, applying this to his own
purpose, demanded of him that desired to learn who was his
neighbour, and saith, "Which of these three seemeth to
thee to have been this man's neighbour? He answered,
He that shewed mercy.   Then said the Lord, Go thou,
and do the like[3]."   As if he should have said: Like as the
Samaritan judged even his enemy to be his neighbour, and
dealt friendly with him, when he stood in need of his friendship; so see that thou take every one that needeth thy help
to be thy neighbour, and do him good.   Aurelius Augustine
therefore, according to the right sense of the scripture, said:
"We take him to be our neighbour, to whom we shew mercy
when need requireth; or to whom we should shew mercy, if
at any time he should need[4]."   We Switzers do most properly express it, when we call our neighbour *Den nachsten*

[1 Rom. viii. 28.]   [2 tuberibusque, Lat.]   [3 Luke x. 29—37.]
[4 Ut videlicet eum esse proximum intelligamus, cui vel exhibendum est officium misericordiæ si indiget, vel exhibendum esset si indi-
geret.—August. de Doct. Christ. Lib. i. cap. 30, Par. 1531, Tom. iii.
col. 4.]

menschen; that is, any man, without difference, whosoever by The man
next to us. hap shall light into our company.   Moreover, in our country speech we will call our neighbour, *Der abenmensch, namlich* Any one
that is a man
as well as
we. *ein yeder der so wol ein mensch ist als wir :* meaning thereby any man whatsoever, whether he be our friend or enemy. Hereunto belongeth that saying of Lactantius, in the eleventh chapter of his sixth book : " Why makest thou choice of persons ? why lookest thou so narrowly on the limbs ?   Thou must take him to be a man, whosoever beseecheth thee therefore, that he may think thee to be a man.   Give to the blind, to the impotent, to the lame, to the comfortless ; to whom unless thou be liberal, thou shalt die undoubtedly[5]."   Again he saith : " If so be we will rightly be called by the name of men, then must we in any case keep the law of civil humanity.   And what else I pray you is it to keep humanity, but therefore to love a man because he is a man, and the very same that we ourselves are[6] ?"   The Lord in the gospel verily, speaking of the love of our neighbour, saith : " Love your enemies, bless them that curse you, do good to them that hate you, pray for them that hurt you[7]."   And again : " Give to every one that asketh of thee.   And if you love them that love you, what thank is that to you ?   For sinners also love them of whom they are loved[8]."   So then every man, whosoever standeth in need of our aid, both is and is to be counted our neighbour.

And yet, all this notwithstanding, there is no cause but An order
and measure
in loving. that there ought to be an order, a measure, and decent regard in love and well-doing.   For rightly said St Augustine, in the twenty-seventh chapter of his book *de Doctrina Christiana :* " No sinner, in that he is a sinner, is to be loved[9]."   And in the twenty-eighth chapter : " All men are to be loved alike ; but since thou canst not do good to all men, therefore thou

[5] Quid personas eligis? quid membra inspicis? Pro homine tibi habendus est, quisquis ideo precatur, quia te hominem putet. . . . Largire cæcis, debilibus, claudis, destitutis : quibus, nisi largiare, moriendum est.—Lactant. Div. Inst. VI. 11, Lugd. Bat. 1660. p. 583.   More correctly translated, " to whom unless thou be liberal, *they must die.*"   P.]

[6] Conservanda est igitur humanitas, si homines recte dici velimus. Id autem ipsum, conservare humanitatem, quid aliud est, quam diligere hominem, quia homo sit et idem quod nos sumus ?—Ibid. p. 581.]

[7] Matt. v. 44.]   [8] Luke vi. 30, 32.]

[9] Omnis peccator, in quantum peccator est, non est diligendus.—De Doct. Christ. I. 27, Opp. Tom. III. fol. 4.]

must especially do good to them, to whom thou art, as it were by lot, more nearly joined, by opportunity either of time, of place, or of any other thing whatsoever[1]." And this did Paul, before Augustine, teach, where he saith: "Whoso-ever worketh not, let him not eat[2]." And again: "While we have time, let us work good to all men; but specially to them of the household of faith[3]." And in another place he commandeth us not to bestow unto others, and to lack our-selves at home; but rather he chargeth every one to have a godly care of his own house. The place is known in the fifth chapter of the first epistle to Timothy.

How our neighbour must be loved.

Now since I have declared who is our neighbour, let us see also in what sort this neighbour of ours ought to be loved. Our neighbour must be loved simply, without any coloured deceit, with the very self-same love wherewith we love our-selves, or that wherewith Christ hath loved us. For in all things we must stand our neighbour in stead, and do him pleasure, so far as the law of humanity shall be found to re-quire. In this declaration there are four things more fully to be noted.

The love of our neigh-bour must be sincere.

First, that love of our neighbour that is looked for at our hands ought to be so sincere, as that it be without all manner guile, deceit, and coloured craft. For there are many to be found, that have the skill to talk to their neighbours with sugared tongues, and to make a face as though they loved them, when as indeed they do utterly hate them, meaning nothing else but with fawning words to beguile them, that thereby they may work the things that they desire. Paul and John, therefore, the apostles of Christ, go about earnestly to sever hypocrisy from love. For Paul saith: "Let not your love be feigned." Again: "The end of the command-ment is love of a pure heart, and a good conscience, and faith not feigned[4]." On the other side, John crieth out, saying: "My babes, let us not love in word, nor in tongue, but in deed and in verity[5]." Moreover, in this sincerity we

[1 Omnes autem homines æque diligendi sunt. Sed cum omnibus prodesse non possis, his potissimum consulendum est, qui pro locorum et temporum vel quarumlibet rerum opportunitatibus constrictius tibi quasi quadam sorte junguntur.—c. 28, ib.]

[2 2 Thess. iii. 10.]   [3 Gal. vi. 10.]

[4 Rom. xii. 9; 1 Tim. i. 5.]   [5 1 John iii. 18.]

contain a free, willing, and merry cheerfulness, that nothing may seem to be done unwillingly or by compulsion. For Paul saith: "Let every man do with a good purpose of mind, not of trouble or necessity; for God requireth a cheerful giver[6]."

Secondarily, it is to be looked for of us, that we should love our neighbour as ourselves. For the Lord hath said, "Love thy neighbour as thyself[7];" that is, most entirely, and as dearly as by any means thou mayest. For there is not any affection that is of more force or vehemency than self-love is. Neither was it the Lord his mind, that the love of our neighbour should be any whit lesser than the love that we bear to ourselves: but rather by this he gave us to understand, that we ought to bestow on others as ardent love as may be, to wit, the very same affection that we bear to ourselves and our own estate; and that we ought to be ready to do good to other, or to keep them from harm, with the same care, faith, and diligence, with the same zeal and goodwill, wherewith we provide for ourselves or our own safety. Whereupon the Lord in another place saith: "Whatsoever thou wouldest have done to thyself, that do thou to another. And whatsoever thou wouldest not have done to thyself, do not thou the same to another[8]." And herein doth the Lord require two things at our hands; not to hurt, and to do good. For it is not enough not to hurt a man, but also to do him good, so much as lieth in us to do. For we ourselves desire not only to keep ourselves from hurt, but to do ourselves good also.

We must love our neighbour as ourself.

But if so it be, dearly beloved, that ye do not yet sufficiently understand the manner how we ought to love our neighbour; then mark, I beseech you, the third part of my description of this love, where I said, that we ought to love our neighbour with that same love wherewith the Lord Christ loved us. For in the gospel after St John the Lord saith: "This is my commandment, That ye love one another, as I have loved you[9]." So then, here ye have the manner of our love: we must love our neighbours as Christ hath loved us. But in

We must love our neighbour as Christ hath loved us.

[6 2 Cor. ix. 7.   non ex molestia, Lat. and Erasmus; Vulgate, ex tristitia.]

[7 Matt. xxii. 39.]   [8 Matt. vii. 12.]

[9 ch. xv. 12.]

what sort hath Christ loved us? Here again in the gospel he saith: "No man hath greater love than this, that a man bestow his life for his friends[1]." So then, such must the manner of our love toward our neighbour be, as that we shall not doubt to give our life for our neighbour. And if so it be then, that for our neighbour's sake we owe the loss of our life, there is nothing verily that we owe him not, considering that to a man nothing is more dear than life: for sooner will he lose all that he hath than once to put his life in jeopardy. Whereupon the apostle John crieth out, and saith: "Hereby perceive we love, because he laid down his life for us: and we ought to lay down our lives for the brethren[2]." This is easy to be understood by reason of the most evident example. Let us pray earnestly and continually to the Lord, that we may indeed fulfil the thing that we do manifestly understand by the word of God, lest peradventure the same apostle condemn us, who saith: "Whoso hath this world's good, and seeth his brother have need, and shutteth up his compassion from him, how dwelleth the love of God in him[2]?"

How we ought to stand our neighbour in stead. And now let us also declare the fourth and last manner, how we ought to stand our neighbour in stead, and how to do him good in shewing our dutiful love and civil humanity. That hath the Lord already very finely[3] set out in the very same parable wherein he taught us who is our neighbour: for he hath briefly, and yet very evidently, touched all the points of the love that we owe to our neighbour. First, the Samaritan, at the sight of the wounded man, was moved with pity. There is therefore required of us a merciful motion of pity, so to regard other men's calamities as though they were our own: it is looked for at our hands, that we should be as sorrowful-minded for another man's trouble, as he that feeleth the misery, according to that saying of the apostle: "Be mindful of them that are in bonds, as bound with them; and of them which suffer adversity, as though ye yourselves also, being in the body, suffered adversity[4]." Secondarily, the Samaritan passeth not by, but cometh unto him; he doth not

[1 Ibid. v. 13.]   [2 1 John iii. 16, 17.]
[3 eleganter, Lat.]
[4 Heb. xiii. 3.   velut ipsi quoque versantes in corpore, Lat. and Erasmus. The Genevan Testament renders: As if ye were afflicted in the body.]

with sorrowful words wish health to the wounded, and so, letting him lie, depart to dispatch his own affairs : for James the
apostle saith : " If a brother or sister be naked, and destitute
of daily food, and one of you say unto them, Depart in peace,
be ye warmed and filled ; and yet notwithstanding give them
not those things that are needful to the body, what shall it
profit[5] ?"   The Samaritan therefore cometh unto him, setteth
to his hand, and sheweth the skill that he hath (which was
not much, I wis[6]) to heal the seely[7] mangled man.   He doth
not loathe and turn his face from the ill-favoured colour, bloody
matter, corrupted filth and stench of his wounds ; he bindeth
them up himself, not letting them alone for another to do.
He maketh not his excuse, that he is no physician ; but doth
what he can in that necessity, using such medicine as for the
time present he had in a readiness, till more conveniently he
might come by better.   Wine and oil he had taken with him
when he began his journey, which in that necessity he
doth use ; and that not very inconveniently, because wine
purgeth wounds, and oil doth make them supple.   Moreover,
whatsoever he hath, that doth he employ to the seely man's
behoof, and to do him ease doth even disease himself[8] : for
he alighteth from the back of the beast whereon he rode, and
maketh him to serve the maimed man's necessity.   He also
with his own hands lifteth up from the ground the man that
was too weak to stand, and setteth him on the beast.   And
lastly, he himself becometh his guide to lead the way, not
suffering any other to take charge over him.   For when as
he could not readily bring him to his own house, yet did he
convey him into a common inn : where again he spareth not
for any cost or pains-taking ; for he himself taketh charge of
the miserable man, because in common inns sick folks, for the
most part, are slenderly looked unto.   But when his earnest
business calleth on to make haste in his journey, he taketh
out so much money as he doth think to be sufficient till his
return, and giveth it to the inn-keeper[9].   And not being
therewithal content, he giveth to his host an especial charge

[5] James ii. 15, 16.]
[6] quando meliorem (artem) non didicerat, Lat.]
[7] Seely, i. e. weak.]
[8] suum etiam genium defraudans, Lat.]
[9] hospiti meritorio, Lat.]

of the sick man; and also bindeth himself for him, saying: Whatsoever more than this thou shalt lay out about things necessary for his recovery, thou shalt not lose one mite; for at my return I will pay thee all again to the uttermost farthing. So then he promiseth to return, and therewithal declareth that he shall not be quiet until he see him thoroughly healed of all his wounds. Ye have here, dearly beloved, in this the Lord's parable, a most godly and absolute example of love: for the Samaritan doth liberally and willingly employ his whole service upon his needy neighbour's necessity. We therefore owe ourselves wholly and all that we have to our neighbour's behoof; which if we bestow on him, then do we fulfil the duties of love and civil humanity.

The pith of charity.

To this we will yet add some testimonies of the scripture, that thereby we may more fully understand the very innermost pith of love; if yet peradventure any thing may seem to be wanting in that which hitherto I have alleged. Paul therefore, writing to the Corinthians, saith: " Love suffereth wrong, and is courteous; love envieth not; love doth not frowardly; love swelleth not, dealeth not dishonestly, seeketh not her own, is not provoked to anger, thinketh not evil, rejoiceth not in iniquity, but rejoiceth in the truth, suffereth all things, believeth all things, hopeth all things, endureth all things[1]." And again, the same apostle in his epistle to the Romans saith: " Love striveth to go before in giving honour to other; love distributeth to the saints' necessity; is given to hospitality, speaketh well of her persecutors, and curseth not them that persecute her; love rejoiceth with them that do rejoice, and weepeth with them that weep, and applieth itself to the weaker sort's infirmity[2]." And again: " Owe nothing to any man, but to love one another. For he that loveth another

Love the fulfilling of the law.

hath fulfilled the law. For this, Thou shalt not commit adultery, Thou shalt not steal, Thou shalt not kill, Thou shalt not bear false witness, Thou shalt not lust, and if there be any other commandment, it is comprehended briefly in this saying, namely, Thou shalt love thy neighbour as thyself. Love worketh no ill to his neighbour; therefore the fulfilling of the law is love or charity[3]."

Works of mercy.

Hitherto also pertaineth the works of mercy, which as they

[1 1 Cor. xiii. 4—7.   patiens est, Lat.]
[2 Rom. xii. 10, 13—16.]   [3 Rom xiii. 8—10.]

flow out of love, so are they rehearsed of the Lord in the
gospel after Matthew, and are especially these that follow : To
feed the hungry, to give drink to the thirsty, to harbour the
harbourless[4] and strangers, to cover or clothe the naked, to
visit the sick, and to see and comfort imprisoned captives[5].
Hereunto Lactantius, *Lib. Institut.* vi. cap. 12, hath an eye,
where he saith : " The chiefest virtue is to keep hospitality,
and to feed the poor : to redeem captives also is a great and
excellent work of righteousness : and as great a work of
justice is it, to save and defend the fatherless and widows, the
desolate and helpless, which the law of God doth every where
command.   It is also a part of the chiefest humanity and a
great good deed, to take in hand to heal and cherish the sick,
that have nobody to help them.   Finally, that last and
greatest duty of piety is the burial of strangers and of the
poor[6]."   Thus much hitherto touching the duty of civil humanity, which true love sheweth to his neighbour in necessity.

But it is not enough, my brethren, to understand how we   An exhorta-
ought to love our neighbour (though we ought often to repeat   tion to love.
it), but rather we must love him exceedingly, and above that
that I am able to say.   Let us hear the apostle, who with a
wonderful goodly grace of speech, with a most excellent, exquisite, and holy example of Christ doth exhort us all to the
shewing of charity to our neighbour, and saith : " If therefore
there be any consolation in Christ, if any comfort of love, if
any fellowship of the Spirit, if any compassion and mercy,
fulfil ye my joy, that ye be like-minded, having the same
love, being of one accord and mind : let nothing be done
through strife or vain-glory, but in meekness let every man
esteem one the other better than himself ; look ye not every
man on his own things, but every man also on the things of
others.   For let the same mind be in you that was in Christ

[4] colligere vagos, Lat.]   [5] Matth. xxv. 35, 36.]

[6] Præcipua virtus est hospitalitas, &c.   Captivorum redemptio
magnum atque præclarum justitiæ munus est. . . . Non minus magnum
justitiæ opus est, pupillos et viduas, destitutos et auxilio indigentes,
tueri atque defendere : quod adeo universis divina lex illa præscribit.
Ægros quoque, quibus defuerit qui assistat, curandos fovendosque
suscipere, summæ humanitatis et magnæ operationis est. . . . Ultimum
illud et maximum pietatis officium est peregrinorum et pauperum
sepultura.—Lactant. Div. Instit. Lib. vi. cap. 12, Opp. Lugd. Bat.
1660. pp. 585—588.]

Jesus; who, being in the form of God, thought it no robbery
to be equal with God, but made himself of no reputation,
taking on him the form of a servant; and made in the likeness of men, and found in figure as a man, he humbled himself, made obedient unto death, even the death of the cross.
Wherefore God also hath highly exalted him, and given
him a name which is above every name, that in the name of
Jesus every knee should bow, of things in heaven, and things
in earth, and things under the earth, and that every tongue
should confess, that the Lord Jesus Christ is the glory of God
the [1]Father[2]." To him alone be honour and power for ever
and ever. Amen.

[1 quod Dominus sit Jesus Christus ad gloriam Dei Patris, Lat.]
[2 Phil. ii. 1—11.]

THE END OF THE FIRST DECADE OF SERMONS.

THE
SECOND DECADE OF SERMONS,

WRITTEN BY

HENRY BULLINGER.

OF LAWS, AND OF THE LAW OF NATURE, THEN OF THE LAWS OF MEN.

THE FIRST SERMON.

THE sum of all laws is the love of God and our neighbour; of which and every part whereof because I have already spoken in my last sermon, the next is, that now also I make a particular discourse of laws, and every part and kind thereof. Let us therefore call to God, who is the cause and beginning of laws, that he through our Lord Jesus Christ will vouchsafe with his Spirit always to direct us in the way of truth and righteousness.

A heathen writer, no base [3] author, I wis, made this definition of law; that it is an especial reason, placed in nature, commanding what is to be done, and forbidding the contrary [4]. And verily the law is nothing but a declaration of God's will, appointing what thou hast to do, and what thou oughtest to leave undone. The beginning and cause of laws is God himself, who is the fountain of all goodness, equity, truth, and righteousness. Therefore all good and just laws come from God himself, although they be, for the most part, published and brought to light by men. Touching the laws of men, we must have a peculiar consideration of them by themselves.

For of laws, some are of God, some of nature, and some of men. As concerning God's law, I will speak of it in my second sermon: at this present I will touch first the law of nature, and then the law of men.

What law is.

The division of laws.

[3 non obscurus, Lat.]
[4 Lex est ratio summa, insita in natura, quæ jubet ea quæ facienda sunt, prohibetque contraria.—Cicero, de Leg. I. 6.]

[BULLINGER.]

13

The law of
nature.

Conscience.

Nature.

The law of nature is an instruction of the conscience, and, as it were, a certain direction placed by God himself in the minds and hearts of men, to teach them what they have to do and what to eschew.   And the conscience, verily, is the knowledge, judgment, and reason of a man, whereby every man in himself, and in his own mind, being made privy to every thing that he either hath committed or not committed, doth either condemn or else acquit himself.   And this reason proceedeth from God, who both prompteth and writeth his judgments in the hearts and minds of men.   Moreover, that which we call nature is the proper disposition or inclination of every thing.   But the disposition of mankind being flatly corrupted by sin, as it is blind, so also is it in all points evil and naughty.   It knoweth not God, it worshippeth not God, neither doth it love the neighbour; but rather is affected with self-love toward itself, and seeketh still for its own advantage.   For which cause the apostle said, "that we by nature are the children of wrath."   Wherefore the law of nature is not called the law of nature, because in the nature and disposition of man there is of or by itself that reason of light exhorting to the best things, and that holy working; but for because God hath imprinted or engraven in our minds some knowledge, and certain general principles of religion, justice, and goodness, which, because they be grafted in us and born together with us, do therefore seem to be naturally in us.

Let us hear the apostle Paul, who beareth witness to this, and saith: "When the Gentiles, which have not the law, do of nature the things contained in the law; they, having not the law, are a law unto themselves; which shew the works of the law[1] written in their hearts, their conscience bearing them witness, and their thoughts accusing one another, or excusing, in that same day, when the Lord shall judge the secrets of men by Jesus Christ according to my gospel[2]."   By two arguments here doth the apostle very evidently prove, that the Gentiles are sinners.   For first of all (lest peradventure they might make this excuse, and say, that they have no law) he sheweth, that they have a law; and that, because they transgress this law, they are become sinners.   For, although they had not the written law

[1] opus legis, Lat.]   [2] Rom. ii. 14—16.]

of Moses, yet notwithstanding they did "by nature the things contained in the law." The office of the law is to disclose the will of God, and to teach thee what thou hast to do and what to leave undone. This have they by nature; that is, this know they by the law of nature. For that which followeth maketh this more plain: "They, when they have no law, are to themselves a law:" that is, they have in themselves that which is written in the law. But in what sort have they it in themselves? This again is made manifest by that which followeth: "For they shew the work of the law written in their hearts." But who is he that writeth in their hearts, but God alone, who is the searcher of all hearts? And what, I pray you, writeth he there? The law of nature, forsooth; the law, I say, itself, commanding good and forbidding evil, so that without the written law, by the instruction of nature, that is, by the knowledge imprinted of God in nature, they may understand what is good and what is evil, what is to be desired and what is to be shunned. By these words of the apostle we do understand, that the law of nature is set against the written law of God; and that therefore it is called the law of nature, because it seemeth to be, as it were, placed or graffed[3] in nature. We understand, that the law of nature, not the written law, but that which is graffed[3] in man, hath the same office that the written law hath; I mean, to direct men, and to teach them, and also to discern betwixt good and evil, and to be able to judge of sin. We understand, that the beginning of this law is not of the corrupt disposition of mankind, but of God himself, who with his finger writeth in our hearts, fasteneth in our nature, and planteth in us a rule to know justice, equity, and goodness.

Then also the apostle maketh his second argument, whereby he proveth the Gentiles to be guilty of sin; and this argument he fetcheth from the witness-bearing of their conscience. For the conscience, being instructed by the law of nature, doth accuse and condemn the evil committed; because this conscience only and alone is instead of a thousand witnesses. And again, it excuseth, that is, it absolveth and acquitteth them, if nothing be committed contrary to the law. But although in this present life we do set light by the judgment of our conscience; yet verily we may not then despise

[3 grafted, 1577.]

13—2

or lightly pass over the conscience's accusations, when the Lord shall come with justice and equity to judge the world. So then by all this it followeth, that all nations are sinners; whom unless the Son of God, the common and only Saviour and deliverer of all the world, do cleanse from their offences, it cannot be but that all nations must needs perish in their sins.

Two espe-
cial points of
the law of
nature.

But now we come again to the law of nature, of which there are two points especially for you to be put in mind of. The first is, Acknowledge God, and worship him : the second is, Keep or maintain society and friendship among men. Touching the first, we have these words of Christ his apostle: "Whatsoever may be known of God is manifest among them" (to wit, among the Gentiles) ; "for God hath shewed it to them. For his invisible things, being understood by his works, through the creation of the world are seen ; that is, both his eternal power and Godhead : so that they are without excuse ; because that, when they knew God, (notwithstanding) they glorified him not as God, neither were thankful[1],"

The Gentiles
knew God.

&c. So then, the Gentiles knew God; yea, they knew whatsoever might be known of God. But what teacher had they, or what master ? They had God to their master. In what order taught he them, or out of what book ? Not out of the written books of Moses, or the prophets; but out of that great and large book of nature. For the things that are not seen of God (in which sort are his everlasting eternity, his virtue, power, majesty, goodness, and Godhead), those he would have to be esteemed of according to the visible things, that is, the things which he hath created. For God's eternal Godhead is known by man's creation, by the continual moving of heaven, and the perpetual course of rivers : for it must needs be, that he is most mighty which sustaineth all these things, which moveth, strengtheneth, and keepeth all things from decay, and which with his beck shakes the whole world. Finally, who doth not see the goodness of him which suffereth the sun to rise upon the good and the evil? But to what intent revealeth he these things to the Gentiles ? To the intent, forsooth, that they may acknowledge him to be God, that they may glorify and worship him as God, and be thankful to such a benefactor. When therefore they do not

[1 Rom. i. 19—21.]

this, they are inexcusable, and perish deservedly for their unbelief and unthankfulness' sake. So then it is manifest, that the law of nature doth expressly teach, that there is a God which is to be acknowledged and reverently worshipped.

Touching the latter of these two especial points (that is, for the preserving of friendship and society among men) the Lord in the Gospel saith: "Whatsoever ye would that men should do to you, do ye the same to them[2]." This sentence did Alexander Severus the Emperor turn and express thus: "Whatsoever thou wouldest not have done to thyself, that do not thou to another." Which saying he loved so well, that he commanded it to be written up in his palace and common houses of office[3]. Moreover, to that general law belong these that follow: "Live honestly: hurt not another: give every man his own[4] : provide things necessary for life, and keep it from distress." *Friendship and society of men to be preserved.*

But now, because the law of nature is made opposite to the written law of God, it is requisite that it be answerable also to the law of God: let us therefore see what the wise men and lawgivers of the Gentiles have left in writing to countervail the ten commandments[5], and how far their writings are answerable to the law of God. *The law of nature answerable to the written law.*

Pythagoras, in St Cyril's first book *contra Julianum*, writeth thus of God: "God verily is one; and he too is not, as some do imagine, without the government of the world; but, being wholly in every place of it, doth view all the generations in the whole compass thereof, and is himself the moderation of all ages, the light of his own virtues, the beginning of all works, the light in heaven, the father of all things, the life and quickening of all things, and lastly, the moving of all the circles[6]." See, here Pythagoras confesseth that there is *I. Of God.*

[2 Matt. vii. 12.]

[3 Clamabat (Alexander) sæpius quod a quibusdam sive Judæis sive Christianis audierat, et tenebat; idque per præconem, cum aliquem emendaret, dici jubebat, *Quod tibi fieri non vis, alteri ne feceris.* Quam sententiam usque adeo dilexit, ut et in palatio et in publicis operibus præscribi juberet.—Æl. Lamprid. in Vit. Alexandri Severi apud Hist. August. Scriptores. Hanov. 1611. pp. 352, 3.]

[4 Honeste vivito; Alterum ne lædito; Suum cuique tribuito. Lat. See Early Writings of Hooper, Parker Soc. ed. page 275, note 2.]

[5 quod respondeat Decalogo, Lat.]

[6 Πυθαγόρας γοῦν φησὶν, Ὁ μὲν Θεὸς εἷς· αὐτὸς δὲ οὐχ, ὥς τινες

but one God, who is the maker, preserver, and governor of
all things, the father of all, and the light and life of all
things.   Zaleucus, in the preface of his laws, writeth as followeth : " It is necessary that all men, which inhabit any city
or region whatsoever, be throughly persuaded that there are
gods ; which is evident to be seen by the contemplation of
heaven and all the world, and by the goodly disposition and
order of that that is therein : for it is not convenient to
think that these are the works of fortune or man's ability.
Then also the gods must be worshipped and honoured, as
they that are the causes of all good things that are done to
us by any manner of means.   Every one, therefore, must do
his best to have his mind purely cleansed from all evil.   For
God is not honoured of a wicked man ; he is not worshipped
with sumptuous cost, neither is he delighted with the sight
of solemn tragedies, as a wicked man is ; but his delight is in
virtue, and in a mind that purposeth to do good works and
righteousness.   Wherefore every one must endeavour himself,
as much as he may, both to do well and will well, if he desire
to have God to his friend[1]," &c.   Cicero, in his second book
de Natura Deorum, saith : " The best worshipping of the
gods, and the most holy and pure religion is, always to
honour them with a pure, perfect, and uncorrupted mind
and voice[2]."

ὑπονοοῦσιν, ἐκτὸς τᾶς διακοσμήσιος· ἀλλ᾿ ἐν αὐτῷ ὅλος ἐν ὅλῳ, τῷ κύκλῳ
ἐπισκοπῶν πάσας γενεάς· ἔστι κρᾶσις ὦν τῶν ὅλων αἰώνων, καὶ φῶς τῶν
αὐτοῦ δυνάμεων καὶ ἔργων, ἀρχὰ πάντων, ἐν οὐρανῷ φωστὴρ, καὶ πάντων
πατὴρ, νοῦς καὶ ψύχωσις τῶν ὅλων κύκλων, πάντων κίνασις.—Cyril.
Alexandr. Contra Julian. Lib. I. Tom. VI. p. 30, ed. Paris. 1638.   See
also Early Writings of Bp Hooper, Parker Soc. ed. p. 285.]

[1 Τοὺς κατοικοῦντας τὴν πόλιν καὶ τὴν χώραν πάντας πρῶτον πεπεῖσθαι
χρὴ καὶ νομίζειν θεοὺς εἶναι, καὶ ἀναβλέποντας ἐς οὐρανὸν καὶ τὸν κόσμον
καὶ τὴν ἐν αὐτοῖς διακόσμησιν καὶ τάξιν· οὐ γὰρ τύχης οὐδ᾿ ἀνθρώπων
εἶναι δημιουργήματα· σέβεσθαι δὲ τούτους καὶ τιμᾶν, ὡς αἰτίους ὄντας
ἀπάντων ἡμῖν ἀγαθῶν, τῶν κατὰ λόγον γιγνομένων. Ἕκαστον οὖν ἔχειν καὶ
παρασκευάζειν δεῖ τὴν αὐτοῦ ψυχὴν πάντων τῶν κακῶν καθαράν· ὡς οὐ
τιμᾶται θεὸς ὑπ᾿ ἀνθρώπου φαύλου, οὐδὲ θεραπεύεται δαπάναις οὐδὲ τραγῳ-
δίαις τῶν ἁλισκομένων, καθάπερ μοχθηρὸς ἄνθρωπος· ἀλλ᾿ ἀρετῇ καὶ προαιρέσει τῶν καλῶν ἔργων καὶ δικαίων. Διὸ ἕκαστον δεῖ εἰς δύναμιν ἀγαθὸν
εἶναι, καὶ πράξει καὶ προαιρέσει, τὸν μέλλοντα ἔσεσθαι θεοφιλῆ.—Zaleucus
ap. Stobæi Florileg. ed. Gaisford. Oxon. 1822.   Vol. II. pp. 197, 8.]

[2 Cultus autem Deorum est optimus, idemque castissimus atque
sanctissimus, plenissimusque pietatis, ut eos semper pura, integra,

Seneca also, in his fifth book *ad Lucil.* saith: "Our usual custom is to teach men how the gods are to be worshipped. Let us give commandment, that on holy days no man set perchers[3] or taper light before the gods; for they are as much delighted with lights, as men half smouldered have pleasure in smoke. Let us forbid these morning greetings, and solemn kneelings at the temple-doors. This more than needing fiddle-faddle smacks somewhat of ambition. He worshippeth God that knoweth God. Let us forbid to bring napkins and rubbers to Jupiter, and to hold a looking-glass to Juno. God seeketh not such service. Why so? Because he himself, forsooth, doth serve and supply all men's necessities. He is present every where, and at hand with all men. Let every man hear therefore how he ought to worship God as he should. He shall never verily be sufficiently clear from troublesome superstitions, unless he in his mind think of God as he should do; that is, that he hath all things, that he giveth all things, and that he bestoweth benefits freely, not looking for any recompence at all. What is the cause that the gods do good? Their nature, forsooth. He is deceived, whosoever thinketh that they either will or possibly can do harm: they can neither take wrong nor yet do wrong: for to do harm and to suffer harm are coupled together. The chiefest and most excellent nature of all is the nature of them which are themselves exempt from peril, and are not by nature hurtful to others. The first point of worship due to the gods, is to believe that there are gods; then to give them the majesty due unto them, and to ascribe to them their goodness, without the which their majesty is none at all; to confess that they are they that govern the world, that they rule all things as their own, that they do generally look to the safeguards of all mankind, and sometime too are careful for peculiar men. They neither do nor have any evil at all. But some they chastise, keep under, and punish sometime by whipping, in hope to make them good. Wilt thou please the gods, and make them thy friends? Be good thy-

incorrupta et mente et voce veneremur.—Cic. de Nat. Deor. Lib. II. 28.]

[3 The larger sort of wax candles, which were usually set upon the altar.—Bailey apud Johnson in voc. See also Calfhill's Answer to Martiall, Parker Soc. ed. p. 300.]

self then.   He hath sufficiently worshipped them, whosoever
hath imitated them in goodness[1]."

The ethnics'
sentences
are in some
places
maimed.   In these words of Seneca, although notable indeed, and
agreeable to true religion, I find default notwithstanding of
two things.   The first is, because not so seldom as once[2] he
maketh mention of gods, when as nevertheless in another
place he doth frankly confess, that God is one in substance
and no more[3].   Neither dare I undertake for him, that he
spake after the manner of the scripture, which calleth God
Elohim, as if you should say " gods," because of the mystery
of the most reverend Trinity[4].   And yet I know very well,

[1 Quomodo sint Dii colendi solet præcipi. Accendere aliquem lucer-
nam Sabbatis prohibeamus, quoniam nec lumine Dii egent, et ne
homines quidem delectantur fuligine. Vetemus salutationibus matutinis
fungi, et foribus assidere templorum. Humana ambitio istis officiis
capitur: Deum colit qui novit. Vetemus lintea et strigiles Jovi ferre, et
speculum tenere Junoni. Non quærit ministros Deus. Quidni? Ipse
generi humano ministrat. Ubique et omnibus præsto est. Audiat
licet quemadmodum se gerere in sacrificiis debeat, quam procul resilire
a molestiis ac superstitionibus, nunquam satis profectum erit, nisi
qualem debet Deum mente conceperit, omnia habentem, omnia tribu-
entem, beneficia gratis dantem. Quæ causa est Diis benefaciendi?
Natura. Errat si quis putat illos nocere velle ; non possunt : nec acci-
pere injuriam queunt nec facere : lædere enim lædique conjunctum
est. Summa illa ac pulcherrima omnium natura, quos periculo exemit,
nec periculosos quidem fecit. Primus est Deorum cultus Deos credere : deinde reddere illis majestatem suam, reddere bonitatem, sine
qua nulla majestas est; scire illos esse qui præsident mundo; qui
universa vi sua temperant, qui humani generis tutelam gerunt, interdum curiosi singulorum. Hi nec dant malum, nec habent. Ceterum
castigant quosdam, et coercent, et irrogant pœnas, et aliquando specie
[Bulling. text. *spe*] boni puniunt. Vis Deos propitiare? Bonus esto.
Satis illos coluit, quisquis imitatus est.—Senec. Opp. Par. 1607.
Epist. ad Lucil. 95, p. 427.]

[2 Subinde, Lat.]

[3 Bullinger quotes the passsge (from de Benef. lib. iv. cap. 8) in
his treatise *de Origine Erroris*, cap. viii. p. 36. Tigur. 1539.]

[4 Hoc ipsum nomen (Elohim) non semel in sacris jungitur verbis
singularibus, quemadmodum mox ab ipso Genesis initio legis, In
principio creavit Dii cœlum et terram. Nam ברא, *Bara*, creavit,
singulare est, אלהים, *Elohim*, plurale; notaturque Trinitatis mysterium:
ut sit sensus, Deus ille trinus in principio creavit cœlum et terram.
Verum hac de re docte disputavit Petrus Galatinus.—Bullinger. de Orig.
Error. Tigur. 1539, cap. i. p. 5.]

that learned men of our religion have gone about to prove, even by the testimonies of the Gentiles, that the Gentiles also did acknowledge the mystery of the Trinity.   The second is, that (for as much as I can see) Seneca, with the other wise men of the Gentiles, doth not expressly set down and teach the sound trust and confidence that should be had in God.

Moreover, there was not among the Romans any image of God in any temple that they had for the space of one hundred and seventy years after Rome was builded.   For Plutarch, in the life of Numa Pompilius, saith : " As for the decrees that Numa made touching images of the immortal gods, how like are they almost in every point to the doctrine of Pythagoras !   Pythagoras thought that that first beginning (he meaneth God) is not subject to sense or any troublesome affection, but is an invisible and uncreated Spirit.   And on the other side, Numa forbade the Romans to think that the shape of God hath the likeness of a man, or else the figure or simi-litude of any living thing.   Neither was there among them of the old time any painted or fashioned image of God : but in the first hundred and seventy years they builded temples, and set up houses for service to be done in unto the gods, but bodily similitudes they did not make ; even as if it were a detestable thing to liken the better unto the worse, and as though God could not otherwise be perceived, but by reason and knowledge only [5]."   The very same doth Marcus Varro testify touching the Romans, in the thirty-first chapter of Augustine's book *de Civitate Dei*.   For he saith, that " the Romans worshipped the gods a hundred and seventy years without any images at all ;" and going further he addeth this ; " Which if it had endured till now, the gods verily should have been more purely reverenced.   Neither doubteth he to conclude that place with these words, and to say, that

2.
The Gentiles against idols.

[5] Ἔστι δὲ καὶ τὰ περὶ τῶν ἀφιδρυμάτων νομοθετήματα παντάπασιν ἀδελφὰ τῶν Πυθαγόρου δογμάτων.   Οὔτε γὰρ ἐκεῖνος αἰσθητὸν, ἢ παθητὸν, ἀόρατον δὲ καὶ ἀκήρατον καὶ νοητὸν ὑπελάμβανεν εἶναι τὸ πρῶτον· οὗτός τε διεκώλυσεν ἀνθρωποειδῆ καὶ ζωόμορφον εἰκόνα θεοῦ Ῥωμαίους νομίζειν.   Οὐδ' ἦν παρ' αὐτοῖς οὔτε γραπτὸν οὔτε πλαστὸν εἶδος θεοῦ πρότερον· ἀλλ' ἐν ἑκατὸν ἑβδομήκοντα τοῖς πρώτοις ἔτεσι ναοὺς μὲν οἰκοδομούμενοι, καὶ καλιάδας ἱερὰς ἱστῶντες, ἄγαλμα δ' οὐδὲν ἔμμορφον ποιούμενοι διετέλουν· ὡς οὔτε ὅσιον ἀφομοιοῦν τὰ βελτίονα τοῖς χείροσιν, οὔτ' ἐφάπτεσθαι θεοῦ δυνατὸν ἄλλως ἢ νοήσει.—Plutarch. in Vit. Numæ. Lond. 1729. Tom. I. p. 141.]

they which first brought in images among the people, diminished devout fear, and augmented foolish error, in the cities where they governed; wisely judging thereby that the gods may easily be despised under the fondness of imagined likenesses[1]," &c.

3.
The name of God highly esteemed.

Now, as concerning the name of God, how much the Gentiles did set by it, it is evident to be seen by the great religion that they had in taking or giving an oath. There is extant to be seen a notable discourse of this in the eighteenth chapter of the seventh book of Gellius; where among the rest this is to be found written: "An oath among the Romans hath been had and kept holy and uncorrupted: which is declared by many laws and customs[2]." And if so be that among the Gentiles any man should speak opprobriously against God, he was reputed faulty, most sharply to be punished.

4.
The Gentiles keepers of religion.

Furthermore, the Gentiles had their religion[3], their festival-days, ceremonies, and priests of their religion. Melchizedech and Jethro were notable priests of the Gentiles. And although Paul doth flatly say, that "the things which the Gentiles offered were not offered to God, but to devils[4];" yet notwithstanding, because they had in reverence religion and holy ceremonies, they did thereby declare, that God had printed in the minds of men a familiar knowledge of reverence[5] and religion, which afterward is corrupted by false doctrine and wrong opinions touching God and his holy service.

5.
The honouring of parents.

For the honouring of parents and magistrates, for the bringing up of children, and touching the duty of children, there are excellent precepts and sentences of the wiser sort of Gentiles. Hierocles, among his other writings, saith: " I

[1 Dicit (Varro) etiam, antiquos Romanos plusquam annos centum et septuaginta Deos ine simulacro coluisse. Quod si adhuc, inqui mansisset, castius Dii observarentur.—Nec dubitat eum locum ita con cludere, ut dicat, Qui primi simulacra Deorum populis posuerunt, eo civitatibus suis et metum dempsisse et errorem addidisse, prudente existimans Deos facile posse in simulacrorum stoliditate contemni —Augustin. Opp. Par. 1531. Tom. v. fol. 57.]

[2 Jusjurandum apud Romanos inviolate sancteque habitum ser vatumque. Id et moribus legibusque multis ostenditur.—Aul. Gell Noct. Attic. Lib. VII. cap. 18. init.]

[3 sua sacra, Lat.]   [4 1 Cor. x. 20.]
[5 cultus, Lat.]

ny man shall call his parents certain second or earthly gods,
e shall not do amiss; considering that, for the nigh affinity
etwixt us, they ought to be (if it be lawful so to say) more
o be honoured of us than the gods themselves.   And it is
ecessary to be persuaded, that we must with a continual
eadiness of mind do our endeavour to repay the benefits re-
eived at their hands with the like again.   And although we
hall do very much for them, yet notwithstanding all will be
oo little in comparison of that we ought to do[6]."   And so
orth as followeth.   For sooner will the time fail me, than
hat I can conveniently rehearse this, and the like belonging
ereunto, out of heathen writers: neither did I purpose to
eckon up all.

Against murder, wrong, and injury, very severe laws have
een made by the Gentiles.   From them also came the law
alled *Lex Julia*, against adultery and detestable lusts[7].   They
rdained excellent laws for the contracting and observing of
natrimony.   And the word of truth doth expressly declare,
hat the Chananites were wiped away because of their incest
n marriage and horrible lusts. Levit. viii.   Lycurgus also,
Solon, and the Romans, did publish laws for the restraint of
utrageous expenses in riotous persons[8].   And here, of pur-
ose, I overpass that which is naturally engraffed in all men,
he begetting (I mean) and nourishing of their issue and
ffspring.

6.
Murder and adultery.

Against theft, deceit, and usury, for the lawful getting
nd possessing of goods, for the distributing of riches, and

8.
Theft.

[6 Λεκτέον περὶ τούτων (i. e. γονέων), οὓς δευτέρους καὶ ἐπιγείους τινὰς
εοὺς εἰπὼν οὐχ ἁμάρτοι τὶς ἕνεκά γε τῆς ἐγγύτητος, εἰ θέμις εἰπεῖν, καὶ
εῶν ἡμῖν τιμιωτέρους.   Προλαβεῖν δὲ ἀναγκαῖόν ἐστι, ὡς μόνον μέτρον
ῆς πρὸς αὐτοὺς εὐχαριστίας ἡ διηνεκὴς καὶ ἀνένδοτος προθυμία πρὸς τὸ
μείβεσθαι τὰς εὐεργεσίας αὐτῶν· ἐπείτοι γε πολὺ καταδεέστερα, κἂν πάνυ
ολλὰ πράξωμεν ὑπὲρ αὐτῶν.—Hierocl. ap. Stobæi Floril. ed. Gaisford.
Oxon. 1822. Vol. III. p. 125.]

[7 This word is substituted for that used by the translator.—In
he time of Augustus a lex was enacted (probably about B.C. 17)
ntitled *Lex Julia de adulteriis coercendis*.   The chief provisions of
his law may be collected from the Digest (48 tit. 5), and from Paulus
Sentent. Recept. ii. tit. 26. ed. Schultius).   Smith's Dict. of Gr. and
Rom. Antiq. sub voc. Adulterium.]

[8 See Smith's Dict. of Greek and Rom. Antiq. sub voc. Sum-
uariæ leges; and Plutarch's lives of Lycurgus and Solon.]

for bargaining, the Gentiles have very commendable laws
That saying of Ausonius is notably known:

> If greedy gaping after gain
> To get another groat
> Makes usury dispatch apace
> To cut the poor man's throat[1].

9.
Lies.
False wit-
nesses.

All the Gentiles in their writings do worthily commend
the truth; and do, by all means they can, cry out on and
condemn lying, slandering, and all such kind of knavery.
The law of the twelve tables is, that a false witness should be

A hill in
Rome.
Catana, a
town in
Sicily.

cast headlong down from the top of Tarpey[2]. Charondas
Catanæus, among other excellent sayings of his own, hath
this also: "Let every one," saith he, "love honesty and
truth, and hate dishonesty and lying; for they are the
marks whereby virtue is known from vice. We must therefore begin with children, while as yet they are little ones,
and inure ourselves to chastise them if they delight to lie,
and to make much of them for telling the truth; that thereby
the best and fruitfullest branch of virtue may be graffed in
every several mind, and so be turned as it were into their
nature[3]."

10.
Concupis-
cence.

The wiser sort of the Gentiles do utterly condemn concupiscence and evil affections: which the poet in his satires
blameth as the root of all mischief, where he saith:

> From thence almost comes every cause
> Of mischief; for no vice,
> That reigns in man, so many times
> Could frantic heads entice
> To mingle poison privily
> To stop another's breath,

[1]   si turpia lucra
Fœnoris, et velox inopes usura trucidat.
                    Auson. Idyll. xv. ed. Lond. 1823. Vol. ii. p. 593. P.]

[2 Si falsum testimonium dicassit, saxo dejicitor.—See also A.
Gellius, Noct. Attic. Lib. xx. 1, 14; and Works of Becon, Parker Soc.
ed. Vol. i. p. 391.]

[3 Τιμάτω δὲ ἕκαστος τὸ καλὸν καὶ τὸ ἀληθὲς, καὶ μισείτω τὸ αἰσχρὸν
καὶ τὸ ψεῦδος· ταῦτα γὰρ ἀρετῆς σημεῖα καὶ κακίας. Διὸ χρὴ συνεθίζειν
ἐκ παίδων, κολάζοντας μὲν τοὺς φιλοψευδεῖς, φιλοῦντας δὲ τοὺς φιλαλήθεις,
ἵν' ἐμφυσιῶται ἑκάστῳ τὸ κάλλιστον καὶ σπερματωδέστατον τῆς ἀρετῆς.
—Charondas ap. Stobæi Florileg. Vol. ii. p. 220.]

Or else in armour openly
   To work his rival's death,
   As beastly raging lust hath done[4].

So then by all this we may easily gather, that even in the Gentiles' minds also were graven a certain knowledge of God, and some precepts whereby they knew what to desire, and what to eschew: which notwithstanding they did corrupt, and make somewhat misty, with the evil affections and corrupt judgments of the flesh. For which cause God also, beside the law of nature, did ordain other means to declare his will; I mean, the lively tradition of the fathers, the answers of angels, the voices of prophets[5], wonderful miracles, and written laws which he published by wise and very devout patriarchs[6]. All these did God ordain to be a help to the law of nature. Whatsoever therefore is to be found among the Gentiles agreeable to truth and honesty, that is to be referred to God, the author of all goodness: and on the other side, whatsoever is contrary to the truth, that must be attributed to the corrupt nature and evil affections of mankind.

In all this that I have said ye have to note especially, that here I speak of knowledge, and not of ability. The knowledge of the law is, after a sort, manifest in the Gentiles; but the consent, the will, and ability to fulfil the law is weak, and not easy to be found in them[7]. Wherefore, as we affirm that the understanding of the law must be inspired from heaven; so also we say that ability to fulfil the law must of necessity be given of God above. Nature without grace is herein without force and effect. But whereas some of the Gentiles bear the name and praise of righteousness (as Melchizedech, Job, Jethro, and other more), they have that not of their own ability, but of the grace of God: as by the history of Job we may evidently gather by probable arguments. Wherefore, if any of the Gentiles be saved, then are they

Nature, without grace, of none effect.

[4   Inde fere scelerum causæ, nec plura venena
            Miscuit, aut ferro grassatur sæpius ullum
            Humanæ mentis vitium, quam sæva cupido
            Immodici census.
                                 Juvenal. Sat. XIV. 173—6.]

[5 *Oracula* is Bullinger's one word, which the translator has rendered, *the voices of prophets.*]

[6 per homines sapientissimos et religiosissimos, Lat.]

[7 et infirma est et implicatissima, Lat.]

saved, not by the works of nature, or their own deserts, bu
by the mercy of God in our Lord Jesus Christ.

Moreover, the law of nature is not graffed of God in man
to the intent that it, without grace and Christ, should work
man's salvation; but rather, to teach us what is good and wha
is evil, thereby to convince us to be sinners, and without ex
cuse before the Lord. Paul verily, proving that the Gentile
by the law of nature are guilty of sin, as well as the Jews by
Moses' law, doth shew that in Christ alone, the Son of God
is justification, life, and all good else. Thus far touching th
law of nature.

Laws of
men.

The laws of men (for my promise was, that in my secon
part I would speak of them) are those which are by me
ordained and published to the preservation of the common
weal and[1] church of God. Touching these they are of diver

Laws of
policy.

kinds. For there are politic laws, there are ecclesiastica
laws, and men's traditions. Politic laws are those which th
magistrate, according to the state of times, places, and per
sons, doth ordain for the preserving of public peace and civi
lity. Of this sort there are an innumerable company o
examples in the civil law and constitutions of the emperor
especially of Justinian. All which ought to come as near a
may be to the laws of God and nature, and not to be con
trary to them, or to have any smack of impiety or crue
tyranny. To such laws St Peter willeth us to obey, when
he saith: "Submit yourselves unto all manner ordinance o
man for the Lord's sake; whether it be to the king, as havin
the pre-eminence, or unto rulers, as they that are sent by
him for the punishment of evil doers, but for the praise o
them that do well." For although the apostle by ordinances
or men's constitutions, doth inclusively mean the kings an
magistrates themselves, as in the second clause of the sentenc
he doth immediately declare; yet, notwithstanding, he dot
bid us therefore obey good laws and just, because by them
the magistrates support and rule the commonweal. More
over, just and honest politic laws are an help to love an
tranquillity; do preserve fellowly society among men[3]; d

[1] vel, Lat. or.]
[2] See Schleusner, Lex. N. T. in voc. κτίσις. §. 5.]
[3] hominum societatem, Lat.]

defend the good, bring inordinate persons into better order; and lastly, do not make a little only to the setting forward of religion, but do also abrogate evil customs, and utterly banish unlawful mischiefs. Hereof we have examples in the deeds of Nabuchodonosor, Cyrus, Darius, Artaxerxes, and other princes more. But touching the magistrate's power, his laws, and office, I will speak of them in another place.

Ecclesiastical laws are those which, being taken out of the word of God, and applied to the state of men, times, and places, are received and have authority in the church among the people of God. I call these ecclesiastical laws, and not traditions of men, because, being taken out of the holy scriptures, and not invented or brought to light by the wit of man, they are used of that church which heareth the voice of the Shepherd alone, and knoweth not a stranger's tongue. The congregation cometh together to hear the word of God, and unto common prayers, at morning, at evening, and at such appointed hours as are most convenient for every place and every people; and that the church holdeth as a law. The church hath solemn prayer times[4], holy days, and fasting days, which it doth keep by certain laws. The church, at certain times, in a certain place and appointed order, doth celebrate the sacraments according to the laws and received custom of the church. The church baptizeth infants; it forbiddeth not women to come to the Lord's supper: and that it holdeth as a law. The church, by judges conveniently appointed, doth judge in causes of matrimony, and hath certain laws to direct them in such cases. But it deriveth these, and all other like to these, out of the scriptures; and doth for edification apply them to the estate of men, times, and places: so that in divers churches ye may see some diversity indeed, but no discord or repugnancy at all.

Ecclesiastical laws.

Furthermore, ecclesiastical laws have their measure and certain marks, beyond which they may not pass; to wit, that nothing be done or received contrary or differing in any jot from the word of God, sounding against charity and comeliness, either in little or much; that lastly, this rule of the apostle may be effectually observed, " Let all things be done decently, according unto order, and to the edification of the church[5]." If therefore any man shall go about, under a

Superstitious laws.

[4 supplicationes, Lat.]   [5 1 Cor. xiv. 3, 40.]

coloured pretence of ecclesiastical laws, to bring in, and pop
into the mouths of the godly[1], any superstitious, busy[2], and
unseemly traditions of men, which withal do differ from the
scriptures; their part shall be, first to try that deceit of theirs
by the rule of God's word, and then to reject it.

Men's tradi-
tions.

There remain now the traditions of men, which have
their beginning, are made and invented, of men, at their own
choice; of some foolish intent, or some fond affection of mankind; contrary or without the holy scriptures: of which sort
you shall find an infinite number of examples; I mean, the
sects, the dominion[3], and single life of spiritual men, the
rites and sundry fashioned customs used in their church.
Touching all which the Lord in the gospel, citing the prophet Esay, saith: "Why transgress ye the Lord's commandment for your own tradition? Ye hypocrites, rightly did
Esaias prophesy of you, where he saith, This people cometh
nigh unto me with their mouth, and with their lips they
honour me, but their heart is far from me: but they worship
me in vain, teaching doctrines the precepts of men[4]." The
blessed martyr Cyprian, alluding to these words of Christ,
Epistolarum, Lib. I. Ep. 8, saith: "It is corrupt, wicked,
and robbery to the glory of God, whatsoever is ordained by
the giddy madness of men's heads, to the violating of God's
disposition. Depart as far as may be from the infective con-
tagiousness of such fellows, and seek by flight to shun their
talk, as warily as an eating canker or infecting pestilence;
for the Lord forewarneth and telleth you, that they are blind
leaders of the blind[5]." Paul also in his epistle to Titus saith:
"Rebuke them sharply, that they may be sound in the faith;
not taking heed to Jewish fables, and commandments of men
turning from the truth." I do of purpose here let pass the
words of Paul in his second chapter to the Colossians, because
the place is known of all men.

[1 piis obtrudere, Lat.]   [2 operosas, Lat.]

[3 regnum, Lat.]

[4 Matt. xv. 7—9. docentes doctrinas præcepta hominum, Lat.
Erasmus', not the Vulgate, rendering.]

[5 Adulterum est, impium est, sacrilegum est, quodcunque humano
furore instituitur, ut dispositio divina violetur. Procul ab hujusmodi
hominum contagione discedite, et sermones eorum velut cancer et
pestem fugiendo vitate, præmonente Domino et dicente: Cæci sunt
duces cæcorum.—Cypr. Opp. Ep. 43, pag. 83, Oxon. 1682.]

I will not trouble you, dearly beloved, with too large and busy[6] an exposition hereof. For I suppose that this little that I have said, touching the laws of nature and of men, (I mean laws politic, ecclesiastical, and mere traditions of men,) are sufficient to the attentive and faithful hearers, who at their coming home do more diligently think of every point by themselves, and also read the places of scripture often cited by me, and devoutly expounded[7]. The Lord for his mercy grant, that we do never despise the admonitions of nature's law graffed in our hearts, nor yet be entangled in men's traditions; but that we, in walking lawfully in upright politic laws and holy ecclesiastical ordinances, may serve the Lord: to whom be all glory, honour and dominion, for ever and ever   Amen.

OF GOD'S LAW, AND OF THE TWO FIRST COMMANDMENTS OF THE FIRST TABLE[8].

THE SECOND SERMON.

THE law of God, openly published and proclaimed by the Lord our God himself, setteth down ordinary rules for us to know what we have to do, and what to leave undone, requiring obedience, and threatening utter destruction to disobedient rebels. This law is divided into the moral, ceremonial, and judicial laws: all which parts, and every point whereof, Moses hath very exquisitely written, and diligently expounded. The moral law is that which teacheth men manners, and layeth down before us the shape of virtue[9]; declaring therewithal how great righteousness, godliness, obedience, and perfectness God looketh for at the hands of us mortal men. The ceremonial laws are they which are given concerning the order

What the law of God is.

The moral law.

The ceremonial law.

[6] operosiore, Lat.]
[7] ac religiose excussis, Lat. This refers to the *hearers*, and not to the *preacher*. The words should be rendered,—and devoutly weigh and test them.]
[8] seu Decalogi, Lat. omitted.]
[9] virtutum formas, Lat.]

[BULLINGER.]   14

of holy and ecclesiastical rites and ceremonies, and also touching the ministers and things assigned to the ministery and other holy uses.   Last of all, the judicial laws give rules concerning matters to be judged of between man and man, for the preservation of public peace, equity, and civil honesty. Touching the two latter of these, I will speak of them in place convenient.   At this time I mean to discourse upon the moral law.

The judicial law.

The law was even before Moses' time.   First of all, therefore, let no man think, that before Moses' time there was no law, and that the law was by Moses first of all published.   For the self-same especial points of the moral law, which Moses setteth down in the ten commandments, were very well known to the patriarchs, even from the beginning of the world.   For they worshipped the one true God alone for their God, whom they reverenced, and called upon him.   Jacob took away with him the Syrian idols of Laban out of his house[1], and hid them in Bethel under an oak or terebinth tree, which was nigh to Sichem[2].   Abraham, in taking an oath, used always a reverend fear, and a spiced conscience[3]; whereby it followeth, that to him the name of the Lord was holy, and not lightly taken[4].   All the holy fathers did both diligently and devoutly solemnize and observe holy rites and sacrifices.   Cham hath his father's curse, because he did unreverently behave himself toward his father. Cain is reproved for murdering his brother.   Noe giveth commandment not to shed blood.   Joseph is highly commended for refusing to lie with another man's wife; I mean, the wife of his master.   Ruben is rebuked, because he did with incest defile his father's bed.   Jacob was not angry without a cause with Laban his father-in-law, when he suspected him of theft.   All the patriarchs have utterly condemned liars and false witnesses, as well as evil lusts and concupiscence.   Wherefore the patriarchs ever, from the beginning of the world even until Moses' time, were not without the precepts of the ten commandments, although they had them not graven in tables or written in parchments.   For the

[1 aufert e sua familia, Lat.   The translator misrepresents Bullinger's meaning by rendering,—took away *with him*.]

[2 Gen. xxxv. 4.]

[3 sacrosancta erat jurisjurandi religio Abrahamo, Lat.]

[4 celebre, Lat.]

Lord with his finger writ them in their hearts[5], which the
lively tradition of the fathers did exquisitely garnish and reverently teach. The law is every where the same, and the
will of God is always one, because God is but one and is
never changed. Nevertheless, the commandments were first
of all set down in tables by God, who was the beginner and
writer of them ; and after that again were written into books
by Moses.

Likewise also the old and holy patriarchs, that were
before Moses, did not want the ceremonial and judicial laws.
For they had their priests, I say, their fathers of every
kindred or household ; they had their ceremonies, their altars
and sacrifices ; they had their solemn assemblies, and purifi-
cations. They had their laws for succession in heritage, for
the division and possession of goods, for bargaining and contracts, and for the punishing of evil doers. All which Moses
gathered together into a certain number of decreed laws ;
setting down many things more plainly than they were before,
and ordaining many things which the patriarchs were either
altogether without, or else had used in another order : of
which sort were the tabernacle, the holy vessels, the ark of
the covenant, the table, the candlestick, the altar for burnt-
offerings and for incense, the Levitical priesthood, the holy
vestments, with the feasts and holy-days, and whatsoever else
is like to this : all which verily are abrogated by Christ, as
in place convenient I mean to declare. But for because
manners cannot consist, if the ten commandments be broken,
therefore the moral law, although it have properly the name
of a law, is notwithstanding not abrogated or broken[6]. For
the ten commandments are the very absolute and everlasting
rule of true righteousness and all virtues, set down for all
places, men, and ages, to frame themselves by. For the sum
of the ten commandments is this, to shew our love to God,
and one love another ; and this doth the Lord require at all
times, and every where, of all kind of men[7].

The patriarchs before Moses had the ceremonial and judicial laws.

The moral law endureth still.

[5 See above, page 46.]

[6 ut proprie legis nomen obtinuit, ita nunquam abrogatur, Lat.]

[7 Porro Decalogus significat librum seu expositionem et volumen
decem capitum præceptorum vel articulorum, Lat. omitted by the
translator. Moreover the Decalogue means a book, or exposition and
collection, of commandments under ten chief heads.]

The majesty and dignity of the moral law. Moreover, this is to be noted touching the dignity of the moral law contained in the ten commandments; that, whereas all the ceremonial and judicial laws were revealed of God to Moses by the angels, and by Moses to the people; and that again by Moses, at God's commandment, they were inserted into written books; yet notwithstanding the moral law of the ten commandments was not revealed by man, or any means of man, but by God himself at the Mount Sina: who there, among other mighty and marvellous wonders, did openly, in a public and innumerable assembly of men and angels, rehearse them word for word, as they are now to be seen. Furthermore, they were written not by the hand of Moses, but with the finger of God, in tables, not made of matter easy to be dissolved[1], but made of stone to endure for ever. Those tables also were kept, as the most precious treasure, in that ark, which of the tables of the covenant (containing in them the chief articles of the eternal league) was named the ark of

Sanctum sanctorum, the most holy place in the temple of God. the covenant: which ark again was laid up in the holy of holiest. All which circumstances tend to nothing else, but to commend unto us the excellency of the ten commandments, and to warn us to reverence that God which published this moral law, as him that is the Lord of heaven and earth, and which at his own will and pleasure doth order the disposition of all the elements against disobedient rebels. These circumstances also do admonish us, that even now, in our time also, we have to esteem of the ten commandments, as of the dearest jewels to be found in all the world. For the holy reliques, that are remaining in the church of Christ, are the ten commandments, the apostles' creed, the Lord's prayer, and lastly, the whole contents of the sacred bible[2]. Touching the proclamation or first edition of the ten commandments, we have a wonderful large discourse of Moses, Exod. xix. and Deut. iv. and v. chap.

Two tables of God's law. Now the tables, whereinto the ten commandments of God's law be disposed, are in number two; whereof the first containeth four commandments, and the latter six. For the last commandment, which some divide into twain, is in very deed

[1 non cereas, Lat. not of wax.]

[2 Cf. Bullinger's Comment. in 2 Epist. Petri, cap. i. 12—15. p. 59. (published 1534) and Argument. Epist. ad Galat. ad finem. p. 340. (published 1535).

but one alone and undivided[3]. For first the Lord doth
generally command and say, "Thou shalt not covet:" and
then he descendeth particularly, and doth by enumeration
reckon up the things that we must not covet; to wit, our
neighbour's wife, his house, his lands, his cattle, and his substance. Beside that too, this doth argue that it is so, because,
according to the Hebrew disposition, this commandment is
altogether one whole verse, not divided into twain[4]. With
this division of ours agree Joseph. *Antiq.* Lib. iii. cap. 5[5];
Origenes *in Exod.* Hom. 8[6]; Ambros. *in* vi. *cap. Epist. ad
Ephes.*[7] But the Master of Sentences, having divided this last
commandment into twain, doth therefore place in the first
table three commandments and no more[8]. He did, perad-

He putteth
three in the
first table, and
seven in the
last, which
added toge-
ther do make
up ten.

[3 Cf. Calvin. Instit. Lib. ii. cap. 8, §. 12. Becon's Works, Parker
Soc. ed. Vol. ii. pp. 59, 60.]

[4 Exod. xx. 17.]

[5 Μωϋσῆς (τοὺς λόγους τοῦ Θεοῦ) ἐν ταῖς δύο πλαξὶν γεγραμμένους
κατέλιπεν ...... Διδάσκει μὲν οὖν ἡμᾶς ὁ πρῶτος λόγος, ὅτι Θεός ἐστιν εἷς,
καὶ τοῦτον δεῖ σέβεσθαι μόνον· ὁ δὲ δεύτερος κελεύει, μηδενὸς εἰκόνα ζώου
ποιήσαντας προσκυνεῖν· ὁ τρίτος δέ, ἐπὶ μηδενὶ φαύλῳ τὸν Θεὸν ὀμνύναι· ὁ δὲ
τέταρτος, παρατηρεῖν τὰς ἑβδομάδας, ἀναπαυομένους ἀπὸ παντὸς ἔργου· ὁ δὲ
πέμπτος, γονεῖς τιμᾶν· ὁ δὲ ἕκτος, ἀποσχέσθαι φόνου· ὁ δὲ ἕβδομος, μὴ
μοιχεύειν· ὁ δὲ ὄγδοος, μὴ κλοπὴν δρᾶν· ὁ δὲ ἔνατος, μὴ ψευδομαρτυρεῖν·
ὁ δὲ δέκατος, μηδενὸς ἀλλοτρίου ἐπιθυμίαν λαμβάνειν.—Joseph. Antiq.
Jud. Lib. iii. capp. 4 and 5, Amst. 1726. Tom. i. p. 129.]

[6 Hæc omnia simul nonnulli putant unum esse mandatum. Quod
si ita putetur, non complebitur decem numerus mandatorum ....
Est ergo primum mandatum, Non erunt tibi Dei alii præter me.
Secundum vero, Non facies tibi idolum, &c.—Origen. Opp. ed. Bene-
dict. Par. 1733. Tom. ii. p. 157.]

[7 Quia prima quatuor mandata ad Deum pertinent, hæc in prima
tabula contineri subintelliguntur; cetera ad hominem .... Hæc
sex mandata in secunda tabula videntur scripta, quorum primum est,
Honora patrem et matrem, &c.—Ambros. Opp. ed. Bened. Par. 1690.
Tom. ii. Append. p. 249. Comment. in Ep. ad Ephes. cap. vi. verse
3.—But these Commentaries are generally admitted not to be the
work of Ambrose. See James, on the Corruption of Scripture, Councils, and Fathers, Lond. 1843. p. 26.]

[8 Habet decalogus decem præcepta... quæ sic sunt distributa, ut
tria quæ sunt in prima tabula pertineant ad Deum ...... septem quæ
sunt in secunda tabula ad dilectionem proximi. Primum in prima
tabula est, Non habebis deos alienos. Non facies tibi sculptile, &c.
Hæc Origenes dicit esse duo mandata, sed Augustinus unum.—Pet.
Lombard. Lib. iii. Distinct. 37. Par. 1575. fol. 293.—The title of

venture, follow Augustine herein, who, *Quæst. in Exod.* 71, and *Epistola ad Januarium* 119[1], doth also reckon up but three commandments of the first table alone; which he did in respect of the mystical Trinity. And yet, this notwithstanding, he doth not overslip the commandment for abandoning and not worshipping of images; for, undoubtedly, he had always in his mind those words of the Lord in the gospel, where he saith: "Verily I say unto you, though heaven and earth do pass, one jot or tittle of the law shall not pass, till all be fulfilled. Whosoever, therefore, shall break one of the least of these commandments, and shall teach men so, he shall be called the least in the kingdom of heaven." The same Augustine again, in *Quæstionibus Veteris et Novi Testamenti,* Lib. i. cap. 7, maketh four commandments of the first table, and six of the second[2]. And again, he differeth not much from the same order in his third book *ad Bonifacium, &c.*[3]

What the two tables of the law do contain.

Now touching these commandments, the Lord hath divided them into two several orders or tables because of the several difference of matters handled in either of them. For the first of the two appertaineth to God, the second unto man. The first teacheth us what we have to think concerning God, and the

---

Distinct. 40 is, De sexto et septimo præcepto secundæ tabulæ; and there the *sixth* commandment is, Non desiderabis uxorem proximi tui; and the *seventh,* Non concupisces domum proximi tui, &c. fol. 300.]

[1 Quæritur, decem præcepta legis quemadmodum dividenda sint. ... Mihi tamen videntur congruentius accipi tria illa, et ista septem, quoniam Trinitatem videntur illa, quæ ad Deum pertinent, insinuare diligentius intuentibus.—August. Quæst. super Exod. Opp. ed. Par. 1531. Tom. iv. col. 32.—Hinc est quod etiam in tribus primis præceptis decalogi, quæ ad Deum pertinent (cetera enim septem ad proximum pertinent, id est, ad hominem, quia in duobus præceptis tota lex pendet), tertium ibi de observatione Sabbati positum est: ut in primo præcepto Patrem intelligamus, ubi prohibetur coli aliqua in figmentis hominum Dei similitudo ... ne quisquam Filium Dei verbum ... putaret esse creaturam, sequitur aliud præceptum, Non accipies in vanum nomen Dei tui. Spiritus autem sanctus, in quo nobis illa requies tribuitur, &c.—Id. Ep. Januar. 119. Tom. ii. col. 110.]

[2 Hæc quatuor verba sunt de decem; ista ad Deum proprie pertinent. Hæc sunt in prima tabula scripta: deinde in secunda tabula hæc (6) continentur.—Tom. iv. fol. 150.]

[3 Tom. vii. fol. 185. On this subject of the division of the Decalogue, see also Early Writings of Hooper, Parker Soc. ed. pages 349—351; and Calvin. Instit. Lib. ii. cap. 8. §. 12.]

worship due unto him; that is, it teacheth us the perfect way to live uprightly and holily in the sight of God. The second is the rule whereby we have to learn our duty toward our neighbour; which also teacheth us humanity, directing us in the way to live peaceably and civilly one with another. And in these two tables are so nearly contained all and every duty looked for at men's hands, that there cannot so much as one jot be added more by all the wise men of the world, concerning a godly life and civil behaviour, which is not contained in these ten commandments.

The first commandment of the ten hath the Lord himself expressly spoken in these very words that follow: " I am the Lord thy God, which brought thee out of the land of Egypt, out of the house of bondage: thou shalt have none other gods before me." This commandment standeth of two branches; the very first whereof also containeth divers matters. For first of all, God doth simply offer himself to us, and precisely set down what he will be to us-ward, thereby declaring what he is to all men[4]. Whereupon we again do gather what he, on the other side, doth look for at our hands, and what our duty is to him. Thirdly and last of all, he addeth an evident proof of that, where he said that he is our God.

The first commandment.

In the beginning he crieth out and saith: " I am the Lord thy God." Wherein he declareth what he is, and what he will be unto all men. These words are like to the words of the covenant which God made with Abraham, and in Abraham with all faithful believers: " I am," saith the Lord, " a strong God, and I am Schaddai;" as who should say, *Saturnus a saturando*[5], which is, " to fill." For God is the abundant fulness[6] that satisfieth all men and all things: he

The sense is this, I am a strong God, and the fulness of all things.

[4 exponit nobis qualis sit erga homines, imo qualis erga nos esse velit, Lat. Yea, what he desires to be to us.]

[5 Appellatur (Dominus) etiam Saturnus, quia omnes suas creaturas exsaturat.—Bullinger. de Origine Erroris, cap. VIII. p. 36. Tigur. 1539. Saturnus autem est appellatus, quod saturetur annis.—Cic. de Nat. Deor. Lib. II.]

[6 Copiæ cornu, Lat. On this Divine name שַׁדַּי, Bullinger thus gives his opinion in his book, De Origine Erroris, cap. 1. p. 5: Magis mihi placet Rabbi Mosis Maimonis filii sententia, quam Petrus Galatinus hisce ferme verbis exponit: Nomen Schaddai compositum est ex verbis דַּי Daii, quod est, *sufficit;* et ex litera שׁ, quæ idem pollet quod אֲשֶׁר, *qui:* ut Schaddai idem sit quod, *qui sufficit,* vel *qui suffi-*

is the everlasting well of all good things, which never is
drawn dry. And that doth Jeremy declare at large in the
second chapter of his prophecy. All which verily God in
effect comprehendeth in these few words: "I am the Lord
thy God." 'I, I say, which speak to thee from within the
fire, I, and none other.' Here is expressly meant the unity
of God. We are here taught to acknowledge one God, and
no more; to stick to one, and not to suffer our hearts fantas-
tically to dream of many[1]. "I am thy Lord, I am thy God."
He is a Lord, because he alone hath the rule over all creatures;
all things are subject to him as to their Lord; all things do
bend and obey him, if once he do but beck. He, as Lord
alone, doth govern and uphold all things that are[2]. So then
in this one word is contained the wisdom of God, his virtue,
his power, and infinite majesty. *Deus,* which word we use
for "God," is, peradventure, derived of the Hebrew word
Daii, which signifieth sufficiency or full ability[3]. For God
alone, of himself, is unto himself most perfect blessedness and
absolute felicity: he is also sufficiently able to minister all
things most abundantly to all them that seek after him in
truth sincerely, being of himself most liberally wealthy to all
that call upon his name. Therefore in this branch the sufficient and full ability, the liberality, the goodness and mercy
of God, are to be noted: but most especially in this that he
saith, "I am thy God; thy God, I say." For God is not
good to himself alone, but even unto us also. He desireth to

---

ciens aut sufficientia est. Hæc Galat. Poterit itaque Deus appellari
Saturnus. Ut enim a die fit diurnus, sic a saturando dicitur Saturnus.
. . . . . Itaque licebit nunc summam illam vim ipsum Deum appellare
et Schaddai et Saturnum et Copiæ cornu. See also Early Writings of
Bp. Hooper, ed. Parker Soc. p. 293.]

[1 *non corda pluribus dividere,* Lat.]

[2 Est enim cœli et terræ et omnium quæ in eis sunt Conditor,
Rector, Conservator, Rex et Princeps summus et maximus, Lat. omitted
by the translator. For he is of heaven and earth, and of all things
which are therein, the Creator, Ruler, Preserver, and supreme and
highest King and Prince.]

[3 A Græco vocabulo deflexa ac transumpta est forte et Latinorum
vox *Deus;* nisi cui verisimilius videatur tractam esse ab Hebraica ‏די‎,
Daii.—Bullinger. de Orig. Error. cap. 1. p. 5. From Heb. ‏די‎ (enough,
sufficiency,) the Greeks likewise derived their Δὶς, Gen. Διὸς, &c. (whence
Lat. Deus, dius, divus.)—Parkhurst, Heb. Lex. in voc. ‏די‎.]

pour and bestow himself wholly, with all his goodness and gifts
of grace, upon the faithful and sincere believers. He is no nig-
gard, he is not envious, he rejoiceth and is glad to bestow and
divide himself among us abundantly, and to our comfort; to
fill us with the enjoying of himself at all times and seasons,
but especially in time of our necessity. And God verily saith
expressly "thy God," and not your God, that thereby every
one of us may understand, that the eternal, most mighty, and
holy God both is and will be the God and Lord of every
particular man; that is, that he is and will be the keeper,
deliverer, redeemer, the unmeasurable mountain and bottomless sea[4] of all good gifts of body and soul, to all them that
either are or else ever shall be.

By this now, in the second place, we have to gather what
the good and gracious Lord requireth again at our hands, and
what our duty to him both is and ought to be. For this,
where he saith "thy God," betokeneth an evident relation.
For if he will be mine, then I again of duty must be his.
He will be my Lord and my God; therefore must I again of
duty make account of, and worship him, as my Lord and my
God. Wherefore in this commandment there is required at
our hands, that we do not only acknowledge the true God to
be the true God, and so to stay there; but also, that we do
take and account him for our God, our Lord, our King, our
Creator, our Preserver, and our Father; and that we do
attribute to him his property, to wit, that he is one alone,
the only fountain and giver of all good things, that he liveth,
and is eternal, righteous, true, holy[5], happy, merciful, mighty,
most excellent and chief of all. Let us therefore stick to
him alone, let us obey him in all things, let us put our trust
in him, let us call on him alone, let us repute him to be the
giver of all good things, and crave all good gifts of him; let
us thank him for all benefits whatsoever we receive, let us reverence him, and lastly, honour him in fear sincerely, in love
most ardently, and in hope as constantly as may be. For
hereunto belong those sentences in the books of Moses and
the holy gospel: "Thou shalt honour the Lord thy God, and
him alone shalt thou serve[6]." And again: "Follow ye the

What this command-ment re-quireth of us.

[4 acervum et mare, Lat.]
[5 beatus, Lat.]
[6 Deut. vi. 13; Matt. iv. 10.]

Lord your God, fear him, keep his commandments, hearken to his voice, serve him, and stick to him[1]." The Lord himself also in the Psalm crieth out and saith : " Offer to the Lord the sacrifice of praise, and pay thy vows unto the Highest. And call upon me in the day of trouble[2]," &c.

The true God is our God.

And now, touching the demonstration, whereby he declareth that he hath been, is, and will be the God and Lord of us all, of our fathers, and of our children that come after us ; the proof thereof is most evident by our[3] delivery out of Egypt. Therein are contained all the virtues of God ; his wisdom, his goodness, his righteousness, his truth, his power, and what not ? He declareth that he is the Lord in heaven and in earth, in all elements and all creatures. His people the Israelites doth he graciously deliver, defend, with sundry gifts adorn, and mightily preserve, even in despite and maugre all the heads of the whole Egyptian kingdom[4]. And on the other side, he doth by sundry means very terribly, yet notwithstanding justly, punish the Egyptians ; and last of all, together with their king, he overwhelmeth them in the Red Sea. By this one miracle of the Lord's the Israelites might have gathered, as God is almighty and the mightiest of all, so also that he would be their God, as heretofore he had been the God of their fathers. For by this wonder he did declare what he was then, and of how great power and goodness he is even at this day among us, and also what he will be in all ages, even unto the end. To us that live in these days the deliverance, which we have obtained by Jesus Christ our Lord, is far more fresh in memory ; who hath not delivered us from the bondage of any Egyptian kingdom, nor from the tyrannous hands of any earthly Pharao, but hath set us free from the power of darkness, of sin, death, and the devil. Whereby we gather, that as the eternal, true, excellent, high, and holy God is most mighty, so also he is our God ; that he wisheth well to us, and that he careth for and loveth us, according to that saying of the apostle : " Who spared not his own Son, but gave him for us all, how can it be but that

The mystery of our redemption

with him he will give us all things[5] ? " Verily, the mystery

[1 Deut. xiii. 4.]   [2 Psal. l. 14, 15.]

[3 *our* is not in the original Latin.]

[4 vel invito et fremente toto regno Ægypti, Lat.]

[5 Rom. viii. 32.]

of our redemption by our Lord Jesus Christ is manifestly contained in the first precept of the ten commandments. For it is evident, that the Israelites' free departure out of Egypt was a type or figure of the delivery of the whole compass of the earth, and of all the kingdoms of the world, which should be wrought by Christ our Lord, who hath now already set all the world free from the bondage of sin and hell. But if any man doubt of this, let him diligently consider with himself the meaning of the ceremony and sacrament of that bodily deliverance, I mean, the very passover. For what is he that knoweth not that the paschal lamb did in a figure represent Christ our Redeemer? Are Paul's words unknown, who saith, "Christ our passover is offered up[6]?" Have not all the apostles and John Baptist called our Lord "the Lamb of God which taketh away the sins of the world[7]?" The words of the prophet Esay also, in his fifty-second chapter, are apparently known; where he compareth the delivery of Israel out of Egypt with the redemption of all the world wrought by Christ from the slavery of sin. Wherefore, in this first precept of the ten commandments is contained the mystery of Christ our Lord, and our salvation: so that, as often as those words of God shall be recited in our ears, we ought not so much to set our eyes and minds upon the ancient delivery of Israel out of Egypt, as upon the new and latter redemption, which we have by Christ Jesus, thereby to quicken our hope, and not to despair, but that the most excellent and mighty God both is and will be our God, as heretofore he hath been theirs.

by Christ contained in the first commandment.

The latter branch of this first commandment flatly forbiddeth us, and every one of us, to have any strange gods; that is, it taketh from us all extraordinary means to seek the safeguard of our lives, where the working finger of God is not, and whatsoever else may be either devilishly devised or unadvisedly chosen beside the very word of God. And therefore the Lord useth a most vehement or earnest kind of speaking: for saith he, "Thou shalt not have any other gods before me[8]." See, he saith, Thou shalt not have, and thou shalt not have before me, or before my face, or with me, or

Strange gods are forbidden.

[6 1 Cor. v. 7.]
[7 John i. 29; Acts viii. 32; 1 Pet. i. 19; Rev. v. 6.]
[8 coram me, Lat.]

by me. We Germans say, *Zu mir; oder nabĕnd mir; oder lass michs nit sahen vor meinen augen.* For so do fathers speak in their anger, when they do earnestly forbid a wicked and heinous thing. See, say they, that thou do it not before mine eyes for me to see it. But now God is present every where; God seeth all things; yea, he beholdeth our hearts, and hidden secrets of our hearts. We must not therefore in any case, either openly or privily, have any strange gods: that is, none of us must make account of any creature, either in heaven or earth, as of our God; none of us must attribute God's properties to his creatures, nor yet the things which we of duty do owe to God himself. The properties of God are these; to be all over[1] and every where, to see all, to know all, to be able to do all, to give life, to deliver, and cleanse from sins, to save, preserve, to justify, to sanctify, and whatsoever else is like to these. On the other side, our duty to him is, to reverence God, to call on God, to fear God, to worship God, to hope in God, to stick to God, to hear God, to believe God, and to obey God.

Strange gods, what they are.

The strange god therefore is that which is not God properly and by nature; yea, it is whatsoever we do make to ourselves to be our God beside the very living and eternal God, wherein we trust, wherein we hope, whereon we call, which we do love and fear, whereon we settle and fasten our minds, whereupon we do depend, whereof we make account as of our treasure, help, and safeguard, both in prosperity and our adversity. When Rahel asketh children of Jacob, she hath this answer at his hand: "Am I God, which have made thee barren[2]?" And again, when Joram king of Israel had by Naaman received letters from Benhadad, king of Syria, requesting to cleanse the leprosy, he rent his clothes for anger, and cried out, saying: "Am I God, that I can kill, and restore to life again[3]?" Let God alone, therefore, be our God, that is, our life and safeguard, our help and refuge, our protection and deliverance, our hope and love, our fear, our dread, our trembling, and all. These if we do attribute to others, and not to God alone, then shall we make other gods to ourselves. Moreover, whatsoever is not ordained by God

[1] ubique, Lat.]
[2] Gen. xxx. 2.   Num pro Deo sum, Lat. and Vulgate.]
[3] 2 Kings v. 7.]

‍imself, that is in the scriptures many times called strange, ‍or other. In that sense it is said, that strange fire was car‍ried into the tabernacle[4]; to wit, not that fire which God had ‍commanded for to kindle. In the Proverbs she is called a ‍strange woman[5], whose company the Lord hath not allowed ‍thee to use. They therefore are strange gods, whom we ‍have made to ourselves to hang on, and to seek aid of, when ‍God, notwithstanding, hath not appointed them to have the ‍charge over us. Wherefore the very saints themselves, ‍triumphant now in heaven with Christ our King, shall be re‍puted for strange gods; the saints themselves, I say, not in ‍respect of themselves, but to us they shall be strange gods in respect of us, which judge very fondly of them, and bestow on them the honour due to God, in worshipping and calling upon them, as we should worship and call upon our tutors and defenders[6]. The very devils and devilish men shall be strange gods, if we for fear shall stand in awe of them more than of God, to whom indeed our fear is due. The stars, the planets, and signs in the firmament shall be strange gods, if we, being deceived with the mathematicals[7], shall wholly hang on them, and in all our doings evermore have regard to the impressions of the sky, directing every minute of our lives to the course of the stars. Likewise, if we shall honour and love money or men with honour or love due unto God, then shall this money and men of ours be imputed to us for strange gods. King Asa is blamed (2 Paral. xvi.[8]) for putting too much confidence in physic and physicians: physic[9] and physicians therefore may be abused, and made strange gods. The Jews are rebuked by the Lord in Esay, chap. xxx. for trusting too much in the Egyptians, their confederates: confederates

Conjurors and witches.

[4 Levit. x. 1.]

[5 ch. ii. 16.]

[6 pro tutelaribus. See Becon's Works, Parker Soc. ed. Vol. I. pp. 138, 9; Calfhill's Answer to Martiall, pp. 19, 20; and Works of Bp. Jewel, Vol. II. pp. 922, 3.]

[7 i. e. astrologers. Sequitur lauta illa Astrologia seu Mathematica, &c.—Luther. in Decem Præcepta. Opp. Witeb. 1582. Tom. I. p. 3. Olim Genethliaci et similes pro Mathematicis se venditarunt.—Calvin. Opp. Amstel. Tom. I. p. 353. See also Early Writings of Bp. Hooper, Parker Soc. ed. p. 330; Bingham. Orig. Eccles. Book XVI. chap. 5. §. 1.]

[8 2 Chron. xvi. 12.]

[9 Herbæ, Lat.]

therefore may be abused, and made strange gods. But mos
of all are condemned here the leagues and covenants mad
with the devil by witchcraft, to have him at commandment
Those blessings also which of right ought rather to be calle
cursings, I mean, superstitious exorcisms or conjurations, ar
utterly to be rejected; wherein also this is blameworthy, tha
the name of the most high God is horribly abused and take
in vain. But what is he, that can exactly reckon up every
particular thing wherein this first commandment is transgressed, considering that in it is taught the perfect rule of
godliness, which is the inward worship done to God; to wit,
to acknowledge God, to believe him, to think rightly of him,
to call upon him, to cleave unto him, and in all things to obey
him?

The second precept of the ten commandments is: "Thou
shalt not make to thyself any graven image, nor any likeness
of those things which are in heaven above, or in the earth
beneath, or in the water under the earth; thou shalt not bow
down to them, nor worship them: I am the Lord thy God,
strong, and jealous, visiting the fathers' sins in the children
unto the third and fourth generation of them that hate me,
and shewing mercy unto thousands to them that love me, and
keep my commandments." In the first commandment the
Lord did teach and draw out before our eyes the pattern of
his inward worship and religion: now here, in the second, he
amendeth that which might be amiss in the outward rites and
ceremonies. If we could have rightly judged of God, and
have kept (as devoutly as we should) the first commandment,
then should there have been no need of the second: but, because God knew our disposition and nature, he doth therefore
expressly forbid the thing that otherwise we would have done.
For many there are which think, that God ought to be pourtrayed in some similitude or likeness, and to be worshipped
with some bodily or visible reverence, in offering gold, silver,
pearls, ivory, and precious things of price. Wherefore the
general end of this commandment is, to draw them from
those gross imaginations and carnal worshippings of God, who
as he is an incomprehensible power and an eternal spirit, so
can he not be resembled to any corruptible similitude: he
will be worshipped in spirit and holiness. Under the name
of the idol, or imagined likeness, is contained all the outward

The second command-ment of God.

The end of the com-mandment is to draw us from strange and foreign worship-pings.

reverence done thereunto: when therefore the idols are forbidden, together with them is also forbidden all outward honour irreligiously exhibited to the true and very God. For wheresoever an idol is, there must the idolaters set him up a pillar[1], place him in a seat, erect him an altar, and build him a temple. And all these again require keepers and overseers, ministers or priests, sacrifices and offerings, ceremonies, furnitures, holy-days, cost and labour that will never be ended. In this sense did the prophets say, that idolatrous images were endless labours and infinite miseries[2]: for after images are once received, there is no end or measure of expenses and toil. This doth experience teach to be true.

Now to proceed: this commandment standeth of three several parts. For first of all, God flatly forbiddeth to make a graven image, or other kind of idol; that is, God doth utterly forbid to set up or hallow to him any image, of what shape or substance soever it•be. For as God will not, so indeed he cannot, be expressly represented in any manner of likeness. Now, in this commandment are reckoned up in a manner all the similitudes of those things, whereunto we are wont in pourtraying to liken our pictures. Thou shalt not, saith he, fashion like unto God any shape or figure of those things which are in heaven; which are, I say, above us. Above us are the celestial bodies, the sun, the moon, the planets, the stars, and divers birds of sundry fashions: in all which figures and shapes almost no small number of the Gentiles did solemnly honour and reverently worship the name of God. Thou shalt not liken unto God, saith he, any shape or fashion of those things that are in the earth. In the earth are men, beasts, herbs, shrubs, trees, and such-like. Now it is manifest that the Gentiles worshipped God under the likeness of men and beasts. Cornelius Tacitus, writing of the Germans, saith: " But by the greatness of the visible

God forbiddeth a graven image.

[1 basim, Lat.]

[2 Bullinger refers to the word עֶצֶב, which signifies both *trouble* and an *idol*. And in Psal. xvi. 4, the word עַצְּבוֹתָם is rendered by the Chaldee Paraphrast and others, *their idols*, and by the English version and others, *their sorrows*. And Bucer remarks in loc. עַצְבוּת *molestias* significat; at עֲצַבִּים pro idolis sæpissime usurpatur.—See also Calvin. Comment. in loc. cit. ed. Calvin. Translat. Soc. Vol. i. note 1; and Hooper's Early Writings, p. 43, Parker Soc. ed.]

That is, the
sun, moon,
and stars.
celestial bodies they do conjecture and verily think, that the
gods are neither inclosed in walls, nor yet in favour resem-
bling men's visages; and therefore do they hallow woods and
groves, calling that hidden mystery by the name of the gods,
which with outward eyes they see not, but with inward reverence alone[1]." Lo, here, our ancestors worshipped God in
the likeness of trees and woods: which, nevertheless, men are
forbidden here to do, even as also we are prohibited to worship our God in the likeness of any thing that is in or under
the water. The Philistines worshipped God in the image of
a fish; for Dagon their God bare the shape of a fish[2].
Egypt honoured God in the similitude of serpents[3]. All
which, and many other, Paul knitteth up together in the
first to the Romans, where he argueth against the Gentiles,
and saith: "Their foolish heart was blinded: when they
counted themselves wise, they became fools, and turned the
glory of the incorruptible God unto the likeness, not only of
a mortal man, but also of birds, and of four-footed beasts,
and of creeping beasts." Against this madness is the first
part of the law directly given.

The cause
why God will
not be likened
to any thing.
But now, the cause why God will not be represented in
any visible or sensible image is this[4]. God is a spirit; God
is unmeasurable, incomprehensible[5], unspeakable, all over and
every where, filling heaven and earth, eternal, living, giving
life unto and preserving all things; and lastly, of a glorious
majesty exalted above the heavens. But what is he that can
pourtray a spirit in any image or substance? God is an incomprehensible[6] power, quickening and preserving all and every

[1 De Mor. Germ. c. ix. Ceterum nec cohibere parietibus deos,
neque in ullam humanioris speciem adsimulare, ex magnitudine cœlestium arbitrantur: lucos ac nemora consecrant, deorumque nominibus
appellant secretum illud, quod sola reverentia vident. They think it
not consistent with the greatness of celestial beings, &c.]

[2 Marinum (i. e. piscis) ei (Dagoni) corpus; humana vero facies,
manus, item et pedes.—Selden de Dis Syris, Syntag. ii. cap. 3. et
add.]

[3 The worship of the serpent was in her (Egypt's) early history an
important and conspicuous part of her idolatry.—Deane, on the Worship of the Serpent, chap. 2. §. 1.]

[4 in promptu causa est, Lat.]

[5 incircumscriptibilis, Lat.]

[6 immensa potentia, Lat.]

thing. But David, describing images, saith: "The idols of the heathen are silver and gold, the works of men's hands. They have ears, and hear not; noses have they, and smell not. They have hands, and handle not; feet have they, and walk not; neither is there any voice in the throat of them [7]." Wherefore, if these be compared to God, how like, I beseech you, are they unto him? To go about, therefore, to express God in any visible likeness is the next way to dishonour God, and to bring him into contempt. God's eye beholdeth all things; idols see nothing. God's ears hear all things; idols hear nothing. By God all things live, move, and are preserved; the idols themselves neither live, nor move, and, unless they be upheld by the men that make them, they fall and are dashed in pieces. An idol breatheth not; God giveth to other [8] a breathing spirit. How then, and wherein, are these twain alike? In substance, or in shape? If ye say, in substance; I answer, Is God then of gold, of silver, or of wood? If in shape; mine answer is, Hath the invisible power of God then put on visible and mortal members? How greatly therefore did the Anthropomorphites [9] offend herein? If then there be no similitude of God, how cometh it to pass, I beseech you, that images and idols be called the likeness and pictures of God? Among us he that calleth another an idol or an image, doth seem to have spoken it too too despitefully [10] in reproach of the other: for we know that idols are counterfeits of men [11], and not men indeed; and therefore do we call him an image, that is a sot, a fool, a dolt, an idiot, and one that hath no wit, nor knoweth any more than he heareth of other. Why then henceforward should we any more call images the likeness of God? God is living: images are monuments of dead men; as Salomon [12], the author of the book of Wisdom, saith: "God is glorious, and heaven and earth are full of the glory of his majesty; but idols are with-

They were heretics, affirming, that God hath members like to mortal men.

[7 Ps. cxv. 4—7.]

[8 omnibus, Lat.]

[9 For traces of these heretics, see Mosheim's Eccles. Hist. Cent. 4. book 2. part 2. ch. 5. §. 23; and Cent. 5. book 2. part 2. ch. 2. §. 10. note 9; and ch. 5. §. 20. ed. Soames, 1845.]

[10 magna affecisse contumelia, Lat.]

[11 speciem falsam hominis referre, Lat.]

[12 The name, Solomon, is not in the original Latin.]

out all glory, and subject to the scoffs and mocks of men[1]."
Images are tokens of absent friends: but God is present
always and everywhere. And the signs or tokens, which
God did of old ordain and give to his people, were not simply
the signs and images of God, but tokens of God's presence,
signifying that God, who by nature is a spirit, and invisible,
incomprehensible, and unmeasurable, is present still among
them. Such a token was the cloud, the smoke, the fire, and
finally, the very ark of the covenant, which also the cherubin
did cover with their wings, signifying thereby that no mortal
man could look God in the face; and that therefore the soul,
and the mind, and the spirit, ought by contemplation to be
lifted up into heaven, there to behold him. For to Moses,
who notwithstanding is said to have seen God face to face, it
was said, "No man shall see me and live[2]." When once we
are deceased, then shall we see him as he is, according to the
sayings of the blessed evangelist John[3]. So then these, I
say, are the causes, why the Lord will not have himself represented or pourtrayed in any matter or likeness.

Hereunto now do appertain the places of scripture, and
testimonies of the men that are the chiefest pillars of true
religion and godliness, of Moses, Esay, and Paul. Moses in
Deuteronomy saith: "The Lord spake unto you from the midst
of the fire: and a voice of words ye heard, but likeness saw
ye none, but heard the voice only. Take good heed therefore
unto yourselves, as pertaining unto your souls (for ye saw no
manner of image in that day), lest ye mar yourselves by
making you a graven image, the likeness of any manner of
figure, whether it be the picture of man or woman; the likeness of any manner of beast that is on the earth; or the
likeness of any manner of feathered fowl that flieth in the air;
or the likeness of any manner of worm that creepeth on the
earth; or the likeness of any manner of fish that is in the
waters beneath the earth: yea, and lest thou lift up thine
eyes unto heaven, and when thou seest the sun, the moon,
and the stars, with all the host of heaven, thou shouldest
begin to worship them and reverence them, and shouldest
worship and serve the things which the Lord thy God hath
made to serve all nations under the whole heaven. Take

[1 Wisd. xiv. 15.]
[2 Ex. xxxiii. 20.]   [3 1 John iii. 2.]

heed, therefore, that ye forget not the appointment[4] of the Lord your God, which he hath made with you, and that ye make you no graven image, nor the likeness of any thing that the Lord thy God hath forbidden thee[5]." This hath Moses thus far.

Esaias also, in his fortieth chapter, saith: "Behold, all people" (to wit, compared to God) "are in comparison of him as a drop of a bucketful, and are counted as a little dust sticking on the balance, and weighing nothing at all. Yea, the isles are to him as a very little thing. Libanus is not sufficient to minister fire to his offering, and all the beasts thereof are not enough for one sacrifice. All people in comparison of God are reckoned as nothing; in respect of him they are less than nothing, and as that that is not. To whom then will ye liken God? or what similitude will ye set up to him? Shall the carver make him an image? and shall the goldsmith cover it with gold, or cast it into a form of silver plates? Moreover, shall[6] the poor man, that he may have somewhat to set up, choose a tree that is not rotten, and seek out a cunning workman to carve thereout an image, that moveth[7] not? Know ye not this? heard ye never of it?" And again: "It is he that sitteth upon the circle of the world, whose inhabiters are, in comparison of him, but as grasshoppers. It is he that spreadeth out the heavens like a curtain; he stretcheth them out as a tent to dwell in. It is he that bringeth princes to nothing, and maketh the judges of the earth as though they were not. To whom now will ye liken me, and to whom shall I be like? saith the Holy One. Lift up your eyes on high, and consider who hath made those things, which come out by so great heaps, and he calleth them all by their names." And so forth. Thus much out of Esaias[8].

Moreover, Paul, the apostle of Christ, disputing at Athens of true religion, saith: "God that made the world and all that therein is, seeing that he is Lord of heaven and earth,

[4 fœderis, Lat.]   [5 Deut. iv. 12, 15—19, 23.]
[6 In the original Latin the verbs in these three sentences are *not* the future tense, nor are the sentences interrogatory. But the two former are interrogatory in the Vulgate.]
[7 ne moveatur loco, Lat.]
[8 Isai. xl. 15—23, 25, 26.]

dwelleth not in temples made with hands, neither is worshipped
with men's hands, as though he needed any thing; since he
himself giveth life and breath to all and everywhere, and
hath made of one blood all nations of men, to dwell on all
the face of the earth, and hath determined the times before
appointed, and also the limits of their habitation, that they
should seek the Lord, if perhaps they might have felt, and
found him; though he be not far from every one of us: for
by him we live, and move, and have our being; as certain of
your own poets have said, For we are also his offspring. Forasmuch then as we are the offspring of God, we ought not to
think that the Godhead is like to gold, or silver, or stone
graven by art or man's device[1]."

These testimonies are so evident, and do so plainly declare
that which I purposed, that I need not for the further exposition of them to say any more. They were great causes
therefore, that moved St Augustine precisely to pronounce it
to be horrible sacrilege for any man to place in the church
the image of God the Father, sitting in a throne with bended
hams; because it is detestable for a man so much as to conceive such a likeness in his mind. His very words I have
rehearsed in the eighth Sermon of my first Decade[2], where I
had occasion to speak of the right hand of the Father, and to
teach you what it is to sit at the Father's right hand.

All other
images are
forbidden
to be wor-
shipped.

Now, touching other images also, which men erect to creatures or to the heathen gods, they are no less forbidden than
the pictures of God himself. For if we may not hallow an
image to the true and very God, much less shall it be lawful
for us to erect or consecrate an idol to a strange or foreign
god. Man in his mind doth choose himself a god, and of
his own invention deviseth a shape or figure for it, which
lastly he frameth with the workmanship of his hands: so
that it may truly be said, that the mind conceiveth an idol,
and the hand doth bring it forth. But the Lord, in the first
commandment, forbad us to have any strange gods. Now, he
that neither hath, nor chooseth to himself, any strange or
foreign gods, doth not in his imagination devise any shape
for them, and so consequently erecteth no images. For he
thinketh it a detestable thing to make an image to the true
and very God; he is persuaded that it is a wicked thing to

[1 Acts xvii. 24—29.]   [2 See page 150.]

choose himself a foreign god; and therefore he judgeth it to be most abominable to place the picture of a foreign god in the church or temple of the true and very God. And that is the cause that in the church before Christ his time we do not read, that any images were erected to any saints, whereof at that time there were a great number, (suppose) of patriarchs, judges, kings, priests, prophets, and whole troops of martyrs, matrons, and modest widows. The primitive church also of Christ his apostles had no images, either of Christ himself, or of other saints, set up in their places of public prayer, nor in their churches. The deed of Epiphanius is very well known, which he committed at Anablatha in Syria. It is written in Greek in an epistle to John Bishop of Jerusalem, and translated into Latin by St Hierome. He rent the vail that hung in the temple, bearing in it the image of Christ or some other saint; testifying therewithal, that it is against christian religion, for the picture of a man to hang in the church of God[3]. St Augustine in *Catalogo Hæreseων* maketh mention of one Marcella, a follower of Carpocrates his sect, which worshipped the images of Jesu, Paul, Homer, and Pythagoras, with falling down prostrate before them, and offering incense unto them[4]. Very well and wisely, therefore, did Erasmus of Roterodame, being deeply seen in the works of ecclesiastical writers, when he had wittily spoken many things touching the use of images in churches, at the last also add this, and say: "There is no decree, no not so much as of men, which commandeth that images should be in churches. For as it is more easy, so is it less perilous, to take all images quite and clean out of the churches, than to be able to bring to pass that, in keeping them still, measure should not be exceeded, nor superstition covertly cloked. For admit that (as some say) the mind be clean from all superstition; yet notwithstanding it is not

[3 Quando—venissem ad villam quæ dicitur Anablatha,—inveni velum pendens in foribus—ecclesiæ, tinctum atque depictum, et habens imaginem, quasi Christi, vel sancti cujusdam.—Cum ergo hoc vidissem, in ecclesia Christi contra auctoritatem scripturarum hominis pendere imaginem, scidi illud.—Epiphan. Opp. Par. 1622. Tom. II. fol. 317.]

[4 Sectæ ipsius (i. e. Carpocratianorum) fuisse traditur socia quædam Marcellina, quæ colebat imagines Jesu et Pauli et Homeri et Pythagoræ, adorando incensumque ponendo.—August. Opp. Par. 1531. Tom. VI. fol. 3.]

without a shew of superstition, for him that prayeth to fall
down prostrate before a wooden idol, to have his eyes stedfastly bent upon that alone, to speak to that, to kiss that, and
not to pray at all but before an idol. And this I add, that
whosoever do imagine God to be any other than indeed he
is, they, contrary to this precept, do worship graven images[1]."
And again, in the same catechism, he saith : "Even until the
time of Hierome there were men of sound religion, which
suffered not in the church any image to stand, neither painted,
nor graven, nor woven ; no, not so much as of Christ, because
(as I suppose) of the Anthropomorphites. But afterward the
use of images by little and little crept up and came into the
churches[2]." This hath Erasmus.

No image
must be made
for Christ.

Furthermore, for Christ, our Lord and very God, though
he have taken on him the nature of us men, yet, that notwithstanding, there ought no image to be erected. For he did
not become man to that intent ; but he drew up his humanity
into heaven, and therewithal gave us a charge, that, so often
as we pray, we should lift up the eyes of our minds and
bodies into heaven above. Moreover, being once ascended,
he sent his Spirit instead of himself unto the church, wherein
he hath a spiritual kingdom, and needeth not any bodily or
corruptible things. For he commanded that, if we would
bestow any thing on him or for his sake, we should bestow it
on the poor, and not on his picture or image. And now
since, without all controversy, our Christ is the very true
God, and that the very true God doth forbid to hallow to
him any likeness of man, that is, to represent God in the

[1 Ut imagines sint in templis, nulla præcipit vel humana consti-
tutio. Et ut facilius, ita tutius quoque est, omnes imagines e templis
submovere, quam impetrare, ut nec modus prætereatur, nec admiscea-
tur superstitio. Jam ut animus sit ab omni superstitione purus, tamen
non caret superstitionis specie, orantem ad ligneum simulacrum pro-
cumbere, in hoc intentos habere oculos, ad hoc verba facere, huic
oscula figere, nec orare prorsus nisi coram imagine. Illud addam, quicunque sibi aliusmodi fingunt Deum quam est, contra præceptum hoc
colunt sculptilia.—Erasm. Symbol. Catec. vi. col. 1188. Opp. Lugd.
Bat. Tom. v.]

[2 Usque ad ætatem Hieronymi erant probatæ religionis viri, qui
in templis nullam ferebant imaginem, nec pictam, nec sculptam, nec
textam ; ac ne Christi quidem, ut opinor, propter Anthropomorphitas.
Paulatim autem imaginum usus irrepsit in templa.—Ibid. col. 1187.]

shape of a man; it followeth consequently, that to Christ no image is to be dedicated, because he is the true and very God and life everlasting.

In the second part of this commandment we are taught, how far forth it is unlawful for us to make any image of God, or else of feigned gods; and, if so it be that any make or cause them to be made, how and after what sort then we ought to behave ourselves toward them. Images ought not in any case to be made for men to worship, or otherwise to use as means or instruments to worship God in. But if so it happen, that any man make them to the intent to have them worshipped; then must the zealous and godly disposed despise, neglect, not worship nor honour them, nor yet by any means be brought to do them service. For in this precept are two things set down especially to be noted. The first is, "Thou shalt not bow down to them." To bow down is to cap and to knee, to duck with the head and bend the body, to fall down, to honour, to worship, and to reverence. The saints of old did use to bow down (that is, to bend the knee, to uncover the head, and to fall down) to the magistrates, the prophets, the princes, and teachers of the people, and unto all sorts of reverend men. And that they did partly because God had so commanded, who useth their ministery to common men's commodity; and partly again, because men are the lively image of God himself. But deaf, dumb, and blind idols are wood and stone, whereunto we are forbidden to bend or bow down, howsoever we are made to believe that they do bear the likeness of God. The latter is, "Thou shalt not worship them," or else, Thou shalt not do any service unto them. In this clause is forbidden all the outward and unlawful honour done to God, or to the gods, in the way of religion, nay rather, in the way of superstition, and devilish hallowing of churches, reliques, holy-days, and such-like trash and trumpery [3]. For to serve is to worship, to reverence, to attribute some majesty and divine authority to that which we do worship, to have affiance in, to burn incense, to offer gifts, and to shew ourselves dutifully serviceable to that which we worship. There is no man that knoweth not what it is to serve, and what is meant by service, in matters of religion. We are forbidden,

How far forth it is not lawful to make images.

To bow down, what it is.

To serve, what it is.

[3 superstitione et cultu templorum, sacrorum, feriarum, omnium-que rerum similium, Lat.]

therefore, to run in pilgrimage to idols, yea, though they be the images of God himself. We are forbidden to do them any service, in offering gifts, or attributing unto them any one jot of God's pre-eminence, thereby to bind ourselves to maintain and uphold their unlawful honour, in mingling such superstitions with better points of true religion. This therefore considered (since we may not attribute to images any serviceable honour[1]), I do not see how we can ascribe to them the office of teaching, admonishing, and exhorting, which are the offices and benefits of God's Holy Spirit and word : for Abacuck the prophet, of whose writings Paul did make no small account, hath left in writing words worth remembering. "What profiteth" (says he) "the image ? for the maker of it hath made it : an image and a teacher of lies, though he that made it trusteth therein, when he maketh dumb idols ? Woe unto him that saith to the wood, Awake ; and to the senseless stone, Arise ! Should that teach thee ? Behold, it is covered with gold and silver, and there is no breath in it. But the Lord is in his holy temple ; let all the earth keep silence before him[2]." What could be said more plainly and agreeable to the truth ? Images (saith he) are mere and very lies. But how can that teach the truth, which of itself is nought else but a lie ? There is no moving, there is no life, there is no breath in a picture or image. But the Lord sitteth in his holy temple, where he reigneth, and teacheth, by inspiration and the preaching of his word, the sum of godliness, and where he liveth for ever in the hearts of all his saints and servants. Let therefore all the tongues in the whole world be stopped of them that go about to maintain and uphold superstitious idolatry against the true and living God.

Idols teach not.

Now again in the third part of this commandment the Lord doth briefly knit up the pithy handling of sundry things. For, first, he sheweth that men have no just or lawful cause in turning from God, either to make them strange gods, or else to worship God otherwise than they ought to do. "I am" (saith he) "the Lord thy God," a strong God. If I be the Lord, then shouldest thou of duty serve me, honour me, obey me, and worship me, so as thou dost understand that I do desire to be worshipped and honoured. If I be God, then am I of

We have no cause to choose strange gods.

---

[1] cultum latriæ, Lat.]　　　　[2] Hab. ii. 18—20.]

sufficient ability to minister to all men whatsoever they lack[3]. What canst thou want, therefore, that thou mayest not find in me? why then shouldest thou turn to strange gods? Thou hast no cause at all, undoubtedly, to turn from me. . I am, moreover, a strong God, a mighty, yea, an almighty God and Lord. Thou hast no cause to seek a mightier or wealthier prince than me, by him to be delivered out of my hands, and by his liberality to be farther enriched than thou shalt be by my good gifts and blessings. For I am that true and eternal God, the invincible and almighty Prince of the world, the true and only helper and deliverer, the liberal and bountiful giver of all good gifts or benefits. I am also thy Lord and thy God. Those goods of mine are thine. For I am thine: yea, I am thy helper and deliverer out of all adversities and afflictions. Thou art mine: I have created thee: I live in thee, I do preserve thee. Why then shouldest thou turn away from me, and seek after any strange god whatsoever? What needest thou any more hereafter to hunt after senseless idols? Thou art the church and temple of God. Dost thou not feel and perceive within thyself, that I do dwell in thee, and have thine heart in possession? And what, I pray thee, hath the temple of God to do with godless images?

Then also he descendeth, and doth very severely, yet notwithstanding justly, threaten extreme and terrible revengement. "I am" (saith he) "a jealous God." This may be taken two ways very well, and not amiss. For, first, the sense may be thus: I will not have thee to seek any other gods but me, neither will I have thee admit or receive any foreign or unlawful worshipping of me. The cause is, I am a jealous God, envious against my rival, not suffering mine equal, nor by any means abiding to have a mate. I alone will be loved, I alone will be worshipped; and that too, not after any other fashion than I myself have appointed to be observed. For no man is so ignorant but that he knoweth how God in the scripture doth, by the parable of wedlock[4], figuratively set down the assurance and bond wherein by faith we are bound to God[5]. God is our husband and bridegroom: we are his

God suffereth not a mate.

[3 omnisufficientia sum, Lat.]
[4 humani conjugii, Lat.]
[5 religamur Deo (unde et religionis nomen est), Lat. omitted; from which binding the name, religion, is derived. So Augustine: Ad

wife and chosen spouse. A chaste and faithful wife giveth ear alone to her husband's voice; him alone she loveth, him alone she doth obey, and, him excepted, she loveth no man at all. Again, on the other side, a shameless, faithless adulteress and whorish strumpet, not worthy to be called a wife, seemeth outwardly to stick and cleave to her husband; but privily she maketh her body common to many men, and loveth other more than her husband, and for the most part burneth on them, being cold enough to him-ward. But God is a jealous God, and will be loved and worshipped alone, without any partner to rob him thereof. That is spiritual adultery and whore-hunting, when men do partly love and worship God, and yet notwithstanding do therewithal give reverence to strange and other gods. Against this faithless and double dealing all the prophets cry out most vehemently with words that represent a tyrannous and cruel revengement[1]: for of all other sins that is most detestable. I would to God at this day so many were not persuaded, that this kind of honour is the worship that God maketh most account of!

Or else otherwise the sense of those words may be thus: I will not have thee to seek any other gods but me; I will not have thee worship me according to thine own inventions. The cause is, I am a jealous God; that is, I am easy to be provoked, and will not suffer myself and mine honour to be rejected without due punishment for the contempt. And to this sense he seemeth to draw, where he goeth forward, and doth at large expound how he is jealous: for "I visit," saith he, "the fathers' iniquity in the children unto the third and fourth generation of them that hate me." God therefore is a sharp revenger and a just judge against them that follow after strange gods, or serve God unlawfully or irreligiously, and also against all them that swerve from the law of God. For he thundereth out this bitter punishment, especially against idolaters; but therewithal inclusively he threateneth it to them which break the rest of his commandments. For that which the Lord uttereth here is generally spoken, and is of force and effect against all impiety and unrighteousness of all mankind. But for because God's case is far more excellent

unum Deum tendentes, et ei uni religantes animas nostras, unde religio dicta creditur, &c.—De Ver. Relig. cap. 55.]

[1 plane tragicis vocibus, Lat.]

han man's, they therefore do more heinously offend which break the first table, than they that sin against the second; and thereby do deserve a far more grievous pain and heavy punishment.

Now, whereas we see that the Lord saith, that he will visit, and by inquisition punish, the sins of the fathers in the children unto the third and fourth generation; we must not by and by think that God is unjust, and punisheth another man's fault in afflicting the innocent, that is, in whipping him that did not offend: as the Jews in Ezechiel did wickedly taunt and cavil with God, saying, " The fathers have eaten sour grapes, and the children's teeth are set on edge." But it is not so. " For every man shall bear his own offences; neither shall the son bear or abide the father's sin, nor the father the son's iniquity[2]." This doth the most true God very often and earnestly beat into our heads throughout Ezechiel, and the whole scripture beside. If therefore the children, or childer's children, shall abide in the crooked steps of their fathers, and shall, as their fathers did, do service to idols, and shall think that they shall be safe and remain unpunished because they learned it of their fathers, even as their fathers also were idolaters, and yet flourished in wealth and prosperity; then, I say, I will punish the sin of the fathers in the children: that is, I will sharply revenge the sin that the children have learned of the fathers, and wherein they stiffly stand and abide, being encouraged thereunto by their fathers' example and good fortune; although for the very same sin I did not once touch their fathers before them. And for that cause is this expressly added, " of them that hate me." Hereof have we very many and very evident examples in the books of Kings. The house of Jeroboam is utterly destroyed, because Jeroboam did erect in Israel idolatry and superstition[3]. Immediately after, the whole stock of king Baasa is clean cut off: and Achab's house is pulled up by the roots. At length, the Israelites are made slaves[4] to serve the Assyrians. Solomon, the most mighty, wealthy, wise, and happy king of Juda, because of his idolatry and strange superstition, is of a sudden made a wretch of all

(marginal note:) How God doth visit the fathers' sins in the children.

[2 Ezek. xviii. 2, 20.]
[3 peregrinos cultus, Lat.]
[4 captivi abducuntur in Assyriorum regna, Lat.]

other.   There is none, unless he never read the holy scrip
tures, but doth know what happened to his son Roboam, t
Joram the son of Josaphat, to Achas, Manasses, Jehoiachin
and Zedechias, because of idolatry and foreign worshipping
of God.

Let us therefore firmly hold and believe, that the
threatenings of God are true in effect, and that God is both
a severe and just revenger and punisher of idolaters and
wicked superstitious men, and finally, of all and every wicked
act done by every man.   Although God do sundry time
seem to wicked men to slumber, and not to see them, yet
notwithstanding he doth awake when he thinks good[1], and
payeth home the wicked for all their offences done and past
Although he be long-suffering, yet the righteous Lord doth
not always neglect the godly and oppressed, neither doth he
always wink at ungodliness, and let the wicked be unpunished
for ever: but he giveth them time to repent in, which who
soever do neglect, they do at length feel the greater pain
and sharper punishment, according to the saying of the
apostle: "What, dost thou despise the riches of God's good
ness, suffering[2], and gentleness, not knowing that God's good
ness calleth thee to repentance?   But, according to thy
hardness and heart that cannot repent, thou heapest up to
thyself wrath against the day of wrath, wherein shall be
made manifest the just judgment of God, who shall repay to
every one according to his deeds[3]," &c.

Again, the bountiful Lord promiseth great and large re
wards to them that worship him, and stedfastly persevere in
true godliness and perfect religion.   "I am God," saith he
"shewing mercy, or giving bountifully, unto thousands."   Here
note, that his mercy is greater than his vengeance: for
where he is angry, there he punisheth unto the third and
fourth generation; but where he is mercifully liberal, there
he is bountiful unto many thousands.   For of his goodness
and benefits there is no measure or end; and the mercy of
God is far above all his works.   Here yet again he addeth
two things more: "To them," saith he, "that love me, and keep
my commandments."   Here, I say, he requireth two things at
their hands that are his.   The first is, that they love God

A most large
promise is
made to the
godly wor-
shippers of
the Lord.

[1 justo tempore, Lat.]   [2 tolerantiæ, Lat.]
[3 Rom. ii. 4—6.   Bullinger has used Erasmus' rendering.]

and make account of and take him to be their God : which if they do, then shall there no room be left in the godly for strange or foreign gods. The second is, that they obey God, and walk in his commandments : which if they do, then are all idols and strange worshippings utterly at an end; then doth the Lord by his word reign in the heart of every godly man, whom the bountiful Lord doth liberally bless with all kind of blessings and good gifts. And this clause verily doth especially belong to this commandment, but inclusively also it is referred to all the rest, as by the very words of God we may easily gather. Let us hold and verily think therefore, that the infinite and unspeakable benefits of God are prepared for them that walk in the law of the Lord.

Thus much had I to speak of these two commandments of the first table, which I cannot now again recapitulate, because an hour and a half is already spent, and for that I hope that I have so orderly proceeded in every point, and taught every thing so evidently and plainly, that there is nothing which ye do not very well perceive and understand. Let us now praise the Lord, and thank him for his goodness, for shewing us his ways; and let us pray that we, walking rightly in them, may at the last come to his eternal[4] joys. Amen.

OF THE THIRD PRECEPT OF THE TEN COMMAND-MENTS[5], AND OF SWEARING.

THE THIRD SERMON.

THE third commandment of the first table[6] is thus word for word : " Thou shalt not take the name of the Lord thy God in vain; because the Lord will not let him go unpunished that taketh the name of the Lord his God in vain." In the second commandment the Lord did set down the worship that he would not have, that he misliked of, and did flatly forbid ; to wit, a worldly, earthly, and carnal kind of honour, a base

The third command-ment of God.

[4 cœlestia, Lat.]
[5 primæ tabulæ, seu Decalogi, Lat.]
[6 sive Decalogi, Lat. omitted.]

and vile kind of worship, a service that is directly contrary to the spirit, nature, and majesty of God; that is, to think that God will in shape resemble a man, or any other creature made of earth or corruptible stuff or matter; and then again to worship him under those shapes and figures with corruptible things, that were first ordained and created for the use and behoof of men, and not of God. For God is an eternal Spirit, which goeth all over [1] and preserveth every thing; whom all the most excellent creatures of the whole world, if they were joined together in one, are not able to resemble, nor yet to represent the least jot of excellency in the living God. God is so far from lacking any corruptible things, that he himself supplieth the want of all our necessities. It is a mere folly therefore to set up a percher [2], a taper, or a smoky torch before the maker and giver of light. It is a very toy to offer flesh of beasts to that eternal Spirit, who in the Psalms saith: " All the beasts of the wood are mine, and the cattle in a thousand hills. I know all birds upon the mountains, and in my power are all the beasts of the field. If I be hungry, I need not to tell thee, since the world is mine, and all that is therein [3]."

Now, therefore, in this third commandment the Lord doth very exquisitely, although very briefly, declare the manner how he will be worshipped, that is, in holy reverencing of his holy name. The names whereby God is called are God, God's majesty, God's truth, God's power, and God's justice. Now the charge of this commandment is, not to abuse the name of God, and not to use it in light and trifling matters; but to speak, to think, and judge honourably, reverently, holily, and purely of God and godly things. But the pith and effect almost of the whole lieth herein, that he saith, " the name of the Lord thy God;" to wit, which is thy chief goodness and felicity, thy Creator, thy Redeemer, and thy tender Father. Now note, that the Lord doth not barely forbid to use his name; but he chargeth not to use it lightly or in vain, that is, beyond necessary use or our behoof, and beside the honour and glory of God. Let us see, therefore, how we ought to sanctify the Lord's name, and how we may devoutly use the name of God, and, last of all, so worship him as he himself hath appointed us to do.

How the
Lord's name
is sanctified.

First of all, we have to think of God as of the chief feli-

[1 omnia permeans, Lat.]

[2 See page 199.]

[3 Ps. l. 10—12.]

-ity and infinite treasure of all good things, who loveth us exceedingly with a fatherly affection, always wishing and by all means desiring to have us men saved, and to come to the perfect knowledge of the very truth; whose judgments are true and just, whose works for their excellency are wonderful, and whose words are most true, and truth itself. Then must this holy name of God continually be called upon in prayers, need, and requests: by that alone we must look to obtain whatsoever is needful for our bodies or souls. We must never cease to give thanks to that for all the good benefits that we do or shall receive; for what good soever men have and enjoy, that have they not from elsewhere than from God, the fountain and giver of all. This glory must ever be given to God. If we be nipped with any adversity, let us not by and by murmur against God's good pleasure and his secret judgments; but rather, suffering and submitting ourselves under his mighty and fatherly hand, let us say with the prophet David: "It is good for me, Lord, that thou hast chastened me[4]." Let not us appoint God what he shall do, but wholly and always submit ourselves to his good will and holy pleasure[5]. Let us in all things give God the glory, in praising openly and plainly professing his name and doctrine before kings and princes, yea, and in sight of all the world, so often as occasion shall be given, and the glory of God shall seem to require. Let us not be ashamed of God our Father, of his truth and true religion. Let us not be ashamed of Christ our Redeemer, nor yet of his cross. But let us be ashamed of errors, idolatry, of the world and vanity, of lies and iniquity. Let us holily, reverently, and devoutly, both speak and think of God, his works, and his word. Let the law of God be holy to us, let his gospel be reverend in our eyes; and let the doctrine of the patriarchs, prophets, and apostles be esteemed of us as that which came from God himself. Let us not take the name of the Lord our God into our mouths, unless it be in a matter of weight. Let us not blaspheme, curse, nor lie in the name of the Lord. Let us not use, nay, rather abuse, the name or word of God in conjuring, juggling, or sorcery[6]: for in these things the name of God is most of all abused. Let us

[4 Ps. cxix. 71, as in Vulgate.]
[5 bonæ, sanctæ et justæ ejus voluntati, Lat.]
[6 ad res magicas, ad circulatoriam, ad incantamenta, Lat.]

precisely and holily keep the oath which we have made by the name of the living and eternal God. Let us in all things tell truth, and lie not; that when this world, that will not see, shall be enforced to see so great a reverence and devotion in us to the name of our God, it may be compelled thereby to glorify our Father which is in heaven. And this verily is the godly using of the Lord's name, and the religion[1] wherein our God is very well pleased.

How the
name of God
is abused. Now note by the way, that there are sundry ways whereby we abuse the name of God; and first of all, we abuse it as often as our hearts are without all reverence to God himself; when we do unreverently, filthily[2], wickedly, and blasphemously speak of God, of his judgments, of his word, and of his laws; when we do with scoffing allusions apply God's words to light matters and trifles, by that means turning and drawing the scriptures into a profane and unhonest meaning. Moreover, we do disgrace the name of the Lord our God, when we call not upon his name, but turn ourselves rather to I know not what sort of gods, to man's skill and succour, to things forbidden, to idols, and conjurors[3]; which we fall a-doing then especially, when, being wrapped in misery and calamities, either for our sins, or else because God will try us, we do presently begin to murmur against God, and to accuse his judgments, hardly abstaining from open blasphemy, in grudging to bear the things that for our deserts we do worthily suffer. Hereunto belongeth the abuse of beastly knaves, which do not stick to use the holy name of God in obtaining their filthy lusts, which they call love; and also the naughtiness of them that thereby seek to find and recover the things that are lost, or else are stolen from them. We do unhallow the name of the Lord our God, when we give not to him all honour and glory. We shall, peradventure, do some good deed; there is, perhaps, in us something worthy to be praised: if we, therefore, shall challenge the praise thereof to ourselves, or, at the least, shall pare out a piece of that glory for our own share, and give the rest to God, not referring it all and whole to God the author of all, then do we therein defile the name of God, which ought alone to be praised for ever and ever.

[1 cultus, Lat.]

[2 petulanter, Lat.]

[3 ad magicas artes, Lat.]

Furthermore, if we deny the Lord, or blush at and be ashamed of his holy gospel, because of this wicked world and the naughty men therein; if also we do spot ourselves with a filthy and unclean life, which is to the slander of God's name and the offence of our neighbour; then do we take the Lord's name in vain; yea, we abuse it to his dishonour and reproach. We do abuse the name of the Lord, if we take a solemn oath in a trifle or matter of no effect, or if we do not keep and perform the oath that we have sworn. In our daily talk very often, and almost about godless matters, we are wont to call, and take to witness, the dreadful name of God, having learned it of an ill continuance and custom, or else being stirred up by some evil motion of our naughty mind: we have an innumerable sort of deep and terrible oaths, as wounds, blood, cross, and passion of the Lord, heaven, earth, sacraments, every saint in heaven, and all the devils of hell[4]. Beside all this, we abuse the name of God also sundry and divers ways in telling of lies. The preacher or teacher of the church lieth, when he crieth, "Thus saith the Lord;" whereas the Lord indeed saith nothing so. He maketh the name of God a cloke and a colour to hide his deceit, and doth beguile poor simple souls. The magistrate crieth out, "All power is of God[5];" and so, under pretence of God's name, doth his subjects injury in playing the tyrant and not the magistrate. The common people deceive one another, under the name of the Lord, in contracts and bargaining. And the sturdy rogue, unworthy of alms, will not stickle to stand and make God's name an idle occupation for to get a penny. But who can reckon up all the things, wherein God's name is foully abused? We must all therefore have an eye, that we defile not the name of God, but rather bless it, and holily worship it.

For it followeth in the words of the Lord, what punishment abideth for them that so disgrace his name: "Because," saith he, "the Lord will not let him go unpunished, that taketh his name in vain." And although this commination of the Lord is very horrible indeed, and of itself effectual enough to make the godly sort afraid to pollute the name of God; yet nevertheless I will add one example or twain of

The punishment of them that abuse God's name.

[4 Cf. Becon's Works, Parker Soc. ed. Vol. I. page 359; Latimer, Vol. I. page 231; Hutchinson's Works, page 20.]

[5 Rom. xiii. 1.]

[BULLINGER.]

16

them whom the Lord hath punished for defiling his name.
David crieth out, and saith: " The unrighteous shall not
stand in thy sight, O Lord: thou hatest them that work
iniquity : thou shalt destroy all them that speak lies[1]."   But
how much more likely is it, that the Lord will destroy all
them that speak blasphemy, and abuse his holy name ! Saul,
verily, because he called not upon the Lord in his extreme
necessity, but asked counsel of the pythonisse[2], was compelled
to kill himself with his own hand, after he had seen his
people downright slain by the Philistines, his enemies, and his
sons lie dead in the midst of the people. Ananias lieth to
the Holy Ghost, and defileth the name of the Lord; and, falling down suddenly dead to the ground, down he goeth with
shame enough to the devil of hell[3]. Sanherib blasphemeth
the name of the eternal God before the walls of Jerusalem ;
but anon after he is for his labour bereft of his puissant
army, and in his own god's temple is shot through[4] by his
own sons. Jehoiachim and Zedechias, both kings of Juda
and blasphemers of God's name, are taken captives and slain
by Nabuchodonosor, king of Babylon[5]. Achab, Jezebel, and
the priests of Baal are utterly wiped out by king Jehu, because they, under the colour of God and godliness, blasphemed the name of God, and persecuted the true religion[6].
In the twenty-fourth of Leviticus, he that blasphemed the
name of God was overwhelmed with stones to death.

A pain for
blasphemers
decreed by
an emperor.

And therefore the emperor Justinian, *In Novellis constitu.*
77, writing to the citizens of Constantinople, saith : " Moreover, because, besides unspeakable lusts, some men lash out
cursings and oaths of God, thereby provoking him to anger ;
we therefore exhort them to abstain from cursings and oaths
by his hair and head, and such other words like unto these.
For if reproaches done unto men are not left unrevenged,

[1 Psal. v. 5, 6.]

[2 Saul pythonissam consulit; head-note of Vulgate in 1 Reg.
xxviii.]

[3 migrat ad inferos, Lat.]

[4 sagittis confligitur, Lat.; with the sword, 2 Kings xix. 37; cum
gladio, Vulg.]

[5 2 Chron. xxxvi. 6 ; 2 Kings xxv. 7.   It is not recorded in scripture, although it may be inferred, that these two kings were brought
to death by Nebuchadnezzar's treatment of them.]

[6 1 Kings xxii. ; 2 Kings ix. and x.]

much more is he worthy to be punished, that stirreth God to
anger with his villany.   And for such offences as these do so
many dearths, earthquakes, and plagues come unto men.   We
therefore admonish them to abstain from those crimes : for
whosoever, after this admonition of ours, shall be found faulty
therein, they shall first shew themselves unworthy to be
beloved of men, and, after that too, suffer such punishment as
the law shall appoint.   For we have given in charge to
the right honourable the lieutenant of our royal city to
apprehend the guilty, and to punish them extremely : lest
peradventure at length for such sinners' contempt, and such
heinous offences, not only this city, but also the whole commonweal, be justly destroyed by God's just vengeance[7]."
Thus much writeth he.   Now by this we may gather, that
not the least part of our calamities at these days do happen
unto us because of our detestable cursings and horrible blasphemies, which very few magistrates, or none almost at all,
do go about to redress, or punish as they should do.   The
name of the living God is blasphemed with passing deep and
horrible oaths, of all sorts, of all kinds[8], and all ages; so that
I think verily, that from the beginning of the world there
never was such a blasphemous people as are in this cursed
age of ours.   And therefore are we vexed with unspeakable
and endless calamities.   For God is true, and cannot lie,

[7 Ἐπειδὴ δέ τινες—καὶ βλάσφημα ῥήματα καὶ ὅρκους περὶ Θεοῦ
ὀμνύουσι, τὸν Θεὸν παροργίζοντες· καὶ τούτοις ὁμοίως παρεγγυῶμεν ἀποσχέσθαι τῶν τοιούτων βλασφήμων ῥημάτων, καὶ τοῦ ὀμνύναι κατὰ τριχός
τε καὶ κεφαλῆς καὶ τῶν τούτοις παραπλησίων ῥημάτων· εἰ γὰρ αἱ κατ'
ἀνθρώπων γινόμεναι βλασφημίαι ἀνεκδίκητοι οὐ καταλιμπάνονται, πολλῷ
μᾶλλον ὁ εἰς αὐτὸ τὸ θεῖον βλασφημῶν ἄξιός ἐστι τιμωρίας ὑποστῆναι.—
Διὰ γὰρ τὰ τοιαῦτα πλημμελήματα καὶ λιμοὶ καὶ σεισμοὶ καὶ λοιμοὶ γίγνονται.   Καὶ διὰ τοῦτο παραινοῦμεν τοῖς τοιούτοις ἀποσχέσθαι τῶν εἰρημένων
ἀτοπημάτων—εἰ γὰρ καὶ μετὰ τὴν τοιαύτην ἡμῶν νομοθεσίαν εὑρεθῶσί τινες
τοῖς αὐτοῖς ἐπιμένοντες πλημμελήμασι, πρότερον μὲν ἀναξίους ἑαυτοὺς
ποιοῦσι τῆς τοῦ Θεοῦ φιλανθρωπίας, ἔπειτα δὲ καὶ τὰς ἐκ τῶν νόμων ὑποστή-
σονται τιμωρίας.   Ἐπετρέψαμεν γὰρ τῷ ἐνδοξοτάτῳ ἐπάρχῳ τῆς βασιλίδος
πόλεως τοὺς ἐπιμένοντας ταῖς εἰρημέναις ἀτόποις καὶ ἀσεβέσι πράξεσι—
συνέχειν, καὶ ταῖς ἐσχάταις ὑποβάλλειν τιμωρίαις· ἵνα μὴ, ἐκ τοῦ παραβλέ-
πειν τὰς τοιαύτας ἁμαρτίας, εὑρεθῇ καὶ ἡ πόλις καὶ ἡ πολιτεία διὰ τῶν
τοιούτων ἀσεβῶν πράξεων ἀδικουμένη.—Justin. Auth. Collat. vi. tit. 6 :
Novell. 77. cap. 1, p. 323. Gotting. 1797.]

[8 Sexuum, Lat.]

which saith, that they shall not scape scot free that take his
name in vain.   The men of our time do not only take it in
vain, but do of malice also blasphemously defile it.   I would
to God the magistrates would more sincerely set forth the
worship of God among the people : or else, if this may not
be obtained at their hands, yet then at least that they would
be no worse nor godless than Caiphas, who, when he heard
(as he thought) blasphemy against the name of God, did rent
his clothes[1], and cry, that the blasphemer was worthy to die.
For surely, unless our christian magistrates do become more
sharp and severe against blaspheming villanies, I do not see
but that they must needs be a great deal worse than the
wicked knave Caiphas.   Undoubtedly the Lord is true (as
every one of you must severally think within yourselves),
and he verily will punish in all men the defiling of his name,
but much more the malicious blaspheming of the same.

Of an oath.   This very matter and place do now require, that I also
speak somewhat here of taking an oath, or swearing, which
is done by calling and taking to witness of God's name.   Now,
in the handling of this matter, many things are to be thought
of and considered.   For first of all, I see that some there
are, which doubt whether it be lawful to take an oath or no,
Whether it
be lawful to
swear. because in Matthew the Lord hath said : "Ye have heard
what was said of old, Thou shalt not forswear thyself, but
shalt perform thine oaths unto the Lord ; but I say unto you,
Swear not at all, &c.[2]"   But the Lord's mind in Matthew
was not to take clean away the true and ancient law, but
to interpret it, and to bring it to a sounder sense, because it
was before corrupted and marred by divers forged and counterfeit glosses of the Pharisees.   For the people, being taught
by them, had evermore an eye to keep their mouths from
perjury ; but touching superfluous, unprofitable, and needless
oaths, they had no care at all, not thinking that it was amiss
to swear by heaven and by earth : wherefore the Lord, expounding his Father's law, saith, that all oaths generally are
forbidden, to wit, those wherein the name of the Lord is taken
in vain, and whereby we swear when there is no need at all.
In the meanwhile, he neither condemned, nor yet took clean

[1 Matt. xxvi. 65, 66.]
[2 Matt. v. 33, 34.]

away, the solemn and lawful oath. Now there is great difference between a solemn oath and our daily oaths, which are
nothing else but deep swearings, not only needless, but also
hurtful. But a solemn oath is both profitable and needful.
The law of God and words of Christ do not forbid things profitable and needful, and therefore they condemn not a solemn
and lawful oath. Yea, in the law too is permitted a solemn
oath, where there is forbidden alone the unprofitable using of
the Lord's name. And Christ, our Lord, came not to break
the law, but to fulfil the law. And therefore he, in St
Matthew, did not condemn an oath : unless a man should go
about to prove that the Son taught a doctrine clean contrary
to the doctrine of his heavenly Father ; which is a blasphemy
against the Father and the Son not to be suffered. Moreover,
God himself also sweareth ; which undoubtedly he would not
do, if an oath could not be taken without any sin. For, after
a long exposition of the law, he saith : " Be ye holy, for I
am holy ; be ye perfect, even as your heavenly Father is perfect[3]." We read also, that the holiest men of both the Testaments, by calling and taking to witness the name of God in
matters of weight, did swear, and that they sware without
any sin. An oath therefore in the law of Christ is not forbidden ; and it is lawful for a christian man both to exact and
also to take an oath. I rather, verily, do not see how that
man is worthy to be called a Christian, which, being lawfully required to swear, will seem to refuse it. But of this
I have more fully disputed in another place against the
Anabaptists[4].

Secondarily, we have to consider for what causes we ought
to swear. In many commonweals it is an usual and received
custom to take an oath upon every light occasion ; and for
that cause we see that an oath is lightly set by and very
little esteemed. For what is this but to take the name of
God in vain ? Let magistrates therefore learn and know, that
an oath ought not to be required but in earnest affairs : as
when it standeth for the glory of God, for the safety of our

For what
causes we
ought to
swear.

[3 Levit. xix. 2 ; Matt. v. 48.]
[4 See H. Bullingeri adversus Anabaptistas Libri vi. nunc primum e
Germanico sermone in Latinum conversi per Josiam Simlerum, Tigu-
rinum, Lib. v. cap. 11, pp. 197—202. Tiguri. 1560.]

neighbour, and for the public weal. We must mark therefore, when, and why, the people of God have sworn in the scriptures. Abraham sware, when he made the league and confederacy with Abimelech[1]. The people of God doth very often swear under their kings, in making a covenant with God for the keeping of true religion[2]. They of old time did clear themselves of heinous suspicions by taking of an oath. In Exodus we read: "If any man shall give to his neighbour a beast to keep, and it shall die, or be stolen away, no man seeing it, then shall an oath by the Lord go betwixt them twain, that he hath not laid his hand on his neighbour's thing: which oath the owner of the thing shall take, and the other shall not restore it[3]." For Paul, in the sixth to the Hebrews, saith: "Men verily swear by the greater; and an oath for confirmation is to them an end of all strife." To this end, therefore, let magistrates apply the use of an oath; and let them have an especial regard, in giving an oath, to do it reverently: let the peers of the people[4] keep inviolably that which they swear; and let them take heed that they do not rashly require an oath of light-headed fellows: let them not compare any thing, or think any thing to be equal, to an oath; but let them reverently, and last of all, have their recourse to that, as to the utmost remedy to find out the truth; and therewithal let them use sharp punishment against perjured persons[5]. But woe to the people's princes, if through their wicked negligence an oath be not esteemed! For he, without doubt, will punish them sharply for it, who saith: "Because I will not suffer him to go unpunished that taketh the Lord's name in vain."

What an oath is.

Thirdly, I will tell you what an oath is, and what it is to swear. An oath is the calling or taking to witness of God's name, to confirm the truth of that we say. There is difference betwixt an oath, and that deep kind of swearing, whereby

[1 Gen. xxi. 24.]

[2 2 Kings xxiii. 3 ; 2 Chron. xv. 12—15; Jer. xxxiv. 8—10.]

[3 Exod. xxii. 10, 11.]

[4 proceres populi, Lat.]

[5 Ita minus vilescet in popularium animis juramenti religio, Lat. omitted by the translator. By these means reverence for an oath will not be so much weakened in the minds of their people.]

God is blasphemed and torn in pieces. There is difference, too, betwixt an oath and those bitter speeches wherewith we use to curse and ban our neighbours: they are not worthy, doubtless, to be called oaths. But, for because this word *juramentum* is over largely used for any kind of oath, as well in the worse as better part; therefore the godly and lawful oaths are wisely called by the name of *jusjurandum*[6]. For by adding *jus*, which signifieth the law, we are admonished that that kind of oath is lawful and righteous. Now this taking of God's name to witness hath joined to it a calling on, and avowing ourselves to, God's curse and vengeance. For this is the manner of an oath and order of swearing: I will say, or do, it truly indeed and without deceit, so God may help me. Therefore we put ourselves in danger of God's wrath and vengeance, unless we do truly and indeed both speak and do the thing that we promised to do or speak. A very deep and solemn promise-making is this, than the which verily there is not a greater to be found in the world. Here also must be considered the circumstances and ceremonies in swearing. For our ancestors of old were wont to lift their hand up unto heaven, and to swear by the name of the Lord. The Lord our God dwelleth in heaven. We therefore do manifestly declare, that, as in the judges' eyes we lift our hand to heaven, even so in our minds we do ascend, and swear in the presence and sight of God; yea, we give our hand, and plight our faith, to God there, in taking an oath by the name of God. This ceremony used Abraham, the singular friend of God, and father of the faithful[7], when he was wont to swear.

I need not therefore to proceed any further, for to declare whether we ought to swear by the name of God alone, or else by the names of saints, or else by laying the hand upon the holy Gospel. For it is manifest, that the faithful must swear by the only eternal and most high God: touching which thing we have most evident precepts, commanding us to swear by the name of the Lord, and again, forbidding us to swear by the names of strange gods. Of the first sort are these: "Thou shalt fear the Lord thy

Circumstances and ceremonies in swearing.

How we ought to swear.

[6 Jusjurandum est affirmatio religiosa.—Cic. de Offic. Lib. III.]
[7 pater fidei, Lat.—See Gen. xiv. 22.]

God, thou shalt serve him, and swear by his name.'
Deut. sixth and tenth chapter. Also the Lord himself in
Esay saith : " To me shall every knee bend, and by me shall
every tongue swear[1]." And again, in the sixty-fifth chapter
the same prophet saith : " He that will bless himself shall
bless in the Lord, and he that will swear shall swear by the
true and very God." Of the latter sort too are these testimonies of the holy scriptures : Exod. xxiii., " All that I have
said keep ye, and do ye not once so much as think of the
names of strange gods, neither let them be heard out of your
mouth." And Josue, in the twenty-third chapter, saith: "When
ye shall come in among these nations, see that ye swear not by
the name of their gods, and look that ye neither worship nor
yet bow down unto them." In the fifth of Jeremy the Lord
saith : " Thy sons have forsaken me, and sworn by other gods
which are no gods indeed : I have filled them, and they have
gone a whoring," &c. Moreover, the prophet Sophony
bringeth in the Lord speaking and saying : " I will cut off
those that worship and swear by the Lord, and swear by
Malchom[2]," that is, by their king and defender. And no
marvel though he do threaten destruction to them that swear
by the names of creatures : for an oath is the chief and
especial honour done to God, which therefore cannot be divided
to other. For we swear by the highest, whom we believe
to be the chiefest goodness, the giver of all good things,
and the punishing revenger of every evil deed. But and
if we swear by the names of other gods, then verily shall
we make them equal to God himself, and attribute to them
the honour due to him. And for this cause the blessed
martyr of Christ, Polycarpus, chose rather the flames of fire
than to swear by the power and estate of Cæsar. The
story is to be seen in the fourth book and fifteenth chapter
of Eusebius[3].

An oath is the special honour done to God.

[1 Isai. xlv. 23.]

[2 Zephan. i. 4, 5.—Malkom regem significat. Propheta usurpavit
pro divo aliquo sive patrono deoque tutelari.—Bullinger de Origine
Erroris, cap. xii. p. 54, Tigur. 1539.]

[3 Ἐπιμένοντος δὲ πάλιν αὐτοῦ (τοῦ ἡγουμένου) καὶ λέγοντος, Ὄμοσον
τὴν Καίσαρος τύχην, ὁ Πολύκαρπος, Εἰ κενοδοξεῖς, φησὶν, ἵνα ὀμόσω τὴν
Καίσαρος τύχην, ὡς λέγεις προσποιούμενος ἀγνοεῖν ὅς τις εἰμὶ, μετὰ παρρησίας
ἄκουε· Χριστιανὸς εἰμί.—Euseb. Hist. Eccles. Lib. IV. cap. 15. See
also Early Writings of Hooper, Parker Soc. ed. page 478.]

Fourthly, we have to consider how we ought to swear, and what the conditions of a just, a lawful, and an honest oath are. Jeremy therefore saith: "Thou shalt swear, The Lord liveth, in truth, in judgment, and righteousness: and the nations shall bless themselves in him, and in him shall they glory[4]." There are therefore four conditions of a just and a lawful oath. The first is, Thou shalt swear, "The Lord liveth." Here now again is repeated that which hath so many times been beaten into our heads, that we ought to swear by the name of the living God. The pattern of our ancestors' oath was this, "The Lord liveth;" as it is evident by the writings of the prophets. Let us not swear therefore by any other but by God. The second condition is: "Thou shalt swear in truth." So then it is required, that not only the tongue, but also the mind, should swear; lest haply we say, The tongue indeed did swear, but the mind sware not at all[5]. Let us be true and faithful therefore, without deceit or guile; let us not lie, nor go about with subtilty to shift off the oath that once we have made. We Germans express this well, when we say, *On alle gfard*[6], or else, *On gfard;* that is, I will not use any double dealing, but will simply and in good faith perform that I promise. There is an excellent pattern of a false and a deceitful oath in *Auli Gellii Noct. Att.* Lib. VII. cap. 18.[7] The third condition is: "Thou shalt swear in," or with, "judgment;" that is, advisedly, with great discretion, not rashly nor lightly, but with consideration of every thing and circumstance, in great necessity, and cases of public commodity. The fourth condition is: "Thou shalt swear in justice," or righteousness; lest peradventure our oath be against right and equity, that is, lest we sin against righteousness or justice, which attributeth that which is theirs both to God and man;

The conditions of an holy oath.

[4 Jer. iv. 2.]

[5 Reference is here made to the well-known line of Euripides, Hippolyt. 608. ἡ γλῶσσ᾽ ὀμώμοχ᾽, ἡ δὲ φρὴν ἀνώμοτος :—and Bullinger uses the words of Cicero's version: Juravi lingua, mentem injuratam gero.—De Offic. Lib. III. cap. 29.]

[6 ohne alle gefährde.]

[7 The case referred to by A. Gellius is that of the ten prisoners sent by Hannibal to Rome, after the battle of Cannæ; two of whom evaded their oath, and remained in Rome. P.—See also Cic. de Offic. Lib. I. cap. 13, and Lib. III. cap. 32.]

so that our oath do not directly tend against the love of God and our neighbour.

Here, dearly beloved, ye have heard me express in few words (which God himself hath also taught us), how we must swear, of what sort and fashion our lawful and allowable oaths ought to be, and under what conditions they are contained. But now, if we shall swear against these conditions appointed us by God, then shall our oaths and swearings be altogether unlawful: and furthermore, if we shall go about to perform those unlawful and unallowable oaths, then shall we therewithal purchase and incur the heavy wrath of the revenging Lord.

Whether wicked oaths must be performed. Now, in these days it is usually of custom demanded whether we ought to keep or perform wicked or ungodly unjust or evil vows, or oaths; as if, for example, thy oath or vow should directly tend against God, against true religion against the word of God, or the health of thy neighbour?

I will here allege and rehearse the usual accustomed answer, which notwithstanding is very true, and grounded upon examples of holy scriptures, as that that squareth not from the truth the narrow breadth of one small hair[1]. The answer therefore is this: If any man shall swear against the faith and charity, so that the keeping of his oath may tend to the worse, then it is better for him to change his oath than to fulfil it.

It is best to break an ill oath. Whereupon Saint Ambrose saith: "It is sometime contrary to a man's duty to perform the oath that he hath promised, as Herod did[2]." Isidore also saith: "In evil promises break thine oath; in a naughty vow change thy purpose. The thing thou hast unadvisedly vowed, do not perform. The promise is wicked that is finished with mischief[3]." And again, "That oath must not be kept, whereby any evil is unwarily promised. As if, for example, one should give his

[1 veritatique per omnia consentaneam, Lat.]

[2 Est etiam contra officium nonnunquam solvere promissum sacramentum custodire: ut Herodes, &c.—Ambros. de Offic. apud Gratian. Decret. Par. 1583. Decr. sec. par. caus. xxii. Quæst. 4. can. 2 col. 1574.]

[3 In malis promissis rescinde fidem: in turpi voto muta decretum quod incaute vovisti, ne facias. Impia enim est promissio, quæ scelere adimpletur.—Isidor. in Synon. Lib. ii. ap. Gratian. Decret. ibid. can 4. col. 1575. See also Becon's Works, Parker Soc. ed. Vol. i. p. 372.]

ith to an adulteress to abide in naughtiness with her for ver: undoubtedly it is more tolerable not to keep promise, han to remain in whoredom still[4]." Beda moreover saith: If it shall happen, that we at unawares shall with an oath romise anything, and that the keeping of that oath shall be he cause of further evil, then let us think it best upon better dvice to change our oath without hurt to our conscience; and hat it is better, upon such a necessity, for us to be forsworn, han, for avoiding of perjury, to fall into another sin ten times vorse than that. David sware by God, that he would kill he foolish fellow Nabal; but at the first intercession that his rife Abigal, wiser than himself, did make, he ceased to hreaten him, he sheathed his sword again, and did not find imself any whit grieved for breaking his hasty oath[5]." Augustine also saith: "Whereas David did not by shedding of lood perform his promise bound with an oath, therein his odliness was the greater[6]." "David sware rashly, but, upon etter and godly advice, he performed not the thing he had worn[7]." By this and the like it is declared, that many oaths re not to be observed. Now he that sweareth so doth in: but in changing his oath he doth very well. He that hangeth not such an oath, committeth a double sin; first, for wearing as he ought not, and then for doing that he should

[4 Non est observandum juramentum, quo malum incaute promit-tur: veluti si quispiam adulteræ perpetuam cum ea permanendi dem polliceatur. Tolerabilius est enim non implere sacramentum, uam permanere in stupri flagitio.—Isidor. ap. Gratian. Decret. ibid. an. 13. col. 1576.]

[5 Si aliquid forte nos incautius jurasse contigerit, quod obser-atum pejorem vergat in exitum, libere illud consilio salubriore mu-andum noverimus, ac magis instante necessitate pejerandum nobis, uam pro vitando perjurio in aliud crimen gravius esse divertendum. enique juravit David per Dominum occidere Nabal, virum stultum et npium—sed ad primam intercessionem Abigail feminæ prudentis ox remisit minas; revocavit ensem in vaginam; neque aliquid culpæ tali perjurio contraxisse doluit.—Beda in Homil. xliv. in natal. ecoll. S. Joan. ap. Gratian. Decret. ibid. can. 6. col. 1575.]

[6 Quod David juramentum per sanguinis effusionem non implevit, ajor pietas fuit.—Augustin. ap. Gratian. Decret. ibid. can. 3. col. 574. See Becon, Vol. I. p. 374.]

[7 Juravit temere, sed non implevit jurationem majore pietate.— ratian. ibid. can. 4. col. 1575, and August. Serm. Opp. Par. 1531. om. x. fol. 304.]

not. Thus much hitherto have I rehearsed of other men'
words, which all men verily acknowledge to be true and s
indeed. Now by this ye do easily understand, dearly beloved
Monastical
vows. what ye have to think of those monastical vows and priests
oaths, which promise chastity, (no farther, I wis, by thei
leave, than man's frail weakness will suffer them.) "For i
is better," saith the apostle, "to marry than to burn[1]." And
more commendable is it not to perform those foolish, hurtful
and unpure promises, that drive them perforce to filthy uncleanness, than, under the colour of keeping an oath truly, to
lie and to live unchastely, God wot[2].

How religi-
ously we
ought to keep
our oaths. Fifthly and lastly, I have briefly to put you in mind, that
ye endeavour yourselves, by all the means ye may, devoutly
to keep that which ye swear; and therewithal, in few words,
to let you understand what reward is prepared for them that
do religiously and holily keep and observe the holy oath once
solemnly taken. If we love God, if we desire to sanctify his
name, if we take the true God for the very true God, and for
our God; if we will have him to be gentle and merciful to
us-ward, and to be our present deliverer and aider at all
assays; then will we have a most diligent care to swear with
fear devoutly, and holily to keep and perform the oath that
we devoutly make. But unless we do this, then terrible
threatenings and sharp revengement of God's just judgment
are thundered from heaven against us transgressors. The
very heathens shall rise up and condemn us in the day of
judgment. For the Saguntines, the Numantines, and they of
Petilia, chose rather to die with fire and famine, than to break
or violate their promise once bound with an oath[3]. Moreover,
the laws of all wise and civil princes and people do adjudge
perjured persons to die the death. How great offences, how
great corruptions, how great and many mischiefs, I pray you,
do rise through perjuries! They entangle, trouble, disgrace,
mar, and overthrow the estates, both civil and ecclesiastical.
Whosoever, therefore, doth love the commonweal and safeguard of his country; whosoever doth love the church and

[1 1 Cor. vii. 9.]   [2 parum pudice vivere, Lat.]
[3 Liv. Lib. XXI. cap. 14, and XXIII. capp. 20, 30; Florus, Lib. II.
cap. 18; Valer. Max. Lib. VII. cap. 6.   See also early writings of
Hooper, Parker Soc. ed. page 336, and Augustin. de Civit. Dei. Lib.
III. cap. 20.]

ood estate thereof; he will, above all things, have an especial egard to keep religiously the promise of his oath. Now to hose that holily do keep their oaths, the Lord doth promise large reward. For Jeremy saith: "And the nations shall less themselves in him, and in him shall they glory[4]." As if e should say: If the people of Juda shall swear holily and eep their oaths, then will the Lord pour out upon them so great elicity and abundant plenty of all good things, that, when as ereafter one shall bless or wish well to another, he shall say, The Lord shew thee his blessing, as of old he did to the ews." And whosoever shall praise another, he shall say hat "he is like to the Israelites." It is therefore assuredly ertain, that they shall be enriched with all good things, and orthy of all manner praise, whosoever shall inviolably keep heir oaths and promises.

A large reward promised to such as keep their oaths.

Let us endeavour ourselves, my brethren, I beseech you, o sanctify the Lord's name, and to add to this third com-andment your earnest and continual prayers, saying, as our ord Jesus hath taught us, O heavenly Father, hallowed be ny name; or, let thy name be holily worshipped. To him be lory for ever and ever. Amen.

F THE FOURTH PRECEPT OF THE FIRST TABLE[5], THAT
IS, OF THE ORDER AND KEEPING OF THE
SABBATH-DAY.

THE FOURTH SERMON.

THE fourth commandment of the first table is word for ord as followeth: "Remember that thou keep holy the bbath-day. Six days thou shalt labour, and do all thy orks; but on the seventh day is the sabbath of the Lord y God, in which thou shalt not do any manner of work, either thou, nor thy son, nor thy daughter, nor thy man-rvant, nor thy maid-servant, nor thy cattle, nor thy stranger hich is within thy gates. Because in six days the Lord

The fourth precept.

[4 Jer. iv. 2.]   [5 seu Decalogi, Lat. omitted.]

made heaven and earth, the sea, and all that is therein; an rested the seventh day: therefore the Lord blessed the sabbath day, and hallowed it."

The order, which the Lord useth in giving these commandments, is natural and very excellent. In the first precept the Lord did teach us faith and love to God-ward. I the second he removed from us idols and all foreign kind of worship. In the third he began to instruct us in the true and lawful worship of God: which worship standeth in the sanctifying of his holy name, for us to call thereon, and holily and freely to praise it, and to think and speak of it as religiously as he shall give us grace[1]. The fourth commandment teacheth us also the worship due to God, and the hallowing of his holy name; but yet it bendeth somewhat to the outward honour, although, nevertheless, it frameth to the inward religion. For the sabbath doth belong both to the inward and outward service of God. Let us see, therefore, what we have to think that the sabbath is, how far forth the use thereof extendeth, and after what sort we have to worship our God in observing the sabbath. Sabbath doth signify rest and ceasing from servile work[2]. And this here I think worthy to be noted, that the Lord saith not simply, "Sanctify the sabbath;" but, "Remember that thou keep holy the sabbath-day;" meaning thereby, that the sabbath was of old ordained, and given first of all to the ancient fathers, and then again renewed by the Lord, and beaten into the memory of the people of Israel. But the sum of the whole commandment is, Keep holy the sabbath-day. This sum doth the Lord by and by more largely amplify, by reckoning up the very days, and particular rehearsing the whole household, to whom the keeping of the sabbath is given in charge[3].

The sabbath itself hath sundry significations. For first of all, the scripture maketh mention of a certain spiritual and continual sabbath. In this sabbath we rest from servile work, in abstaining from sin, and doing our best not to have

Side notes:
The order of the Lord's commandments.

The sabbath.

The sabbath is spiritual.

[1 "as he shall give us grace," not in the original.]

[2 שַׁבָּת a cessation, rest.—Lee's Hebr. Lex. in voc.]

[3 Postremo adjicitur exemplum quoque ipsius Dei quiescentis et sanctificantis sabbatum. "Lastly is added also the example of God himself resting on the Sabbath-day and sanctifying it." Omitted by the translator. P.]

ur own will found in ourselves, or to work our own works; but, in ceasing from these, to suffer God to work in us, and wholly to submit our bodies to the government of his good Spirit. After this sabbath followeth that eternal sabbath and everlasting rest, of which Esay, in his 58th and 66th chapters, speaketh very much, and Paul also, in the fourth to the Hebrews. But God is truly worshipped, when we, ceasing from evil, and obeying God's holy Spirit, do exercise ourselves in the study of good works. At this time I have no leisure, neither do I think that it is greatly profitable for me, to reason, as largely or as exquisitely as I could, of the allegorical sabbath, or spiritual rest. Let us rather, my brethren, in these our mortal bodies, do our endeavour, with an unwearied good-will of holiness, to sanctify the sabbath, that pleaseth the Lord so well.

Secondly, the sabbath is the outward institution of our religion. For it pleased the Lord, in this commandment, to teach us an outward religion and kind of worship, wherein he would have us all to be exercised. Now, for because the worshipping of God cannot be without a time, therefore hath the Lord appointed a certain time, wherein we should abstain from outward or bodily works; but so yet that we should have leisure to attend unto our spiritual business. For for that cause is the outward rest commanded, that the spiritual work should not be hindered by the bodily business. Moreover, that spiritual labour among our fathers was chiefly spent about four things; to wit, about public reading and expounding of the scriptures, and so consequently, about the hearing of the same; about public prayers and common petitions; about sacrifices, or the administration of the sacraments; and lastly, about the gathering of every man's benevolence. In these consisted the outward religion of the sabbath. For the people kept holy day, and met together in holy assemblies; where the prophets read to them the word of the Lord, expounding it, and instructing the hearers in the true religion. Then did the faithful jointly make their common prayers and supplications for all things necessary for their behoof. They praised the name of the Lord, and gave him thanks for all his good benefits bestowed upon them. Furthermore, they did offer sacrifices, as the Lord commanded them, celebrating the mysteries and sacraments of Christ

The sabbath is the outward institution of religion.

their Redeemer, and keeping their faith exercised and in ure: they were joined in one with these sacraments, and also warned of their duty, which is, to offer themselves a lively sacrifice to the Lord their God. Lastly, they did in the congregation liberally bestow the gifts of their good-will to the use of the church: they gathered every man's benevolence, therewith to supply the church's necessity, to maintain the ministers, and to relieve the poor and needy. These were the holy works of God, which while they, having their hearts instructed in faith and love, did fulfil, they did therein rightly sanctify the sabbath and the name of the Lord; that is, they did on the sabbath those kind [of] works[1], which do both sanctify the name of God, become his worshippers, and also are the works indeed that are holy and pleasing in the sight of God. If any man require a substantial and evident example of the sabbath or holy day thus holily celebrated, he shall find it in the eighth chapter of the book of Nehemias: for there the priests do read and expound the word of God, they praise the name of the Lord, they pray with the people, they offer sacrifice, they shew their liberality, and do in all points behave themselves holily and devoutly as they should.

There is time enough allowed to labour in.

Now, lest any peradventure might make this objection and say, Ease breedeth vice[2]; or else, I must labour with my hands to get my living, lest I die with hunger, and my family perish; he answereth, The Lord alloweth thee time sufficient for thy labour, for thee to work in to get a living for thyself and thy household: for six days thou mayest work, but the seventh day doth the Lord challenge and require to be consecrated to him and his holy rest. Every week hath seven days: but of those seven the Lord requireth but one for himself. Who then can rightly complain, I beseech you, or say that he hath injury done unto him? More time is allowed to work in, than to keep holy the sabbath: and he that requireth to have this sabbath kept is God, the maker, the father, and Lord of all mankind.

The master of the house must teach all his family the keeping of the sabbath-day.

Furthermore, the Lord doth precisely command and give a charge to plant and bring in this holy rest, this discipline and outward worship, into the whole family of every several house. Whereby we gather, what the duty of a good house-

[1 ea operabantur opera, Lat.]   [2 otia dant vitia, Lat.]

holder is; to wit, to have a care to see all his family keep holy the sabbath-day; that is, to do on the sabbath-day those good works which I have before rehearsed. And for because the Lord doth know that man's natural disposition is, where it hath the mastery, there for the most part to rule and reign over-haughtily and too too princelike; therefore, lest peradventure the fathers or masters should deal too hardly or rigorously with their households, or hinder them in observing of the sabbath, he doth in express words and exquisite steps of enumeration command them to allow their family, and every one in their family, a resting time to accomplish his holy service. He doth not exempt or except so much as the stranger. He will not suffer nor allow among them the example of such dullheads[3] as say: "Let faith and religion be free to all; let no man be compelled to any religion." For he commandeth to bind the stranger within the gates of God's people, that is, the stranger that dwelleth in their jurisdiction, to the holy observing of the sabbath-day.

Now, this ease or rest is not commanded in respect of itself, (for idleness always hath been found fault withal,) but it is ordained for the aforesaid especial causes. God's pleasure is, that there should be a place and time reserved for religion: which time and place are not open to them that are busy about bodily and outward works. He is not conversant in the congregation, he heareth not the word of God, he prayeth not with the church, neither is he partaker of the sacraments, which at his master's commandment taketh a journey, or in the market selleth his wares, or in the barn doth thrash or winnow his corn, or in the field doth hedge or ditch, or doth stand at home beating the anvil, or else sitteth still sewing shoes or hosen[4]. Faith, therefore, and religion bid thee to give rest to thy servants and family; yea, they command thee to egg and compel them, if they be slow, to the holy and profitable work of the Lord. Moreover, the Lord's mind is, that they which labour should also refresh and recreate themselves:

> For things that lack a resting time
> Can never long endure[5].

Ease or rest.

[3 segnium, Lat.]   [4 caligas, Lat.]
[5 Quod caret alterna requie durabile non est, Lat.—Ovid. Ep. 89.]

[BULLINGER.]   17

Wherefore the bountiful Lord, whose mind is to preserve hi creatures, doth teach a way to keep them, and doth diligentl provide, that his creatures be not too much afflicted by th hard handling or covetousness of their owners. Moses i Deuteronomy addeth the pitiful affection of mercy, saying "Remember, that once thou thyself wast a servant in th land of Egypt[1]." Charity, therefore, and civil humanity d crave a measure to be kept, so that we do not with endles labours overlade and weary our household servants. Moreove it is manifest, that the good man of the house[2], by plantin godliness in his family, doth not a little advance and set for ward his private profit and own commodity: for wicke servants are for the most part pickers[3] and deceitful; where as, on the other side, the godly are faithful, whom in h absence he may trust to govern his house. In the reckonin up of the household also is mention made of beasts an cattle; which is done, not so much because their owner is man and ought therefore to use them remissly and mod rately, as for because beasts cannot be laboured without th working hand of man to guide them: so then men a drawn from the solemnizing of the sabbath-day by helpin their cattle. Wherefore, to the intent that they should n be drawn aside, we are here precisely commanded to allo our cattle that resting time.

The Lord did keep the sabbath-day.

Last of all, the Lord doth add his own example, whereb he teacheth us to keep holy the sabbath-day. "Because saith he, "in six days the Lord made heaven and earth, t sea, and all that in them is, and rested the seventh da therefore the Lord blessed the seventh day, and hallowed it The Lord our God wrought six days in creating heaven a earth, the sea, and all that in them is; and the seventh d he rested, and ordained that to be an appointed time for to rest in. On the seventh day we must think of the wor that God did in the six days: the children of God must call remembrance what and how great benefits they have receiv the whole week, for which they must thank God, for whi they must praise God, and by which they must learn God. V

[1 Deut. v. 15.]

[2 paterfamilias, Lat.; an old term for the master of the house. Toone's Glossary. Cf. Matt. xxiv. 43.]

[3 furaces, Lat.]

must then dedicate to him our whole body and soul; we must consecrate to him all our words and our deeds. As that day the Lord did rest from creating, but he ceased not still to preserve; so we upon that day must rest from handy and bodily works, but we must not cease from the works of well doing and worshipping of God. Furthermore, the heavenly[4] rest was no prejudice at all to the things created: neither shall the holy day, or sabbath, spent in God's service, be any let or hinderance to our affairs or business. For the Lord blessed the sabbath-day; and therefore shall he bless thee and thy house, all thy affairs and business, if he shall see thee to have a care to sanctify his sabbath; that is, to do those works which he hath commanded to be done on the sabbath-day. They therefore do err from the truth as far as heaven is wide, whosoever do despise the religion and holy rest of the sabbath-day, calling it an idle ease, and do labour on the sabbath-day, as they do on working days, under the pretence of care for their family and necessity's sake.

The Lord blessed the sabbath-day.

For all these things must we apply to ourselves and our churches. It is most sure, that to Christians the spiritual sabbath is given in charge especially and above all things. Neither is it to be doubted, but that the good Lord's will is, that even in our churches at this day, as well as of the Jews of old, there should be kept and appointed order in all things, but especially in the exercising of outward religion. We know that the sabbath is ceremonial, so far forth as it is joined to sacrifices and other Jewish ceremonies, and so far forth as it is tied to a certain time: but in respect that on the sabbath-day religion and true godliness are exercised and published, that a just and seemly order is kept in the church, and that the love of our neighbour is thereby preserved, therein, I say, it is perpetual, and not ceremonial. Even at this day, verily, we must ease and bear with our family[5]; and even at this day we must instruct our family in the true religion and fear of God. Christ our Lord did no where scatter abroad the holy congregations, but did, as much as he could, gather them together. Now, as there ought to be an appointed place, so likewise must there be a prescribed time, for the outward exercise of religion, and so, consequently, an holy rest. They of the primitive church,

The Christian sabbath.

The Sunday.

[4 quies divina, Lat.]   [5 parci familiæ, Lat.]

therefore, did change the sabbath-day, lest, peradventure they should have seemed to have imitated the Jews, and still to have retained their order and ceremonies[1]; and made their assemblies and holy restings to be on the first day of sabbaths[2], which John calleth Sunday[3], or the Lord's day[4] because of the Lord's glorious resurrection upon that day. And although we do not in any part of the apostles' writings find any mention made that this Sunday was commanded us to be kept holy; yet, for because, in this fourth precept of the first table, we are commanded to have a care of religion and the exercising of outward godliness, it would be against all godliness and christian charity, if we should deny to sanctify the Sunday: especially, since the outward worship of God cannot consist without an appointed time and space of holy rest.

I suppose also, that we ought to think the same of those few feasts and holy days, which we keep holy to Christ our Lord, in memory of his nativity or incarnation, of his circumcision, of his passion, of the resurrection and ascension of Jesus Christ our Lord into heaven, and of his sending of the Holy Ghost upon his disciples[5]. For christian liberty is not a licentious power and dissolving of godly ecclesiastical ordinances, which advance and set forward the glory of God and love of our neighbour. But for because the Lord will have holy days to be solemnized and kept to himself alone, I do not therefore like of the festival days that are held in honour of any creatures. This glory and worship is due to God alone. Paul saith: "I would not that any man should judge you in part of an holy day, or of the sabbaths, which are a shadow of things to come[6]." And again: "Ye observe days, and months, and years, and times; I fear lest I have laboured in you in vain[7]." And therefore we at this day,

(marginal note) Christmas day, New-year's day, Good-Friday, Easter day, Ascension day, Whit-sunday.

[1 See Ignatii, Epist. ad Magnes. cap. 8 and 9.]

[2 prima sabbati, Lat.]　　　　　　　　[3 Rev. i. 10.]

[4 haud dubie, Lat.; omitted.]

[5 Nostra ecclesia ante annos, ni fallor, 12, plura habuit festa: sed abrogatis his solum retinuit diem Dominicam, et festa Christi, Nativitatis videlicet, Circumcisionis et Ascensionis D. Adjecit et missionem Spiritus Sancti superioribus propter celebrationem cœnæ D.——Bullinger. Ep. ad Calvin. in Calv. Opp. Tom. IX. p. 63. Ed. Amstel. dat. Tigur. 29 August. MDLI.]

[6 Coloss. ii. 16, 17. See authorised version, marginal reading.]

[7 Galat. iv. 10, 11.]

hat are in the church of Christ, have nothing to do with the Jewish observation; we have only to wish and endeavour to have the christian observation and exercise of christian religion to be freely kept and observed.

And yet, as the hallowing of the Jewish sabbath, so also the sanctifying or exercise of our Sunday, must be spent and occupied about four things, which ought to be found in the holy congregation of Christians, if their Sunday be truly sanctified and kept holy as it should be. First, let all the godly saints assemble themselves together in the congregation. Let there in that congregation so assembled be preached the word of God; let the Gospel there be read, that the hearers may learn thereby what they have to think of God, what the duty and office is of them that worship God, and how they ought to sanctify the name of the Lord. Then let there in that congregation be made prayers and supplications for all the necessities of all people. Let the Lord be praised for his goodness, and thanked for his inestimable benefits which he daily bestoweth. Then, if time, occasion, and custom of the church do so require, let the sacraments of the church be religiously ministered. For nothing is more required in this fourth commandment than that we should holily observe, and devoutly exercise, the sacraments, and holy, lawful, profitable, and necessary rites and ceremonies of the church. Last of all, let entire humanity and liberality have a place in the saints' assembly; let all learn to give alms privately, and relieve the poor daily, and to do it frankly and openly, so often as opportunity of time and causes of need shall so require. And these are the duties, wherein the Lord's sabbath is kept holy even in the church of Christians; and so much the rather, if to these be added an earnest good will to do no evil all the day long.

The sanctification of the christian sabbath.

This discipline now must be brought in and established by every householder in all our several houses, with as great diligence as it was with the Jews. Touching which thing I have nothing to say here, since I have before so plainly handled this point, as that ye perceive that it agreeth even to the church of us that are Christians. This one thing I add more; that it is the duty of a christian magistrate, or at leastwise of a good householder, to compel to amendment the breakers and contemners of God's sabbath and worship. The peers of

The office of every householder.

Numb. xv.

Israel, and all the people of God, did stone to death (as the Lord commanded them) the man that disobediently did gather sticks on the sabbath-day[1]. Why then should it not be lawful for a christian magistrate to punish by bodily imprisonment, by loss of goods, or by death, the despisers of religion, of the true and lawful worship done to God, and of the sabbath-day? Verily, though the foolish and indiscreet magistrate[2] in this corrupted age do slackly look to his office and duty; yet notwithstanding, let every householder do his endeavour to keep his several family from that ungodly naughtiness; let him punish them of his household by such means as he lawfully may. For if any one householder dwell among idolaters, which neither have, nor yet desire to have or frequent, the christian or lawful congregations; then may he in his own several house gather a peculiar assembly to praise the Lord, as it is manifest that Lot did among the Sodomites; Abraham, Isaac, and Jacob, in the land of Canaan, and in Egypt. But it is a heinous sin and a detestable schism, if the congregation be assembled, either in cities or villages, for thee then to seek out byways to hide thyself, and not to come there, but to contemn the church of God and assembly of saints: as the Anabaptists have taken an use to do.

The abuses of the sabbath-day.

Here therefore I have to reckon[3] up the abuses of the sabbath-day, or the sins committed against this commandment. They transgress this commandment, that cease not from evil works, but[4] abuse the sabbath's rest to the provoking of fleshly pleasures. For they keep the sabbath to God, but work to the devil, in dicing, in drinking, in dancing, and feeding their humours with the vanities of this world, whereby we are not only drawn from the company of the holy congregation, but do also defile our bodies, which we ought rather to sanctify and keep holy. They sin against this precept, which either exercise any handy occupation on the sabbath-day, or else lie wrapt in bed and fast asleep till the day be almost spent, not once thinking to make one of God's congregation. They offend in this precept, that awe their servants to work, and by appointing them to other

[1 Numb. xv. 32—36.]
[2 si cesset demens et ebrius magistratus, Lat.]
[3 paucis recensendi, Lat.]   [4 imo, Lat.]

business do draw them from the worship of God, preferring other stinking things[5] before the honour due to God. And they, above all other, offend herein, which do not only not keep holy the sabbath-day themselves, but do also, with their ungodly scoffs and evil examples, cause other to despise and set light by religion; when they do disdain and mock at the holy rites and ceremonies, at the ministery, ministers, sacred churches[6], and godly exercises. And herein, too, do both the good-men and good-wives offend, if they be slack in their own houses to call upon and to see their families keep holy the sabbath-day. Whosoever do contemn the holiness of the sabbath-day, they give a flat and evident testimony of their ungodliness and light regard of God's mighty power.

Furthermore, the keeping or despising of the sabbath doth always carry with it either ample rewards or terrible threats. For the proof whereof, I will recite unto you, dearly beloved, the words of Jeremy, in his seventeenth chapter. "Thus hath the Lord said unto me," saith he; "Go, and stand under the gate of the sons of the people, through which the kings of Juda go in and out, and under all the gates of Jerusalem, and say unto them: Take heed for your lives, that ye carry no burthen upon you on the sabbath-day, to bring it through the gates of Jerusalem, and that ye bear no burthen out of your houses on the sabbath-day: look that ye do no labour therein; but keep holy the sabbath-day, as I commanded your fathers. Howbeit, they obeyed me not, neither hearkened they unto me, but were obstinate and stubborn, and would not receive any correction. Nevertheless, if ye will hear me, saith the Lord, and bear no burthen through this gate upon the sabbath, but hallow the sabbath, so that ye do no work therein; then shall there go through the gates of this city kings and princes that shall sit upon the throne of David; they shall be carried upon chariots, and ride upon horses, both they and their princes: there shall come men from the cities of Juda and the land of Benjamin, which shall bring sacrifices, and shall offer incense and thanksgiving in the house of the Lord. But if ye will not be obedient unto me to hallow the sabbath, so that ye will bear your burthens through the gates upon the sabbath-day; then will I set fire upon the gates of Jerusalem, which shall burn up the great

Promises and threatenings added to the sabbath-day.

[5] res putidas, Lat.]   [6] scholas sacras, Lat.]

The empe-
ror's law for
the keeping
of the sab-
bath.

houses thereof, and shall not be quenched." Very justly,
therefore, did the devout princes, Leo and Anthemius, writing
to Arsemius, their lieutenant, in these words give charge :
" That the holy days, ordained in honour of the high God's
majesty, should not be spent in any voluptuous pleasures,
nor be unhallowed with troublesome exactions. We therefore do decree and ordain, that the Lord's day, or Sunday, as it hath always been accounted well of, so it shall
still be had in estimation ; so that upon that day no office of
the law shall be executed, no man shall be summoned, no man
arrested for suretyship, no man attached, no pleading shall be
heard, nor any judgment pronounced," &c.   And by and by
after again : " Neither do we, in giving this rest of the holy
day, suffer any man to wallow in any kind of wanton pleasures
at all.   For on that day stage-plays are not admitted, nor
fencers' prizes, nor bear-baitings ; yea too, and if it happen
that the solemnizing of our birth-day fall upon the Sunday,
then shall it be deferred till the next day after.   And we
have determined, that he shall sustain the loss of his dignity,
and have his patrimony confiscate, whosoever shall on the sabbath-day be present at any sight or play, or what summoner
soever of any judge whatsoever shall, under the pretence of
any business, either public or private, do anything to infringe
the statutes in this law enacted[1]."

And yet, nevertheless, they that are Christians do not for-

[[1] Impp. Leo et Anthemius. A. A. Armasio. P. P. x.—Dies festos,
majestati altissimæ dedicatos, nullis volumus voluptatibus occupari,
nec ullis exactionum vexationibus profanari.   Dominicum itaque
diem semper honorabilem decernimus venerandum, ut a cunctis exe-
cutionibus excusetur ; nulla quenquam urgeat admonitio ; nulla fidei-
jussionis flagitetur exactio ; taceat apparitio ; advocatio delitescat ; sit
ille dies a cognitionibus alienus, &c.—Nec hujus tamen religiosi diei
otia relaxantes, obscœnis quibuslibet patimur voluptatibus detineri.
Nihil eodem die vindicet sibi scena theatralis, aut Circense certamen,
aut ferarum lacrymosa spectacula : etiam si in nostro ortu aut natali
celebranda solennitas inciderit, differatur.   Amissionem militiæ pro-
scriptionemque patrimonii sustinebit, si quis unquam hoc die festo
spectaculis interesse, vel cujuscunque judicis apparitor, prætextu ne-
gotii publici seu privati, hæc, quæ lege hac statuta sunt, crediderit
temeranda.—D. Id. Decembr. Constantinop. Zenone et Martiano
Coss.—Justin. Cod. Lib. III. tit. 22. de feriis. p. 411. Tom. I. Lugd.
1551.]

get the words of Christ in the gospel, where he saith : "The sabbath was made for man, and not man for the sabbath; and that[2] the Son of man too is Lord of the sabbath[3]." The godly do very well know that God ordained the sabbath for the preservation, and not for the destruction, of mankind; and that therefore he doth dispense with us for the sabbath, as often as any urgent necessity or saving of a man shall seem to require it. Touching which matter our Saviour Christ himself hath fully satisfied the faithful in the 12th of Matthew, and the 6th and 13th chapters after St Luke. In such things, verily, Christians may use their liberty to occupy themselves in on the sabbath-day[4]. Since the priests and Levites are held excused, which do in the temple openly both kill, slay, burn, and boil beasts, in making their sacrifices, so that they are not thought to break the sabbath-day, because they may without offence to God, even on the sabbaths, dress and make ready the things serving to the outward worship of the Lord; so likewise may we on the sabbath dress and make ready meat and other necessaries which our bodies cannot lack. We may also minister physic to the sick, visit the weak, and help the needy, that so we may preserve the creature of God. Herein did our Saviour give us an example to follow, who did on the sabbath work the deeds of charity and mercy. We have more than one example of his to be seen in the gospel, but especially in Luke vi. and xiii. and John, the fifth chapter. If then on the sabbath-day it be lawful to draw out of a pit a sheep or an ox in danger of drowning, why should it not be lawful likewise on the sabbath to underset with props a ruinous house that is ready to fall? Why should it not be lawful on the sabbath-day to gather in, and keep from spoiling, the hay or corn, which, by reason of unseasonable weather, hath lain too long abroad, and likely to be worse if it stay any longer? The holy emperor Constantine, writing to Elpidius, saith: "Let all judges in courts of law, and citizens of all occupations, rest upon the Sunday, and keep it holy with reverence and devotion. But they that inhabit the country may freely and at liberty attend on their tillage upon the sabbath-day. For oftentimes it falleth out, that they cannot upon another day so commodiously sow their seed, or plant their vines; and

The sabbath made for man, and not man for the sabbath.

To plough land on the sabbath-day.

[2 proinde, Lat.]　　　　　　[3 Mark ii. 27, 28.]
[4 Certe in his versatur libertas Christiana, Lat.]

so, by letting pass the opportunity of a little time, they may hap to lose the profit given of God for our provision[1]." Thus saith the emperor. Now we must consider, that he doth not license husbandmen by all kind of toil continually to defile the sabbath-day. For of the countrymen, as well as of the townsmen, are looked for due honour done to God, and the keeping of the fourth commandment: only this must be remembered, that liberty is granted in causes of necessity. But a godly mind and charity shall be excellent dispensers and mistresses to lead us in such cases as these, lest, under the coloured pretence of liberty and necessity, we do deeds not to be borne withal on the sabbath-day, and exercise the works of greedy covetousness, and not of sincere holiness. And thus much had I to say touching the second use of the sabbath-day.

God doth
sanctify or
make holy.

Thirdly, the sabbath hath a very ample or large signification. For it is a perpetual sign that God alone is he that sanctifieth those that worship his name. For thus saith the Lord to Moses: "Ye shall keep my sabbaths, because it is a sign betwixt me and you to them that come after you, to know that I am the Lord which sanctify you;" and so forth, as it is to be seen in the 31st of Exodus, and is again repeated in the 20th of Ezechiel[2]. And to this end doth the Lord mutually apply himself[3], as is before said in the declaration of the sabbath's second use and signification. For God doth by his Holy Spirit sanctify his faithful folk and constant believers: which he declareth unto the church by the preaching of the gospel, bearing witness thereunto and sealing it with his sacraments; so that he commandeth us with continual prayers incessantly to crave of him that glorious sanctification. All which things, verily, are practised and put in use upon the sabbath-days especially, to the intent that we may be sanctified of God, who is the only sanctifier of us all.

Hitherto have I declared unto you, dearly beloved, as

[1 Imp. Constantinus. A. Elpidio. III.—Omnes judices urbanæque plebes, et cunctarum artium officia, venerabili die solis quiescant. Ruri tamen positi agrorum culturæ libere licenterque inserviant: quoniam frequenter evenit ut non alio die aptius frumenta sulcis et vineæ scrobibus commendentur; et ne occasione momenti pereat commoditas cœlesti provisione concessa.—D. Non. Mart. Crispo II. et Constantino II. Coss.—Cod. Just. Lib. III. tit. 12. de feriis. p. 409.]

[2 Exod. xxxi. 13; Ezek. xx. 12.]

[3 mutuam operam confert, Lat.]

briefly as I could, the first table of God's commandments, wherein we have very exquisitely laid down before us the worship due to the name of God. But for because they are not the children of God, which know his mind, but they that do it, let us beseech our heavenly Father so to illuminate our minds, that we may faithfully and indeed worship our Lord and God, who is to be praised world without end. Amen.

OF THE FIRST PRECEPT OF THE SECOND TABLE, WHICH IS IN ORDER THE FIFTH OF THE TEN COMMANDMENTS, TOUCHING THE HONOUR DUE TO PARENTS.

THE FIFTH SERMON.

Now followeth the second table of God's law, which (by the help of God's Holy Spirit) I will declare as briefly unto you as I have already gone through the first. And as the first contained the love of God, so doth the second teach us the charity due to our neighbour; instructing all men what they owe every one to his neighbour, and how we may in this world live honestly, civilly, and in quiet peace among ourselves. For our good God would have us to live well and quietly. But we that will not know how to live well, nor yet obey his good commandments, do with our sins and iniquities never cease to heap upon our own pates an infinite multitude of miserable calamities.

This table containeth six commandments; the first whereof is, "Honour thy father and thy mother, that thy days may be long in the land which the Lord thy God shall give thee." Very well and rightly doth the Lord begin the second table with the honouring of our parents. For after our duty to God, the next is the reverent love that we owe to our parents, of whom, next after God, we have our life, and by whom we are from our infancy brought up with incredible care and exceeding great labour. Now the very order of nature doth require, that the most excellent and dearest things should always have the first and chiefest place.

And that this commandment may the more easily be un-

The fifth precept.

derstood, I mean to divide my treatise thereof into three parts:
In the first whereof I will declare what degrees and kinds of
men are comprehended under the name of parents: secondarily, I will search out what kind of honour that is, and how
far it extendeth, which the Lord commandeth to give to our
parents: and lastly, I will both touch the promise made to
godly children, and thereupon conjecture and gather the punishment appointed for the ungodly and disobedient offspring.

What is meant by the name of parents.

There is none so ignorant but knoweth what parents are.
The Lord our God hath given us them for us to take of them
our beginning of life, that they might nourish and bring us up,
and that of rude and almost brutish things they might make
us very men. Greater are the good turns that parents do for
their children, greater is the cost and labour that they bestow
on them, and greater is the care, grief, and trouble which
they take for them, than any man, however eloquent soever
he be, is able to express. And here is not the name of the
father only, but also the name of the mother in express words
set down in the law, lest she peradventure should seem and
be contemptible without any offence to God, because of the
weakness of her frail sex. The godly and virtuous mothers
do feel and abide more pain and grief in the bearing, bringing
up, and nourishing of their children, than the fathers do. For
no small cause therefore have we the name of the mother
precisely expressed in this commandment. We do also comprehend herein the grandfather and grandmother, the great
grandsire and great granddame, and all other like to these.

Our native country.

In the second place we do contain every man's country wherein
he was born, which fed, fostered, adorned, and defended him.

Magistrates or rulers.

Thirdly, we take princes and magistrates into the name and
title: for the senators and princes are in the holy scriptures
called the fathers and pastors of the people[1]. Xenophon was
persuaded, that a good prince did differ nothing from a good

Guardians or overseers of fatherless children.

father[2]. Fourthly, there are to be reckoned under the name
of parents those guardians, which are usually called overseers
of fatherless children or orphans: for they supply the place
of departed parents, taking upon them the charge and defence

[1 2 Kings v. 13; Isai. xxii. 21, and xliv. 28; Jer. xii. 10, and xxv.
34; Micah v. 5.]

[2 Ἀλλὰ πολλάκις μὲν δὴ, ὦ ἄνδρες, καὶ ἄλλοτε κατενόησα, ὅτι ἄρχων
ἀγαθὸς οὐδὲν διαφέρει πατρὸς ἀγαθοῦ.——Xenoph. Cyrop. Lib. vii.]

of their children, whom they must (for that affection ought to be in them) bring up, defend, and advance, even as they would do to their own and those that they themselves did once beget. Among whom also we must make account of such masters and workmen, as teach them an art or occupation: for of them young men and striplings learn some honest science, for every one to get his living honestly; and by them they are taught good manners, being thereby, after a certain sort, out of rude unpolished stuff made perfect seemly men. Fifthly, the ministers, doctors, and pastors of the churches, are taken for parents, whom Paul himself did call by the name of fathers, not so much for the care and love wherewith they are affected toward the disciples and sheep of Christ his flock, as for because we are by them through the gospel begotten in Christ. In the sixth place, we must think of our cousins and kinsfolks, brother and sister, nephews and nieces, mother-in-law and daughter-in-law, father-in-law and son-in-law, who are by alliance knit together[3], as the members of the body are fastened with sinews. Finally, in the last place, old folks and widows, fatherless children and impotent weak persons, must be reputed among our parents: whose cause and tuition the Lord hath in more places than one commended unto us. So then, my brethren, here ye have heard who they be, that in this first precept of the second table we have to take for our parents, and who and how many are comprehended and commended to us under that name: and now shall ye hear what honour we owe to them, and what the honour is that we should attribute unto them.

To honour, in the scriptures, is diversely taken; but in this treatise it signifieth to magnify, to worship, to esteem well, and to do reverence as to a thing ordained by God; and also to acknowledge, to love, and to give praise as for a benefit received at God's hand, and as for a thing given from heaven, that is both holy, profitable, and necessary. To honour is to be dutiful and to obey; and so to obey, as if it were to God himself, by whom we know that our obedience is commanded, and to whom we are sure that our service is acceptable. Otherwise we have not in any cause to obey either our parents or magistrates, if they themselves shall do, or else command us to do, the things that are wicked and

Marginal notes:
Ministers and pastors of the church.

Cousins and kinsfolk.

Aged persons or old folks.

To honour, what it is.

The honour of God goeth always before.

[3 et conservantur, Lat.; omitted.]

unjust. For still the latter commandments have a relation to those that went before. In the second commandment we learned, that God would visit the sins of the fathers in the children; and therefore children ought not to obey their parents, if they command anything contrary to God, or prejudicial to his law. Jonathan obeyed not his father Saul's commandment, who charged him to persecute David: and therefore is he worthily commended in the holy scriptures. The three companions of Daniel obeyed Nabuchodonosor in all that he said, they loved him, and reverenced him as a most mighty, puissant, and bountiful king; but, so soon once as he charged them to fall to idolatry, they set not a button by his commandment[1]. And St Peter, who taught us the honour and obedience that we owe to our parents and magistrates, when he was commanded by the princes and fathers of the people not to preach Christ crucified to the people any more, did answer them, that "we ought to obey God more than men[2]." But what need I thus to stand reckoning up this, when the Lord himself in one short sentence hath knit up this, and all other like to this? "If any man," saith he, "cometh to me, and hateth not his father and mother, his wife, his children, his brethren and sisters, yea, and his own life, he cannot be my disciple[3]." Furthermore, thou dost honour thy parents, when thou dost not contemptuously despise them, unthankfully neglect them, nor shamefully think scorn of them, if peradventure they happen to fall into adversity. Thou honourest thy parents, when with thine help and counsel thou aidest them in their old age and unwieldy crookedness[4]; when thou easest them in time of their need, or succourest them otherwise in any case else. For that indeed is the true and proper honour due to our parents, the Lord himself bearing witness thereunto in the 15th of Matthew, and concluding that we ought to provide and have a care for our parents, to save and defend them, and wholly to give ourselves and hazard our lives in their behalf.

And now, that this that I have said may be more easily and evidently understood, I will confer and apply this honour to those seven several kinds of men which we do comprehend

[1 tantum non contempserunt, Lat. Dan. i. and iii.]
[2 Acts v. 29.]   [3 Luke xiv. 26.]
[4 confectos diuturna ætate, Lat.]

under the name of parents; that thereby every one may see
what, and how much, honour he ought to bestow upon his
parents, his country, the magistrates therein, and those sorts
of people that are afore named.

Whereas of duty we ought to honour our parents, that
duty is paid, if we do so worshipfully esteem of them, as to
think that they are given to us of God to the end that we
should reverence, love, and always have an eye to them,
although for nothing else, yet only for the Lord's sake; who
is and doth think himself despised, so long as we go on to
contemn our parents and to think vilely of them. Neither
doth it make any matter to us, whether they be worthy or
unworthy, whom the Lord commandeth us to honour. For
be they as they may be, yet notwithstanding they did not,
without the providence of God, chance to be our parents;
in respect of which parentage the lawgiver himself will have
them to be honoured. Whatsoever therefore children shall
have occasion to speak to their parents, let it always savour
of humble reverence and childly affection; and let them with
such affection and reverence obey their parents. If they
seem to us to be somewhat bitter and ungentle, yet let us
wisely wink at, and not seem to know it, by little and little
still declining from the evil, which by force they seem to
compel us unto; and let us so discreetly handle the matter,
that we may give them as small occasion as may be to be
offended at us. We have Jonathas, the son of Saul, to be an
example to us of a godly and obedient child. He did with
great grief and trouble of mind behold his father's madness
upon David, and wrongful dealing against himself; yet did
he for that present discreetly sustain and wisely dissemble it,
finding occasion at another time, and in a place convenient, to
tell him of it: he never aided his father in any conceived
mischief; he clave alway to the just man and righteous
causes; he bewailed his father's stubbornness, and sought not
over boldly to resist him and strive against him, when he
offered to deal by violent extremity with him, but saved himself by flying away; and yet, for all this, he loved his father
never the worse, but prayed still to God for his health and
welfare, shewing himself in all things an obedient son to his
crabbed father. This verily is the duty of a godly son.
This ought every one of us most diligently to follow, in doing
our duty and humble obeisance unto our parents, how froward

The honour due to parents.

or crooked soever they be. Let none give a rough answer
stubbornly; yea, let none so much as mumble an answer or
mutter against his parents. Let none curse, or speak evil of,
his father or mother, unless he will perforce seek the way and
means to make the high and mighty[1] God's curse hang over
and light upon his pate. If haply our parents be poor, if
misshapen in limbs, or otherwise diseased with any infirmity;
let none of us therefore in mockery flout at or disdainfully
despise them. Let us not shew ourselves unthankful to them,
to whom, for their good deeds to us-ward, we are of duty
bound for ever. Let us nourish, cherish, and aid them in all
their necessities: yea, let us wholly bestow ourselves, and all
that we have, to do them good withal. For all that we
possess undoubtedly is theirs; and all that we have we enjoy
by them; for if they were not, then should not we be.

Matt. xv.   Let us here call to remembrance the charge that the Lord,
in Matthew, giveth us touching this commandment[2]. Let us
consider what is meant by the Gentiles' ἀντιπελαργεῖν[3], which
is, to requite one good turn with another; and especially to
nourish and cherish them, by whom thou thyself in thy
youth wast brought up, and tendered[4]. There is, among the
Gentiles, a law extant, worthy to be called the mistress of
piety, whereby it is enacted, that the children should either
nourish their parents, or else lie fast fettered in prison[5]. This
law many men do carelessly neglect, which the stork alone,
among all living creatures, doth keep most precisely. For
other creatures do hard and scarcely know or look upon
their parents, if peradventure they need their aid to nourish

The stork the
ensign of na-
tural love.

them; whereas the stork doth mutually nourish them, being

[1 justissimi, Lat.]

[2 Inspiciatur cap. 15, Lat.; omitted.]

[3 ἀντιπελαργέω, to cherish in turn. Liddell and Scott's Greek
and Eng. Lex. 2nd ed. Oxf. 1845, from πελαργός, a stork. Metaphora a
ciconiis, quæ parentes senio jam confectos nutrire, et fessos ad terga
recipere, dicuntur ab Aristotl. Scapula. in voc. See also, Calvin. Opp
ed. Amstel. Tom. I. p. 496, and Tom. II. p. 608. Early Writings of
Hooper, Parker Soc. ed. page 359, and Erasm. Adag. Chil. p. 282.
Han. 1617.]

[4 ut cum liberi parentes ætate fessos vicissim alunt foventque
Lat.; omitted: as when children requite their aged parents by nourishing and cherishing them.]

[5 See Potter's Archæol. Græc. Book I. chap. 26. Vol. I. p. 181.
Lond. 1813.]

tricken in age, and bear them on her shoulders, when for
feebleness they cannot fly.

There are to be seen among the Gentiles very religious
and excellent sentences touching the honour due unto parents.
Isocrates saith: " Shew thyself such an one to thy parents,
as thou wouldest wish to have thy children shew themselves
to thee[6]." Anaximenes said: " He loveth his father exceedingly well, which doth his endeavour to make him joyful
without any trouble at all[7]." Plato also, in his Laws, thinketh, that " he hath a great treasure in his house, whosoever
doth nourish at home in his house his father or mother, or
any of their parents, in their impotent old age;" and doth
suppose that he needeth "no other picture of any of the gods
to reverence in his house, because he should turn all his care
and diligence to honour his parents[8]." And again, in another
place: " Let us pay," saith he, " to our parents, while they
are alive, the oldest, first, and greatest debts, that we owe
them for our being and bringing up. For every one must
think, that all which he hath is theirs, who did beget and
bring him up; so that, according to his ability, he must supply and minister to them all that he doth possess: first of
all, the external goods of fortune; then, of the body; and
lastly, those that do belong unto the mind; thereby restoring
all that he borrowed, and recompensing them in their old age
for all their old cares and grief sustained for him. It is
seemly also and requisite, that even in words, so long as we
live, we should shew reverence unto our parents: for after
light and foolish words used to them doth commonly come a
terrible plague. For before every man doth Nemesis (the
executrice of judgment) stand, and doth throughly think
upon all their offences. We must therefore give place to our

The Gentiles'
sentences
touching
honour due
to parents.

[6 Τοιοῦτος γίγνου περὶ τοὺς γονεῖς, οἵους ἂν εὔξαιο περὶ σεαυτὸν
γενεσθαι τοὺς σεαυτοῦ παῖδας.—Isocrat. Orat. ad Demonicum. ap. Stobæi
Floril. ed. Gaisford. Oxon. 1822. Vol. III. p. 113.]

[7 Οὗτος γὰρ μάλιστα πάντων φιλοπάτωρ ἐστὶν, ὅστις ζητεῖ δι᾽ οὗ
μηδὲν λυπήσας τὸν πατέρα πλεῖστ᾽ αὐτὸν εὐφράναιτ᾽ ἄν.—Anaximenes,
ibid.]

[8 Πατὴρ οὖν ὅτῳ καὶ μήτηρ ἢ τούτων πατέρες ἢ μητέρες ἐν οἰκίᾳ κεῖνται
κειμήλιοι ἀπειρηκότες γήρᾳ, μηδεὶς διανοηθήτω ποτὲ ἄγαλμα αὑτῷ, τοιοῦτον ἐφέστιον ἵδρυμα ἐν οἰκίᾳ ἔχων, μᾶλλον κύριον ἔσεσθαι· ἐὰν δὴ κατὰ
τρόπον γε ὀρθῶς αὐτὸ θεραπεύῃ ὁ κεκτημένος.—Plato de Legib. Lib.
XI. et ap. Stobæi Floril. ubi supra.]

[BULLINGER.]

18

parents, when they be angry without a cause, or do what
they list, whether it be by word or deed; knowing always,
that the father is rightfully angry with his son, though he be
angry for nothing else but because he thinks that his son
hath done to him the thing that he should not.   Let us,
therefore, erect to our parents, even when they be dead,
monuments seemly for their estate while they were alive:
which if we shall do, then shall we undoubtedly be worthily
rewarded at the hands of the gods[1]."   Thus much hath

*The pains
and travails
of mothers
in childbirth.*

Plato.   St Hierome saith: "Pay to mothers the reverence
that ye owe them, who, serving you with the pain of their
own wombs, do bear the weight of your bodies; and, carrying
about the infant unknown, do, as it were, become servants to
them that shall be born.   At that time the mother hungereth,
not to the filling of her own belly, neither doth she alone
digest and feed upon the meat that she eateth: with the
mother's meat is the babe nourished that lieth within her;
his members are fed with another body's eating; so that the
man that shall be is filled with the morsels that the mother
swalloweth.   What should I rehearse the nourishment that
they give to their children, and the sweet injuries of wayward
infancy, that they take and put up by means of their little
ones?   Why should I speak of the meat digested of the
mother, which, coming from the other parts of her body into

[1 Γονέων δὲ μετὰ ταῦτα τιμαὶ ζώντων, ὡς θέμις ὀφείλοντα ἀποτίνειν
τὰ πρῶτά τε καὶ μέγιστα ὀφειλήματα, χρεῶν πάντων πρεσβύτατα· νομίζειν δὲ, ἃ κέκτηται καὶ ἔχει, πάντα εἶναι τῶν γεννησάντων καὶ θρεψαμέ-
νων πρὸς τὸ παρέχειν αὐτὰ εἰς ὑπηρεσίαν ἐκείνοις κατὰ δύναμιν πᾶσαν,
ἀρχόμενον ἀπὸ τῆς οὐσίας, δεύτερα τὰ τοῦ σώματος, τρίτα τὰ τῆς ψυχῆς,
ἀποτίνοντα δανείσματα ἐπιμελείας τε καὶ ὑπερπονούντων ὠδῖνας παλαιὰς
ἐπὶ νέοις δανεισθείσας, ἀποδιδόντα δὲ παλαιοῖς ἐν τῷ γήρᾳ σφόδρα κε-
χρημένοις. Παρὰ δὲ πάντα τὸν βίον ἔχειν τε καὶ ἐσχηκέναι χρὴ πρὸς αὐτοῦ
γονέας εὐφημίαν διαφερόντως, διότι κούφων καὶ πτηνῶν λόγων βαρυτάτη
ζημία· πᾶσι γὰρ ἐπίσκοπος τοῖς περὶ τὰ τοιαῦτα ἐτάχθη Δίκης Νέμεσις
ἄγγελος. Θυμουμένοις τε οὖν ὑπείκειν δεῖ καὶ ἀποπιμπλᾶσι τὸν θυμὸν,
ἐάν τ' ἐν λόγοις ἐάν τ' ἐν ἔργοις δρῶσι τὸ τοιοῦτον, ξυγγιγνώσκοντα ὡς
εἰκότως μάλιστα πατὴρ υἱεῖ δοξάζων ἀδικεῖσθαι θυμοῖτ' ἂν διαφερόντως.
Τελευτησάντων δὲ γονέων ταφὴ μὲν ἡ σωφρονεστάτη καλλίστη, μήθ'
ὑπεραίροντα τῶν εἰθισμένων ὄγκων μήτ' ἐλλείποντα ὧν οἱ προπάτορες
τοὺς ἑαυτῶν γεννήτας ἐτίθεσαν. . . . Ταῦτ' ἂν ποιοῦντες καὶ κατὰ ταῦτα
ζῶντες ἑκάστοτε ἕκαστοι τὴν ἀξίαν ἂν παρὰ θεῶν καὶ ὅσοι κρείττονες
ἡμῶν κομιζοίμεθα.—Plato de Legib. Lib. IV. et ap. Stobæi Floril.
Vol. III. p. 116.]

er paps, is turned there into milk and moisture, to fill the
reak and tender jaws with thin and liquid food for nourishment? By nature the infants are compelled to take of their
mothers that which they drink; and when as yet their tooth-
less gums are not able to bite, then do they with the labour-
ing of their lips draw that from their mother's breasts that
they need not to chew. The mother's dug doth serve the
child, and still attendeth upon the swathled babe; her hands
to hold, and her back to bend, are ready still to dandle the
suckling's limbs, that she loves full well, God wot. The
mother desireth often and earnestly to have her youngling
grow, and wisheth full many a time to see him a man. For
these so many and so great good deeds ought the child, once
come to age, to apply himself to do her service with a good
and ready mind and heart. Let nature's debt be paid; let
them that follow have their due. Pay, child, that which
thou owest, and shew thy bounden duty by all manner of
service, whatsoever it be; because no man is able to pay to
his parents so much as he oweth them [2]." Thus far out of
Jerome.

Now touching the country wherein every one is born and
brought up; every man doth well esteem of it, love it, and

*For the ho-
nouring of
our country.*

[2 Matribus quoque debitam impendite reverentiam, quæ, vobis
eri labore servientes, pondus vestri corporis tolerant; atque ignotam
portantes infantiam, famulatum quendam exhibent nascituris.   Illo
tempore non sibi tantum mater esurit, nec acceptos sola digerit cibos.
materno victu alitur et ille qui latet, ejusque membra alterius comes-
tone pascuntur; ut homo futurus alienis morsibus saturetur.   Quid
sa memorem nutrimenta, et teneræ infantiæ dulces injurias, quas
tritoris affectus de suis parvulis sumit?   Quid cibos in matre con-
ctos, qui fœmineis manantes ex membris lacteum solvuntur in succum,
fauces invalidas liquido sapore perfundunt?   Cogente natura su-
unt infantes de matre quod bibant, et dente non nato hoc sibi curren-
us labris eliciunt, quod non sit necesse mordere.   Serviunt materna
steris pectora, serviunt ipsis incunabulis, manus et terga membris
vota lactentium gratos artus accipiunt.   Optat mater parvulum
escere; optat cito videre majorem.....His tot tantisque præceden-
us factis—matri tota debet alacritate serviri.   Reddatur naturæ
bitum; reddatur et posteris quod debetur.   Exsolve, fili, quod
bes, et officia debita qualicunque exhibe famulatu, quia parentibus
mo potest reddere quod debetur.—Hieron. Opp. Par. 1706. Tom.
p. 97. Epist. de Honorandis Parentibus.   The Benedictine editors
nsider that this treatise is not Jerome's.]

18—2

Fighting in
defence of
our country.

wish to advance it; every man doth deck it with his virtu
and prowess; every one doth help it with all sorts of benefits
stoutly defending it, and valiantly fighting for it, if need be
to save it from violent robbers. What is, I pray you, mor
to be delighted in, than the good platform of a well ordere
city, wherein there is (as one did say) the church we
grounded; wherein God is rightly worshipped; and wherei
the word of God in faith and charity is duly obeyed, so fa
forth as it pleaseth God to give the gift of grace; wherei
also the magistrate doth defend good discipline and uprigh
laws; wherein the citizens are obedient and at unity amon
themselves, having their assemblies for true religion and ma
ters of justice; wherein they use to have honest meetings i
the church, in the court, and places of common exercise
wherein they apply themselves to virtue and the study o
learning, seeking an honest living by such sciences as man
life hath need of, by tillage, by merchandise, and other hand
occupations; wherein children are honestly trained up, paren
recompensed for their pains, the poor maintained of alms, an
strangers harboured in their distress? There are therefo
in this commonweal virgins, married women, children, o
men, matrons, widows, and fatherless children. If any (b
the naughty disposition of nature) transgress the laws, the
are worthily punished; the guiltless are defended; peac
justice, and civility doth flourish, and is upheld. Now wh
is he, that can abide to behold[1] such a commonweal, th
country where he is born and bred up, to be troubled, vexe
torn, and pulled in pieces, either by seditious citizens o
foreign enemies? In civil seditions and foreign wars a
virtue and honesty is utterly overthrown, virgins defile
matrons uncivilly dealt withal, old men derided, and religi
destroyed. Wherefore the valiant captain Joab, being read
to fight against the Syrians in defence of his country, spea
eth to his brother Abisai, saying: "If the Syrians be strong
than I, then shalt thou help me; but if the sons of Amm
be too strong for thee, then will I come and aid thee. B
courageous therefore, and let us fight lustily for our peop
and for the cities of our God: and let the Lord do the thi
that is good in his own eyes[2]." Moreover Judas Machabe

[1 æquis et patientibus oculis videat, Lat.]
[2 2 Sam. x. 11, 12.]

a man among the Israelites worthily esteemed, and a famous warrior, and singularly affected toward his country, encouraging his soldiers and countrymen against their enemies, said: "They come upon us wrongfully in hope of their force, to spoil and make havoc of us, with our wives and children; but we fight for our lives and liberty of our laws, and the Lord will destroy them before our faces." The people also among themselves, exhorting one another, do cry out and say: "Let us take this affliction from our people, and let us fight for our nation and our religion[3]."

Let not any man make an objection here, and say: "Tush, these are works pertaining to the law, which we, that are of the church of Christ, have nothing to do withal." For the apostle Paul, speaking to the Hebrews, as concerning christian faith, doth say: "These through faith did subdue kingdoms, wrought righteousness, were valiant in fight, and turned to flight the armies of aliants[4]." Now, since our faith is all one, and the very same with theirs, it is lawful for us, as well as for them, in a rightful quarrel by war to defend our country and religion, our virgins and old men, our wives and children, our liberty and possessions. They are flatly unnatural to their country and countrymen, and do transgress this fifth commandment, whosoever do (under the pretence of religion) forsake their country afflicted with war, not endeavouring to deliver it from barbarous soldiers and foreign nations, even by offering their lives to the push and prick of present death for the safeguard thereof. St John saith: "By this we know his love, because he gave his life for us; and we ought to give our lives for the brethren." The hired soldiers[5], who fight unlawful battles for pay of wages, and sell their bodies for greediness of money, shall judge the men that leave their country in peril and danger. For the one put loss of life and limbs in adventure for gain of a few odd crowns; whereas the other dainty fools and effeminate

[marginal notes: Heb. xi. · 2 Cor. iv. · 1 John iii.]

[3 1 Macc. iii. 20—22, 43.]

[4 Hebr. xi. 33, 34.]

[5 "In 1549, he (Bullinger) by his influence hindered the Swiss from renewing their league with Henry II. of France, representing to them, that it was neither just nor lawful for a man to suffer himself to be hired to shed another man's blood, from whom himself had never received any injury."—Chalmers' Biogr. Dict. Vol. VII. p. 280.]

hearts will not hazard the loss of a limb for their religion, ma
gistrates, wives, children, and all their possessions.   What, I
beseech you, shall those traitors to their country say in tha
day, wherein the Lord shall reward the lovers and the unnatura
traitors of their country and countrymen; when before thei
eyes they shall see the Gentiles to excel them in virtue and

Lovers of
their coun-
try.

love to their country-people[1]?   Publii Decii, the father and
the son, gave their lives freely for the safeguard of the com
monweal, and died willingly for the love of their country[2]
Codrus, the natural and loving king of the Athenians, when he
understood by the oracle of Apollo that Athens could not be
saved but by the king's death, and that therefore the enemie
had given commandment that no man should wound the king
this Codrus laid aside his kinglike furniture, and, clothing him
self in base apparel, rushed into the thickest of his enemies
and found the means by egging to provoke one of them perforc
to kill him[3].   The two brethren, called Phileni, chose rather t
lengthen their country with a mile of ground than to prolon
their lives with many days; and therefore did they suffe
themselves to be buried alive[4].   But what suffer we for th
health and safeguard of our country?   Hierocles saith: " Ou
country is as it were a certain other god, and our first an
chiefest parent.   Wherefore he, that first called our countr
by the name of *patria*, did not unadvisedly give it that nam
but called it so in respect of the thing which it was indeed
for *patria*, ' our country,' is derived of *pater*, ' a father
and hath his ending or termination in the feminine gende
thereby declaring, that it taketh the name of both the parent
And this reason doth covertly lead us to think that our cou
try, which is but one, ought to be reverenced and loved as we
as both our parents, jointly knitting them together, to mak
them equal in honour[5]."

[1 Curtius Romanus adolescens nobilissimus in hiatum fori inger
tem sese præcipitem dedit, ut sua morte spontanea servaret patriam
Lat.; omitted by the translator.   Curtius, a most noble Roman youth
cast himself headlong into a vast gulph in the forum, that by h
voluntary death he might preserve his country.—Liv. Lib. VII. cap. 6

[2 Liv. Lib. VIII. cap. 9, and Lib. X. cap. 28.]

[3 Justin. Lib. II. cap. 6.   Vell. Patercul. Hist. Rom. Lib. I. cap. :
Valer. Max. Lib. V. cap. 6.]

[4 Sallust. de Bell. Jug. p. 333. Lugd. Bat. 1654.]

[5 Ἔστι γὰρ ὡσανεὶ δεύτερός τις θεὸς αὕτη (i. e. ἡ πατρὶς) νὴ Δί

Furthermore, we must make our earnest prayer for the We must
pray for our
country. safeguard of our country. Babylon was not the country of the Jews; but yet, for because the Jews for their sins were banished by God to Babylon for the space of seventy years, Babylon was counted to them instead of their country. And therefore saith the prophet Jeremy: "Build up houses, and dwell therein; plant gardens, and eat the fruit thereof; marry wives, and beget sons and daughters, and give them in marriage, that they may get children. Seek the peace of that city to which I do carry you, and pray to the Lord for it; because your peace and safeguard is joined to the peace thereof." Chapter twenty and nine. Traitors to their country therefore sin exceedingly, whom the laws of the realm do command for their foul offence to be hanged and quartered.

Touching the magistrate and his office, I mean to speak of For the
honour due
to magis-
trates. them in another place: so much as it is necessarily requisite for this present time St Peter uttereth, where he saith, "Fear God, honour the king[6]." Let us therefore acknowledge and confess, that the magistrate's office is ordained of God for men's commodity, and that God by the magistrate doth frankly bestow on us very many and great commodities. The peers[7] do watch for the common people, if they do rightly discharge their office, not shewing themselves to be detestable tyrants; they judge the people, they take up controversies, they keep justice in punishing the guilty and defending innocents, and, lastly, they fight for the people. And for the excellency of their office, which is both the chiefest and the most necessary, God doth attribute to the magistrate the use of his own name, and calleth the princes and senators of the people gods[8], to the intent that they by the very name should be put in mind of their duty, and that the subjects might thereby learn to have them in reverence. God is just, good, righteous, and one which hath no respect of persons: and such an one

ρῶτος καὶ μείζων γονεύς· παρ' ὃ δὴ καὶ ὁ τοὔνομα τῷ πράγματι τιθέμενος οὐκ ἀνεντρεχὲς ἔθετο, παρασχηματίσας μὲν τῷ πατρὶ, θηλυκῶς δ' ἐξενεγκὼν, ἵν' οἷον μίγμα τυγχάνοι, τῆς τε τοῦ πατρὸς καὶ τῆς μητρώας. καὶ δὴ οὗτος μὲν ὁ λόγος ὑπαγορεύει πατρίδα τιμᾶν, ἐπίσης τοῖς δυσὶ ὀνεῦσι τὴν μίαν.—Hierocles ap. Stobæi Floril. ed. Gaisford. Vol. II. p. 75, 76.]

[6 1 Pet. ii. 17.]   [7 principes, Lat.]
[8 Psal. lxxxii. 1, 6; John x. 34, 35.]

ought the good judge or magistrate to be. Monks and
heremites[1] do praise their profession or solitary life, extolling
it above the skies; but I think verily, that there is more true
virtue in one politic man, who governeth the commonweal and
doth his duty truly, than in many thousands of monks and heremites[1], who have not so much as one word expressed in the holy
scriptures for the defence of their vocation and vowed order
of living: yea, I am ashamed that I have compared the holy
office of magistrates with that kind of people, in whom there
is nothing found worthy to be compared with them, insomuch
as they fly from the labour and ordinance that God hath made
profitable for their people and countrymen. Truly, if the
prince do faithfully discharge his office in the commonweal, he
heapeth up to himself a number of very good works and
praise that never shall be ended. Therefore the magistrate
must be obeyed, and all his good and upright laws. No
sedition or conspiracies ought in any case to be moved against
him. We must not curse or speak evil of the magistrate.
For God himself in his law doth charge us, saying: "Thou
shalt not speak evil of the gods, nor curse the prince of the
people[2]." If he chance at any time to sin, let us behave ourselves toward him as to our father; of whom I have spoken
a little before.

Against seditious rebels.

It happeneth oftentimes, that magistrates have a good
mind to promote religion, to advance common justice, to defend the laws, and to favour honesty; and yet notwithstanding, they are troubled with their infirmities, yea, sometimes
with grievous offences: howbeit, the people ought not therefore to despise them and thrust them beside their dignity.
David had his infirmities, albeit otherwise a very good
prince. By his adultery he endamaged much his people and
kingdom: and, for to make his trouble the more, Absolom
sinned grievously[3], and went about to put him beside his
crown and kingdom. So likewise in other princes there are no
small number of vices, which nevertheless neither move nor
ought to move godly people to rebellious sedition, so long as
justice is maintained and good laws and public peace defended

---

[1 Anachoretæ, Lat.]   [2 Ex. xxii. 28.]
[3 Peccavit tamen graviter Absolon, qui, &c., Lat. Yet Absalom
sinned, &c.]

We ought to pray earnestly and continually for the magistrate's welfare. We must aid him with our help and counsel, so oft as need shall serve and occasion be given. We must not deny him our riches or bodies to assist him withal. The saints did gather their substance in common to help the magistrate, so oft as public safeguard did so require. The Israelites of all ages did always fight for their judges, for their kings and other magistrates; and so did all other people upon good advice taken: and likewise, on the other side, did the princes fight for the people. I would therefore that those offices of godly naturalness were of force and did flourish even at this day in all kingdoms, cities, and commonweals. Let every nation give to his magistrate that which by law, or by custom, or by necessity, it oweth him. For Paul the apostle saith: "Give to every one that which ye owe; tribute to whom tribute belongeth, custom to whom custom, fear to whom fear, and honour to whom honour is due." Rom. xiii.

Now, for because the guardians or overseers of orphans do supply the room of parents, and execute the offices of deceased parents to the children that remain, they do worthily deserve to have the reward that is due to parents, whether it be love, reverence, thanks, or obedience. The same also do I judge touching workmen and masters of sciences, who, for the fatherly affection, love, good-will, faith, and diligence shewed to their scholar or apprentice, ought mutually of their scholars to be regarded as a master; to be reverenced, feared, and hearkened unto, as a loving father. But in these unhappy days of ours it is abominable to see the negligence of masters in teaching their scholars, and intolerable to behold the peevish rudeness of untoward scholars. Let masters therefore learn here to shew themselves to be fathers, not being otherwise affected toward their scholars than toward their own children. Let them teach their apprentices their science or occupation, and train them up in manners and all points of civility, with the very same care and diligence that they use in bringing up their own. On the other side, let youths learn to break their natural ingraffed rudeness, and to bridle their youthful lusts; let them learn to be humble and subject, to keep silence, to reverence, to fear, to love, and obey their masters. Let them always remember, that their

The honour due to guardians and masters of occupations.

The office or duty of masters and scholars.

masters are given them of God, and therefore that God is
despised in their contemned masters. Let them be diligent,
earnest, and trusty in their work. Let them give their
masters cause to perceive their earnest desire and ready
good-will, that they bear to him, their occupation, and principles of their science. Let every one think upon, and diligently practise indeed, the things that their master teacheth
by word of mouth. Let them not grudge to watch and
take pains. Let not the masters be grieved, so often as they
be asked how to do a thing, to shew it readily in every
point as it should be done[1]. Unthankfulness and lack of
diligence in the scholar doth many times make the master
unwilling and negligent to teach him. Observe this, and, in
the rest, fear God, and have an eye to sound religion. When
thou art abroad, come not in company of blasphemous and
riotous toss-pots[2]; behave thyself honestly, provoke no man
to anger, despise no man, speak ill of no man, desire peace
and quietness, honour all men, and strive to do good to every
one. When thou art at home, help forward thy master's
commodity; do not endamage him nor his affairs; if any man
either hurt, or doth go about to hinder him, give him warning of it betimes; seek to appease, and hide as much as thou
canst, all occasions of falling out and chidings; whatsoever
thou hearest at home, do not blab it abroad, and make no
tales at home of that that thou hearest abroad. Be silent,
quiet[3], chaste, continent, temperant, trusty in deeds, true in
words, and willing to do any honest and household business.
Beware of them by whom evil suspicions and offences may
chance to arise. Do not over-boldly dally with thy master's
wife or daughters, nor yet with his maidens; do not stand
familiarly talking with them in sight or secretly. Imagine
thou (as it is indeed) that thy master's wife is thy mother,
his daughters thy sisters; whom to defile, it is a filthy and
villanous offence. Let every young man be neat, not nasty;
gentle, just, content with a mean diet, not licorice-lipped nor

[1 The translator seems here to have missed Bullinger's meaning.
The Latin is: Sit gratus fideliter docenti magistro, ut sæpius roganti
de modo agendi dignetur fideliter indicare omnia. Bullinger still
declares the duty of the apprentice to his master, and *not* of the
masters to their apprentices.]

[2 luxuriosorum, Lat.]　　　　　　　　[3 pacificus, justus, Lat.]

dainty-toothed[4].   But why stay I hereabout so long?   Let
every young man be persuaded and keep in memory, that
his duty is to keep himself chaste from filthy defilings, to
obey and not to rule, to serve all men, to learn always, to
speak very little, not to brag of any thing over arrogantly,
not to answer tip for tap[5], but to suffer much and wink
thereat.

For the honouring of ministers of the churches, which The honour
due to minis-
ters of the
churches.
are the pastors, teachers, and fathers of christian people,
many things are wont to be alleged by them who covet
rather to reign as lords, than to serve as ministers, in the
church of Christ.   But we, which are not of that aspiring
mind, do acknowledge, that they are given us by the Lord,
and that the Lord by them doth speak to us.   I speak here
of those ministers which tell us not a headless tale of their
own dreams[6], but preach to us the word of truth: for of
them the Lord in the gospel saith, "He that heareth you
heareth me, and he that despiseth you despiseth me[7]."
Wherefore the ministery is of the Lord, and through it he
worketh our salvation.   And therefore must we obey the
ministers which do rightly execute their office and ministery;
we must think well of them; we must love them and continually pray for them; and since they sow to us their heavenly things, we must not deny them the reaping of our
bodily and temporal things.   "For the labourer is worthy of 1 Cor. ix.
Matt. x.
his reward."   And since the Roman president among the
Jews did not deny it, but aided the apostle Paul against the
pretended[8] murder and open wrong of the Jewish nation; a Acts xxiii.
xxiv. xxv.
christian magistrate, verily, ought not to deny his assistance
and defence to the godly ministers of Christ and the churches.
Hereunto belong the testimonies of St Paul, that may be
alleged.   In the last chapter of his first epistle to the Thessalonians he saith: "We beseech you, brethren, to know
them which labour among you, and have the oversight of
you in the Lord, and admonish you; that ye may have them

[4 non palato delicato et moroso, Lat.]
[5 non responsare, Lat.   Shakspeare has *tap for tap*.   King Henry
IV. Part 2. Act II. Scene 1.—Tip, to strike lightly.   Wilson's Dict.]
[6 qui non sua nobis adferunt somnia, Lat.]
[7 Luke x. 16.]
[8 conceptum, Lat.]

in reputation through love for their work, and be at peace
with them[1]." Again, to the Hebrews he saith : " Obey them
that have the rule over you, and give place unto them; for
they watch for your souls, as they that shall give account
for them, that they may do it in joy, and not in trembling ;
for that is unprofitable for you[2]." For how many and great
calamities have fallen upon kingdoms and peoples for the

The contempt
of the minis-
ters of God's
word.

contempt of God's word and his ministers, many examples
can teach us; but that especially, which in the last chapter
of the second book of Chronicles is set down in these words :
" The Lord God of their fathers sent to them by his messengers, rising up betimes, and sending ; for he had compassion
on his people, and on his dwelling-place. But they mocked
the messengers of God, and despised his words, and jested at
his prophets, until the wrath of God arose against his people,
and till there was no remedy."

Like unto this are the words of the Lord in the gospel,
where he saith : " I send unto you prophets and wise men,
some of whom ye shall scourge and kill, that all the righteous
blood may light upon you, which hath been shed upon the
earth ; from the blood of the righteous Abel, unto the blood
of Zacharias, the son of Barachias, whom ye slew between
the temple and the altar ;" and so forth : for the place is
known to you all, dearly beloved, and is to be seen in the
twenty-third chapter after St Matthew. We must beware
therefore, in any case, that we do not despise God, who
speaketh to us in his word by his servants the prophets.

The honour
due to our
kinsfolks.

We owe, by the force of this commandment, all love,
reverence, help, comfort, and humanity to our kinsfolks and
alliance. In this commandment[3] are they condemned that
shew themselves to be ἄστοργοι[4], that is to say, men without
all natural affection and friendly love to their own blood and
kinsfolks. There is a certain natural affection, good-will, love,
and pitiful mercy (which the scripture calleth the " bowels of

[1 chap. v. 12, 13. pacem habete cum illis, Lat., Erasmus' version.
"And be at peace with them," Tyndale's Test. 1525, and Cranmer,
1539.]

[2 Hebr. xiii. 17.]

[3 sicut et Apostolicis scriptis, Lat. ; omitted by the translator. As
also in the Apostolical writings.]

[4 Rom. i. 31.]

mercy[5]") in the father and mother toward their children, in brother toward brother, and in cousins toward kinsfolks and friends of their alliance. We have notable examples hereof set down in the scriptures, of Abraham's love toward his son Isaac, and of Joseph's affection toward his father Jacob and his brethren, but especially toward Benjamin his brother by one mother. Mothers and daughters-in-law have a notable example to follow in Noemi and Ruth. Mothers and daughters-in-law (for the most part) do bear a deadly hate the one to the other, which is the cause of much mischief in the houses where they be. Let them learn therefore by this pretty example[6] how to behave themselves on both parts. Let the mother-in-law think the daughter-in-law to be her own daughter; and let the daughter-in-law honour and reverence her mother-in-law, even as if she were her own mother. Many things must be winked at on both sides, many things must be taken in good part, and many things put up with a quiet mind. Many things must be forgiven; and they must both have their ears stopped against tattling tale-bearers and wrongful suspicions. Concord in every house is the greatest treasure that may be, and discord at home is the most perilous and endless mischief that can be invented. Paul his words, touching good turns and honour to be given to our kinsfolks, are very well known, and extant to be seen in the fifth chapter of his first epistle to Timothy.

Last of all also, there is to be found in the word of God a peculiar law for the honouring of old men, which biddeth us to rise before the hoary and grey-haired head[7]. Old men therefore are to be honoured, whom we must worthily magnify, and in whom we must acknowledge the singular grace of God in giving them long life, and that by long and continual experience of all things they have attained to much wit or wisdom, whereby they are able to help us with their counsel. They therefore ought to be praised, that all men may understand[8], that grey hairs are a crown of glory[9]. Moreover, if aged impotent persons are driven into need, then must our abundance supply their necessity. To be short, we must not

For the honour due to old men.

[5 quæ scriptura viscera vocat, Lat. See Gen. xliii. 30; 1 Kings iii. 26; 2 Cor. vii. 15, marg.]

[6 lepido exemplo, Lat.]   [7 Levit. xix. 32.]

[8 et prædicent, Lat.; omitted.]   [9 Prov. xvi. 31.]

deny to old men any duty of humanity wherewith we may pleasure them. In the same sort, also, there are here commended unto us widows, orphans, wards, poor men, strangers, sick and miserable people. And for that cause did the devout and good men of old bestow their goods liberally to the refreshing of old men, widows, fatherless children, and poor silly[1] creatures. Those goods at this day are called church goods, or ecclesiastical contributions[2]: which, undoubtedly, are very well bestowed, if they be laid out on them for whom they were given. In the emperor's constitutions we may see that there were common houses and substance builded and appointed for all sorts of needy people: for there is mention made of houses for fatherless children, of hospitals for old men, of spittles for beggars, of places for sick men, and nurseries for children[3]. Among us, at these days, there are hospitals and monasteries[4], very many whereof have several places appointed for orphans, old men, poor people, impotent creatures, sick persons, and infants. They therefore do commit an unappeasable offence, whosoever bestow to other uses the substance and places ordained for old and poor people, and lash out (they care not how prodigally) in riot and lustiness the alms bestowed upon poor silly souls.

And now hitherto have I declared how our parents ought to be honoured, and they which are contained under the name of parents.

The promise made to those that worship their parents, and threatenings against such as despise their parents.

There is now remaining the third and last part of our present treatise, wherein we have to see what God promiseth to them that honour their parents religiously; whereby we have to gather, what peril hangs over the heads of them that wickedly neglect and irreligiously despise their parents. The Lord in the law therefore saith: "That thy days may be long in the land which the Lord thy God shall give thee." The meaning of which saying is: Honour thy father and thy mother, that thou mayest for many days enjoy the possession of the land which thou shalt have in testimony of my favour

Marginal note: Church goods.

[1 silly, i. e. weak.]   [2 facultates ecclesiasticæ, Lat.]

[3 Orphanotrophiorum, Gerontocomiorum, Ptochotrophiorum, Nosocomiorum, et Brephotrophiorum, Lat. See also Bucer's Script. Anglic. de Regno Christi, p. 82. Basil. 1577. These are often mentioned in Novell. Justinian.]

[4 Cœnobia et Hospitalia, Lat.]

to thee-ward.   These words do properly belong to the Jews.
But very well and truly doth a godly minister of Christ,
writing upon this place, say: "Because the whole earth is
blessed to the faithful, we do nothing amiss, when we reckon
this present life among the blessings of God.   Wherefore this
promise appertaineth as well to us as to the Jews, because the
prolonging of this present life is a testimony of God's especial
favour[5]."   He promiseth assuredly to them that do religiously
honour their parents, in what land soever they dwell, all
kind of blessings, felicity, and store of temporal things, with
a sweet prolonging of this present life.   For Paul, interpreting this in the sixth chapter of his epistle to the Ephesians,
saith: "That it may go well with thee, and that thou mayest
live long upon the earth:" meaning any land whatsoever,
and promising a temporal blessing of the Lord.

We therefore gather hereupon, that the contrary is threatened and set as a penalty upon the heads of those that disobediently despise their parents.   By examples, and other
places of the scripture, this shall be made more manifest.
Cham is cursed of his father Noe for behaving himself unreverently toward him, even in his drunkenness[6].   Joseph is
exalted to the chiefest dignity in Egypt, because from his
childhood he honoured God and reverenced his father Jacob.
Solomon, in the seventeenth chapter of his Proverbs, saith:
"Whosoever rewardeth evil for good, evil shall not depart from
his house."   Again: "He that despitefully taunteth his father,
and despiseth the old age of his mother, shall be confounded
and left in reproach."   "The son that leaveth to keep the discipline of his father, shall think of talk of wickedness."   "Whoso
curseth his father or mother, his light shall be put out, and
the balls of his eyes shall see nought but darkness."   For
they are monsters and no men, that are unnatural toward
their parents; and especially they which do not only neglect
and despise them, but also beat and uncourteously handle
them.   Such fellows doth the Lord command to be slain, as

[5 Quia tota terra fidelibus benedicta est, præsentem vitam inter
Dei benedictiones merito reponimus.   Quare ad nos similiter spectat
ista promissio, quatenus scilicet divinæ benevolentiæ documentum
nobis est præsentis vitæ duratio.—Calvin. Instit. Lib. II. cap. 8. § 37.
Tom. IX. p. 101. Amst. 1667.]

[6 Gen. ix. 25.]

people unworthy to see the light, because they forget and will
not acknowledge, that by the means of their parents they
came into the world. "He that curseth father or mother,"
saith the Lord, "let him die the death." And again: "He
that striketh his father or mother, let him die the death[1]."
There is none of you which knoweth not the law, called *Lex
Pompeia*[2], against such as kill their parents. It is not amiss
here to hear what the gentile writers say touching this
matter. Homer saith:

> He did not nourish as he should
> His aged parents dear;
> Therefore the gods did from his youth
> Cut off the jolliest year[3].

And the ancient poet Orpheus saith:

> God sits above, and sees the sons
> That do themselves apply
> To do their fathers' hests, and those
> That shamelessly deny
>
> Them to obey; and as he doth
> Bless th' one with sundry gifts,
> So, for to vex the other, he doth
> Devise a thousand drifts:
>
> For though despised parents die,
> Yet do their ghosts remain,
> And are of force upon the earth,
> To put their sons to pain[4].

[1 Ex. xxi. 15, 17.]

[2 Lex Pompeia de Parricidiis; passed in the time of Cn. Pom-
peius: "He who killed a father or mother, grandfather or grandmother, was whipped till he bled, sewn up in a sack with a dog, cock,
viper, and ape, and thrown into the sea," &c.—See Smith's Dict.
of Gr. and Rom. Antiquities, 286, a. P.; and Early Writings of
Bp. Hooper, Parker Soc. ed. p. 368.]

[3
                                        οὐδὲ τοκεῦσι
θρέπτρα φίλοις ἀπέδωκε, μινυνθάδιος δέ οἱ αἰὼν
ἔπλεθ'.   Hom. Il. Lib. XVII. 301. P.]

[4
Ζεὺς δ' ἐφορᾷ γονέων ὁπόσοι τίουσι θέμιστας,
ἠδ' ὅσοι οὐκ ἀλέγουσιν ἀναιδέα θυμὸν ἔχοντες.
καὶ τοῖς μὲν πρόφρων τε καὶ ἤπιος ἐσθλὰ δίδωσι,
τοῖς δὲ κακὰ φρονέων νεμεσίζεται ἐμμενὲς ἀεί·
δειναὶ γὰρ κατὰ γαῖαν ἐρινύες εἰσὶ τοκήων.
Orpheus ap. Stobæi Floril. ed. Gaisford. Vol. III. pp. 111, 112.]

Moreover, the tragical poet, Euripides, hath:

> To him, that while he lives doth love
> His parents to obey,
> Whether he live, or else do die,
> God is a friend alway[5].

And Menander, the comical poet, saith:

> The wretch is worse than mad, that with
> His parents falls at odds[6]:
> For wise men greatly reverence them,
> And honour them as gods[7].

Virgil also, among other horrible vices which are punished in hell with eternal and unspeakable pains, doth say:

> Here they that did their brethren hate,
> While life on earth did last,
> Or beat their parents, &c.

And immediately after:

> He did his country sell for gold,
> And made a tyrant king;
> For bribes he made and marr'd his coun-
> try's laws and every thing[8].

And Horace in his Odes saith:

> It is a sweet and seemly thing,
> In country's cause to die[9].

And Silius Italicus hath:

> Doubt not of this; forget it not,
> But keep it in thy mind:
> It is a detestable thing
> To shew thyself unkind

[5   Ὅστις δὲ τοὺς τεκόντας ἐν βίῳ σέβει,
          ὅδ' ἐστὶ καὶ ζῶν καὶ θανὼν θεοῖς φίλος.
                    Eurip. Heracl. ap. Stobæi Floril. Vol. iii. p. 107.]
[6 Δίκας γραφόμενος πρὸς γονεῖς μαίνῃ, τάλαν.—Menand. ap. Sto-
bei Floril. Vol. iii. p. 112.]
[7 Θεοὶ μέγιστοι τοῖς φρονοῦσιν οἱ γονεῖς.—Menand. Sentent. Mo-
l. Lugd. 1817.]
[8   Hic, quibus invisi fratres, dum vita manebat,
          Pulsatusve parens, &c.
          Vendidit hic auro patriam, dominumque potentem
          Imposuit, fixit leges pretio atque refixit.
                              Virg. Æn. vi. 608, 9, 21, 22.]
[9   Dulce et decorum est pro patria mori.
                              Hor. Od. Lib. iii. 2, 13.]

[BULLINGER.]
                                                                    19

> Unto thy native country soil;
> For no such sin remains
> In hell to be tormented there
> With utter endless pains,
> As that: so doth experience teach[1].

These testimonies have I cited to this end and purpose, that by these, dearly beloved, ye may gather the heinousness of this offence, which the very Gentiles themselves do so grievously cry out against and utterly condemn. Cain slew his brother Abel, but thereby he gat his reward; to be marked with a perpetual blot of ignominy and reproach. Semei did intolerably rail upon David, his ordinary magistrate; and therefore was he punished according to his deserts[2]. Absalom rebelled unnaturally against his father David; but, being wrapped by the hair to a tree, and hanging betwixt heaven and earth, he is horribly thrust through with a javelin[3]. The Lord called them that slew the prophets by the name of adders' brood and sons of the devil[4]. As for them that have reproachfully dealt with old men, or troubled widows, they have not gone unpunished. For the

Exod. xxii.

Lord in the law saith: "Thou shalt not afflict the widow nor fatherless children: but if ye do go on to afflict them, they shall undoubtedly cry to me, and I will hear them; and my wrath shall wax hot, and I will slay you with the sword, and your wives shall be widows, and your children fatherless." Thus much hitherto.

Eph. vi.

St Paul, alleging this law in his epistle to the Ephesians, doth very aptly apply it to our learning and comfort. For he saith: "Children, obey your parents, for this is right: honour thy father and mother, which is the first commandment in promise, that thou mayest prosper and live long on earth. Fathers, provoke not your children to wrath, but

[1]   Jamque hoc (ne dubites) longævi, nate, parentis
        Accipe, et æterno fixum sub pectore serva:
        Succensere nefas patriæ; nec fœdior ulla
        Culpa sub extremas fertur mortalibus umbras.
        Sic docuere senes.

                                          Sil. Ital. Punic. Lib. vii. 553.]
    [2 2 Sam. xvi. 5—8; 1 Kings ii. 8, 9, 36—46.]
    [3 2 Sam. xv. and xviii. 14.]
    [4 Matt. xxiii. 33; John viii. 38—44.]

bring them up in instruction and information of the Lord."
In these words he telleth the parents their duty, as well as
the children.   Three things he doth require at the hand of
the parents; that is, to bring up their children, to instruct
them, and to correct them.   For it is the parents' office to
nourish, to feed, and bring them up, till they be grown
to age, that, being once dispatched from hanging on their
parents any longer, they may get their livings with their
own labour and travail.   It is the parents' office to teach and
instruct their children.   That teaching or instructing consisteth in three things,—in religion, in manners, and skill of an
occupation.

The duty of parents to their children.

Now touching religion, it hath certain principles, rudi-
ments, I say, and catechisms to teach by: secondly, it hath
the scriptures setting out the word of God, with a full exposition of all things belonging to God: it hath also mysteries,
holy signs and sacraments, to teach and to learn by.   If the
householder be conversant among a people which honoureth
the true religion, and hath received the lawful worship of
God, with true, faithful, and godly ministers and teachers of
Christ his church, let him give charge and see that his children go to the holy congregation, there to be instructed in
religion by the public preacher.   Yet nevertheless, let the
father at home examine his children, and know what they
have learned by hearing the sermon.   Let both the father
and mother also at home privately do their endeavour to
teach their children the ten commandments, the Apostles'
Creed, and the Lord's prayer; and let them teach them a
brief and ready rule out of the scriptures for the understanding of the sacraments.   Let them often and many times
cause them to repeat the catechism, and beat into their heads
such sentences as are most necessary to put them in memory
of their faith and duty of life.   But if so it be, that the
householder have his dwelling with a people that persecuteth
the christian faith and doctrine, which hateth the true and
lawful worship of God's name, and cannot abide the congregation and ministers of Christ, (as it happeneth in the Turkish
captivities and troublesome persecutions of our days;) then
shall he take heed and keep himself from idolatry: neither
shall he in his own person go, nor suffer his family to come,

Children are to be instructed in religion.

Counsel and advice given to house- holders in captivity.

19—2

to those ungodly assemblies, but shall rather in his own house
at home instruct them in true religion, first in the catechism,
and then in deeper divinity.   Moreover, so oft as the case
and necessity shall require, he must freely and openly profess
Christ and his gospel.   For it is apparently evident by the
epistles of Paul and other histories, that such churches were
in private houses of great cities in the time of the apostles
and thickest of those hot and ancient persecutions[1].   Neither
is it likely that the Jews in their captivity at Babylon, although they lacked the outward use of sacrifices, were altogether without all worship of God.   Although Daniel did
not sacrifice, yet did he at certain hours in the day-time
worship God in his own house[2].   The house of Cornelius at
Cesarea was the church, wherein Peter preached in a very
good and ecclesiastical assembly or congregation; and he,
because Joppe had no church for him to pray in, went up to
the higher part of the house to make his prayers there[3].
Neither is it to be doubted, but that the eunuch of queen
Candace's nobility, of whom mention is made in the Acts of
the Apostles, did ordain a church in Æthiopia[4].   And let
them be persuaded, which are without the public and lawful
use of the sacraments, that that shall not be imputed to their
default, which is committed, not by them, but by another's
offence.   For even in such a case can the Lord work well
by his Spirit in the minds of his people.   But where as[5], by
the grace of God, liberty is given for the congregation to
assemble, and to hear the free, sincere, and true preaching
of the gospel, and lastly, to celebrate the sacraments, there
must those private and domestical churches be broken up and
come to an end : not for because the house of a godly householder is not, nor remaineth still, a church ; but for because
the hearing of God's word, prayer, and the celebrating of the
sacraments, ought to be public and common to all the saints.

[1 Rom. xvi. 5; 1 Cor. xvi. 19; Coloss. iv. 15; Philem. 2.   Bingham, Orig. Eccles. Book VIII. cap. 1. §. 13, and 14; Staveley's Hist. of
Churches, chap. 3. pp. 26—34. Lond. 1712]

[2 Dan. vi. 10.]   [3 Acts x.]

[4 Acts viii. 27, &c., and Euseb. Eccles. Hist. Lib. II. cap. 1. Vol.
I. p. 85. ed. Burton. Oxon. 1838.]

[5 i. e. where: ubi, Lat.]

For those assemblies by stealth, which the Anabaptists use, and all other sectaries, are both worthily and utterly condemned.

And now let us hear the testimonies of scripture, which command all householders to instruct holily their family in the true religion, and to declare to their children the meaning of the sacraments. Moses in the sixth of Deuteronomy saith: "Hear, Israel, the Lord our God is Lord only[6]: therefore shalt thou love the Lord thy God with all thy heart, with all thy soul, and with all thy might. And these words, which I command thee this day, shall be in thy heart. And thou shalt shew them unto thy children, and shalt talk of them when thou art at home in thine house, and as thou walkest by the way, and when thou liest down, and when thou risest up. And thou shalt bind them for a sign upon thy hand, and they shall be as frontlets between thine eyes[7]." And again: "When thy son asketh thee in time to come, saying, What mean these testimonies, ordinances, and laws, which the Lord our God hath commanded us? Then thou shalt say unto thy son: We were Pharaoh's bondmen in Egypt, and the Lord brought us out with a mighty hand, and shewed signs and mighty wonders before our eyes; and brought us out from thence, and gave us all these precepts and statutes to do and to fear the Lord our God." Hereunto belongeth a great part of the seventy-eighth Psalm. And in the thirteenth of Exodus the Lord doth say again: "Sanctify to me all the first-born. And when thy son shall ask thee in time to come, saying, What is this? Thou shalt say to him, The Lord slew all the first-born of Egypt, and therefore I sacrifice unto the Lord all the males that open the matrix." Also in the twelfth chapter God, or Moses in God's name, expounding the mystery or sacrament of the passover, said[8]: "When your children ask you, saying, What manner of service is this that ye do? ye shall say, It is the sacrifice of the Lord's passover, which passed over the houses

<aside>Precepts for the instructing of our children and family.</aside>

[6 unus est, Lat.]

[7 Scribes quoque ea super postes domus tuæ et in portis tuis, Lat. omitted by the translator. "And thou shalt write them upon the posts of thy house, and on thy gates."]

[8 inter alia, Lat.]

of the children of Israel," &c. These testimonies are sufficiently evident, and need no further exposition. I will now,
therefore, add to these the other things, which parents have
to teach their children.

The child must be taught manners.

Let the father instruct his children in manners. We all
from our birth are clownish and rude; and all children have
unseemly and uncivil manners: which evil is made double as
much by evil custom and clownish company. Let the parents,
therefore, teach their children manners betimes, which may
adorn them at home, and become them abroad. Let him
instruct him how to behave himself decently in his going and
gesture of his body; how in the church, how in the market,
how at the table, how in men's companies, and in all other
places of company. There are excellent pretty books set out
for that purpose, so that I need not stand to discuss to you
the particularities thereof.

Children must learn an occupation.

Lastly, let the father place his children with expert and
cunning[1] workmen, to teach them some handycraft whereby
to get their living another day. But first, he must make
trial of their wits, to see whereunto every one is best apt,
and wherein he doth most delight. For "cunning will never
be come by, where good will is wanting in him that must
learn it[2]." If thou hast any fit for learning, thou shalt do a
good and godly deed, to train them up to the ministery of the
church, or some other office that standeth by learning. But
of all other those parents are to be found fault withal, that
bring up their children in lazy idleness. For, although there
be left unto them huge heaps of treasure, yet in three or four
odd hours all may be wasted and come to nought. Whereunto, then, shall your dainty idle gentleman trust, what shall
he do, when there is nothing left but his bare carcass, that is
a lump of clay not good for any thing[3]? The inhabiters of
Massilia would not admit any into the number of citizens, but
such as had learned an occupation to live by[4]. For to a city
there is no greater a plague than an unprofitable citizen. But
who, I pray you, may be thought to be a worse citizen than

[1 fidis et peritis, Lat.]
[2 Invita Minerva nihil feliciter perfeceris, Lat.—P.]
[3 Quo tunc confugiet miser tellurisque inutile pondus? Lat.]
[4 Valer. Max. Lib. II. cap. 6. § 7.]

he that, being accustomed to ease and delicateness, and of a sudden by some mishap or else by prodigal riotousness being deprived of them both, and driven to extreme poverty, is compelled, perforce, to seek out unlawful[5] shifts to get more wealth again? Furthermore, they of old had a proverb worthy to be remembered of us[6] at this time: "Every land maintaineth art[7]." "By this sentence they meant, that learning and science is the surest preparation for every journey. For they cannot be taken away by thieves, but whithersoever thou goest, they bear thee company, and are no burden for thee to bear[8]." If therefore mishap do spoil thy children of the wealth that thou leavest them; if thou hast taught them an occupation, it is enough for them to live by. Kings are deprived of their prince-like dignity, and put beside their exceeding riches; so that it is no marvel though kings' inferiors be spoiled of their wealth, and banished their countries. Dionysius of Syracuse is reported for his tyranny to have been thrust beside his seat: but, having lost his kingdom, he departed to Corinth, where he set up a school, and taught children their grammar and music, whereby in that necessity he got his living[9]. He had been hard bested verily, and in a miserable taking, if he had never learned any thing, but had settled his hope upon dignity and riches: vain hope had been his destruction; for he had died in extreme beggary. Thus much touching the bringing up of children in learning or knowledge of some occupation.

I have, in that which is behind, to speak somewhat Of correction. touching the correction of those that are contained under the name of children. This correction consisteth partly in words, and partly in stripes. In both there must be had a middle-mean and measure, that nothing be done outrageously[10]. Let not the admonition that is given in words be bitterer than the fault deserves. Let it nip for the time present; but, being

---

[5] injustissimas planeque seditiosas rationes, Lat.]

[6] omnibus parentibus, Lat.]

[7] Artem quævis alit terra, Lat.—Erasmi. Adag. Hanov. 1617. col. 368, a.]

[8] The quotation is from Erasmus' Adag. in loc. cit.]

[9] Erasmi Adag. in loc. cit.; Justin. Lib. xxi. cap. 5; Cic. Tusc. Quæst. iii. 12.]

[10] ne quid nimis, Lat.]

past, let it be spoken of no more. Continual chiding breeds
contempt. Thou shalt find some children also, with whom
gentle dealing will somewhat prevail[1]. And, unless thou do
sometime praise them and speak well of that which they do,
although peradventure not so well done as thou wouldest
require, thou shalt perceive that utter desperation will take
away hope and courage clean from them. I think it not
good with too heavy a burden to overawe such children as
are willing to bear. Stripes must not be bestowed but for
some great offence, and that too, not in the father's anger,
but moderately; not to mar, but to amend them. Let the
parents always remember that golden saying of St Paul,
" Fathers, provoke not your children to anger[2]." For the
best wits are hurt by too much rigorousness. Salomon, where
he speaketh of moderate correction, saith : " The rod and
correction giveth wisdom ; but the child that runneth at random bringeth his mother to shame." Again : " Chastise thy
son, and thou shalt be at quiet, and he shall bring pleasure
unto thy soul[3]." These words of his do utterly condemn the
father's cockering[4], and the mother's pampering, which is the
marring of very many children. For the parents offend God
as much in too much cockering their children, as they do in
overmuch punishing of them. Heli in the scriptures is ill reported of for doting over his children ; he himself dieth
miserably, and bringeth the shameless wicked knaves, his
sons, to a shameful ending[5]. What is to be thought of that
moreover, that in the twenty-first of Deuteronomy the parents
themselves are commanded to bring their disobedient children
before the judge, and there, by complaint, to sue them to
death ? By this example, which may otherwise seem to be
somewhat too sharp, it pleased God to put other men in
remembrance to keep their children in awe and obedience.
For God is a God of salvation, and not of destruction ; so
that, when disobedient rebels and godless people perish
through their own default, he turneth that destruction of theirs
to the safeguard of his obedient servants. Let parents therefore always remember this saying in the gospel : " It is not

Cockering of children.

[1 plus efficias, Lat.]   [2 Eph. vi. 4.]
[3 Prov. xxix. 15, 17.]
[4 indulgentiam, Lat.]
[5 1 Sam. ii. 29. & iv.]

the will of your heavenly Father, that one of these little ones
should perish. Whosoever offendeth such an one, it were
better for him that a millstone were hanged about his neck,
and that he were drowned in the depth of the sea[6]."

Now, touching the duty of children, I have spoken of it
before in the place where I taught, how and after what sort
parents ought to be honoured. Paul, as it were in one word,
knitteth up much matter, and saith: "Children, obey your
parents in the Lord." He telleth the reason why: "For
that," saith he, "is righteous." And again he addeth the
cause, saying: "For God hath commanded it[7]." Let children
therefore consider and think upon the nightly watchings and
continual labour that their parents took in bringing them
up, and let them learn to be thankful for it, and content
with their present estate. When their parents instruct them,
let them learn attentively, and shew themselves like to godly
Jacob rather than to godless Esau. Let them learn to ac-
custom themselves to good and honest manners. Let them
willingly learn the art or occupation whereunto they are
set. Let them yield and submit themselves to their parents'
correction. Let them not stir up or provoke their parents to
anger. Let them choose to learn wit, and obey their parents,
of their own mind and accord, rather than to be driven to it
by beating and brawling. If parents at their departure leave
little behind them for their children to inherit, let not the
good children therefore speak ill by the dead. If thy father
hath taught thee any art or occupation, he leaveth for thee a
sufficient inheritance. Thriftiness, also, and moderate spend-
ing, is a very great revenue[8]. If thy father hath well and
honestly taught thee good manners, and trained thee up in
the true wisdom and perfect religion, then hath he bequeathed
thee a patrimony sufficient for to maintain thee. For what
else are exceeding great riches, left to a fool or irreligious
fellow, but a sword in a madman's hand? Thou art left
wealthy enough by thy father's legacy, if that thou art
godly, painful, heedful, and honest. For goods gotten by
the sweat of our own brows do for the most part continue

The duty of children.

[6 Matt. xviii. 14, 6.]
[7 Ephes. vi. 1, 2.]
[8 Frugalitas ac parsimonia magnum est vectigal, Lat. Cf. Erasm.
Adag. Chiliad. fol. 269. *a.* Parsimonia summum vectigal.]

longer, and prosper better with us, than those which other
leave unto us.

We have again, dearly beloved, spent an hour and a half
in handling this matter touching the honour due unto parents.
I have stayed you longer than of right I should have done,
but ye shall impute it to the love and good will I bear to the
matter. I am not ignorant how necessary this argument is,
almost to all men : and therefore stick I the longer upon it.
For I endeavour myself, not only to teach you things profitable and necessary, but also to beat them into your memories
so much as I may, to the end that ye never forget them.
God grant you all a fruitful increase of his holy word, which
is the seed that is sown in your hearts.   Let us pray, &c.

OF THE SECOND PRECEPT OF THE SECOND TABLE, WHICH IS IN ORDER THE SIXTH OF THE TEN COMMANDMENTS, THOU SHALT NOT KILL: AND OF THE MAGISTRATE.

THE SIXTH SERMON.

JUSTICE and innocency are very well joined to[1] the
higher power and magistrate's authority ; and in this sixth
precept both public and private peace and tranquillity are
hedged in and inclosed against open tumults and secret dis-
cords.   And since the life of man is the most excellent thing
in the world, whereupon all other things, of how great price
soever they be, do wait and attend ; and finally, since the
body of man is more worth than all other gifts whatsoever ;
the very natural order doth seem to require, that the sixth
commandment should be placed next, which God himself
hath plainly expressed in these few words, " Thou shalt not

The sixth
precept.

kill[2]."   For in this precept justice and innocency are commanded and commended unto us, wherein also it is provided,
that no man hurt another's life or body ; and so in this pre-

[1 subjungitur, Lat.]

[2 Exod. xx. 13.—duabus duntaxat vocibus proditum, Non occides,
Lat.]

cept charge is given to every one to maintain peace and quietness.

Now here are to be observed the steps that lead to murder; wherein we must consider the kinds and causes of hurting and annoying. For the Lord doth not simply forbid murder, but all things else whereon murder doth consist. All egging on, therefore, and provoking to anger is utterly forbidden; slanderous taunts and brawling speeches are flatly prohibited; strife, wrath, and envy, are plainly commanded to be suppressed. And in this sense we have Christ our Lord himself interpreting this law, where in the Gospel after Matthew he saith: "Ye have heard it said of old, Thou shalt not kill; whosoever killeth shall be in danger of judgment. But I say unto you, that whosoever is angry with his brother unadvisedly shall be in danger of judgment. And whosoever shall say unto his brother, Racha, shall be in danger of a council. But whosoever shall say, Thou fool, shall be in danger of hell fire." Thou seest here, therefore, that anger, slander, brawling, and all other tokens of a mind moved to utter ill words, are flatly forbidden. What then must thou do? Thou must, forsooth, come into charity again with him whom thou hast offended; thou must lay aside all wrath and envy, unless thou hadst rather have all the honour that thou dost to God[3] be imputed for sin unto thee, and that, peradventure, thou wouldest choose rather utterly to be condemned. For our Lord goeth on in the gospel, and saith: "If therefore thou bring thy gift unto the altar, and there rememberest that thy brother have any thing against thee, leave there thy gift before the altar," (he speaketh to them, who as then had their temple standing, their altar remaining, and burnt-offerings in use; we, at this day, have another manner of worshipping God,) "and go thy way; first be reconciled to thy brother, and then come and offer thy gift." And again: "Agree with thine adversary quickly, whiles thou art in the way with him; lest at any time the adversary deliver thee to the judge, and the judge deliver thee to the minister, and thou be cast into prison. Verily, I say unto thee, thou shalt not depart from thence until thou hast paid the utmost farthing[4]." But for because

[3 cultum, quem Deo exhibes.]
[4 Matt. v. 23—26.]

so few of us obey this sound and wholesome doctrine of the Lord's, thereby it cometh to pass, that so many great and troublesome tumults happen among men. For small is the substance of them that obey the word of God, but great is the rest and quietness of their consciences. And what pleasure, I pray you, do infinite riches bring to man, since with them a man cannot likely be without troublesome cares of mind, great turmoils and lack of a quiet life? This law therefore, which tends to no other end, but to teach man the way to lead a sweet and pleasant life, doth wholly take from the mind of man such immoderate affections as anger and envy are, two the most pestilent evils that reign among men.

As concerning anger, I mean not at this present to speak over busily, even as also I have determined to be brief touching envy. Of anger many men have uttered many profitable sentences: and yet there is an holy kind of anger, which the scripture disalloweth not; so that, unless a man be angry in that sort, he shall never be a good and godly man. For a good man hath a zeal of God, and in that godly zeal he is angry at the iniquity and naughtiness of mankind; whereof there are many examples to be seen in the scriptures: and this anger doth stomach the sin committed, rather than the person who doth commit the sin. For the good servant of God hateth nothing in the wicked man's person, but his very sin; so that, if the wicked cease once to sin, he will leave to hate or be angry therewithal any longer. This anger is utterly condemned then, when it springs of evil and corrupt affections; when no just cause is given, but that he, which is offended, doth in his anger either fulfil his affection, or else hurt or determine to hurt him with whom he is angry. A great evil it is, and a fruit, which when it is sown doth yield and bring forth one mischief upon another's neck. And therefore doth the apostle of Christ counsel all men not to give any place to anger; and if so be it happen that it enter into our minds, and stick there awhile, yet that we suffer it not to catch fast hold, or take deep root therein. "Be angry," saith he, "and sin not. Let not the sun set upon your anger, and give no place to the devil[1]." For this is the apostle's meaning: if so it happen, that ye be angry, yet sin not; that is, yet bridle your anger. Neither doth the apostle bid

Of anger.

[1 Eph. iv. 26, 27.]

us to be angry, but willeth us not to let our anger to continue long, nor to break out to the working of injury. And παρορ-γισμός (which word Paul useth) signifieth anger indeed, but yet, more rightly, the stirring or provoking to anger ; so that thereby we have to understand, that to him, which is by injury provoked to anger, although he be somewhat grieved and touched at the quick, that grief ought to be but of short continuance : neither must we in any case suffer our adversary[2], the devil, to fasten his foot in our hearts, who doth through anger by little and little creep into our minds, and by continual wrath doth work out envy, by which he doth captivate and pervert the whole man, with all his senses, words, and works.

For envy is anger grown into custom by long continu- *Of envy.* ance, which doth for the most part vex, burn, and (mangle him that doth[3]) envy, more than the party which is envied ; although the envious doth never cease to devise mischief against the man whom he doth envy. It is an endless evil, which doth not admit any remedy to take it away. And therefore did the Gentiles bait and canvass it to and fro with wonderful pretty quips and pithy sentences[4]; some of which I will not be ashamed here to rehearse, to the intent that counterfeit Christians, addicted to envy, may be ashamed of it, if peradventure they will learn to blush, when they find themselves touched by heathens and paynims.

Virgil saith :

> In heart, where envy's seed takes root,
>   There grows a poisoned grain,
> Which dries and drinks from every limb
>   The blood of every vein ;
> And sucks and soaks the marrow bones,
>   Until they feeble wax;
> (Such is th' envenom'd poison's force,)
>   And yet no bone it cracks[5].

[2] calumniator, Lat. This exposition of St Paul's words is taken almost verbatim from Erasmus' Annot. in loc.]

[3] invidentem fere torquet, urit, et excarnificat, Lat. The words between brackets are accidentally omitted in the translation.]

[4] Gentes id exagitarunt miris modis, Lat.]

[5]   Livor tabificum malis venenum
        Intactis vorat ossibus medullas,
        Et totum bibit artubus cruorem.
            Epigr. de Livore. Virgil. Opp. Basil. 1613, p. 1981.]

And therefore saith Horace:

> The Sicil tyrants never found
> A more tormenting hell,
> Than envy was, &c.[1]

Silius Italicus crieth out:

> Ill-favour'd envy, ugly hag,
> And dogged end
> Of mortal men, that never could'st
> Abide to lend
> One word to praise praise-worthy deeds,
> But swell'st to see
> Small things increase, and low things grow
> To high degree[2].

Ovid, speaking of envy, describeth it thus:

> Within did devilish envy sit,
> And eat the flesh of snakes,
> To feed the humour of her vice
> With such kind loathly cates:
> With face of tallow-caked hue,
> And body lean like death,
> With squint eyes turn'd nine sundry ways,
> With rusty stinking teeth.
> Her bitter breast was overspread
> With gaid[3] as green as grass;
> Her tongue, that ceas'd not to say ill,
> With venom poison'd was.
> She never laugh'd, unless it were
> When grief made others weep;
> And fretting care within her heart
> Did keep her eyes from sleep.
> She sees, and pines away to see,
> The good success and state
> Of men that prosper on the earth:
> And so her deadly hate
> Is to herself a deadly plague.

[1]   Invidia Siculi non invenere tyranni
         Majus tormentum.

                                     Hor. Ep. I. 2, 58.]
[2]   O dirum exitium mortalibus! O nihil unquam
      Crescere, nec magnas patiens exsurgere laudes,
      Invidia!

                              Sil. Ital. Punic. Lib. XVII. 188.]
[3 Gaid, withes.   Shaw's Gaelic and English Dict. in voc.]

> Where as she goes, she mars the corn
>   That grows upon the ground;
> She makes on trees that blossoms bear
>   There can no fruit be found;
> And with her breath she doth infect
>   Whole houses, realms, and towns[4].

Since, therefore, that envy is so great an evil, and that the Lord commandeth to keep ourselves from it, therein doth appear the Lord's goodness to us-ward; and thereby we may gather how good and profitable his law is, which tendeth, and is given, to none other end, but to set us at liberty from so great a mischief. And here, by the way, we do perceive, that our fault, and not the waywardness of God, is the cause, why many in this world are never at peace and quietness, but are exceedingly vexed with continual torments. For as they cease not to envy the estate of other, so with their anger they disquiet more than themselves, and do at last duly aby[5] and worthily suffer the deserved punishment of their wicked deeds.

And this law doth not only forbid and restrain the mo- *All hurting is forbidden.* tions and evil affections of the mind by wrath, anger, and envy; but doth also give commandment against all manner hurt that riseth by them. Harm and hurt is done by sundry means; by beating, by violent thrusting, by overthrowing, by pulling, and troubling, although in doing so thou dost not wound thy neighbour. But thy sin is the greater, if thou

[4   videt intus edentem
Vipereas carnes, vitiorum alimenta suorum,
Invidiam.——
Pallor in ore sedet, macies in corpore toto:
Nusquam recta acies: livent rubigine dentes;
Pectora felle virent: lingua est suffusa veneno;
Risus abest, nisi quem visi movere dolores.
Nec fruitur somno, vigilacibus excita curis:
Sed videt ingratos, intabescitque videndo,
Successus hominum: carpitque et carpitur una;
Suppliciumque suum est.——
Quacumque ingreditur, florentia proterit arva,
Exuritque herbas, et summa cacumina carpit;
Afflatuque suo populos, urbesque, domosque
Polluit.
                              Ovid. Met. Lib. ii. 768, &c.]
[5 luunt poenas, Lat.]

givest him a wound after what sort soever, either with wea-
pon, or by any means else.   And again, thou sinnest yet
more grievously, if thou dost quite cut off, or otherwise break,
any limb of his body; if thou puttest out his eyes, or dashest
a tooth out of his head.   So then the better that the limb is
that thou cuttest off, or puttest out of joint, the greater is the

The law of
like for like.

sin, and more grievous thine offence.   From whence, without
doubt, the law called *lex talionis*[1] took the beginning, which
commandeth to cut off the hand of him, which did cut off
another's hand; and to pluck out the eye of him, which did
put out another man's eye.

The manners
of killing.

Now also, the manner of killing must not be overpassed.
The Lord saith, "Thou shalt not kill."   We kill divers
ways: either we ourselves do the deed, or else we use the
help of other to strike the stroke; it is done either privily or
openly.   And in this sort again there are very many fashions:
for we commit murder sometime by holding our peace, sometime by dissembling, by giving ill counsel, by consenting, by aid-
ing, or egging forward to evil.   Another peradventure would
not do the thing that he doeth, but because he seeth that
thou hastenest him on; but because he knoweth he shall
please thee thereby; and because he perceiveth that thy help
upholdeth him.   Although, therefore, that thou with thine
own hand strike not the stroke, yet the murder, that another
committeth by thy setting on, shall be imputed to thee as
well as if thou thyself hadst killed the man.   And no marvel,
since John, the apostle and evangelist, calleth hatred manslaughter[2].

The causes
of murder.

Moreover, here are to be touched the causes of murder,
or doing of mischief.   For hereupon standeth, and from
hence cometh, the mischievous deed and foul offence.   Murder is committed, and the neighbour endamaged, either un-
wittingly, or else upon pretended[3] malice.   It is done un-
wittingly, where as, when a man purposeth another thing, by
ill hap, or, as I should rather say, by the providence of God,
murder doth ensue.   As for example; when my mind is to
discharge a gun against a buck, meaning to kill the beast, by

[1 See Smith's Dict. of Greek and Rom. Antiq. sub voc. *talio*.
Arnold's Hist. of Rome.   Chap. xiv. § 2. Vol. i. p. 286. Lond. 1840.]

[2 1 John iii. 15.]

[3 i. e. designed, premeditated.]

hap I strike a man, who unawares to me was in the same wood, cutting timber: or else where as upon simplicity I give my friend a draught of poison, where mine intent was to have given him a medicine to recover his health. For such chances as these hath the Lord in the law[4], and among all nations, prepared sanctuaries for men to flee to, as places of refuge. Sanctuaries. Murders proceed of pretended malice, when I, being blinded with private greediness, do go about to take from another man that which is his, and for resistance do kill him, if he yield it not to me. Of that sort are many wars and foughten battles now-a-days; and of that sort are robberies and murders committed by the highways' side. That also is pretended murder, when I, for injury that another man doth me, do revenge myself by killing him; or else, when I, being mad with anger, or overcome with wine, do murder the man, whom otherwise, if I were not in that ill-favoured taking, I would make much of and love very heartily.

But now, how foul and detestable an offence murder is, that proceedeth of malice, I think it expedient for me to declare to you, and you to mark in this that followeth. For the consideration thereof, being throughly scanned, must needs undoubtedly work so in the hearts of men, that fewer murders shall be committed, and that every one shall endeavour himself the more, by suppressing anger, to preserve mankind, who is the holy similitude of God himself. The very deed of murder itself fighteth directly and disobediently against the eternal God, who is the life and salvation of the world. For murder destroyeth the very image of God; because man is created to the similitude and likeness of God. If a man should of purpose deface[5] the image of the king or prince, set up at their commandment, he should be accused of treason committed: in how great danger is he then, that doth destroy a man, which is the reasonable, lively, and very picture of God himself! We read that Theodosius the emperor did determine to destroy a great number of the citizens of Antioch, for none other cause but for overthrowing of the image that was set up for the honour of Placilla Augusta. But hereunto is added, that one Macedonius, an hermit, came to the emperor's messengers, and said: "O my friends, go say to the emperor, Thou art not an emperor only, but also a man.

How great an offence murder is.

[4 Numb. xxxv. 11, &c.]   [5 everteret in foro, Lat.]

Do not thou cruelly destroy the image of God. Thou angerest
thy Maker, when thou killest his image. Consider with thyself, that thou art sorry for an image of brass. Now it is
evident to all men what difference there is betwixt a thing
that is dead, and that which hath life and a reasonable soul.
Moreover, it is an easy matter instead of one brasen image to
set up more: but it is unpossible to restore one hair to them
that once are slain[1]." Finally, murder is clean contrary to
the nature of man. For man cherisheth himself, and flesh
destroyeth not itself, but preserveth and nourisheth itself so
much as it may. But all we men, as many as live, are of
one lump, and of the same substantial flesh: and to kill a man
therefore is against man's nature. Furthermore, all men are
the children of one father, of one stock, and of the same progeny: murder therefore is directly against civil humanity, and
is a plague that reigns among men. And doth not the Lord
our Redeemer also require charity of all men, which must so
abound, that we may not stick to die for our neighbour? To
kill our neighbour, therefore, is flatly repugnant to christian
religion. And take this by the way too; that the blood of
man, shed by murder, crieth out of the earth to heaven for
revengement: for to Cain, when he had slain his brother, it
was said, "The voice of thy brother's blood crieth out of the

[1 Ὁ δῆμος (τῆς Ἀντιόχου πόλεως) τὴν χαλκὴν εἰκόνα τῆς πανευφήμου
Πλακίλλης ... κατήνεγκέ τε καὶ ἐπὶ πολὺ τῆς πόλεως κατέσυρε μέρος. Ταῦτα
πυθόμενος ὁ βασιλεὺς, καὶ χαλεπήνας ... ἐμπρήσειν ἠπείλει καὶ καταλύσειν
καὶ εἰς κώμην τὸ ἄστυ μετασκευάσειν. Μακεδόνιος δὲ ὁ θειότατος ... ἐν
ταῖς τῶν ὁρῶν κορυφαῖς διαιτώμενος ... τῆς χλανίδος θατέρου (τῶν ἀποστα-
λέντων ἀπὸ τοῦ βασίλεως) λαβόμενος, ἀμφοτέρους ἐκ τῶν ἵππων καταβῆναι
κελεύει. Ὁ δὲ, τῆς θείας σοφίας ἐμφορηθεὶς, τοιοῦσδε πρὸς αὐτοὺς ἐχρήσατο
λόγοις· Εἴπατε, ὦ φίλοι ἄνδρες, τῷ βασιλεῖ· οὐ βασιλεὺς εἰ μόνον, ἀλλὰ
καὶ ἄνθρωπος· μὴ τοίνυν μόνην ὅρα τὴν βασιλείαν, ἀλλὰ καὶ τὴν φύσιν
λογίζου· ἄνθρωπος γὰρ ὤν, ὁμοφυῶν βασιλεύεις. Κατ᾽ εἰκόνα δὲ θείαν καὶ
ὁμοίωσιν ἡ τῶν ἀνθρώπων δεδημιούργηται φύσις· μὴ τοίνυν ὠμῶς οὕτος καὶ
ἀπηνῶς τοῦ Θεοῦ τὴν εἰκόνα κατασφαγῆναι κελεύσῃς· παροξυνεῖς γὰρ τὸν
δημιουργὸν, τὴν ἐκείνου κολάζων εἰκόνα. Σκόπησον γὰρ, ὡς καὶ σὺ χαλκῆς
ἕνεκα δυσχεραίνων εἰκόνος ταῦτα ποιεῖς. Ὅσον δὲ τῆς ἀψύχου διαφέρει ἡ
ἔμψυχός τε καὶ ζῶσα καὶ λογικὴ, δῆλον ἅπασι τοῖς γε νοῦν ἔχουσι. Πρὸς
δὲ τούτοις λογισάσθω κάκεινα, ὡς ἡμῖν μὲν ῥάδιον ἀντὶ τῆς μιᾶς εἰκόνος
πολλὰς δημιουργῆσαι χαλκᾶς· αὐτῷ δὲ πάμπαν ἀδύνατον μίαν γοῦν τῶν
ἀναιρεθέντων δημιουργῆσαι τρίχα.—Theodorit. Eccles. Hist. Lib. v. cap.
20. Ed. Reading. Cantab. 1720, pp. 219, 220. See also Calfhill's
Answ. to Martiall. Parker Soc. ed. p. 22.]

earth, and is come up to me." For bloodshed verily pol-
luteth and maketh the ground accursed whereon it is shed,
and is not cleansed again, nor easily appeased, until it do also
drink the guilty blood of them which spilt before the guiltless
blood of innocents. Lastly, murders procure and mark the
committers thereof with endless spots of reproachful infamy;
and, that which is worst of all, it bringeth unto them
everlasting damnation. Wherefore Salomon in his proverbs
saith: "My son, if sinners entice thee, consent not unto
them. If they say, Come with us, we will lay wait for blood,
and will lurk privily for the innocent without a cause; We
will swallow them up like the grave quick, and whole as
those that go down into the pit; We shall find all manner of
costly riches, and fill our houses with the prey; Cast in thy
lot among us; we will all have one purse: My son, walk
not thou with them, but rather pull back thy foot from their
ways. For their feet run to evil, and are hasty to shed
blood[2]." Now David saith, that "the blood-thirsty man,
and the hypocrite, are abominable to the Lord[3]."

From this law is exempted the magistrate ordained by
God, whom God commandeth to use authority and to kill,
threatening to punish him most sharply, if he neglect to kill
the men whom God commandeth to be killed. This sixth
commandment of the law, therefore, doth flatly forbid upon
private authority to kill any man: but the magistrate killeth
at God's commandment, when he putteth to death those
which are by law condemned for their offences, or when in
defence of his people he doth justly and necessarily arm himself to the battle. And yet the magistrates may offend in
those two points two sundry ways. For either they do by
law, that is, under the coloured pretence of law, slay the
guiltless, to satisfy their own lust, hatred, or covetousness;
as we read, that Jezebel slew the just man Naboth, with the
Lord's prophets[4]: or else by peevish pity and foolish clemency do let them escape scot-free, whom the Lord commanded them to kill; as Saul and Achab are reported to
have sinned in letting go the bloody kings whom God commanded to be slain[5]. And Salomon, in the seventeenth of his

The magistrate may kill.

[2 Prov. i. 10—16.]   [3 Psal. v. 6.]
[4 1 Sam. xv; 1 Kings xx. 42.]
[5 1 Kings xxi. & xviii. 13. Hooper's Early Writ. ed. Park. Soc. p. 475.]

Proverbs, doth testify, that the Lord doth as greatly hate the magistrate that acquitteth a wicked person, as him that condemneth an innocent man[1]. The magistrates also in making or else repelling war do offend two ways in this sort: for either they do unjustly themselves make war upon other men, and entangle their people therein; or else they suffer foreign enemies to rob and spoil the people committed to their charge, and do not with such force as they may keep off and defend[2] that open wrong and manifest injury. Both these offences are of sundry sorts, and therewithal so great that they can hardly be purged. Thou readest therefore, that the holy kings of Israel did never make war upon anybody, unless the Lord commanded them. And they again fought for their people, and suffered them not to be led away captive, as miserable bond-slaves. For so did the blessed patriarch Abraham follow upon and pursue those four kings, nay, rather cutthroat robbers of the east, and recovered by force of arms Lot, Lot's substance, and the people of Sodom that were carried away[3]. And such wars as these are taken in hand, either for the recovery, or else for the confirmation, of peace: so that the magistrates that make war in such a cause are rightly and indeed the children of God, because they are peace-makers; for all peace-makers are the children of God.

What the magistrate is.
And now this place and argument do require, that I speak somewhat touching the office or authority of the magistrate: which (by God's help) I will assay to do, not that I mean or can allege all that may be said thereof, but that which shall seem most properly to declare the meaning of it, and is most necessary for this present treatise[4].

[1 Prov. xvii. 15.]

[2 i. e. repel, keep off.—Johnson. So in Early Writings of Hooper, Parker Soc. ed. p. 107.]

[3 Gen. xiv. 14—16.]

[4 The mischievous tenets of the Anabaptists rendered so necessary in the age of Bullinger the setting forth of the true doctrine concerning civil magistracy. A summary proof of this necessity is thus given by Melancthon: Saepe et olim et recens fuerunt hypocritae supersti tiosi et fanatici, qui ... magistratuum functiones, judicia, leges forenses legitimas poenas, imperia, bella legitima, militiam damnaverunt. Tales furores olim sparserunt Marcion et Manichæi;—circumtulerunt et simi les errores ante trecentos annos Flagelliferi, ut vocabantur; et hoc

Magistratus (which word we use for the room wherein Magistratus, the magistrate is) doth take the name *a magistris populi designandis,* " of assigning the masters, guiders, and captains of the people." That room and place is called by the name of " power" or " authority," by reason of the power that is given to it of God. It is called by the name of "domination," for the dominion that the Lord doth grant it upon the earth. They are called princes that have that dominion: for they have a pre-eminence above the people. They are called consuls, of counselling; and kings, of commanding, ruling, and governing the people. So, then, the magistracy (that I may henceforward use this word of the magistrate's power and place) is an office, and an action in executing of the same. Aristotle defineth a magistrate to be a keeper of laws[5]. Plutarch, in that book wherein he sheweth that learning is required to be in a king, among other things saith: " Princes are the ministers of God for the oversight and safeguard of mortal men, to the end that they may partly distribute, and partly keep, the good things that he doth liberally give, and frankly bestow upon them[6]." The magistracy, by the scriptures, may be defined to be a divine ordinance or action, whereby the good being defended by the prince's aid, and the evil suppressed by the same authority, godliness, justice, honesty, peace, and tranquillity, both public and private, are safely preserved. Whereby we gather, that to govern a commonweal, and to execute the office of a magistrate, is a worship and service to God himself. God verily is delighted therein. For the office of a magistrate is a thing most excellent, and abounding with all good works, as in my former sermon I have declared.

Now there are three kinds of magistracies or governments Three kinds of commonweals; the monarchy, the aristocracy, and the of magistrates. Monarchy.

nostro tempore Anabaptistæ passim vagantes adhuc circumferunt hos errores.—Melanc. Loc. Com. Erlang. 1838. Vol. i. pars 2. p. 138.]

[5 Ἔστι δὲ ὁ ἄρχων φύλαξ τοῦ δικαίου.—Aristot. Eth. Lib. v. cap. 6. Polit. iii. c. 16, Aristotle calls magistrates, νομοφύλακας καὶ ὑπηρέτας τὶς νόμοις.]

[6 Ἀληθέστερον δ' ἄν τις εἴποι τοὺς ἄρχοντας ὑπηρετεῖν Θεῷ πρὸς ἀνθρώπων ἐπιμέλειαν καὶ σωτηρίαν, ὅπως, ὧν Θεὸς δίδωσιν ἀνθρώποις καλῶν καὶ ἀγαθῶν, τὰ μὲν νέμωσι, τὰ δὲ φυλάττωσιν.—Plutarch ad Princip. doct.]

democracy[1]. We may call the monarchy a kingdom, wherei
one alone doth by just and upright laws rule all things an
causes in the commonweal. For if that justice and equity
be once neglected, and that this one doth against all righ
and reason rule all the roost, then is he a tyrant, and hi

Tyranny. power is tyranny, that is to say, wrong and injury; which i
a disease of that troubled kingdom, and a vice that is, as i
were, set opposite to be the destruction of that commonwea

Aristocracy. The aristocracy is the superior power of a few peers, wher
a certain number of holy and upright men are chosen to b
the guides and rulers of the people. And this did first begi
by the fall of tyranny: for when men perceived how dar
gerous it was to commit the rule of their whole state into on
man's hand, they altered the order, and gave the charg
thereof to an appointed number of chosen men, who did exce
the common sort in power and authority. But if these chi
or head men use evil means to come to authority, and, neg
lecting the commonweal, do hunt after their own advantage
then is their government not to be called an aristocracy, bu

Oligarchy. an oligarchy, that is, the violent lust of a few, and not th
good and upright government of chosen peers. So then thes
few violent rulers are the contrary to the estate, where u

Democracy. right headmen have the pre-eminence. The democracy ma
be called a commonweal, wherein all the people together bea
the whole sway and absolute authority. And this democrac
began first by the fall of the oligarchy. For when th
people saw that their headmen did abuse their power, an
waxed violent rulers, they displaced them, and kept the au
thority to themselves, meaning that every man should freel
give his voice in matters touching the commonweal. Th
kind of government breaketh out commonly into outrageo
tumults[2], I mean, into seditions and conspiracies: for no ma
will suffer himself to be corrected, while every man wi
challenge to himself full and absolute authority to do wha
he lusteth, because, forsooth, he is one and a member of th
people, in whose hands the whole authority doth consist.

[1 On this subject of the various forms of governments and the
abuses, Bullinger seems to have borrowed from Aristot. Ethic. Li
VIII. cap. 10.]

[2 Systremma, Lat. σύστρεμμα, tumultus e concursu hominum.-
Hederic. Lex.]

Now touching the excellency of these forms or kinds of
government, it maketh not greatly to my purpose to dispute
which ought to be preferred before other.   Many have preferred the monarchy before the rest: but therewithal they
added, "If he which holdeth the monarchy be a good and
upright prince."   Which, nevertheless, is rare to be found.
They also, which were of that opinion, did themselves live
under princes in monarchies.   "But it is dangerous to speak
against Jupiter."   Among many kings of Judah and Israel
thou shalt find a very few good, or at least wise tolerable and
indifferent, princes; whereby we may perceive that the Lord
did not in vain, by the mouth of Samuel, persuade his people
to keep their aristocracy, and to be ruled by their priests and
elders, as God, by Moses and Jethro, the wisest in the world,
had ordained long before.   And yet none can deny, but that
great perils and infinite discommodities are in the aristocracy,
but far more many in the democracy.   But such is the condition of mortal men in this corruptible flesh, that nothing
among them is absolutely and on every side happy[4]; and
therefore that seemeth to them to be most excellent, which,
although it be not altogether without inconveniences and some
kind of vices, doth nevertheless, in comparison of other, bring
fewer perils and lesser annoyance.   But howsoever that case
doth stand, the apostles of Christ do command us to obey the
magistrate, whether he be king, or senate of chosen men.   For
Paul in his epistle to Titus saith: "Warn them to be subject
to rule and power, and to obey magistrates[5]."   For to the
Romans he saith: "Let every soul be subject to the higher
powers: for no power is but of God, and those powers that
are are ordained by God[6]."   Again, to Timothy he saith:
"I exhort you that prayers be made for kings, and for all
that are in authority[7]."   If therefore any man live in a
monarchy, let him obey the king: if in a commonweal of
what title soever, let him be ruled by the consuls, tribunes,

Marginal notes:

A proverb, signifying that it is perilous for a subject to speak against his prince. In English we say, it is ill jesting with saints[3].

The magistrate must be obeyed.

Tit. iii.

[3 The proverb most like this occurs in Ray, as the Italian form of
our English one, "No jesting with edge tools, or with bell-ropes:" viz.
"Tresca con i fanti, et lascia star i santi; i. e. Play with children, and
let the saints alone."—Ray's Proverbs, p. 124.]

[4 Nihil est ab omni parte beatum.   Quoted from Hor. Od. Lib. II.
16. 27.]

[5 Titus iii. 1.]   [6 Rom. xiii. 1.]   [7 1 Tim. ii. 1.]

headmen, and elders of the people. For we ought rather to obey the ordinance of God, than over curiously to dispute of the kinds of governments, which is the better or worse than other.

The causes of
magistrates,
and their be-
ginning. And in all cases truly, the magistrate is very necessary, and cannot be missing among men; yea, he is so necessary, that without the magistrate's help the state of men can hardly prosper, or easily stand. Neither dost thou read, that the state and commonweal of the Israelites was ever at any time in greater danger and peril of undoing, than it was in the middle time betwixt Sampson and Heli, when they were governed by no magistrates, but did every man what he thought good himself[1]. For all men even from their birth are blindly led with self-love, and therefore they seek their own advantage; nothing pleaseth them but what they do themselves, they utterly mislike the deeds and words of other men: yea, such is our fond affection and opinionative sense, that how evil soever our causes are, yet we will not stick to face them out with a card of ten[2], and to colour them with law and equity. He that will stand in denial hereof, did never consider man's disposition. The people of Israel, at their delivery out of Egypt, saw wonderful signs; they were marvellously fed from heaven in the desert, and did every day behold new miracles. But yet, hearken, my brethren, and consider, what Moses, the meekest and gentlest man that ever was, doth say touching this holy people, this people of God, whom God had chosen to be a peculiar people unto himself: "How shall I alone," saith he to the people, "bear your trouble, your burden, and the strifes that are among you[3]?" What

[1 Judg. xvii. 6.]

[2 Causis nostris licet pessimis jus prætexamus et justitiam, Lat. The proverbial expression used by the translator occurs in Shakspeare's Taming of the Shrew, Act II. Scene 1. ad fin. and, earlier still, in Skelton:

　　　Fyrste pycke a quarell, and fall out with him then,
　　　And so outface hym with a carde of ten.——

　　　　　　　　　　　The Bouge of Courte.

The phrase of *a card of ten* was possibly derived, by a jocular allusion, from that of *a hart of ten*, in hunting, which meant a full-grown deer; one past six years of age. Nares's Glossary, in voc. *Card.* I conceive the force of the phrase to have expressed originally the confidence or impudence of one who with a ten, as at brag, faced, or out-faced one who had really a faced card against him.——Ibid. in voc. to *face it.*]

[3 Deut. i. 12.]

may be thought of that moreover, that in the most sure fellowship of the ancient and apostolic church, yea, in those very vessels which were regenerate, the wrangling disposition of flesh did shew itself? For the Greeks murmured against the Hebrews, because their widows in the daily ministry were little regarded[4]. The Corinthians also go to law before heathen judges; and therefore doth Paul very sharply rebuke them, and chargeth them to appoint honest judges among themselves to take up matters betwixt them that were at variance[5]. Let no man therefore make this objection, and say, that the old people of Israel were a carnal people and not regenerate. For we see, that even in the regenerate the relics of flesh remain, which ever and anon, when occasion is offered, do shew forth themselves, and trouble the quiet state of everything. For I will not now say that the greater sort of men do rather follow the flesh than the spirit. And for that cause God, who loveth man, who keepeth and preserveth civility, peace, and human society, hath prepared and applied a medicine against those grievous diseases of men; he hath appointed the magistrate, I say, to step betwixt them that strive with the authority of law and equity, to judge and discuss matters betwixt them that are at variance, to bridle and suppress wrong and affections, and lastly, to save the guiltless and innocents. Whosoever subverteth this ordinance of God, till such time as men do leave their wayward disposition[6], he bringeth utter confusion to every state, and aideth wrongful dealers and violent robbers to oppress and root out the best sort of people. By this verily, which hitherto we have alleged, it is manifestly apparent, that the magistrate is ordained by God for the safeguard of the good, and punishment of the evil; I mean, for the good and quiet state of mortal men. Wherefore we read, that from the beginning there have been magistrates in the world.

The magistrate ordained by God for the good of men.

Hereunto do appertain these testimonies of the holy scripture. Moses in the law calleth the judges Gods, and this "judgment," saith he, "is God's[7]." From whence also Josaphat borrowed that saying, which he spake to the judges, where he saith: "See what ye do: for ye judge not to man, but

---

[4 Acts vi. 1.]   [5 1 Cor. vi. 1—4.]

[6 priusquam homines angelicum recipiant ingenium, Lat.]

[7 Exod. xxii. 28; Deut. i. 17.]

to the Lord, which is with you in the causes which ye judge: let the fear of God therefore be in your hearts[1]." St Peter saith, that we must "obey the magistrate for the Lord's sake, by whom he is ordained to the praise of the good, and terrifying of the evil[2]." And Paul, the teacher of the Gentiles, saith: "There is no power but of God, and the powers that are are ordained by God: and whosoever resisteth the power, resisteth the ordinance of God; and he that resisteth shall receive to himself damnation. For rulers are not fearful to them that do well, but to the evil. For he is the minister of God, revenger of wrath on him that doth evil[3]." The magistrate therefore is of God; his office is good, holy, pleasing God, just, profitable, and necessary for men: and the rulers, which do rightly execute their office, are the friends and worshippers of God; they are his elect instruments, by whom he worketh man's health and safeguard. We have examples hereof in Adam, all the patriarchs, our father Noe, Joseph, Moses, Josue, Gedeon, Samuel, David, Josaphat, Ezechias, Josias, Daniel, and many other after the time of Christ, who rightly executed the office of magistrates.

Now many there are which will have the magistrate to be of two sorts, to wit, either good or bad. The good magistrate is he who, being lawfully ordained, doth lawfully execute his office and duty. The evil magistrate is he which, when he hath by evil means got the authority, doth turn and dispose it as himself lusteth. And hereupon the question is wont to be demanded: Whether an evil, that is, a tyrannical, magistrate, be of God or no? To this I answer, that God is the author of good, and not of evil. For God by nature is good, and all his purposes are good, being directed to the health and preservation, not to the destruction, of us men. Therefore the good and healthful ordaining of the magistrate, without all doubt, is of God himself, who is the author of all goodness.

∨   But here it is requisite, that we make a difference betwixt the office which is the good ordinance of God, and the evil person that doth not rightly execute that good office. If therefore in the magistrate evil be found, and not the good for which he was ordained, that cometh of other causes, and

A good magistrate and a bad.

Whether an evil magistrate be of God or no.

[1 2 Chron. xix. 6, 7.]   [2 1 Pet. ii. 14.]
[3 Rom. xiii. 1—4.]

the fault thereof is in the men and persons, which neglect God and corrupt the ordinance of God, and not in God, nor in his ordinance: for either the evil prince, seduced by the devil, corrupteth the ways of God, and by his own fault and naughtiness transgresseth God's ordinance, so far, that he doth worthily deserve the name of devilish power, and not divine authority;—(we have an example hereof in the magistrate of Jerusalem: for although he were able to refer the beginning of his power by degrees unto Moses, and so unto God himself who did ordain it; yet, for because he taketh the Saviour in the garden and bindeth him, to his servants it is said, "Ye are come out as it were to a thief with swords and staves; when I was daily with you in the temple, ye stretched not forth your hands against me; but this is even your hour, and the power of darkness[4]." Lo, here he calleth the ordinary magistrate the power of the devil, when he abuseth his power. What could be more evidently spoken? But here ye must mark, that the reproach was in the person, and not in the office. Likewise also the Roman empire was ordained by God, as by the visions of Daniel it is clearly evident: and yet, when Nero, not without God's ordinance, bare the sway in the empire, whatsoever he did as king and emperor, contrary to the office of a good king, that did he not of God, but of the devil: for whereas he hung up and beheaded the apostles of Christ[5], moving a bloody persecution against the church, that sprang not from elsewhere than from the devil, the father of murder. So then, verily, we ought not at any time to defend the tyrannical power, and say that it is of God: for tyranny is not a divine, but a devilish, kind of government; and tyrants themselves are properly the servants of the devil, and not of God:) or else otherwise, some people do deserve by their wicked deeds to have, not a king, but a tyrant. So then the people's sin is another cause that evil magistrates are found in commonweals. In the meanwhile, the king is of the Lord, and sometimes he makes an hypocrite reign. Wherefore the evil magistrate is of God, even as also seditions, wars, plagues, hail, frost, and other miseries of mankind come from the Lord, as punishment of

[4 Luke xxii. 52, 53.]
[5 Paul is said to have been *beheaded*, and Peter *crucified*, at Rome, under Nero.—Euseb. Hist. Eccles. Lib. II. cap. 25.]

sin and wickedness, which the Lord hath appointed to be executed, as he himself saith: "I will give them children to be their kings, and infants shall rule them; because their tongue and heart hath been against the Lord[1]." Likewise the Lord stirred up the cruel kings of Assyria and Babylon against his city and own peculiar people, whose living was not agreeable to their profession.

How the oppressed must behave themselves under tyrannical princes.

But now, how and after what sort subjects ought to be affected toward such hard, cruel, and tyrannical princes, we learn partly by the example of David, and partly by the doctrine of Jeremy and the apostles. David was not ignorant what kind of man Saul was, a wicked and merciless fellow: yet, notwithstanding, he fled to escape his hands; and when he had occasion given him once or twice to kill him, he slew him not, but spared the tyrant and reverenced him as though he had been his father[2]. Jeremias prayed for Joachim and Zedechias, wicked kings both, and obeyed them until they came to matters flatly contrary to God's religion[3]. For where I spake touching the honour due to parents, there did I by the scriptures prove, that we ought not to obey the wicked commandments of godless magistrates, because it is not permitted to magistrates to ordain or appoint any thing contrary to God's law, or the law of nature. Now the Acts of the Apostles teach us in what sort the apostles did behave themselves in dealing with tyrannical magistrates. Let them, therefore, that are vexed with tyrants, and oppressed with wicked magistrates, take this advice to follow in that perplexity. First, let them call to remembrance, and consider, what and how great their sins of idolatry and uncleanness are, which have already deserved the revenging anger of their jealous God: and then let them think, that God will not withdraw his scourge, unless he see that they redress their corrupt manners and evil religion. So then first, they must go about and bring to pass a full reformation of matters in religion, and perfect amendment of manners amiss: then must they pray continually that God will vouchsafe to pull and draw his oppressed people out of the mire of mischief, wherein they stick fast. For that counsel did the Lord himself, in the eighteenth after

[1 Isai iii. 4, 8.]
[2 1 Sam. xxiv. and xxvi.]
[3 Jer. vii. 16, and xiv.]

Luke, give to those that are oppressed, promising therewithal assured aid and present delivery. But what and how the oppressed must pray, there are examples extant in the ninth of Daniel, and in the fourth chapter of the Acts of the Apostles. Let them also, whose minds are vexed, call to remembrance the sayings of Peter and Paul, the chief of the apostles. "The Lord," saith Peter, "knoweth how to deliver his from 2 Pet. ii. temptation, as he delivered Lot." Paul saith: "God is faith- 1 Cor. x. ful, and will not suffer his to be tempted above their strength; yea, he will turn their temptations unto the best[4]." Let them call to mind the captivity of Israel, wherein God's people were detained at Babylon by the space of seventy years: and therewithal let them think upon the goodly comfort of the captives, which Esay hath expressed from his fortieth chapter unto his forty-ninth. Let us persuade ourselves, that God is good, merciful, and omnipotent, so that he can, when he will, at ease deliver us. He hath many ways and means to set us at liberty. Let us have a regard only, that our impenitent, filthy, and wicked life do not provoke the Lord to augment and prolong the tyrants' cruelty. The Lord is able, upon the sudden, to change the hearts of princes (for "the hearts of kings are in the hands of the Lord, as the rivers of water, to turn them which way he will[5]"), and to make them, which have been hitherto most cruelly set against us, to be our friends and favourable to us; and them which have heretofore most bloodily persecuted the true religion, to embrace the same most ardently, and with a burning zeal to promote it so far as they may. We have evident examples hereof in the books of the Kings, of Esdras, and Nehemias, and in the volume of Daniel's prophecy. Nabuchodonosor, whose purpose was to toast with fire and utterly to destroy the martyrs of God for true religion, was immediately after compelled to praise God, because he saw the martyrs preserved: and he himself doth by edicts given out publicly proclaim and set forth the only true God and his true religion[6]. Darius, the son of Assuerus[7], suffereth Daniel

---

[4 imo tentationibus etiam felicem concedet eventum, Lat. 1 Cor. x. 13. So Erasmus expounds; dabit et exitum bonum.—Annotat. in loc. cit.]

[5 Prov. xxi. 1.]   [6 Dan. iii.]

[7 See Prideaux. Connect. Vol. I. pp. 72, 104, 122, ed. Mc Caul. 1845. See also above, page 51, note 3.]

to be cast into the lions' den: but straightway he draweth him out again, and shutteth up Daniel's enemies in the same den, to be torn in pieces by the famishing beasts. Cyrus, the puissant king of Persia, advanceth true religion: Darius, son of Hystaspes, whose surname was Artaxerxes[1], did by all means possible aid and set forward the godly intent of God's people in building up again their city and temple. Let us not doubt therefore of God's aid and helping hand. For God sometime doth utterly destroy, and sometime he chasteneth, untoward tyrants with some horrible and sudden disease: as it is evident that it happened to Antiochus[2], Herod the Great[3], and to his nephew, Herod Agrippa[4], to Maxentius[5] also, and other enemies of God and tyrants over men[6]. Sometime he stirreth up noble captains and valiant men to displace tyrants, and set God's people at liberty; as we see many examples thereof in the books of Judges and Kings. But lest any man do fall to abuse those examples, let him consider their calling by God: which calling if he have not, or else do prevent, he is so far **Killing of** from doing good in killing the tyrant, that it is to be feared **tyrants.** lest he do make the evil double so much as it was before. Thus much hitherto. Now I return to that which by my digression remaineth yet unspoken of.

The election of magistrates. Here I have to speak somewhat touching the election of magistrates: and first, to whom the choice and ordering of **Who ought to choose them.** the magistrate doth belong; secondarily, whom and what kind of men it is best to choose to be magistrates; and lastly, the manner and order of consecrating those which once are chosen.

Touching the election of magistrates, to whom that office should belong, no one and certain rule can be prescribed.

[1 The Artaxerxes, who so much befriended the Jews in the days of Ezra and Nehemiah, and whom, no doubt, Bullinger means, was Artaxerxes Longimanus. Yet the Jewish tradition makes Darius Hystaspis to be Artaxerxes, and Bullinger, perhaps, followed it.— See Prideaux. Con. Vol. I. pp. 201, 244. ed. Mᶜ Caul, 1845.]

[2 Prideaux's Connect. Vol. II. p. 189.]

[3 Ibid. p. 613. Euseb. Eccl. Hist. Lib. I. cap. 8.]

[4 Acts xii. 21—23, *grandson* of Herod the Great;—nepoti, Lat.— Euseb. Eccles. Hist. Lib. II. cap. 10.]

[5 Gibbon's Decline and Fall, &c. Vol. II. chap. xiv. p. 232. ed. 1820. Euseb. Eccles. Hist. Lib. IX. cap. 9.]

[6 See Jewel's Works.—Parker Soc. ed. pp. 977—8.]

For in some places the whole commonalty doth choose their peers[7]; in other places the peers do choose the magistrates; and in other places princes come to it by succession and birth. In discussing which of these orders should be the best, it were but folly to make much ado. For to every kingdom and every city is worthily left their country fashion, unless it be altogether too too corrupt, and not to be borne withal. But where princes come to it by birth, their earnest prayer must be made to the Lord, that he will grant them to be good.

Now for the good election of magistrates, the Lord himself declareth whom and what kind of men he will have to be chosen, in these very words: "Look over all the people, consider them diligently, and choose from among them men of courage, such as fear God, speakers of truth, and haters of covetousness, and make them rulers over thousands, rulers of hundreds, rulers of fifties, and rulers of tens, to judge the people at all seasons[8]." Four things the Lord requireth in a good governour. First, that he be a man of courage, of strength or force, that is, which hath ability to do the thing whereunto he is appointed. That ability consisteth in mind rather than in body. For it is required, that he be not a fool, but wise and skilful in that which he hath to do: because the office of a captain is to know how to set his army in order of battle, rather than to fight himself; as also the duty of a surveyor of works is to know how buildings must be erected, rather than to work himself; or as a chariot-man ought rather to know how to guide his cart in driving, than to draw it himself. And therewithal too, there is demanded a boldness of stomach to dare to do the thing that he already knoweth; for constancy and sufferance are very needful in every captain. In the second place that is set down, which indeed is the first; let him fear God, let him be religious, and not superstitious. No idolater preserveth the commonweal, but rather destroyeth it; and a wicked man defendeth not truth and true religion, but persecuteth and driveth them out of his jurisdiction. Let this magistrate of ours therefore be of the right religion, sound in faith, believing the word of God, and knowing that God is present among men and doth repay to whom he list according to their deserts. And for that cause Justinian, the emperor, in *Novellis Constitutionib.* 109, doth freely confess that all

What kind of men ought to be chosen to be magistrates, and the description of a good magistrate.

The magistrate must be sound in religion.

[7 optimates, Lat.]   [8 Exod. xviii. 21.]

his help is of God; and that therefore it is convenient, that
the making of all laws should depend upon him alone. Immediately after he saith: "It is known very well to all men, that
they in whose hands the empire was before it came to us, and
especially that Leo of worthy memory, and the most sacred
prince Justin our father, did in their constitutions flatly forbid
all heretics to be admitted soldiers in any warfare, or dealers
in matters concerning the commonwealth, that the less occasion might be given, by receiving them into the fellowship
of war or handling of public affairs, for any to think that
they corrupt the members of God's holy catholic and apostolic
Church. And this decree do we establish[1]." Thus saith the
emperor. And the godly man verily prayeth to God, and receiveth wisdom at the Lord's hand. And where the princes
are God's friends, and have often conference with God, there
is hope that those commonweals shall prosper and flourish.
But, on the other side, there must needs be feared an unhappy
end of that commonweal, where the enemies of God have the
pre-eminence. Thirdly, there is required of him, which must
be chosen and called to be magistrate, that he be true in word
and deed, so that he be not found to be an hypocrite, a liar, a
deceiver, a turncoat, nor one which out of one mouth doth
blow both hot and cold; but faithful, simple, a plain dealer,
and blameless. He must not be more liberal in promising
than in performing. He must not be one that setteth light by
an oath, not a false swearer, nor a perjured man. Fourthly,
because many that are in office desire riches, and seek to increase their wealth by bribes, the Lord removeth such from
the magistracy, and forbiddeth good magistrates to be covetous: yea, he doth expressly charge them to hate and abhor

[1 Μίαν ἡμῖν εἶναι βοήθειαν ἐπὶ παντὶ τῷ τῆς ἡμετέρας πολιτείας τε καὶ
βασιλείας βίῳ τὴν εἰς Θεὸν ἐλπίδα πιστεύομεν· εἰδότες ὅτι τοῦτο ἡμῖν καὶ
τὴν τῆς ψυχῆς καὶ τὴν τῆς βασιλείας δίδωσι σωτηρίαν· ὥστε καὶ τὰς
νομοθεσίας τὰς ἡμετέρας ἐκεῖθεν ἠρτῆσθαι προσήκει . . . . Ἴσασι τοίνυν
ἅπαντες, ὡς οἱ πρὸ ἡμῶν βεβασιλευκότες, καὶ μάλιστα Λέων ὁ τῆς εὐσεβοῦς
μνήμης, καὶ Ἰουστῖνος ὁ τῆς θείας λήξεως ἡμῶν πατήρ, ἐν ταῖς ἑαυτῶν
διατάξεσι, τοῖς αἱρετικοῖς ἅπασιν ἀπηγόρευσαν ὥστε μηδεμίαν αὐτοὺς μετ-
ιέναι στρατείαν, μήτε δὲ τὴν οἱανοῦν ἐπὶ δημοσίαις φροντίσι μετουσίαν
ἔχειν· ὅπως ἂν μὴ προφάσει τῶν στρατείων τῶν τε δημοσίων ἐπιταγμάτων
τῷ τῆς ἁγίας τοῦ Θεοῦ καθολικῆς καὶ ἀποστολικῆς ἐκκλησίας μέρει φανεῖεν
λυμαινόμενοι· καὶ ἡμεῖς δὲ αὐτὸ τοῦτο πεπράχαμεν.—Justin. Anth. Collat
VIII. tit. 9. Novell. 109. Præfat. p. 431. Gotting. 1797.]

it; as he doth also, in another place, not only forbid them to take bribes, but also command them to shake off and rid their hands of all rewards[2]. Covetousness and greedy desire of bribes are the very plagues that choke good magistrates. By covetous men and takers of bribes law, judgment, liberty, justice, and the country itself, is set to sale and sold to the devil for money. And now, though in this place the Lord hath named only the most pestilent mischief of all other, yet there is no doubt but that he doth inclusively debar all other vices and evils of that sort, commanding them to be strange and far off from the good magistrate and godly governor. Those vices are pride, envy, anger, dicing, surfeiting, drunkenness, whoredom, adultery, and whatsoever else is like to these.

This place is made more manifest by conferring it with other places in the law of God. Moses, in Deuteronomy, saith to the people: "Bring men of wisdom, of understanding, and Deut. i. of an honest life, according to your tribes[3]." Three things here again doth the wise man, Moses, require in them that are to be appointed magistrates in his commonweal. First, saith he, let them be wise. But the beginning of wisdom is the fear of the Lord. Let them therefore be ordained magistrates, that are friends to God and true religion; let them be wise, and not foolish idiots. Secondarily, they must be men of understanding; that is, men of experience, who by long and continual exercise in handling of matters are able at the first brunt to deal in all cases according to the law. Lastly, they must be men of honest report, whose life and sound conversation are by their deeds perfectly tried and sufficiently witnessed of unto the people: and finally, they must be such as bear authority, and not be despised as rascal and vile knaves.

In the book of Numbers also Moses saith: "Let the God Numb. xxvii. of the spirits of all flesh set a man over the congregation, which may go in and out before them, and lead them in and out, that the congregation of the Lord be not as sheep without a shepherd[4]." By these words of the holy prophet we learn who are to be chosen, and how they are to be chosen, into the office of magistrates. Moses prayed to the Lord for a fit and a convenient man: and we therefore must pray to

[2 Isai. xxxiii. 15.]   [3 Deut. i. 13.]
[4 Numb. xxvii. 16, 17.]

[BULLINGER.]

God, who searcheth all men's hearts, that he will vouchsafe to send such men to be our magistrates as are meet for that room and calling. The outward shew doth many times deceive us, and we judge him to be a good and godly man who is indeed a notable hypocrite. God alone doth know the mind: we must beseech him, therefore, that he suffer us not in our choice to err or choose amiss. Let him be thought the best and meetest for the purpose, who is instructed with the Holy Spirit of God. Furthermore, he that is appointed to that office must still be the first and the last, and always at one end in all matters of weight and public affairs. Some unprofitable and idle drones there are, that drive other forward, and after the first onset do themselves take their ease. And some wicked fellows there are, which will appoint other what to do, but will themselves do nothing of that which by right belongs unto their office. The guide of the people must be a man of choice elected to be magistrate, whose care is day and night to have an eye that the flock of the Lord be not scattered, endangered, nor utterly destroyed. And thus have I hitherto told you what kind of men they ought to be, to whom the charge is to be committed over the Lord's people.

The manner of consecrating magistrates.

Last of all, touching the manner of consecrating magistrates, sundry cities and countries have sundry customs. Let every country freely retain their own usual order. I for my part think best of that manner of consecrating, wherein sumptuous pomp is little or none, but what reason and decency seem to allow. The best and most profitable way is, in consecrating them that are once chosen, to use a certain moderate ceremony, and that too in the face of all the people, that every one may know who they be that are the fathers of the people, to whom they owe honour, whom they ought to obey, and for whose health and welfare they ought to pray. The people of God had a certain prescribed ceremony, which we read that they used in consecrating their kings and magistrates: and it is certain that it was profitably and for good causes first invented, and then commanded by God himself[1].

The rest that is yet behind to be spoken touching the magistrate I mean to defer until to-morrow. And now to end with thanksgiving, let us praise the Lord, &c.

[1 a Deo inventum atque traditum, Lat.]

OF THE OFFICE OF THE MAGISTRATE[2], WHETHER THE
CARE OF RELIGION APPERTAIN TO HIM OR NO,
AND WHETHER HE MAY MAKE LAWS AND
ORDINANCES IN CASES OF RELIGION.

THE SEVENTH SERMON.

THE first and greatest thing, that chiefly ought to be in
a magistrate, is easily perceived by the declaration of his
office and duty.   In my yesterday's sermon I shewed you
what the magistrate is, how many kinds of magistrates there
are, of whom the magistrate had his beginning, for what
causes he was ordained, the manner and order how to choose
peers[3], and what kind of men should be called to be magistrates.   To this let us now add what the office and duty of a
magistrate properly is.

The whole office of a magistrate seemeth to consist in *The magis-*
these three points; to order, to judge, and to punish: of *trate's office.*
every one whereof I mean to speak severally in order as
they lie.   The ordinance of the magistrate is a decree made
by him for maintaining of religion, honesty, justice, and public
peace: and it consisteth on two points; in ordering rightly
matters of religion, and making good laws for the preservation
of honesty, justice, and common peace.   But before I come
to the determining and ordering of religion, I will briefly, and
in few words, handle their question which demand, whether
the care of religion do appertain to the magistrate as part of
his office or no?   For I see many that are of opinion, that
the care and ordering of religion doth belong to bishops alone[4],
and that kings, princes, and senators ought not to meddle
therewith.

But the catholic verity teacheth, that the care of religion *Whether the*
doth especially belong to the magistrate; and that it is not in *care of re-*
his power only, but his office and duty also, to dispose and *ligion belong
to the magis-
trate.*

[2 quæ ordinet, Lat.; omitted.   What he may regulate.]
[3 proceres, Lat.]
[4 Cf. Becon's Works, Vol. II. p. 303. Parker Soc. ed.   The Ro-
mish arguments on this topic are alleged and discussed by Melancthon.
—Corp. Reform. Tom. III. No. 1520. pp. 240—58.]

advance religion.　For among them of old their kings were priests; I mean, masters and overseers of religion.　Melchizedech, that holy and wise prince of the Canaanitish people, who bare the type or figure of Christ our Lord, is wonderfully commended in the holy scriptures: now he was both king and priest together.　Moreover, in the book of Numbers, to Josue, newly ordained and lately consecrated, are the laws belonging to religion given up and delivered.　The kings of Juda also, and the elect people of God, have for the well ordering of religion (as I will by examples anon declare unto you) obtained very great praise: and again, as many as were slack in looking to religion are noted with the mark of perpetual reproach.　Who is ignorant, that the magistrate's especial care ought to be to keep the commonweal in safeguard and prosperity?　Which undoubtedly he cannot do, unless he provide to have the word of God preached to his people, and cause them to be taught the true worship of God, by that means making himself, as it were, the minister of true religion.　In Leviticus and Deuteronomy the Lord doth largely set down the good prepared for men that are religious and zealous indeed; and reckoneth up, on the other side, the evil appointed for the contemners of true religion.　But the good magistrate is commanded to retain and keep prosperity among his people, and to repel all kind of adversity.　Let us hear also what the wise man, Salomon, saith in his Proverbs: "Godliness and truth preserve the king, and in godliness his seat is holden up."　"When the just are multiplied, the people rejoice; and when the wicked ruleth, the people lamenteth.　The king by judgment stablisheth his dominion, but a tyrant overthroweth it.　When the wicked increase, iniquity is multiplied, and the just shall see their decay.　Where the word of God is not preached[1], the people decay; but happy is he that keepeth the law[2]."　Whereby we gather, that they, which would not have the care of religion to appertain to princes, do seek and bring in the confusion of all things, the dissolution of princes and their people, and lastly, the neglecting and oppression of the poor.

Furthermore, the Lord commandeth the magistrate to make trial of doctrines, and to kill those that do stubbornly teach

Levit. xxvi.
Deut. xxviii.

[1 quando non est visio, Lat.; cum prophetia defecerit, Vulg.]
[2 Prov. xx. 28; xxix. 2, 4, 16, 18.]

against the scriptures, and draw the people from the true God. The place is to be seen in the thirteenth of Deut. God also forbade the magistrate to plant groves, or erect images : as is to be seen in the seventeenth of Deut. And by those particularities he did insinuate things general; forbidding to ordain, to nourish, and set forth superstition or idolatry ; wherefore he commanded to advance true religion : and so consequently it followeth, that the care of religion belongeth to the magistrate. What may be thought of that moreover, that the most excellent princes and friends of God among God's people did challenge to themselves the care of religion as belonging to themselves ; insomuch that they exercised and took the charge thereof, even as if they had been ministers of the holy things ? Josue in the mount Hebal caused an altar to be builded, and fulfilled all the worship of God, as it was commanded of God by the mouth of Moses[3]. David, in bringing in and bestowing the ark of God in his place, and in ordering the worship of God, was so diligent, that it is wonder to tell. So likewise was Salomon, David's son. Neither do I think that any man knoweth not how much Abia[4], Josaphat, Ezechias, and Josias, laboured in the reformation of religion, which in their times was corrupted and utterly defaced. The very heathen kings and princes are praised, because, when they knew the truth, they gave out edicts for the confirmation of true religion against blasphemous mouths. Nabuchodonozor, the Chaldean, the most mighty monarch of all the world, than who I doubt whether any more great and mighty did reign in the world, publisheth a decree, that he should be torn in pieces, and his house made a jakes, whosoever spake reproachfully against the true God which made both heaven and earth. The place is extant in the third chapter of Daniel's prophecy. Darius Medus, the son of Assuerus, king Cyrus his uncle, saith : " I have decreed that all men in the whole dominion of my kingdom do fear the God of Daniel :" as is to be seen in the sixth of Daniel. Cyrus, king of Persia, looseth the Jews from bondage, and giveth them in charge to repair the temple, and restore their holy rites again[5]. Darius Persa, the son of Hystaspes, saith : " I have decreed for every man which changeth

[3] Josh. viii. 30, &c.]   [4] Asa, in the Latin original.]
[5] Ezra i.]

any thing of my determination touching the reparation of the
temple, and the restoring of the worship of God, that a beam
be taken out of his house, and set up, and he hanged thereon,
and his house to be made a jakes[1]." The very same Darius[2]
again, who was also called Artaxerxes, saith: "Whosoever
will not do the law of thy God (Esdras), and the law of the
king, let judgment straightway pass upon him, either to death,
or to utter rooting out, or to confiscation of his goods, or imprisonment[3]." All this we find in the book of Esdras.

An answer to an objection.

The men, which are persuaded that the care and ordering
of religion doth belong to bishops alone, do make an objection, and say, that these examples, which I have alleged, do
nothing appertain to us which are Christians, because they
are examples of the Jewish people. To whom mine answer
is: The men of this opinion ought to prove, that the Lord
Jesus and his apostles did translate the care of religion from
the magistrate unto bishops alone: which they shall never be
able to do. But we, on the other side, will briefly shew, that
those ancient princes of God's people, Josue, David, and the
rest, were Christians verily and indeed; and that therefore
the examples which are derived from them and applied to
christian princes, both are and ought to be of force and effect
among us at this day. I will in the end add also the prophecy of the prophet Esay, whereby it may appear, that even
now also kings have in the church at this day the same office
that those ancient kings had in that congregation which they
call the Jewish church. There is no doubt but that they ought
to be accounted true Christians, which, being anointed with
the Spirit of Christ, do believe in Christ, and are in the sacraments made partakers of Christ. For Christ (if ye interpret
the very word) is as much to say as "anointed." Christians
therefore, according to the etymology of their name, are

1 John ii.

anointed. That anointing, according to the apostle's interpretation[4], is the Spirit of God, or the gift of the Holy Ghost.
But St Peter testifieth, that the Spirit of Christ was in the

[1 Ezra vi. 11.]

[2 This is not Darius Hystaspis, but Artaxerxes Longimanus.—Prideaux. Connect. Vol. I. p. 249. ed. McCaul. 1845. But, by some
writers, Artaxerxes Longimanus is called also Darius.—See Works of
Bp. Pilkington, Parker Soc. ed. p. 14.]

[3 Ezra vii. 26.]   [4 1 John ii. 20, 27.]

kings and prophets[5]. And Paul affirmeth flatly, that we have the very same Spirit of faith[6] that they of old had; and doth moreover communicate our sacraments with them, where he saith, that they were baptized under the cloud, and that they all drank of the spiritual rock that followed them, which rock was Christ[7].

Since then the case is so, the examples, truly, which are derived from the words and works of those ancient kings, for the confirmation of faith and charity, both are and ought to be of force with us. And yet I know that every thing doth not consequently follow upon the gathering of examples. But here we have, for the making good of our argument, an evident prophecy of Esay, who foretelleth that kings and princes, after the times of Christ and the revealing of the gospel, should have a diligent care of the church, and should by that means become the feeders and nurses of the faithful. Now it is evident what it is to feed and to nourish; for it is all one as if he should have said, that they should be the fathers and mothers of the church. But he could not have said that rightly, if the care of religion did not belong to princes, but to bishops alone. The words of Esay are these: "Behold, I will stretch out my hand unto the Gentiles, and Isai. xlix. set up my token to the people; and they shall bring thee thy sons in their laps[8], and thy daughters on their shoulders. And kings shall be thy nursing fathers, and queens thy nursing mothers; they shall fall before thee with their faces flat upon the earth, and lick up the dust of thy feet," &c. Shall not we say, that all this is fully performed in some christian princes? Among whom the first was the holy emperor Constantine, who, by calling a general council, did determine to establish true and sincere doctrine in the church of Christ, with a settled purpose utterly to root out all false and heretical phantasies and opinions. And when the bishops did not go rightly to work by the true rule and touchstone of the gospel and of charity, he blamed them, upbraiding them with tyrannical cruelty, and declaring therewithal what peace the Lord had granted by his means to the churches: adding moreover, that it were a detestable thing, if the bishops, forgetting to thank God for his gifts of peace, should go on among them-

Constantine the great.

[5 1 Pet. i. 11.]
[7 1 Cor. x. 2—4.]
[6 2 Cor. iv. 13.]
[8 in gremio, Lat.]

selves to bait one another with mutual reproaches and taunting libels, thereby giving occasion of delight and laughter to wicked idolaters; when as of duty they ought rather to handle and treat of matters of religion. For (saith he) the books of the evangelists, apostles, and oracles of the ancient prophets, are they which must instruct us in the understanding of God's holy law. Let us expel, therefore, this quarrelling strife, and think upon the questions proposed, to resolve them by the words of scripture inspired from above[1]. After him again,

Gratian, Va-
lentinian, and
Theodosius. the holy emperors, Gratian, Valentinian, and Theodosius, make a decree, and give out the edict in these very words: " We will and command all people, that are subject to our gracious empire, to be of that religion, which the very religion, taught and conveyed from Peter till now, doth declare that the holy apostle Peter did teach to the Romans[2]." And so forward.

By this, dearly beloved, ye perceive how kings and princes, among the people of the new Testament, have been the foster-fathers and nourishers of the church; being persuaded that the care of religion did first of all and especially belong to themselves.

Osias the
leper. The second objection that they make is the leprosy of Osias king of Juda, which he gat by challenging to himself the office of the priest, while he presumed to burn incense on the incense-altar[3]. They object the Lord's commandment, who bad Josue stand before Eleazar the priest, and gave the king

[1 Βασιλεὺς ὁ πανεύφημος τοὺς περὶ τῆς ὁμονοίας τε καὶ συμφωνίας προσενήνοχε λόγους, τῆς τε τῶν τυράννων ἐκείνων ἀναμιμνήσκων ὠμότητος, καὶ τῆς ἐπ᾽ αὐτοῦ θεόθεν παρασχεθείσης ἐντιμοτάτης εἰρήνης· καὶ ὡς δεινὸν εἴη καὶ ἄγαν δεινὸν, τῶν πολεμίων καταλυθέντων καὶ μηδενὸς ἀντιτείνειν τολμῶντος, ἀλλήλους βάλλειν, καὶ τοῖς δυσμενέσιν ἡδονὴν καὶ γέλωτα προξενεῖν, ἄλλως τε καὶ περὶ θείων διαλεγομένους πραγμάτων, καὶ τοῦ παναγίου πνεύματος τὴν διδασκαλίαν ἀνάγραπτον ἔχοντας· εὐαγγελικαὶ γάρ, φησι, βίβλοι καὶ ἀποστολικαὶ, καὶ τῶν παλαιῶν προφήτων τὰ θεσπίσματα, σαφῶς ἡμᾶς ἃ χρὴ περὶ τοῦ θείου φρονεῖν ἐκπαιδεύουσι. Τὴν πολεμοποιὸν οὖν ἀπελάσαντες ἔριν, ἐκ τῶν θεοπνεύστων λόγων λάβωμεν τῶν ζητουμένων τὴν λύσιν.—Theodorit. Eccles. Hist. Lib. I. cap. vii. Ed. Reading. Cantab. 1720. pp. 26, 27.]

[2 Cunctos populos, quos clementiæ nostræ regit imperium, in tali volumus religione versari, quam divinum Petrum apostolum tradidisse Romanis religio usque ad hunc ab ipso insinuata declarat, &c.— Grat. Valent. et Theod. Edict. in Corp. Jur. Civil. a Gothof. Amst. 1663. Cod. Lib. I. Tit. i. 1. Tom. II. p. 1.   See also, page 34 above.]

[3 2 Chron. xxvi. 18, 19.]

in charge to receive the book of the law at the Levites' hands[4]. But our disputation tendeth not to the confounding of the offices and duties of the magistrate and ministers of the church, as that we would have the king to preach, to baptize, and to minister the Lord's supper ; or the priest, on the other side, to sit in the judgment-seat, and give judgment against a murderer, or by pronouncing sentence to take up matters in strife.   The church of Christ hath, and retaineth, several and distinguished offices[5] ; and God is the God of order, and not of confusion.   Hereunto tendeth our discourse, by demonstration to prove to all men, that the magistrate of duty ought to have a care of religion, either in ruin to restore it, or in soundness to preserve it ; and still to see that it proceed according to the rule of the word of God.   For to that end was the law of God given into the king's hands by the priests, that he should not be ignorant of God's will touching matters ecclesiastical and political, by which law he had to govern the whole estate of all his realm.   Josue, the captain of God's people, is set before Eleazar indeed ; but yet he hath authority to command the priests, and, being a politic governor, is joined as it were in one body with the ecclesiastical ministers. The politic magistrate is commanded to give ear to the ecclesiastical ruler, and the ecclesiastical minister must obey the politic governor in all things which the law commandeth. So then the magistrate is not made subject by God to the priests as to lords, but as to the ministers of the Lord : the subjection and duty which they owe is to the Lord himself and to his law, to which the priests themselves also ought to be obedient, as well as the princes.   If the lips of the priest err from the truth, and speak not the word of God, there is no cause why any of the common sort, much less the prince, should either hearken unto, or in one tittle reverence the priest.   "The lips of the priest," saith Malachi, " keep knowledge, and they seek the law at his mouth ; because he is the messenger of the Lord of hosts[6]."   To refuse to hear such priests is to repel God himself.   Such priests as these the godly princes of Israel did always aid and assist ; false priests they did disgrade ; those which neglected their offices they

The several offices of the magistrates and of the ministers must not be confounded.

[4 Numb. xxvii. 22 ; Deut. xvii. 18.]
[5 officia distincta, Lat.]
[6 Mal. ii. 7.]

rebuked sharply; and made decrees for the executing and right administering of every office.

Of Salomon we read, that he put Abiathar beside the priesthood of the Lord[1] (that he might fulfil the word of the Lord, which he spake to Heli in Silo), and made Zadok priest in Abiathar's stead.   In the second book of Chronicles it is said : " And Salomon set the sorts of priests to their offices, as David his father had ordered them, and the Levites in their watches, for to praise and minister before the priests day by day, as their course did require[2]."   In the same book again, Joiada[3] the priest doth indeed anoint Joas king ; but, nevertheless, the king doth call the priest, and give him a commandment to gather money to repair the temple.   Moreover, that religious and excellent prince, Ezechias, called the priests and Levites, and said unto them : " Be ye sanctified, and sanctify ye the house of the Lord our God, and suffer no uncleanness to remain in the sanctuary.   My sons, be not slack now, because the Lord hath chosen you to minister unto himself[4]."   [5]He did also appoint singers in the house of the Lord, and those that should play on musical instruments in the Lord's temple.   Furthermore, king Ezechias ordained sundry companies of priests and Levites, according to their sundry offices, every one according to his own ministery. What may be said of that too, that even he did divide to the priests their portions and stipends throughout the priest-hood ?   The same king gave charge to all the people to keep holy the feast of passover, writing to them all such letters as priests are wont to write, to put them in mind of religion and hearty repentance.   And after all this there is added : " And the king wrought that which was good, right, and just before the Lord his God[6]."   When princes therefore do order religion according to the word of God, they do the thing that pleaseth the Lord.   This and the like is spoken again by[7] the godly prince Josias.   Who therefore will hereafter say, that the care of religion belongeth unto bishops alone ?

[1 1 Kings ii. 27.]   [2 2 Chron. viii. 14.]
[3 2 Chron. xxiv.]   [4 2 Chron. xxix. 5, 11.]
[5 Idem rex mox jubet sacerdotes sacrificare Domino, Lat. ; omitted.   "The same king presently commandeth the priests to sacrifice to the Lord." P.]
[6 2 Chron. xxxi. 20.]   [7 by, i. e. concerning; de, Lat.]

The christian emperors, following the example of the an-   Princes have appointed orders for religion.
cient kings as of their fathers, did with great care provide for
the state of true religion in the church of Christ.   Arcadius
and Honorius did determine that, so often as matters of religion were called in question, the bishops should be summoned
to assemble a council[8].   And before them again, the emperors
Gratian, Valentinian, and Theodosius, established a law,
wherein they declared to the world what faith and religion
they would have all men to receive and retain, to wit, the
faith and doctrine of St Peter: in which edict, also, they
proclaimed all them to be heretics which thought or taught
the contrary; allowing them alone to be called catholics,
which did persevere in St Peter's faith[9].   By this we gather,
that the proper office of the priests is to determine of religion
by proofs out of the word of God, and that the prince's duty
is to aid the priests in advancement and defence of true religion.   But if it happen at any time that the priests be slack
in doing their duty, then is it the prince's office by compulsion to enforce the priests to live orderly according to their
profession, and to determine in religion according to the word
of God.   The emperor Justinian, in *Novellis Constitut.* 3,
writing to Epiphanius, archbishop of Constantinople[10], saith:
" We have, most reverend patriarch, assigned to your holiness
the disposition of all things that are honest, seemly, and
agreeable to the rule of holy scriptures, touching the appointing and ordering of sacred bishops and reverend clerks[11]."
And in the seventeenth constitution he saith: " We give
charge and commandment, that no bishop have licence to sell
or make away any immovables, whether it be in houses or

[8 Episcopos convenit agitare, Lat.—Impp. Arcad. et Honor. A. A.
Apollodoro Proc. Afric.—Quotiens de religione agitur, episcopos convenit judicare, &c.—Dat. 13 Kal. Septemb. Patavi. Theodoro. V. C.
Cons.—Cod. Theodos. de religione. Lib. XVI. Tit. 11. p. 527. Par.
1607.]

[9 See above, page 35.]

[10 regiæ urbis archiepiscopum, Lat.]

[11 Ἤδη μὲν κοινῷ τε καὶ ἡγεμονικῷ νόμῳ, πρός τε τὴν μακαριότητα τὴν
σὴν πρός τε τοὺς λοιποὺς ἁγιωτάτους πατριάρχας γεγραμμένῳ, τὰ περὶ τῆς
χειροτονίας τῶν εὐαγῶν ἐπισκόπων καὶ εὐλαβεστάτων κληρικῶν ... διετυ-
πώσαμεν ἅπερ ἡμῖν ἐδόκει καλῶς τε καὶ προσηκόντως ἔχειν, καὶ τῶν ἱερῶν
κανόνων ἀξίως.—Justin. Auth. Collat. I. Tit. 3. Novell. 3. p. 18. Præfat.
Gotting. 1797.]

lands, belonging to the churches[1]." Again, in the fifty-seventh
constitution, he forbiddeth to celebrate the holy mysteries in
private houses[2]. He addeth the penalty, and saith: "For
the houses, wherein it is done, shall be confiscate and sold for
money, which shall be brought into the emperor's exchequer[3]."
In the sixty-seventh constitution, he chargeth all bishops not
to be absent from their churches: but if they be absent, he
willeth that they should receive no commodity or stipend of
the provincial stewards, but that their revenue should be
employed on the church's necessities[4]. In the hundred and
twenty-third constitution, the lieutenants of every province
are commanded to assemble a council for the use and defence
of ecclesiastical laws, if the bishops be slack to look thereunto[5]. And immediately after he saith: "We do utterly
forbid all bishops, prelates, and clerks, of what degree soever,
to play at tables, to keep company with dice-players, to be
lookers on upon gamesters, or to run to gaze upon may-games
or pageants[6]." I do not allege all this as canonical scriptures,
but as proofs to declare, that princes in the primitive church
had power, official authority, and a usual custom, granted by
God, (as Esay did prophesy,) and derived from the examples

[1 Ἡμεῖς οὖν ... θεσπίζομεν ... μήτε ἄλλον μηδένα πανταχοῦ μήτε
πατριάρχην μήτε ἐπίσκοπον ... ἄδειαν ἔχειν ἐκποιεῖν πρᾶγμα ἀκίνητον ἐν
οἰκίαις ἢ ἐν ἀγροῖς.—Justin. Auth. Collat. II. Tit. 1. Novell. 7. cap. 1.]

[2 Justin. Auth. Collat. v. Tit. 12. Novell. 58. p. 269.—περὶ τοῦ ἐν
ἰδιωτικοῖς οἴκοις ἱερὰν μυσταγωγίαν μὴ γίνεσθαι.]

[3 ... πρὸς τῷ καὶ τὴν οἰκίαν αὐτὴν τὴν ἐν ᾗ τοιοῦτό τι πράττεται γίνεσθαι δημοσίαν, καὶ ὑπὸ τὸ ἱερώτατον ἔρχεσθαι ταμεῖον.—Ibid. p. 270.]

[4 Κἀκεῖνό γε μὴν θεσπίζομεν, ὥστε κατὰ τὸν ἤδη παρ' ἡμῶν φοιτήσαντα
νόμον τοὺς θεοφιλεστάτους ἐπισκόπους ταῖς ἑαυτῶν ἐκκλησίαις προσκαρτε-
ρεῖν ... εἴπερ ἀπολειφθείη ὁ θεοφιλέστατος ἐπίσκοπος τῆς ἐκκλησίας τῆς
αὐτοῦ πλείονα χρόνον, μηδεμίαν αὐτῷ στέλλεσθαι δαπάνην ἐκ τῆς χώρας,
ἀλλ' ἐκείνην μὲν περὶ πράξεις εὐσεβεῖς καὶ περὶ τὴν ἁγιωτάτην ἐκκλησίαν
δαπανᾶσθαι.—Justin. Auth. Collat. v. Tit. 22. Novell. 67. cap. 3. p.
294.]

[5 ... προνοούντων τοῦ τοιούτου οὐ μόνον τῶν κατὰ τόπον ὁσιωτάτων
ἐπισκόπων καὶ τῶν ὑπ' αὐτοὺς κληρικῶν, ἀλλὰ καὶ τῶν πολιτικῶν καὶ τῶν
στρατιωτικῶν ἀρχόντων, καὶ τῶν ὑπ' αὐτοὺς τάξεων, καὶ τῶν κατὰ τόπον
ἐκδίκων·—Justin. Auth. Collat. IX. Tit. 6. Novell. 123. cap. 44. p. 512.]

[6 ... ἀπαγορεύομεν δὲ τοῖς ὁσιωτάτοις ἐπισκόποις καὶ πρεσβυτέροις ...
καὶ παντὶ ἄλλῳ οἱουδήποτε εὐαγοῦς τάγματος ἢ σχήματος καθεστῶτι ταβλί-
ζειν, ἢ τῶν τὰ τοιαῦτα παιζόντων κοινωνοὺς ἢ θεωρητὰς γίνεσθαι, ἢ εἰς
οἱανδήποτε θέαν τοῦ θεωρῆσαι χάριν παραγίνεσθαι.—Ibid. cap. 10. p. 496.]

of ancient kings, to command bishops, and to determine of religion in the church of Christ.

As for them which object the church's privilege, let them know, that it is not permitted to any prince, nor any mortal man, to grant privileges contrary to the express commandments and very truth of God's word. St Paul affirmed that he had power given him to edify, but not to destroy[7]. I am the briefer, because I will not stand to prove that they are unworthy of indifferent[8] privileges, which are not such as[9] priests and Christ his ministers should be, but are soldiers rather and wicked knaves, full of all kind of mischief. Among other things in the canon law, *Distinct*. 40, we find this written: "See to yourselves, brethren, how ye sit upon the seat: for the seat maketh not the priest, but the priest the seat: the place sanctifieth not the man, but the man the place. Every priest is not a holy man, but every holy man is a priest. He that sitteth well upon the seat, receiveth the honour of the seat: but he that sitteth ill upon the seat, doth injury unto the seat. Therefore an evil priest getteth blame by his priesthood, and not any dignity[10]." And thus much thus far touching this matter.

Since now that I have declared unto you, dearly beloved, that the care of religion doth belong to the magistrate too, and not to the bishops alone, and that the magistrate may make laws also in cases of religion; it is requisite, that I inquire what kind of laws those are that the magistrates may make in matters of religion. There is no cause why the king or magistrate should suppose, that power is given to him to make new laws touching God, the worship of God, or his holy mysteries; or to appoint a new kind of true justice

[7 2 Cor. xiii. 10.]

[8 Æquis, Lat.]

[9 non sunt hoc quod audiunt, Lat.; are not that which they are called.]

[10 Videte ergo quomodo sedetis super cathedram: quia non cathedra facit sacerdotem, sed sacerdos cathedram; non locus sanctificat hominem, sed homo locum; non omnis sacerdos sanctus, sed omnis sanctus sacerdos. Qui bene sederit super cathedram, honorem accipit ab illa; qui male sederit, injuriam facit cathedræ: ideoque malus sacerdos de sacerdotio suo crimen acquirit, non dignitatem.—Corp. Jur. Can. Decret. I. Pars. Distinct. 40. xii. Joan. Chrysost. id est, Autor. Op. Imperf. in Matt. Hom. 43. ad c. 23. ed. Par. 1687. p. 54.]

and goodness. For as every magistrate is ordained of God, and is God's minister, so must he be ruled by God, and be obedient to God's holy word and commandment, having evermore an eye unto that, and depending still upon that alone. The scripture, which is the word of God, doth abundantly enough set down all that which is proper to true religion : yea, the Lord doth flatly forbid to add to or take anything from his holy word. The magistrate therefore maketh no new laws touching God, and the honour to be given to God; but doth religiously receive and keep, doth put in ure and publish, those ancient laws in that kingdom which God hath allotted him unto. For hereunto appertaineth the giving of the book of God's law unto the kings of Israel[1], that they might learn thereby the way to do the things which they of duty ought to see done. To Josue the Lord doth say : " See that thou dost observe and do according to all the law that Moses my servant commanded thee : thou shalt not turn from it either to the right hand or to the left. Neither shall the book of this law depart out of thy mouth, but occupy thy mind therein day and night, that thou mayest observe and do according to all that is written therein. For then thou shalt make thy way prosperous, and then thou shalt do wisely[2]." Devout and holy princes therefore did do their faithful and diligent endeavour to cause the word of God to be preached to the people, to retain and preserve among the people the laws, ceremonies, and statutes of God ; yea, they did their best to spread it to all men as far as they could, and, as time and place required, to apply it holily to the states and persons : on the other side, they were not slack to banish and drive away false doctrine, profane worshippings of God, and blasphemies of his name, but settled themselves utterly to overthrow and root it out for ever. In this sort (I say) godly magistrates did make and ordain devout laws for the maintenance of religion. In this sort they bore a godly and devout care for matters of religion.

Schools.   The cities which the Levites had to possess were of old their schools of Israel. Now Josue did appoint those cities for studies' sake, and the cause of godliness[3]. King Ezechias was no less careful for the sure payment and revenue of the

[1 See Deut. xvii. 18, 19 ; 2 Kings xi. 12.]
[2 Josh. i. 7, 8.]   [3 Josh. xxi.]

ministers' stipends than he was for the restoring and renewing of every office[4]. For honour and advancement maketh learning to flourish, when need and necessity is driven to seek out sundry shifts : beggary setteth religion to sale, much more the invented lies of men's own mouths. Josaphat sendeth senators and other officers with the priests and teachers through all his kingdom[5] : for his desire was by all means possible to have God's word preached with authority and certain majesty, and, being preached, to have it defended and put in ure to the bringing forth of good works. King Josias doth, together with idolatry and profane worshippings of God, destroy the false priests that were to be found, setting up in their steads the true teachers of God's word, and restoring again sincere religion[6] : even as also king Joas, having rebuked the Levites, did repair the decayed buildings of the holy temple[7]. I am not able to run through all the scriptures, and rehearse all the examples in them expressed : let the godly prince or magistrate learn by these few what and how he ought to determine touching laws for religion.

On the other side, Ahia, the Silonite, saith to Jeroboam : "Thus saith the Lord : Thou shalt reign according to all that thy soul desireth, and shalt be king over Israel. And if thou hearken unto all that I command thee, and wilt walk in my ways, and do that is right in my sight, that thou keep my statutes and my commandments, as David my servant did; then will I be with thee, and build thee a sure house[8]." But the wretch despised those large promises, and rejecting God's word, his temple at Jerusalem, and his lawful worship, refusing also the Levites, he made him priests of the dregs and rascal sort of people ; he built himself new temples, which he decked, nay, rather disgraced, with images and idols, ordaining and offering sacrifices not taught in God's word, by that means inventing a certain new kind of worshipping God and a new manner of religion. And although his desire was to seem to be willing to worship God, yet is he by God condemned for a wicked man. Hearken, I pray, the sentence of the Lord, which he denounceth against him : "Thou hast done evil," saith Ahia, as the Lord had taught him, "above all that were

Devisers of new-fangled worships are cursed of God.

[4 2 Chron. xxxi.]   [5 2 Chron. xvii. 7—9.]
[6 2 Kings xxiii.]   [7 2 Kings xii.]
[8 1 Kings xi. 38.]

before thee. For thou hast gone and made thee other gods
and molten images, to provoke me, and hast cast me behind
thy back. Therefore I will bring evil upon the house of
Jeroboam, and will root out from Jeroboam even him that
pisseth against the wall, and him that is in prison and forsaken
in Israel, and will take away the remnant of the house of
Jeroboam, as one carrieth away dung till all be gone." And
all these things were fulfilled according to the saying of the
Lord, as the scripture witnesseth in these words: " When
Baasa was king, he smote all the house of Jeroboam, and left
nothing that breathed of that that was Jeroboam's." But the
very same king, being nothing the better or wiser by another's
mishap and miserable example of his predecessor, sticketh not
to continue to teach the people, to publish and defend the
strange and foreign religion, contrary to the word of God,
which Jeroboam had begun. But what followed thereupon?
Forsooth, the Lord by the preaching of Hanani the prophet
doth say unto him: " Forasmuch as I exalted thee out of the
dust, and made thee prince over my people Israel, and thou
hast walked in the way of Jeroboam, and hast made my
people Israel to sin, to anger me with their sins; behold
I will root out the posterity of Baasa, and the posterity of his
house, and will make thy house like the house of Jeroboam."
Which was performed (as the scripture saith) by Simri, captain
of the host of Israel: for he destroyed king Hela, the son of
Baasa, when he was drunken, and all his posterity[1]. Amri
succeeded in the kingdom, who was the father of Achab, that
mischievous cut-throat, whom the Syrians slew in fighting
a battle[2]. After him reigned his sons Ochosias and Joram.
But when they left the religion taught in the word of God to
follow the new tradition of king Jeroboam, and had thereunto
added the worshipping of the shameful idol Baal, they were
utterly (at last) destroyed by the means of Jehu, a very just
although a rigorous prince[3]. The offspring of Amri reigned
about the space of forty years, not without the shedding of
much innocent blood; but it was at last destroyed, when the
measure of iniquity was fulfilled, and was utterly plucked up
at the roots by the just judgment of Almighty God[4].

[1 1 Kings xiv. 9, 10; xv. 29; xvi. 2, 3, 9—13.]
[2 1 Kings xxii. 34.]   [3 2 Kings ix. and x.]
[4 The reigns of Ahab, Ahaziah, and Jehoram take up 37 years.]

Let all princes and magistrates therefore learn by these wonderful and terrible examples to take heed to themselves how they devise any new religion, or alter the lawful and ancient manner of worshipping, which God himself hath ordained already. Our faithful Lord is our good God, who hath fully, simply, and absolutely set down in his word his true religion and lawful kind of worship, which he hath taught all men to keep alone and for evermore: let all men therefore cleave fast unto it, and let them die in defence thereof, that mean to live eternally. They are punished from above, whosoever do add to, or take away anything from, the religion and kind of worship first ordained and appointed of God. Mark this, ye great men and princes of authority. For the keeping or not keeping of true religion is the root from whence abundant fruit of felicity, or else utter unhappiness, doth spring and bud out. He therefore that hath ears to hear, let him hear. Let no man suffer himself to be seduced and carried away with any coloured intent, how goodly to the eye soever it be, which is indeed a mere vanity and detestable iniquity. To God obedience is much more acceptable than sacrifices are. Neither do the decrees of the Highest need any whit at all our fond additions[5].

Here followeth now the second part of the magistrates' ordinance, which consisteth in making good laws for the preservation of honesty, justice, and public peace; which is likewise accomplished in good and upright laws. But some there are who think it mere tyranny to lay laws on free men's backs, as it were a yoke upon necks not used to labour; supposing that every one ought rather to be left to his own will and discretion. The apostle indeed did say, "The law is not given for the just, but for the unjust[6]:" but the cause, why the law is not given to the just, is because he is just; for the just worketh justice, and doth of his own accord the thing which the law exacteth of every mortal man. Wherefore the law is not troublesome to the just man, because it is agreeable to the mind and thoughts of upright livers, who do embrace it with all their hearts. But the unjust desireth nothing more than to live as he lusteth: he is not conformable in any point to the law, and therefore must he by the law be kept under,

Laws are necessary for kingdoms, good and requisite for commonwealths.

[5 emblematis, 1 at.]
[6 1 Tim. i. 9.]

and bridled from marring himself and hurting other. So then,
since to good men the laws are no troublesome burden but an
acceptable pleasure, which are also necessary for the unjust,
as ordained for the bridling of lawless and unruly people; it
followeth consequently, that they are good and profitable for all
men, and not to be rejected of any man. What may be said
of that, moreover, that God himself, who did foresee the disposition of us men, what we would be, and hath still favoured
the true liberty which he desired always to have preserved
among his people, as one that ever meant them good, and
never did ordain the thing that should turn to their hinderance
or discommodity; that God himself (I say) was their lawgiver,
and hath not suffered any age at any time to live as people
without a law? Yea too, those commonweals have been happy
always, that have admitted laws, and submitted themselves to
be governed by laws; when as, contrarily, those kingdoms
have of all other been most miserable, and torn in pieces
by civil dissensions and foreign enemies, which, having banished
upright laws, did strive to maintain their own kind of freedom,
their uncontrolled dealing and licentious liberty, that is, their
beastly lust and uncivil rudeness. Good laws therefore are for
the health and preservation of the people, and necessary for
the peace and safeguard of commonweals and kingdoms.

Wherefore it is a wonder to see the folly of some Christians,
since the very heathens have given so honest report of laws
and lawgivers. They took their lawgivers for gods, confessing thereby that good laws are the gift of God[1]. But the gift
of God cannot be superfluous and unprofitable. Plutarch
called laws the life of cities[2]. Demosthenes did expressly confess that laws are the gifts of God[3]. Cicero named laws the
bonds of the city (because without laws it is loosed and
dispersed), the foundation of liberty, and the well-spring of
justice and perfect honesty[4]. For laws undoubtedly are the

[1 ΑΘ. Θεὸς ἤ τις ἀνθρώπων ὑμῖν, ὦ ξένοι, εἴληφε τὴν αἰτίαν τῆς τῶ
νόμων διαθέσεως;   ΚΛ. Θεὸς, ὦ ξένε, θεὸς, ὥς γε τὸ δικαιότατον εἰπεῖν.—
Plato de Legib. Lib. I. in init.]

[2 Εἴπερ οὖν οἱ νόμους καὶ πολιτείας ἀναιροῦντες τὸν βίον ἀναιροῦσι τὸ
ἀνθρώπινον, &c.—Plutarch. adv. Colot. in fin.]

[3 Πᾶς ἐστὶ νόμος εὕρημα μὲν καὶ δῶρον θεῶν.—Demosth. Orat. adv
Aristog.]

[4 Hoc enim vinculum est hujus dignitatis, qua fruimur in repub-

strongest sinews of the commonweal, and life of the magistrates : so that neither the magistrates can without the laws conveniently live and rule the weal public, nor the laws without the magistrates shew forth their strength and lively force. The magistrate therefore is the living law, and the law is the dumb magistrate[5]. By executing and applying the law, the law is made to live and speak : which those princes do not consider that are wont to say, *Wir sind das recht,* "We are the right, we are the law." For they suppose that they at their pleasure may command what they list, and that all men by and by must take it for law. But that kind of ruling, without all doubt, is extreme tyranny. The saying of the poet is very well known, which representeth the very words of a tyrant :

I say, and it shall be so ;
My lust shall be the law[6].

The magistrate is a law endued with life.

The prince, indeed, is the living law, if his mind obey the written laws, and square not from the law of nature. Power and authority, therefore, is subject unto laws ; for unless the prince in his heart agree with the law, in his breast do write the law, and in his words and deeds express the law, he is not worthy to be called a good man, much less a prince. Again, a good prince and magistrate hath power over the law, and is master of the laws, not that they may turn, put out, undo, make and unmake, them as they list at their pleasure ; but because he may put them in practice among the people, apply them to the necessity of the state, and attemper their interpretation to the meaning of the maker.

They therefore are deceived as far as heaven is wide, which think for a few privileges, of emperors and kings granted to the magistrate to add, diminish, or change some point of the law, that therefore they may utterly abolish good laws, and live against all law and seemliness. For, as no

To put to and take from laws.

ca ; hoc fundamentum libertatis ; hic fons æquitatis : mens, et animus, et consilium, et sententia civitatis posita est in legibus.—Cic. rat. pro A. Cluent.]

[5 Referring to that saying of Cicero's, (de Legg. Lib. III. cap. 1.) Magistratum legem esse loquentem, legem autem mutum magistratum.]

[6 Hoc volo, sic jubeo ; sit pro ratione voluntas.—Juv. Sat. VI. 23.—P.]

emperors or kings are permitted to grant any privileges contrary to justice, goodness, and honesty; so, if they do grant any such privilege, it ought not to be received or taken of good subjects for a good turn or benefit, but to be counted rather (as it is indeed) their utter destruction and clean overthrow. Among all men, at all times and of all ages, the meaning and substance of the laws touching honesty, justice, and public peace, is kept inviolable: if change be made, it is in circumstances, and the law is interpreted as the case requireth, according to justice and a good end. The law saith, "Let no man kill another: let him that killeth another be killed himself." That law remaineth for ever unchangeable, neither is it lawful for any man at any time to put it out or wipe it away. And yet the rigour of the law may be diminished, and the law itself favourably interpreted: as, for example, if a man kill one whom he loveth entirely well and kill him by chance, and not of set purpose or pretended malice, so that, when he hath done, he is sorry for it at the very heart, and would (if it were possible) buy his life again with whatsoever he hath to give for it; in such a case the killer ought not to be killed, and therein the magistrate may dispense with the rigour of the law. Another beareth a deadly and continual grudge[1] to one, whom he killeth, and goeth about to colour the matter under the pretence of hap and misfortune: for he sought occasion, that he might for himself have a show of chance-medley[2]. In such a case as this the magistrate cannot change any jot of the law, but must needs kill him whom the meaning of the law commandeth to kill. I could allege more examples like unto these; but my care is, of purpose, so much as I may, not to be too tedious unto you with too long discourse. By this that I have spoken it is apparently evident that laws are good and not to be broken, and how far forth they do admit the prince's ἐπιείκειαν[3], that is, the prince's moderation, interpretation, limitation, or dispensation, lest per

[1 Vatiniano odio, Lat. Vatinius, in quem acerrime M. Tullius invectus est, in tantum odium populi Romani pervenerat, jam detectis illius flagitiis, ut in proverbium cesserit, Odium Vatinianum.—Erasm. Adag. Chiliad. Hanov. 1617. p. 551. *Odium.*]

[2 casus fortuiti, Lat.]

[3 cf. Aristot. Ethic. Lib. v. cap. 10.]

adventure that old and accustomed proverb be rightly applied unto them, " Law with extremity is extreme injury [4]."

Hitherto I have declared that laws are good, profitable, necessary, and not to be broken: it remaineth now to tell what and what kind of laws the magistrate ought most chiefly to use for the ordering and maintaining of honesty, justice, and public peace, according to his office. Some there are whose opinion is, that the magistrate ought not to use any written laws, but that he should rather give sentence as he thought best according to natural equity, as the circumstances of place, time, persons, and cases do seem to require. Other some there are that do their endeavour to thrust into all kingdoms and commonweals the judicial laws of Moses. And some there are which, having once rejected the law of Moses, will have no judgment given in law, but what is derived out of the laws of heathen princes. But since they that have the pre-eminence and magistrate's authority are men either good or bad; and since that, even in the best men, covetousness, anger, hatred, favour, grief, fear, and other affections, are rife to be found; to whom, I pray you, have they committed the commonweal, which, rejecting all written statutes and certain laws, would have every man that is a magistrate to give judgment as he himself thinketh best? Have they not committed their commonweal to the rule of a beast? But what shall I say then of evil men that are in authority, since in the best men things are so amiss? As good were a kingdom subject to the furies of hell, as bound to the judgments of naughty men. But we will (say they) have them give judgment according to the equity of nature's law, and not after the lust of their corrupt affection. Mine answer is to that; that they will give judgment as affection leadeth them without controlment, and say that they judged by natural equity. They cannot, they will say, judge otherwise, nor otherwise understand the pith of the matter. They think that best which they have determined, and nothing is done contrary to conscience; and thou for thy labour shalt be called *Coram nobis* [5]

What manner of laws the magistrate ought to use.

Written laws are needful.

[4 Summum jus summa injuria, Lat. — Erasm. Adag. Chiliad. p. 619. *Rigor*.]

[5 te in jus vocabunt, Lat.   The colloquial phrase of the translator occurs in Latimer's Works, Parker Soc. ed. Vol. II. p. 348, and commonly in Foxe: see Acts and Monuments, Vol. v. pp. 291, 537. ed. 1838.]

for daring find fault with their sentence in judgment. And so shall the just man perish, barbarous affections shall have the upper hand, and naughty men rule all the roost. Yea, and admit we grant all men are good that are called to be magistrates; yet diversity of opinions, that will rise in giving of judgment, will stir up among them endless brawls and continual troubles. If all things therefore be well considered, the best way by a great deal is to put written laws in ure.

Let us learn this by the example of our eternal, wise, excellent, and mighty God, who gave to the Jews, his peculiar people, such laws as at his commandment were set down in writing. The magistrate hath otherwise business enough to judge, that is, to apply and confer the causes with the laws; to see how far and wherein they agree or disagree; and to judge who hath offended against the law, and who have not transgressed the law.

The law of Moses is not to be enforced upon kingdoms and countries.

Now it is to be marked, that in Moses' judicial law there are many things proper and peculiar to the Jewish nation, and so ordained, according to the state of the place, time, and persons, that, if we should go about to thrust on and apply them all to other nations, we should seem to shew ourselves more than half mad. And to what end should we bring back and set up again among the people of God[1] the offscourings of the heathen that were cast out a great while ago? The apostles of our Lord Jesus Christ did bind or burden no man with the laws of Moses; they never condemned good laws of the heathens, nor commended to any man naughty laws of the Gentiles; but left the laws, with the use and free choice of them, for the saints to use as they thought good. But therewithal they ceased not most diligently to beat into all men's heads the fear of God, faith, charity, justice, and temperance; because they knew that they, in whose hearts those virtues were settled, can either easily make good laws themselves, or pick and choose out the best of those which other men make. For it maketh no matter whether the magistrate pick out of Moses' Jewish laws, or out of the allowable laws of the heathen, sufficient laws for him and his countrymen, or else do keep still the old and accustomed laws which have before been used in his country, so that he have an eye to cut off such wicked, unjust, and lawless laws, as are found to be thrust in among the better sort. For I suppose that

[1 in forum populi Dei, Lat.]

upright magistrates ought to take off curiosity and new invented novelties. "Seldom," saith the proverb, "is the crow's eye picked out without troublesome stirs[1]:" and curious men's new laws are for the most part worse than the old, that are broken by them and utterly abolished.

A proverb used when one will make them blind that were before him, and disannul that which wise men have allowed.

Furthermore, all laws are given for ordering of religion or outward worship of God, or else for the outward conversation of life and civil behaviour. Touching the laws of religion, I have spoken of them before. For civil and politic laws, I add thus much, and say, that those seem to be the best laws, which, according to the circumstance of every place, person, state, and time, do come nearest unto the precepts of the ten commandments and the rule of charity, not having in them any spot of iniquity, licentious liberty, or shameless dishonesty. Let them, moreover, be brief and short, not stretched out beyond measure, and wrapped in with many expositions: let them have a full respect to the matter whereto they are directed, and not be frivolous and of no effect.

Civil laws; what manner of laws they be.

Now mark, that politic laws do for the most part consist in three especial and principal points—honesty, justice, and peace. Let laws therefore tend to this end, that discipline and honesty may be planted and maintained in the commonweal, and that no unseemly, licentious, and filthy act be therein committed. Let law forbid all uncleanness, wantonness, lightness, sensuality, and riotousness, in apparel, in building, in bibbing and banquetting. Let wedlock be commanded by law to be kept holy. Let stews and brothel-houses be banished the realm. Let adulteries, whoredoms, rapes, and incests, be put to exile. Let moderate feastings be allowed and admitted. Let thriftiness be used, which is the greatest revenue that a man can enjoy[2]. Briefly, whatsoever is contrary to honesty and seemliness, let it by law be driven out and rejected.

Laws of honesty.

Let justice by laws be strongly fortified. Let it by laws be provided, that neither citizen nor foreigner be hurt or hindered in fame, in goods, in body, or life[3]. Let upright laws be made

Laws of justice and equity.

[1] Undecunque fluxerit, perinde valere videtur, *Cornicum oculos configere,* quasi dicas, novo quodam invento veterum eruditionem obscurare.—Erasm. Adag. Chiliad. p. 504. *Mira nova.*]

[2] See above, page 297, note 8.]

[3] Lædens alium violenter vel insidiose puniatur secundum leges, Lat.; omitted by the translator. Whoever injures another by violence or treacherously, let him be punished according to law.]

for the obtaining of legacies and inheritances, for the performing of contracts and bargains, for covenants and agreements, for suretiships, for buying and selling, for weights and measures, for leases and things let to hire, for lending and borrowing, for pawns in mortgage, for use, commodity, and usury of money. Let order be taken for maintenance of peace between the father and his children, betwixt man and wife, betwixt the master and the servant; and, to be short, that every man may have his own. For my meaning is not here to reckon up particularly every several point and tittle of the law.

Laws of peace and unanimity. Lastly, means must be made by giving of laws, that peace may be established, whereby every man may enjoy his own. All violent robberies and injuries must be expelled; privy grudges and close conspiracies must not be thought of. And war must be quieted by wisdom, or else undertaken and finished with manly fortitude.

But, that we may have such a magistrate and such a life, the apostle commanded us earnestly to pray, where he saith: "I exhort you that, first of all, prayers, supplications, intercessions, and giving of thanks, be made for all men; for kings and for all that are in authority, that we may live a quiet and peaceable life in all godliness and honesty[1]."

I am now again compelled to end my Sermon before the matter be finished. That which remaineth I will add tomorrow. Make ye your earnest prayers, with your minds lift up into heaven, &c.

[1] 1 Tim. ii. 1, 2.]

OF JUDGMENT, AND THE OFFICE OF THE JUDGE; THAT
CHRISTIANS ARE NOT FORBIDDEN TO JUDGE: OF
REVENGEMENT AND PUNISHMENT: WHETHER
IT BE LAWFUL FOR A MAGISTRATE TO KILL
THE GUILTY: WHEREFORE, WHEN, HOW,
AND WHAT THE MAGISTRATE MUST
PUNISH: WHETHER HE MAY
PUNISH OFFENDERS IN
RELIGION OR NO.

THE EIGHTH SERMON.

I SPAKE yesterday, dearly beloved, of the magistrate's
ordinance: there are yet behind other two parts of his office
and duty, that is, judgment and punishment; of both which,
by the help of God, I mean to speak as briefly as may be.
Give ye attentive ear, and pray ye to the Lord to give me
grace to speak the truth.

Judgment is taken in divers significations; but in this pre- *What judg-
sent treatise it importeth the sentence of judges brought in*
ment is.
betwixt men at variance; which sentence is derived out of the
laws, according to right and equity, as the case put forth of
the parties required, and is pronounced to the intent to take
up[2] the strife betwixt them at variance, and to give to every
man his own.   For at sessions or assizes parties appear and
sue one another for some inheritance or possession, which
either party affirmeth to be his by law, laying for themselves
whatsoever they can to prove and shew what right and title
they have to the thing.   All which the judges do diligently
hear and perfectly note; then they confer the one with the
other, and lay them with the law; lastly, they pronounce
sentence, whereby they give the possession to the one party,
and take it from the other.   The like reason is also in other
cases and matters.   And this is judgment; yea, this, I say, is
the execution of justice.   But this kind of quieting and setting
parties at one is very mild in comparison of revengement and
punishment, which is not executed with words and sentences,
but with swords and bitter stripes.   And good cause why it

[2 ut dirimat, Lat.]

should be so, since there be divers causes, whereof some cannot be ended but with the sword, and some more gently with judgment in words. But herein consisteth the health and safeguard of the kingdom or commonweal.

Judgment and punishment pertain to the magistrate, as depending upon his office. Judgment and punishment therefore are in the magistrate the most excellent offices, although peradventure they seem to be somewhat hard and cruel. But unless this which seemeth to be cruelty be put in ure, all ages, states, and sexes shall feel the smart of crueller things, and that which is most cruel indeed. For it is not cruelty, but rather just severity, which (as the Lord commandeth) is put in ure for the safeguard of the guiltless and preservation of peace within the realm and commonweal. Put case there were a commonweal well furnished with most absolute laws for politic manners and matters of religion : suppose also, that in the same commonweal there were no magistrate to execute, and as it were to father[1] those laws, by his authority to bring and reduce all the deeds and sayings of men to the trial of those laws ; and that therefore every man breaketh forth to what kind of life he list himself, and doth what he will: tell me, I pray you, what good do those written laws to the men of that country ? Believe me, forsooth, not one halfpenny worth of good[2]. The best part therefore of the magistrate's duty consisteth in upright judgment and punishing revengement. And those two points require a man of courage and princely stomach ; whom the Lord in his law describeth lively, and telleth what kind of man he would have him to be, and what the office is whereto he is called : which description I will rehearse and expound, because therein the judge's person is chiefly touched.

The judge's office is described. Moses, at the Lord's commandment, saith to the judges "Hear the cause of your brethren, and judge righteously betwixt every man and his brother, and the stranger that is with him. Ye shall have no respect of any person in judgment, but ye shall hear the small as well as the great: ye shall not fear the face of any man, for the judgment is the Lord's[3]." The holy prophet in these words toucheth two things chiefly; he declareth what the judge's office is; and what vices or diseases do infect the judge, that he cannot fulfil his office as he ought to do.

[1 qui tueatur, Lat.]   [2 nihil prorsus, Lat.]
[3 Deut. i. 16, 17.]

Now touching the office of a good judge, the first point thereof is, that he repel no man, but hear every one, the small, the great[4], the citizen, the stranger, the known and unknown. And he must hear the parties willingly, diligently, and attentively. Herein there is admitted no sluggishness of the judge, nor a mind busied about other matters. Judgment before the matter be decided is utterly excluded, because it carrieth away the mind of the judge before the matter is known. The thing itself crieth out, that the matter must first be heard and well understood, before the magistrate proceed to judgment. And the common proverb saith, "Let the other party be heard too[5]." Very wisely said that judge, which told one that made a complaint, "That with the one ear he heard him, and kept the other ear for him upon whom the complaint was made[6]." Herein we contain the perfect knowledge of the judge, and say, that he must not make too much haste in cases unknown, since he must judge them by the thing itself, and not by the parties, secret tales, and privy accusations. Secondarily, let him judge, saith he, yea, let him judge uprightly. To judge is to determine and pronounce truly and justly, according to the laws, what is good, what is evil, what is right, and what is wrong. We Switzers say, *Urteilen, oder erteilen, oder richten;* as if one should say, to distinguish a thing throughly considered, and to plane and make straight a crooked thing. Parties blinded with affections make straight things crooked, which the judge by applying the rule of equity and law doth straighten again; so that to judge is to straighten and to make plain. Moreover, to judge is, by defending and punishing, to keep in liberty. The magistrate doth judge, therefore, when he defendeth the innocent, and bridleth the hurtful person. But he must judge justly, that is, according to justice, and agreeably to the laws, which give to every man that that is his. The judge doth judge unjustly, when of a corrupt mind he pronounceth sentence contrary to all law and equity.

The office of a good judge is to hear and know,

The judge must judge justly.

[4 inquilinum, Lat.; omitted.]

[5 Audiatur et altera pars, Lat.]

[6 Λέγεται δὲ καὶ τὰς δίκας διακρίνων ἐν ἀρχῇ τὰς θανατικὰς, τὴν χεῖρα τῶν ὤτων τῷ ἑτέρῳ προστιθέναι τοῦ κατηγόρου λέγοντος, ὅπως τῷ κινδυνεύοντι καθαρὸν φυλάττηται καὶ ἀδιάβλητον.—Plutarch. in Vit. Alexandri. Lond. 1723. Tom. IV. p. 60. See also Early Writings of Bp. Hooper, Parker Soc. ed. page 408.]

Now therefore we have to consider the vices which

usually are wont to reign in judges. The vices that are
in judges be many, and the diseases of their minds are
sundry: but two special diseases there are, and chief of
all the rest. The one of these two vices, which so infecteth the minds of judges that they cannot execute their

office as they should, is the accepting of faces, or respect of
persons; that is, when the judge in giving judgment hath not
his eye set upon the things themselves, or upon the causes or
the circumstances of the causes as they are indeed; but hath a
regard either of dignity, excellency, humility, poverty, kindred, men of honours, letters[1], or some such like stuff. The
Lord excludeth this evil, and saith: " Ye shall judge justly; ye
shall have no respect of any person in judgment; ye shall hear

the small as well as the great." The other disease of these
twain is fear; a very vehement affection of the mind, which
disturbeth the very best and most excellent counsels, and
choaketh up virtue before it come to light. Under fear we do
contain hope also, I mean, of commodity; and so by that
means by fear we understand the corruption of bribes. The
judge that stands in fear to lose his life or goods, or is afraid
to displease a nobleman, or is loath to lose the common people's good will; he also that taketh bribes, or is in hope to be
rewarded at one of the parties' hands, doth pervert equity and
advance iniquity. The Lord saith therefore, Ye shall not fear
any mortal man: ye shall not look for any reward at any
man's hand. He addeth the reason why: Because the matter
is not yours, neither were ye called in to do your own business;
but the judgment is the Lord's. The will and law of God
therefore must be respected. For God is able to defend just
judges from the unjust hatred of any, whatsoever they be, and
against all wrong and open violence. Moreover, where it is
said that the judgment is the Lord's, thereby are the judges
warned that they ought to imitate the example of the most
high God. But what, and of what sort, that example of God

is, the same Moses, in the first of Deuteronomy[2], expresseth and
saith: " God doth accept neither person nor gift; he doth
justice for the fatherless and widow, and loveth the stranger to

[1 vel clientelam is the Latin, which is here translated, men of
honours, letters.]

[2 It is Deut. x. 17—19.]

give him meat and clothing; and therefore shall ye love the stranger." And so must godly judges do in the judgment which is God's. Josaphat, without all doubt a very godly prince, speaking to them whom he had made judges, did say: "Take heed what ye do; for ye execute not the judgments of man, but of God, which is with you in judgment, Let therefore the fear of the Lord be upon you, and take heed, and be diligent. For there is no unrighteousness with the Lord our God, that he should have any respect of persons, or take any reward." 2 Chron. xix.

To these I will yet add a few places of the holy scripture more, which shall partly make manifest those that went before, and partly expound and more plainly express the office of the judge. In Deuteronomy we read: "The judges shall judge the people with equity and justice. Thou shalt not pervert judgment, nor have respect of persons, nor take a reward: for a reward doth blind the eyes of the wise, and perverteth the words of the righteous. Thou shalt do judgment with justice, that thou mayest live and possess the land[3]." Again, in Exodus we find: "Thou shalt not follow a multitude to do evil, neither shalt thou speak in a matter of justice according to the greater number for to pervert judgment. Neither shalt thou esteem a poor man in his cause. Keep thee far from false matters, and the innocent and righteous see thou slay not; for I will not justify the wicked. Thou shalt take no rewards, for rewards blind the seeing, and pervert the words of the righteous." In Leviticus also we have this: "Ye shall do no unrighteousness in judgment; thou shalt not favour the person of the poor, nor honour the mighty, but in righteousness shalt thou judge thy neighbour." Again: "Ye shall do no unrighteousness in judgment, in meteyard, in weight, or in measure. True balances, true weights, a true epha, and a true hin, shall ye have. I am the Lord your God," &c. I suppose verily, and am thus persuaded, that in these few words of the Lord our God are comprehended all that which profound philosophers and lawyers of great learning do scarcely absolve in infinite books and volumes of many leaves. Beside all this, the most holy prophet Jeremy crieth to the king, and saith: "Keep equity and righteousness, deliver the oppressed from the power of the violent; do not grieve nor oppress the Exod. xxiii.

Levit. xix.

Jer. xxii.

[3 Deut. xvi. 18—20.]

stranger, the fatherless, or the widow, and shed no innocent blood." Thus much touching the office of judges.

But in the eyes of some men this our discourse may seem vain and fruitless; unless we do also refute their objections, whereby they endeavour to prove, that pleadings and law-matters are at an end, because the Lord in the gospel saith: "To him that will sue thee at the law and take away thy coat, let him have thy cloke also." And again: "While thou art yet with thine adversary upon the way, agree with him quickly, lest he deliver thee to the tormenter[1]." They add, moreover, the strifes in the law, which St. Paul the apostle, in the sixth chapter of his Epistle to the Corinthians, doth flatly condemn. To all which objections mine answer is this: As the doctrine of the evangelists and apostles doth not abrogate the private ordering of particular houses, so doth it not condemn or disannul the public government of common-weals. The Lord, in the gospel after St Luke, chideth with and repelleth the young man who desired him to speak to his brother for an equal division of the inheritance betwixt them. He blamed him, not for because he thinketh ill of him that claimeth an equal division, or that part of the inheritance that is his by right; but because he thought that it was not his duty, but the judges' office, to deal in such cases. The words of our Saviour in that place are these: " Who hath appointed me a judge between you, and a divider of land and inheritance[2]?" And again, as we read in the gospel, "If any man will sue thee at the law, and take away thy coat, give him thy cloke also;" so, on the other side, against this doing of injury there is nothing more busily handled and required in all the evangelical doctrine than charity and well-doing: but a good deed is done in nothing more than in judgment and justice. Since, therefore, that judgment was invented for the practising and preserving of justice and up-right dealing, it is manifest, that to judge in matters of controversy is not forbidden in the gospel. The notable prophets of the Lord, Esay and Zachary, cry out, and say;

" Cease to do evil, learn to do good; seek after judgment, help the oppressed, and plead the cause of the fatherless and widow." " Execute true judgment, shew mercy and loving-

[1 Matt. v. 40. 25.]
[2 Luke xii. 14.]

kindness every man to his brother. Do the widow, the father-less, the stranger, and poor, no wrong." They sin, therefore, that go on to hinder judgment, and to thrust judges beside their seats; for, as they pull away from the true God no small part of his worship, so do they open a wide gate to wrong, robbery, and oppression of the poor.

The Lord, I grant, commanded that which our adversaries have alleged; meaning thereby to settle quietness among his people: but because the malice of men is invincible, and the long-suffering of seely [3] souls makes wicked knaves more mis-chievous, therefore the Lord hath not forbidden nor condemned the moderate use of judgments in law. Moreover, we read in the Acts of the Apostles, that Paul did oftener than once use the benefit of judgment, not for money or goods, but for his life, which he endeavoured to save and defend from them that lay in wait to kill him. Neither consented he to the unjust judgment of Festus, the president, but appealed to Cæsar [4]: and yet we know, that Paul did not offend therein against the doctrine of the gospel of Christ. The same Paul, in his Epistle to the Corinthians, did not absolutely condemn the Corinthians for going to law about things belonging to their living; but because they sued and troubled one another before heathen judges. It is good and seemly, without doubt, to suffer wrong with a patient mind; but, because it pleaseth the Lord to ordain judgment to be a mean of help and succour to them that are oppressed with injury, he sinneth not at all that seeks to keep himself from wrong, not by private re-vengement, but by the upright sentence of judges in law. And therefore did the apostle command the Corinthians to choose out to themselves among the faithful such judges as might take up temporal matters in controversy betwixt them that fell at variance.

Thus have I declared unto you the second part of the magistrate's office, which consisteth in judgment. I will now therefore descend to the exposition of the third and last part, which comprehendeth revengement and punishment. For the magistrate, by his office, beareth the sword; and therefore is he commanded by God to take revengement for the wrong

Of revenge-ment taken by the ma-gistrate.

[3 Seely, meek: innocuorum, Lat.]
[4 Acts xxv. 11.]

The sword.

done to the good, and to punish the evil. For the sword is God's vengeance, or instrument, wherewith he strikes the stroke to revenge himself upon his enemies for the injury done unto him; and is in the scripture generally taken for vengeance and punishment. The Lord in Jeremy crieth out, and saith: "I call a sword upon all the dwellers upon earth[1]." Again, in Ezechiel: "The sword is sharp and ready trimmed to kill the sacrifice." And again: "I will give my sword into the hands of the king of Babel[2]." The kings of Egypt were of their people called Pharaos, as who should say, Revengers[3]. But the sword in the magistrate's hand is to be put unto two uses: for either he punisheth offenders therewith for doing other men injury, and for other ill deeds; or else he doth in war therewith repel the violence of foreign enemies abroad, or repress the rebellions of seditious and contentious citizens at home.

Whether it be lawful to kill and punish offenders.

But here again another objection is cast in our way by them which say that, according to the doctrine of the gospel, no man ought either to kill or to be killed, because the Lord hath said, "Resist not the evil[4];" and again to Peter: "Put up thy sword into thy sheath. Every one that taketh the sword doth perish by the sword[5]." My answer to this is: that throughout all the scripture private revengement is utterly forbidden; but that that is done openly by authority of the public magistrate is never found fault withal. But that was private and extraordinary vengeance that the apostle Peter was about to have taken, considering that he was called to be a preacher of the word of God, not to be a judge, a captain, or a man of war. And against private and extraordinary revengement is that sentence rightly pronounced: "Every one that taketh the sword shall perish by the sword."

But that public vengeance and the ordinary use of the sword is not prohibited by God in the church of Christ, I prove by this testimony of the holy apostle. Paul in the twelfth to the Romans hath taught what and how much the perfect-

[1 Jer. xxv. 29.]

[2 Ezek. xxi. 9; xxx. 24.]

[3 פָּרַע "apparently, *avenged.* Comp. Syr. ܦܪܰܥ, retribuit. Judg. v. 2."—Lee's Hebr. Lex. in voc.]

[4 Matt. v. 39.]

[5 Matt. xxvi. 52.]

ness of the gospel requireth of us, and among the rest thus he saith: "Dearly beloved, revenge not yourselves, but rather give place unto wrath: for it is written, Vengeance is mine, and I will repay." But because this might be argued against, and this objection cast in his way, Then, by this means, the long-suffering of Christians shall minister matter enough to murder and manslaughter; he doth therefore immediately after in the next chapter add: "The magistrate is the minister of God to thy wealth, to terrify the evil doers. For he beareth not the sword in vain: for he is God's minister, revenger of wrath to him that doeth evil." We gather therefore by this doctrine of the apostle, that every one of us must let God alone with taking of vengeance, and that no man is allowed to revenge himself by his own private authority. But public revengement, wrought by the ordinary magistrate, is nowhere forbidden. For that God which said to us, "Vengeance is mine, I will repay," doth grant to the magistrate authority to exercise and put that vengeance in ure, which he doth claim as due to himself: so that the magistrate's duty is to punish with the sword the wrongful dealings of wicked men, in the name and at the commandment of God himself. Therefore, when the magistrate punisheth, then doth God himself, to whom all vengeance belongeth, punish by the magistrate, who for that cause is called by the name of God. Moreover, it is written: "Thou shalt not suffer a witch to live[6]." Again: "A wise king will scatter the wicked, and turn the wheel upon them[7]." And again: "He that justifieth the wicked, and he that condemneth the just, they are both abominable in the sight of the Lord[8]."

Neither do we lack examples to prove, that some have incurred the heavy wrath and displeasure of the Lord for their foolish pity in sparing them whom the Lord commanded to strike with the sword. I speak of Saul and Achab[9]. Again, on the other side, there are innumerable examples of most excellent princes, which testify and bear witness of the praise that they deserved for punishing of lewd and wicked offenders. For the prince sinneth not, nor is blame-worthy any whit at all, which killeth or otherwise punisheth the guilty and ungracious man: and for that cause we find in the law so often repeated,

Foolish pity.

[6 Exod. xxii. 18.]   [7 Prov. xx. 26.]
[8 Prov. xvii. 15.]   [9 1 Sam. xv; 1 Kings xx.]

[BULLINGER.]

23

" His blood be upon himself." But if the blood of the guilty
be not shed, then that is imputed as a fault, and laid to
the magistrate's charge; because he, neglecting his office, hath
pardoned them that were not worthy to be forgiven, and by
letting them go hath left the innocent unrevenged. For he
is made partaker of the injury done, and shedding of the
innocent's blood, which he leaveth unrevenged, by letting the
murderer go untouched, on whose neck the Lord gave charge

Severity is
not cruelty.

to let the sword fall. The just severity of the upright
magistrate in punishing naughty men is not (as it is falsely
judged) extreme cruelty. But overthwart and peevish pity
that spareth offenders which are not worthy to live among
men, is utter and mere cruelty indeed. For when the magistrate letteth them go unpunished and at ease, which with
their naughty deeds have deserved death, he doth thereby
first of all, give occasion and courage to like offenders to go
on and increase in their mischievous wickedness : for they see
their own faults borne withal in other men. Secondarily, the
men that are not as yet altogether drowned in the mire of
wickedness, but are every hour tempted and provoked to
naughtiness, will at the last leave to have scruple of conscience,
and give their consent to yield to mischief : for they see
that mischievous merchants[1] are gently dealt withal. Lastly,
offenders set free without any punishment do for the most
part become little better : yea, they became twice worse than
they were before ; and the increase of his sin shall at length
compel thee to kill him for many murders, whom thou
wouldest not kill for the murder of one, whereby thou
mightest have saved many guiltless men whom that cut-
throat, since his first pardon, hath villainously slain. They
therefore send wolves and bears among the common people
that let such rakehells[2] escape unpunished.

For what
causes God
commanded
to kill of-
fenders.

Since, now, that I have declared the right use of the
sword, and proved that the magistrate hath power to revenge
men's injuries, and to kill heinous offenders ; let us go on
to consider what the causes be for which God commanded
to punish transgressors ; let us see, also, when they ought to
be punished ; and lastly, what kinds of punishment or penalties the magistrate must use.

[1 facinorosos, Lat.]   [2 nebulones nefarios, Lat.]

The especial causes, for which the Lord doth openly command to punish offenders, are for the most part these that follow. The Lord resisteth force with force, and worketh the safeguard and salvation of men; he revengeth them that suffer wrong, and restoreth again whatsoever may be restored. He declareth his justice also, which rewardeth every one according to his deeds; and therefore he wipeth out reproachful deeds with a reproachful death. He putteth offenders in mind of their crime, and therewithal, for the most part, doth give them sense of repentance unto salvation. For if the wicked do acknowledge his fault, and repent himself of his ill deed, and believe in Christ with all his heart, his sin is forgiven him and he is saved: as we have an evident example Luke xxiii. in the thief that was crucified, whose punishment was an occasion of his salvation; but from the other this salvation was far off, because he did not believe in Christ, and would not be warned by the pain that he felt for his offence to repent for his sins, and to call to God for mercy. Furthermore, by public judgment and open execution all other men may take example to learn to beware of like offences, unless they will suffer like horror of torments.

But let not the magistrate execute any man until he When the magistrate ought to punish offenders. know first perfectly, whether he that is to be punished hath deserved that punishment that the judges determine; and whether God hath commanded to punish that offence, that is, whether by God's law that is condemned, which is to be punished. The truth thereof shall be manifestly known, either by the proper and free confession of the man accused, or by the probable testimonies brought in and gathered against the defendant, or by conferring the laws with the offences of him that is to be punished. So then the magistrate may not punish virtue, true religion, nor good, honest, and godly men: for he is ordained of God to terrify, not the good, but offenders.

Now, touching the manner and fashion of punishment, The kinds of punishment. I think it not best over curiously to dispute. Let every nation or city retain still their penalties and order of punishing, unless peradventure their country-custom smack somewhat of rigour and extreme cruelty. For no wise man denieth but that the kind of punishment must be tempered according to the rule of justice and equity. The kinds of punishment are

Diminutio capitis, a kind of judgment whereby one is put out of the king's protection or condemned to bondage.

exile or banishment, bondage[1], loss of goods, imprisonment and fetters, scourges, marks with burning irons, loss of limbs, and, lastly, death itself, by killing with the sword, by burning, hanging, drowning, and other such means as every nation useth of custom.   Neither is the scripture without a pitiful beadrow[2] of miserable torments.   For in the book of Esdras we read: "And whosoever will not do the law of thy God, (Esdras), and the law of the king, let judgment straightways pass upon him, whether it be to death, or banishment, or loss of goods, or imprisonment[3]."   This do I add not unadvisedly, because of them that are of opinion that such torments ought not so much as once to be named among christian people.

Discretion and clemency of the judge.

But measure and discretion must be used of the judges in punishing offenders, so that heinous faults may be plagued with grievous punishment, lesser crimes may be nipped with smaller penalties, and the smallest and light offences punished more lightly.   That sentence in God's law ought to be remembered, "According to the fault, so shall the punishment be[4]:" where also the judge must have a consideration of his clemency and pity.   Oftentimes the kind[5] and age excuseth the party accused.   The circumstances, being rightly weighed, do sometime excuse the deeds that otherwise are of themselves not all of the best.   The judge also must inquire after and diligently consider the former life of the man accused; for which, if it fall out to have been good and honest, then doth he deserve some favour and mercy, unless the offence for which he is troubled be so heinous that it can admit no sparkle of pity. But godliness or the fear of God, with pouring out of prayers unto the Lord and a diligent and lawful examination of the deed or word, that is, of the fault committed, is the best rule for the judge to follow in choosing his time when to use pity,

[1 Diminutio capitis, Lat. "A Roman citizen possessed *libertas*, *civitas*, and *familia*: the loss of all three, or of libertas and civitas (for civitas included familia) constituted the maxima capitis diminutio."— Smith's Dict. of Gr. and Rom. Antiq. voc. *caput*.]

[2 catalogo, Lat.]   [3 Ezra vii. 26.]

[4 Deut. xxv. 2. The last sentence, "according to his fault, by a certain number," is in the Vulgate, "Pro mensura peccati erit et plagarum modus;" which are the words that Bullinger quotes, and which are rendered in the Douay Version, "According to the measure of the sin shall the measure also of the stripes be."]

[5 sexus, Lat.]

and when to deal with extreme rigour. For otherwise decent clemency is most praiseworthy before God and men.

I have shewed you, dearly beloved, that the magistrate both may and of duty ought to punish offenders; then, for what causes the Lord will have them to be punished; and, lastly, how, when, and how much, they are to be punished. It remaineth now for me to declare wherefore, and for what offences, they are to be punished: which I mean to lay down in one word, and briefly too. All words and deeds which are contrary to the laws of God and the magistrate, that is, all things that are done mischievously against the laws, are to be punished: but laws are made either for religion or politic government; and politic government consisteth in honesty, justice, and peace. Therefore the magistrate must punish and keep under all them which do disturb, afflict, trouble, destroy, or overthrow honesty, justice, public peace, or private tranquillity betwixt man and man. Let him punish dishonesty, ribaldry, filthy lust, whoredom, fornication, adultery, incest, sodomy, riotousness, drunkenness, gluttony, covetousness, cozening, cutting usury, treason, murder, slaughter of parents, sedition, and whatsoever is like to these. The law of the Lord, published by the ministery of Moses, doth in the eighteenth and twentieth of Leviticus reckon up a beadrow[6] long enough of such offences as are to be punished. And lest perhaps any man may think, that at this day that which Moses hath rehearsed is utterly abolished, let him give ear to St Paul, who saith: "To the just the law is not given, but to the unjust, and to sinners, to unholy and unclean, to murderers of fathers and murderers of mothers, to manslayers, to whoremongers, to them that defile themselves with mankind, to man-stealers, to liars, to perjured men, and if there be any other thing contrary to sound doctrine[7]." But apostates, idolaters, blasphemers, heretics, false teachers, and mockers of religion, do offend against the laws of religion, (and therefore ought they to be punished by the magistrate's authority[8].)

But the question hath been, and is yet at this day, in controversy, whether it be lawful for a magistrate to punish any man in his jurisdiction for the contempt of religion or blaspheming of the same? The Manichees and Donatists were of opinion that no man ought to be compelled, much less to be

What is to be punished in offenders.

Whether the magistrate may punish for the breach of religion.

[6 catalogum, Lat.]   [7 1 Tim. i. 9, 10.]
[8 This is added by the Translator. P.]

killed, for any religion; but that every man ought to be left
to his own mind and judgment. And yet the scripture doth
expressly command the magistrate not to spare false prophets;
yea, rebels against God are commanded by holy laws and
judges to be killed without mercy. The places are extant to
be seen in the holy scriptures; the one in the thirteenth of
Deuteronomy, the other in the seventeenth of the same book.
In Exodus this same is set down for a rule: "Whosoever
sacrificeth to any God, but to the Lord alone, let him be
rooted out[1]." In Leviticus, the blasphemer is slain and overwhelmed with stones[2]. In the book of Numbers, the man
is slain that did unhallow the sabbath-day[3]. And how many,
I pray you, did God's revenging sword destroy of that calvish
people that did erect and worship the calf in the wilderness[4]?
Helias at mount Carmel killed whole hundreds of false prophets in a solemn set and appointed sacrifice[5]. Eliseus, at the
Lord's commandment, anointed Jehu king, to the end that he
might root out the house of Achab, and kill at once all Baal's
priests[6]. Joiada the priest slew Athalia[7], and good king Josias
destroyed together the wicked and stubborn priests of all high
places[8]. St Augustine, *Tractatu in Joan.* 11, disputing against
the Donatists, doth prove by the example of Nabuchodonozor,
that Christian princes do justly punish the Donatists for despising Christ and his evangelical doctrine. Among other
things he saith: "If king Nabuchodonosor did glorify God
for delivering three children out of the fire; yea, and glorified
him so much that he made a decree throughout his kingdom
for his honour and worship: why should not the kings of our
days be moved so to do, which see not three children saved
from the flame alone, but themselves also delivered from
the fire of hell, when they behold Christ, by whom they are
delivered, burnt up in Christian men, and when to a Christian
they hear it said, Say thou that thou art no Christian? This
they will do, and yet this they will not suffer. For mark
what they do, and see what they suffer. They kill souls;
they are afflicted in body. They kill other eternally, and do
complain that they themselves do suffer a temporal death[9]."

[1 Exod. xxii. 20.]   [2 Lev. xxiv. 10—16.]
[3 Numb. xv. 32—36.]   [4 Exod. xxxii.]
[5 1 Kings xviii.]   [6 2 Kings ix.]
[7 2 Kings xi.]   [8 2 Kings xxiii. 20.]
[9 Si Nabuchodonozor rex laudavit et prædicavit et gloriam dedit

Thus much hath Augustine. In the new Testament we have most evident examples of Peter and Paul, Christ's greatest apostles: the one whereof slew Ananias and Sapphira, for their lying hypocrisy and feigned religion[10]; the other struck Elymas the sorcerer blind, and bereft him of his eyes[11]. Neither is there one hair's difference to choose, whether a man be killed with a sword or with a word[12]. For to kill is to kill, by what means or with what instrument soever it be done. God wrought that by his apostles, and doth the like by the magistrate also. For vengeance is God's, who giveth it to the magistrate and chief men to be put in ure and execution upon wicked offenders. There are to be seen many laws made by holy Christian princes for the state of religion, which give an especial charge to kill idolaters, apostates, heretics, and godless people. I will recite unto you, dearly beloved, one law among many, made by the holy emperor, Constantine the Great. For in an epistle, intituled *ad Taurum P. P.*, he saith: "It pleaseth us that in all places, and throughout every city, the temples be out of hand shut up, and liberty denied to wicked men to have access thither to commit idolatry. We will also and command all men to be restrained from making of sacrifice. And if so be it happen that they offend herein, our pleasure is that they be slain with the sword, and the slain man's goods to be confiscate. And we have decreed that the rulers of the provinces shall suffer like punishment, if they neglect to punish the offenders[13]." The very same almost

Deo, quia liberavit de igne tres pueros, et tantam gloriam dedit, ut decretum mitteret per regnum suum, Quicunque dixerint, &c., quomodo isti reges non moveantur, qui non tres pueros attendunt liberatos de flamma, sed seipsos liberatos de Gehenna, quando vident Christum, a quo liberati sunt, exsufflari in Christianis, quando audiunt dici Christiano, Dic te non esse Christianum? Talia facere volunt, et saltem talia pati nolunt. Nam videte qualia faciunt, et qualia patiuntur. Occidunt animas, affliguntur in corpore. Sempiternas mortes faciunt, et temporales se perpeti conqueruntur.—Opp. Par. 1531. Tom. IX. fol. 22. P.]

[10 Acts v.]   [11 Acts xiii. 11.]

[12 gladio, poculis, an verbis, Lat.]

[13 Imp. Constantinus. A. ad Taurum. P. P. I. Placuit omnibus locis atque urbibus universis claudi protinus templa, et accessu vetito omnibus licentiam delinquendi perditis abnegari. Volumus etiam cunctos sacrificiis abstinere. Quod si aliquid forte hujusmodi perpe-

do Theodosius and Valentinianus by proclaimed edicts command *in Codice Theodosiano*, tit. 2. And Valentinianus and Martianus *in Codice Justiniano*, tit. 2. Lib. I.[1] Lastly, without all controversy, adulterers, murderers, rebels, deceivers, and blasphemers, are rightly punished, and not against religion. Wherefore it followeth consequently, that false prophets and heretics are by good right slain: for they are deceivers, blasphemers, and man-quellers[2].

What moderation must be had in punishing.

But in the execution of this punishment there must a great consideration be had and observed; first, of the persons; then, of the errors; and, lastly, of the penalties. For in persons there is great diversity: because there are some standard-bearers, and heady grand captains, which are stout, hypocrites, and full of tongue, and therefore the aptest for to seduce; who, falling headlong without amendment to their own destruction, do with themselves draw other into danger. They must by all means be bridled and kept under, as plagues to the church; lest, like a canker, they spread all over. Again, there are some silly seduced souls, made fools by other men, which err not of malice nor stubborn stomach, but do repent and amend in time. These the magistrate must not straightway condemn, but pray to the Lord, and bear with their error, and teach them in the spirit of gentleness, until they be brought to a better mind.

Moreover, in erroneous doctrines some are more intolerable than other some are. Some there be so wicked and blasphemous, that they are unworthy to be heard, much less to be done[3]. Some there are which do directly and openly tend to the overthrow of the commonweal, unless they be in time appeased and resisted. But those crimes that are brought in and accused, ought first to be by the scripture and manifest truth convinced to be such as they are said to

traverint, gladio ultore sternantur, facultates etiam peremti fisco decernimus vindicari. Et similiter puniri rectores provinciarum, si facinora vindicare neglexerint.—D. Prid. No. Mar. Arbitrione et Lolliano Coss. Justin. Cod. Lib. I. Tit. ii. p. 100. Lugd. 1551. Tom. I.]

[1 Impp. Theod. et Valentin. A. A. Isidoro P. F. P. Cod. Theod. Lib. XVI. Tit. x. p. 526. Par. 1607.—Impp. Valentin. et Mart. A. A. Palladio. P. P. VII. Lib. I. Tit. ii. Cod. Justin. Tom. I. Lugd. 1551. p. 102.]

[2 homicidæ, Lat.]

[3 nedum ferri, Lat.]

be.　When the truth is known, and manifest proofs of scripture alleged, then is it lawful most sharply to punish those blasphemers of God and overthrowers of the church and commonweal.　But a light and easier penalty must be set on the heads of them whose offence consisteth in light and smaller errors: for some do err so, that by their error God is not blasphemed, the church not subverted, nor the commonweal in any danger at all.　Where, by the way, every one must think of that saying of the apostle: "Bear ye one another's burden[4]."　And again: "The weak in faith receive ye, not to the doubtfulness of questions[5]."

Furthermore, in punishment and penalties there is great difference.　They that err stubbornly, and do their endeavour to draw in and keep other men in their errors, blasphemers, troublers, and subverters of churches, may by law be put to death.　But it followeth not thereupon, that every one which erreth must therefore by and by suffer loss of his life.　The things, that by threats and fault-finding[6] may be remedied and amended, must not be punished with sharper correction.　A mean in every thing is always the best.　There is a penalty by payment of money.　There are prisons for them to be shut up into, which are corrupted with the poison of false doctrine and lack of belief, lest peradventure they infect others with their contagious disease.　There are also other means to punish the body, whereby to keep them under that err from the truth, to keep them from marring those that are sound, and to preserve themselves that they perish not utterly, but that through repentance they may fall to amendment.　But the fear of God, justice, and the judge's wisdom shall by the circumstances make him perceive how he ought to punish the naughty doctrine and stubborn rebellion of malicious seducers, and how to bear with the foolish, light belief of silly seduced men, grounded upon simplicity, and not envenomed rancour.

Earnest and diligent admonition is given too late, when the fault is already committed, and is so detestable that it ought straightway to be plagued with the sword: let the

Admonition before punishment.

[4 Gal. vi. 2.]

[5 Rom. xiv. 1.—non ad dijudicationes disceptationum, Lat.; Erasmus' rendering.]

[6 increpationibus, Lat.]

magistrate, therefore, always have an eye to admonish them in time, that are to be warned to take heed of a fault. For earnest admonitions are earnestly commended to men in authority to use to their subjects, when they begin to work any broil. Moreover, godly and wise magistrates have many times pardoned unwitting offenders, whom they saw ready to repent upon giving of warning. The Lord in the gospel biddeth us admonish a sinner; then, if he repent, to pardon his fault; but if he reject a fair warning once given him, then to punish him so much the sharper[1]. And Josue, before he made open war to be proclaimed upon the children of Reuben, did first by embassage command them to dig down the altar, which they seemed to have made contrary to the law of the Lord[2]. The emperor Justinian also granted pardon to them which repented, and turned to a sounder opinion, *Constitut.* 109.[3] Moreover, Josias did not utterly kill all them that were wrapped in error and idolatry, but those especially that were incurable, and would not recant. The magistrate therefore must wisely moderate the matter, and be very circumspect in punishing offenders.

Objections answered.

I cannot here wink and slyly pass over the objections, that some men make against that which hitherto I have said touching punishment; to wit, that the apostle Paul hath not commanded to kill or punish an heretic after the first and second admonition, but to avoid him[4]; again, that faith is the gift of God, which cannot be given or engraffed in any man by rigour of the sword; also, that no man is to be compelled: he that constraineth may make an hypocrite; but a devout and zealous man he cannot make: and lastly, that the apostles required no aid of kings either to maintain or set out the religion of Christ, or else to punish blasphemous railers and enemies of God's word. To all this I answer thus: Paul, when he wrote his epistle to Titus, did write to an apostle: in that epistle, therefore, he instructeth an apostle how to behave himself according to his duty toward an heretic past all reco-

---

[1 Matt. xviii. 15—17.]   [2 Josh. xxii.]

[3 Ἔξεστι δὲ αὐταῖς, τῆς βελτίονος γινομέναις γνώμης, καὶ τὴν ὀρθὴν καὶ ἀληθινὴν ἀσπαζομέναις πίστιν ... τῶν τοιούτων ἀπολαύειν δωρεῶν τε καὶ προνομίων.—Justin. Auth. Collat. VIII. Tit. x. Novell. 109. cap. 2. p. 432. Gotting. 1797.]

[4 Tit. iii. 10.]

very. If he had written to Sergius Paulus, or any lieutenant[5], he would undoubtedly have taught him his office. For the same Paul, standing before Sergius Paulus, then prince of Cyprus, did by his deeds declare unto him the duty of a magistrate: for first, he did not only most sharply rebuke the false prophet Elymas, then forsake his company, eschew and shun him, as the apostle John did Cerinthus[6], but strake him also with bodily blindness.

I grant and confess, that faith is God's gift in the heart of Faith is the gift of God. man, which God alone doth search and know. But men are judged by their words and deeds. Admit, therefore, that the erroneous opinion of the mind may not be punished; yet notwithstanding, wicked and infective profession and doctrine must in no wise be suffered. Verily, no man doth in this world punish profane and wicked thoughts of the mind: but if those thoughts break forth into blasphemous words, then are those blaspheming tongues to be punished of good princes. And yet by this I say not, that godliness lieth in the magistrate to give and bestow. Justice is the very gift of God, which none but God doth give to men: but who is so foolish as to gather thereupon, that unjust men, robbers, murderers, and witches are not to be punished, because the magistrate by punishment cannot bestow righteousness upon unrighteous people? We must therefore make a difference betwixt faith, as it is the gift of God in the heart of man, and as it is the outward profession uttered and declared before the face of men. For while false faith doth lurk and lie hid within the heart, and infecteth none but the unbeliever, so long the unbelieving infidel cannot be punished: but if this false and forged faith, that so lay hid, do once break forth to blaspheme, to the open tearing of God and the infecting of his neighbours, then must that blasphemer and seducer be by and by plucked under, and kept from creeping to further annoyance. Not to suppress such a fellow as this, is to put a sword in a madman's hand to kill unwise and weakly men.

Faith is the gift of God; but, where he bestoweth faith, he useth means to give it by: those means he will not have us to neglect. An householder knoweth that faith is the gift

[5] præsidem aliquem, Lat.]

[6] Euseb. Eccles. Hist. Lib. IV. cap. 14. Milner's Church History, Cent. i. chap. 13. Vol. I. p. 102, ed. 1834.]

of God; and yet notwithstanding, he instructeth his children in the word of truth, he chargeth them to go to church, to pray for faith, and to learn it at the preacher's mouth. A good father would think much, yea, he would not think well of it, if his son should say: Father, I pray you, teach me not, send me not so much to church, and beat me not if I be not there; for faith is the gift of God, which whipping cannot bring me to. Then what man can quietly abide to hear that faith is the gift of God, and that therefore no man ought for faith, that is, for the corruption of faith and open blasphemy, to suffer any punishment?

Whether it be lawful to compel one to faith.

And yet Petilian, in the eighty-third chapter of St Augustine's second book *contra Petiliani literas*, crieth out, and saith: "God forbid, and far be it from our conscience, to compel any man to our religion[1]." Shall we, therefore, go on to speak the words of heretics, or to say, that the Lord God in the scriptures hath planted hypocrisy, where with threats and punishment he hath driven men to goodness? David saith: "It is good for me, Lord, that thou hast chastised me[2]." And Jeremy saith: "Thou hast chastised me, O Lord, and I am chastised, like an untamed heifer[3]." But if no man ought to be compelled to goodness, to what intent doth Solomon (the wisest of all men) so many times command to chastise children? "He that spareth the rod hateth the child," saith he; "Thou indeed dost strike him, but with the rod thou deliverest his soul from death[4]." Daily experience, and the disposition of men, do plainly teach, that in men there are most vehement affections, which, unless they be remedied and bridled betimes, do both destroy them in whom they be, and other men too, who at the first might easily with light punishment have been preserved. Men in their madness despise compulsion and chastising punishment; but, when they come to themselves again, and see from how great evils they are delivered by those that compelled them, then they rejoice that to their health they were chastised, and praise the compulsion which before they despised.

[1 Augustine says, Noli ergo dicere, Absit, absit a nostra conscientia, ut ad nostram fidem aliquem compellamus. Facitis enim ubi potestis.—Opp. Par. 1531. Tom. VII. fol. 29. P.]

[2 Ps. cxix. 71.]   [3 Jer. xxxi. 18.]

[4 Prov. xiii. 24; xxii. 14.]

Let us hear what Augustine doth think and teach hereof, whose experience in this matter was very much. In his forty-eighth Epist. *ad Vincentium contra Donatist. de vi coercendis hæreticis*, he writeth thus: " My opinion sometime was, that no man ought by force to be compelled to the unity of Christ; that we ought to deal by words, fight in disputations, and overcome with reason, lest peradventure we should have those to counterfeit themselves to be catholics, whom we knew to be open heretics. But this opinion of mine was not confuted with the words of my gainsayers, but with the examples of those which shewed the contrary. For first, mine own city (Hippone) was objected against me; which, when as sometime it held wholly with Donatus, was by the fear of the imperial laws converted to the catholic unity; and at this day we see it so greatly to detest the naughtiness of your heretical stomachs, that it is thought verily that your heresy was never within it. And many more places by name were reckoned up unto me, that, by the effect of the thing itself, I might confess, that in such a case as this that may be rightly understood where it is written: 'Give a wise man occasion, and he will be the wiser[5].'" And again: " Not every one that spareth is a friend; nor every one that striketh is an enemy. Better are the stripes of a friend than the voluntary kisses of an enemy. It is better to love with severity, than to deceive with lenity. He that bindeth a frenzy man, and waketh him that is sick of the lethargy, doth trouble them both, and yet he loveth them both. Who can love us more than God himself doth? and yet, as he teacheth us mildly, so he ceaseth not to terrify us to our health. Thinkest thou that no man ought to be compelled to righteousness, when thou readest that the goodman

[5 Nam mea primitus sententia erat, neminem ad unitatem Christi esse cogendum; verbo esse agendum, disputatione pugnandum, ratione vincendum, ne fictos catholicos haberemus, quos apertos hæreticos noveramus. Sed hæc opinio mea non contradicentium verbis, sed demonstrantium superabatur exemplis: nam primo mihi opponebatur civitas mea, quæ cum tota esset in parte Donati, ad unitatem catholicam timore legum imperialium conversa est; quam nunc videmus ita hujus vestræ animositatis perniciem detestari, ut in ea nunquam fuisse credatur: ita aliæ multæ, quæ mihi nominatim commemorabantur; ut ipsis rebus agnoscerem etiam in hac causa recte intelligi posse, quod scriptum est, Da sapienti occasionem, et sapientior erit.—Opp. Tom. II. fol. 34. P.]

of the house said to his servants, 'Whomsoever ye find, compel them to come in;' when thou readest that he, that was first called Saul and afterward Paul, was constrained by the violent force of Christ, which compelled him to know and keep fast the truth of the gospel[1]?" And the same Augustine again, in Epist. *ad Bonifacium comitem* 59, saith : "Where is that now that they were wont to cry and say, that it is at every one's free choice to believe, or not to believe? Whom did Christ constrain? whom did he compel? Lo, here they have the apostle Paul for an example : let them confess in him, that Christ first compelled him, then taught him; first struck him, and afterward comforted him. And it is wonderful how he, which by the punishment of his body was compelled to the gospel, did after his entering in labour more in the gospel than all they that were called by word alone : and whom the greater fear compelled to charity, his charity, once perfect, did cast out all fear. Why then should not the church therefore compel her lost children to return, since the lost children have compelled other to their destruction[2]?"

Again, in the same epistle, the same Augustine saith : "Whereas some, which would not have upright laws ordained

[1 Non omnis qui parcit amicus est, nec omnis qui verberat inimicus. Meliora sunt vulnera amici, quam voluntaria oscula inimici. Melius est cum severitate diligere, quam cum lenitate decipere... Qui phreneticum ligat, et qui lethargicum excitat, ambobus molestus, ambos amat. Quis nos potest amplius amare quam Deus? Et tamen nos non solum docere suaviter, verum etiam salubriter terrere non cessat ... Putas neminem debere cogi ad justitiam, cum legas patrem familias dixisse servis, Quoscunque inveneritis cogite intrare; cum legas etiam ipsum primo Saulum, postea Paulum, ad cognoscendam et tenendam veritatem magna violentia Christi cogentis esse compulsum?—Aug. Ep. 48. ad Vincentium Opp. Par. 1531. Tom. ii. fol. 33. P.]

[2 Ubi est quod isti clamare consueverunt, Liberum est credere vel non credere? Cui vim Christus intulit? Quem coegit? Ecce habent Paulum apostolum: agnoscant in eo prius cogentem Christum et postea docentem, prius ferientem et postea consolantem. Mirum est autem quomodo ille, qui poena corporis ad evangelium coactus intravit, plus illis omnibus qui solo verbo vocati sunt in evangelio laboravit; et quem major timor compulit ad caritatem, ejus perfecta caritas foras misit timorem. Cur ergo non cogeret ecclesia perditos filios ut redirent, si perditi filii coegerunt alios ut perirent?—Opp. Tom. ii. fol. 42. P.]

against their ungodliness, do say, that the apostles did never require any such things of the kings of the earth; they do not consider, that that was another time (not like to this), and that all things are done in their due time and season. For what emperor did at that time believe in Christ, to serve him by making laws in defence of religion against ungodliness? when as yet that prophecy was in fulfilling, 'Why did the heathen rage, and the people imagine a vain thing? The kings of the earth stood up, and the rulers took counsel against God and against his Christ.' For as yet that was not begun which followeth in the Psalm, where it is said: 'And now understand, ye kings, and be ye learned, ye that judge the earth; serve him in fear and rejoice in trembling.' But how do kings serve God in fear, but by forbidding and punishing with devout severity those things which are done against God's commandments? For in that he is a man, he serveth him one way; but in that he is a king, he serveth him another way: because in that he is a man, he serveth him by living faithfully; but in that he is a king, he serveth him by establishing convenient laws to command that which is just, and to forbid the contrary:—as Ezechias served him, by destroying the groves and temples of idols, and those high places that were erected against the Lord's commandment: as Josias served him, by doing the like: as the king of Ninivie served him, by compelling the whole city to please and appease the anger of the Lord: as Darius served him, by giving the idol into Daniel's power to be broken in pieces, and by casting his enemies in among the lions: as Nabuchodonosor served him, by a terrible proclamation, which forbade all men within his dominion to blaspheme the true and very God. In this therefore should kings serve God, in that that they are kings, by doing those things which none can do but kings. Wherefore, when as in the apostles' times the kings did not as yet serve the Lord, but imagined a vain thing against the Lord and against his Christ, that the prophet's sayings might be fulfilled, there could not as then, I say, any laws be made to forbid ungodliness, but counsel be rather taken to put ungodliness in practice. For so the course of times did turn, that both the Jews should kill the preachers of Christ, thinking that thereby they did God good service; and that the Gentiles also should fret and rage

The apostles required no aid of the magistrate for the maintenance of religion against the adversaries of the same.

against the Christians, and make the martyrs' constancy overcome the flames of fire. But afterward, when that began to be
fulfilled which is written, ' And all the kings of the earth shall
worship him, all nations shall serve him ;' what man that were
well in his wits would say to kings, ' Tush, take ye no care
how, or by whom, the church of your Lord is defended or
defaced within your kingdom ; let it not trouble you to mark
who will be honest, and who dishonest within your dominion?'
For since God hath given man free will, why should adultery
be punished, and sacrilege left untouched ? Is it a lighter
matter for the soul to break promise with God, than a woman
with a man ? Or, for because those things which are not
committed by contempt, but by ignorance of religion, are to be
more mildly punished, are they therefore to be utterly neglected ? It is better (who doubteth ?) for men to be brought
to the worshipping of God by teaching, rather than for to be
compelled to it by fear or grief of punishment : but because
these are the better, they, which are not such, are not therefore to be neglected. For it hath profited many men (as we
see by experience) first to have been compelled with fear and
grief, that afterward they might either be taught, or follow
that in deed which they had learned in words[1]."

[1 Quod enim dicunt qui contra suas impietates leges justas con-
stitui nolunt, non petisse a regibus terræ apostolos talia, non considerant
aliud fuisse tunc tempus, et omnia suis temporibus agi. Quis enim
tunc in Christum crediderat imperator, qui ei pro pietate contra im-
pietatem leges ferendo serviret, quando adhuc illud propheticum com-
plebatur, Quare fremuerunt gentes et populi meditati sunt inania;
astiterunt reges terræ et principes convenerunt in unum adversus
Dominum et adversus Christum ejus? Nondum autem agebatur, quod
paulo post in eodem Psalmo dicitur, Et nunc, reges, intelligite, erudimini
qui judicatis terram : servite Domino in timore, et exultate ei cum
tremore. Quomodo ergo reges Domino serviunt in timore, nisi ea,
quæ contra jussa Domini fiunt, religiosa severitate prohibendo atque
plectendo? Aliter enim servit quia homo est, aliter quia etiam et rex
est. Quia homo est, ei servit vivendo fideliter : quia vero etiam rex
est, servit leges justa præcipientes et contraria prohibentes convenienti
vigore sanciendo : sicut servivit Ezechias, lucos et templa idolorum,
et illa excelsa quæ contra præcepta Dei fuerant constructa, destruendo:
sicut servivit Josias, talia et ipse faciendo : sicut servivit rex Ninivi-
tarum, universam civitatem ad placandum Dominum compellendo :
sicut servivit Darius, idolum frangendum in potestatem Danieli dando,
et inimicos ejus leonibus ingerendo : sicut servivit Nabuchodonosor,

Hitherto I have rehearsed the words of St Augustine's answer to the objections of them which are of opinion, that by no law disobedient rebels, seduced people, and deceivers, ought to be punished in cases of religion.

I see my hope doth fail me, wherein I thought that I could have been able in this sermon to have made an end of all that I had to say touching the magistrate. But I perceive that here I must stay, unless I should go on, dearly beloved, and be too tedious unto you all. I mean to-morrow, therefore, to add the rest that is yet behind. Make ye your humble prayers unto the Lord upon your knees, and then depart in peace.

de quo jam diximus, omnes in regno suo positos a blasphemando Deo lege terribili prohibendo. In hoc ergo serviunt Domino reges, in quantum sunt reges, cum ea faciunt ad serviendum illi, quæ non possunt facere nisi reges. Cum itaque nondum reges Domino servirent temporibus apostolorum, sed adhuc meditarentur inania adversus eum et adversus Christum ejus, ut prophetarum prædicta omnia complerentur, non utique tunc possent impietates legibus prohiberi, sed potius exerceri. Sic enim ordo temporum volvebatur, ut et Judæi occiderent prædicatores Christi, putantes se officium Deo facere, sicut prædixerat Christus ; et gentes fremerent adversus Christianos, et omnes potentia (patientia) martyrum vinceret. Postea vero quam cœpit impleri quod scriptum est, Et adorabunt eum omnes reges terræ, omnes gentes servient illi ; quis mente sobrius regibus dicat, 'Nolite curare in regno vestro a quo tueatur (teneatur) vel oppugnetur ecclesia Domini vestri : non ad vos pertineat in regno vestro, quis velit esse sive religiosus sive sacrilegus. ... Cur enim, cum datum sit divinitus homini liberum arbitrium, adulteria legibus puniantur, et sacrilegia permittantur ? An fidem non servare levius est animam Deo, quam fœminam viro ? Aut si ea, quæ non contemptu sed ignorantia religionis committuntur, mitius vindicanda, numquid ideo negligenda sunt ? Melius est quidem (quis dubitaverit ?) ad Deum colendum doctrina homines duci, quam pœnæ timore vel dolore compelli. Sed non quia isti meliores sunt, ideo illi, qui tales non sunt, negligendi sunt. Multis enim profuit, quod experimentis probavimus, prius timore vel dolore cogi, ut postea possint doceri, aut quod jam verbis didicerant opere sectari.—Opp. Tom. II. fol. 42. P.]

OF WAR; WHETHER IT BE LAWFUL FOR A MAGISTRATE
TO MAKE WAR. WHAT THE SCRIPTURE TEACHETH
TOUCHING WAR. WHETHER A CHRISTIAN MAN
MAY BEAR THE OFFICE OF A MAGISTRATE.
AND OF THE DUTY OF SUBJECTS.

THE NINTH SERMON.

To the right of the sword, which God hath given to the
magistrate, doth war belong: for in my last sermon I taught
you, that the use of the sword in the magistrate's hand is
twofold, or of two sorts. For either he punisheth offenders
therewith; or else repelleth the enemy that spoileth or would
spoil his people, or cutteth off the rebellious purposes of his
own seditious citizens.

Whether it
be lawful for
a magistrate
to make
war.

But many make a doubt whether it be lawful for a magistrate to make war or no [1]. And it is marvel to see them as
blind as beetles in a matter of itself as plain as may be. For
if the magistrate doth by God's law punish offenders, thieves,
and harmful persons; and that it maketh no matter whether
they be few or many in number, as I declared in my yesterday's sermon; even by the same law may he persecute,
repel, and kill rebellious people, seditious citizens, and barbarous soldiers, who, under the pretence of war, do attempt
that openly which thieves and robbers are wont to do privily.
The prophet, I confess, did among other things prophesy of
us Christians, and say: "They shall turn their swords into
spades, and their javelins into scythes [2]:" for Christians have
peace with all men, and do altogether abstain from armour;
for every one doth that to another which he would wish to
have done to himself. But, for because all are not so minded,
but that many unruly persons, wicked thieves, and oppressors
of the poor, do live and dwell among honest and good-mean-
ing men, as wild beasts among harmless creatures; therefore
God from heaven hath given the sword into the magistrate's
hand, to be a defence for harmless people against unruly

[1 Of these doctrines of the Anabaptists, Latimer also makes mention, Parker Soc. ed. Vol. I. pp. 495, 6. See also Bullinger. adv. Ana-
baptist. Lib. v. cap. 10.]

[2 Isai. ii. 4.]

cut-throats. But we read not in any place that we are forbidden to suppress and kill wolves, wild boars, bears, and
such other beasts that do annoy and prey upon men or cattle.
What let then should there be why we should not, by lawful
war begun in a good quarrel, repel the unjust injury of violent
robbers, since thieves, robbers, barbarous soldiers, and seditious citizens, do differ little or nothing from wild beasts? The
scripture, verily, doth not vouchsafe to call them by any other
names than by the names of beasts. Hereunto consenteth
the common sense of nature; and herewithal agreeth the
doctrine of faith and religion. " If it be possible," saith the
apostle, " as much as lieth in you, live quietly with all men;
not revenging yourselves." See here, " as much as lieth in
you," saith he, and, " if it be possible :" otherwise, he addeth
immediately after : " The magistrate beareth not the sword in
vain[3]." He meaneth, for them that trouble all things, and
do annoy the men which do desire to live at peace. And this
is confirmed by the examples of the most holy and excellent
men that have been in the world, which have taken war in
hand for the defence of their country and harmless countrymen; as I have already declared out of St Paul's Epistle to
the Hebrews, when as in the exposition of the fifth precept
I shewed what honour every man doth owe to his country[4].

I will add to these some reasons of St Augustine, uttered
contra Faustum Manichæum, Lib. XXII. cap. 74. " Neither
let him," saith he, " marvel or be astonied at the wars made
by Moses; for because even in them too he followed God's
commandment, not like a tyrant, but like an obedient servant.
Neither did God rage with cruelty, when he commanded
those wars; but justly paid home them that deserved it, and
terrified those that were worthy of it. For what is blame-
worthy in war? Is it to be blamed that they do die which
once must die, that they which live may rule in peace? To
find fault with that is rather a cowardly touch, than the part
of a religious Christian. Desire to hurt, cruelty in revenging,
an unappeased stomach, bruteness in rebelling, greediness to
rule, and whatsoever else is like to these, are the things that
in war are worthy to be blamed, and by right of law to be
sharply punished. Against the violence of injurious enemies,
at the commandment either of God himself or any other lawful

[3 Rom. xii. 18; xiii. 4.]   [4 See before, p. 277.]

power, even good men are wont to take war in hand; since
their state in the world is such, that politic order doth justly
bind the magistrate in such a case to command it, and the
subjects to obey it. Otherwise John, when the soldiers came to
him to be baptized, saying, 'And what shall we do?' would have
answered them, and said: Cast off your armour, forsake your
soldier's life, strike, wound, or kill nobody. But, because
he knew that while they did so, as soldiers in the war, they
were not man-quellers, but ministers of the law, not revengers
of their own injuries, but defenders of the commonweal, he
said unto them, 'Strike no man, do no man injury; be content with your wages.' But because the Manichees have of
use blasphemed or spoken against John, let them hear the
Lord Jesus Christ himself commanding to give to Cæsar that
stipend which John did say the soldier should be content
withal. 'Give,' saith he, 'to Cæsar that which is Cæsar's, and
to God the things that do belong to God.' For to this end
is tribute paid, that the soldier in the war may have his pay
out of hand for his pain. Very well, therefore, when the
centurion said, 'And I am a man set under power, having
soldiers under me; and I say to one, Go, and he goeth, and to
another, Come, and he cometh, and to my servant, Do this, and
he doeth it,'—did the Lord commend his faith, and not command him to forsake his soldiership[1]." Hitherto also apper-

[1 Nec bella per Moysen gesta miretur aut horreat, quia et in illis
divina secutus imperia, non sæviens, sed obediens fuit: nec Deus, cum
jubebat ista, sæviebat, sed digna dignis retribuebat, dignosque terrebat.
Quid enim culpatur in bello? An quia moriuntur quandoque morituri,
ut dominentur in pace victuri? Hoc reprehendere timidorum est, non
religiosorum. Nocendi cupiditas, ulciscendi crudelitas, impacatus atque
implacabilis animus, feritas rebellandi, libido dominandi, et si qua
similia, hæc sunt quæ in bellis jure culpantur, quæ plerumque ita culpantur ut etiam jure puniantur. Adversus violentiam resistentium,
sive Deo sive aliquo legitimo imperio jubente, gerenda ipsa bella
suscipiuntur a bonis, cum in eo rerum humanarum ordine inveniuntur,
ubi eos vel jubere tale aliquid, vel in talibus obedire juste ordo ipse
constringit. Alioquin Joannes, cum ad eum baptizandi milites venirent,
dicentes, Et nos quid faciemus? responderet eis, Arma abjicite, militiam istam deserite, neminem percutite, vulnerate, prosternite neminem.
Sed quia sciebat eos, cum hæc militando facerent, non esse homicidas
sed ministros legis, et non ultores injuriarum suarum sed salutis pub-
licæ defensores, respondit eis, Neminem concusseritis, nulli calumniam
feceritis, sufficiat vobis stipendium vestrum. Sed quia Manichæi

taineth that which followeth in the same 75th chapter and 76th next after. But I do of purpose willingly bear somewhat with you, not meaning by overlong rehearsing of too many sentences to be tedious unto you.

Thus hitherto I have shewed you that it is lawful for the magistrate for to make war. Where, by the way, also we gather, that the subjects do lawfully, without any offence to God, take armour to battle, when they take it in hand at the magistrate's bidding. But if the magistrate's purpose be to kill the guiltless, I declared in my former sermons that then his people ought not to obey his wicked commandments.

Let the people obey the magistrate when he commandeth them to war.

Let the magistrate therefore have an eye to himself, that he abuse not his lawful authority. And although the magistrate be licensed to make war for just and necessary causes; yet, notwithstanding, war is a thing most full of peril, and draweth with itself an endless troop of mischievous evils. By war the just judgment of God doth plague the men whom his fatherly warning could never move; but among them many times, too, the guiltless feel the whip. In war, for the most part, soldiers misuse themselves, and thereby incur God's heavy displeasure: there is no evil in all the world that war upholdeth not. By war both scarcity of every thing and dearth do arise: for highways are stopped, corn upon the ground is trodden down and marred, whole villages burnt, provision goeth to wrack, handicrafts are unoccupied, merchandise do cease, and all do perish, both rich and poor. The valiant strong men are slain in the battle; the cowardly sort run away for their lives to hide their heads, reserving themselves to be tormented with more exquisite and terrible kinds of cruel punishments: for wicked knaves are promoted to dignity, and bear the sway, which abuse mankind like savage beasts. Hands are wrung on every side; widows and children

War, a thing full of peril and danger.

Joannem aperte blasphemare consueverunt, ipsum Dominum Jesum Christum audiant, hoc stipendium jubentem reddi Cæsari, quod Joannes dicit debere sufficere militi. Reddite, inquit, Cæsari quæ Cæsaris sunt, et Deo quæ Dei sunt. Ad hoc enim tributa præstantur, ut propter bella necessario militi stipendium præbeatur. Merito et illius centurionis dicentis, Et ego homo sum sub potestate constitutus, habens sub me milites, et dico huic, Vade, et vadit; et alii, Veni, et venit; et servo meo, Fac hoc, et facit; fidem laudavit, non illius militiæ desertionem imperavit.—Opp. Par. 1531, Tom. vi. fol. 89. P.]

cry out and lament; the wealth, that hath been carefully
gathered to help in want to come, is spoiled and stolen away;
cities are rased, virgins and unmarriageable maidens are shamefully deflowered, all honesty is utterly violated, old men are
handled unreverently, laws are not exercised, religion and
learning are nothing set by, godless knaves and cut-throats
have the dominion: and therefore in the scriptures war is
called the scourge of God. For with war he plagueth incurable idolaters, and those which stubbornly contemn his word;
for that was the cause why the city of Jerusalem with the
whole nation of the Jews was utterly destroyed; "because
they knew not the day of their visitation" (as the Lord in the
gospel saith), but went on to kill the Lord's apostles, bringing
on upon their own necks "the shedding of all the blood, from
the righteous Abel unto Zacharias[1]." For murder, idolatry,
incest, and detestable riot, we read that the Canaanites were
rased out and cut off[2]. The Moabites, as Esay witnesseth,
were quite overthrown for cruelty, inhumanity, and contempt
of the poor[3]. The men of Ninivy did by war unjustly vex
other nations, making havoc of all, to fill their greedy desire:
and therefore, saith the prophet Nahum, other men measured
to them with the same measure that they had measured to
other before[4]. Micheas, in his sixth chapter, affirmeth flatly
that God sendeth war upon unjust men for their covetousness
and false deceit. In Jeremy arrogancy and pride, in Esay
riot and drunkenness, are said to be the causes of war[5].

But the evil and misery that war bringeth with it sticketh
so fast to commonweals and kingdoms, where it once hath hold,
that it cannot be removed, taken away, or shaken off, at our
will and pleasure, by any worldly wisdom, by any league-
makings, with any wealth, by any fortifications, by any power
or manhood; as it is to be seen in the prophet Abdias[6]. Our
sincere turning to God alone is the only way to remedy it, as
Jeremy testifieth in his fifth chapter. Now this turning to the
Lord consisteth in free acknowledging and frank confession of
our sins, in true faith for remission of sins through the grace
of God and merit of Christ Jesus: secondarily, it consisteth
in hatred and renouncing of all unrighteousness, in love of

*War is the
scourge of
God.*

[1 Luke xix. 44; Matt. xxiii. 34—38.]   [2 Lev. xviii. 27, 28.]
[3 Isai. xvi.]   [4 Nahum iii. 19.]
[5 Jer. xiii. 9; Isai. v.]   [6 Obad. 3, 4, 8, 9.]

justice, innocency, charity, and all other virtues; and, last of all, in earnest prayers and continual supplications.

Again, thou mayest see perhaps, that some by war have no small commodity, profit, and inestimable riches, with very little loss or no damage at all. Such was the war which the Israelites had with the Canaanites under their captain Josue. But I would not that gaping after gain should draw any man from right and equity. And many times the magistrates suppose that their quarrel is good, and that of right they ought to make war on others and punish offenders; when as notwithstanding the righteous God by that occasion draweth them on into peril, that their sins may be punished by the men in whom they did purpose to have punished some grievous crime. We have evident examples hereof in the scriptures. The eleven tribes of Israel in a good quarrel made war on the Benjamites, purposing to revenge the detestable crime that a few wicked knaves had horribly committed, wherein the whole tribe bare them out and upheld them, being partners thereby of their heinous offence: but twice the Israelites were put to the worse, and the wicked Benjamites had the upper hand in the battle[7]. In the time of Heli the Israelites minded to drive the tyrannous rule of the idolatrous Philistines out of their country; but they are slain, the ark of God is taken, and carried into the cities of their idolatrous enemies[8]. Likewise that excellent prince Josias is overthrown and slain by the Chaldees, because the Lord had purposed to punish and bring evil upon the whole people of Israel, which he would not have so holy a prince his servant to see with his eyes, to his sorrow and grief[9]. Whereby we have to gather, that the truth of religion is not to be esteemed by the victory or overthrow of any people, so that that religion should be true and right whose favourers have the upper hand, and that again be false and untrue whose professors and maintainers are put to the worse: for we must distinguish betwixt religion and the men or persons that keep that religion, which do for other causes suffer the Lord's visitation.

But all this admonisheth us, that the magistrate hath need of the great fear of God before his eyes, both in making and

War for profit.

They that have the juster quarrel are overcome of the unjust.

[7 Judg. xx.]   [8 1 Sam. iv.]
[9 2 Kings xxii. 20, and xxiii. 29.—"In his days Pharaoh Necho, king of *Egypt*," &c. P.]

repelling wars, lest while he goeth about to avoid the smould-ering coalpit, he hap to fall into the scalding limekiln[1]; or lest, while he supposeth to ease his shoulders of one evil, he doth, by the way whereby he sought ease, heap up either more or far greater evils.   Princes therefore must precisely look into, and throughly examine, the cause of wars, before they

The causes of war.

begin or take them in hand.   The causes are many, and of many sorts; but the chief are these that follow.   For either the magistrate is compelled to send aid and raise the siege of his enemy, which doth environ the garrisons that he hath appointed for the defence of some of his cities; because it were an offence, and part of parricide, to forsake and give over, against oath and honesty, his cities and garrisons that are in extremity : or else the magistrate of duty is compelled to make war upon men which are incurable, whom the very judgment of the Lord condemneth and biddeth to kill without pity or mercy.   Such were the wars as Moses had with the Madianites, and Josue[2] with the Amalechites.   Of that sort are the wars wherein such men are oppressed, as of invincible malice will both perish themselves and draw other to destruc-tion as well as themselves, with those also which, rejecting all justice and equity, do stubbornly go on to persist in their naughtiness.   Such were the Benjamites, which were destroyed by sword and fire of the other eleven tribes.   Such are at this day those arrogant and seditious rebels as trouble commonweals and kingdoms, as of old Absalom was in Israel, and Seba the son of Bochri; of whom mention is made in the second book of Samuel[3].

Wars taken in hand for the defence of religion.

Hereunto appertain the wars that are taken in hand for the defence of true religion against idolaters and enemies of the true and catholic faith.   They err, that are of opinion that no wars may be made in defence of religion.   The Lord, indeed, blamed Peter for striking with the sword, because he was an apostle ; but thereby, notwithstanding, he bade not the magistrate to be negligent in looking to religion, neither for-bad he him to defend and maintain the pureness of faith. For if it be lawful for the magistrate to defend with the sword the things of account, of which sort are liberty, wealth, chas-

[1 ne dum vitant carbonariam, incidant in calcariam, Lat.—Cf. Erasm. Adag. Chiliad. pp. 493, 4. Hanov. 1617.]

[2 a Saule, Lat.—*not* Joshua.]   [3 2 Sam. xx.]

tity, and his subjects' bodies; why should he not defend and revenge the things of greater account, and those which are of greatest weight? But there is nothing of more and greater weight than sincere and true religion is. There is, moreover, a manifest and flat commandment of God touching this matter to be seen in Deuteronomium. For the Lord commandeth that every city, within the jurisdiction of every magistrate, which departeth from God and the worship of God, should be set on with warriors, and utterly rased, if it revolted not from idolatry betimes. The place is extant in the thirteenth of Deut. But if the magistrate be commanded to punish apostates by war, then is it lawful for him by war to defend the Church in danger to be drawn by any barbarous prince from true religion unto false idolatry. Josue would by war have suppressed the Reubenites with their confederates for building an altar against God's commandment. Judas Machabeus fought for the people of God against the people and soldiers of king Antiochus, who purposed to tread down the Jewish religion, which at that time was the true worship of God, and perforce to make all men receive and profess his heathenish superstition. Likewise also Paul commended greatly those Jewish captains or judges, which by faith withstood and turned away foreign enemies' invasions. And Paul himself did war in Cyprus against Elymas the false prophet, and struck him with blindness: he addeth the reason why he struck him blind, which he fetcheth from the keeping of religion, and saith: "Ceasest thou not to pervert the right ways of the Lord? &c." Act. xiii. For the same Paul again forty men do lie in wait, supposing, if he were once made away, that a good part of the preaching of the gospel would then come to an end, and that thereby the Jewish religion (which, notwithstanding, was utterly false) should have been set up and maintained for truth. But Paul was not negligent to remedy this case, neither turned he the other cheek to have that stricken too; but earnestly and humbly requireth delivery and defence, which he requested not of a christian magistrate (when as yet there was none), but of a Roman centurion: neither did he once gainsay him, when he saw that he chose out four hundred footmen and seventy horsemen, whom he placed in order of battle array, to conduct him safely from Hierusalem to Antipatridis: and by that means was Paul, the vessel of election, preserved by an armed

Since he asked aid of heathens, he would a great deal sooner have required it at the hands of christian magistrates, if as then there had been any.

band of Italian soldiers[1]. Of the Armenians, whom Maximinus the emperor did tyrannously oppress, Eusebius in the ninth
book and eighth chapter of his Ecclesiastical History saith:
"The people of Armenia, having been long time both profitable and friends to the people of Rome, being at length compelled by Maximinus Cæsar to change the use of Christian
religion (whereunto the whole nation was most holily bent) into
the worship of idols, and to honour devils instead of God, of
friends became enemies, and of fellows adversaries; and preparing by force of arms to defend themselves against his
wicked edicts, do of their own accord make war upon him, and
put him often to much trouble and business[2]." Thus saith he.
It is lawful, therefore, for the magistrate to defend his people
and subjects against idolaters, and by war to maintain and
uphold true religion.

Like to this there is another cause why the magistrate
may take war in hand. For either some barbarous enemy
invadeth the people committed to thy charge, tearing and
spoiling them most cruelly, like a wolf in a flock of sheep;
when as notwithstanding thou didst not first provoke him
thereunto by injury, but also after his causeless beginning
thou hast offered equal conditions of peace to be made: in
such a case as this the magistrate is commanded to stand
forth like a lion, and to defend his subjects against the open
wrong of merciless cut-throats: (so did Moses, when he fought
against Arad, Sehon, and Og, kings of the Amorites[3]: so did
Josaphat, when he fought against the Ammonites and inhabitants of mount Seir[4]: so did David, when he understood[5] the
war made on him by the Syrians:) or else the magistrate
doth aid his confederates (for the magistrate may make league
with the nations about him, so that thereby nothing be done
against the word of God), when by tyrants they be wrongfully
oppressed. For so did Josue deliver the Gabionites from the

[1 Acts xxiii.—Romanorum militum, Lat.]

[2 Τούτοις προσεπανίσταται τῷ τυράννῳ ὁ πρὸς Ἀρμενίους πόλεμος, ἄνδρας
ἐξ ἀρχαίου φίλους τε καὶ συμμάχους Ῥωμαίων· οὓς καὶ αὐτοὺς Χριστιανοὺς
ὄντας, καὶ τὴν εἰς τὸ θεῖον εὐσέβειαν διὰ σπουδῆς ποιουμένους, ὁ θεομισὴς
εἰδώλοις θύειν καὶ δαίμοσιν ἐπαναγκάσαι πεπειραμένος, ἐχθροὺς ἀντὶ φίλων
καὶ πολεμίους ἀντὶ συμμάχων κατεστήσατο.—Euseb. Hist. Eccles. Lib. IX.
cap. 8.]

[3 Numb. xxi.]   [4 2 Chron. xx.]

[5 propellens, Lat.—2 Sam. viii.]

siege of their enemies, and Saul the men of Jabes Galaad, fighting for them against Nahas, a prince full of tyranny[6]. In such cases as these magistrates and princes do lawfully make war, and their soldiers and subjects do rightly obey them; yea, they do with great glory die a happy death, that die in so just a quarrel, as for the defence of religion, of the laws of God, of his country, wife, and children. They therefore that enter into warfare to sustain the troublesome toil of battle, must not set their minds upon gain or pleasure, wherein they look, when peril is past, to lie still and wallow : but justice, public peace, defence of truth and innocency, must be the mark for them all to shoot at : to the intent, when the wicked are vanquished, the victory obtained, and the enemies put to flight, slain out of hand, or brought to better order, that then religion may flourish, judgment and justice may be exercised, the Church upheld, the ceremonies, rites, ordinances, and discipline thereof maintained, study and learning cherished, the poor provided for, widows and children defended and cared for ; that all sorts may live in quiet peace, that old men in reverence, maidens in chastity, and matrons in honesty, may serve God, praise God, and worship God, without fear or danger. This was the mark whereto our fathers Abraham, Moses, Josue, David, and other valiant men of famous memory[7], did direct the eyes of their bodies and minds : upon this only their hearts were settled, so often as they warred and went to battle against ungodly tyrants in defence of the church and commonweal : to whom, and to all other valiant and godly soldiers, eternal praise is duly given of all the church and faithful saints. But to fearful and cowardly soldiers, to wicked, covetous, and blaspheming warriors, to riotous knaves, and unconstant traitors, by whose cowardice, gluttony, lust, and unnatural treason, excellent kingdoms do come to nought[8], and flourishing commonweals are quite overthrown, is reproach and infamy worthily due : for God himself hath cursed such knaves for evermore.

The commendation of war and warriors.

Therefore it is not lawful to make any war, unless it be against open enemies, and wicked men that are incurable. The wars are unjust, that men do make upon their own fellows,

Unjust wars.

[6 Josh. x. ; 1 Sam. xi.]

[7 denique beatæ recordationis patres nostros, Lat. P.]

[8 hodie, Lat., omitted ; at this day.]

against innocent persons, or people in whom there is hope of amendment. Those wars also are unjust, that are not begun by lawful means for matters of weight. All things must first be assayed, before it come to be tried out by battle. Other men's territories must not be desired: the liberty of other people or thine own subjects must not be repressed: thou must not follow any affection, which may withdraw or seduce thy mind; of which sort are desire of rule, covetousness, greediness of gifts, envy, and other affections like unto these. War is to commonweals a remedy indeed, but perilous and dangerous, even as lancing or cutting is to the members. The hand is poisoned, and the arm in danger to be envenomed too, whereby the whole man perhaps may be cast away: but yet thou cuttest not off thy hand until, when thou hast tried all other medicines, thou dost plainly perceive that no other means can remedy the sore but cutting off alone. Likewise, when all helps fail, then at the last let war begin; so yet, nevertheless, that the prince do remember to begin with war before all help and hope of recovery be utterly past [1].

The word of God hath made laws of war. For the word of God is so far off from finding fault with war begun upon a just quarrel, that it doth both make laws of war, and sheweth a number of examples of upright wars, of wise and worthy warriors. The laws of war are recited in the 20th chapter of Deuteronomy, both profitable and necessary, and therewithal so evident, that they need no words of mine to expound them. Moreover, in every place of the scripture these laws of war are still bidden to be kept. First of all, the chief and uppermost place must be given to religion in every camp and garrison: for the Lord himself hath appointed priests and ministers of true religion to attend and serve in wars. Secondarily, let upright laws be of force in camps abroad, as well as in cities at home: let soldiers live honestly, justly, and rightly, as order and discipline are wont to require when as they are in the city at home. For that saying cometh not of God, but of the devil, which is commonly spread abroad, Let laws in war be hushed and still [2]. Thirdly, let him that is chosen to be guide and general of the war be godly, just, holy, valiant, wise, and fortunate; as, among them of old, were Josue, David, Judas Machabeus, Constantine,

[1 ut meminerint tamen principes, Ne quid sero nimis, Lat.]
[2 Sileant inter arma leges, Lat.—See Cic. pro Mil.]

Theodosius[3], and many more.   To all this there must be
added a chosen band of tried men : for choice of soldiers
must be made, unless perhaps the army do consist in a troop
of bastards and unskilful men, of perjured and blaspheming
knaves, of cut-throats and rakehells, of drunkards and glut-
tons, and a beastly drove of filthy swine.   Victory consisteth
not in the multitude of men, but in the grace of God and
a chosen band.   The proverb is common which saith, " Where
a multitude is, there is confusion."   Great and innumerable
armies are a let to themselves very greatly ; as we do learn
by daily experience, and as examples of every age do testify
to us.   Moreover, loiterers in camps are always reproved.
Let the christian soldier, therefore, be idle at no time ; let
him ever be busy, and still doing something : let him be
courageous, faithful to his country, ready to take pains, obedient to his captains, fit to take time when occasion is offered,
and evermore occupied in warlike discipline ; no effeminate
milksop, but of manly stomach ; not cruel and merciless, but
severe and pitiful, as time requireth.   What he may preserve,
that let him not destroy.   But, above all things, let him not
forget or think scorn, both in peril and out of peril, evermore
to make his prayers and supplications to God his Saviour.
In God's name let him begin all things ; without God let him
attempt nothing : in adversity, and when he hath the overthrow,
let not his courage quail, nor his heart and hope forsake him ;
in prosperity let him not be puffed up with pride and arrogancy, but let him give thanks to God, and use the conquest
like a merciful victor : let him wholly depend upon God's helping hand, and desire nothing rather than the defence of the
commonweal, laws, religion, justice, and guiltless people.

The description of a christian soldier.

Many, I know, will marvel to see me require at the
hands of a soldier the things that seem to be enough, as the
common saying is, to be looked for of a right good and godly
man ; as though, indeed, that none could be soldiers but irreligious and naughty men.   Soldiers, I confess, are for the
most part such kind of fellows : but what fruit, I pray you,
reap we at this day of so evil seed?   The Turks overrun
and spoil us ; we are to all the heathen a jesting-stock to

[3 Mascelzer, Lat. ; omitted by the translator.—See Gibbon, Decl.
and Fall. chap. xxix. ; and Universal Hist. Ancient Hist. Vol. xvi. p. 473.
Lond. 1748. Book iv. chap. 5.]

laugh at; kingdoms decay and are made subject to devilish Mahometism, and every day we are wrapped in more mise-

What man-
ner of soldiers
the ancient
Christians
were in
times past.
ries than other[1]. But what kind of soldiers they of old were, which went to the war from out of the church or congrega-tion of the Christians, we may easily gather even by that one history, worthy the remembrance, which Tertullian to Scapula setteth down thus: "Marcus Aurelius also in his wars with the Germans, by the prayers which christian sol-diers made unto God, obtained showers of rain in that great drought. At what time have not droughts been turned away by our prayers and fastings? Then the people crying out for joy to the God of gods, and the emperor himself, under

The Latin
copy hath,
*Et qui solus
potens*,
by which I
think he
meant the
emperor.
the name of Jupiter, confessed the wonderful working of our God[2]." Thus much Tertullian. But Eusebius, in his Eccle-siastical History, hath more largely and fully set down the same history, and saith: "Histories report that Marcus Aure-lius, brother to Antoninus Cæsar, making war upon the Ger-mans and Sarmatians, when his army was in danger to be lost with drought, being at his wits' end because he knew not what way to seek for remedy in that distress, did at the last light upon a certain legion wherein christian soldiers were, whose prayers God heard, when they, as the manner of our men is, had upon their knees cried out unto him; so that on a sudden, when no man looked for it, with the pouring down of sufficient showers, the thirst of the army that then was in danger, for which the Christians had made supplica-tions, was presently quenched; but their enemies, that hovered there to have been their destruction, were stricken and scat-tered with thunder and fire in lightning from heaven: which deed is reported by heathen historiographers; but that it was obtained at the prayers of our men, they do not report: for with them the other miracles, which are done by our men, have no place of credit. But among our men Tertullian

---

[1 See Works of Becon, Parker Soc. ed. Vol. I. p. 239.]

[2 Marcus quoque Aurelius in Germanica expeditione christianorum militum orationibus ad Deum factis imbres in siti illa impetravit. Quando non geniculationibus et jejunationibus nostris etiam siccitates sunt depulsæ? Tunc et populus adclamans Deo deorum, qui solus potens, in Jovis nomine Deo nostro testimonium reddidit.—Tertul. ad Scapulam. cap. 4. pag. 162. Tom. III. ed. Semler. 1829. Bullinger's quotation reads: et qui solus potens.]

maketh mention hereof; and among the Greeks Apollinaris, Legio ful-
minea. who also affirmeth, that for the miracle of that notable deed that legion's name was changed by the emperor, and called The Legion of Thunder. Tertullian addeth, that the letters of Marcus the emperor are yet to be had, wherein the full and manifest truth of this matter is plainly declared[3]."

Hitherto Eusebius. Whereby we gather that christian soldiers of old were not only given to prayer, but to justice also, and holiness of living. For who knoweth not that James the apostle said, "The earnest prayer of a righteous man availeth much: Elias was a man under infirmities even as we are, and he prayed in his prayer, and the heavens gave rain, and the earth brought forth her fruit[4]?" It is most evident, therefore, that soldiers of old were very godly and religious men. Our soldiers at these days, because they are far from religion, yea, because they are enemies to true religion, do, instead of victory, suffer overthrows abroad, and loss and destruction of their cities at home. And worthily do commonweals suffer such plagues for trusting so much in such wicked soldiers. For to trust them is all one as if they should put

[3 Τούτου δὴ ἀδελφὸν Μάρκον Αὐρήλιον Καίσαρα λόγος ἔχει, Γερμανοῖς καὶ Σαρμάταις ἀντιπαρατεταττόμενον μάχῃ, δίψει πιεζομένης αὐτοῦ τῆς στρατιᾶς, ἐν ἀμηχανίᾳ γενέσθαι, τοὺς δὲ ἐπὶ τῆς Μελιτινῆς οὕτω καλουμένης λεγεῶνος στρατιώτας, διὰ πίστεως ἐξ ἐκείνου καὶ εἰς δεῦρο συνεστώσης, ἐν τῇ πρὸς τοὺς πολεμίους παρατάξει γόνυ θέντας ἐπὶ γῆν, κατὰ τὸ οἰκεῖον ἡμῖν τῶν εὐχῶν ἔθος, ἐπὶ τὰς πρὸς τὸν Θεὸν ἱκεσίας τραπέσθαι. Παραδόξου δὲ τοῖς πολεμίοις τοῦ τοιούτου δὴ θεάματος φανέντος, ἄλλό τι λόγος ἔχει παραδοξό- τερον ἐπικαταλαβεῖν αὐτίκα· σκηπτὸν μὲν εἰς φυγὴν καὶ ἀπώλειαν συνελαύ- νοντα τοὺς πολεμίους, ὄμβρον δὲ ἐπὶ τὴν τῶν τὸ θεῖον παρακεκληκότων στρατιάν, πᾶσαν αὐτὴν ἐκ τοῦ δίψους μέλλουσαν ὅσον οὔπω διαφθαρή- σεσθαι, ἀνακτώμενον. Ἡ δὲ ἱστορία φέρεται μὲν καὶ παρὰ τοῖς πόρρω τοῦ καθ᾽ ἡμᾶς λόγου συγγραφεῦσιν .... Τοῖς μὲν ἔξωθεν ἱστορικοῖς, ἅτε τῆς πίστεως ἀνοικείοις, τέθειται μὲν τὸ παράδοξον, οὐ μὴν καὶ ταῖς τῶν ἡμετέρων εὐχαῖς τοῦτο ὡμολογήθη γεγονέναι· τοῖς δέ γε ἡμετέροις, ἅτε ἀληθείας φί- λοις, ἁπλῷ καὶ ἀκακοήθει τρόπῳ τὸ πραχθὲν παραδέδοται. Τούτων δ᾽ ἂν εἴη καὶ Ἀπολινάριος, ἐξ ἐκείνου φήσας τὴν δι᾽ εὐχῆς τὸ παράδοξον πεποιη- κυῖαν λεγεῶνα οἰκείαν τῷ γεγονότι πρὸς τοῦ βασιλέως εἰληφέναι προσηγορίαν, Κεραυνοβόλον τῇ Ῥωμαίων ἐπικληθεῖσαν φωνῇ. Μάρτυς δὲ τούτων γένοιτ᾽ ἂν ἀξιόχρεως ὁ Τερτυλλιανός .... Γράφει δ᾽ οὖν καὶ αὐτὸς λέγων, Μάρκου τοῦ συνετωτάτου βασιλέως ἐπιστολὰς εἰσέτι νῦν φέρεσθαι, ἐν αἷς αὐτὸς μαρτυρεῖ ἐν Γερμανίᾳ ὕδατος ἀπορίᾳ μέλλοντα αὐτοῦ τὸν στρατὸν διαφθεί- ρεσθαι ταῖς τῶν Χριστιανῶν εὐχαῖς σεσῶσθαι.—Euseb. Hist. Eccles. Lib. v. cap. 5.]

[4 James v. 16—18.]

confidence in the very devils, whom these soldiers do, for the most part, exceed in all kind of filthiness, uncleanness, cruelty, and villainy.

Examples of war and captains out of the scripture.
But now the word of God doth set before our eyes an innumerable sort of examples almost of holy and upright wars, and of excellent kings and captains. Abraham, our father, setting forward with a very small army, pursueth the four most puissant kings or robbers of the world; he overthroweth and putteth them to flight; and, having recovered his people, and restored to them their substance again, he giveth the thanks to God, as to the author of that unlikely victory[1]. Moses and Josue destroyed about thirty-nine kings; they punished severely the unspeakable wickedness of all those nations; and planted the people committed to their charge in the land which God had promised to give them. The Judges of the people of Israel had notable wars against the heathens and infidels, whereby they brake the tyranny of those wicked men, unlawfully usurped among God's people, restoring them again to their liberty and religion. The prophet Samuel is here to be numbered among the notable captains of God's people. Jonathas, Saul's son, was a worthy captain, and a singular example of a godly man. Than David none was more excellent or worthy to be praised. In war he vanquished the Philistines, the Idumites, the Syrians, and a good part of the East beside; by war he revenged injuries; by war he maintained his liberty, and kept God's people from a number of mischiefs: and yet, notwithstanding, he that warred thus is said to be a man according to God's heart's desire, and the father of our Lord Jesus Christ touching his flesh or his humanity[2]. In David's posterity thou mayest find many excellent warriors and valiant captains, Abia, Asa, Josaphat, Amasia, Osia, Ezechias, and other more. Among these Judas Machabeus hath not the last nor least place of all, who fought very stoutly for the law, religion, and people of God, and died at the last in the midst of the battle, in defence of religion and his country quarrel. I will not add to these the examples of Constantine, Gratian, Theodosius, and other more that were excellent in feats of war. Of these and other writeth St Augustine in the end of his fifth book *de*

[1 Gen. xiv.]
[2 1 Sam. xiii. 14; Rom. i. 3.]

Civitate Dei[3], and Orosius very largely in the seventh book of his history unto the end of the 28th chapter[4]. This is sufficient for godly magistrates. Hitherto have I discoursed of war to be made by the magistrate, and the use of the sword in the magistrate's hand; touching which I gave some notes by the way in that sermon wherein I expounded the Fifth Commandment.

This being thus ended, I have now to prove that christian men may bear the office of a magistrate; which treatise I mean therefore to take in hand, because our mad-headed Anabaptists, and some other builders of a devised commonweal[5], by gainsaying that which hitherto we have alleged, do go about to prove that a Christian may not bear the office of a magistrate: their reason is, because Christians, as they say, may not strive in law, nor kill any man, nor recover by war things violently taken away, nor revenge any injury that is done unto them. And although these causes of theirs be answered every one in his fit and several place; yet will I briefly gather here together a few substantial arguments, by which a politic and christian man may understand, contrary to the madness and dreams of the Anabaptists, if he be called to bear rule and authority, that then he both may, and of duty ought, to serve the Lord his God in taking upon him and executing the office of a magistrate. For, whereas they feign that the doctrine of the gospel doth utterly cut off all kind of defence, and whatsoever else belongeth to the defence of christian men's goods and bodies, that is nothing so, and they are deceived as far as heaven is wide: for the truth doth teach us clean contrary.

For whatsoever things are ordained by God for a means of men's safeguard and good estate, they are so far from misbecoming and being unseemly for a christian man, if he

A christian man may be a magistrate.

Respublica Utopiana.

[3 Chap. xxv. "De prosperitatibus, quas Constantino Imp. Christiano Deus contulit," and xxvi. "de fide et pietate Theodosii Augusti."—Opp. Par. 1531. Tom. v. fol. 69. P.]

[4 a 28 cap. ad finem usque, Lat.—Pauli Orosii adv. Paganos Histor. Libri Septem. Mogunt. 1615. In the chapters of the 7th Book from the 28th are related the successes of Constantine, Gratian, Theodosius, &c.]

[5 Utopianæ reipublicæ extructores, Lat.—See Preface of Hooker's Eccles. Pol. Vol. I. p. 183. Oxf. 1820.]

use them and apply himself unto them, that, if he refuse and neglect, he cannot rightly be called a true Christian. For the first and greatest care of every Christian is, by all means that he may, to set forward and maintain the health and safeguard of all sorts of men. But the magistrate is not ordained by any man, but by God himself, for the health and wealth of all mankind; as it is expressly witnessed by the prophets and apostles, but by Paul especially in the 13th to the Romans. Who then cannot thereby perceive that a Christian may praiseworthily execute a magistrate's office?

Furthermore, no man will deny, I know, that a christian man's faith is, not in words only, but in deeds also, to give a proof of justice and mercy, by all means to care for public peace and tranquillity, to do judgment with justice, to defend the fatherless, widows, and children, and to deliver poor oppressed people. Neither doth he contemn, flee from, nor reject, occasion, places, and means, by which he may put those good works in ure. And therefore a Christian refuseth not the place or office of a magistrate: for the magistrate's office is to do judgment with justice, and to provide for public peace.

Moreover, it is undoubtedly true, as before we have declared, that Moses, Samuel, Josue, and David, are not excluded from the name of Christianity: but since they were in authority and bare the names of magistrates, what let is there, I pray you, why a true christian man may not[1] bear the office of a magistrate in his commonweal? What may be thought of this, moreover, that in the new Testament certain notable men are well reported of, who, when they were in authority, were not put beside their offices because they were Christians and of a sound religion? Touching Joseph of Arimathea, thus we read in Luke: "And, behold, there was a man named Joseph, a counsellor," (Mark saith, "a noble Honestus senator[2]), who was a good man and a just; the same had not senator. consented to the counsel and deed of them; which was of Arimathea, a city of the Jews, which waited also for the kingdom of God[3]." Mark here, I beseech you, how notable a testimony this man hath here. Joseph is a counsellor or

[1 vel hodie, Lat., omitted; at this day too.]

[2 The Vulgate has, "nobilis decurio;" but "honestus senator," which Bullinger adopts, is the rendering of Erasmus in Mark xv. 43.]

[3 Luke xxiii. 50, 51; Mark xv. 43.]

senator; yea, and that more is, a noble senator too: he sat in the senate, and among those judges which did condemn our Saviour Christ; but, because he consented not to their deed and judgment, he is acquited as guiltless of that horrible murder. The same is said to have been a good man and a just, and of the number of them that look for the kingdom of God; that is, of the number of those which of Christ are called Christians: and yet, nevertheless, he was a counsellor or senator, and that too[4] in the city of Jerusalem. A Christian therefore may lawfully bear the office of a magistrate. Hereunto belong the examples of the Æthiopian treasurer, Acts viii.; of Cornelius the centurion, Acts x.; and of Erastus the chamberlain[5] of Corinth, Rom. xvi. 2 Tim. iv. But our desire is to have the Anabaptists prove and declare out of the scriptures that which they object here, in saying that these men, being once converted to the faith, did straightway put off their robes of estate, and lay aside their magistrate's sword[6]. For we have a little before, by the words of St Augustine upon John Baptist's answer[7], (who did himself also preach the gospel,) already proved, that the soldiers that were baptized were not put beside their office, nor commanded by John to give over armour and cease to be soldiers.

They object, again, that the Lord conveyed himself privily away, when the people were minded to have made him a king[8]: which, say they, he would not have done, but because by his example he would commend humility to all Christian people; and, as it were, thereby to command them, not to suffer the charge to rule any commonweal to be laid on their necks. They add, moreover, these sayings of the Lord: "My kingdom is not of this world." Again: "Kings of nations have dominion over them; but ye shall not be so[9]." But they understand not that the cause, why the Lord conveyed himself away, was for the fond purpose of the foolish people, which went about, by making him a king, not to do

The Lord conveyeth himself away, while the people would have made him a king.

[4] et manet, Lat.]

[5] quæstor ærarius, Lat.—Erasmus' rendering.]

[6] deposuisse trabeam et gladium, Lat.]

[7] See page 372.]

[8] John vi. 15.—creare et salutare regem, Lat.]

[9] John xviii. 36; Luke xxii. 25.]

the will of God, but, being blinded with affections, to seek to bring those things to pass that were for the ease and filling of their bellies. For insomuch as he had fed them miraculously a little before, therefore they thought that he would be a king for their purpose, who was able to give his subjects meat without any cost or labour at all. Furthermore, our Lord came not to reign on the earth after the manner of this world, as the Jews imagined, and as Pilate feared, who dreamed the Messias should reign as Salomon did: and for that cause the Lord doth rightly say, "My kingdom is not of this world." For he is ascended into heaven, and sitteth at the right hand of his Father, having subdued all kings to himself, and all the world beside, wherein he reigneth by his word and his Spirit, and which he shall come to judge in the end of the world. And although Christ denieth that his kingdom is of this world, yet, notwithstanding, he never denied that kings and princes should come out of the world into the church, to serve the Lord therein, not as men alone, but as kings and men of authority. But kings cannot otherwise serve the Lord as kings, but by doing the things for which they are called kings[1]. And unless that Christians, when they are once made kings, should continue in their office and govern kingdoms according to the rule and laws of Christ, how, I beseech you, should Christ be called "King of kings, and Lord of Lords[2]?" Therefore, when he said, "Kings of nations have dominion over them, but so shall not ye be;" he spake to his apostles, who strove among themselves for the chief and highest dignity: as if he should have said, Princes, which have dominion in the world, are not by my doctrine displaced of their seats, nor put beside their thrones; for the magistrate's authority is of force still in the world, and in the church also. The king or magistrate shall reign; but so shall not ye: ye shall not reign, ye shall not be princes, but teachers of the world and ministers of the churches. Thus briefly I have answered to the Anabaptists' objections, which in other places also I have many times confuted somewhat more largely. By this that here I have said, I think I have sufficiently proved, that a christian man can not only, but ought of duty also, to take upon him the office of a magistrate, if it be lawfully offered unto him.

My kingdom is not of this world.

But so shall not ye.

[1 See page 367.] [2 Rev. xix. 16.]

Now, before I make an end of the discourse of this place, I will briefly add what the duty of subjects is, and what every man doth owe to his magistrate. First of all, the subjects' duty is, to esteem honestly, reverently, and honourably, not vilely nor disdainfully, of their magistrates or princes. Let them reverence and honour them as the deputies and ministers of the eternal God. Let them abroad also give them the honour that is usually accustomed in every kingdom and country. It is a foul thing for subjects to behave themselves undecently towards their lords and men of authority. But a false, a light, or ill opinion, once conceived, breedeth a contempt of the things and persons, touching whom that opinion is once taken up. Some evident testimonies of scripture, therefore, must be gathered and graffed in every man's heart, that thereby a just estimation and worthy authority of magistrates and officers may be bred and brought up in all people's minds. Here, by the way, let princes and magistrates take heed to themselves, that by a spotted and unseemly life they make not themselves contemptible and laughing-stocks, and so by their own default lose all their authority among the common people. The Lord our God, verily, vouchethsafe to attribute his own name to the princes and magistrates of the people, and to call them gods. Exod. xxii.; Psalm lxxxii. The apostles called them the deputies and ministers of God. 1 Peter ii.; Rom. xiii. But who will not think well of gods, and them which are the deputies and ministers of God, by whom God worketh the wealth of the people? He that despiseth him that is sent, despiseth him that sendeth[3]. He that honoureth the deputy seemeth to give more honour to him that appointed the deputy than to him that is the deputy. Moreover, Salomon in the sixteenth of his Proverbs saith: " Prophecy is in the lips of the king; therefore his heart shall not go wrong in judgment[4]." And in the eighth of the Preacher: " I must keep the king's commandment because of the oath that I have made to God for the same[5]." Again, Proverbs xxiv.: " My son, fear thou the Lord and the king, and keep no company with them that

Of the duty of subjects.

[3 Luke x. 16.]
[4 Prov. xvi. 10.—divinatio, Lat.]
[5 Eccles. viii. 2.—et rationem habere juramenti Dei, Lat.]

slide back from the fear of them[1]: for their destruction shall rise suddenly." And Paul said: "Whosoever resisteth the power, resisteth the ordinance of God; but they that resist shall receive judgment to themselves[2]." Of this sort I have rehearsed certain testimonies in the exposition of the fifth precept.

Secondarily, let subjects pray for their princes and magistrates, that the Lord may give them wisdom, knowledge, fortitude, temperance, justice, upright severity, clemency, and all other requisite virtues, and that he will vouchsafe to lead them in his ways, and to preserve them from all evil; that we may live under them in this world in peace and honesty. This doth Paul require at the hands of subjects, in the second chapter of his first epistle to Timothy, and Jeremy, in the twenty and ninth of his prophecy. I have in another place recited their very words; therefore at this time I let them pass. The minds of many men are herein very slow and careless, and that is the cause many times why they feel the things that willingly they would not, and bear the burdens, with grief enough, that otherwise they should not; and worthily too: for if they would but do their duty willingly, in praying for their magistrate earnestly, their case undoubtedly would be far better than it is. But how fervent a desire they in the primitive church had to pray for their magistrate, we may gather even by these words of Tertullian, in the thirtieth chapter of his Apology: "We pray always," saith he, "for all emperors, desiring God to give them long life, a sure reign, a safe house, valiant armies, faithful counsellors, honest subjects, a quiet world, and whatsoever else a man or emperor may desire[3]."

Obedience to magistrates' laws.

Let the people also obey the good and upright laws of their princes or magistrates; yea, let subjects obey them holily, reverently, and with a devout mind; not obeying their laws as the laws of men, but as the laws of the ministers and

[1 Qui defectores sunt, Lat.] [2 Rom. xiii. 2.]
[3 Precantes sumus omnes semper pro omnibus imperatoribus, vitam illis prolixam, imperium securum, domum tutam, exercitus fortes, senatum fidelem, populum probum, orbem quietum, et quæcunque hominis et Cæsaris vota sunt.—Tertul. Apol. cap. xxx. Tom. v. p. 62. ed. Semler.]

deputies of God himself: for Peter biddeth us obey them for the Lord; and Paul saith, "We must not obey them for anger only, but for conscience sake also[4];" that is, we must not obey the magistrate only for fear, lest our contempt and disobedience do breed our punishment; but we must obey him, lest we sin against God himself, and so our own conscience do argue our wickedness. But in the fifth commandment I proved by testimonies and examples out of the scriptures, that we ought not to obey godless magistrates, so oft as they command any wicked thing, which is flatly contrary to the word of God. The apostles and faithful men of the primitive church did choose rather to be shut up in prison, to be sent in exile, to be spoiled of their substance, to be cast to wild beasts, to be killed with the sword, to be burnt with fire, and to be strangled, than to obey any wicked commandments. That blessed martyr, bishop Polycarpus, answered the Roman proconsul, and said: "We are taught to give to princes, and to the powers that are of God, such honour as is not contrary to true religion[5]." And St John Chrysostom said to Gaina: "It is not lawful for a godly emperor to assay any thing contrary to God's commandments[6]."

Lastly, let subjects pay tribute to their magistrates; yea, let them, if necessity so require, not stick to bestow their bodies and lives for the preservation of their magistrate and country, as I have already taught you in the fifth commandment. The Lord in the gospel doth simply say, "Give to God that which belongeth to God, and to Cæsar that which belongeth to Cæsar[7]." They therefore are worthily blamed, that pinch, grudge at, or defraud the magistrate of any part of his tribute. Taxes and tributes are due to the magistrate, as the hire of his labour, and as it were the sinews of public tranquillity and commonweal. For "who goeth to warfare

---

[4 1 Pet. ii. 13; Rom. xiii. 5.]

[5 Πολύκαρπος ἔφη ... δεδιδάγμεθα ... ἀρχαῖς καὶ ἐξουσίαις ὑπὸ Θεοῦ τεταγμέναις τιμὴν κατὰ τὸ προσῆκον τὴν μὴ βλάπτουσαν ἡμᾶς ἀπονέμειν.— Euseb. Hist. Eccles. Lib. iv. cap. 15.]

[6 Ὁ δὲ μέγας Ἰωάννης ἀντέλεγε φάσκων, οὐκ ἐξεῖναι βασιλεῖ τῶν θείων κατατολμᾶν, εὐσεβεῖν γε προαιρουμένῳ.—Theodorit. Eccles. Hist. Lib. v. cap. 32. ed. Reading. Cantab. 1720, p. 232. Bullinger gives the history more at length in his treatise de Script. Sac. Author. &c. fol. 123. Tigur. 1538.]

[7 Luke xx. 25.]

of his own proper cost[1]?" Every man liveth by that labour
wherein he is occupied. The prince taketh pains in governing the commonweal, and preserving it in peace; he neglect-
eth his own private and household business, whereby he should
live, and provide things necessary for himself and his family,
by looking and attending on his country's affairs: it were
against reason, therefore, but that he should be fed and main-

Common cost or treasures. tained upon the public treasure and cost of his country. It
is requisite, also, that kingdoms and commonweals be suffici-
ently furnished with money and substance to help in distress,
either of war, famine, fire, and other miseries[2]; or else to the
setting up again of men fallen into poverty, or putting away
of greater calamities. I say nothing now touching the keeping in reparation of common buildings, as the city-walls, bul-
warks, trenches, ditches, gates, bridges, highways, wells, con-
duits, judgment-halls, and market-places, with many more of
the same sort. There are also certain common persons, as
serjeants, watchmen, and such like, which are to be nourished
and maintained of the common cost and treasury; and, unless that money be still at hand and in readiness, there can
no kingdom nor any commonweal stand long in assurance.
They, therefore, that grudge to pay tribute deny the hire of
the magistrate's labour, and go the next way to work to subvert the commonweal, and to bring it to nought. The men
that in the commonweal's affairs (as some of custom be) are
negligent and careless, sin not against any one lord, but
against the whole commonweal: and therefore thou mayest
see that such slothful workmen are seldom times enriched with
the good blessings of God.

But now here, by the way, all magistrates and princes
must be admonished to love the people subject to their
charge and government, to bear with them bountifully, and
not to nip them with immoderate exactions: which is easily
done, if they themselves will be thrifty, and keep themselves
moderately from riotous gluttony and over sumptuous pride.
Let a good prince consider what a sin it is to have his
palace abound in riotousness and surfeiting, while his cities
and towns are tormented and pined with famine and hunger.
Let magistrates consider that tributes and subsidies are not
the private goods of them in authority, but the public sub-

[1 1 Cor. ix. 7.]   [2 calamitatibus publicis, Lat.]

stance of the whole commonweal. God hateth pillers and
robbers. God abhorreth immoderate exactions. God curseth
polling tyrants; but blesseth profitable and moderate magistrates. But, in peace and war, agreement and concord are
much more available than money unjustly gotten; and stronger
is that kingdom, and firmer that commonweal, which is upheld
by the love and agreement of the prince and commonalty,
although the common treasure there be very small, than that
country or city which hath innumerable riches heaped up
together and wrung out of the citizens' entrails, when as
continual grudge and ill-will makes the prince and people at
continual variance. I say no more here than the very truth
is; experience of all ages is a witness that it is so.

Thus much hitherto have I laid down before your eyes,
dearly beloved, as briefly as I could, touching the magistrate;
taking occasion upon the sixth commandment, "Thou shalt
not kill," and declaring to what end and purpose God did
ordain him, what his duty is toward his subjects, and what
his subjects' duty is toward him. Now let us pray, and beseech the Lord that he will grant both to magistrates and
subjects to walk worthily in their vocations.

OF THE THIRD PRECEPT OF THE SECOND TABLE, WHICH IS IN ORDER THE SEVENTH OF THE TEN COMMANDMENTS: THOU SHALT NOT COMMIT ADULTERY OF WEDLOCK; AGAINST ALL INTEMPERANCE; OF CONTINENCY.

THE TENTH SERMON.

THE nearest to our life and body is every one's several
mate in wedlock; for by wedlock two bodies are joined
together[3], and are made one: for the Lord said, "And two
shall be one flesh[4]." In this third precept, therefore, which is
next after the forbidding of murder, commandment is given
for the holy keeping of honourable wedlock, and for the true

[3 conjugio enim conjunguntur, Lat. P.]
[4 Gen. ii. 24; 1 Cor. vi. 16.]

sanctifying of the body against adulteries, wandering lusts, and all incontinency.   Wedlock is prepared to this end and purpose, that honesty and chastity may flourish among good men, and children may be brought up in the fear of the Lord. This commandment again is briefly expressed in as few

The seventh precept.

words as may be : " Thou shalt not commit adultery[1]."   In the exposition of this commandment, by the help of God's good Spirit, I will first speak of holy matrimony; then, of adultery; thirdly, I will shew you what is contained under the name of adultery ; and lastly, I will make an end with a treatise of continency.

What wedlock is.

Wedlock, which is also called matrimony, is an alliance or holy joining together of man and woman, coupled and brought into one by mutual consent of them both, to the intent that they, using all things in common betwixt themselves, may live in chastity, and train up their children in the fear of the Lord. The gospel verily calleth wedlock a joining together which God hath made: for Christ said, " What God hath joined together, let no man separate[2]." Neither is it lawful to make any other the author of matrimony than God himself. God did, by the mean and ministry of his angels and chosen men, appoint other good and necessary ordinances for mankind's commodity ; but he himself did immediately, without the ministry of any person, ordain matrimony ; he himself did establish and ratify it with laws for the purpose; he himself did couple the first married folks ; and he, being the true high priest indeed, did himself bless the couple then whom he did join together.

The excellency or dignity of marriage.

By this we may easily gather the excellent dignity of marriage or matrimony. For God did ordain it; yea, he ordained it in paradise, when man as yet was free from all kind of calamities. Adam, when he was in the great felicity of paradise, seemed not yet to live commodiously nor sweetly enough, except a wife were given to be joined unto him. " It is not good," saith God, " for man to be alone ; I will make him a helper to tarry or dwell with him[3]." For God brought to Adam all living creatures, which he had created, for him to name them : but among them all there was no-

---

[1 Exod. xx. 14.—duobus exprimitur verbis, Non mœchaberis, Lat.]
[2 Matt. xix. 6.]
[3 Gen. ii. 18.—adjutorium, quod ei cohabitet, Lat.]

thing that Adam had lust unto; his mind and nature did utterly abhor to be coupled with any of them. God therefore, casting Adam into a dead sleep, doth out of his side, as he slept, frame up a woman; which so soon as Adam set his eye upon, when she was brought unto him by God who had made her, he straightway crieth, that this was such a one as he desired, that this was such a one as he could love, and wherewith his nature could very well agree. "This now," saith he, "is bone of my bones, and flesh of my flesh." I have found, saith he, I have found an help fit for me, which hath part of my flesh, of my blood, and my very substance. From hence riseth and yet remaineth that natural proneness of men toward women: when, on the other side, overthwart mingling and meddling of cursed men with beasts, contrary to man's nature, was long ago destroyed by fire; which shewed that God did abhor it. The Lord moreover said: "A man shall forsake his father and his mother, and cleave to his wife, and two shall be one flesh[4]." But in the exposition of the fifth commandment we perceived, how much God doth set by the love and good-will of children to their parents, and what a charge he giveth to children to honour them. It must needs be, therefore, that wedlock is a most heavenly ordinance, since it is preferred before the honouring of parents: and yet, nevertheless, it is so preferred, as that, by the law of matrimony, the precept for the honour due to parents may not be abolished; but that thereby married folks may know to behave themselves so, if their parents go about to breed discord betwixt them and their spouses, that then they suffer not themselves for their parents' words to be severed, but in all things else to honour them as they should.

The holy patriarchs kept the law of matrimony, and reverenced wedlock very devoutly[5]. For no small parcel of the first and most excellent book of the bible, called Genesis, is spent in rehearsing the marriages of holy men. Neither is Moses, the peerless servant of God ashamed to make mention of the business and works of wedlock as pure and excel-

[4 Gen. ii. 24; Mark x. 7, 8.]

[5 Nec puduit sanctum dei Spiritum multis recensere et describere matrimonia ipsorum, Lat. Nor was the Holy Spirit of God ashamed to recount and describe their marriages in many words.—Omitted by the translator.]

lent, which seem to many at this day to be foul and filthy. Christ himself (who, being the very natural Son of God, was himself born in wedlock, although of a pure and uncorrupted virgin) did honour and commend the knot of matrimony, while he did vouchsafe to shew his first miracle at a wedding; which was such a miracle, as did declare that the Lord is able to make the bitterness of marriage sweet, and the scarcity thereof abound with plenty. As the apostles were married men, according to the examples of the patriarchs, kings, princes, priests, and prophets[1]; so Paul, the chief of all the apostles, crieth out and saith : " Wedlock is honourable among all and the bed undefiled: but whoremongers and adulterers God will judge[2]." He saith, that wedlock is honourable among all men: he meaneth, all nations; for very few people shall you find that do not greatly commend the state of marriage. Xenophon thinketh, that among all God's ordinances scant any one can be found that is more commendable or profitable than wedlock is[3]. Musonius, Hierocles[4], and other ancient sages think marriage to be so necessary to live well and conveniently, that the life of man without marriage seemeth to be maimed. Even they (the heathens I mean) do make the evils and discommodities of marriage to consist in the married folks, and not in marriage. For marriage of itself is good; but many use not well the thing that is good, and therefore they feel the smart of their foul abuse worthily. For who knoweth not, that the fault of drunkenness is not to be referred to wine, which is the good and wholesome creature

[1 Bullinger, in his treatise de Scriptur. Authorit. et de Episcop. Instit. et Funct. establishes this statement by Euseb. Eccles. Hist. Lib. III. cap. 30, and Lib. v. cap. 24, and Lib. VIII. cap. 10; and Tripart. Hist. Lib. I. cap. 10, and Lib. IX. cap. 38. See also Jewel's Works, pp. 882, 3, and Original Letters, Vol. I. pp. 116, 146, and Becon's Works, Vol. III. p. 235. Parker Soc. ed.]

[2 Hebr. xiii. 4.]

[3 Ἐμοὶ γάρ τοι, ἔφη φάναι, καὶ οἱ θεοὶ, ὦ γύναι, δοκοῦσι πολὺ διεσκεμμένως μάλιστα τὸ ζεῦγος τοῦτο συντεθεικέναι, ὃ καλεῖται θῆλυ καὶ ἄρρεν, ὅπως ἔτι ὠφελιμώτατον ᾖ αὐτῷ εἰς τὴν κοινωνίαν.—Xenoph. Œcon. cap. vii. p. 39. Tom. v. ed. Schneider. Oxon. 1813.]

[4 Ὥστε ὁ ἀναιρῶν ἐξ ἀνθρώπων γάμον ἀναιρεῖ μὲν οἶκον, ἀναιρεῖ δὲ πόλιν, ἀναιρεῖ δὲ σύμπαν τὸ ἀνθρώπειον γένος. Musonius.—οἶκός τε ἡμιτελὴς μὲν τῷ ὄντι ὁ τοῦ ἀγάμου, &c.—Hierocles ap. Stobæi Floril. ed. Gaisford. Oxon. 1822. Vol. III. pp. 8, 10.]

of God, but to the excessive bibbing and over-great greediness of man, which abuseth God's good creature? "That which cometh out of the heart of man," saith the Lord in the gospel, "and not that which goeth in by the mouth, defileth the man[5]." Hereunto belongeth that saying of Paul, the apostle of Christ, where he attributeth sanctification to wedlock ; "for the bed," saith he, "is undefiled :" and in another place he testifieth, that "the unbelieving husband is sanctified by the believing wife[6] :" he affirmeth also, that children born in wedlock are holy or clean. Moreover, the same Paul maketh Christ an example of love betwixt man and wife, and shadoweth the mysteries of Christ and the church by the colour of wedlock: he figureth, I say, a heavenly thing by an holy type that God doth allow[7]. Whereupon in another place the same apostle doth say, that their doctrine is a very "doctrine of devils," which forbid men to marry[8]. And so, consequently, it followeth, that that is an heavenly doctrine, proceeding from God, which permitteth marriage freely to all men, and doth commend and reverence it.

The excellency and dignity of matrimony being thus understood, let us now seek out and look on the causes for which God hath ordained marriage for men to embrace. God, according to his natural goodness, directeth all his ordinances to the great good and abundant commodity of mortal men : and therefore it followeth, that he ordained matrimony for the preservation of mankind, to the end that man's life might be pleasant, sweet, and thoroughly furnished with joys suffi- cient. But all these causes may be reduced into the number of three. First, God himself doth say, "It is not good for man to be alone ; let us make him an help therefore to be before him," or to dwell with him[9]. So, then, the first cause why wedlock was instituted is man's commodity, that thereby the life of man might be the pleasanter and more commodious; for Adam seemed not to live half happily nor sweetly enough, unless he had a wife to join himself unto : which wife is not in the scriptures called an impediment or necessary evil, as certain poets and beastly men who hated women have fool-

The causes of marriage.

[5 Matt. xv. 11, 17, 18.]
[6 1 Cor. vii. 14.—intercedente matrimonio, Lat. ; omitted.]
[7 Eph. v. 22, &c.]   [8 1 Tim. iv. 1, 3.]
[9 Gen. ii. 18.]

The wife is
the arm of
her husband.
ishly jangled; but she is the help or arm of the man. Antipater, an heathen writer, *in Sermone de Nuptiis*, doth
wonderfully agree with this saying of the scripture, and
expresseth plainly what kind of help and what manner of arm
the wife is to her husband. "Whosoever," saith he, "hath
not had trial of wife and children, he is utterly ignorant of
true mutual good-will. Love in wedlock is mutually shewed,
when man and wife do not communicate wealth, children, and
hearts alone, as friends are wont to do; but have their bodies
in common also, which friends cannot do. And therefore
Euripides, laying aside the deadly hate that he bare to
women, writ these verses in commendation of marriage:

> The wife that gads not, gigglot[1] wise,
> With every flirting gill[2],
> But honestly doth keep at home,
> Not set to gossip still,
> Is to her husband in his cares
> A passing sweet delight;
> She heals his sickness all, and calls
> Again his dying sprite.
> By fawning on his angry looks
> She turns them into smiles;
> And keeps her husband's secrets close,
> When friends work wily guiles.

"For like as a man, having one hand or one foot, if by any
means he get himself another, may thereby the more easily
lay hold on what he listeth, or go whither he will; even so
he that hath married a wife shall more easily enjoy the
healthful pleasures and profitable commodities of this present
life: for married folks for two eyes have four, and for two
hands as many more, which being joined together, they may
the more easily dispatch their handy business. Again, when
the one's two hands are wearied, the hands of the other supply
their room, and keep their work in a forwardness still.
Marriage therefore, which, instead of one member, is by
increase compact of twain, is better able to pass through the
course of this world than the single and unwedded life[3]."

[1 gigglot: a wanton; a lascivious girl.—Johnson's Dict.; Shakspeare, Measure for Measure, Act v. Sc. 1.]

[2 gill, (from *gillian*, the old English way of writing Julian, or Ju-
liana): the appellation of a woman in ludicrous language.—Ibid.]

[3 Συμβέβηκε δὲ καὶ τὸν μὴ πεῖραν ἐσχηκότα γαμετῆς γυναικὸς καὶ

Thus much out of Antipater. Hierocles also in his book *De Nuptiis* saith: "To live with a woman is very profitable, even beside the begetting of children: for, first, she doth welcome us home, that are tired abroad with labour and travail; she entertaineth us serviceably, and doeth all she may to recreate our weary minds; she maketh us forget all sorrow and sadness: for the troublesome cases of our life, and generally of care and business, while we are occupied in matters abroad, in bargaining in the country, or among our friends, are not easily suffered to be troubled with our domestical and household affairs; but when we have dispatched them, and are once returned to our wives at home, so that our minds are at quiet, and we restored to our ease and liberty, then are our cumbersome businesses well lightened and eased, whereby they cease to trouble us any longer. Neither is a wife troublesome undoubtedly, but lighteneth things that are troublesome to us; for there is nothing so heavy that a man and wife, living in concord, are not able to bear, especially if they be both willing to do their endeavour[4]." And so forth.

τέκνων ἄγευστον εἶναι τῆς ἀληθινωτάτης καὶ γνησίου εὐνοίας.... Οὐ γὰρ μόνον τῆς οὐσίας καὶ τῶν φιλτάτων πᾶσιν ἀνθρώποις τέκνων καὶ τῆς ψυχῆς, ἀλλὰ καὶ τῶν σωμάτων οὗτοι μόνοι κοινωνοῦσι.... καὶ ὁ Εὐριπίδης εἰς ταῦτα ἀποβλέψας, καὶ ἀποθέμενος τὴν ἐν τῷ γράφειν μισογυνίαν, ταῦτ᾽ εἴρηκεν·

Γυνὴ γὰρ ἐν νόσοισι καὶ κακοῖς πόσει
ἥδιστόν ἐστι, δώματ᾽ ἢν οἰκῇ καλῶς,
ὀργήν τε πραΰνουσα καὶ δυσθυμίας
ψυχὴν μεθιστᾶσ᾽· ἡδὺ καὶ ἀπάται φίλων....

Ὁμοιότατον γάρ ἐστιν, ὡς εἴ τις μίαν ἔχων χεῖρα ἑτέραν ποθὲν προσλάβοι, ἢ ἕνα πόδα ἔχων ἕτερον ἀλλαχόθεν ἐκτήσατο. Ὡς γὰρ οὗτος πολὺ ἂν ῥᾷον καὶ βαδίσαι οὗ θέλοι, καὶ προσαγάγοιτο· οὕτως ὁ γυναῖκα εἰσαγόμενος ῥᾷον ἀπολήψεται τὰς κατὰ τὸν βίον σωτηρίους καὶ συμφερούσας χρείας. Ἀντὶ γοῦν δύο ὀφθαλμῶν χρῶνται τέσσαρι· καὶ ἀντὶ δύο χειρῶν ἑτέραις τοσαύταις, αἷς καὶ ἀθρόως πράττοι ἂν ῥᾷον τὸ τῶν χειρῶν ἔργον. Διὸ καὶ ἐὰν αἱ ἕτεραι κάμνοιεν, ταῖς ἑτέραις ἂν θεραπεύοιτο· καὶ τὸ σύνολον δύο γεγονὼς ἀνθ᾽ ἑνός, μᾶλλον ἂν ἐν τῷ βίῳ κατορθῷ.—Antipater ap. Stobæi Floril. Vol. III. pp. 17—19.]

[4 Ἔπειτα καὶ πρὸ γενέσεως τέκνων λυσιτελὴς ἡ μετὰ γυναικὸς συμβίωσις. Πρῶτον μὲν γὰρ ἀποτετριμμένους τοῖς θυραίοις καμάτοις ὑποδέχεται θεραπευτικῶς ἀναλαμβάνουσα, καὶ μετ᾽ ἐπιμελείας ἀνακτωμένη πάσης· ἔπειτα τῶν ὄντων δυσχερῶν ἐν τῇ διανοίᾳ λήθην ἐντίθησι. Τὰ γὰρ σκυθρωπὰ τοῦ βίου, περὶ μὲν τὴν ἀγοράν, ἢ τὸ γυμνάσιον, ἢ τὸ χωρίον, ἢ καθόλου πάσης μερίμνης ἀσχολίας, καὶ περὶ τοὺς φίλους τε καὶ συνήθεις διατρίβουσιν ἡμῖν, οὐκ ἔστι πρόχειρα τοῖς ἀναγκαίοις ἐπιπροσθούμενα περισπασμοῖς· ἀνεθεῖσι

The begetting and bringing up of children.

The second cause why matrimony was ordained is the begetting of children for the preservation of mankind by increase, and the bringing of them up in the fear of the Lord: for the Lord blessed Adam and Eva, saying, "Increase and multiply, and replenish the earth." Paul the Apostle in his Epistle to Titus saith: "Speak to the elder women, that they may teach honest things, that they may make the younger women to be sober-minded, to love their husbands, to love their children, to be discreet housekeepers, good, obedient to their husbands." And again, to Timothy: "Adam was not deceived, but the woman was seduced; notwithstanding, through bearing of children she shall be saved, if they continue in faith, and charity, and holiness with modesty[1]." But the begetting of children were altogether unprofitable, if they were not well brought up; for she that loveth her children indeed doth bring them up in the fear of the Lord: which bringing up is no small commodity to the commonweal and church of God. The glory also and worship of God is greatly augmented, when as by wedlock there doth spring up a great number of men that acknowledge, call upon, and worship God as they ought to do.

The bed in wedlock undefiled.

The third cause why matrimony was ordained the Apostle Paul expresseth in these words: "To avoid whoredom, let every man have his own wife, and every woman her own husband. It were good and expedient for a man not to touch a woman," and to live single[2]; but because this is "not given to all men[3]," as the Lord in the gospel testifieth, and that concupiscence of the flesh doth, for the most part, burn the greatest sort of men, the Lord hath appointed marriage to be, as it were, a remedy against that heat; as the Apostle in another place witnesseth, saying, "Let them marry which

δ' ἐκ τούτων, εἴς τε τὴν οἰκίαν ἐπανελθοῦσι, καὶ οἷον εὐσχόλοις τὴν ψυχὴν γενομένοις, ἐμπελάζει καιρῷ χρώμενα τούτῳ τοῦ ἀνιᾶν ἡμᾶς, ὅτ' ἄν γε ἔρημος εὐνοίας καὶ μονήρης ὁ βίος.... Οὐ γὰρ ἡ γυνὴ, μὰ Δία, βάρος ἢ φορτίον ἐστί ... ἀλλ' ἥδε μὲν κἂκ τῶν ἐναντίων κοῦφόν τι καὶ ῥᾶστα φέρεσθαι δυνάμενον, μᾶλλον δὲ καὶ τῶν ὄντως ἐπαχθῶν καὶ βαρέων κουφιστικόν. Οὐδὲν γὰρ οὕτω φορτικόν ἐστι τῶν ὄντων, ὥστε μὴ ῥᾷστον εἶναι συμφρονοῦσί γε ἀνδρὶ καὶ γυναικὶ, καὶ κοινῇ φέρειν αὐτὸ βουλομένοις.—Hierocles ap. Stobæi Floril. Vol. III. pp. 12—14.]

[1 Titus ii. 3—5; 1 Tim. ii. 14, 15.]
[2 1 Cor. vii. 2, 1.]
[3 Matth. xix. 11.]

cannot abstain; for it is better to marry than to burn[4]." By this we learn, that the natural company of a man with his own wife is not reputed for a fault or uncleanness in the sight of God. Whoredom is uncleanness in the eyes of the Lord, because it is directly contrary to the law of God: but God hath allowed wedlock and blessed it; therefore married folks are sanctified by the blessing of God through faith and obedience. Neither lack we here any evident arguments and testimonies of Paul to prove it by; for to the Hebrews he said, " Wedlock is honourable among all men, and the bed undefiled; but whoremongers and adulterers God will judge[5]." The Apostle here spake very reverently; and by "the bed" he understood the natural company of a man with his wife, which he saith plainly is undefiled. What God hath made *Acts x.* clean who shall call unclean? Who can deny that to the *Tit. i.* clean all things are clean? Paphnutius, therefore, both bishop and confessor, judging rightly of this, did in the Nicene council say openly, that "the lying of a man with his own wife is chastity[6]." Neither was the most modest apostle ashamed to make laws betwixt a man and his wife; for to the Corinthians he saith, " Let the husband give to the wife due *1 Cor. vii.* benevolence; likewise also the wife to the husband. The wife hath not the power of her own body, but the husband; likewise also the husband hath not the power of his own body, but the wife. Defraud ye not the one the other, except it be with both your consents for a time, that ye may give yourselves to fasting and to prayer; and afterward come together again, that Satan tempt you not for your incontinency." These words of the Apostle are so evident, that they need no exposition at all. In the same Epistle again he saith, " If thou marriest a wife, thou sinnest not." And again, "If a virgin marry, she hath not sinned[7]." Now what is more excellent, pure, and holy, than virginity is? But a virgin sinneth not, if she change virginity for holy matrimony. Very well therefore doth Chrysostom in a certain homily say,

---

[4 1 Cor. vii. 9.]   [5 Hebr. xiii. 4.]

[6 Ἀναστὰς δὲ Παφνούτιος ὁ ὁμολογητὴς ἀντεῖπε· τίμιον δὲ τὸν γάμον ἀποκαλῶν, σωφροσύνην δὲ τὴν πρὸς τὰς ἰδίας γυναῖκας συνουσίαν.—Sozomen. Eccles. Hist. Lib. I. cap. 23. See also Early Writings of Hooper, Parker Soc. ed. page 376.]

[7 1 Cor. vii. 28.]

[BULLINGER.]

26

"The first degree of chastity is unspotted virginity; the second is faithful wedlock[1]." St Augustine also calleth marriage chastity or continency: the place is to be seen in the 19th and 20th chapters, *de bono conjugali*[2], and in the 199th epistle[3]. This is the head from whence doth spring the greatest part of public honesty; for God alloweth wedlock,

Honesty. but disalloweth fornication and all kind of uncleanness. It pleased him by his ordinance to exclude all uncleanness from his believing servants. Let the saints therefore, but magistrates especially, have an especial eye not to be slack in promoting holy wedlock, but diligent to punish severely all filthy fornication and other uncleanness.

This have I hitherto rehearsed somewhat largely out of the holy scripture, to the intent I might prove to all men, that wedlock is holy, and that therefore no man can be

No man forbidden to marry. defiled with the moderate, holy, and lawful use thereof; and so, consequently, that marriage is permitted to all sorts of men. For the apostle saith: "Let a bishop be the husband of one wife; let him rule his own house well, and have faithful children[4]." For it is manifest, by the testimonies of scripture and ecclesiastical writers, that the apostles of Christ and other apostolical teachers of the primitive church were married men, and had wives and children[5]. Neither is there anything, next after corrupt doctrine, which doth more infect the church of Christ, and subvert all ecclesiastical discipline, than if the ministers of the churches, which should be lights of the whole congregation, be fornicators or adulterous persons. That offence especially, above all other, is an hinderance and blot to all kind of honesty. But touching this I purpose not at this time to discourse so largely and fully as I might.

[1 Nam primus est gradus castitatis sincera virginitas: secundus autem fidele conjugium.—Chrysost. Opus Imperf. in Matt. Hom. xxxii. p. 133. Tom. vi. Par. 1724. But this work is not Chrysostom's.]

[2 Restat ut videamus, utrum saltem continentes nostri conjugatis illis patribus comparandi sint, &c. And, Nuptiis sanctorum patrum, non quas nuptias, sed quam continentiam comparem quæro," &c.—De Bon. Conj. capp. 19, 20. Opp. Par. 1531. Tom. vi. fol. 165. col. 1.]

[3 Tom. ii. fol. 156. col. 3. P.]

[4 1 Tim. iii. 2, 4; Titus i. 6.]

[5 See Bullinger. de Episcop. Instit. et Funct. fol. 96—8. Tigur. 1538; and Jewel's Works, Park. Soc. ed. pp. 882, 3.]

To this I add, that the band of wedlock is indissoluble and everlasting, that is to say, such a knot as never can be undone. For of two is made one flesh and one body, which if you sever, you do utterly mar it. " What God hath joined together, therefore, let not man separate[6]." They therefore do make a slaughter of this body, that do commit adultery. For the laws of God and men admit a divorcement betwixt a man and his adulterous wife. And yet, let not any less or lighter cause dissolve this knot betwixt man and wife, than fornication is. Otherwise God, which in the gospel hath permitted the less, doth not forbid the greater, to be causes of divorcement. And in the primitive church, the epistles and constitutions of christian princes do testify, that once committing of fornication was no cause of divorcement. Of which I have spoken in another place.

The knot of wedlock is indissoluble.

But that this holy knot may be the surer, it is available, that marriages be made holily, lawfully, and with discretion, in the fear of the Lord. Let them not be unwillingly agreed unto and made up by compulsion. First, let the good liking of their consenting minds be joined in one, whom the open profession of mutual consent and outward hand-fasting must afterward couple together. Let them be matched together, that are not severed by alliance of blood and nighness of affinity. Let them be coupled in one, that may marry together by the laws of God and their country, with the consent and counsel of their friends and parents. Let them, which mind marriage, have a sincere heart purposely bent to seek their own safeguard and continual felicity; that is, to respect only the will and pleasure of God, and not admit any evil affections as counsellors to make up the marriage betwixt them. Hierocles, in his book *De nuptiis*, saith: " It is mere folly and lack of wit which make those things, that of themselves are easy to be borne, troublesome, and make a wife a grievous clog to her husband. For marriage to many men hath been intolerable, not because the wedded state is, by default of itself or own proper nature, so troublesome or cumbrous; but for our matching as we should not, it falleth out as we would not, and causeth our marriages to be grievous and noisome. To this end, verily, our daily marriages do commonly come. For they marry wives usually, not for the

How matrimony must be contracted.

[6 Matth. xix. 6.]

26—2

begetting of children or society of life: but some for a great
dowry, some for a beautiful body; and some, being seduced
by such kind of causes, as it were men abused by unfaithful
counsellors, have no regard to the disposition and manners of
their spouse, but marry at adventures, to their own decay
and utter destruction[1]." Hereunto belongeth Plutarch's admonition to parents, in his treatise of bringing up of children,
where he counselleth men to bestow such wives on their sons
as are not much wealthier nor mightier than their children.
For a very pithy saying is that usual proverb, "Marry a
wife of thine own degree[2]." To be short, let the fear of
God, the word of God, and earnest prayer poured out to God,
be always annexed to the beginning of marriages.

Against poly-
gamy, or
the having of
many wives.
But it is not convenient, that in lawful matrimony any
more should be than two alone, to be joined together under
one yoke of wedlock. For the use of many wives, which
our fathers usurped without any blame, may not stablish
polygamy for a law among us at these days. The time of
correction[3] is now come to light, and Messias now is come into
the world, who teacheth all rightly, and reformeth things
amiss. He therefore hath reduced wedlock to the first prescribed rule and law of matrimony. "Two," saith the Lord,
"shall be one flesh." And the apostle saith: "Let every
man have his own wife, and every woman her own husband[4]."
The multitude of Salomon's concubines therefore appertain

[1 Βαρὺ δέ ἐστιν ὡς ἀληθῶς ἀφροσύνη καὶ δύσοιστον τοῖς αὐτὴν κεκτη-
μένοις, ὑφ' ἧς δὴ καὶ τὰ φύσει κοῦφα γίνεται βαρέα, τά τε ἄλλα καὶ γυνή.
Τῷ ὄντι γὰρ καὶ συχνοῖς δή τισιν ἀφόρητος ἐγένετο ὁ γάμος, ἀλλ' οὐχὶ παρ'
ἑαυτῷ, οὐδὲ τῷ φύσει τοιάνδε τὴν μετὰ γυναικὸς εἶναι κοινωνίαν· ἀλλ' ὅτ'
ἂν γαμῶμεν ἃς μὴ δεῖ, μετὰ τοῦ καὶ αὐτοὶ παντάπασιν ἀπειροβίως διακεῖσθαι
καὶ ἀπαρασκεύως ἔχειν πρὸς τὸ ἀγαγεῖν ὡς χρὴ τὴν ἐλευθέραν ἄγεσθαι, τὸ
τηνικαῦτα συμβαίνει χαλεπὴν καὶ ἀφόρητον γίνεσθαι τὴν κοινωνίαν. Ἀμέλει
καὶ ταύτῃ χωρεῖ τοῖς πολλοῖς ὁ γάμος. Οὐ γὰρ ἐπὶ παίδων γένεσιν καὶ
βίου κοινωνίαν ἄγονται γυναῖκας· ἀλλ' οἱ μὲν διὰ προικὸς ὄγκον, οἱ δὲ δι'
ἐξοχὴν μορφῆς, οἱ δὲ δι' ἄλλας τινὰς τοιουτοτρόπους αἰτίας, αἷς χρώμενοι
κακοῖς συμβούλοις, οὐδὲν περὶ τῆς διαθέσεως καὶ τοῦ ἤθους τῆς νύμφης
πολυπραγμονήσαντες, ὄλεθρον αὐτῶν θύουσι τὸν γάμον.—Hierocles ap.
Stobæi Floril. Vol. III. p. 15.]

[2 Ἐγγυᾶσθαι δεῖ τοῖς υἱοῖς γυναῖκας μήτε εὐγενεστέρας πολλῷ μήτε
πλουσιωτέρας· τὸ γὰρ, τὴν κατὰ σαυτὸν ἔλα, σοφόν.—Plutarch. de Liberis
Educand. See also Erasm. Adag. Chiliad. Hanov. 1617. p. 124. col. 2.]

[3 correctionis tempora, Lat.——Heb. ix. 10.]

[4 1 Cor. vi. 16, and vii. 2.]

not to us. We have not to follow the example of Jacob, who married two sisters. And yet, notwithstanding, the word of truth condemneth not the second, third, or many marriages which a man maketh, when his wife is deceased. For that saying of the apostle is general to all men, and endureth in all ages: "Let them marry, that cannot abstain; for it is better to marry than to burn[5]." Which sentence is taken out of these words in the gospel: "All men cannot receive this saying, save they to whom it is given. For there are some chaste, which were so born out of their mother's womb; and there are some chaste, which were made chaste of men; and there are some chaste, which have made themselves chaste for the kingdom of heaven's sake. He that is able to receive it, let him receive it[6]." Let him therefore, that cannot receive it, marry a wife, so often as necessity compelleth him thereunto.

The second and third marriages after the first wife.

But now, especially, it standeth us in hand to know, how married folks must behave themselves, what they must do in wedlock, to what end they must direct their deeds and thoughts, and how they ought to be affected toward that holy ordinance of God Almighty. Touching which thing I will not speak much, but briefly note out the most necessary points, to give all men occasion to think with themselves, and call to mind both more and greater matters which I leave untouched.

The reverend behaviour which is required in the estate of marriage.

First of all, let married folks be throughly persuaded and assuredly certain, while they live in matrimony, that they are in the work of God, that they please God, and do an acceptable thing in the sight of the Lord, because of God's word wherein he blessed that kind of life, and sanctified all wedded people, which by faith do live in that work and ordinance of the living God. Therefore, when married couples do patiently suffer the troubles that follow the married life, while they labour faithfully, while they do those things decently which belong to the charge and office of married people; as, while the wife doth love her husband, while she doth dutifully obey him, while she doth bring forth her children with grief and pain, and, when they are brought forth, doth diligently nourish them, and labour to bring them up; while the husband doth love his wife, while he doth mutually help

[5 1 Cor. vii. 9.]   [6 Matth. xix. 11, 12.]

✓ her, and faithfully in all things shew himself a careful father for his family and household; in doing these things they please God no less than they do when they go to church to hear the word of God and to worship the Lord. For these works of wedlock are reputed for good works, as well as giving of alms, justice, and making of peace. Married folks therefore have need especially of true faith in God, the author of wedlock: for by wedlock in faith they shall please the Lord. This our monks[1] could not abide to hear of, although the word of God doth urge it upon them; they ceased not to magnify their counterfeit holiness and hypocritical vows.

Married folks must be faithful. Secondarily, it is required at the hands of wedded couples to be mindful of the faith which they give and take, that they do not falsely deceive one another, but holily keep the promise that they make and troth that they plight, and to keep it sincerely both in body and mind. Let neither of them lust after the body of a stranger, nor conceive an hatred or loathsomeness of their wedded spouse. And thy body, thou that art a married man, is not thy body, but thy wife's; as also thy wife's body is not thy wife's, but thine. Thou stealest and dost commit a robbery, if thou take away another body's goods; and, when thou hast conveyed it from the proper owner, dost give it to another. Let the mind of wedded mates be unspotted, and the body untouched. Every one, when he first cometh to solemnize wedlock by the holy ceremony ordained for that purpose, doth promise with an oath in the name of the Lord before God and the church, that he will use the company of no woman but her, that he will cleave to, love, and cherish her alone without any other. This faith once given whosoever doth violate, he is falsely forsworn, and is a breaker of a godly promise and God's holy truth.

They must dwell together with knowledge. Neither is it sufficient for thee to be faithful, unless thou be courteous or tractable toward thy wife, and dwell with her "according to knowledge," as St. Peter saith[2]. Let the husband be the head of the wife, to wit, her adviser and counsellor, her ruler and guide, her sweet yokefellow and admonisher in all her affairs, her assured aid and faithful defender. Let the wife be obedient unto her husband, even as we see the members obey the head: let her yield herself to her husband to be

[1 Hæc non urserunt monachi, quæ tamen jubentur urgere, Lat. P.]
[2 1 Pet. iii. 7.]

ruled and governed; let her not despise his honest counsels and indifferent commandments[3]. Let them think that they twain are one body, or the members of one body. And therefore let them learn by the government of this mortal body, how to behave themselves in the guiding of wedlock. The worthier members do not despise the more unworthy limbs, but do rather honour them, lighten their labour, and aid and help them. Again, the more unworthy limbs are in love with the worthier, not envying their pre-eminence any whit at all. One member breaketh not or hurteth another; but all do mutually cherish themselves, and defend one another from harm and injury. Such a mutual knitting together, and working, and love, and charity, and good-will, and fellowship, let there be betwixt man and wife. For to that end the woman was taken out of the man's body, that the husband should cherish (his wife) his own body. And for that cause the apostle saith : Ephes. v. "So must husbands love their wives, even as their own bodies. He that loveth his wife doth love himself; for no man at any time hath hated his own flesh, but loveth and cherisheth it, as the Lord doth the church." What may be said to that, moreover, that the apostle, in the very same place, hath made the Son of God and the holy Church an example for married folks to follow in keeping of wedlock; requiring at the husband's hand to love his wife, even as Christ hath loved the church; and of the wife to reverence her husband and to love him again, as the church doth Christ? Than which example there is none in the world more holy and effectual. For there is no love greater than the love of Christ toward his church, neither is there any love more chaste than that which the church doth bear to Christ. It is therefore required at the hands of wedded mates mutually to bear most ardent and holy love the one to the other. Let them use all things in common : let them be partakers both of the same prosperity and the same adversity. Let them both draw under one yoke, and bear betwixt them one another's burden. Briefly, let them twain be the members of one and the very same body. I have more at large set down these offices of man and wife in my treatise which is called "The Institution of Christian Matrimony[4]."

[3 æqua dogmata, Lat.]
[4 See Becon's Works, Parker Soc. ed. Vol. i. p. 29, n. 2.]

Lastly, let them bring up their children in holy discipline
and the fear of God, to the health of their own house and the
whole commonweal. Paul saith : "I would have the younger
women marry, to get children, and to govern the house; for
that is honest and acceptable before God[1]." But touching
the bringing up of children, I have already spoken in the fifth
Sermon of this Decade. Now, the very begetting of children
alone is very profitable both to every private or particular
house, and also to the commonweal : for here I will not stand
to shew, that the honour and glory of God is very greatly
augmented, if children be not only begotten, but also brought
up in the fear of God and knowledge of his word. Hierocles
saith : "I confess that marriage is profitable, especially because it bringeth children forth, which is indeed a goodly
fruit: for they, being of our very blood, do while we are
in health aid us in all our affairs; and in old age, when years
come upon us, they succour us well with all that they may :
they are familiar companions of our joy in prosperity, and in
adversity are our partners in sorrowing with us for our heavy
mishaps[2]." And so forth. Antipater also saith : "Man,
which is endued with a civil disposition to maintain society,
must augment his country and commonwealth with increase of
children : for cities could not have been preserved by any
means at all, unless the head men of every city, and the sons
of noble gentlemen, seeing their ancestors wither and fall
away like goodly leaves of a fair tree, had married in time
convenient, and left behind them children as worthy plants, to
succeed in their country, thereby to make it flourish for ever ;
doing their best, so far as they could, to keep it from the
assaults and conquests of enemies and strangers. They therefore, shooting at nothing more than to defend and assist their
country, both in their lifetime and when they were dead, did
think it most necessary and especially convenient to marry and
be married, desiring thereby both to do all things that nature

---

[1] 1 Tim. v. 14.]

[2] Φημὶ τοίνυν καὶ σύμφορον εἶναι τὸν γάμον, πρῶτον μὲν ὅτι θεῖον ὡς
ἀληθῶς φέρει καρπὸν τὴν παίδων γένεσιν, οἳ παραστάται μὲν ἡμῖν οἷον συμ-
φυεῖς ἔτι καὶ αὐτοῖς ἐρρωμένοις ἐν ἁπάσαις γίγνονται πράξεσιν· ἀγαθοὶ δὲ
ἐπίκουροι κάμνουσιν ὑφ' ἡλικίας καὶ γήρᾳ πιεζομένοις, οἰκεῖοι μὲν ἐν εὐπρα-
γίαις εὐφροσύνης κοινωνοί, συμπαθεῖς δὲ ἐν τοῖς ἐναντίοις καιροῖς διάδοχοι
τῶν ἀνιαρῶν.—Hierocles ap. Stobæi Floril. Vol. III. p. 12.]

requireth, and also those that touch the health and increase of their country, and most of all the worship of God, &c.³"

Since therefore that lawful matrimony is of so great effect, and so available to live well and happily, the faithful do not without cause begin their marriages with religion and religious rites. The Lord, verily, did presently in the beginning⁴ bless the first marriage of our parents, Adam and Eve, and did himself couple them in wedlock. Whereupon the church of God hath received a custom, that they which join in marriage, before they dwell together, go into the temple of the Lord, where, after prayer made in the midst of the congregation, they are joined together, and blessed by the minister of God in the name of God himself. Wherefore in wedlock the first and chiefest things that be required, are the earnest and continual prayers of the married folks to God, that he will vouchsafe to make the husbands wise, religious, modest, gentle, honest, painful sufferers⁵, and lovers of their wives; and that it will please him to make the wives obedient, meek, chaste, faithful lovers of their husbands and children, housewives, and fruitful⁶. For no one man is able to declare all the evils that come even of one corrupt and naughty marriage. Through it whole houses are wonderfully disquieted, all wealth and honesty do utterly decay, the children are bastards, God is offended and provoked to anger, and an endless mischief brought to the whole commonweal. God, therefore, must be earnestly beseeched to bless all married people, that both the glory of his holy name, and the

Marriages must be begun with religion.

[³ ... Ταῦτα δὲ δὴ κατανενοηκὼς ὁ εὐγενὴς, καὶ ὡς φύσει πολιτικὸν γενόμενον, συναύξειν τὴν πατρίδα δεῖ. Καὶ γὰρ οὐκ ἂν ἄλλως δύναιντο αἱ πόλεις σώζεσθαι, εἰ μὴ οἱ βέλτιστοι ταῖς φύσεσι τῶν πολιτῶν, ἢ τῶν γενναίων παῖδες, τῶν προτέρων καθαπερεὶ φύλλων καλοῦ δένδρου ἀπομαραινομένων καὶ ἀπορρεόντων, οὗτοι καθ' ὥραν γαμοῖεν, καθαπερεὶ τινας γενναίους βλαστοὺς διαδόχους τῇ πατρίδι καταλιπόντες, οἳ θάλλειν αὐτὴν ἀεὶ ποιοῖεν, καὶ τὴν ἀκμὴν ἀΐδιον φυλάττοιεν, καὶ ὅσον ἐφ' ἑαυτοῖς μηδέποτ' εὐεπίθετον τοῖς ἐχθροῖς, στοχαζόμενοι τοῦ καὶ ζῶντες καὶ μεταλλάξαντες ἀμύνειν τῇ πατρίδι καὶ βοηθεῖν, τῶν ἀναγκαιοτάτων καὶ πρὸ τῶν καθηκόντων νομίζουσι τὸ συγκραθῆναι εἰς γάμον, πᾶν μὲν τὸ τῇ φύσει ἐπιβάλλον σπεύδοντες ἐπιτελεῖν, πολὺ δὲ μάλιστα τὸ εἰς τὴν τῆς πατρίδος σωτηρίαν καὶ αὔξησιν ἀνῆκον, καὶ ἔτι μᾶλλον εἰς τὴν τῶν θεῶν τιμήν.—Antipater ap. Stobæi Floril. Vol. III. p. 16.]

[⁴ protinus ab initio, Lat.]   [⁵ patientes, Lat.]
[⁶ œconomicas, Lat.]

commonweal's prosperity, may thereby daily increase more and more.

Against
adultery.

I am now come to speak of adultery, which is a sin whereby the husband goeth to another woman, or the wife turneth aside after another man, to whom they make common the use of their bodies, which are not their own bodies now, but their mates' in wedlock. Some there are that flatter themselves, and are of opinion, that they are not culpable of adultery, if they have the company of any unbetrothed maiden, or one that is unmarried; or if a woman play the harlot with an unwedded man: they will have it (in God's name[1]) to be fornication, and not adultery. But the scripture teacheth the contrary. Thou goest to another woman, thou art an adulterer: thou breakest thy faith, thou art forsworn: thy body is not thine, but thy wife's; when therefore thou bestowest thy body on another, thou committest adultery. If thou, being wedded, dost lie with a married wife, thou doublest the sin of thine adultery. This offence was plagued with most sharp punishment even in the beginning almost, and as soon as the world was created. Pharao, the king of Egypt, commanded Sara, Abraham's wife, to be taken away and carried to his palace, that he might use her as his wife; thinking verily that she had been Abraham's sister. But

Gen. xii.

the scripture saith, "The Lord vexed Pharaoh and all his house with great plagues, because of Sara, Abraham's wife." Lo, here the king of Egypt is punished with grievous plagues for his adultery; and yet he knew not that Sara was Abraham's wife: how great plagues therefore are prepared for the men that wittingly and willingly, without all shame, commit adultery! To Abimelech, king of the Philistines, the Lord

Gen. xx.

doth say, "Lo, thou shalt die, because of the woman which thou hast taken away from her husband." And yet this king also had taken away Sara, not knowing that she was Abraham's wife. Joseph, being provoked to adultery by his

Gen. xxxix.

master's wife, doth simply say, "How should I do this great wickedness, and sin against God?" Every word doth bear some weight: for adultery is an heinous sin. Whereupon in

Job xxxi.

the book of Job we find these words of Job himself: "If mine heart have been deceived by a woman, or if I have laid

[1 Not in the original Latin.]

wait at my neighbour's door[2]; then let my wife be another man's harlot, and let other men have to do with her. For this is a wickedness and sin that is worthy to be judged to death : yea, it is a fire that utterly should consume and root out all mine increase." Job saith that he hath not only not committed adultery, but that he hath not so much at any time as once given the attempt to defile another man's wife. He confesseth that adultery is a sin, and so grievous an offence, that it doth deserve to have the adulterer's wife to be defiled with adultery. He addeth, that adultery is a fire that utterly consumeth and devoureth all things ; and, lastly, that it is a sin to be judged, and punished by death.

Moreover, Salomon, the wisest of all men, saith : " May a man take fire in his bosom, and his clothes not be brent[3]? *Prov. vi.* Or can one go upon hot coals, and his feet not be brent? Even so he that goeth in to his neighbour's wife, and toucheth her, cannot be unguilty. Men do not utterly despise a thief that stealeth to satisfy his soul, when he is hungry ; but if he may be gotten, he restoreth again seven times as much, or else he maketh recompence with all the substance of his house: but whoso committeth adultery with a woman, he lacketh understanding; and he that doeth it, destroyeth his own soul. He getteth himself a plague and dishonour, and his reproach shall never be put out. For the jealousy and wrath of the man will not be entreated; neither accepteth he the person of any mediator, nor receiveth any gifts, how great soever they be." In these words of Salomon many things are to be noted. First, as it cannot otherwise be, but that fire must burn the garment wherein it is carried; so no man can commit adultery without damage and danger of further punishment. Secondarily, comparison is made betwixt a thief and an adulterer : not that theft is thereby defended; but because thieves, although they be infamous, do seem yet to sin a great deal less than adulterers do. For a thief may make satisfaction by restoring the worth of the thing that he stole to him from whom he stole it away ; but for adultery no amends can be made. And what is he that would not

[2 nimirum ut corrumperem uxorem ejus, Lat.; omitted by the translator: namely, with the intent of corrupting his wife.]

[3 brent, i. e. burnt.]

rather wish to have thieves ransack his chest, and take away his substance, than to have his wife, his darling, defiled with adultery? Moreover, Salomon calleth the adulterer mad, and without understanding. Adultery is judged to be a sin worthy of death and endless infamy. For the Lord in the law doth not say only, "Thou shalt not commit adultery;" but in another place also goeth on, and addeth, "And he that committeth adultery with another man's wife, even he that committeth adultery with his neighbour's wife, let both the adulterer and the adulteress be slain." Levit. xx. And this punishment of adultery by death was not abrogated or changed by the very Gentiles; for the Roman law *Lex Julia* is very well known, how it commanded adulterers to be put to death[1]: which law was of force in the time of St Hierome, as we may gather by the history which he wrote of an adulteress, at the chopping off of whose head seven strokes were given[2].

Neither is it marvel, undoubtedly, that adultery was among them of old, and is yet at this day, according to the laws[3], to be punished by death; for upon that one many sins do depend. First of all, the adulterer is a perjured man; for he hath broken and violated the faith, which he gave openly, before God and the face of the congregation, by calling to witness the most holy and reverend Trinity, when the minister of Christ did solemnise the marriage, and couple him to his wife, by giving hand in hand. Secondarily, the adulterer hath committed theft and robbery; for when the adulteress doth make her body common to another man, then doth she set to sale, defile, and mar, not her own, but her husband's body. Thirdly, bastards born in adultery do oftentimes

[1 "The Lex Julia, passed about B. C. 17, did not inflict the punishment of death on either party; and in those instances under the emperors, in which death was inflicted, it must be considered an extraordinary punishment, and beyond the provisions of the Julian Law. By a constitution of Constantine, confirmed by Justinian, the offence in the adulterer was made capital. The Julian Law, however, *permitted the father in certain cases* to kill the adulterer and adulteress."— Dict. of Gr. and Lat. Antiq. s. v. *Adulterium.* P.]

[2 Hieron. Epist. xvii. ad Innocentium de muliere septies percussa. Par. 1706. Tom. IV. col. 23—26.]

[3 See Becon's Works, Parker Soc. ed. Vol. II. p. 649; and Early Writings of Bp. Hooper, p. 376.]

enjoy an equal part of inheritance with the right-begotten
children; which cannot be without great wrong done to the
lawful heirs and legitimate offspring: for they are against
all right robbed of their due inheritance, whereof an equal
portion is given to him to whom by law no parcel is due.
Lastly, beside all these, innumerable mischiefs do spring of
adultery. Since therefore that it is a serpent with so many
heads, both the laws of God and men do rightly punish
adulterers with loss of life.

But some jolly fellows there are, forsooth[4], that of adul- David's
tery do make but a sport. They are persuaded that David's adultery.
adultery doth make on their side; and that place of scripture where we read, that the Lord was favourable to the
adulteress that was taken even as the deed was in doing.
Why do not these merry conceited men consider how severely
the Lord did punish David for that offence? The bloody
house[5] of David was immediately after defiled with filthy
incest. For Amnon doth perforce deflour his sister Thamar.
And straightway, upon the neck of that again, his house is
defamed by most cruel parricide, while Absalom in a banquet
murdered his brother Amnon. The very same Absalom also,
David's son, defileth or defloureth his father's wives, and that
openly too, laying all fear of God and shame aside. He
driveth his father out of his kingdom, and hasteneth on to
shorten his days. All which calamities David confesseth
that he doth worthily sustain, for the adultery and murder by
him committed. Lastly, many thousands of his people were
slain in the battle; David himself is hardly and with much
ado restored to his kingdom; and afterward, being restored,
he repented his sin all the days of his life[6]. Now it is
marvel if adulterers, considering these punishments, will go
on yet to allege the example of David in defence of their
naughtiness. Our Saviour did not come into the world to be The Lord
a judge, but a saviour; neither did he in any place usurp adultery.
the right of the sword. Who, therefore, will make any
marvel at it, to see the adulteress not condemned by him to
be stoned to death? Yet he said: "Hath no man condemned
thee[7]?" as if he minded not to have resisted the law, if

[4 Si diis placet, Lat.]   [5 funesta domus, Lat.]
[6 2 Sam. xi—xix.]   [7 John viii. 10.]

judgment had once passed upon her. For he came not to be a patron to adulterers, nor to break the law, but to fulfil it. But if it like adulterers well, that the adulteress was not condemned of the Lord, then let them also like that sentence, wherewith the history is ended, when the Lord saith : "Go thy ways, and sin no more." Let them, therefore, leave off to defile and destroy themselves with filthy adultery.

What other things are forbid under the title of adultery.

The Lord in his law hath expressly named adultery alone ; but therewithal he doth inclusively understand all kinds of lust and luxury, and all things else which do edge forward and stir up fire in men to wantonness, which he forbiddeth as severely as adultery itself. The Lord in the gospel doth not only forbid the outward work of adultery, but the very affection also and wanton lust of the heart and mind. "Ye have heard," saith he, "that it was said to them of old, Thou shalt not commit adultery. But I say unto you, That whosoever looketh on a woman to lust after her, hath committed adultery already with her in his heart[1]." In the same place he teacheth us to pluck out our eyes, and cut off our hands, that is, to extinguish unclean affections that rise in our minds, while yet they be young and begin to bud, lest peradventure they break out from thoughts to deeds. So then in this precept every unclean thought, all ribald talk, and filthiness of bodily deeds, are utterly forbidden.

Fornication.

In this precept is forbidden fornication, or that kind of whorehunting, which is said to be the meddling of a single man with an unmarried woman. This kind of whoredom is thought of many either to be a very small offence, or none at all. But such kind of men doth the devil hearten on, bewitch, and by all those ill thoughts drive on to commit that sin ; when as the doctrine of the evangelists and apostles Acts xv. doth teach us the contrary. For the apostles, in that synodal epistle, which they sent from Hierusalem to all nations, 1 Pet. iv. do expressly name and forbid fornication. St Peter reckoneth fornication among those filthy sins, from which he would 1 Cor. x. have Christians to be most clear. St Paul saith, "Flee fornication." Again, "Let us not be defiled with fornication, as some of them committed fornication, and fell in one day three and twenty thousand[2]." Fornication doth directly

[1 Matt. v. 27, 28.]   [2 1 Cor. vi. 18 and x. 8.]

fight with the covenant of God, whereby he is joined to us, and we to him: and whoredom also spoileth God of his glory, and doth most filthily pollute the temple of the Lord. Let us hear what the apostle Paul saith touching this matter: 1 Cor. vi. "Know ye not that your bodies are the members of Christ? shall I therefore take the members of Christ, and make them the members of an harlot? God forbid. What, know ye not that he that is coupled to an harlot is one body? For two, saith he, shall be one flesh. But he that is coupled to the Lord, is one spirit. Flee fornication. Every sin that a man doeth is without the body; but he that committeth fornication sinneth against his own body. What, know ye not that your body is the temple of the Holy Ghost which is in you, whom ye have of God, and ye are not your own? for ye are bought with a price." Therefore fornication shutteth fornicators out of the kingdom of God. For the same apostle saith: "Neither whoremongers nor adulterers Ephes. v. shall inherit the kingdom of God." And therefore in another place he suffereth not fornication to be so much as once named among Christians[3]; so far was he[4] from admitting stews and brothel-houses among God's people. Moreover, whoredom doth fill the whole body with sundry diseases: it depriveth whore-haunters of all their goods and substance; it bringeth them to poverty and extreme misery, and driveth them at last to utter desperation. It overthroweth their fame and good name with shame and ignominy: the view whereof is lively expressed in the holy scriptures by the example of Samson, the strongest man among all the Israelites. Salomon, therefore, the most wise of all other, doth very fitly, in time and place convenient, admonish all men to fly the enticing baits and flattering allurements of whorish strumpets. For the end of them is deadly poison, and they throw a man down headlong into a bottomless pit of endless miseries[5].

By this law also that kind of whoredom is prohibited, Rapes forbidden. which consisteth in defloration of virgins, and violent rapes, by which children are perforce defiled and carried from their

[3 Eph. v. 5, 3.]

[4 servus Jesu Christi. Lat. So far was the servant of Jesus Christ, &c.]

[5 Prov. vii. 23, &c.]

parents. There is difference betwixt a rape perforce, and the deflouring of a maid done without violence. Sichem defiled Dina, the daughter of Jacob; and although he desired to have the defloured maid to his wife, and to change his religion, yet notwithstanding he himself is slain by Levi and Simeon, the brethren of Dina; his city is rased and filled with the blood of murdered men, whose goods were ransacked and laid open to spoil. The history is extant in the thirty-fourth chapter of Genesis. For the rape which Roderichus, king of the Goths in Spain, committed upon the daughter of Julianus, a lieutenant, all Spain in a manner was mingled with fire and blood. For Volaterranus, in his second book of his Geography, saith: "Roderichus reigned three years, whose filthy lust brought an end, as well to the name, as to the quiet kingdom, of the Goths in Spain, by means of the Saracens that invaded their land. For when it fell out, that he had defloured the daughter of one Julianus, a lieutenant of that part of Mauritania that is called Tingitana, private grief did prick her father to seek revengement, whereto he used the commodity of the place. Wherefore Julianus doth privately call the Saracens out of Africa; who, in the year of grace 714, under the conduct of their captain Muzta, being sent by Mirmemolinus their king at that time, entering in through the straits of Morocco, did in two years' space subdue all Spain almost, except Asturia: in the space of which time it is reported that seven hundred thousand men on both sides were destroyed by that war; wherein also the king, which had defloured the virgin, with all his nobility, was utterly slain[1]."

Asturia, a country in Spain, between Galatia and Portugal.

[1] Roderychus tres annos regnavit; cujus fœda libido finem attulit Gothorum non tam generi quam pacifico imperio, Saracenis supervenientibus. Nam cum filiam cujusdam Juliani præfecti, qui Tingitanam administrabat provinciam, vitiasset, dolor domesticus patrem ad ultionem sollicitavit, loci fretum commoditate. Quare Julianus clam ex Aphrica Saracenas evocat: qui anno salutis 714 duce Muza, misso a Mirammelino eorum tunc rege, per angustias Herculei freti ingresso, biennii spatio omnem fere Hispaniam occupant præter Astures. In quo temporis spacio dicuntur ad septies centena hominum millia in eo bello utrinque absumpta.—Volaterrani Commentar. Urban. Geograph. Lib. II. p. 17, Basil. 1559. The author of the modern part of the Universal History, (Vol. XVI. p. 87, Lond. 1782) observes on this account, in a note: "The reign of Roderic was so short and so full of troubles, and his own personal character in other respects so fair,

In Israel, for the Levite's concubine, whom the citizens of Gibea of the tribe of Benjamin had violently ravished, were twenty-five thousand Benjamites slain, beside them which perished from among the other eleven tribes, whose number amounted to forty thousand men[2]. Neither is it unknown to any, that the kings were expelled out of the city of Rome, and Troy, being wearied with ten years' war, (which troubled both the east and west,) was at the last utterly sacked and clean overthrown, because Tarquinius had perforce ravished Lucretia, and Alexander Paris had stolen out of Greece Menelaus his Helena, another man's wife[3]. Every age almost doth minister an innumerable sort of such like examples. For the most just God hath always by evident examples declared, how greatly he is offended with deflourers of virgins and ravishers of women. And for that cause are laws and very sharp punishments ordained and appointed for such lascivious knaves. Rapes and such villainies committed perforce the laws do punish with loss of life; but to him that doth deflour a maid not violently the Lord doth say, "Marry and endow her[4]." Other laws appoint other penalties: touching which more is spoken in the civil law.

Moreover, incest is especially prohibited. They call in- Incest. cest an unlawful meddling of a man with a woman against the honour of blood and affinity. For "cestus" signifieth the marriage-girdle, which the bride did wear, to shew that the marriage was just and lawful[5]. We Germans call this sin by the name of "Bloutschand;" whereby we signify the sin committed in corrupting or defiling our own blood or kindred. In Leviticus, after the degrees of blood, in which we are forbidden to marry, the Lord doth presently add : "In all these be not ye defiled : for in all these things are the nations defiled, which I cast out before you. And hereby the land is defiled, and I have visited the iniquity thereof upon it, and the

that nothing can be more improbable with respect to him than this imputation."]

[2 Judges xx.]

[3 See also Early Writings of Hooper, Parker Soc. ed. p. 354.]

[4 Deut. xxii. 28, 29.]

[5 ab *in* priv. et *castus.* Facciol. Alii ducunt ab *in*, et *cesto*, Veneris cingulo, quo amor maritalis in legitimis nuptiis conciliari putabatur.— Holyoke's Dict. in voc. 1677.]

land hath spewed out the inhabitants thereof. Ye shall therefore keep my statutes and mine ordinances, and shall not do
any of all these abominations. For whosoever shall do so, he
shall be cut off from among his people[1]." And in the twentieth
chapter of Leviticus he hath appointed death to be the punishment of incest; which is not changed by the civil laws or
imperial constitutions.

Sodomy.

The abominable sin of sodomy, and meddling with beasts,
also is plainly forbidden: against which we have most evident
and express laws set down in the eighteenth and twentieth chapters of Leviticus. We have also a very severe, but yet a most
just, punishment laid by God himself upon the pates of the detestable Sodomites: for with fire and stinking brimstone sent
down from heaven he consumed those filthy men to dust and
ashes; which ashes he washed away with the waves of the Dead
Sea, because he would not have so much as the very cinders to
remain of so wicked men. Moreover, their whole cities and
fruitful fields were burnt with fire. For it was not requisite[2]
that any one jot of the substance of those most wicked men
should remain undestroyed. The place where those cities sometime were situated is at this day overflown with water, and
called the Dead Sea. Whereby we do consequently gather,
that the most just God will not spare the Gentiles, entangled
in the very same sin, although for a time he wink at and dissemble it. Fire shall destroy both them and theirs; and they
themselves shall for ever burn in hell, where nothing shall
remain of them but a reproachful memory. For in the Revelation[3] of our Lord Jesus Christ to his apostle John we read:
"And fire came down from God out of heaven, and devoured
them; and the devil, which deceived them, was cast into a
lake of fire and brimstone, where the beast and the false
prophet shall be tormented day and night for evermore."
Apoc. xx.

Allurements
forbidden.

Furthermore, all things else are forbidden, that do incite
or allure us to unlawful lusts; which baits are the over-nice
pranking and decking the body, evil and wanton company,
gluttony, surfeiting, and drunkenness. For Ezechiel, among
the rest of his prophecies, saith: "This was the iniquity of

[1 Lev. xviii. 24—29.]
[2 oportebat, Lat.]
[3 in Theologia Domini nostri Jesu Christi, Lat. See p. 170, n. 6.]

Sodom, pride, gluttony, abundance of all things, and idleness[4]." Men are provoked to lust either by hearing or reading of dishonest ditties and bawdy ballads; or by looking
on and beholding wanton dances, unseemly sights, ribald talk,
and filthy examples. They therefore are by this law reproved, which wink at or cherish, which are the bawds or
bringers together of adulterous persons. Unto the wicked
the Lord in the Psalms doth say: "Why dost thou take my   Psal. 1
covenant in thy mouth, whereas thou hatest to be reformed,
and dost cast my words behind thee? When thou sawest a
thief, thou consentedst unto him; and hast been partaker with
the adulterers," &c. The just Lord therefore doth punish
all these offences in wicked men, every one according to the
greatness of the sin. For some sins are far more heinous
than other some are. He is an adulterer, that in his mind
doth lust after another man's wife: but he sinneth more
grievously, if he endeavour to finish in deed his wicked
thought; he offendeth yet more deeply, if he do the deed;
and sinneth most of all, if, after once, he fall unto it again.
Likewise the adulterer sinneth; so doth the bawd, and he also
that upholdeth his adultery. The whoremonger sinneth
deeply; but he that defileth himself with incest sinneth more
grievously; and he most heinously of all, that in meddling
with beasts committeth filthy sodomy. So then in this seventh precept charge is given for the maintenance of shame-
facedness, modesty, sobriety, temperancy, chastity, public
honesty, and true holiness of soul and body.

The next is for me to say somewhat now touching conti-   Of continency. By abstinence we refrain from other men's goods, and   nency.
take from no man the thing that is his. Some there are that
will have temperancy to extend farther than continency; for
they will make the one to be but a part of the other[5]. I, in
this treatise, do simply make continency the contrary to intemperancy or incontinency. For continency is a virtue or
power of the mind received from the Spirit of God, which
suppresseth affections, and doth not in any wise permit unlawful pleasures. This is conversant and doth shew itself in

[4 Ezek. xvi. 49.]
[5 Temperantia est rationis in libidinem atque in alios non rectos
animi impetus firma et moderata dominatio. Ejus partes sunt con-
tinentia, clementia, modestia.—Cic. de Orat. Lib. II. cap. 60.]

the common and usual talk of men, in pleasures that are allowed, in apparel, in buildings and dwelling-houses, in meat and drink, and in other things also. I at this present will only examine those points of continency which are already rehearsed.

The continency or the bridling of the tongue.

First of all, it is required of us to keep in our tongue, and not to let it loose at random to the blaspheming of God's glory or hurt of our neighbour. Let the talk of a christian man be honest, profitable, and seasoned with salt; let it be unacquainted with scoffing, lightness, lying, ribaldry, and filthiness. St James in the third chapter of his epistle hath spoken sufficiently of the tongue's properties. In his first chapter also he saith: "Let every man be swift to hear, slow to speak, and slow to anger." And Paul saith: "Let no filthy communication proceed out of your mouth, but that which is good to edify withal, as oft as need is, that it may minister grace unto the hearers; and grieve not the Holy Spirit of God, by whom ye are sealed unto the day of redemption[1]." And again: "Let not fornication, or any uncleanness, or covetousness, be once named among you, as it becometh saints; neither filthiness, nor foolish talking, neither jesting, which are not seemly; but rather giving of thanks. Let no man deceive you with vain words; for for such things cometh the wrath of God upon the children of disobedience[2]." For in another place he citeth this sentence out of Menander, and saith: "Ill words corrupt good manners[3]." Moreover, a man's mind is bewrayed by his talk; for "of the heart's abundance the mouth doth speak[4]." If therefore in any thing, then in tongue especially, it behoveth Christians to be sober and continent.

Granted pleasures.

The Lord, I confess, hath granted man the use of certain pleasures. For he may lawfully, without offence to God, clothe his body with garments soberly, thereby to keep his limbs from cold. God hath and doth allow the embracings of man and wife in holy wedlock. He granteth choice of a dwelling-place conveniently situated against the untemperateness of the air, and biddeth us not to wander, like beasts and

[1 Eph. iv. 29, 30.   quoties opus est, Lat.   Erasmus' rendering.]
[2 Eph. v. 3, 4, 6.]
[3 1 Cor. xv. 33.]
[4 Matt. xii. 34.]

cattle, through fields and desolate woods. He hath, for our necessity and pleasant feeding, allowed us the use of meat and drink. He granteth us quietness, ease, and sleep, which doth wonderfully refresh the strength, that is decayed and tired with pains. Therefore, so often as a godly man doth enjoy them, doth use them, and is delighted with the honest pleasure of them, let him give thanks to God, and use them moderately in the fear of the Lord. For in so doing he sinneth not against the Lord: but by the abuse of those things, by unthankfulness for them, and by immoderate using of them, he doth offend his God and maker.

For what is allowed or permitted to married folks I have already declared in this very sermon: so that I need not here again to repeat it unto you. Solomon saith: "Be glad with the wife of thy youth; let her be as the beloved hind and pleasant roe; let her love always refresh thee, and be thou still delighted therein[5]," &c. In the meantime, let every one refrain from all abuse and intemperancy: and, if necessity at any time require it, let man and wife lie asunder, as Paul doth counsel them[6]; or else let them give ear to the prophet Joel, who saith: "Proclaim an holy fast, gather the people together; let the bridegroom come forth of his chamber, and the bride out of her closet[7]."

Our garments must be cleanly and honest, according to our country fashion, to cover and become us, unless our country fashion be too far out of order: there must be in them no hypocritical sluttishness, beyond-sea gauds, newfangled toys, nor unseemly sights[8]. The chief apostles of Christ, Peter and Paul, were not ashamed in their epistles to write somewhat largely touching the manner and ordering of women's apparel; because that kind of people do most of all bend to that foolish bravery. Let every faithful body think what is seemly for them to wear, not so much by their degree in dignity or condition of riches, as by their religion. Excess in every thing is discommended in Christians. And to what end do we jag and gash[9] the garments that are sewed

Continency in apparel.

1 Pet. iii.
1 Tim. ii.
Tit. ii.

[5] Prov. v. 18, 19.]
[6] 1 Cor. vii. 5.]
[7] Joel ii. 16. de velo suo, Lat. But edit. 1587 reads, *his* closet.]
[8] nihil peregrinum, leve et indecorum, Lat.]
[9] discindere, Lat.]

together to cover our bodies, but that thereby we may, as it were, by a most fond and ridiculous anatomy, open and lay forth to the eyes of all men what kind of people we are in our inward hearts, jagged (God wot) and ragged[1], vain, light, and nothing sound? And a linen or woollen garment doth as well cover and become the body, as damasks and velvets[2], the cost whereof doth overlade thy purse with expenses to buy them, and mis-shape thee like an ill-favoured picture, when thou wearest them upon thee[3].

Continency in buildings.

In buildings God forbiddeth not cleanliness and necessary cost, but sumptuous expense and gorgeous excess. For these over-brave buildings are seldomtimes finished without extorting wrong and over-great injury done to the poor. Jeremy bringeth in the Lord speaking against the king of Judah, and saying: " Woe to him that buildeth his house with unrighteousness, and his parlour with the goods that are wrongfully gotten; which never recompenseth his neighbour's labour, nor payeth him his hire; who saith to himself, I will build me a wide house and gorgeous parlours; who causeth windows to be hewn therein, and the ceilings and joists maketh he of cedar and painteth them with sinoper[4]. Thinkest thou to reign now that thou hast inclosed theeself with cedar? Did not thy father eat and drink and prosper well, as long as he executed justice and equity[5]?" Let none of us, therefore, build sumptuous houses by robbing the poor of their hire for their labour. Let every one dwell in a house agreeable to his profession, degree, and condition. St Hierome condemneth sumptuous cost even in churches and temples[6]. Neither do I see what gorgeous buildings bring to a man, but mischief and misery. Lord[7], how unwillingly do we die and depart

[1] discissi videlicet, laceri, Lat.]

[2] holoserica, Lat.]

[3] quæ te non decent, et luxuriosa sunt, Lat.]

[4] Vulg. *sinopide;* a red stone found in Sinopis in Pontus.—Plin. Hist. Nat. Lib. xxxv. cap. 5. § 13.   Usus, si lignum colorare libeat.]

[5] Jer. xxii. 13—16.]

[6] Hieron. Ep. xxxiv. ad Nep. de Vit. Cler. Par. 1706. Tom. iv. col. 263.   See Bullinger de Scriptur. Sanct. Authoritate, &c. Lib. ii. fol. 115. Tigur. 1538. and de Orig. Error. cap. 21. fol. 102. Tigur. 1539.]

[7] This expression is not in the original Latin.]

from goodly dwellings, whereby we double the fear of death and terror of sickness! The patriarchs, verily, did dwell in tents, whereby they witnessed that they were pilgrims, and sought another country, the heavenly Hierusalem[8].

Continency in meat and drink is not the loathing of wine and victuals, but the moderate using of them to supply our necessity, and not to cloy us with gluttony. God in the scripture doth condemn gluttony, surfeitings, riotous after-banquets, and drunkenness, which he forbiddeth most of all: for of drunkenness do spring endless miseries and innumerable mischiefs, grievous diseases, poverty, and pinching beggary. Solomon saith: "Who hath woe? who hath sorrow? who hath strife? who hath brawling? who hath wounds without a cause? who hath red eyes? even they that follow the wine, and seek excess thereof[9]. Look not thou upon the wine, how red it is, and what a colour it giveth in the glass. It goeth down sweetly, but at the last it biteth like a serpent, and poisoneth like an adder[10]." I will not rehearse all which I could allege out of heathen writers against surfeiting and drunkenness. Solomon alone in that one sentence containeth a great deal of matter. Moreover, he that heareth not Christ, whom is it likely that he will give ear unto in all the world? Now Christ, in the gospel, by the parable of the rich glutton[11] doth marvellous evidently set forth the woeful end of insatiable paunches[12]. In the same gospel also he taketh occasion to touch the surfeitings and drunkenness of our age, (I mean the age which is immediately before the judgment-day,) where he saith: "As it happened in the days of Noe and Lot; they did eat and drink, even until the day that Noe entered into the ark, and that Lot departed from among the Sodomites; and then incontinently the deluge came, and fire and brimstone poured down from heaven, and destroyed them all[13]." Again, he addeth: "Take heed to yourselves, lest at any time your hearts be overcome with surfeiting and drunkenness and cares of this life; and so that day come upon you at unawares. For

Continency in meat and drink.

Christ against drunkenness.

[8 Heb. xi. 9, 10, 13—16.]
[9 qui veniunt inquisitum ubi misceatur, Lat.]
[10 Prov. xxiii. 29—32.]
[11 Luke xvi. 19, &c.]
[12 epulones, Lat.]
[13 Luke xvii. 26—29.]

as a snare shall it come upon all them that dwell upon the face of the whole earth. Watch ye therefore, at all times praying, that ye may escape all these things, and stand before the Son of man[1]." And I would to God that all men would not write this golden, heavenly, and divine admonition of our Saviour in their halls and dining-parlours only, but in their several hearts also. For since drunkenness hath in these our days so good entertainment with all degrees, estates, kinds[2], and ages, we do daily feel the woeful miseries that God doth threaten to drunkards in the fifth and twenty-eighth chapters of Esay's prophecy. And it is to be feared greatly, that the day of the Lord shall suddenly light upon an innumerable sort of drunkards, to their endless pain and utter destruction. Let him hear, therefore, which hath ears to hear.

Saint Martin's doctrine of continency.

Some say that this Martin was abbot of the monastery of Dumia.

Neither can I here refrain, but needs must recite unto you, dearly beloved, that which St Martine, the bishop, not of Tours in France, but of Dumia [in Germany,] who flourished in the days of Justinian the emperor, did write to Miro, king of Gallicia, touching the ordering and leading a continent life: "If (saith he) thou dost love continency, cut off superfluity, and keep under thine appetite. Consider with thyself, how much nature requireth, and not how much lust desireth. Bridle thy concupiscence, and cast off the alluring baits that serve to draw on hidden pleasures. Eat without undigested surfeiting, and drink without drunkenness. Neither glut thyself with present delicates, nor long after deintrels[3] hard to be come by. Let thy diet be of cates good-cheap, and sit not down for pleasure, but for meat. Let hunger, not sauces, provoke thee to eat. Pay but little for pastimes to delight thee, because thy only care should be to leave such pleasures, that thereby thou, in fashioning thyself to the example of God, mayest, as much as thou canst, make haste to reduce thyself from the body to the spirit. If thou lovest continency, then choose not a pleasant but a wholesome dwellingplace; and make not the lord to be known by the gorgeous house, but the house by the honest landlord. Boast not thyself of that which thou hast not, nor that which thou hast, neither covet to seem more than thou art. But rather take heed that thy poverty be not uncleanly, nor thy niggishness filthy, nor thy

[1 Luke xxi. 34—36.]   [2 sexus, Lat.]
[3 daintrel, a delicacy.—Webster's Dict. 1831.]

simplicity contemptible, nor thy lenity fearful; and though thy estate be poor, yet let it not be in extreme misery. Neither be out of love with thine own degree, nor wish after the estate of another man's life. If thou lovest continency, avoid dishonest things before they happen, and fear no man above thine own conscience. Think that all things are tolerable, dishonesty excepted. Abstain from filthy talk, the liberty whereof doth nourish unshamefacedness. Love rather profitable communication than merry conceits and pleasant talk, and set more by the blunt-spoken truth than by fair soothing speeches. Thou mayest sometime mingle mirth with matters of weight ; but it must be done moderately, without the hurt or detriment of thine estate and gravity : for laughter is blameworthy, if it be immoderately used, childishly squeaked, or taken up by fits, as women are wont to do. Esteem not saucy scoffing, but civil mirth with courteous humanity. Let thy conceits of mirth be without biting, thy sports not without profit, thy laughter without unseemly writhing of thy mouth and visage, thy voice without shrieking, and thy pace in going without hasty shuffling. Let not thy rest be idleness; and when other play, take thou some holy and honest thing in hand. If thou art continent, take heed of flattery, and let it grieve thee as much to be praised of naughty men, as if thou were praised for thine own naughty deeds. Be the gladder for it, if thou displeasest evil men, and impute the evil opinions which naughty men have of thee for the best praise that can be given thee. The hardest work of continency is to put away the soothing courtesies of dissembling flatterers, whose fawning words undo the mind with pleasant sensuality. Presume not too much upon thyself, neither be thou arrogant. Submit thyself so far as thou mayest keep thy gravity ; and yet make not thyself a footstool or cushion for every man to lean on. Be told of thy faults willingly, and suffer thyself gladly to be reprehended. If any man for a cause be angry with and chide thee, acknowledge thy fault, and let his chiding profit thee: but if he chide thee without any cause, think that thereby he would have profited thee. Fear not sharp, but sugared, words. Do thou thyself eschew all sorts of vices, and be not an over-busy searcher-out of other men's faults : be thou no sharp fault-finder, but an admonisher without upbraiding, so that still thy warning may bear the shew of

cheerful mirth : and condescend easily to pardon the error.
Neither praise nor dispraise any man overmuch. Be still, and
give ear to them that speak, and be ready to instruct them
that do hearken : to him that asketh give a ready answer, to
him that despiseth thee give place easily, and fall not out
to chiding and cursing. If thou art continent, have an eye to
the motions of thy body and mind, that they be not unseemly :
and set not light by them because nobody seeth them; for it
maketh no matter if no body see them, so thou thyself dost
spy and perceive them. Be moveable, not light; constant,
not stubborn. Be liberal to all men, fawning on no man :
familiar with few, and upright to every one. Believe not
lightly every rumour, accusation, or conceived suspicion. Despise vainglory, and be no sharp exactor of the goods that
thou hast. Use few words thyself, but suffer them that speak.
Be grave, not rough, nor contemning the merry nature. Be
desirous and applicable to be taught wisdom : impart what thou
knowest to him that demandeth without any arrogancy, and
desire to learn the things that thou knowest not without
hiding thine ignorance. A wise man will not change his
common country fashion, nor make the people gaze on him
with new-found devices[1]."

[1 Continentiam si diligis, circumcide superflua, et in arctum desideria tua constringe. Considera tecum quantum natura poscat, et non
quantum cupiditas expetat. Impone concupiscentiæ tuæ frœnum et
modum, omniaque blandimenta, quæ occultam voluptatem trahunt,
rejice. Ede citra cruditatem, bibe citra ebrietatem. Nec præsentibus
deliciis inhærebis, nec desiderabis absentes. Victus tibi ex facili sit;
nec ad voluptatem, sed ad cibum accede. Palatum tuum fames ex-
citet, non sapores. Desideria tua parvo redime, quia hoc tantum curare
debes, ut desinant; atque, quasi ad exemplar compositus divinum, a
corpore ad spiritum, quantum potes, te festina reducere. Si continentiæ
studes, habita non amœne, sed salubriter : nec dominum esse velis no-
tum a domo, sed domum a domino. Non tibi ascribas quod non eris,
nec quod es, nec major quam es videri velis. Hoc magis observa, ne
paupertas tibi immunda sit, nec parsimonia sordida, nec simplicitas
neglecta, nec lenitas languida : et si tibi res exiguæ sunt, non tamen
sint angustæ. Nec tua defleas, nec mireris aliena. Si continentiam
diligis, turpia fugito antequam accidant; nec quenquam alium vere-
beris plusquam te. Omnia tolerabilia præter turpitudinem crede. A
verbis quoque turpibus abstineto, quia eorum licentia impudentiam
nutrit. Sermones utiles magis quam facetos et amabiles ama, rectos
potius quam obsecundantes. Miscebis interdum seriis jocos, sed tem-

Thus much have I hitherto recited touching continency out of the writings of the blessed bishop, Martine of Dumia. We, for our parts, must pray to the Lord, that he will vouch-safe to bestow on us his holy Spirit, by which the force of continency in all things may take root in our hearts, to the bringing forth of fruit in our deeds, agreeable to the prescript rule of this commanded continency. For, unless the Holy

peratos et sine detrimento dignitatis ac verecundiæ. Nam reprehen-sibilis risus est, si immodicus, si pueriliter effusus, si muliebriter fractus. Non erit tibi scurrilitas, sed grata urbanitas. Sales tui sint sine dente, joci non sine utilitate, risus sine cachinno, vox sine clamore, incessus sine tumultu. Quies tibi non desidia erit; et cum ab aliis luditur, tu sancti aliquid honestique tractabis. Si continens es, adulationes evita, sitque tibi tam triste laudari a turpibus, quam si laudaris ob turpia. Lætior esto quoties displices malis, et malorum de te existi-mationes malas veram tui laudationem ascribe. Difficillimum con-tinentiæ opus est assentationes adulatorum repellere, quorum sermones animum voluptate resolvunt. Non eris audax, nec arrogans. Sub-mittes te, non projicies, gravitate servata. Admoneberis libenter, et reprehenderis patienter. Si merito objurgabit aliquis, scito quia pro-fuit: si immerito, scito quia prodesse voluit. Non acerba, sed blanda, timebis verba. Esto vitiorum fugax ipse, aliorum vero neque curiosus scrutator, neque acerbus reprehensor; sed sine exprobratione correptor, ita ut admonitionem hilaritate prævenias; et errori facile veniam dato. Nec extollas quenquam, neque dejicias. Dicentium esto tacitus auditor, audientium promptus receptor: requirenti facile responde, contem-nenti facile cede, ne in jurgia execrationesque discedas. Si continens es, animi tui motus corporisque observa, ne indecori sint; nec illos ideo contemnas, quia latent: nam nihil differt, si nemo videat, cum tu ipse illos videas. Mobilis esto, non levis; constans, non pertinax. Cunctis esto benignus, nemini blandus, paucis familiaris, omnibus æquus; rumoribus, criminibus, suspicionibus minime credulus vel malignus. Vanæ gloriæ contemptor, et bonorum, quibus præditus es, non acerbus exactor. Rari sermonis ipse, sed loquentium patiens. Severus, non sævus, sed hilarem non aspernans. Sapientiæ cupidus et docilis, quæ nosti sine arrogantia postulanti imparties; quæ nescis, sine occultatione ignorantiæ tibi postula impartiri. Non conturbabit sapiens mores publicos, nec populum in se vitæ novitate convertet.— D. Martini Episcopi Dumiensis formula honestæ vitæ, sive de quatuor virtutibus cardinalibus liber unus, ap. Max. Biblioth. Vet. Patr. Lugd. 1677. Tom. x. fol. 383.—This Martin, a monk born in Pannonia, be-came abbot and bishop of Dumium, (*not in Germany*, the transla-tor's mistake,) and finally bishop of Braga in Portugal, A. D. 563—583. —Mosheim's Eccles. Hist. ed. Soames. Cent. VI. Book 2. part 2. chap. 2. p. 37, note 4. Bingham's Antiq. B. IX. chap. 6. § 16.]

Ghost do quicken and inspire us, we do in vain give ear to so many and so good commandments; and, unless we live and lead a temperate and a sober life, we are utterly unworthy to bear the name of Christians.

Of fasting.   To this place also doth the treatise of fasting belong; which I mean to handle in as few words as conveniently can be. Christian fasting is a discipline, ordering, and chastening of the body for the present necessity, which we begin and keep of our own accord, without compulsion, and wherewith we humble ourselves in the sight of God, by drawing from the body the matter that setteth the flesh on fire, thereby to make it obey the spirit. For so long as we mortal men do live in this body, the flesh doth still resist the spirit; and most of all rebelleth then, when we with delicates do pamper the body. Wherefore fasting doth draw from the body every evil which stirreth up and strengtheneth it against the good commandments of God's holy Spirit.

Two kinds of fastings.   Now the necessity for which we keep this fasting is of two sorts, public and private. We fast for the public or common necessity, when some calamity doth either oppress, or else hang over the head of the church. Of such a manner of fasting we see examples in the second chapter of Joel, and in the third of Jonas his prophecy: which very same order in fasting was used in the time of our Lord's apostles, as it is evidently extant in the Acts of the Apostles[1]. And this kind of fasting doth seem to have differed very little, among them of old, from a general mourning; yea, it seemeth altogether to have been nothing else but a kind of lamenting. In the scriptures every book is full of examples, which teach and instruct us how the holy saints did humble themselves in the sight of God with true repentance for their sins and offences. Private necessity is that for which every particular man doth fast, when he feeleth himself to be vexed with bodily concupiscence, that thereby he may take from the flesh the flame and fuel, lest the body at last be fired and burned. For the Lord in the gospel said, that the children of the bride-chamber do fast when the bridegroom is taken from them[2], that is, in a hard and dangerous time. The marriage doth signify the bond whereby we are knit to Christ in faith and the Holy

[1 Acts xiii. 3. and xiv. 23.]
[2 Mark ii. 19, 20.]

Ghost. This yet notwithstanding, the godly man doth still rejoice[3]. He doth with giving of thanks and temperance both eat and drink so much as is sufficient, and is delighted also in these external gifts of God : but when he feeleth that the bridegroom is ready for to depart, or that he is now already almost departed out of his heart; that is, when he feeleth that the spirit is extinguished by the flesh's wantonness, and that faith doth once begin to be cold; then doth he settle himself to prayer, and doth appoint a solemn fasting, thereby either to keep the bridegroom still, or else to pull him back being ready to depart.

But neither public nor private fastings can abide to be enforced: for they will not be compelled, but desire to proceed of a free, cheerful, and voluntary mind. Unwilling men do nothing well. God requireth a cheerful giver. Moreover, let fastings be moderated according to the quality of places, persons, perils, and temptations : if they be not continual, yet let them be often, till such time as we be delivered and rid utterly of them. Let them be without superstition and feigned hypocrisy, as our Lord in the sixth of St Matthew's gospel hath taught us. Herewithal do the words of St Hierome agree very well, which he wrote to Nepotianus, touching fasting, as followeth : " Prescribe to thyself so long a time to fast in as thine ability will suffer thee to bear. Let thy fastings be pure, uncorrupt, simple, moderated, and not superstitious. What availeth it to eat no oil, and to seek out such seldom fond cates as are hard to be come by, as figs, pepper, nuts, dates, pure flour for overfine bread, and honey ? The gardens, with digging for novelties, are turned over and over, because we will not eat common cribble[4] bread; and so, while our dainty mouths seek after delicates, our souls are pulled from the kingdom of heaven. I hear, moreover, that some men there are, which (contrary to nature) refuse to drink water and feed upon bread; but suck up and swallow very costly suppings, dainty herb-broths, and the juice of beets, not out of a cup, but out of a shell. O shame ! blush we not at such fond toys, and are

Of what quality and kind our fastings must be.

[3 Hoc integro, perpetuo gaudet pius, Lat. This remaining unbroken, the godly man continually rejoices.]

[4 cribble, coarse flour, or meal.—Webster's Dict.]

we not ashamed of such superstition[1]?" Thus much saith Hierome. And it is evident, that even at this day this vice is especially received among our wealthy and religious men.

The end of fastings.   But the end of christian fastings are, that the church, or sinner, should submit and humble themselves before the Lord, that the flesh should be obedient and subject to the spirit, that the flesh should not hinder the sinner to work righteousness, and that the intent and mind of him that prayeth should be the more earnestly bent toward God. For fasting is of the number of those works which of themselves are not absolute and perfect, but have another meaning, for which they are ordained to another end and purpose: therefore fasting is a certain help to the prayers and virtues of godly men. Whereupon in the prophets we find, that the fastings of the Jews displeased the Lord: for they did nought else but fast alone; that is, they did at a certain and appointed time abstain from their usual manner of eating, but they restrained not themselves from sin and wickedness, but let their flesh have the bridle at will, when as indeed they should have ceased to have pampered it, that thereby it being the weaker, the spirit might be the stronger to do and fulfil all sort of good works. And therefore saith the Lord: "I have not chosen such a manner of fasting;" and the rest, as it followeth in the fifty-eighth chapter of Esay, and in the seventh and eighth chapters of Zachary's prophecy.

The true fast.   The apostle Paul, verily, doth expressly say, that "meat commendeth us not to God: for neither if we eat, have we anything the more; neither if we eat not, have we anything the less[2]." He therefore doth not fast truly, which doth

[1 Tantum tibi jejuniorum modum impone, quantum ferre potes. Sint tibi pura, casta, simplicia, moderata, et non superstitiosa jejunia. Quid prodest oleo non vesci, et molestias quasdam difficultatesque ciborum quærere, carycas, piper, nuces, palmarum fructus, similam, mel, pistacia? Tota hortorum cultura vexatur, ut cibario non vescamur pane; et dum delicias sectamur, a regno cœlorum retrahimur. Audio præterea quosdam, contra rerum hominumque naturam, aquam non bibere, nec vesci pane; sed sorbitiunculas delicatas et contrita olera, betarumque succum, non calice sorbere, sed concha. Proh pudor! non erubescimus istiusmodi ineptiis, nec tædet superstitionis?— Hieron. Opp. Par. 1706. Epist. XXXIV. ad Nepot. de Vit. Cler. Tom. IV. pars 2. col. 264.]

[2 1 Cor. viii. 8. Erasmus' rendering.]

abstain only, at a certain appointed time, from certain manner of meats; but he, which doth therefore refrain from the pleasures of the flesh, that thereby he may make it subject to the spirit, and do the works of faith and charity, which are acceptable in the sight of the Lord. If therefore thou dost desire to fast a true fast, eat, drink, and sleep, and take heed to thy body, that it wax not insolent; fast from all sin, eat not the meat of malice, taste not the juncats[3] of lust and pleasure, and be not set on fire with the wine of wantonness. Fast from evil deeds, abstain from evil words, and refrain thyself from naughty thoughts. For Basil also saith: "True fasting consisteth in freeness from vices, in continency of tongue, in suppressing of anger, in cutting off concupiscence, backbiting, lying, and perjury[4]," &c. But even as the good works themselves, which are done by faith, do not merit the kingdom of heaven (for that glory is due to the merit of Christ alone); even so fasting, which is an aid and help to good works, doth not meritoriously deserve the kingdom of God.

But now I see a doubtful disputation arise among the most divines of this our age, touching the time and manner of fastings, and also of the choice of meats. Some there are which affirm and uphold the fasts of Lent[5], and embering days, and such other, to be the fasts which God hath appointed. There are that say, thou hast not fasted, if by any means thou taste any flesh: and there are which prescribe and appoint some certain hours to fast in. But I, for my part, see not any such doctrines to be taught us in the scriptures. For the Lord in the gospel kept not any of their devised fasts, when he fasted forty days; but did altogether abstain from all kinds of meat, even as Moses and Helias had also done: wherefore he by that deed of his did not give us any law to fast so. Moreover, the Lord in the gospel doth evidently teach, that the thing, which entereth in by the mouth, doth not defile the man, but that which issueth out from his heart[6].

Of the manner and time of fasting, and of the choice of meats.

[3 epulas, Lat.]

[4 ἀληθὴς νηστεία ἡ τοῦ κακοῦ ἀλλοτρίωσις, ἐγκράτεια γλώσσης, θυμοῦ ἐποχὴ, ἐπιθυμιῶν χωρισμὸς, καταλαλιᾶς, ψεύδους, ἐπιορκίας.—Basil. Hom. II. de Jejunio, T. II. p. 15. Paris. 1722.]

[5 stata jejunia quadragesimæ, quatuor temporum, Lat. See Bingham's Orig. Eccles. Lib. XXI. cap. 1. and cap. 2. § 1.]

[6 Matt. xv. 11, 18.]

"To the pure are all things pure[1]." And Paul saith: "I know, and am persuaded through the Lord Jesus Christ, that nothing is common of itself; but to him that thinketh that any thing is common, to him is it common." Again: "Let not him which eateth despise him which eateth not; nor let him which eateth not judge him which eateth: for him that eateth the Lord hath taken[2]." Moreover, the place is evident, which the same Paul writeth in the fourth chapter of his first epistle to Timothy, where he affirmeth, that the forbidding of meats is a "doctrine of devils." Neither needeth any man here to tell us any whit of the Tatians and Encratites[3]; for they did slander the good creatures of God. Paul speaketh of them who, although they do not utterly condemn meat and marriage, do yet notwithstanding forbid the use of meat.

Difference in fastings.

Furthermore, we do not read that any laws were ordained in that age which followed next after the preaching of the apostles, which did command and prescribe any time and order of fasting, or choice of meats. I will rehearse unto you, dearly beloved, the words of Irenæus the martyr, which in the Ecclesiastical History of Eusebius are to be found word for word, as they are here set down: "The controversy is not only touching Easter-day, but also touching the manner of fasting. For some do think that the fast ought to be kept but one day only, other two, other more, and some whole forty days; so that, counting the hours of the night and day, they make a day. Which difference of observing the times is not now first of all in our age begun, but was brought in a great while ago (as I suppose) of them, which did not simply keep that which was taught from the beginning, but, either by negligence or unskilfulness, fell afterward into a worse use and custom. And yet notwithstanding, all these, though they jarred in the observation of times, were nevertheless and are

[1] Titus i. 15.]
[2] Rom. xiv. 14, 3.]
[3] The Tatiani or Tatianists, who were also called Encratitæ, or *abstainers*, were the followers of Tatian in the second century of the Christian era. They held *matter* to be the source of all evil, and therefore discarded all the external comforts and conveniences of life, and fasted rigorously.—Mosheim. Eccles. Hist. Book I. Cent. II. part 2. chap. 5. § 9. Vol. I. p. 195. ed. Soames. See also Early Writings of Hooper, Parker Soc. ed. p. 375.]

agreeable with us; neither hath the discord about fasting broke our concord in faith[4]." Thus much Irenæus. Moreover, Socrates Constantinopolitanus in the ninth book and thirty-eighth chapter of his[5] Tripartite History witnesseth, that about the year of our Lord 453, in the reign of Theodosius the younger, the same diversity was in the church, and setteth it down in these words following: " Furthermore, they have not the same kind of abstinence from meat. For some do altogether abstain from living creatures; some among living creatures do eat fish only; some with fish do feed on fowls also, saying, that they (as Moses saith) have their substance of water; some are known to abstain from herbs and eggs; some do feed of dry bread only; some not so much as that: some, fasting nine hours, do then without difference use any kind of meat: and innumerable customs are found among sundry men." Now the very same Socrates, shewing his opinion upon that diversity, doth say: " And for because no ancient writing is found touching this thing, I think that the apostles left it free to every man's judgment, that every one may work, not by fear or necessity, the thing that is good[6]." Thus far Socrates. The fasts of Christians, therefore, ought

The Latin copy hath caulis, *which I turn* herbs: *it may also be taken for roots.*

Fastings must be

[4 Οὐδὲ γὰρ μόνον περὶ τῆς ἡμέρας ἐστὶν ἡ ἀμφισβήτησις, ἀλλὰ καὶ περὶ τοῦ εἴδους αὐτοῦ τῆς νηστείας. Οἱ μὲν γὰρ οἴονται μίαν ἡμέραν δεῖν αὐτοὺς νηστεύειν, οἱ δὲ δύο, οἱ δὲ καὶ πλείονας· οἱ δὲ τεσσαράκοντα ὥρας ἡμερινάς τε καὶ νυκτερινὰς συμμετροῦσι τὴν ἡμέραν αὐτῶν. Καὶ τοιαύτη μὲν ποικιλία τῶν ἐπιτηρούντων οὐ νῦν ἐφ' ἡμῶν γεγονυῖα, ἀλλὰ καὶ πολὺ πρότερον ἐπὶ τῶν πρὸ ἡμῶν, τῶν παρὰ τὸ ἀκριβὲς, ὡς εἰκὸς, κρατούντων, τὴν καθ' ἁπλότητα καὶ ἰδιωτισμὸν συνήθειαν εἰς τὸ μετέπειτα πεποιηκότων. Καὶ οὐδὲν ἔλαττον πάντες οὗτοι εἰρήνευσάν τε, καὶ εἰρηνεύομεν πρὸς ἀλλήλους, καὶ ἡ διαφωνία τῆς νηστείας τὴν ὁμόνοιαν τῆς πίστεως συνίστησι.—Euseb. Histor. Eccles. Lib. v. cap. 24. ed. Burton.]

[5 Not *his*, but the history compiled from him and others.]

[6 Sed etiam ciborum abstinentiam non similem habent. Nam alii omnino ab animatis abstinent: alii ex animantibus pisces solummodo comedunt: quidam cum piscibus vescuntur et volatilibus, dicentes hæc secundum Mosen ex aqua habere substantiam: alii vero etiam caulibus et ovis abstinere noscuntur: quidam sicco tantummodo pane vescuntur: alii neque hoc. Alii, usque ad nonam jejunantes horam, sine discretione ciborum reficiuntur. Et innumeræ consuetudines apud diversos reperiuntur. Et quia nulla lectio de hoc invenitur antiqua, puto apostolos singulorum hoc reliquisse sententiæ, ut unusquisque operetur non timore, non necessitate, quod bonum est.—Hist. Tripart. ap. Cassiodori Opp. Lib. ix. cap. 38. Tom. v. p. 348. Rotomag. 1679.]

[BULLINGER.]

28

free, and not
bound to
laws.
to be free, and not bound to laws. Apollinus, a certain
ancient and ecclesiastical writer, disputing against Montanus,
the heretic, saith : "This is he which taught that marriages
are undone, and which first of all hath appointed laws for
men to fast by [1]."

And verily, to go about to set down to all men and
nations one manner of fasting in one appointed time, one
prescribed order and choice of meat, is a mere folly, and
a brain-sick kind of madness. For, according to the choice of
air, so are men's bodies of sundry temperatures, and one kind
of meat doth not stir men of sundry complexions to one kind
of affection. The most godly way, therefore, and profitable
order for the church is, that all pastors in every congregation
should teach sobriety, temperancy, and the true fast indeed:
not presuming to prescribe any laws for the choice of meats or
times, but leaving that free to every man and nation, who undoubtedly will have an especial eye to temper themselves from
the things by which they perceive that their health [2] will be
endangered ; but most of all in the time when the flesh be-
ginneth to wax over wanton, or when some great peril hangeth
over their head. For the time of fasting is not prorogued till
an appointed number of years or days be expired, but till the
looseness or wantonness of the flesh, temptations, or motions,
be utterly bridled. Fastings being so ordered, as they be the
exercises of godliness, obtain great praise indeed in the church
of the Lord.

The sum of
the seventh
precept or
command-
ment.
Thus much hitherto touching fasting. Now, to shut up
this seventh precept, I say it forbiddeth all intemperance, it
commandeth holiness, and the clean and lawful use of all the
members of the whole body. And therefore in this short
precept there is contained a good part of the doctrine of
Christ and his apostles. For Paul to the Thessalonians saith :
"We beseech you, brethren, and exhort you by the Lord
Jesus, that ye increase more and more, as ye have received of
us how ye ought to walk, and to please God. For ye know

[1 Auctor Euseb. Ecclesiast. Hist. Lib. v. cap. 18, Lat.   Οὗτός
ἐστιν ὁ διδάξας λύσεις γάμων, ὁ νηστείας νομοθετήσας.—Euseb. Hist.
Eccles. Lib. v. cap. 18. ed. Burton. The writer is *Apollonius.*—Routh,
Reliq. Sacr. Tom. I. p. 466. Oxon. 1846. See also Calvin. Comment.
in I. Ep. ad Tim. cap. IV. v. 3. Tom. VII. p. 455. ed. Amst.]

[2 Suæ integritati, Lat.]

what commandments we gave you by the Lord[3] Jesus. For this is the will of God, even your holiness; that ye should abstain from fornication; that every one of you should know how to possess his vessel[4] in holiness and honour; not in the lust of concupiscence, as the Gentiles, which knew not God. God is a revenger of all such, as we have forewarned you and testified. For God hath not called us unto uncleanness, but unto holiness[5]." And straightway after again: "The God of peace sanctify you throughout, that your whole spirit, and soul, and body, may be preserved blameless in the coming of our Lord Jesus Christ[6]."

I have again, my brethren, passed beyond the appointed time of an ordinary sermon, staying you longer than I am wont to do. Pardon this fault; for, I hope, I have not troubled you, almost two whole hours, without profiting you any whit at all. Make your prayers now, and depart in peace. By the help and will of God I will, within these few days, add the rest of the ten commandments. The grace of our Lord and Saviour Jesus Christ be with you all. Amen.

[3 Dominum nostrum, Lat. our Lord.]

[4 suum inquam corpus, Lat. omitted by the translator:—I mean, his body.]

[5 1 Thess. iv. 1—7. immunditiæ causa, Lat. Erasmus' rendering.]

[6 1 Thess. v. 23. The rendering in Cranmer's Bible is more agreeable with Bullinger's text: viz. "So that in nothing ye may be blamed in the coming of our Lord Jesus Christ."]

ERRATA.

PAGE	NOTE	LINE	FOR	READ
10	2	1	*hæc*	*hanc*
138	2	8	*regis*	*regio*
—	—	12	*lationis*	*latronis*
202	1	2	*ine*	*sine*

ADDENDA.

15 note 7   line 8 παθόντα,

—   —   12 ἢ τρεπτὸν,

29 line 9   " sat at the right hand of God," should have been noted as an interpolation of the Translator's.

53   13   of the Saviour : ab ipso Salvatore, Lat.

54   33   Mark,

64   21   dele², and insert [Matt. xv. 9.]

83 note 5   The definition is taken from Budæi Comment. Ling. Græc. p. 103.

91   3   cf. Tertull. adv. Praxean. cap. 10. Tom. II. p. 161. ed. Semler. Hal. Mag. 1828, which passage, no doubt, Bullinger had here in his mind, as he has referred to it also in his Exposit. Epist. ad Roman. iv. 20, 21. p. 47. Tigur. 1537.

112 line 32   So in his Expos. Epist. ad Rom. iii. 26. p. 35, Bullinger writes : Hactenus exposuit (Paulus) fidem, videlicet in Christum, id est, ipsum Christum Jesum, Dei filium, cui fidimus, veram esse pii hominis justitiam.

123 note 4   line 13. Of this treatise Bullinger himself says in his Comment. in Lucam. Lib. I. p. 17. Tigur. 1546.—quæ S. Cyprianus, *sive is Ruffinus est,* scripsit.

129 line 22   cf. Augustine's Enarrat. in Psalm. cit.

154   9   See Pearson on the Creed. Art. 7. p. 455. Vol. I. and Vol. II. p. 365. Oxf. 1820.

158   23   Symbolum secundo conditum disertis verbis in hunc modum confitendum docet : πιστεύω εἰς τὸ Πνεῦμα τὸ ἅγιον τὸ Κύριον, τὸ λαλῆσαν διὰ τῶν προφητῶν εἰς μίαν καθολικὴν καὶ ἀποστολικὴν ἐκκλησίαν, hoc est, Credo in Spiritum sanctum Dominum, qui loquutus est per prophetas in unam catholicam et apostolicam ecclesiam. Audis unum atque eundem esse Spiritum, qui per prophetas loquator in unam generalem ecclesiam, olim quidem a prophetis, nunc ab apostolis, verbo veritatis, qui Sancti Spiritus instinctus est, collectam. Bullingeri Comment. in 1 Epist. Petri. cap. i. p. 11.

195   36   See Erasmi Adag. Chili. p. 500, conscientia mille testes.

212 note 2   See an anecdote of Celio Secundo Curio in M'Crie's Hist. of Reform. in Italy, p. 102. Lond. 1827.

320 line 1   cf. Bp. Hooper's Early Writ. ed. Park. Soc. p. 78.

350   5   These were the Anabaptists' objections. See Bullinger. adv. Anabapt. Lib. v. cap. 4.

THE
EIGHTH ANNUAL REPORT
(FOR THE YEAR 1848.)
OF
The Parker Society,
INSTITUTED A.D. 1840.

FOR THE PUBLICATION OF

THE WORKS OF THE FATHERS AND EARLY WRITERS OF THE REFORMED ENGLISH CHURCH.

PRESENTED TO THE GENERAL MEETING, MAY THE 21st, 1849.

> " He (*Archbishop Parker*) was a great collector of ancient and modern writings, and took especial care of the safe preservation of them for all succeeding times; as foreseeing, undoubtedly, what use might be made of them by posterity; that, by having recourse to such originals and precedents, the true knowledge of things might the better appear."
> " As he was a great patron and promoter of good learning, so he took care of giving encouragement to printing—a great instrument of the increase thereof."
>
> *Strype's Life of Archbishop Parker.*

The Council of the Parker Society have to lay before the Members the following Report of the proceedings of the past year:—

The total receipts, from all sources, for the year just closed were £5983, 16s. 1d.; the total payments £6357, 7s. 8d., leaving a balance against the Society of £373, 11s. 7d., which comprises several payments for books in progress, to appear in future years.

The books for the year 1848 which have been circulated among the Subscribers were four in number:—1st. A third portion of Bishop Jewel's works; containing his celebrated Apology, both in the original Latin, and in Lady Bacon's English Translation; also, a part of the Defence of the Apology.

2nd. Doctrinal Treatises of Tyndale, the martyr, and translator of the Scriptures.

3rd. A portion of the Writings of Bradford; containing various Sermons, Meditations, and other Tracts, by that honoured martyr.

4th. Fulke's Answer to Stapleton, Martiall, and Sanders; being a supplement to Calfhill's work, published in 1846.

A small edition of the Latin originals of the Letters printed in two parts in 1846 and 1847, has been issued to those who paid the specified additional subscription.

For the year 1849, the following books are in preparation:—

1st. Another portion of Tyndale's Works.

2nd. A volume of Bullinger's Decades, a work of great importance, having been prescribed by the Convocation of 1586 as a manual for the clergy.

3rd. Selections from the Writings of Bishop Bale.

4th. A translation of Whitaker's valuable Disputation on Holy Scripture. These volumes, it is confidently expected, will have been circulated among the members before Christmas.

In reference to future proceedings, the Council feel that they may now speak more definitely than they have hitherto ventured to do. A wish has frequently been expressed by subscribers, to know how long the series of re-publications was likely to last; but, in the early stages of their progress, the Council could only point out certain works which they felt it desirable to print, and promise that pains should be taken to issue these as speedily as circumstances, with a due regard to the creditable editing of them, would allow. Now, however, when much has been accomplished, and many volumes have been presented to the subscribers, the Council can more easily define what remains to be done. They are sure that the members will agree with them in deeming the works of Bishop Jewel, and of Archbishop Whitgift, of the highest importance, which it would be a discredit to the Society to leave unfinished. To complete Jewel and to publish Whitgift must, therefore, be a main object. Simultaneously with these may proceed the remaining volumes of Tyndale, Bradford, and Hooper, of which portions have already appeared. There are also in forward preparation Archbishop Parker's Correspondence, Rogers on the Articles, the remainder of Bullinger's Decades, the Reformatio Legum, Nowel's Catechisms, with a few other valuable treatises and documents. The precise time of completing these must of course depend upon the support the Council continue to receive; but it may be stated with confidence, that about four years will suffice to place the works they have enumerated in the hands of the subscribers, who will then possess a series of the most important character.

If these volumes have been more generally controversial than some persons expected, the Council would remind their friends that a peculiar value must always attach to them as evidence of the opinions of men to whom, under God, we owe the deliverance of our Church from the foreign yoke under which she had for centuries laboured, and who compiled and settled those formularies which are her present standards of doctrine. On every point connected with the doctrine and discipline of the Church the opinions of such men must be of incalculable interest. They were her defenders against external and internal assailants; they were the expounders of the truths which they had contributed to embody. Of course it is not intended to assert that the private writings of any divines, however venerable and eminent, can claim a public authority; but public standards may indisputably be illustrated by the contemporaneous writings of their compilers, and the spirit in which they were conceived, and the sense they were designed to convey be hence better understood.

And it is to be observed, that the writers of the Reformation era demand respect, not only for the circumstances under which they wrote, but because they were the distinguished men of an age neither unlearned nor un-adorned with genius of the highest order; besides, they were men, not only of natural endowments, but of primitive zeal and piety. They, many of them, obtained the martyr's crown, and are, therefore, worthy to be had in everlasting remembrance. Their faults, in a great measure, were those of the system in which they had been nurtured, or of the period in which they lived; their graces were the peculiar and excellent gift of Him who raises up and strengthens His own instruments for the great work He is accomplishing in the earth: they were honoured by Him, they should be honoured and esteemed by us

The Council feel grateful to God that they have been enabled to put forth the works of so many of these men, that they have been permitted so far to complete their original design; and they would earnestly solicit from the members such continued support, as that they may not have to leave undone that which yet remains.

ABSTRACT OF THE CASH ACCOUNT OF THE PARKER SOCIETY,

FOR THE YEAR 1848.

RECEIVED.	£	s.	d.
Balance brought from 1847	94	11	11
Subscriptions received for 1848, and previous Years	5155	18	6
Amount received on Consols account	676	8	4
" " Exchequer Bill account	56	17	4
Balance due to Treasurer	373	11	7
Total	**£6357**	**7**	**8**

PAID.	£	s.	d.
Paid for Printing and Paper of the books for 1848	3752	12	3
For Binding and Delivery	1118	18	2
For Editorial Expenses	769	1	3
For Insurance from Fire	5	12	6
Library	11	17	3
For Printing Plans, Reports and Circulars, and for Advertisements	83	5	6
For Rent of Office, Salary of Secretary, and Wages of Clerks and Porters	448	13	6
Books purchased to complete Sets	54	15	3
For Furniture and Fittings	6	5	6
For Stationery and Account Books	6	11	9
For incidentals, including postage, carriage, coals, and various petty expenses	99	14	9
Total	**£6357**	**7**	**8**

HENRY POWNALL.   } Auditors.
FRANCIS LOWE.

LAWS OF THE PARKER SOCIETY.

I.—That the Society shall be called THE PARKER SOCIETY, and that it objects shall be—first, the reprinting, without abridgement, alteration, or omission, of the best Works of the Fathers and Early Writers of the Reformed English Church, published in the period between the accession of King Edward VI. and the death of Queen Elizabeth: secondly, the printing of such remains of other Writers of the Sixteenth Century as may appear desirable (including, under both classes, some of the early English Translations of the Foreign Reformers); and thirdly, the printing of some manuscripts of the same Authors, hitherto unpublished.

II.—That the Society shall consist of such a number of members, being subscribers of at least One Pound each annually, as the Council may determine; the subscription to be considered due on the First day of January in each year, in advance, and to be paid on or before such a day as the Council may fix; sufficient notice being given of the day appointed.

III.—That the Management of the Society shall be vested in a President, a Treasurer, a Librarian, and a Council of twenty-four other subscribers, being members of the established Church, of whom not less than sixteen shall be Clergymen. The Council and Officers to be elected annually by the subscribers, at a General Meeting to be held in the month of May; and no persons shall then be proposed who are not already members of the Council, or Officers, unless their names shall have been transmitted to the Secretaries on or before the 15th of April in the current year, by nominations in writing, signed by at least five subscribers. And that there be three Secretaries appointed by the Council; also that the Council have power to fill all vacancies during the year.

IV.—That the accounts of the receipt and expenditure of the Society shall be examined every year, previously to the General Meeting by four Auditors, two of them selected from the Council, and two appointed by the preceeding General Meeting.

V.—That the funds shall be expended in the payment of the expenses incurred in producing the works published by the Society, so that every member not in arrear of his or her annual subscription, shall receive a copy of every work published by the Society during the year, for each sum of One Pound subscribed, without any charge for the same; and that the number of copies printed in each year, shall be limited to the quantity required for the number actually subscribed for.

VI.—That every member of the Society who shall intimate to the Council a desire to withdraw, or who shall not pay the subscription by the time appointed, shall cease to be a member of the Society; and no Member shall at any time incur any liability beyond the annual subscription.

VII.—That, after the commencement of the proceedings, no rule shall be made or altered excepting at a General Meeting, and after notice of the same has been communicated to the members by circulars, or by advertisement in two London daily newspapers, at least fourteen days before the General Meeting.

VIII.—Donations and Legacies will be thankfully received; the amount of which shall be expended by the Council in supplying copies of the publications to clerical, or other libraries, destitute of funds to purchase the same, and for such other purposes, connected with the objects of the Society, as the Council may determine.

THE FOLLOWING NAMES, AMONG OTHERS, ARE IN THE LIST OF SUBSCRIBERS TO

The Parker Society.

HER MOST GRACIOUS MAJESTY ADELAIDE, QUEEN DOWAGER.
HIS ROYAL HIGHNESS THE PRINCE ALBERT.
HIS MAJESTY THE KING OF PRUSSIA.
HER ROYAL HIGHNESS THE DUCHESS OF KENT.

HIS GRACE THE LORD ARCHBISHOP OF CANTERBURY.—HIS GRACE THE LORD ARCHBISHOP OF YORK.

His Grace the Duke of Devonshire.—His Grace the Duke of Manchester. —His Grace the Duke of Sutherland.—His Grace the Duke of Roxburghe. The most Honourable the Marquesses of Bute, Cholmondeley, Conyngham, Downshire, Northampton, Ormonde, and Salisbury.

The Right Honourable the Earls of Cavan, Chichester, Clancarty, De Grey, Essex, Galloway, Howe, Jermyn, Nelson, Rosse, and Spencer.

The Right Honourable Lord Viscounts Adare, Alford, Campden, De Vesci, Fordwich, Hill, and Lorton.

The Right Honourable and Reverend Lords Charles Thynne, John Thynne, Arthur Hervey, Wriothesley Russell, The Right Honourable Lord George A. Hill, Lord Lindsay, Lord Henry Cholmondeley, Lord Edward Chichester, &c., &c.

The Right Honourable and Right Reverend the Lord Bishop of London.— The Right Reverend the Lords Bishops of Durham, Winchester, Chester, Chichester, Ely, Hereford, Lichfield, Lincoln, Llandaff, Manchester, Oxford, Peterborough, Ripon, Rochester, St. Asaph, and of Worcester.

The Right Honourable and Right Reverend the Lords Bishops of Clogher, of Meath, and of Killaloe and Clonfert.—The Right Reverend the Lords Bishops of Down and Connor, of Ossory and Ferns, and of Cashel and Waterford.

The Right Reverend the Lords Bishops of Australia, Bombay, Calcutta, Capetown, Colombo, Guiana, Melbourne, Newcastle, Toronto, and of Tasmania.

The Right Reverend the Bishops of Delaware, Georgia, Maryland, New Jersey, Ohio, South Carolina, and of Virginia.

The Right Honourable the Lords Ashley, (President), Bolton, Calthorpe, Farnham, Lindsay, Littleton, Rayleigh, and Teignmouth.

Her Grace the Duchess Dowager of Argyle.—Right Honourable the Countess of Annesley.—Right Honourable Viscountess Valentia.— Right Honourable Lady Ward, &c.

The Right Honourable the Lord Chief Justice of Ireland.—The Right Honourable Lord Justice Clerk, Scotland.—The Honourable Mr. Justice Jackson, The Chevalier Bunsen.—The Right Honourable Henry Goulburn, M.P. for the University of Cambridge.—The Right Honourable W. E. Gladstone, M.P. for the University of Oxford, &c.

The Very Reverend the Deans of Chester, Durham, Gloucester, Manchester, Norwich, Peterborough, Salisbury, and Winchester.—The Deans and Chapters of Lichfield, Worcester, Limerick, Raphoe, Tuam, &c.

The Very Reverend the Deans of Clogher, Cloyne, Connor, Cork, Derry, Cashel, Elphin, Emly, St. Patrick, Ossory, Kildare, and Kilmacdaugh.

The Honourable and Worshipful T. W. Law, Chancellor of Bath and Wells. —The Worshipful H. Raikes, Chancellor of Chester, E. T. M. Phillips, Chancellor of Gloucester, F. R. Sandys, Chancellor of Ossory, Marsham Argles, Chancellor of Peterborough, and J. N. Woodroffe, Chancellor of Cork.

The Venerable Archdeacons Berners, Bevan, Brown, Buckle, Davys, Hare, Hill, Hodson, Hoare, Law, Mac Donald, Philpot, Spooner, C. Thorp, Henry Williams, William Williams of New Zealand, R. J. Wilberforce.

The Venerable Archdeacons Bell, Beresford, Creery, Digby, Mant, Monsell, Oldfield, Power, Stopford, Strean, Stuart, Verschoyle, and St. George.

Reverend Dr. Plumtre, Master of University Coll., Oxford, and Vice Chancellor of the University.—Reverend Dr. Phelps, Master of Sidney Sussex Coll. Cambridge.—Reverend Dr. Philpot, Master of Catherine Hall, Cambridge. —Reverend Dr. Archdall, Master of Emmanuel Coll. Cambridge.— Reverend Dr. Tatham, Master of St. John's Coll. Cambridge.—Reverend Dr. Symons, Warden of Wadham Coll. Oxford.—Reverend Dr. Fox, Provost of Queen's Coll. Oxford.—Reverend Dr. Cotton, Provost of Worcester Coll. Oxford.—Reverend Dr. Jeune, Master of Pembroke Coll. Oxford.—Reverend Dr. Thackeray, Provost of King's Coll. Cambridge. —Reverend Dr. Ainslie, Master of Pembroke Hall, Cambridge.—Reverend Dr. French, Master of Jesus Coll. Cambridge.—Dr. King, President of Queens' Coll. Cambridge.—Reverend Dr. Webb, Master of Clare Hall, Cambridge.—Reverend Dr. Cramer, Principal of New Inn Hall, Oxford.—Reverend E. Cardwell, Principal of St. Alban's Hall, Oxford.

The Reverend Dr. Sadleir, Provost of Trinity Coll. Dublin.—The Venerable Archdeacon Thorp, Warden of the University of Durham.—The Very Reverend Dr. Lee, Principal of the University of Edinburgh.—Reverend J. Wheeler, President of the University of Vermont, U.S.—Reverend Dr. Hawtrey.—Reverend Dr. Williamson, late Head Master of Westminster School.—Reverend Dr. Tait, Head Master of Rugby School, &c., &c.

LIBRARIES.—The Royal Library, Berlin.—Balliol Coll. Oxford.—Gonville and Caius, Pembroke, and Queens' Coll. Cambridge.—Wadham, and Worcester Coll. Oxford.—Trinity Coll. Dublin.—University of Edinburgh.—King's Coll. London.—Advocates' Library, and Library of the Writers to the Signet, Edinburgh.—St. Bees' Coll.—Cathedrals of Chester and Cashel.— The London Institution.—The London Library.—The Chetham Library, Manchester ; and many other Collegiate, Public, and School Libraries, &c.

THE COUNCIL AND OFFICERS FOR 1849-50.

President.
THE RIGHT HONOURABLE LORD ASHLEY, M.P., L.L.D., &c.

Treasurer.
SIR WALTER R. FARQUHAR, BART.

Council.
REV. R. G. BAKER.—REV. C. BENSON, Canon of Worcester.—REV. E. BICKERSTETH.—JOHN BRIDGES, ESQ.—JOHN BRUCE, ESQ.—REV. GUY BRYAN.—REV. RICHARD BURGESS.—REV. T. TOWNSON CHURTON, Fellow of Brasenose College, Oxford.—HON. WILLIAM COWPER.—REV. W. HAYWARD COX, Oxford.—REV. J. W. CUNNINGHAM.—REV. THOMAS DALE, Canon Residentiary of St. Paul's.—REV. W. GOODE.—REV. JOHN HARDING.—REV. T. H. HORNE, Canon of St. Paul's.—JOSEPH HOARE, ESQ.—REV. J. JACKSON.—HON. ARTHUR KINNAIRD.—REV. DR. OLLIVANT, Regius Professor of Divinity in the University of Cambridge.—HENRY POWNALL, ESQ.—REV. JOSIAH PRATT.—REV. M. M. PRESTON.—REV. DR. ROBINSON.—REV. DANIEL WILSON.

General Secretary and Librarian.

REV. JOHN AYRE.

Editorial Secretary.
REV. JAMES SCHOLEFIELD, Regius Professor of Greek in the University of Cambridge.

Secretary for General Business.
WILLIAM THOMAS, ESQ., at the Office of the Parker Society, 33, Southampton Street, Strand, London.

Auditors.
HON. A. KINNAIRD, REV. R. E. HANKINSON, H. POWNALL, ESQ., and F. LOWE, ESQ

Bankers.
MESSRS. HERRIES, FARQUHAR, AND CO., No. 16, St. James's Street.

REGULATIONS FOR DELIVERY OF THE BOOKS PUBLISHED BY THE SOCIETY.

I.   They will be delivered, free of expense, at the office, or within three miles of the General Post Office, London.

II. They will be sent to any place in England beyond the distance of three miles from the General Post Office, by any conveyance a member may point out. In this case the parcels will be booked at the expense of the Society, but the carriage must be paid by the members to whom they are sent.

III. They will be delivered, free of expense, at any place in London which a member resident in the country may name.

IV. They may remain at the office of the Society until the members apply for them; but in that case, the Society will not be responsible for any damage which may happen from fire, or other accident.

V.   They will be sent to any of the Correspondents, or Agents of the Society, each member paying the Correspondent or Agent a share of the carriage of the parcel in which the books were included. Arrangements are made for the delivery on this plan, in many of the cities and large towns where a sufficient number of members reside; *and it will be esteemed a favour if gentlemen who are willing to further the objects of the Parker Society, by taking charge of the books for the members in their respective neighbourhoods, will write to the Office on the subject.*

VI. They will be delivered in Edinburgh and Dublin as in London, and forwarded from thence to members in other parts of Scotland and Ireland, in the same manner as is mentioned above with respect to England.

A List of the Works

ALREADY PUBLISHED BY THE PARKER SOCIETY.

For 1841.
The Works of Bishop Ridley.
The Sermons and other Pieces of Archbishop Sandys.
The Works of Bishop Pilkington.
The Works of Roger Hutchinson.

For 1842.
The Examinations and Writings of Archdeacon Philpot.
Christian Prayers and Meditations.
Letters of Bishop Jewel, and others, translated from the Originals in the Archives of Zurich (1st Series).
The Writings of Archbishop Grindal.
Early Writings of the Rev. T. Becon, Chaplain to Archbishop Cranmer, and Prebendary of Canterbury.

For 1843.
Fulke's Defence of the English Translation of the Bible.
Early Writings of Bishop Hooper.
Writings of Archbishop Cranmer on the Lord's Supper.
The Catechism and other pieces of Becon.

For 1844.
The Liturgies, Primer, and Catechism of the Reign of Edward VI.
Writings of Bishop Coverdale.
Sermons of Bishop Latimer.
The Flower of Godly Prayers, and other pieces of Becon.

For 1845.
Second Series of Letters from the Archives of Zurich.
Remains of Bishop Latimer.
Writings of Bishop Jewel.
Devotional Poetry of the Reign of Queen Elizabeth.

For 1846.
Remaining Portion of Bishop Coverdale's Writings.
Original Letters relative to the Reformation.
Remains of Archbishop Cranmer.
Calfhill's Answer to Martiall's Treatise on the Cross.

For 1847.
A further Portion of Bishop Jewel's Works, including the latter part of his Answer to Harding, his Exposition on the Epistles to the Thessalonians, and other Pieces.
Liturgies and Occasional Services of the Reign of Queen Elizabeth.
The concluding Portion of the Original Letters relative to the Reformation.
Norden's Progress of Piety.

For 1848.
A third Portion of Bishop Jewel's Works, containing his Apology and the 1st part of the Defence.
A Volume of Bradford.
A Volume of Tyndale.
Fulke's Answer to Martiall and Stapleton.

The Books preparing for 1849, are:—

Whitaker's Disputation on Holy Scripture.
Bullinger's Sermons.
Bishop Bale's Select Writings.
Tyndale, 2nd Portion.